ROMAN BRITAIN

PLANTAGENET SOMERSET FRY

ROMAN BRITAIN

History and Sites

DAVID & CHARLES
Newton Abbot London

BARNES & NOBLE BOOKS
Totowa, New Jersey

To the many hundreds of amateur and independent archaeologists and historians who, in local societies or as individuals, make so many important contributions to the advancement of archaeological and historical knowledge, but whose work is too often inadequately recognised, and sometimes not recognised at all.

British Library Cataloguing in Publication Data

Somerset Fry, Plantagenet
  Roman Britain.
  1. Great Britain–History–Roman period, 55B.C.–
  A.D.449
  I. Title
  936.1′04   DA145

ISBN 0-7153-8267-5

Library of Congress Cataloging in Publication Data

Somerset Fry, Plantagenet, 1931–
  Roman Britain.

  1. Great Britain—History—Roman period, 55 B.C.—
  449 A.D.   2. Historic sites—Great Britain—Guide-books.
  3. Great Britain—Description and travel—1971-   —Guide-
  books.   4. Romans—Great Britain.   I. Title.
  DA145.S685 1984   936.2′04 83-21412
  ISBN 0-389-20439-0

This edition first published in 1984
in Great Britain
by David & Charles (Publishers) Limited
Brunel House   Newton Abbot   Devon

First published in the USA in 1984 by
Barnes & Noble Books
81 Adams Drive, Totowa, New Jersey, 07512

Typesetting by Typesetters (Birmingham) Limited
Edgbaston Road, Smethwick, Warley, West Midlands
and printed in Great Britain
by Butler & Tanner Limited, Frome and London

PREFACE

The study of Britain in Roman times has advanced enormously in the past twenty years or so. There has been a steady outflow of books on the occupation in general and on numerous aspects of it in particular, and these have been eagerly devoured, as it were, by an enthusiastic public anxious to enlarge its knowledge of this formative period of British history. The justification for adding this work to the literature on the subject lies in the need to spread more widely some of the vast amount of information that has been accumulated over the years about the numerous sites of Roman occupation. There have been gazetteers, some of them excellent, but they confine themselves to visible remains. What about the hundreds of sites that are no longer visible but which are none the less still there, under later buildings or deeply ploughed fields, or those no longer there, washed away by the sea or cut away by the quarrymen, but about which details are known and recorded? This is the sort of information that the Roman Britain enthusiast wants. He or she can, of course, get it from academic institutions, university libraries, learned journals with site reports and so forth, but these are not all easily accessible. The gazetteer in this book digests a considerable quantity of this information, and at the same time lists the numerous sources from which it came, thus pointing the serious student directly towards further research. It is the first such gazetteer, yet with over a thousand sites representing all the main areas of interest – forts, towns, villas, farms, industrial settlements, potteries, mines and temples – the list is selective rather than complete.

The preparation of this book took several years. Extensive work was done in city and university libraries, notably the University Library, the Library of the Museum of Classical Archaeology and Wolfson College Library, all at Cambridge, the Central Library of the city of Cambridge, the Suffolk County Library at Bury St Edmunds and the library of the Institute of Archaeology at London University, and to the staff of all these I am enormously grateful for help and services too numerous and comprehensive to mention in detail. A large number of sites were visited, and I should like to say thank you very much indeed to so many excavation leaders who let me look at their sites and who discussed points with me. I should also thank many other archaeologists, not necessarily specialising in Roman Britain, but who yet had important advice to give and valuable points to make.

Two people deserve special gratitude. Professor John Wacher, Professor of Archaeology at the University of Leicester, very kindly read the text of the introductory section of the book, a summary of the history of the Roman occupation, and I owe him a very great debt for an invaluable list of comments and corrections, nearly all of which I have been delighted to incorporate. For such errors as may remain, I am alone responsible. Ms Janet Douglas, lately of St Catharine's College, Cambridge, carried out a remarkable job on the gazetteer, notably on the principal sites in Roman Britain, and I am extremely grateful for the swiftness and skill with which she helped me to get it finished.

To Wendy Galletti and Anne Meldrum, my gratitude for so capably handling the typing of my illegible manuscript, to Anthony Lambert and to Sue Banfield for editing the book for publishing, and to my wife Fiona, as always, for reading the text critically, making many valuable suggestions and helping me to prepare the index.

Whatever virtues the book may have, they are greatly enhanced by the line drawings and plans, all sensitively prepared by the artist Graham Sumner, who specialises in drawings related to Roman Britain. The plans are for the most part understandably simple and factual, but the drawings are works of art, and I owe him a great debt.

Finally, I cannot sufficiently thank Professor David Williams, President, and the Fellows of Wolfson College, Cambridge, for giving me temporary senior membership of the college and so providing me with indispensable facilities and a unique environment in which to write the great part of this book.

Plantagenet Somerset Fry
Wolfson College, Cambridge

CONTENTS

1
BEFORE CAESAR

When the Romans came to Britain, they entered not a barbarian land with a primitive culture, as was once thought, but a group of isles peopled by a variety of tribes with many centuries of growth and technology behind them. If these tribes, particularly those in mainland Britain, had had the will to unite in the face of danger from outside, and if they had understood the sense of order and discipline that motivated the Romans and had gone some way towards matching it, the Roman conquest might never have taken place. But it did happen, and Britain became absorbed into a Roman European empire whose northern border was approximately the line of the Rhine and Danube rivers. Although the inclusion of Britain into the empire was to prove a costly exercise, as one or two Roman authors complained,[1] it became an integral and necessary component in the northern defences of the empire.

The existence of Britain was known to Mediterranean traders for several centuries before the first invasion of Julius Caesar in 55BC. Carthaginians, perhaps even their ancestors the Phoenicians, had obtained tin directly by sea from Cornwall. There were commercial links between Britain and north and west Gaul probably as early as 600BC. In the late fourth century BC (in the days of Alexander the Great), the merchant explorer Pytheas, who came from the Greek colony Massilia (Marseilles), visited Britain. He is credited with examining Cornish tin streaming processes, sailing in a ship round the whole of the British Isles and writing an account of his travels which was used by later authorities such as Diodorus the Sicilian (c80–29BC). By the second century BC Britain and the Mediterranean were trading on a regular basis both by sea and by overland routes. Yet the average Roman knew nothing of Britain beyond its location, which was across the 'ocean' and so outside his interest or comprehension. When Caesar was campaigning in Gaul in the 50s BC, he learned of the Britons through the assistance they were giving to their cousins, his Gallic enemies, and this supplied the motive for taking a closer look at the remote territory beyond the sea, the shape and size of which were only vaguely understood by a handful of specialists.

Britain had had the hallmarks of civilisation for thousands of years, and both landscape and archaeology have revealed a variety of splendid examples of Stone Age technological skills, such as Maes Howe chambered tomb and Skara Brae Neolithic village (the Orkneys), Newgrange passage graves (Ireland), Grimes Graves flint mines (Norfolk), Windmill Hill causewayed enclosure (Wiltshire), Cairnpapple Hill (Lothian, Scotland) and Bryn Celli Ddu (Anglesey, Wales) henge monuments, Avebury standing stones and Stonehenge circle (both in Wiltshire). The metal ages that followed have yielded numerous artefacts of great skill and beauty, which can be seen in museums up and down Britain. Some time in the second millennium there emerged the first hillforts: community enclosures erected on hilltops or coast promontories and defended by earth banks revetted with timber or stone, built to protect farms and those who worked on them. As the second millennium gave way to the first, iron technology, already known in Europe, began to reach Britain and very gradually superseded the softer alloy, bronze. We do not know which immigration of peoples brought iron to Britain, but the story of the Iron Age is bound up largely with the Celtic peoples, one of the most remarkable group of peoples ever to walk across the stage of world history, who emerged in the ninth and eighth centuries BC in Britain as a result of invasion and from more peaceful immigration. They are with us and in us in Britain still.

The Celts were a random collection of Indo-European peoples who wandered from central Russia into Europe during the European Bronze Age. They brought new breeds of horses, which they rode bareback or using a simple saddle cloth, with bridle and bit made of bronze or iron. They also used horses to pull ploughs, waggons and carts, and in due course chariots as well. Their horses were a significant advance upon the animals already in use in Europe and they gave the Celts immense advantages, not least in warfare. Their warrior chiefs were buried in timber chambered tombs, sometimes with the chiefs' worldly goods – even their waggons, weapons and horsegear (but not the horses). The Celts brought with them their techniques of iron working, which were more advanced than the rudimentary skills already practised in the lands of Europe north of the Alps. They spoke two basic languages which, with little modification,

10

have survived as living languages, namely, P-Celtic (which became Welsh) and Q-Celtic (Irish); it is likely that most of the people understood both tongues.

The Celts spread out into several parts of Europe, including Austria, Germany, Bohemia, Switzerland, France and the Iberian peninsula. They also came to Britain, not only as invaders but also as traders. For a long time they dominated Europe – even invading Italy in the fourth century BC – but they were checked. The first period of identifiable development in Europe was in Austria, where in the eighth and seventh centuries BC they prospered through salt mining and iron working. This is known as the Hallstatt phase from the name of a village in the Austrian Alps where a major cemetery of their leading men was found in the 1860s. Hallstatt was a centre of salt production. Hallstatt people began to emigrate to Britain in the seventh century BC, and artefacts of this period have been found in many areas, chiefly on or near the coast (eg Llyn Fawr and Scarborough). This phase coincides roughly with the Early Iron Age (or Iron Age A). It should be noted, however, that the different phases of the Iron Age in Britain are extremely difficult to trace, and any generalisation lays itself open to argument. The phases are often classified as Iron Age A (Early), Iron Age B (Middle) and Iron Age C (Late), but A, B and C are not measures of time applicable everywhere: A precedes B, but in some areas lasts longer than in others; B may start where A has not finished; here and there, C may not start at all.

The Hallstatters were great builders of hillforts, taking over the cruder Late or Middle Bronze Age types and improving them or constructing them afresh. They also began to build the first rectangular houses to appear in Britain. The predominance of the Hallstatters, however, seems to have given way in the sixth and fifth centuries BC in Europe to new centres of Celtic power further west. One was in Switzerland, and much evidence of its existence was found at the immersed village of La Tène, on the banks of the river Thièle where it leads into Lake Neuchâtel. The La Tène Celts began to arrive in Britain in the fourth century BC and are often classified as Iron Age B people (though remember the cautions expressed above). They were more aggressive than their predecessors, and they fought vigorously for the space they wanted in Britain. They captured hillforts and enlarged and strengthened them. The earlier forts generally had only one defending rampart and ditch; the La Tène people turned them

Reconstruction of an Iron Age round house, based on a house found in excavations at Pimperne, Dorset. This was erected at the Butser Iron Age Farm, Hampshire, under the direction of Dr Peter Reynolds

into bivallate or multivallate types, with complex gate systems as at Maiden Castle in Dorset.

Outside the hillforts, the La Tène Celts erected new settlements for the communities which worked the more intensive farms that they developed. They may also have introduced the British round house – they certainly built round houses that were larger and more sophisticated than their predecessors. They may also have established the well-known Celtic field system: the lynchet, the rectangular field whose borders were formed by the earth scooped up as a result of ploughing, generally measuring between a half and one and a half acres and usually located on the slopes of downlands, as at Fyfield Down (Wiltshire), Maen y Bardd (Gwynedd, Wales) and Windover Hill (Sussex). These Celtic fields were farmed intensely: two crops were harvested in succession in one year on many of them. Ploughing was improved by the use of iron-tipped ploughshares. Greater food production stimulated population growth, and Caesar commented that he found the island well populated, the countryside thickly studded with homesteads and the cattle very numerous.[2]

By the closing years of the second century BC Britain had evolved into a tribal society with a number of kingdoms (of a kind) controlled by aristocracies and headed by kings or chiefs who were probably elected. At this time, fresh immigrations of Celts began to arrive from Europe and to settle in the south-east. They were the Belgic people from northern France, Iron Age C folk, producing modified La Tène ironwork and pottery; they were more warlike than their 'hosts' in Britain upon whom they planted themselves by force, particularly in the later immigrations. They came in several waves, between about 120 and 50 BC, and they displaced the rulers and noblemen in the areas in which they settled. The history of the first century BC – and the earlier years of the first century AD – is marked by intense rivalry between Belgic and non-Belgic tribes.

The Belgae brought major changes to south-east Britain, particularly to the lands below the Thames. Their iron technology was more advanced. They introduced the potter's wheel, the rotary quern for grinding flour and the light-weight, fast-moving chariot. They established the first towns in any real sense (*oppida*, as the Romans called them), which were large areas for close living and industrial working, chosen as a rule for the natural defensiveness of the site which was complemented by intricate dyke systems, as at Colchester, Silchester and St Albans. They introduced coinage, in gold, silver and bronze, some of it modelled on Greek and Roman types with which they were familiar in Europe. And they buried their chiefs in splendid tombs filled with grave goods which in some discovered instances included all the drinking vessels, flagons and other apparatus associated with a bumper funeral feast, as at Lexden near Colchester.

The arrival of the Belgae in a sense marks the end of British pre-history, for thereafter Britain comes within the embrace of recorded history (in the accounts of Greek and Roman authors), its coinage begins to bear the names of individual chiefs and its activities figure in inscriptions. The Belgic aggression in Britain also marks the beginning of the end of British independence – not far behind the Belgae came the Romans.

NOTES
1. Appian, *Roman History*, preface, S5.
2. Caesar, *De Bello Gallico* V, 12.

The man who started it all – Caius Julius Caesar. A bust executed in his time or shortly afterwards.

2
THE EXPEDITIONS OF JULIUS CAESAR

Julius Caesar's first expedition to Britain is one of the key events in British history. Its date, 55BC, is almost as well known as that other famous invasion date, AD1066. But Caesar's expedition across a hitherto unfamiliar sea (except to Roman traders), and into a land whose dimensions and geography were only hazily guessed at, was a landmark in his own career. When it was reported in Rome, it was to prove one of the most sensational pieces of news ever announced. The Senate, probably a majority of which was hostile to Caesar, voted a *supplicatio* (public thanksgiving) of twenty days – up to then the longest in Roman history. It is important to see the expedition, therefore, and its follow-up in the next year, 54BC, through Roman eyes,[1] and to grasp why Caesar launched them. Most important of all, we have to appreciate their results, around which a great deal of controversy still lingers, to some extent maintained as part of a wider argument about Caesar's overall achievement.[2] As to the events of the expeditions, there is less room for dispute, as they were described in detail by Caesar himself in probably the most pellucid account of military adventures ever written by one actually in command.[3]

By the 60s BC, the republican system of government at Rome was manifestly breaking down. Since the 80s BC, the state had endured several periods of autocratic rule by successful army commanders able to force through their policies by virtue of the armies at their backs. Elections to the magistracies had become a farce: the winners were generally those with the biggest financial backing used flagrantly for bribery. The Senate no longer commanded popular support or respect. This was partly due to its weak-kneed connivance at the extortionate and repressive administration of Roman governors and officials in the provinces. Armed gangs roamed the streets of the capital, making themselves available to rival political groups to

15

generate rioting for the right price. Consuls who failed to get useful measures passed by the Senate had to take them to the popular Assembly via the tribunes. Although they were passed, more often than not this was accompanied by street warfare, bloodshed and even murder.

In 60BC, Caesar stood for the consulship for 59, and won.[4] He had the support of the two most influential and powerful men of the day, Gnaeus Pompeius Magnus (Pompey), then Rome's foremost general, and M. Licinius Crassus, probably the richest man in the city. Together they formed what later became known as the First Triumvirate. It was a simple arrangement by which each promised not to take any political step without the approval of the others. As long as they stayed together, the Triumvirate was unassailable. It ensured a period of stability not enjoyed for a generation or more.

Caesar's term as consul was one of decisive importance. He introduced several valuable reforms, notably measures to stop extortion in the provinces, to prevent governors and their staffs fleecing their subjects, while his land bill redistributed state-held lands in Campania and granted them to veterans of Pompey's army and to the urban poor of Rome. As his term came to an end, he was allotted as his proconsular province the territory of Cisalpine Gaul, that is, Gaul south of the Alps, for five years. The Senate added Transalpine Gaul. This opened up enormous opportunities for Caesar, by now confident that he was the man to reconstruct the ailing state even if he had not yet worked out how he would do it. Beyond the Alps were vast, unconquered lands where enormous wealth and great military prestige could be won. As he set off for Gaul, his enemies in the Senate, many of whom were prone to dismiss him as a military lightweight, rubbed their hands gleefully as they confidently expected he would not return alive. They had wanted to prosecute him once his term was over for the measures passed while he was consul, not for the sake of Rome but for their own selfish ends, but the Triumvirate prevented it.

In a series of campaigns over the next two years, Caesar showed himself to be a commander of the first rank. He astonished his enemies and his colleagues alike by the rapidity of his movements and his ability to change plans at very short notice to meet emergencies. By 56BC he had overcome Gaul as far as Aquitaine, Brittany and what is now Belgium, and had reached the Rhine. Almost the whole Celtic group of tribes was within his grasp. What was he to do next?

During the campaigns, particularly those against the Veneti in

Brittany and the Belgae in northern Gaul, Caesar was well aware that many of the tribes, notably the Atrebates (a Belgic tribe), were being helped by detachments of British Celts. Nobles he had defeated in Gaul but who had refused to surrender in person had taken refuge in Britain, and had doubtless sounded out their kinsmen as to whether they would continue to support resistance to Roman rule in Gaul. Britain therefore posed a serious threat to the stability of his newly won province. There was another consideration: if Gaul was now conquered, in theory he should return to Rome; but if he returned he would lose the immunity from prosecution – and persecution – which all proconsuls as well as consuls in office enjoyed. He knew his enemies in Rome were bent on his destruction. The time had come, therefore, for another meeting of the Triumvirate, and the three men held a conference at Lucca, just outside Italy, in Caesar's province of Cisalpine Gaul, an event celebrated by a coin bearing the word *Concordia*. It was attended by about a hundred and twenty senators who had made the journey from Rome, who were not invited to alter, even if they were allowed to comment on, the arrangements that were made. These included the consulship for Pompey and Crassus for 55BC, followed by a proconsular command for Pompey in Spain and Crassus in Syria (so that he might wage war on the Parthians), both for five years. Caesar's command in Gaul was to be extended for a further five years, up to late 50 or early 49BC.

One is bound to ask why Caesar should need a second term in Gaul. It is a moot point, but it seems reasonable to infer that he raised the problem of the British who remained undefeated, who could – and probably would – stir up fresh difficulties in Gaul. An expedition against them would ensure that they experienced directly the might and power of Rome to act as a deterrent. For good measure, Caesar also drew attention to the danger that German tribes behind the Rhine might encroach upon eastern Gaul (he proved right, as it turned out). Caesar's enemies in Rome – no doubt dismayed that far from wrecking his career in a military disaster in Gaul, he and his army had in fact fought a series of campaigns crowned with success – now breathed sighs of relief that though they could not yet exact their revenge by a prosecution, Caesar would at least be out of the way and might still come to grief.

Assuming that a decision was made in 56BC that some sort of adventure must be launched against the British, it is likely that Caesar decided it need not be his first priority. As it happened, the movement of the Germans on the east side of the Rhine across the river into Gaul, sometime early in the winter of 56BC, pushed the British project into the background. Caesar had to deal with a serious situation, but by the summer of 55BC he had defeated the Germans and crossed the Rhine (over a timber bridge fabricated by his engineers in less than ten days, an astonishing engineering feat) and cowed the immediate Trans-Rhenish tribes into submission. Now he could turn to Britain. Though admitting in his book (*De Bello Gallico* IV, 20) that he had left it very late in the season (he does not say if he had hoped to do something much earlier), he was determined to establish some sort of presence in the island that year.

By August 55BC he had arrived with Legio VII and Legio X in the Pas de Calais, and ships were being assembled in harbours between Calais and Boulogne. In the middle of August he sent one of his officers, Gaius Volusenus, in a fast-rowing warship to reconnoitre the east Kent coast for a suitable harbour in which to land the fleet and shelter the ships. Volusenus returned a week later, having examined the coast from about Hythe round via North Foreland to the Isle of Sheppey.[5] This included the Wantsum channel which then separated the Isle of Thanet from the mainland and which would have provided a good shelter. At about midnight on the 26 (or 27) August, Caesar set sail with his legions (amounting to about ten thousand men) in eighty transports. There is argument as to whether he embarked from Boulogne or from Wissant, about fifteen miles north. His cavalry, in another eighteen transports harbouring at Ambleteuse some eight miles north of Boulogne, failed to catch the tide and left a day or two later.

In the last days before the embarkation, Caesar had sent Commius, (an Atrebatic noble whom he had made King of the Gallic Atrebates after he had defeated them in 57BC and with whom he had maintained good relations) over to Britain to try to persuade the tribes in the south to come peacefully to terms with Rome. He believed that Commius had some influence there, but when Commius reached Kent he was instantly put in chains.

By the morning of the 27 (or 28) August, Caesar was off Dover. Possibly he could see the British hillfort occupying the site of the medieval castle which is there today.[6] Certainly he noticed throngs of warriors along the cliffs. He steered north-eastwards hugging the coast as far as some point between Deal and Walmer, probably near the latter, and at about tea-time (British!) he ordered the transports to be run ashore. The British had guessed his intentions and had moved along the shore to meet his forces as they landed. The Romans had to run their ships into the shore where the water was deep, which meant that they had to jump down into the sea and wade ashore. To begin with, this alarmed the men until, in Caesar's own words, 'the man who carried the eagle of the Tenth Legion . . . shouted out to his colleagues in a loud voice, "Come on, men! Jump in! You don't want to lose your eagle to the enemy, do you? I'm certainly going to do my duty to my country and to my commander"' (*De Bello Gallico* IV, 25). He was followed by the rest of the men and before many minutes, Romans and Britons were fighting in the shallows on the shore. At first it was a desperate battle, since the Romans had not yet been able to form themselves into their accustomed ranks, and the British horsemen repeatedly charged at the legionaries. Then, Roman military organisation reasserted itself and the units made determined charges, putting the British to flight. At this point, Caesar would have hurled in his cavalry to complete the rout, but the eighteen transports had not arrived; indeed, they never did arrive.

The Britons fled inland and a little later sent a delegation to Caesar seeking terms, offering hostages and promising to obey whatever he directed. Among the hostages was Commius. Caesar accepted their promises not to renew hostilities, received the hostages and advised the Britons to get back to their fields. He consolidated his forces and built a camp, probably behind Walmer, though no trace of it has yet been found. On the 31 August, two disasters struck when a storm blew up in the Straits of Dover. The eighteen transports of cavalry, which had not joined Caesar because on their first attempt to get across the Channel they had been driven back to Gaul by changing winds, set out again, but were scattered by the storm. The storm also broke up most of Caesar's ships anchored off Walmer, destroying many and rendering the remainder waterlogged. For a moment, the Romans were in serious difficulties, stranded on an unexplored island populated by hostile Celts who were greatly encouraged by their plight. Caesar says that the chiefs began to conspire to renew warfare, to cut the Romans off from food supplies. He reacted with his customary energy and optimism. Reckoning that the British would need some days in which to assemble and equip enough forces to have any chance of defeating the legions, he organised forage parties to bring in supplies of food greatly in excess of immediate needs, and put men to the job of rebuilding and repairing the damaged ships and

Model of a British war chariot based on finds by Sir Cyril Fox at Llyn Cerrig Bach in Anglesey (*By permission of The National Museum of Wales*)

constructing new ones. Within a few days, all but twelve of the ships were seaworthy again.

Then there was another setback. While they were reaping corn, men of Legio VII were ambushed by a force of British warriors, some on horseback, some on foot, some in chariots. The dust clouds stirred up by the chariots alerted Caesar from the camp that the legion was in difficulty. He dashed out of camp with a detachment and, as he came upon the British, they called off their attack and withdrew. Caesar describes British chariot drill at this engagement in *De Bello Gallico* (IV, 33) and it is worth giving in full in the fine translation by Rex Warner:[7]

> The tactics employed by these charioteers are as follows: First, they drive in every direction, hurling their javelins. Very often the sheer terror inspired by the galloping horses and the noise of the wheels throws their opponents into a state of confusion. They then make their way through the squadrons of their own cavalry, leap down from the chariots and fight on foot. Meanwhile, the drivers retire a little from the battle and halt the chariots in a suitable position so that, if those who are now fighting on foot are hard pressed by the enemy, they will have an easy means of retreating to their own lines. So, in their battles they combine the mobility of cavalry with the stamina of infantry. Daily training and practice have brought them to a remarkable state of efficiency. They are able, for example, to control their horses at full gallop on the steepest slopes, to pull them up and turn them in a moment, to run along the pole, stand on the yoke and dart back again into the chariot.

20

The men of Legio VII had been unnerved by these tactics, but were greatly relieved at the sudden appearance of their commander-in-chief. The Roman forces returned to camp where they were joined by Commius who had been back to Gaul to collect a small troop of about thirty cavalry. (Caesar's cavalry had not yet been able to reassemble after the storm in the Channel.) Wet and stormy weather set in again, which the British used as cover for bringing forward an army of infantry and cavalry right up to the Roman camp. Although outnumbered, Caesar decided to give battle; it was essential for the reputation of the Roman army that its legions should always be seen to be ready to face larger forces and demonstrate that these could be beaten by superior discipline and manoeuvre. So it proved, and the British were defeated; but Caesar was again unable to turn his victory into a rout, for want of pursuing cavalry. The British, however, appeared to have got the message: they sent a fresh delegation to seek peace. Caesar demanded that they should send twice the number of hostages as before. Then he ordered his men to assemble their kit, break camp and prepare to return to Gaul. On or about the 25 September, as the autumnal equinox approached with its attendant winds, he set sail with his ships.

Caesar's first expedition has been described by some authorities prone to 'Caesar-bashing' as a failure – 'bungled', abortive or unimportant.[8] A more reasonable view based on the known facts is that it was a qualified success.[9] It depends, of course, upon what were Caesar's objectives. If it was his aim to conquer the island, or even a significant part of it, then he did fail; but he makes no suggestion that this was his aim in his otherwise frank and detailed commentaries (in which he was not unwilling to admit mistakes). If he set out merely to impress the southern British with Roman military capability, then he achieved this.[10] Moreover, the expedition gave him a considerable amount of first-hand experience of the British in their native environment, how they fought their battles, particularly their chariot warfare which he was to experience again the following year. Most important of all, the expedition furnished him with a dramatic achievement with which to delight his allies and even impress his enemies in Rome. The Senate responded to the despatches he sent on his return to Gaul by decreeing a public thanksgiving of an unprecedented twenty days.

The Roman army had certainly acquitted itself well in Britain. When it is remembered that almost a century later, another Roman army about to embark from the north-west coast of Gaul for Britain mutinied rather than set sail, the men of Caesar's Legio X can be forgiven for their momentary reluctance to jump into the water at Walmer. Thereafter, the men displayed the same bravery and resource that had characterised their campaigning throughout Gaul, to which Caesar again and again refers in most complimentary terms. And the officers and legionaries, as well as their commander-in-chief, profited enormously from the experience. They could make a second assault on Britain with confidence.

Caesar reveals his intention to invade Britain again the next year in his commentaries (*De Bello Gallico* V, 1). Soon after his return to Gaul, it became clear that the British were going to break their agreements; few of the hostages promised were sent. No doubt Caesar expected British agents to step up their trouble-making with their Gallic kinsmen, and this may be why he left the bulk of his army in the Belgic area for the winter with orders to rebuild and enlarge the fleet while he left to go south to Cisalpine Gaul.[11] When he returned to Boulogne in the summer of 54BC, he found a formidable invasion fleet of some eight hundred ships ready to sail. Five legions and two thousand cavalry were assembled, together with sufficient animals and supplies. After some delays which were later to affect his whole programme in Britain, the fleet sailed from Boulogne (Portus Itius) on the 6 or 7 July, at dusk, reaching a point somewhere between Deal and Sandwich (further north than in 55BC) the next morning. Again, we do not know the exact location of the landings, nor have any traces been discovered of the base camp Caesar put down. A Romano-British temple at Worth was excavated earlier this century and found to have underneath it the remains of a pre-Roman shrine. Worth is close to a bay which it is known was used by ships trading between Britain and Gaul before Caesar's time as well as afterwards, and the shrine may have been situated in or near a settlement there, which would have offered a suitable place for a marching camp.

The huge fleet was anchored on an open shore of soft sand ('*in littore molli*' *De Bello Gallico* V, 9) under the command of Q. Atrius, with ten cohorts (about five and a half thousand men) and three hundred cavalry. This time, there was no opposing army waiting to attack, and Caesar led his legions straightaway inland on an overnight march of about twelve miles. Then, as the Romans approached a ford across the Great Stour (at the future site of Canterbury), as the sun rose, they came upon the British with cavalry and chariots. There was a skirmish, and the British withdrew into a hillfort surrounded by trees, most of its entrances already blocked by horizontally placed logs. The hillfort, about a mile west of Canterbury, has been identified as Bigbury. The Romans broke into the fort by means of their well-tried device of the *testudo* (tortoise), that is, rows of locked shields held over the heads of men underneath who scooped up a ramp of earth over the ditch in front of the hillfort rampart. The British fled, and Caesar consolidated his position by constructing a camp near the fort. The next day, news was brought that the fleet had been badly knocked about in a storm the night before, many transports being driven hard on to the shore, crashing into each other in the process. About forty ships were lost, many more damaged, but all except the forty could be repaired. It was serious enough for Caesar to return to base where he detailed the craftsmen among his troops to repair the damage, and then to fortify the base camp.

The news of the fleet's troubles encouraged the British to turn back towards Bigbury. When Caesar returned to his camp there with his forces, he discovered that the British had marshalled a large army and chosen a warlord, Cassivellaunus, chief of the Catuvellauni, a Belgic tribe that occupied territory in an arc through Buckinghamshire, Hertfordshire, Cambridgeshire and Essex, that is, north of the Thames.[12] It required some swallowing of pride by the Kentish Britons, for up to then, they and other British tribes in the south-east had been at loggerheads with the Catuvellauni who were bent on building a large kingdom in the southern part of the country.

Under their new leadership, the British repeatedly attacked Caesar's forces as they pressed forward westwards towards the Medway. The attacks were beaten off. At or near Boughton, Caesar began to construct his third marching camp. Then, as happened in 55BC, when the legions were ordered out of camp to forage for supplies, they were attacked, but this time the Romans were accompanied by their cavalry and they were able to turn on the British with great force and drive them off. The cavalry pursued them for some distance, giving the charioteers no opportunity to stop their vehicles and get down to fight. This was probably in the neighbourhood of Whitehill, near Ospringe. The British determination collapsed and their troops dispersed. As Caesar put it, the British never fielded their whole army against him again.

It is not clear whether Cassivellaunus had appeared in person in these operations, or had delegated command, backing the troops on the spot with promises of help from his kingdom as required. But as soon as the British had been routed at Whitehill (if that is the site of the last battle), they left Kent more or less open to the invader. Caesar decided to deal with Cassivellaunus wherever he was, and headed towards his kingdom. His actual route is not known, but a possible route has been conjectured by C. F. C. Hawkes and Sonia Hawkes, who suggest that after Whitehill he marched to the Medway, crossed a ford probably a few miles north of Aylesford and went on along the lower ground to the north of the North Downs, swinging north-west into what is now London, aiming to cross the Thames perhaps at or near Wandsworth.[13] When he reached the south bank at the crossing, he saw on the north bank a substantial British force drawn up for battle, protected by rows of sharp stakes which covered the bank and, according to information from deserters, more rows were under the water (placed there at low tide). Without hesitation Caesar sent his army across, cavalry in front, and they splashed through with tremendous verve and were upon the British before the latter could react. The Romans then scattered them into the forests of Hertfordshire.

Cassivellaunus now saw that pitched battle with Caesar was out of the question but he had no intention of giving up the struggle against Rome. As Caesar marched through the scrub and marsh of the Brent valley west of the larger Lea valley, northwards towards Hertfordshire, Cassivellaunus kept up a guerilla war against his columns, dashing in and out of thickets and copses, sending in his chariots to harass Caesar's cavalry. Where was Caesar going? We might suppose it was towards Cassivellaunus' headquarters but Caesar implies that he did not know where that was.[14] Perhaps not, but he must have known it was in West Hertfordshire or south Bedfordshire somewhere. Or was Caesar heading towards the territory of the Trinovantes to the east of the Lea? They were one of the tribes that had been at loggerheads with the Catuvellauni.

During the march, Caesar received a deputation from the Trinovantes (who occupied Essex, and parts of Suffolk, Cambridgeshire and Hertfordshire). They reminded him that before leaving Gaul he had received their prince, Mandubracius, who had fled to him for protection after being dispossessed by Cassivellaunus. Now they begged Caesar to return Mandubracius and set him on his rightful throne and to compel Cassivellaunus to recognise him. Caesar does not say but we may assume that he had Mandubracius with him. Quick to see that an arrangement with the Trinovantes would incommode Cassivellaunus on his eastern flank, he agreed to the request and asked for hostages and grain supplies in return, both of which were immediately delivered. The formal protection of the Trinovantes encouraged several other tribes, which had their own problems with the Catuvellauni, to surrender to Caesar and ask for protection, among them the Segontiaci, the Ancalites, the Bibroci and the Cenimagni; the last-named may be the same as the Iceni, a tribe occupying Norfolk and part of High Suffolk. The offers were accepted. It was Roman foreign policy when dealing with collections of tribes in one land to divide them, playing one or more off against the others. For Caesar, the offers anticipated the policy and left him free to concentrate on the primary objective, the seeking out and the reckoning with Cassivellaunus. There was a bonus. The tribes were able to tell him more or less precisely where the headquarters of Cassivellaunus, his *oppidum*, was situated. *Oppidum* in British terms meant stronghold, ie a wooded area fortified with ditch and rampart. In Cassivellaunus' case the *oppidum* was surrounded by marshy ground. Moreover, it was not very far from the spot where this conference was taking place.

Armed with this information, Caesar set forth and found that the *oppidum* was indeed heavily defended. Disposing his forces in two parts, he assaulted it from two sides and in a short struggle captured it, taking numerous prisoners and many cattle. Cassivellaunus escaped via a rear postern. He had already sent urgent requests to four chiefs in the south (Caesar gives their names, Cingetorix, Carvilius, Taximagulus, Segovax, and says they were all kings in Kent) to assemble forces and attack the Roman base camp near Worth. They did so but were heavily repulsed. Among the captured was a British noble called Lugotorix. News of that defeat reached Cassivellaunus quickly and, on hearing it, he sent a delegation to Caesar offering to surrender, using the services of Commius as intermediary. Caesar accepted, since he had already decided not to winter in Britain but to return to Gaul with all possible haste, before the autumnal equinox. He anticipated that there might be risings in Gaul and he had left Labienus in command with too few forces with which to contain more than localised trouble.

The terms Caesar imposed upon Cassivellaunus were not perhaps as harsh as the Catuvellauni might have expected: more hostages to be delivered, an undertaking not to encroach further upon the Trinovantes and to respect the restored kingship of Mandubracius, and this time a tribute, or tax (*vectigal*), to be paid yearly to the Roman People.

The hostages were delivered and Caesar returned to the Kent coast – by what route we do not know. There, he and his army embarked for Gaul, probably on the 29 August. He reached Gaul the next day, though the whole transport operation clearly took a further few days. A day or two before he left, he had written to Cicero that he 'had settled Britain, taken hostages but no booty [tribute, however, imposed] . . .'.[15]

What did the second expedition achieve? Caesar says nothing in his commentaries, but writes to Cicero that Britain is settled. What was the extent of the tax, and for how long was it paid? Strabo (c64BC–AD21) suggests in his *Geography* (II, v) that it was no longer being paid by the end of the century. Suetonius (cAD69–150), in his *Lives of the Twelve Caesars* (Divus Julius, 25), says that Caesar 'exacted a large sum of money as well as hostages . . .'. Strabo also suggests there was booty and that it included slaves. Tacitus (cAD55–120) wrote '*potest videri ostendisse posteris, non tradidisse*', which can be rendered '. . . [Caesar] can be seen to have opened up Britain to those who followed him, but not to have handed it to them' (*Agricola*, 13). What matters in the story of Roman Britain is that if we accept that Caesar's principal motive in invading the island was to discourage the British from aiding their kinsmen in Gaul, his objective was certainly achieved. There is no evidence that the British joined in the great Gallic revolt led by Vercingetorix in 53–2BC. Indeed, Caesar lists the tribes that made up the confederation against him, and actually gives the numbers of men contributed (*De Bello Gallico* VII, 25), and British tribes do not figure in the list. He makes no further reference to them in his commentaries, not even after the pacification of Gaul, which suggests that he was satisfied with the arrangements he had made in Britain.

Britain was not a new Roman province in the usual sense of the term – that was to come a century or so later – but the first steps towards making it one were taken by Caesar: the permanent tax on it gave Britain a kind of provincial status. Caesar moved on to other things and played no further part in the history of the island.

Although there were to be no more military expeditions to Britain for ninety-seven years after Caesar's second invasion, the idea was mooted several times. Dio Cassius suggests three occasions on which Augustus, Caesar's heir, planned an invasion, in 34, 27 and 26BC, presumably to consolidate his uncle's arrangements. The *Panegyricus Messallae* names a possible commander-in-chief for one attempt, and the poet Horace foretells the annexation in his third book of *Odes*, presumably because he heard that it was being planned. This is interesting because Tacitus is quite definite that Augustus chose to put the annexation 'on ice'.[16]

From the military angle, the British were left alone until AD43, but the years between were not wasted, so far as Rome was concerned. There is evidence of steady development of trade via Gaul between the Roman empire and the tribes in the south-east of Britain, notably the Trinovantes (eg Italian wine amphora sherds dating from this period have been found in southern Britain). On the diplomatic front, the Roman government was kept well informed of the changing patterns of British politics and the in-fighting between one tribe and another. On the whole, relations between the Romans and at least some of the British developed constructively.

In the revolt of Vercingetorix in 52BC, the Atrebatic chief Commius, who had been an ally of Caesar a few years before, went over to the other side, notwithstanding many exceptional favours he had received from Caesar personally (*De Bello Gallico* VII, 76). Even after the collapse of the revolt, Commius sought to continue the war by conspiring with German tribes. Caesar's second-in-command, Titus Labienus, ordered a squad to take Commius and put him to death, but Commius escaped a trap set for him and fled to Britain to join the British Atrebates who had settled in lands south of the Thames in what is now Berkshire and parts of Hampshire and Sussex. Commius may have brought many followers with him: certainly there was a migration of Gallic Atrebates to the area at this time. Coins bearing his name (as COMMIOS) have been found in these parts, which suggest he became chief of the Atrebates in Britain, or at least of those in the Berkshire–Hampshire–Sussex enclave.

Commius was succeeded by his son, Tincommius, possibly in about 25BC, who also struck coins, some inscribed with TINC or COMMI F(ilius), son of Commius. Tincommius appears to have eschewed his father's anti-Roman attitude and in about 15BC probably agreed a treaty with Augustus. He was driven out of his kingdom by a brother, Eppillus, at the beginning of the first century AD, which is attested by the appearance of coins of the latter, inscribed variously REX, COMMI F and dated to this time. Tincommius appealed to Augustus for help but this was refused, and the emperor appears to have recognised Eppillus' usurpation, probably because the latter undertook to maintain friendship with Rome. Some of Eppillus' coins bear the inscription CALLEV, which is Calleva, the name of one of the Atrebatic *oppida*, later developed into a Romano-British town, Calleva Atrebatum (Silchester, on the Berkshire–Hampshire border, south-west of Reading). Goods were exported from the Roman world to Calleva as early as the last years of the first century BC, which suggests there was a commercial clause or two in the treaty. Eppillus himself was ousted in the first decade of the first century AD by a younger brother (or half-brother), Verica, who also minted coins with his name, and with REX and COMMI F. He is the same as the king Berikos named by Dio Cassius as the British chief who appealed to emperor Claudius in AD41 or 42.[17] Verica ruled the Atrebates for more than thirty years but was eventually driven out by the two sons of the great Catuvellaunian chief, Cunobelinus, of whom more below. Eppillus, meanwhile, did not appeal to Rome but instead entered Kent, deposed its king Dubnovellaunos (possibly not the only Kentish king) and took over his territory. Dubnovellaunos fled to Essex where he appears to have ruled for a short time over the Trinovantes whose king Addedomaros had just died – or whom Dubnovellaunos had first deposed.[18] Dubnovellaunos did not last long: he was ousted by Cunobelinus in about AD10, perhaps earlier. It is to the Catuvellauni that we now turn.

Cassivellaunus, the chief of the Catuvellauni, defeated by Caesar in 54BC, appears to have kept at least to part of the arrangements dictated to him. Tribute continued to be paid to Rome and he left the Trinovantes alone. But in about 20BC he died and was succeeded by Tasciovanus, his son (or grandson). He was the first Catuvellaunian chief to issue coins bearing his name (TASC, TAS, TASCIO), and in some cases also the name of his capital at Verlamion (VER). Some also bore the title RIGON or RICON which may be a Celtic word for 'rex' (king). He ruled probably into the first decade of the first century AD. He felt none of the constraints imposed upon his father (or grandfather) by Caesar and his reign was marked by a steady and almost unnoticed (by Rome) policy of expansion. By the time of his death, the Catuvellauni were overlords not only of their own Hertfordshire territory but also of lands in Buckinghamshire, Oxfordshire, Bedfordshire, Northamptonshire, Cambridgeshire, Middlesex and parts of Essex. Catuvellaunian coins of this period have also been found in Kent and in the northern parts of the Atrebatic kingdom. This may be in part due to trade and interchange of coinage, but the possibility of Catuvellaunian occupation cannot be ruled out. Their expansion into Essex brought them into conflict with their old rivals, the

Trinovantes, whose integrity Caesar had guaranteed.

Tasciovanus retained his capital at Ravensburgh for the first years but it is clear that some time at the end of the first century BC he moved it to Verlamion (Prae Wood), a site above the valley of the Ver where fragments of enclosing dykes and earthworks are still visible both on the ground and from the air. From the grave goods (silver cups, bronze vessels, amphorae etc.) buried with Catuvellaunian nobles at such places as Welwyn and Hertford Heath, it is also clear that the new capital prospered in its trading with the empire. Tasciovanus died some time in the first decade of the first century AD. By that date his son Cunobelinus had begun to share power with him; he was already striking named coins at Camulodunon in Essex, the tribal capital of the Trinovantes. This bears out that war between the Catuvellauni and the Trinovantes had been renewed and that the former had won some kind of suzerainty over the latter. Cunobelinus' activities coincided with the appalling disaster that befell the Romans in Germany in AD9 when three legions under P. Quinctilius Varus were trapped and destroyed by the German chief, Arminius, in the Teutoberger Forest; Cunobelinus timed his assault upon a Roman ally (the Trinovantes) with little fear of retribution from Rome.

Soon after the death of Tasciovanus (or perhaps before it) Cunobelinus consolidated his position over the Trinovantes by constructing a new tribal city next door to Trinovantian Camulodunon, letting the earlier town run down. Although Verlamion retained its importance for a time, and early in his reign Cunobelinus began to

Both sides of a gold stater of Cunobelinus, minted at the Trinovantian capital of Camulodunon (*Charles Seely, Colchester and Essex Museum*)

mint coins there as well, it is clear that the new city in Essex was to be a new capital for the Catuvellauni, attested by the quantity of imported goods found in Camulodunon which date from the second, third and fourth decades of the first century AD. We have seen that the Catuvellauni were spreading their power through the south-east of Britain and the question arises why the Roman government was willing to allow this empire building at the expense of peoples with whom Rome had friendly relations. The question becomes more important when we consider the fact that one of Cunobelinus' brothers, Epaticcus, installed himself with an administration at Calleva, probably in about AD25, and struck coins, which must have entailed the expulsion of Verica, a pro-Roman, who moved south to rule the Hampshire and Sussex parts of his Atrebatic kingdom. Verica may also have had some sway in Kent, perhaps in those parts where his brother (or half-brother) Eppillus was not ruling, though even here Catuvellaunian encroachments seem to have taken place, for coins of Cunobelinus appear in many Kentish finds.

The picture of south-east Britain for the period leading up to the invasion of AD43 is one of two main powers, the Catuvellauni and the Atrebates (the latter probably in alliance with the lesser Cantii in Kent) existing tenuously side by side, both trading vigorously with the empire via the sea ports and estuaries of Essex, Kent, Sussex and Hampshire, notably exporting grain, cattle, gold, silver, iron, hides, slaves and hunting dogs and importing ivory, amber, glass, pottery, wine and oil.[19] Verica remained staunchly pro-Roman but Cunobelinus was heading towards a break with the lingering obligation to Rome, though at no time did Cunobelinus challenge the Roman government to military confrontation. The situation might possibly have remained stable for some time – certainly as long as the newly found prosperity of the Catuvellauni continued to flourish as a result of the economic links with Rome – but in his last years Cunobelinus was troubled by the growing ambitions of two of his sons, Togodumnus and Caratacus. From about AD35, both were egging their father on to extend the Catuvellaunian 'empire'. Togodumnus invaded the lands of the Dobunni occupying Cotswold country and parts of the west Midlands, installing a puppet ruler, Bodvoc. Catuvellaunian forces began also to encroach upon the southern lands of the Iceni, a non-Belgic people occupying Norfolk, High Suffolk and parts of the east Cambridgeshire fens. Caratacus, meanwhile, had succeeded (or possibly deposed) his uncle, Epaticcus, at Calleva and was pressing down upon Verica's Atrebatic land. The two sons then urged their brother, Adminius, who was probably governing Hertfordshire and Bedfordshire from Verlamion, to advance northwards into lands of the Coritani, a Midlands people who had *oppida* at Old Sleaford, Leicester and, it appears from recent investigation, Lincoln, and who by AD35 may have already arranged some kind of alliance with the Romans. Adminius was pro-Roman and refused to wage war, which was no doubt the reason why his two brothers drove him out of Britain in AD39–40. He fled to Gaul to seek protection from the emperor Gaius (Caligula), then assembling forces for an expedition to German territory. Suetonius records Adminius' expulsion but gives no reasons for it.[20]

The emperor Gaius, whom legend has portrayed as a monster of cruelty and madness, decided to respond to Adminius and ordered preparations for an immediate invasion of Britain. By this time Cunobelinus was either already dead or had fallen completely under the influence of his two headstrong sons, and the detente between the Catuvellauni and Rome was over. The emperor assembled his forces on the shore in the neighbourhood of Boulogne, and then, quite suddenly, called off the whole exercise. 'Collect sea shells in your helmets' was the preposterous instruction issued to his legions, if Suetonius is to be believed.[21] More probably, it was the troops that refused to brave the Channel (they were certainly to do so in AD43, see p 36). Suetonius also records that Gaius erected a lighthouse upon the shore to commemorate a 'victory', but this is more likely to have been as an ancillary to the invasion base.

Preparations for the invasion will have involved a lot of people in a great deal of work. The advance forces which were to embark in the transports will have been provided with carefully estimated back-up (see chapter 10). They would have set out from properly laid out and provisioned bases, as was the custom in Roman military adventures. Reliable communications will have been set up: reserves of men, ships, vehicles, horses, rations, utensils, tools, armaments, siege equipment, even bullion for pay, will have been allowed for. If all these preparations were carried out, which we may assume, they will have taken months. They will also have taken as long to dismantle, if indeed they ever were. Whatever happened, numerous officers will have had first-hand experience of the logistics of invasion.

The invasion may have been scratched, but the idea was not dismissed. A number of factors conspired to ensure that before long the attempt would have to be made again. Gaius was murdered by his own Praetorian Guard in AD41. His successor was his uncle Claudius, a thoughtful, scholarly man whose physical disabilities (from birth) had earned him years of ridicule at court but probably saved him from the excesses of his mad nephew. Claudius was an authority on Roman history, particularly military history, and had accompanied his brilliant brother, Germanicus, on campaign. Undoubtedly he dreamed of a successful military adventure that would justify the army's faith in him, for it was the army that had raised him to the purple. The belligerent activities of the sons of Cunobelinus threatened not only to turn the whole of southern Britain into one anti-Roman confederation, they also endangered the security of Gaul – and thus the north-west frontier of the empire – and they jeopardised trade. Togodumnus and Caratacus would have to be stopped, and the time for diplomacy had passed. The emperor Gaius had in four years of extravagance seriously depleted the imperial revenues and fresh sources were needed. Private speculators, always on the look out for new areas to exploit, believed that Britain held great riches, especially precious metals, and were doubtless making a case for the desirability of military intervention.[22] Then, sometime in AD41–42, Caratacus expelled Verica, the Atrebatic king, from his kingdom and drove him to seek help from Rome. It was a flagrantly hostile act against the empire. When Verica, now an old man, appealed to Claudius, the emperor put an end to speculation and uncertainty and ordered the repreparation of a major invading force to cross the Channel to Britain. It was AD43.

NOTES
1. The poet Catullus (c84–54BC) first put Caesar's invasion of Britain into Roman literature in the last months of his life:
   Nile stains the Ocean with his hue
   Or cross the skyey Alps to view
   Great Caesar's trophies, Gallic Rhine
   And savage Britain's far confine.
2. Some modern scholars, anxious to discredit Caesar's unique career and achievements, employ what they regard as his failure in Britain to reinforce their case.
3. The two invasions are narrated in Caesar's *De Bello Gallico* ('Gallic War') IV, 20–38 and V, 8–23.
4. The career of Caesar, which is outside the scope of this work, can be studied in any of the authoritative biographies listed in the Bibliography.
5. Hawkes, C. F. C. (1977) pp 152–6.
6. Some of the hillfort ramparting was adapted as part of the outer defences of the later castle, and can be seen today.
7. Warner, R. (1960) p 85.
8. Legg, Rodney. (1983)

9. Frere, S. S. (1978) p 47; Salway, P. (1981) p 31.
10. This is suggested by his words: '. . . if the season left no time for actual campaigning, it would still be of great advantage to him merely to have visited the island' (*De Bello Gallico* IV, 20).
11. He even gave the shipwrights instructions on how to adapt the vessels to cope with English Channel tides, and to make them wider and lower in the beam so that they could be run on to the shingle with the larger cargoes they would have to carry. They were also to have sails and oars (*De Bello Gallico* V, 1).
12. There has recently been some argument as to whether the Catuvellauni were a Belgic tribe or a Marnian tribe, that is, a Celtic people from an immigration before the arrival of the first Belgic people. Those interested should consult Rodwell, W. '*Oppida*: the beginnings of urbanization in Barbarian Europe', in Cunliffe, B. and Rowley, T. (eds) *British Archaeological Reports* (1976), S11; Frere, S. S. 'Invasion and response: the case of Roman Britain', in Burnham, B. and Johnson, H. B. (eds) *British Archaeological Reports* 73 (1979); and the excellent summary of the arguments by J. S. Wacher in his *Coming of Rome* (Routledge & Kegan Paul, 1981).
13. I am here following Hawkes, C. F. C. (1977) p 164, though Frere, S. S. (1978) p 54, n 7, gives a suggestion that it may have been further east, perhaps as far as Tilbury.
14. Nor do we for certain. Wheathampstead was long favoured after Mortimer Wheeler's work of 1935-6, but Ravensburgh, about ten miles north-west, is now more than a possibility (Hawkes, C. F. C. [1977] pp 173-4).
15. Cicero passed on the information in a letter to his banker friend, Atticus (*Ad Atticum* IV, 18).
16. Dio Cassius, xlix, 38.2; liii, 22.5; liii, 25.2; *Panegyricus Messallae*, 147-9; Horace, *Odes* L, xxi, 15; Tacitus, *Agricola* 13.
17. Dio Cassius, lx, 19.1.
18. Addedomaros now seems to be the king buried in the tumulus at Lexden, outside Camulodunon, whose grave was discovered in 1924, containing armour, bronze ornaments etc.
19. Strabo, *Geography* IV, v, 2-3.
20. Suetonius, *Lives of the Twelve Caesars*, Gaius, xliv.
21. Suetonius, *Lives of the Twelve Caesars*, Gaius, xlvi.
22. Tacitus, *Agricola*, 12: '. . . Britain yields gold, silver and other metals to make it worth conquering . . .'

3
CONQUEST

There were several top-level Roman generals whom Claudius could choose to lead the invasion force. He selected Aulus Plautius, who was related to him by marriage (or, more accurately, by divorce, for Plautius was cousin to the emperor's first wife, Urgulanilla). Plautius was nearly 60 years old. Consul in AD29, and currently governor of the restive province of Pannonia (Austria and West Hungary) on the Middle Danube, he was a commander used to dealing with 'barbarians'. On receiving the appointment, he set out for northern France with Legio IX *Hispana* to join with three more legions from the Rhineland already there or on the way. The four legions were to form the main army. Legio II *Augusta*, coming from Strasbourg, was under the command of Titus Flavius Vespasianus (later emperor from AD69 to 79), and Legio XIV *Gemina* from Mainz and Legio XX *Valeria* from Neuss were under Vespasian's brother, Flavius Sabinus, and Gnaeus Hosidius Geta, though we do not know which of the two each commanded. The four legions were supplemented by large auxiliary forces. The army totalled about forty thousand men. Each legion consisted of about 5,100 troops, in 9 cohorts of 480, comprising 6 centuries of 80 men each and the first (leading) cohort of 800. There was a special cavalry force of unknown size, but possibly 500, and it was, to begin with, under the command of Aulus Didius Gallus, who in AD52 was to become governor of Britain. The auxiliaries made up the remaining 19,000 troops.

The great army assembled near Boulogne. Some of the support forces and the stores were already there (from the cancelled expedition of Gaius), and no doubt a great part of the paperwork of the planning had only to be taken down from the shelves and quickly perused by a staff of specialists who knew what to do. Meanwhile, the corps of engineers, blacksmiths, carpenters, armourers, medical men, provisioners, pay clerks and so forth, all of whom were also trained legionaries, accumulated the baggage and special equipment they were to need in Britain and prepared it for loading into the holds of the transports. Commissariat staff packed up quantities of clothes, boots, weapons, spades, tools, food, wine jars and everything else invading armies needed.

The centurions in the legions checked that their men had all their regulation equipment. The legionary was basically a foot soldier and he wore thick-soled studded sandals or hob-nailed shoes (see chapter 10). He was dressed in a segmented iron, or leather edged with iron, corselet under which he wore a sleeveless woollen tunic. He wore a bronze helmet with a projecting neck-guard at the back and a toughened head-piece. He carried a rectangular shield curved to fit the body, made from layers of plane plywood, covered with calf skin and fitted with a metal central boss, its edges rimmed with metal. He carried a *pilum* or two, a heavy throwing javelin about 2m (7ft) in length, whose long, thin, iron shaft below the head bent downwards when the javelin stuck in an opponent's shield, immobilising it. He also carried a short, stabbing sword, excellent for close fighting in which the British (and Gallic) long, slashing sword was ineffective. While on the march, the legionary carried everything he needed on his back: armour, stakes for a trench, saw, basket, spade, axe, cooking pot and a supply of corn, as well as weapons and shield. All this weighed

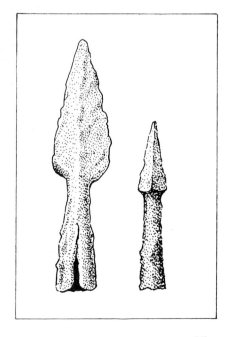

Spearhead and dart

35

over 22.5kg (50lb). Dressed and loaded up, the legionary had to be ready to jump off his invasion transport the instant it ran ashore and to enter into the fray as he splashed on to the wet sand. The heavier baggage, like tents and component parts of siege equipment such as *ballista*, catapults etc, some of which were mounted on wheels when in action, were carried on waggons or by baggage animals.

Sometime during the preparations, the army mutinied. Whether it was on the shores at Boulogne as the legionaries were preparing to board the transports, or whether it was among legionaries from the Rhineland bases who simply refused to budge any further along the roads to northern France when they heard where they were going, we do not know. But the authorities are clear that the men would not cross the Channel. They were terrified: the 'ocean' was the northern limit of the empire and it would be tempting providence to go beyond. Some of the men will have been among the ranks assembled at Boulogne by Gaius in AD 39–40. Aulus Plautius was at a disadvantage. He did not know the Rhineland legions, nor the staff already in northern France, and he was no popular hero like Caesar who once quelled a mutiny with a single word. So he sent an urgent message to Claudius at Rome. The emperor responded by sending one of his principal secretaries of state, the former slave Narcissus, a loyal advisor of intelligence and cunning. Narcissus reached the mutinous army and began to harangue the men. They were at first mortally offended by the spectacle of a freed slave standing upon a general's rostrum. 'Get down off that tribunal, you Greek yobbo!', one or two of the men yelled[1]. Then they began to laugh when they saw the funny side of the situation, mocking the man with cries of 'Io! Saturnalia!', a reference to All Fools' Festival (which it was), when slaves assumed their masters' clothes and roles. The men felt ashamed of their cowardice and clamoured to embark. Aulus Plautius addressed them, perhaps reminding them that many of their ancestors were among those who had gone over to Britain with great Caesar in 55 or 54BC and they had not flinched.

Taking into account the time for Plautius' message to reach the emperor, for Narcissus to get ready, leave for Gaul and reach the army, perhaps two months will have been wasted. But early in May, or even later, the great armada set sail, in three squadrons, slightly separated one from another, so as to divide the British resistance forces they expected to meet on the Kent coast. It was for long thought that the legions landed at three places, Lympne, Dover and Richborough.

Now, it is generally agreed that Richborough received the main force.[2] A subsidiary force sailed south-westwards as far as Chichester to make contact with the pro-Roman Atrebates whose king, Verica, had been expelled the year before.

Plautius was pleasantly surprised to find no British forces waiting to repel his landings. The British, having been prepared for an earlier landing, had heard about the mutiny, thought it would result in an abandonment as in the time of Gaius and had withdrawn their forces from the coast. The Romans established a beachhead and quickly put down a base camp a little way inland; traces of its defensive ditches still remain.

Once the landings were accomplished, Plautius wasted no time. The legions assembled into marching order and advanced westwards. It is possible they headed for Bigbury and then veered north-west directly towards the river Medway, taking a straight route north of the Downs which later became part of the stretch of Watling Street between Dover and London. Somewhere along the way the invaders clashed with both Togodumnus and Caratacus, separately, whom they defeated. Then they pushed on to the river on whose east banks at or near Rochester they stopped. On the other side, British forces were massing. Meanwhile, to protect their rear, the Romans built a small fort at Reculver on the north-west of the Wantsum Channel, eight to nine miles from Richborough. Probably the invasion transports were harboured in this channel, safe from the sort of storms that had wrecked Caesar's ships in 55 and 54BC (see pp 19, 23), and in a good position for a rapid withdrawal to Gaul if needed. But there was no cause to withdraw. Plautius was preparing to cross the Medway when a delegation of the Dobunni (called the Bodunni by Dio Cassius, but obviously the same) arrived, offering to surrender; they did not like their subordination to the Catuvellauni. It was an encouraging sign. Plautius took his forces over the river, sending out in front auxiliaries specially trained to cross rivers fully armed. The ensuing battle lasted two days, but at the end the British were on the run back towards the Thames in London, 'near where the river enters the sea and forms a large pool at high tide',[3] which probably means near London Bridge. Here they crossed and rallied their forces for the next engagement.

What followed is not clear. Dio Cassius records that the Romans got into difficulties and Plautius sent for help from the emperor, still in Rome and waiting to hear how the invasion was proceeding. What were the difficulties? The Romans could not have failed to get across the Thames. Skirmishes with the British are reported. In one of them, Togodumnus was killed. This must have crippled British morale, though Dio Cassius says it stiffened their resolve. Plautius is said to have become alarmed at the resistance and sent for help, but this overlooks the fact that Claudius was determined from the start to take some personal role in the conquest of Britain. Clearly, Plautius decided the right moment had come to send for Claudius to be present at what must before long be a major confrontation. Plautius will have used the interval waiting for the emperor to strengthen any bridge across the Thames or construct a new one (probably the remains of which were found 45–55m (50–60yd) east of the present London Bridge)[4] to facilitate the traffic of troops and supplies into Essex. Doubtless he also knew that Claudius would be bringing elephants with which to overawe the Catuvellauni. Claudius arrived in mid-August, with fresh troops and with the elephants, and together emperor and commander led the Roman army straight across the south Essex flats towards the Catuvellaunian capital, Camulodunon. Resistance was slight; the British may already have been badly mauled by Roman detachments during the waiting period. Caratacus had already fled westwards to Wales; he knew there was little he could do in Essex now that Togodumnus was dead.

Dio Cassius says that Claudius remained only sixteen days in Britain.[5] This is too short a time in which to march from the Kent coast (with elephants), join up with Plautius, cross the Thames, proceed to Camulodunon, be hailed as *imperator* several times en route by the troops (which must mean he was nominally in command in several skirmishes), and then take the capital, level the inner defences and enter the town in triumph in an imperial car flanked by his elephants. He then received delegations from several British kings offering to surrender and made treaties with them, probably of different terms in each case, before returning to his ships in Kent. Suetonius says six months elapsed between the time Claudius left Rome on receipt of Plautius' message and his return there after reducing a large part of Britain to submission.[6] If it took two months to reach Kent and two months to return to Rome (a reasonable assumption), then his activities in Britain occupied eight weeks or so, which seems more realistic. Before Claudius left, he imposed a settlement upon the territories so far won or absorbed (roughly those below the line Camulodunon – Portsmouth or Southampton) and came to terms with other tribes which had offered friendship. Among the latter were the southern Atrebates of Sussex and Hampshire (formerly ruled by Verica who may at this point have been restored); the Iceni in Norfolk, High Suffolk and East Cambridgeshire, ruled by more than one chief, including perhaps Antedios and Prasutagus (whose wife was Boudica); the Brigantes of Northumbria and the Pennines under their queen Cartimandua; the Dobunni under Bodvoc and Corio and perhaps the Coritani.

The Claudian arrangement was intended to be permanent; the southern part of Britain (*proxima pars Britanniae*) was, according to Tacitus, to be 'gradually shaped into a province, a process that was to be capped with an early *colonia* of veterans'.[7] Claudius disarmed the defeated tribes and ordered them to hand their weapons to Plautius. The kingdoms which had chosen to remain loyal to Rome were made 'client kingdoms'. This was a Roman device introduced in Republican times by which the government used rulers of territories technically within the empire (who had been granted a kind of 'subordinate freedom' to keep their thrones) to govern their lands on behalf of the Senate and People of Rome, and rulers of territories outside but generally bordering the empire, who were expected to remain loyal to Roman interests. The device saved the need to introduce a complex and costly civilian government staffed by Romans, when the locals could do the job under suitable guarantees. Client kings were expected to collect tribute, keep order and sometimes to provide troops for imperial armies. They had the illusion, if not always the reality, of independence. As a rule, the arrangement lasted only as long as the king lived, for it was negotiated with him as an individual. On his death, the kingdom normally passed directly under Roman rule, as a province, with a governor, and the attendant apparatus of colonial government (see chapter 11). There were, of course, exceptions.

Soon after Claudius had gone, Plautius proceeded with the next phases of his conquest, and at the same time put in hand the first measures for bringing the settled areas under Roman provincial organisation. Very early on in his governorship (AD43-7), a fort was constructed at what is now the village of St Michael's, adjacent to St Albans, beside the river Ver. This was presumably to keep an eye upon the Catuvellauni and their former capital, Verlamion (Prae Wood). A legionary fortress was also started in what was later the western part of the Roman city at Colchester. We have scant evidence for other Plautian foundations, but there must have been marching camps, forts and stations in Essex, Hertfordshire and Cambridgeshire at least, and perhaps elsewhere in the south Midlands and south-east (eg Chelmsford, Godmanchester etc). Plautius also turned his attention to the southern and more westerly parts of Britain. He had already sent Vespasian with Legio II on a path south of the Thames, probably down through Surrey and Sussex, to receive the submission of the friendly Atrebates. Vespasian then swung into Hampshire. As likely as not, he had started out before Claudius arrived. Suetonius records that he 'fought thirty battles, subjugated two war-like tribes, and captured more than twenty towns, beside the entire Isle of Wight . . . earning triumphal decorations.'[8] One of these tribes was the Durotriges, who occupied Dorset, south Wiltshire and south-west Somerset (bordering upon the lands of the Dobunni), and perhaps edging into Devonshire, most of which was occupied by the Dumnonii. The Durotriges were an Iron Age B people that had been overcome by Belgic Celts in the first century BC and were characterised by their fondness for constructing hillforts (eg Hengistbury Head, Hod Hill, Hambledon Hill and Maiden Castle). The other tribe is not known but could have been an offshoot of the Atrebates occupying west Hampshire, with a capital at Winchester (*Venta Belgarum*), probably Oram's Arbour in the west part of the present city, or the Dumnonii in Devon.[9] Vespasian forged westwards, and splendid evidence of his battles with the Durotriges is manifest in the excavations at Maiden Castle in west Dorset under Sir Mortimer Wheeler (1934–7). A *ballista* bolthead, lodged in the vertebrae of the skeleton of a British defender of the east gate of the hillfort, was found and both bolt and vertebrae are in the Dorchester Museum. Another find was a heap of rounded stones within the hillfort enclosure, which had been an ammunition store for British slingers.

Vespasian's campaign probably took up to three years, and in that time he set down marching camps, perhaps a fort or two and other military installations. There are several possibilities: store buildings at Fishbourne, military timber buildings at Chichester, a 29 acre (12ha) camp near Wimborne (Lake Farm), a naval base at Hamworthy, Poole, and structures in the Iron Age hillforts at Hod Hill and Waddon Hill, and even at Exeter with a naval base at Topsham. Any of these could have been initiated during the campaigns of Vespasian. When Vespasian left Britain in AD46, it is likely that Rome had obtained control of all the southern counties from Kent to Dorset.[10]

Meanwhile, Plautius, with the other three legions, achieved the conquest of most of the lowlands of Britain, bounded roughly by a belt of territory from Bath and Bristol to Lincoln, perhaps to the Humber, through which a major Roman road was later built, called the Fosse Way. Below this belt, the kingdoms of the Iceni, the Dobunni and possibly the Coritani had already formed alliances on Roman terms, leaving only pockets of resistance to be overcome, and it seems that these were satisfactorily crushed by AD47, the year in which Plautius' term ended. It was probably Legio IX that took care of the north-west part of East Anglia, the Fens and Lincolnshire, attested by the discovery of a very early 26 acre (10.5ha) fortress at Longthorpe, suggesting a base not for a whole legion (Legio IX was eventually to have its legionary fortress at Lincoln) but for part, say, one or two vexillations plus auxiliaries, and dating to about AD44-8. Other forts, or smaller forts for smaller military units, of about the same period were Godmanchester (Cambridgeshire) and Great Casterton (Leicestershire). The other two legions operated in East Anglia (Legio XX, based at Colchester) and in the Midlands–Cotswolds (Legio XIV), perhaps helping to construct the fort at Cirencester unless this was begun by northern units of Vespasian's Legio II. Forts may have been put down at this time also at Towcester (Northamptonshire), Leicester (certainly), Mancetter (Warwickshire) and Alcester (Warwickshire), suggesting an intensive consolidation of gains, secured with the protective south-west–north-east frontier belt, from which further offensive activity could be mounted. Future work will doubtless enable us to accept other forts as being begun, perhaps even completed, during this period.

In AD47 Aulus Plautius left Britain for a well-earned triumphal *ovatio* at Rome where the emperor personally came to the gates to welcome him. His successor in Britain was an equally experienced general, P. Ostorius Scapula, whom Tacitus regarded as a fine soldier. Fortunately, we have a good account of Ostorius' term as governor in a surviving part of Tacitus' *Annals* (xii, 31–40). This is the major primary source, and some of it can be supported by archaeology.

In the hiatus between Plautius' departure and Ostorius' arrival, British tribes from Wales, probably the Silures from the south and the Ordovices from the middle and north, launched an assault upon the protective belt with such disruptive effect that Tacitus described the situation greeting Ostorius as chaotic. This was probably an exaggeration. The tribes may have been led – almost certainly they were inspired – by Caratacus who emerged after four years' absence from the historical limelight. Ostorius was equal to the danger, and immediately sent forces to drive them out.

It has long been debated whether the initial intention of Claudius had been to occupy only the lowland part of Britain. Plautius left once he had established a *limes*, or boundary, which conveniently coincided for much of its length with a great belt of limestone hills from Somerset to Lincolnshire and Yorkshire, separating the low from the higher ground. His successor accepted the *limes* to begin with, for once he had dealt with the raids, he turned back into the embryo Roman province and began to organise it, which appears to have involved building more forts and stations. He also decided on an action which was to cost Rome dear: he ordered all the tribes within the *proxima pars Britanniae* – people who had already declared their loyalty – to surrender their arms. This entailed a thorough search in every town and village, possibly a systematic house-to-house check. To the Celts the bearing of arms was a highly prized right. Their war leaders believed their weapons were inherited by gods, and everyone who had a weapon looked upon it as a relative, or ally, at all events a friendly being that would act in concert with him who wielded it. Great skill and care were lavished on the decorating of weapons. To many, they were the most valuable possessions they owned – when they went to their graves, they were buried with their weapons beside them. To take away a Celt's weapons was to take away his manhood. It was tactless of Ostorius to disarm those who had resisted Rome, lost and come to terms: it was far worse to extend the penalty to people who had voluntarily allied themselves to Rome, in peace. Among them, the Iceni took particular exception, and they rebelled, and it is likely that they persuaded the Trinovantes, their neighbours to the south, to join them. Somewhere in East Anglia, at a 'battlefield . . . protected by a rustic earthwork, with an approach too narrow to give access to cavalry', they confronted the governor's forces, made up of dismounted cavalrymen (Tacitus, *Annals* xii, 31). Ostorius' men rushed the ramparts, clambered over and fought a desperate battle with the Iceni whose position turned into a trap from which they could not escape. The battle was probably fought at Stonea Camp, near March, in the Cambridgeshire Fens.

The defeat of the Iceni was sharp and decisive, and it discouraged others from following them into rebellion. But it generated a deep sense of grievance in their hearts, and they were not to forget it thirteen years later when another and graver offence was perpetrated upon them by Rome. Prasutagus, one of the group of Iceni chiefs who

Aerial view of the earthworks at Stonea in Cambridgeshire, which may be the Iron Age fort attacked by Ostorius Scapula in AD 47/48 (*Cambridge University Collection*)

negotiated with Claudius in AD43, appears to have distanced himself and his followers from the revolt, for we find that in AD48 he is the only king of the Iceni, undoubtedly a reward for non-intervention. By this time he had married Boudica, a princess from another tribe, Icenian or possibly Coritanian.

Ostorius had pacified the Iceni and felt sufficiently secure of the continued loyalty of the others to advance out of the province against the Welsh tribes who were renewing war. The centre of British resistance was probably in south-east Wales, the land of the Silures, whom Caratacus may have been invited to lead; Ostorius' more immediate aim was to deal with another tribe, the Deceangli, who occupied the Cheshire Gap and north-east Wales and who were threatening the Cornovii, a friendly people just north-west of the *limes*. With Legio XIV he ravaged their territory and advanced almost 'to the sea facing Ireland', according to Tacitus (*Annals* xii, 32), though he must have meant the Isle of Anglesey or the Isle of Man. It is

43

possible that on this north Wales campaign he put down the beginnings of the 46 acre (18.5ha) fortress recently discovered at Rhyn near Chirk, close to the Shropshire–Clwyd border. The first fort at Chester (*Deva*) and the earliest at Metchley in Warwickshire and Wroxeter in Shropshire may also date from this time (AD48–9). A disturbance among the Brigantes, a client kingdom, compelled Ostorius to return quickly to restore order, which he did by punishing the ringleaders.

The suppression of the Deceangli and the Brigantes did not deter the other Welsh tribes from their activities. As soon as Ostorius had quelled the Brigantes, he resumed the war against the Welsh hillmen, this time in Silures country. To suppress them, a brigade garrison had to be established. This may be the date (AD49) when a fortress was established at Kingsholm, Gloucester, to which part, if not all, of Legio XX was sent from Colchester, which in turn was secured by the settlement of veteran troops, to make the first *colonia* in Britain. From Kingsholm, Ostorius moved into south Wales in pursuit of Caratacus, who evacuated it for the more mountainous terrain of central Wales, the land of the Ordovices, which he knew would present more obstacles to the Roman occupiers. It is possible that Ostorius sent for additional support from Legio XIV, with a vexillation stationed at the new fort at Wall (*Letocetum*) in Staffordshire and perhaps another at Kinvaston a few miles west, both well placed for a direct advance into mid Wales.

Tacitus (*Annals* xii, 33) records that in AD51 Caratacus decided to risk all in a battle. He chose a site:

> . . . where numerous factors – notably approaches and escape routes – helped him and impeded us [the Romans]. On one side were steep hills. Wherever the gradient was gentler, stones were piled into a kind of rampart. And at his front there was a river with no easy crossing. The defences were strongly manned.

The site is still not identified for certain but a number of suggestions have been made. If the river is the Severn, one possibility is slightly west of Caersws in Powys where earthwork remains are supportive. The battle was a disaster for the British. By the familiar use of the *testudo* (see p 23), the Romans easily captured their positions and scattered the enemy into the hills. Caratacus escaped, though his wife and daughter were captured. He fled to Queen Cartimandua of the Brigantes who decided that it was not worth breaking her treaty with Rome by giving him sanctuary, and he was handed over to Ostorius who sent him on to Rome with his family. There, his fame had preceded him, and Romans were curious to see the British chief who had eluded the legions for eight years. Claudius treated him well. After allowing Caratacus and his family to be paraded through the city, at the end of which Caratacus made an impassioned plea that the emperor should make himself famous by sparing them, Claudius released them. It was probably at this time that Caratacus, marvelling at the great buildings of Rome, said to Claudius, 'With such wonderful possessions here, why do you covet our humble British tents?'[11] Why indeed!

Back in Britain, the struggle continued. Ostorius, warmed no doubt by the honorary triumph awarded him by the emperor, soon found that the capture of Caratacus redoubled the resistance of the British, especially the Silures. The army erected more forts and marching camps, among them perhaps Clyro fort in Powys, Clifford fort in Herefordshire and possibly Abergavenny in Gwent.

> Battle followed battle. They were mostly guerilla fights, in woods and bogs. Some were accidental – the results of chance encounters. Others were planned with calculated bravery . . . the Silures were exceptionally stubborn. They were enraged by a much-repeated saying of the Roman commander that they must be utterly exterminated . . . (Tacitus, *Annals* xii, 39).

Tacitus was admitting something of the less attractive side of Roman policy towards rebellious or difficult tribes: a ruthlessness that had earned them undying hatred in the past and would do so again.

Ostorius died suddenly in AD52, worn out by his campaigning – and the Silures were still not overcome. Soon afterwards, in the interval between his death and the arrival of his successor, A. Didius Gallus, a legion, or part of it (possibly Legio XX), was defeated and the Silures began to raid the province almost unchecked. Didius, who had been cavalry commander in AD43 and then gone on to campaign in Moesia (Bulgaria) and in the kingdom of the Bosphorus (Crimea and Black Sea coast), responded vigorously to the deteriorating situation he found. A vexillation fort at Usk in Gwent (later a legionary fortress) can be dated to this period (as probably can others), built to consolidate the western front of the province. At the same time, difficulties began to occur among the Brigantes. Cartimandua fell out with her husband Venutius, who saw himself as a successor to the role of Caratacus. In the ensuing civil war, Cartimandua asked for Roman help. Didius intervened and after a number of engagements restored order, though

Venutius was to trouble the Romans in later years (see pp 71–2). We do not know whether it was Legio IX or Legio XIV that went to her aid, but at this time it seems that the legionary fortress at Wroxeter (*Viroconium*) was begun, for use by Legio XIV, which had been operating in Wales, which points to Legio IX for the Brigantian fracas. The remainder of Didius' term was confined to limited advances over the *limes* when the opportunity arose. Didius retired in AD57 and was succeeded by Q. Veranius, a commander with experience in mountain campaigning. There is a hint from Tacitus (*Annals* xiv, 29) that Veranius planned a major offensive against the British and was confident that he would bring the whole province under control. What did he mean by the whole province? We can probably assume he meant Wales, where the difficulties remained unresolved. But Veranius died within a year, in which his advances and his achievements, if any, are unrecorded. His successor, in AD58, G. Suetonius Paullinus, evidently concurred with the offensive policy, for his first act was to advance into Wales. Suetonius was one of the foremost military commanders of the whole empire, and might well have subdued the entire region but for the interruption of the rebellion of Boudica, queen of the Iceni, which threatened to drive the Roman forces and colonists right out of Britain altogether.

Hitherto, the story of the first fifteen years of Roman occupation in Britain has been a military one. Little is known of the quieter, more domestic picture, but it is clear that the first serious moves towards 'Romanisation' were made. Steps were taken to establish settlements for retired soldiers in the island, to encourage the British to develop their own towns and to build new ones and to link the various centres of Roman military, civilian and commercial organisation by means of roads. The *colonia* at Colchester had been established by Claudius in AD48–9. Ostorius founded the first *municipium* at St Albans and it was called *Verulamium*. It was not settled by veterans but its inhabitants had Latin rights. Other towns began to be developed, such as London, Chelmsford (*Caesaromagus*), Canterbury (*Durovernum Cantiacorum*), Winchester (*Venta Belgarum*), Chichester (*Noviomagus Regnensium*) and Silchester (*Calleva Atrebatum*). The lead mines of the Mendip Hills in Somerset had been opened and ingots were being exported to Europe by sea from Clausentum in Southampton Water.[12] Various stone quarries were being operated very early, notably those at Purbeck in Dorset,[13] Northamptonshire and Bath, and the earliest tile-making industries (one at Silchester) and Roman-sponsored potteries

46

(one at Colchester) had begun. The salt industry was regenerated, notably in Fenland, and a start had been made upon the road network, Watling Street and the Fosse Way being perhaps the largest projects completed or partly completed.

NOTES

1. Dio Cassius, LX, 19 (with liberties taken by the author).
2. Richborough was at the south-east end of the narrow channel, the Wantsum, which separated the Isle of Thanet from Kent.
3. Dio Cassius, lx, 20.
4. Milne, G. (1982) pp 271–6.
5. Dio Cassius, lx, 21.5.
6. Suetonius, *Claudius*, 17.
7. ie, Colchester. Tacitus, *Agricola*, 14.
8. Suetonius, *Vespasian*, iv.
9. Recent excavations at Exeter have shown that the legionary fortress for Legio II was begun in the late 50s AD, which supports the view that Vespasian reached that far between AD43 and 46 and set down some buildings. This is strengthened by the discovery of a permanent fort (cAD55–65) further westwards in Cornwall, at Nanstallon.
10. Vespasian's service in Britain as legion commander is discussed in Eichholz, D. 'How long did Vespasian serve in Britain?', *Britannia* iii (1972) pp 149–63.
11. Dio Cassius, lxi, 33.
12. Dated ingots of the period were found en route from Somerset to Clausentum.
13. Some inscriptions of the period discovered at St Albans and Chichester were in Purbeck marble.

4
RESENTMENT AND REVOLT

We cannot assume that any of the British tribes liked the Roman occupation, whether they were defeated tribes that had terms imposed upon them or were client kingdoms who had some measure of independence. The Iceni had been considerably relieved by the Roman invasion because it removed the pressure of the Catuvellauni along their borders in East Anglia, and this may have encouraged their leaders to submit to Claudius at Colchester in AD43. But within five years they had risen against the occupying forces. The Brigantes had fallen out among themselves in the mid 50s AD over whether to continue 'kowtowing' to Rome or to join the cause being kept alive by the Welsh tribes. There may have been other risings, individually not serious enough to earn even a footnote in the Roman histories. Some kind of disturbance appears to have occurred at South Cadbury in Somerset, in territory of the Dobunni or Durotriges, in about AD60, and it may have been a rising.[1] Clearly, there was a cauldron of grievances simmering throughout the province, and sooner or later some tribes would come together to organise revolt. This ought not to have surprised the Romans – but by all accounts it did.[2] To us, in hindsight, we may wonder more at the secrecy with which the Iceni were able to plan and start the revolt of AD60–1, the support they managed to enlist and the degrees of frightfulness that characterised its course, not only on their side but also on the part of the Romans.

What were the grievances, and why did the trouble begin with the Iceni? 'The Romans did not recognise that there were areas of the known world where they had no legal or moral right to be, and where Roman authority did not run if they could physically enforce it.' Professor Salway's comment aptly encapsulates Rome's colonial policy throughout her imperial history.[3] It meant – no less – that people who were not Romans were not entitled to any consideration whatever, whether they were allies, client kingdoms or conquered peoples. It was quite justifiable to oppress nations, break treaties or exterminate tribes. This is broadcast in their literature. Leaving aside the ethics, the Roman attitude was one that could only make sense if it were backed by limitless military superiority. Of course, there were individual imperial commanders and governors who were more moderate, more humane and more anxious to win the co-operation of the conquered than others, but Romans never gave up the belief that right was always on their side. The British tribal chiefs were perfectly well aware of this attitude, and they knew that they had only two choices: submit and hope for the best, or resist, if necessary to the point of extinction.

Those that did submit were assured of their independence, provided that they collected the tribute, maintained order and raised recruits for Roman armies when asked, but the relationships between these chiefs and Rome were essentially unstable. Undoubtedly, the disarming of the tribes by Ostorius in AD48 seriously undermined any reliance the chiefs had hitherto placed upon the good faith of the Romans. The Icenian king, Prasutagus, probably made sole ruler after the AD48 revolt because he took no part in it, seems to have been co-operative enough with Rome, and he piously hoped that after his death his kingdom would remain free. He even willed a major part of his wealth to the emperor (Nero) to that end. Cogidubnus, king of Sussex, likewise found that his client kingship worked satisfactorily, for Tacitus (*Agricola*, 14) comments upon his continued loyalty to Rome. He may also have been rewarded with the palace at Fishbourne; but these were probably exceptions.

The Trinovantes, whose capital at Camulodunon had been taken from them by Cunobelinus earlier in the century and who had been reduced to servitude, had looked to Claudius to restore their status. He obliged, but a few years later Ostorius attempted to move them to Chelmsford (*Caesaromagus*), first evacuating the early military fort (erected CAD43–4); but it was a centre they did not want. They had other grievances. One was that in the new *colonia* at Colchester they were being pressed into building, among other things, a temple dedicated to Claudius, to subsidise, as it were, a new religion to be imposed upon them. Tacitus (*Annals* xii, 31) records that the colonists enslaved or imprisoned them, appropriating their land and wealth. The Catuvellauni, meanwhile, were divided. Some supported the Roman occupation, and these were largely those allowed to occupy the new *municipium* at St Albans (*Verulamium*) (who were to pay the price of 'collaborating' with Rome during the Boudican revolt). Among the other Catuvellauni it is likely that there was a new generation that was growing up determined to avenge the earlier defeats of their fathers. Among the Brigantes, Venutius may be presumed to have continued his anti-Roman attitude and attempted to stir up discontents among the people still ruled by his wife, Cartimandua. The whole province, meanwhile, had also been groaning under another and universal grievance – Roman taxation.

The system of government imposed upon Britain was the same as in most Roman provinces (see chapter 11). The emperor appointed a governor, or *legatus* (legate), from the ranks of the Senate. In the case of Britain, which had a substantial military establishment (forty thousand or more officers and men) the legate was an ex-consul (though this depended upon the number of legions). He was responsible for military and civil administration, and was commander-in-chief of the imperial armed forces (the navy also played a role in Roman Britain, see chapter 10). The finances of the province, however, were managed by a separate official, the *procurator* or financial secretary, with his own staff. As a rule he was chosen from a lower class of people, the *equites* or businessmen's class (outside the Senate), and he was directly responsible to the emperor. The *legatus* and the *procurator* were expected to keep an eye on the possible excesses of one another, but this often meant that the two reached a mutual understanding to keep out of each other's spheres – the reverse of what was intended.

If the province was directly governed by the *legatus* and the finances controlled by the *procurator*, then the burdens upon the native people were heavy. There were many different taxes: land tax, property tax, customs dues, imposts upon agricultural products and more. The native people also had to contribute to the cost of the 'privilege' of having Roman occupying forces in their land. This was a severe drain upon local resources. Many people found that they had to borrow money and there were always Roman bankers and speculators ready to lend it at high interest rates, for themselves or on behalf of Roman investors living in Italy or elsewhere (see p 54). If the collecting of taxes and the supervision of moneylending were in the hands of a firm and honest *procurator*, then the burdens were just about bearable. But when in about AD58 a new *procurator*, Decianus Catus (or Catus Decianus in some sources) arrived in Britain, the province was to get a taste of Roman extortion at its worst. These were not the only burdens. The *legatus* could conscript natives for the army. He could press people into building and civil engineering projects like roads, canals, bridges, public and private buildings. The Trinovantes were pressed into constructing the temple to Claudius. He could commandeer supplies of corn and other food for the army, and order farmers to deliver cattle and other livestock. If he encouraged natives to improve their towns or obliged them to fortify them, although he might provide free technical advice, he expected the local authorities or private magnates to pay for the work. The British were – and still are – a nation of grumblers, but they had much to grumble about in AD 58.

In AD 58, Gaius Suetonius Paullinus took up his governorship. He was probably in his early sixties, with a long career of military service to his credit. Only a year or two before Aulus Plautius came to Britain, Suetonius was winning his military laurels as governor of Mauretania (now Morocco and Algeria) where he led Roman legions into the Atlas Mountains and successfully reduced the hillsmen who had been harassing Roman lowland settlements for years. He returned to Rome for well-earned honours and was appointed consul. His career between about AD 42 and 58 is unknown, but as Tacitus puts him on a level with Rome's greatest general of the day, Corbulo, and calls him *egregius* (illustrious), we may assume that he distinguished himself again in other areas. Tacitus (*Agricola*, 16) also comments upon Suetonius' undue severity, which he repeats in his *Annals* (xiv, 38). He was probably chosen by Nero because of his experience in the Atlas Mountains (and perhaps other arduous and successful campaigns too), as an appropriate commander to carry out the unfulfilled promises of Veranius in Wales.

It is clear that on his arrival he headed straight for the Midlands where he probably held a major strategic conference with the commanders of Legio XIV and Legio XX and their senior staff, perhaps at the new legionary fortress at Wroxeter (*Viroconium*). The Silures and the Ordovices were still unsubdued and he may have devoted his first year's campaigning against them. In AD 59 he decided to prepare for an all-out assault upon north Wales, including the Isle of Anglesey (Mona). The latter was an obvious target: its rich cornfields provided enough food not only for the islanders but also for most of the north Wales mainland (in later centuries it came to be known as the Granary of Wales). It was known to be a refuge for British leaders and warriors defeated in the campaigns in southern Wales, and it was the centre of druidism, whose priests were (or claimed to be) spiritual leaders of

51

Celtic resistance to Rome and who were taking over the military direction of the struggle. If Suetonius knew that the island was also rich in copper (notably in the Parys mountain area), it provided another motive for invasion.

The invasion of Anglesey required considerable preparation. Suetonius moved up to Chester where a fort had already been erected, probably in the 50s. The site was close to a good natural harbour on the river Dee. A road linking Chester with Wroxeter would have been needed and this may mark the beginning, if not the completion, of the stretch from Wroxeter to Chester [Margary 6a: Watling Street (west) via Whitchurch (*Mediolanum*) where a fort was built contemporaneously (and was later covered by the Roman town)]. Flat-bottomed transports were constructed on the estuary of the Dee. From Chester, Suetonius planned to launch a two-pronged offensive westwards: one along the coastal flats north of the Snowdon mountain range to the Bangor district (as yet no fort has been found there, but there is one at Caerhun in the Conwy valley, of later date) and the other along the southern side of the mountains towards the west coast. When north Wales had been overcome by these encircling movements, he would invade Anglesey, destroy the druids and hope to frighten the remaining unconquered parts of Wales into submission. This was the strategy and it seemed sound. Suetonius appears to have taken for granted that the province below the *limes* was quiet and could be left largely to the native civilian authorities. Legio IX was in East Anglia and the east Midlands, while Legio II was controlling the south-west (based at Exeter). The financial arrangements were in what he believed to be the capable hands of Decianus Catus: it seemed safe to launch the assault into Wales.

The campaign was only partly successful. It took two winters to conquer the tribes and establish strong forts (Tacitus, *Agricola*, 14). However, by early in the year AD61 he was ready to send the army across to Anglesey. The infantry went across the Menai Strait in the transports which had been brought along the north Wales coast, and the cavalry followed. On the shores of the island, the Romans could see the dense throngs of the British. Among them dashed women in black clothes, their hair dishevelled, waving torches and uttering horrible shrieks. Here and there stood druids, lifting their hands to Heaven, pouring forth dreadful curses (Tacitus, *Annals* xiv, 29–30). As the ships ground to a halt on the Anglesey shingle, the legionaries leaped ashore – and for an instant stood still in their tracks, electrified momentarily by the shrieking women. Then, urged on by their centurions, they carried the standards onwards and 'bore down their opponents, enveloping them in the flames of their own torches'. It was all over quickly. Suetonius stationed garrisons throughout the island. He demolished the sacred groves of oak trees in which the druids were wont to practise their hideous rites. In doing so, he is said to have torn out every oak tree from its seat and burned it.[4]

Suetonius and his senior officers were congratulating one another and the troops were celebrating their victory when despatch riders on fast horses arrived at the commander-in-chief's tent, bringing the most shattering news. The Iceni, under the leadership of their fiery queen, Boudica (Prasutagus' widow), had broken into revolt, other tribes had joined them and a vast throng of a hundred thousand angry British warriors and their wives and children had tramped down the eastern side of East Anglia to Colchester. There, in a vigorous assault of two days, they had taken the city, burned it, destroyed the great proportion of its buildings, including the new temple of Claudius, and butchered the entire population of some twenty thousand settlers and officials. Flushed with their grisly success, the host had started to move on down the road to Chelmsford, heading for London or St Albans. The message did not say which.

There was one crumb of comfort in the dismal report. News had got through to Q. Petillius Cerialis, commander of Legio IX, who had two vexillations plus auxiliary cavalry at Longthorpe fort (but where were the other vexillations?). Petillius set out at once with these troops towards Essex to intercept the host, but the messenger was not to know that this force had already been severely defeated somewhere in Cambridgeshire by a detachment sent out by Boudica, and that Petillius himself had barely escaped with his life.

What had happened? Suetonius might well ask, for the revolt took him completely by surprise. While in Wales, regular intelligence reports will have been keeping him informed of the situation throughout the rest of the province. Roman military and political intelligence was the most highly organised the world had seen. As a rule there was not much about a province that was kept from its governor; quite often the governor would hear of revolts even before they had moved beyond the planning stage. But Boudica's rebellion had achieved one of its major objectives before the governor had heard a thing. Today it seems unbelievable that she could have marshalled and moved a force of a hundred thousand (or even half that number if the report is exaggerated) down the road from near Norwich towards Colchester without attracting the attention of spies.

The grievances already outlined were cause enough for rebellion, but it took the rapacity and brutality of the new procurator to ignite the spark that set it off. Decianus Catus is one of those characters who flit briefly across the stage of world history, leaving behind only a bad name. It was given him by his countryman, Tacitus, who blamed him for the revolt: 'His rapacity drove the province to war' (*Annals* xiv, 32). Rapacity among procurators had in republican days been common until Julius Caesar, in his first consulship and again when he was dictator, introduced measures to curb it. On the whole, the provincial procurators under the first emperors were more honest and careful, but it is possible that the criminal extravagances of Gaius had so depleted the imperial revenues that some pressure was put on the provinces to yield greater annual returns, which would have unfortunate results where procurators were already inclined to harshness. We must assume that Decianus Catus began his term in AD57-8 in this brutal and greedy vein, and if so, it was inexcusable for Suetonius not to attempt to curb his excesses. There must have been appeals to the governor when Decianus Catus took it on himself to proclaim that subsidies paid by Claudius to friendly British notables at the time of the settlement of AD43, not intended to be repayable, were now to be paid back after all. What action did he take when the philosopher, Seneca, tutor and advisor to Nero, who had loaned forty million sesterces (many thousands of pounds) to British people, now suddenly called in the loans through agents who became very unpleasant indeed when they were not repaid promptly?[5] Neither Tacitus nor Dio Cassius tells us which of the tribes endured these injustices. Matters came to a head when the Icenian king, Prasutagus, died in AD60.

Everyone in the Icenian kingdom knew that Prasutagus had made the emperor joint heir to his personal fortune and that on his death the client kingdom would come under direct Roman rule. What they did not expect was that the procurator would immediately send in gangs of slaves to seize property and money from the Iceni or that troops of soldiers would tramp through the towns and villages enforcing martial law before taking over the kingdom. A posse arrived at the palace of Prasutagus, which may have been near Norwich, and made for Boudica who was with her two daughters, perhaps still in mourning.[6] One of the slaves insulted her or made advances to one of the girls, which Boudica will have risen to. She was seized and flogged, while some of the soldiery pursued the daughters and raped them. It was an appalling outrage, and news of it spread like wildfire throughout East Anglia. It was the signal for revolt, and everywhere the tribes rose, the warriors took up their weapons and the charioteers got ready their vehicles, all putting themselves under the leadership of the affronted queen. This fiery widow was described by Dio Cassius as tall in stature, terrifying to look at, fierce in the glance of her eye and harsh of voice. A great mass of tawny hair tumbled down to her hips. Around her neck glistened a large golden necklace, and she wore a tunic of many colours over which a thick mantle was clasped with a brooch.[7] This was her invariable attire; and, as Tacitus explained (*Agricola*, 16), the British were quite accustomed to women leaders.

Marshalling an army of many thousands probably on the plains below Caistor St Edmund, Boudica harangued them in a fiery speech variously recorded by the historians, in which she reassured them that they outnumbered several times anything the Romans could send against them. They should remember their ancestors and not be deflected by any initial defeat for they could come back again and again until victory was won. They should take advantage of the absence of the governor in Wales, over two hundred and fifty miles away, and it would take him two weeks or more to bring back his army to East

Iron Age gold alloy torc found at Bawsey in Norfolk. This could be the kind of torc worn by Boudica (*Norfolk Museums Service*)

Anglia. The meeting cheered and clapped. The assembly must have been an impressive sight. The leaders were wearing their finest clothes. Celtic battle dress has been described by Diodorus Siculus: the shields were as tall as the men, beautifully decorated to each individual's favoured style, some with embossed bronze animal motifs; their bronze helmets were crested with animal figures and sported horns.[8] They may also have worn breast plates of a type of chain mail.

Then – forward! The host began to move, slowly and ponderously, in ramshackle order, for the British did not have the discipline and marching drill of the Roman legionaries. Probably the host made no more than five to six miles a day, perhaps much less, but on the way more thousands of angry tribesmen, Trinovantes, Catuvellauni, Coritani maybe, joined the column as it headed for its first target – Colchester, *colonia* of twenty thousand Roman settlers and their families, hated by the Trinovantes for their arrogance. From Caistor to Colchester there was a route, possibly finished by AD60 (Margary 3d and 3c) about fifty-three miles long, and the host may have followed this. It is nearly straight and it makes sense. The host pressed on and camped on rising ground just outside the *colonia* which, denuded a few years earlier of Legio XX, lay undefended, its walls having been pulled down.[9]

The settlers were thoroughly alarmed at the sight of the host, now swelled to a hundred thousand or more. Though there was a small garrison, they were quite unprepared. They sent urgently to Decianus Catus in London for reinforcements, but he could only spare two hundred men and they were not properly equipped. Meanwhile, some of the British in the town began falsely reassuring the settlers: there was nothing to worry about. Tacitus described a 'fifth column'. Then, as the colonists' leaders considered what to do, advance units of Boudica's host appeared on the outskirts.

News of the great march had reached Petillius Cerialis, commander of Legio IX who was at Longthorpe with a vexillation or two. He responded at once, mustering about two thousand men, infantry and cavalry, and started out for Colchester, probably along the road from Chesterton to Godmanchester (Margary 2b) which was part of Ermine Street, intending to fork left on Margary 24 towards

Tombstone of the Moesian auxiliary cavalryman, Longinus Sdapezematygus, now at Colchester Museum. It was damaged in the sack of Camulodunon by Boudica in AD61

Part of the wall of a house in the *colonia* Camulodunon (Colchester), destroyed in the Boudican assault of 61.

Colchester, but he was ambushed north of Godmanchester (where he would perhaps have gathered up more troops stationed at the Claudian fort) by forces sent by Boudica to check him.[10] A fierce battle ensued and his infantry was cut to pieces, but he escaped with the cavalry and headed back to the safety of Longthorpe (why not to the Godmanchester fort?). Colchester was completely isolated. Boudica could do what she liked with it – and she destroyed it.

When the host entered the town, the defenders fled to the stone temple of Claudius – the only building strong enough to withstand destruction by fire – and made ready to fight it out. The thousands of unarmed men and their families who had not been evacuated were left to shift for themselves – and they did not get far. The host set fire to the wooden buildings and the town was burned to the ground, evidence for which has been revealed in excavation, notably in the present High Street, in the form of burnt clay, sherds, melted glass, shattered oil lamps and broken shop goods (all in Colchester Museum). The British besieged the temple and took it in two days. Colchester had fallen. No one was spared, neither child nor old person, cripple nor pregnant woman. Those killed on the spot were fortunate. Those taken were subjected to every kind of outrage. 'All this they did to the accompaniment of sacrifices, banquets and wanton behaviour' wrote Dio Cassius after describing some of the more revolting atrocities.[11] The destruction seems to have been purposeful. A tombstone of a junior Roman officer, bearing a relief sculpture of him on horseback trampling upon a fallen Briton, was smashed. The officer's face was destroyed, but the face of the Briton was left untouched.

News of the fall of Colchester reached Decianus Catus in London. By now he had gauged the depth of feeling against Rome in general and himself in particular. He must have known that Boudica would head for London to exact revenge and, not relishing the idea of the reprisals he had heard about, he bolted and took ship to Gaul. Boudica, meanwhile, had the initiative still. Both London and St Albans lay open, and she moved against the former first. London was not yet a *colonia* or a *municipium* (see chapter 12) but it was the biggest town in Britain, with prospering commerce and industry in which Romans and natives shared. Its position, tucked away among the serpentine coils of the Thames, gave it a measure of natural defence, but there is no evidence of fortification, and there do not appear to have been any forces stationed there. The inhabitants knew they would be utterly at Boudica's mercy unless reinforcements arrived.

During the assault on Colchester, or immediately afterwards, messengers will have set out to inform Suetonius in north Wales. In the Roman world, couriers could cover fifty, even sixty, miles in a day, and it would have taken under a week to travel to the Menai Strait, a distance of some two hundred and fifty miles, going much of the way along Watling Street.[12] They will have known that Boudica planned to march on London and St Albans, but they may not have known which first. Suetonius had to take his choice, and he sensed that she would go for London because of its wealth and its strategic position, with harbours and bridges. He set out immediately with his cavalry down Watling Street, expecting to cover the two hundred and fifty miles in four or five days (cavalry might be expected to cover about fifty miles a day), ordering Legio XIV and part of Legio XX and auxiliaries to follow at once, also down Watling Street. It would take them ten days or so. He also sent orders to Legio II at Exeter, with vexillations at Kingsholm and/or Cirencester (?), to join the other two legions in the Midlands, either at Wall or at High Cross (*Venonae*) where Watling Street intersects with the Fosse Way. By the time Legio XIV and Legio XX entered the Midlands in the first week, he would have got to London and sized up the position. Suetonius reached London before Boudica, expecting to find other vexillations had got there, and he considered defending it. But there were no troops and he reluctantly decided to leave the inhabitants to their fate, offering to take along with him those who wanted to follow.

Boudica reached London, probably a fortnight after the fall of Colchester and only a day or two after Suetonius had left, and fell upon the town at the east end, probably somewhere near the present Tower of London, heading (as Tacitus put it) for those places where the loot was richest. No quarter was given: no prisoners were taken. The whole population was butchered, as at Colchester: throats were cut, people were hanged, crucified or burned. Excavations at Spitalfields revealed a heap of skeletons that it has been suggested could represent a cartload or two of victims of the sack.[13] The orgy of bloodshed at the two towns reveals the depth of hatred felt by the British, and the momentum of vengeance was carried along relentlessly by a people weighed down with a sorry mixture of memories of the past, real and imagined grievances, fears for the future and a taste for blood and loot. Perhaps Boudica herself was revolted by the worst excesses but was powerless to stop them. St Albans was soon to endure the same fate, with vengeance particularly aimed at those of the Catuvellauni who were 'collaborating' with the oppressors. In a terrible orgy of destruction, the work of years of Roman-inspired building was reduced to ashes. Evidence of the thoroughness of this sack was found by Professor Frere in a remarkable series of excavations.

Looking north west along Watling Street near Copston Magna, Warwickshire (*Cambridge University Collection*)

Boudica's sack of St Albans was a major strategic blunder. It wasted valuable military time, allowing Suetonius several days to catch up with his legions coming down from Wales, accumulate food for a prolonged campaign and concentrate his forces, with their superior mobility and speed, so that they could choose where and when to fight. A good general would have followed Suetonius (at a discreet distance) until he could manoeuvre him into an unfavourable position and compel him to fight.[14] As it was, Suetonius hastened up Watling Street, sending fast riders ahead to stop the legions coming any further south than High Cross (*Venonae*) where they should expect to meet up with Legio II. There were factors operating in his favour at last. Reports of the destruction of St Albans, which involved the murder of many Catuvellaunian Britons as well as Romans, were probably not well received by the Coritani, the Brigantes or other Catuvellauni. None of the authorities suggests that all Britain was behind Boudica. Suetonius was drawing Boudica and her host into hillier countryside which many of them did not know, which would slow them down and where there had in recent years been a lot of Roman activity, fort building, road construction and so forth. And as soon as he joined up with the legions, he would have at his disposal over ten thousand men of the best army in the world. Even at odds of ten to one against – a ratio that seldom daunted good Roman generals – he would have more than a sporting chance.

When he took over the forces at High Cross, or at Wall, he sent out scouts to find possible sites for battle. He was annoyed to find that Legio II had failed to arrive. A message from the temporary commander, Postumus Poenius, at Exeter, said it was not safe to leave. But Suetonius could still muster ten thousand men. Tacitus and Dio Cassius described the battle and the terrain in which it was fought but, maddeningly for us, did not identify the site. We may make a constructive guess. Clearly it was somewhere in the neighbourhood of Watling Street, and surely between Wall and High Cross. Graham Webster[15] has put forward a very acceptable case which it would be churlish to question – certainly until someone else comes up with a more convincing alternative.

Tacitus (*Annals* XII, 34) wrote that Suetonius chose a position in a defile with a wood behind. Webster considered the terrain between Wall and Mancetter (*Manduessedum*), along and closely on either side of the A5 (Watling Street), particularly the stretches of rising ground. At Mancetter, near Atherstone, a ridge of quartzite rock, the object of

What could have been the battle area in the confrontation between Suetonius Paullinus and Boudica in 61. This is taken from a ridge south of Watling Street at Mancetter. There is a wood behind the photographer (see Tacitus's description, p 62)

extensive quarrying over the past two centuries, runs north-westwards along the south side of the small river Anker, meeting Watling Street. Although the quarrying has clearly altered the shape of the ridge, Webster visualises several possible defiles there that satisfy Tacitus's brief description and opts for one which overlooks the site of the Roman fort beside the river at Mancetter, first identified in 1955–6 and confirmed in later, more detailed excavation. Taking this to be the site, the forces of Suetonius could have been drawn up on the northern slopes of the ridge, with the protecting woods behind, looking down on the plain below through which Watling Street runs and where to the left it crosses the river. And in the plain, Boudica's host could have been massed. I have walked this terrain with Webster's plan and it makes good sense.

When Suetonius finally determined his dispositions, he drew up his army in an arc before the wood. In the centre were three formations of legionaries, one behind the other. On either side were two detachments of auxiliaries (foot soldiers in this case) and on the wings were the cavalry. They looked down the slopes into the plains below where Boudica was ordering the host to prepare for battle. Hundreds of chariots were being driven about the available space by drivers anxious to whip up enthusiasm among the Britons. Behind them, women and children were hustling waggons and carts into long lines, end-to-end across the lower part of the plain, effectively sealing off any escape route. Tacitus says they had come to watch the fighting, confident that their men would win the day. No one on the British side seems to have considered the bad position of their forces. No one grasped that when the signal for attack was sounded they would be charging uphill and for quite a distance. Tacitus (*Annals* xiv, 36) reports a heroic speech Boudica made to her huge army. Suetonius addressed his men more tersely: 'Keep together, throw your javelins accurately, knock the enemy over with your shield-bosses and finish them off with your swords. Forget about booty. Win the victory in the field – and you'll get all you want afterwards!'

The signals were given and the throng moved forwards, not in orderly ranks but in a mob-like rush. The Romans remained still and quiet. The British accelerated, but soon found it hard going uphill. The Romans waited till they judged the enemy frontlines were within accurate javelin throw. Then Suetonius ordered the javelins to be hurled and in unison the legionaries lunged forward, loosing a concerted and deadly hail of sharp, iron weaponry. The British were checked. At that moment, the legionaries pulled out their swords and charged downhill, well disciplined and in wedge formations. Backed by auxiliaries behind and on the flanks, they cut a series of huge holes in the dense throng. Up came the swords, jabbing at close quarters like daggers, with murderous effect. The Celtic long swords were no use in fighting like this. The British squirmed and turned in their tracks to avoid them, getting in each other's way, adding to the confusion that was spreading everywhere in their ranks. Then the Roman cavalry charged, in steady formation downhill, diagonally, one squadron to left, the other to the right, at the outer ends. They broke the British army that day, and as the luckless natives turned to flee, they found their outlets blocked by the strings of waggons. Hemmed in on all sides, they were cut down.

It was all over by nightfall. Suetonius, and his solid military machine, which functioned with precision, had turned a desperate crisis in which the whole province tottered on the point of collapse into a remarkable military triumph. Tacitus quotes almost eighty thousand Britons killed, which supports the size of Boudica's army being at least a hundred thousand strong. It is an enormous number of dead by any standards, and probably represented about one-tenth of the total Celtic population of Britain at the time. The Romans lost only four hundred. If these figures are correct, the victory was indeed 'glorious and comparable with bygone triumphs' (Tacitus, *Annals* xiv, 37). When he heard the news, Postumus Poenius at Exeter fell on his sword. What else could he do? – he had cheated his legionaries of the chance to take part.

As for Boudica, there would be no journey to Rome, no parade through the streets, no pardon at the end. No Roman could overlook the butcheries by her host. She fled from the battlefield back to her lands in Norfolk. Then *'Boudica vitam veneno finivit'* (Boudica put an end to her life with poison). With this short sentence, Tacitus abruptly makes his last reference to the great queen; his ensuing paragraphs deal with the phase of the career of Suetonius, clearing up after the revolt. He is no longer interested in the woman who had for a few months produced the greatest threat to the Roman empire since the disaster to Varus and his legions in the Teutoberger Forest in AD9. But Rome had triumphed once again, and Tacitus was a Roman. Dio Cassius reported that Boudica was taken ill and died – his way, perhaps of indicating poison.[16] We can imagine the redoubtable lady recognising that she had lost and could expect no mercy, taking poison, perhaps in a last mug of good British beer, which she drank toasting the gods who had watched over her in her gallant stand for Celtic freedom until they had decreed she had gone too far.

NOTES
1. Evidence of a massacre at the south-west gate of the hillfort at South Cadbury at this period has been adduced, *see* Branigan, K. and Fowler, P. J. (1976) pp 37–40.
2. Tacitus, *Annals* xiv, 30 ('sudden rebellion in the province'); *Agricola*, xiv ('Suetonius exposed himself to a stab in the back'); Dio Cassius, lxii, 1 ('while this . . . was going on at Rome, a terrible disaster occurred in Britain').
3. Salway, P. (1981) p 67.
4. Today it is practically impossible to find an oak tree in Anglesey.
5. Dio Cassius, lxii, 2.1.
6. Prasutagus' palace was probably near Caistor St Edmund, a mile south of Norwich, where after the revolt, a *civitas* capital (*Venta Icenorum*) was founded; but see also my note 4 on p 193 concerning A. T. Gregory's find at Thetford.
7. Dio Cassius, lxii, 2.
8. Diodorus Siculus, *Historical Library* v, 21,5.
9. Crummy, P. 'Colchester: the Roman fortress and the development of the *colonia*', *Britannia* viii (1977) p 65.
10. It is not certain that Petillius was defeated on this stretch of route but it is a reasonable assumption.
11. Dio Cassius, lxii, 7.2.
12. Casson, L. (1974) pp 188–9.
13. Collingwood, R. G. and Myres, J. N. L. (1937) p 168.

14. Whether Suetonius left London and went straight to the Midlands along Watling Street or took a detour to the west of London, then via Silchester and turned right to meet Watling Street at Towcester or elsewhere is not resolved. But Boudica could have followed him along either route.
15. Webster, G. *Boudica* (1978) pp 96–8, 111–12.
16. Dio Cassius, lxii, 12.6.

5

CAMPAIGNS IN WALES AND NORTH BRITAIN

The immediate aftermath of the rebellion was terrible, and it left scars upon the province which took a long time to heal. Suetonius took the sternest measures against the survivors: their lands were ravaged with fire and the sword. Tacitus (*Annals* xiv, 38) adds that the resulting misery was compounded by famine. Farming in East Anglia had come to a standstill during the rebellion; Icenian fields had been left unsown. Despite their early successes, the rebels failed to capture Roman foodstocks to make up the deficiency; and when the revolt was over, there was nothing to harvest.

Meanwhile, the military were everywhere. New forts were begun in the rebel areas, from which to enforce martial law. Among these we can probably include Ashill and Scole in Norfolk, Coddenham and Ixworth in Suffolk, Great Chesterford and Kelvedon in Essex and Water Newton in Cambridgeshire. Existing garrisons were strengthened out of reinforcements from Europe. Two thousand legionaries arrived to replenish Legio IX at Longthorpe and eight auxiliary units and a thousand cavalry, all from Germany, were installed probably at the new fort at Great Chesterford.[1] There is some evidence that he rattled the sword of Rome at tribes who had not been involved in the rebellion. A new fort was erected at Baginton in Warwickshire and existing forts at Great Casterton in Leicestershire and Dorchester in Oxfordshire were strengthened.

Rebellion or not, the province was expected to continue turning in revenue for the Imperial treasury, and sometime soon after the battle near Mancetter, the Roman government sent a replacement for the obnoxious Decianus Catus. He was not a Roman, but a Gaul, C. Julius Alpinus Classicianus, a noble from the territory around Trier which enjoyed Roman provincial government. Classicianus will have arrived in Britain aware of the extortions of Decianus Catus and

Reconstructed eastern gateway at The Lunt fort, Baginton, near Coventry

their consequences, and will have been well equipped to handle the sensitive situation. The received view of some historians of Roman Britain is that Classicianus was a generous and moderate official who reacted strongly against the severity of Suetonius. One even believed that Classicianus 'stood up to Suetonius in his hour of victory as the champion of the British people'.[2] We should be careful before accepting this view without qualification, not least because of Tacitus' comment that Classicianus let his personal dislike of the governor override the interests of the province. Classicianus circulated his view that the British should take comfort from the expectation that a new governor would soon be sent from Rome who would treat the rebels more leniently. While spreading this assurance, he wrote to Rome advocating Suetonius' recall. Nero sent one of his ministers, the ex-slave Polyclitus, to Britain to head an enquiry, hoping (as Tacitus reports) that Polyclitus would be able to reconcile Suetonius and Classicianus as well as help to pacify the British tribes. What Polyclitus reported we do not know, but soon after his return to Rome an excuse was found to recall Suetonius, though he was not disgraced.[3] He was replaced by P. Petronius Turpilianus who had just completed his year as consul at Rome for AD61. It was hoped that he would be 'more merciful'. It appears that he was, and when he returned to Rome in AD63, the island was quiet. The next governor was M. Trebellius Maximus, who held office for almost six years.

These post-rebellion years were less sensational. Further military consolidations were made, more cautiously and probably meeting with less resistance. Forts were built in the West Country, at Nanstallon in Cornwall, at Martinhoe on the north Devon coast (a fortlet), and at Gloucester (a fortress); in the east, a fortress for Legio IX was built at Lincoln, possibly to replace an earlier, smaller military establishment north of the river Witham. The legionary fortress at Usk in Gwent was enlarged to include a supply base in case of renewed hostilities in Wales. It could be that Broxtowe in Nottinghamshire, Littlechester in Derbyshire and Templeborough in South Yorkshire were all raised in these years to help prop the weakening client kingdom of the Brigantes, still ruled by Cartimandua. There were also some significant advances in civilian and domestic administration. The road system was extended. The rebuilding of the *colonia* at Colchester and

A model of the Temple of Claudius at Camulodunon (Colchester)

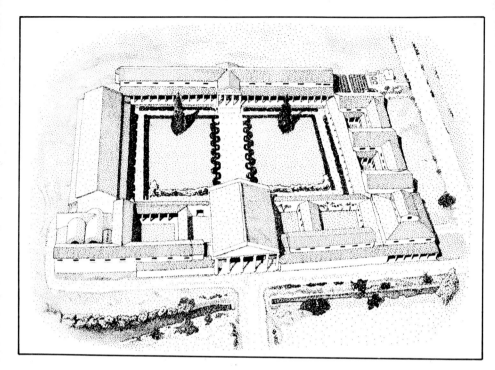

Reconstruction of Fishbourne Palace, near Chichester

the *vicus* at London, both wrecked by Boudica, was started, though we have little firm evidence of progress. The procurator Classicianus is thought to have had his headquarters in London; certainly he died and was buried there.[4] His presence must have been a spur to reconstruction. The destroyed temple that had been dedicated to Claudius at Colchester was rebuilt, or at all events begun again, in these years. And the first villas in the countryside began to be constructed. At Lockleys, near Welwyn in Hertfordshire, a small range of four rooms (one end room divided into two to make five), with a veranda outside added soon afterwards, was built in the mid 60s and later extended in the second and fourth centuries AD. Three larger villas of this period were Angmering in West Sussex, and Eccles and Wingham in Kent; and the first buildings of a major residence went up at Fishbourne in West Sussex, later to become the site of the famous palace of Cogidubnus, so brilliantly excavated by Barry Cunliffe in the late 1960s and early 1970s.

The province was having a tranquil time. Then, in AD68, the empire was rocked by a series of internal crises, the result of the sustained tyranny and misrule of the emperor Nero. Legions in Gaul and Spain rebelled, the infection spread to the Praetorian Guard in Rome, and Nero fled into the countryside where he committed suicide. The legions elected the governor of Spain, Ser. Sulpicius Galba, as emperor, but a few months later he fell foul of the Praetorian Guard in Rome who killed him. He was followed by M. Salvius Otho who, after three months, committed suicide when he heard that Aulus Vitellius, one of Galba's commanders, was marching upon Rome at the head of the legions from Germany. Vitellius was installed in Rome, but gave himself up to vicious living, neglected the state and thus encouraged his own eventual deposition. The troops serving in the East under the command of T. Flavius Vespasianus, whom we have met earlier in his career sweeping through the southern part of Britain, AD43–6, chose him as emperor. It was a popular choice, and in Italy the army deserted Vitellius. He was put to death, and at the end of AD69, Vespasian assumed the imperial purple. The Year of the Four Emperors was over.

In Britain, the legionaries were divided. They were also bored with inactivity or with road building – doubtless even with the climate! They blamed the governor, and under Roscius Coelius, commander of Legio XX, they mutinied. Trebellius was driven out of the island and fled to the doubtful sanctuary of the court of Vitellius in Rome, who replaced Trebellius by despatching to Britain a high-ranking officer who had served under Corbulo. This was Vettius Bolanus, whom Tacitus considered a 'decent' man. We know a little of his achievement in Britain.[5] It was a time of great uncertainty. Legio XIV had been withdrawn by Nero in AD66 for use in the East. Vitellius, contending for the imperial throne, had sent for eight thousand more legionaries from Britain to support his war with Otho. It was a dangerous depletion of the occupation forces; but once he had become emperor, Vitellius sent Legio XIV back to Britain – just in time to assist Vettius in a crisis in the Brigantian kingdom where Cartimandua, the veteran queen, had finally broken with her husband, Venutius, who headed the anti-Roman faction. During the mutiny among the legionaries in Trebellius's term, Venutius took advantage of Roman weakness to rise against his former wife, and this time he was aided by tribes from southern Scotland. Cartimandua appealed to Vettius, but we cannot be sure to what extent he was able to help. Tacitus writes Vettius off as 'paralysed in the face of the foe', but Statius talks about successes against the Caledonians, of building forts and of winning trophies from British chiefs.[6] What does all this lead to?

71

A number of forts in Brigantian territory, and in the land of their neighbours, the Parisi (roughly, the triangle Scarborough–York–Hull), may date from this time: Rossington, near Doncaster, Brough-on·Humber, near Hull, a vexillation fortress at Malton, near Pickering, and the earliest evidence of a military establishment at York itself, later to become the fortress for Legio IX. Cartimandua was helped by Vettius: she was rescued from an unspecified fate. Venutius was ultimately defeated after several battles, but in how many by Vettius and how many by his successor, we do not yet know – but it was the end of the semi-independence of the Brigantes.

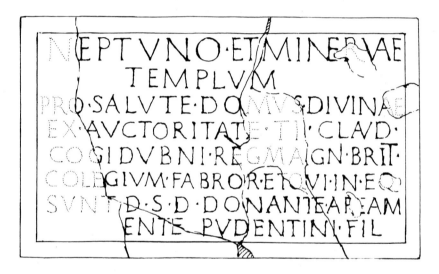

This is an inscription on a slab of Purbeck marble reassembled from fragments found at Chichester in 1723. Suggestions as to what were the missing words on the left side and in parts of the right side have been made by various scholars over the years, the latest by J. E. Bogaers in 1979 (*Britannia* x, pp 243–54). The stone records the dedication of a temple to Neptune and Minerva by a local blacksmiths' guild for the health of the imperial family. Two lines include the wording (translated) '. . . by the authority of Tiberius Claudius Cogidubnus, great king in Britain . . .'.

In *Agricola* xiv, Tacitus wrote that, 'certain states were presented to King Cogidumnus who maintained unswerving loyalty down to our times'. If this Cogidumnus and Cogidubnus are the same, we have a local chief, British or perhaps Gaulish (like Commius?), appointed by Claudius to head a client kingdom in the south, perhaps the Atrebatic kingdom of Verica, with a headquarters near Chichester which is close to Fishbourne where a palace was built after AD75 upon the remains of an early Roman military depot, of 43–4. Tacitus was writing in the 90s. If Cogidubnus lived into the time of Agricola's governorship (78–84), Fishbourne could have been given him by a Roman administration grateful for long service as a loyal client king

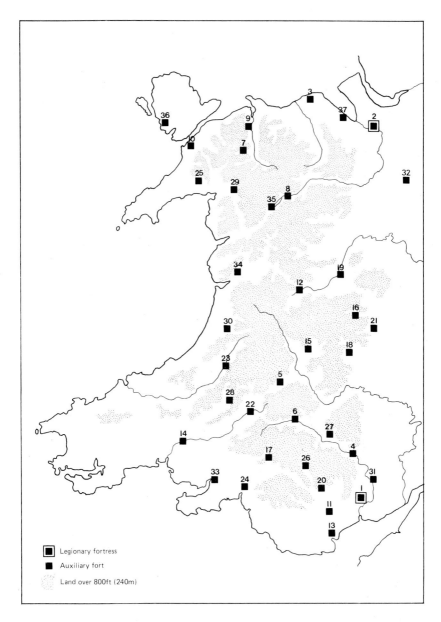

Distribution of Military Sites in Wales in the second half of first century AD
1 Caerleon (legionary fortress) 2 Chester (legionary fortress) 3 Prestatyn 4
Abergavenny 5 Beulah 6 Brecon Gaer 7 Bryn-y-Gefeiliau 8 Caer Gai 9 Caerhun
10 Caernarfon 11 Caerphilly 12 Caersws 13 Cardiff 14 Carmarthen 15 Castell Collen
16 Clun 17 Coelbren 18 Discoed 19 Forden Gaer 20 Gelligaer 21 Leintwardine
22 Llandovery 23 Llanio 24 Neath 25 Pen Llysten 26 Pen-y-Darren 27 Pen-y-gaer
28 Pumpsaint 29 Tomen-y-Mur 30 Trawscoed 31 Usk 32 Whitchurch 33 Loughor
34 Pennal 35 Brithdir 36 Aberffraw 37 Fflint

Vettius' term ended in AD71. Whatever else he had done, he had kept the Roman army intact and had not lost ground. His successor, Petillius Cerialis (whom we have met before during Boudica's revolt) was to start out with advantages not available to Vettius. The empire had been stabilised and at the helm was the tough, popular, astute soldier-statesman, Vespasian, now firmly in control. Petillius was related to the emperor. Dynamic, bold and imaginative, he was the right man to carry out the new policy for Britain, which was to advance northwards and establish a new frontier, ahead of the Brigantian kingdom.[7] He was given an extra legion, Legio II *Adiutrix*, which he stationed at Lincoln, moving Legio IX (his legion during the Boudican revolt) on to York where in due course a 50 acre (20ha) fortress was constructed.

Petillius was governor for three years. In that time it is likely that most of Yorkshire and Lancashire were overcome. Mortimer Wheeler, who excavated a small part of the huge 730 acre (296ha) earthwork enclosure at Stanwick, near Scotch Corner, believed it was the head-quarters of Venutius, where he made his last stand against the Romans.[8] There is some doubt about the actual site of the battle. Petillius may have operated in fanwise expeditions from a base at York, perhaps using Malton and maybe Manchester, too. It has to be remembered that he had also to contend with hostilities in Wales, for the Silures and their allies were still not crushed despite the major victories of Suetonius more than a decade before, and it is possible that Legio II *Augusta*, based no longer at Exeter but now at the new fortress at Gloucester (close to the earlier fortress at Kingsholm), was fully engaged on the Welsh front.

Petillius was succeeded in AD74 by Sextus Julius Frontinus. Tacitus (*Agricola*, xvii) admired him as a great man (*vir magnus*) and credited him with the final subjection of the Silures, a strong and warlike people, beating them in some difficult (ie mountainous) countryside, which could mean the Brecon Beacons, the Black Mountains or the Cambrian Mountains. He is credited today with starting the 60 acre (24ha) legionary fortress at Chester.[9] Frontinus was also responsible for beginning or completing a network of forts and fortlets in Wales, associated with a spreading road system as part of his campaign, which it was planned should once and for all keep down all the Welsh tribes.

South gate at Brecon Gaer fort, Powys (*Janet & Colin Bord*)

The military effort was launched by road, across country and also by seaborne invasion at landings along the south coast, probably at good anchorages at Cardiff, Neath, Barry and Carmarthen. Among the inland forts were Abergavenny (Gwent, the second at this location), Brecon Gaer (Powys), Caerphilly (Mid Glamorgan), Caersws (Powys, second), Castell Collen (Powys), Coelbren Gaer (West Glamorgan), Forden Gaer (Powys), Gelligaer (Mid Glamorgan, first), Llandovery (Dyfed, first), Llanio (Dyfed), Loughor (West Glamorgan), Pen-y-Darren (Mid Glamorgan), Pen-y-Gaer (Powys), Pumpsaint (Dyfed), Trawscoed (Dyfed) and perhaps Pennal (Gwynedd) and Tomen-y-Mur (Gwynedd), though these could be ascribed to Agricola. Frontinus used three of the four British legions, certainly detachments from them, namely, Legio II *Augusta*, Legio II *Adiutrix*, which he moved from Lincoln to Chester, and Legio XX which was still based at Wroxeter. With these resources he must have achieved the conquest of all but the northern part of Wales, that is, the Silures and part of the Ordovices, leaving the last resistance in Gwynedd and Anglesey to be crushed by his successor.

Frontinus also embarked upon several civilian projects in the province. It is in this decade that we see the beginnings of a leap forward in the foundation and development in Britain of towns of two kinds (see chapter 12). These were the *coloniae*, specially built for veteran Roman legionaries and populated by Roman citizens, which were self-governing, run by a council, or *ordo*, and had a city judicial system based upon that functioning in Rome, and the tribal capital towns which either were already tribal capitals (before 'Romanisation') or which were established by tribes (*civitates*) with Roman encouragement and assistance as administrative centres. These were partly self-governing, with magistrates and councils elected from among the native higher classes. The populations were not Roman citizens. We have already mentioned the foundation of the first *colonia* at Colchester. Among the earliest capitals established with Roman help were Cirencester, St Albans (*Verulamium*), Canterbury, Caistor St Edmund (*Venta Icenorum*, Norfolk) and Caerwent (Gwent). Frontinus probably founded Caerwent and Caistor, and almost certainly initiated the *fora* at St Albans (*Verulamium*) and Cirencester. In later years Frontinus was to be Commissioner of Water Works at Rome. He was to write *De Aquis Urbis Romae* (The Water Supply of Rome), two volumes based on his experience as an administrator of civilian amenities, some of which will have been gained in these early

British capitals with which he is associated. His works in Britain were to be resumed and expanded by his successor, Gnaeus Julius Agricola, who took up his appointment in AD78 or (according to some authorities) 77.

The theme of Tacitus' biography of Agricola is essentially how the conquest and settlement of Britain were achieved in a succession of governorships, culminating in the glorious term of office of his father-in-law, Agricola. To heighten the build-up to the climax of what he sees as Agricola's achievement, Tacitus belittles his predecessors one by one, or at best describes them as 'a distinguished' or 'a sound' commander, in a single terse phrase. Only Frontinus receives anything like a just summary. We must steer carefully through this paean about Agricola as it is almost the only literary source we have for the years 78–84 in Britain. Indeed, the only other source comprises two very short paragraphs in Dio Cassius.[10] Archaeology provides substantial back-up to Agricola's activities in northern England and Scotland, but the measure of his success has to be based upon interpretation of the archaeology which is largely limited to the disposition of forts and fortlets and interconnecting road links. Nor should we be influenced by the fact that Agricola's term lasted six years, twice the average term, for that of Trebellius (AD63–9) had been as long.

Agricola was certainly well qualified for the office of governor of Britain, for he had served in the province for two periods, under two earlier governors, as tribune under Suetonius and as commander of Legio XX under Petillius Cerialis. In AD74 he was governor of Aquitania, and in that year was selected for Britain. Leaving aside the effusive descriptions by Tacitus of Agricola's qualities (who, indeed, could have wished for a better son-in-law than the historian turned out to be!), we are probably right in seeing Agricola as a competent and industrious general, a good leader of men, fair, honest and humane, possessing the sort of qualities Rome expected (though did not always get) in her commanders. Promotion was not always solely upon merit: family, wealth, influence and luck played their part. Agricola arrived in Britain to take over from Frontinus (a predecessor who was at least equally competent), who had nearly completed the conquest of Wales. In his first year Agricola overcame the Ordovices, venturing into the Snowdon mountains to fight them on their ground, and 'caesaque prope universa gente' – (in short) wiped them out. The forts constructed at Caer Gai, Caerhun, Caernarfon and Pen Llysten (all in Gwynedd) are seen as part of this campaign, built to control key points in the newly conquered territory which was also watched over by the legions at Chester and Wroxeter. He also invaded the island of Anglesey and took it. The campaigning season of AD79 was devoted to occupying the lands of the Brigantes (Cartimandua had probably died by this time) and then to advancing into the Lowlands of Scotland, marked by the construction of forts, fortlets and linking roads.

The autumn and winter of AD79–80 were spent in further 'Romanisation' of the province; nothing unusual in this except that, as A. H. M. Jones has pointed out, Agricola was the only provincial governor specifically credited in ancient literature with encouraging programmes of urbanisation.[11] We are not supposed to assume that no one else did (ie Frontinus). Tacitus tells us that the winter was devoted to beneficial schemes for the province to get the tribes out of the habit of fighting. Agricola encouraged them to build temples, public squares, market places and new homes, providing grants and loans, praising the British when they carried out projects swiftly and efficiently, and scolding them if they were slack. He persuaded the leading men to have their children educated in *liberalibus artibus* (the liberal arts) and to have them taught Latin to which it seems they took with enthusiasm (*Agricola*, 21). He also got the British to wear the toga. These introductions, however, are said by Tacitus (*Agricola*, 21) to have led the British into bad ways, for they came to enjoy a taste for the baths and prolonged banqueting that were so much a part of Roman life. Archaeology has not yet gone far to substantiate much of this, but in 1955 an inscription from the *forum* at St Albans was found, which bore Agricola's name and which was dated to AD79. But the main achievement of Agricola's governorship (excepting his

A lead ingot found at Chester. It may have been produced at one of the Flintshire lead mines

conquests) was his road building, perhaps begun in this first year of domestic advancement. Although the programme consisted of a network of some 1,300 miles of roads in northern Britain, primarily to assist his military activity by linking over sixty forts and fortlets from Yorkshire–Lancashire to the edge of the Highlands, it had its domestic aspects as well. Encouraging the development of existing capitals and *vici* (small towns) and building new ones (among which can probably be included the capital for the Dumnonii at Exeter, after the legionary fortress there was abandoned in the mid 70s) was accompanied by developing the links between them; roads carried the traffic in people and goods to and fro, ensuring the prosperity of the communities.

We do not know how far into Scotland Agricola penetrated in AD79, but in AD80 his campaigning certainly took the Romans as far as the river Tay – if Tacitus' *Tanaum* (*Agricola*, 22) means 'the Tay' – on a broad front via the Lowlands and across the Forth in Stirlingshire, in two main columns. Four tribes occupied the Lowlands, the Votadini on the east, the Selgovae next to them, the Novantae in Galloway and the Damnonii immediately south of the Forth–Clyde line. These may be the tribes that Tacitus says Agricola confronted. The two columns are thought to have converged in the Forth–Clyde isthmus before moving ahead into Fife. The army suffered more from exceptionally bad weather, storms and winds, than from attack by the tribes who, Tacitus sneers, were too scared to molest the invaders. Agricola then decided to go into winter quarters in southern Scotland, and used the suspension of campaigning to secure the territories so far won and to construct forts in the isthmus, among which may be included Barochan Hill, Camelon and Mollins, and perhaps the first fort at Mumrills too. There is every likelihood that the emperor Titus, who had succeeded his father Vespasian in 79, decided to halt the advance beyond the isthmus as it appeared to be a good, natural frontier. The army had come a long way in a short time and there was much consolidation to do to eliminate the danger of any 'stab in the back'.

Agricola sent forces into what is now Strathclyde and towards Galloway and began the conquest of the Novantae. His campaigns in south-west Scotland and the tightening up of security in the rest of the Lowlands occupied the years 81–2. These operations apparently involved, among other things, an expedition across the sea to locations facing Ireland, which must mean either the islands of Bute, Arran or Islay, or Kintyre, or from Cumbria across the Solway Firth to Dumfries and Galloway, and presumably along the south coast there

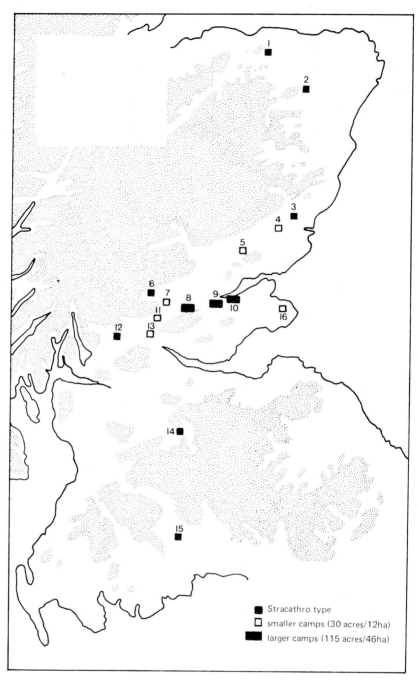

Agricolan marching camps in Scotland 1 Auchinhove 2 Ythan Wells 3 Stracathro
4 Finavon 5 Cardean 6 Dalginross 7 Dornock 8 Dunning 9 Abernethy 10 Carpow
11 Ardoch 12 Menteith 13 Dunblane 14 Castledykes 15 Dalswinton 16 Bonnytown

where Portpatrick is not thirty miles from the Irish coast. Agricola toyed with the idea of invading Ireland; he even calculated that it could be done with only one legion plus some auxiliaries. But the new emperor Domitian (brother of Titus who died in September 81) put an end to this by ordering an advance across the Forth–Clyde isthmus into northern Scotland, the land of the fierce, red-haired, long-limbed Caledonian people, whom Tacitus regarded as quite different from the tribes of the Lowlands. The order is curious; Domitian was planning a major expedition in Germany against the Chatti and the Sugambri (which Suetonius described later as quite unjustified),[12] and appears to have requested Agricola to send detachments from all four British legions to him in Germany, some three thousand or more legionaries, which was bound to weaken Agricola's resources. But in the summer of 83, Agricola advanced across the Forth and into Strathmore, a low-lying valley squashed between the south-eastern foothills of the Grampians and the Ochil and Sidlaw Hills, an easy line of penetration.[13] At the same time, he sent warships carrying extra troops up the North Sea past the Firth of Tay to explore the coast for suitable harbours to land the men. Apparently, this provoked the Caledonians to attack a temporary camp (not yet identified) put up by Agricola for Legio IX, and in the action the camp was broken into and would have been captured but for prompt action by Agricola with a relieving mixed force of cavalry and infantry.

The Caledonians were beaten off, but they were much encouraged by the experience. The Romans were likewise fired with the spirit of battle and longed to bring the war to a head. 'We must drive deeper and deeper into Caledonia and fight battle after battle until we have reached the end of Britain' (*Agricola*, 27). The army moved forward north-eastwards into the Grampian Region and going beyond, possibly setting down camps at Durno, Ythan Wells and Auchinhove. For their part, the Caledonians began to mass for a confrontation. Some thirty thousand warriors from several tribes – old men laden with battle scars and honours, young men 'fresh and green' who had not yet seen fighting – flocked to the colours, putting themselves under the overall leadership of one of the chiefs, Calgacus, a man of outstanding courage. Somewhere, probably on the slopes of the hill of Bennachie, some eighteen miles north-west of Aberdeen, and about four miles from Durno, a great battle was fought.[14] Against the thirty thousand Caledonians, Agricola pitted some eight thousand auxiliary infantry and five thousand cavalry (two thousand of which he held in reserve), while behind the battle lines, detachments from the legions, perhaps numbering some fifteen thousand men, stood or sat to watch the outcome. The two sides were evenly matched, though as it turned out, the legions were not called upon to fight.

After an initial series of furious chariot rushes in the plain, of the kind, no doubt, that the Romans saw in Caesar's and in Suetonius' times, there was an exchange of missiles. Agricola had strung out his forces in a long line below the hills to avoid being outflanked by the ranks of the Caledonians ranged higher up the slopes in positions of advantage. He sent in Batavian and Tungrian cohorts, armed with short, stabbing swords and carrying shields with hard bosses which they used to shove and push while they struck at the enemy's faces, to draw the ranks down into the plain and fight it out at sword point. The cohorts triumphed over the Caledonians whose long swords were unsuitable for close fighting. The auxiliary cavalry, meanwhile, succeeded in dispersing the chariots. Awkward moments followed, however, as the auxiliaries forged uphill, threatened by fresh ranks of Caledonians on the hilltops, but Agricola sent in the reserve cavalry round the back of the Caledonians and broke their attacks. Squeezed now on both sides, the Caledonians disintegrated as an effective fighting force and began to flee, hotly pursued and cut down in their hundreds. Nearly ten thousand Caledonians were killed and the remaining twenty thousand disappeared into the mountains. Tacitus records that the Roman losses amounted to only three hundred and sixty men.

Over the next day or two, Agricola sent out scouts to see if the survivors were planning to regroup for another round, but they found no signs. Confident that he had crushed organised resistance, he withdrew into winter quarters, since it was already the end of the campaigning season. He had a number of Caledonian hostages with him. Before withdrawing, he had sent a fleet northwards to explore the coast and to discourage any other tribes not yet encountered from thinking to challenge the power of Rome. The fleet discovered the Orkney Islands, and then, assisted by favourable winds, sailed round the top of Scotland and down to some point on the western side which they recognised as having seen before, thus actively proving that Britain was an island, which had been known or suspected for well over a century.[15]

The news of the battle, called Mons Graupius, was received in Rome with great enthusiasm. Agricola was awarded triumphal ornaments – and then recalled by the emperor Domitian. Much has been made by several commentators about this recall, following Tacitus' complaint that it was the result of Domitian's jealousy of Agricola's achievement, but this is to overlook that Agricola had already held the governorship for over six years, which was about twice the average term, though equalled by Trebellius. Tacitus himself admits, even boasts, that Agricola 'was in possession of Britain' and that he was able to hand the province 'peaceful and secure' to his successor, which seems an appropriate time to change command (*Agricola* 39, 40). The fact, of course, is that Agricola did not 'possess' Britain entirely, and it was by no means 'secure'. Archaeology has more than amply demonstrated this, as we shall see. Mons Graupius can at best be taken as one tactical success against the Caledonians, two-thirds of whose army survived to fight again. The struggle with Caledonia was not over – it was only just beginning.

NOTES

1. At Chelmsford, a new fort was built to the south of the Roman road, south of the first (Claudian) fort.
2. Collingwood, R. G. and Myres, J. N. L. (1937) p x.
3. He was appointed consul (again) in AD66, and served as a senior commander during the brief reign of the emperor Otho, AD69.
4. His shattered tombstone (now restored) was discovered in London. It is now in the British Museum.
5. From a poem by Statius (*Silvae*, ii) written to the governor's son.
6. Tacitus, *Agricola*, 16; Statius, *Silvae*, ii. Caledonians may mean Brigantians aided by the southern Scottish tribes.
7. The Brigantian client kingdom was the largest in Britain, stretching from the Lancashire–Cumbria coast on the west to the east coast north of Scarborough as far north as Newcastle, and had served as a splendid buffer between the province and the tribes in Scotland. Its disintegration as a result of the break-up between Cartimandua and Venutius compelled the Romans to rethink their British policy. They would have to advance and establish a more northerly frontier, but how far north was not determined.
8. The site had begun as a 17 acre (7ha) British hillfort of the 50s, enlarged in Vettius's time to 130 acres (53ha) and finally expanded by another 600 acres (240ha) a few years later in the time of Petillius. Wheeler, R. E. M. *The Stanwick Fortifications* (1954).
9. Strickland, T. J. (1978) p 7.
10. Dio Cassius, lxvi, 20, 1–2.
11. Jones, A. H. M. (1964) p x.
12. Suetonius, *Domitian*, vi.
13. Dobson, B. 'Agricola's life and career', *Scottish Archaeological Forum* 12. (1981).
14. St Joseph, J. K. 'The camp at Durno, Aberdeenshire, and the site of Mons Graupius', *Britannia* ix (1978) pp 271–87.
15. *De Bello Gallico* iv, 20.

6

THE NORTHERN FRONTIER AND HADRIAN'S WALL

The success at Mons Graupius does not rank among the great victories of Roman arms, and it was in no sense decisive. Indeed, to have let two-thirds of the enemy forces escape must to many Romans have seemed something of a reverse. The triumphal ornaments were more probably awarded to Agricola for accumulated achievements during his six years as governor of Britain. Certainly, apart from his faithful son-in-law and one oblique reference by Dio Cassius, he 'remained uncelebrated by any other surviving ancient author'.[1] This is not altogether surprising when the archaeological record suggests that within five years of Mons Graupius, the Roman frontline had been pulled back below the Forth–Clyde isthmus, over one hundred miles south of the site of the battle – if Bennachie is the true location. Such forts as were built after the battle in conquered Caledonian territory by Agricola's successors – including the legionary fortress of 53 acres (21.5ha) at Inchtuthil, strategically sited beside the Tay as it leads through the Dunkeld Gorge – had been abandoned at the latest by AD90. Inchtuthil – among the largest ever planned in Britain and never completed – was perhaps evacuated by AD87.[2]

There are presently two schools of opinion about the extent of Agricola's skill in fort-siting and building. The first relies historically upon the comments of Tacitus that he chose the sites for camps (*Agricola*, 20), and that:

> . . . there was even time to spare for the establishment of forts. It was observed by experts that no general had ever shown a better eye for ground . . . No fort of his was ever stormed, ever capitulated or was ever abandoned. They were protected against long, protracted siege by supplies renewed every year (*Agricola*, 22).

The innovations in camp and fort design which can be noted in the earlier Flavian period in Britain are attributed largely to Agricola by

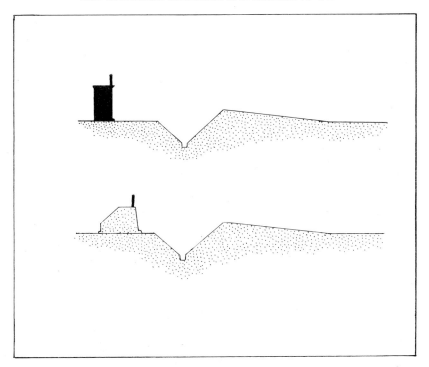

Sections of turf rampart and ditch as reproduced in the experiment at The Lunt fort, Baginton (see p 86)

this school. The second school, on the other hand, sees the innovations to be anonymous, probably the on-the-spot ideas of individual *praefecti castrorum*, and holds that the innovations shown by archaeology cannot be dated closely enough to the Tacitean record without 'a great leap of faith'.[3] On balance, I am inclined to support the second school which suggests, for example, that Inchtuthil was not begun until AD85, after Agricola's recall, and that the forts and watchtowers north of the Forth–Clyde line were likewise post-Agricolan.

Mons Graupius was fought in the autumn of AD84. Soon afterwards, Agricola left for Rome. It may be presumed that his successor, who may have been Sallustius Lucullus (AD85–9), began the construction of forts along or near the road from Camelon to Stracathro – Camelon, Ardoch, Strageath, Bertha, Cargill (near Inchtuthil), Cardean and Stracathro – to hold the lands so far won, and the forts specifically to block the glens ('glen-blockers' as they are affectionately known to many archaeologists) – Drumquhassie, Menteith, Bochastle, Dalginross, Fendoch and the legionary fortress at Inchtuthil. Some of these forts were built beside or incorporating marching camps. It seems a big programme for a few years, but Caesar describes the construction of extensive earthworks and fortifications inside a handful of weeks (*De Bello Gallico*, VII), and Brian Hobley and a team constructed a length of turf rampart for a fort as an experiment in a fortnight.[4] The forts were certainly built to control occupied territory. Were they also intended to be springboards for more offensive strategy, exploring and conquering the Highland massif itself? Breeze has pointed out that the glens were convenient lines for advancing into the massif. We may never know for certain, for the Roman government's policy towards Britain was dramatically affected in about AD86 by serious defeats of Roman armies in south-east Europe. Legio II *Adiutrix*, based at Chester, was withdrawn from Britain altogether to bolster the imperial forces on the Danube, and it was not replaced. A major pullback from the Caledonian war theatre was inevitable, and if there had been any plans to conquer the Highlands, they were shelved. The 'glen-blockers' were abandoned by about AD90, but we are in some difficulty about the other, north-easterly forts, from Camelon to Stracathro, some of which reveal more than one phase of occupation in the Flavian period.

Contemporary with the withdrawal from these northern forts, the Romans appear to have constructed two lines of timber watchtowers, one along the road northwards from Ardoch fort to Strageath fort (evidence of four towers has been found at north Ardoch, Shielhill South, Shielhill North and Westerton, each 3–4sq m (4–5sq yd) standing on four posts and enclosed by double ditches), and eastwards along the road from Strageath towards Bertha fort on the Tay (eleven towers, so far found, at Parkneuk, Raith, Ardunie, Roundlaw, Kirkhill, Muir o'Fauld, Gask House, Witch Knowe, Moss Side, Thorny Hill, Westmuir, of similar dimensions and surrounded by a single ditch and bank).[5] They are often called the Gask Frontier, since the road flanks the south side of Gask Ridge in Strathearn. Most of the Gask towers were about half a mile apart, which provided total cover of the lower ground. If the towers were erected in AD86–7, they would probably have been modelled on similar towers put up after the war against the Chatti in western Bavaria (AD83–5). Their life seems to have been extremely short, for by about AD90 they had been pulled down and burnt. This marks the end of the Flavian I period. Having pulled back behind the Forth–Clyde isthmus (which, it should be noted, had no line of forts such as were later to be erected in the time

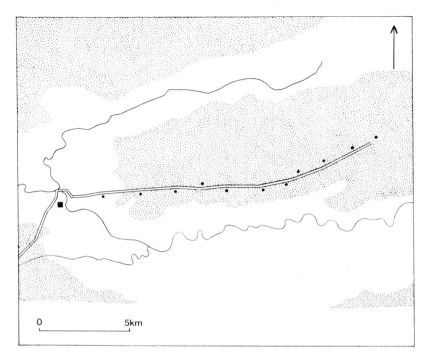

The Gask Frontier towers (*left to right eastwards from Strageath*): Parkneuk, Raith, Ardunie, Roundlaw, Kirkhill, Muio o'Fauld, Gask House, Witch Knowe, Moss Side, Thorny Hill, Westmuir

of emperor Antoninus Pius, in the mid second century), the Roman administration decided to phase a further withdrawal. This appears to have been a gradual process. Most of the forts and fortlets built by Agricola in southern Scotland, were dismantled, leaving a revised frontier along the line of forts (north-east to south-west) from Newstead to Oakwood, Milton, Dalswinton and Glenlochar, all of which were modified in some way. Newstead was rebuilt to a much larger size (13 acres/5ha). At about the same time, Dalswinton was also rebuilt. All this was between the late 80s and early 90s.

In AD96, Domitian, who had become increasingly paranoid and who suspected almost everyone of plotting against him, finally succumbed to assassination, in which his long-suffering wife played her part. His place as emperor was taken by the elderly and much respected senator, M. Cocceius Nerva, breaking for a time the hereditary succession to the purple. Nerva died two years later, having designated the able and popular general, M. Ulpius Traianus (Trajan) as his heir. Trajan was to become one of the greatest warrior-emperors of ancient Rome. At one time, he could boast the long and distinguished title of Imperator Caesar Nerva Traianus Augustus Dacicus Parthicus, the last two names commemorating his great conquests of Dacia and Parthia. His military policy for Rome was essentially expansionist, and yet for Britain he had little interest beyond what resources it might provide for what he believed were better, more rewarding imperial aims. He looked eastwards, and so desired stability in Rome's westerly provinces, and if this meant contraction in Britain, then so be it. Early in the second century, he authorised the withdrawal from Scotland down to the Tyne–Solway isthmus where the Stanegate road, probably built by Agricola, ran. This released forces for his earlier Dacian campaign. It also involved the dismantling of the south Scotland forts. Some of these, Newstead, Dalswinton and Glenlochar included, have revealed evidence in excavation of having been burnt down. We do not know how many were destroyed by assault from the southern Scottish tribes, such as the Selgovae and Novantii, and how many were deliberately fired by the receding Romans. Newstead does seem to have been the victim of a major attack. So as not to leave the 'reduced' province in danger, a new frontier was formed on the base of the Stanegate with the establishment of new forts and the refurbishment of existing ones. At the same time, many of the fortresses and forts throughout Britain were replaced with more permanent buildings of stone. These included the legionary fortresses of Caerleon (c100), Chester (c103) and York (c107–8), as well as forts like Templeborough, Castell Collen and Forden Gaer. The whole process was a gradual one, and not an intensive programme, though Tacitus was to complain '*perdomita Britannia et statim omissa*', that Britain was conquered and immediately lost (*Histories* I, ii). The archaeological record suggests that the army was settling down to a more permanent way of life as a garrison force.

The Stanegate was a major road that ran east–west from Corbridge where the north and south Tyne rivers join to Carlisle (*Luguvalium*) on the river Eden. At Corbridge, it crossed the northerly main route into Scotland, Dere Street, and at Carlisle it crossed the western high road coming up from Lancashire via Ribchester (where the celebrated Ribchester bronze cavalry parade helmet, of the late first century, was found) and Penrith. It is not known how many forts had been built along Stanegate or beside it in Agricola's time or the period immediately following, but the Agricolan constructions appear to be a turf and timber fort at Red House, about a mile west of Corbridge,

Barrack blocks at the legionary fortress of Caerleon, Gwent

altered after Agricola and later destroyed, probably by attack from Scotland in about AD105, a similarly constructed fort at Carlisle (though it is argued this could have been founded by Frontinus), while the first fort at Chesterholm (*Vindolanda*) and the larger, earlier fort at Nether Denton, can be dated to the last years of Domitian. From Carlisle to Nether Denton is thirteen and a half miles, Nether Denton to Chesterholm eleven miles and Chesterholm to Corbridge thirteen and a half miles. There was a possible fifth fort, of the later period of Domitian, at Carvoran, nearly midway between Nether Denton and Chesterholm. This has not been fully investigated, though some interesting discoveries have emerged over the years, notably the Carvoran *modius*, a dry measure of bronze, in perfect condition.

The strengthening of the Stanegate line under Trajan was begun in the first years of the second century, perhaps at the time of, or immediately after, the destruction of Red House fort which itself was not rebuilt but resited about a mile east in Corbridge proper. Chesterholm and Nether Denton were remodelled, and work as yet undetermined was done at Carvoran and no doubt at Carlisle too. New forts of varying sizes were added in the intervals between the first five – (west to east) Brampton Old Church (3½ acres/1.4ha), Throp (fortlet

89

of about 1 acre/0.4ha), Haltwhistle Burn (fortlet of about ¾ acre/0.3ha) and Newbrough (fortlet of about ¾ acre/0.3ha, which some authorities consider may have been a Trajanic fort before its fourth century occupation).[6] These smaller structures are sometimes called 'half-day forts': they are about half a day's march from their larger companions. What was beyond the ends of the Stanegate road it is too early to say for certain, but the discovery of a fort at Washingwells, near Whickham on the Tyne, suggests that the Stanegate system could have been extended eastwards towards the mouth of the Tyne, while at the western end, extensive military works recently excavated indicate that it was continued to an Agricolan fort at Kirkbridge, four miles south of Bowness on the southern bank of the Solway estuary.

The Stanegate frontier was perhaps completed and garrisoned by the second decade, but it was not an adequate barrier against invasion from the north, nor a protection against disaffection among the Brigantes, nor even an effective control of unauthorised movements to and fro across it. There is evidence of fighting in this theatre in both Domitian's last years and in Trajan's time, though it is not yet possible to construct a history. Matters were not helped by the withdrawal of more troops by Trajan, when he removed Legio IX *Hispana* from its

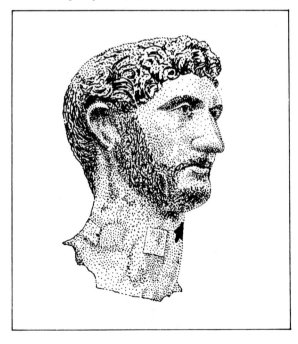

Bust of the Emperor
Hadrian (117–38)

base at York sometime after AD108. Something more permanent had sooner or later to be arranged, and it was Trajan's successor, Hadrian, who devised it.

The concept of a permanent frontier anywhere along the edges of the Roman empire was relatively new. Hitherto, the limits of advance by Roman armies and the bases and roads they put down, represented the frontiers, fluid, short-lived and optimistically regarded as easily expendable. But by the last decades of the first century, it had begun to occur to many Romans that they were not after all going to conquer the whole world. Some frontiers, therefore, had perforce to harden and at first, chains of forts and watchtowers along natural lines like rivers (the Rhine and the Danube) or ridges and hills (the Gask, for example) were considered sufficient to control, but not necessarily to prevent, passage to and fro between the empire and Barbaricum. The Stanegate system, about which there is still a lot to be learned (and along which more excavation would probably be fruitful), may have included watchtowers between forts and fortlets. But sometime between about 105 and 117, there was unspecified trouble in Britain, enough to provoke Hadrian's biographer, Spartianus (S. H. A., *De Vita Hadriani* v, 2), to say that at the beginning of his reign, the British could no longer be kept under control. And there is no evidence that Trajan had made any attempt to do so in his last years.

'He (Hadrian) set out for Britain and there he corrected many abuses and was the first to construct a wall, eighty miles in length, which was to separate the barbarians from the Romans.' Aelius Spartianus leaves us to speculate why the Romans and barbarians needed to be separated. Up to Hadrian's reign, Roman frontiers were normally organised so that peoples on the other side could cross into the empire for legitimate and peaceful purposes, such as trading or visiting relatives and friends, under military supervision by means of patrols between forts and watchtowers. It was rare for outsider tribes to be allowed unchecked passage across the borders. This was understandable, for Roman provinces were frequently in danger of attack from outside, and perhaps there was a tendency to regard all foreign 'travellers' with suspicion until they could prove that their visits were innocent. There was also the question of collecting customs duties. The system was not perfect, but it was helped by the offensive role of the army, constantly on the ready for a further advance into unknown territory.

Hadrian decided, however, to halt the expansion of the empire and fix its borders somewhat behind the limits reached by Trajan. To this end he planned a series of extensive tours of the empire (the first emperor to do so) and he began by visiting Gaul and Britain, setting out in 121 and reaching Britain in 122. There had been disorders in Britain in the first three years of his reign, as well as before it, but these appear to have been dealt with by Hadrian's first appointed governor of Britain, Q. Pompeius Falco. When Hadrian arrived in Britain, he brought with him a new governor, his friend, A. Platorius Nepos, then governor of Lower Germany, together with a replenishing legion for the British garrison, Legio VI *Victrix*. They travelled to the Stanegate 'frontier' where the emperor will have received full details of the unspecified troubles of the previous years. It was now that he decided to build a wall right across the Tyne–Solway isthmus, above the unsatisfactory Stanegate, but incorporating parts of it.

Hadrian's Wall was a substantial structure, even by Roman standards, and by far the greatest of his frontier-building projects. In Africa, for example, he kept the desert tribes out by means of the *Fossatum Africae*, a dry-stone wall interspersed with earth rampart sections, and in Germany, the defence was a timber wall. The British wall was intended to be a monument, as several other of Hadrian's

Hadrian's Wall seen from Cuddy's Crag, near Housesteads (*Reece Winstone*)

major projects were, such as the renovation of the Pantheon of Agrippa and the construction of the building later to be called Castel Santangelo, both in Rome, and the famous villa at Tivoli. In some quarters, he is thought to have been influenced by the amazing Great Wall of China, largely built in the third century BC by Emperor Sh'ih Huang Ti, still much the greatest engineering feat by man. We may go along some of the way with this desire to commemorate himself, but we cannot exclude the possibility that the dangers posed by the Caledonians were actually of such enormous proportions that only a monumental and continuous linear barrier of stone and earth was likely to contain them. The Caledonians had, after all, driven the Romans, or caused them to retreat, right out of Scotland in the last years of the first century. They must have represented a major threat.

Hadrian's Wall is the prime relic of over four hundred years of Roman occupation of Britain. It has been described in the greatest detail,[7] and excavation work continues on its length, producing fresh and often dramatic discoveries.[8] We must confine a description here to the main essentials. The Wall was designed to stretch from Wallsend, east of Newcastle-upon-Tyne, to Bowness-on-Solway, a distance of some seventy-three and a half English miles (eighty Roman miles of 1,620yd). As originally laid down by Hadrian and Platorius and their engineers, it was to begin as a stone wall some 2.75m (9¼ft/10 Roman ft) thick from the east to the river Irthing at Willowford, and thereafter to be a turf rampart wall some 6m (20ft) thick at the base from Willowford westwards to Bowness. The construction did not entirely follow this simple plan. The stretch from Wallsend on the extreme east to Pons Aelius on the Tyne in Newcastle, ended up only 2.25m (7½ft) thick in stone, and was built later in Hadrian's reign. From Newcastle westwards to the North Tyne, some twenty miles, the thickness varied from the full 2.75m (9¼ft) down to as little as 2m (6ft). On average, the Wall was about 4.5m (15ft) tall, with another 1.5–2m (5–6ft) of parapet with crenellations on the stone part, while the turf part of the Wall was on average 3.5m (12ft) tall with a wooden palisade perhaps another 2–2.25m (6–7ft). At the North Tyne, the Wall continued in stone, narrow as far as Willowford on the Irthing, though for some stretches the narrow wall stood on wide foundations (perhaps suggesting that the original intention had been to build the Wall thicker). The reason for this unevenness is not absolutely clear, but may have something to do with the fact that various detachments of legions built separate sections of it, under different supervision.

Part of the extreme east end of Hadrian's Wall, at Wallsend. This fragment was moved from its original site in what is now dockland nearby (*Reece Winstone*)

In front of the Wall, generally about 6m (20ft) north, there was a ditch of widths varying from 7.5 to 12m (25 to 40ft), of almost uniform depth (2.75–3m/9–10ft), with a cleaning slot at the bottom (see p 175). The outer (northern) scarp was higher than the inner scarp. This ditch was almost continuous for the whole length of the Wall, and in places was cut into rock; but there was one stretch without ditch along the ridge of the Whin Sill, and there were other stretches where, because of the hardness of the rock, the ditching was less deep. The stretch of Wall from Newcastle to Willowford was probably completed between 122 and 126, during which time the scheme was altered in several particulars.

The Turf Wall from Willowford to Bowness was completed in the same period but the first five miles westwards from Willowford were converted to a narrow stone wall almost immediately afterwards, some of it perhaps during the period. About two miles of this early stone walling (between the milecastle at Harrow's Scar (no 49) and that at Wall Bowers (no 51), departs from the original Turf Wall and proceeds north-westwards, joining the Turf Wall later on, enabling us to see both turf and stone wall more or less together and to understand the differences. In the interval between the raising of the Turf Wall and the conversion to stone of the five-mile stretch from Willowford

94

westwards, a fort was put down at Birdoswald, with its northern third projecting beyond the Wall. When the five-mile Stone Wall was built, it was steered along the northern side of the fort at Birdoswald. The original Turf Wall (which had a turret, no 49a) was built over. The ditch in front of the Turf Wall (including the five-mile stretch converted to stone) was generally placed about 2m (6ft) or so in front. The remainder of the Turf Wall was converted to stone a generation later, but before about AD180.

Along the Wall a system of forts, fortlets and turrets was constructed. At first, it had been planned that the Wall would contain fortlets every mile (milecastles) with two turrets placed approximately equidistantly between. Milecastles and turrets would be garrisoned with units from the Stanegate forts behind, whose personnel would maintain continuous patrols along the entire frontier. They were to patrol rather than fight. These milecastles were to be built as an integral part of the Wall (stone with elevated stone gates for the stone part, earth with elevated wooden gates for the Turf Wall), their northern sides being the Wall itself. Milecastles were quadrangular, between 15 and 18m (50–60ft) east-west, by 17–23m (56–75ft) north–south, though in some cases the dimensions were reversed, with occasionally a larger milecastle on the Turf Wall.[9] Four of the mile-

Part of the unfinished ditch cut into the rock in front of Hadrian's Wall, at Limestone Corner, near Carrawburgh fort (*National Monuments Record*)

Remains of a barrack block at Milecastle 37 (Housesteads) on Hadrian's Wall. Housesteads, in the care of the National Trust, is open to the public (*Reece Winstone*)

Turret 7b on Hadrian's Wall, at Denton Burn, Newcastle-upon-Tyne

castles were protected by a single ditch, but the others were not. The internal appointments included one or two timber or stone barrack blocks, each for up to thirty-two men, and generally a storehouse and an oven. The gateways opened on the north and south sides. The intermediate turrets, positioned about 480m (540yd) apart between milecastles, were about 6m (20ft) square, and recessed some 2m (6ft) into the Stone Wall. They were two-storeyed, the upper projecting a full storey height above the Wall, reached by an inside stepladder. Turrets were built of stone for both the stone and turf parts of the Wall. Details of the individual milecastles and turrets are noted in the Gazetteer. A good idea of the internal arrangements of a milecastle can be gained from the excellent model at the Corbridge Museum, where there is also a model of a typical Wall turret. Meanwhile, traces of several milecastles and turrets have been excavated, or have survived from Roman times without the need for excavation, and the best visible examples are Cawfields (MC no 42), Housesteads (MC no 37), Poltross Burn (MC no 48) and Harrow's Scar (MC no 49) and turrets at Willowford East (no 48a), Brunton (no 26b) and Coesike (no 33b).

Before the first period of building the Wall (Period IA, AD122–30)

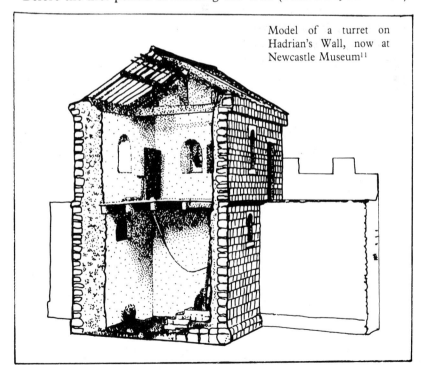

Model of a turret on Hadrian's Wall, now at Newcastle Museum[11]

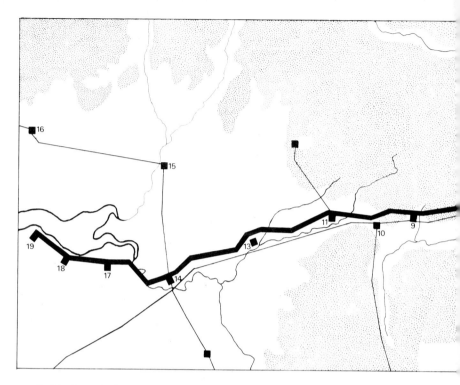

Hadrian's Wall forts and outpost forts (east to west) 1 South Shields 2 Wallsend
3 Benwell 4 Rudchester 5 Haltonchesters 6 Chesters 7 Carrawburgh 8 Housesteads
9 Greatchesters 10 Carvoran 11 Birdoswald 12 Bewcastle (outpost) 13 Castlesteads
14 Stanwix 15 Netherby (outpost) 16 Birrens (outpost) 17 Burgh-by-Sands
18 Drumburgh 19 Bowness

was completed, the scheme was further amended, this time by
constructing major forts along the Wall, thus bringing the legions and
auxiliaries into the frontier zone instead of leaving them in the
Stanegate forts, most of which were abandoned. This was probably
dictated by the fact that the milecastle gateways to the north had
proved hopelessly awkward for large concentrations of troops to pass
through into the 'no-man's land' between the Wall and Scotland.
There was only a short gap in the Housesteads area where construction of the Wall had not been finished. It seems odd that no one in the
army had foreseen this earlier on, for the change of plan was not introduced until the Stone Wall had been completed between Pons Aelius
and the North Tyne at or near Chesters (some twenty-five miles) and
the Turf Wall from Bowness to Birdoswald (about thirty miles). The
scheme was to include fourteen new forts between 3½ and 9½ acres

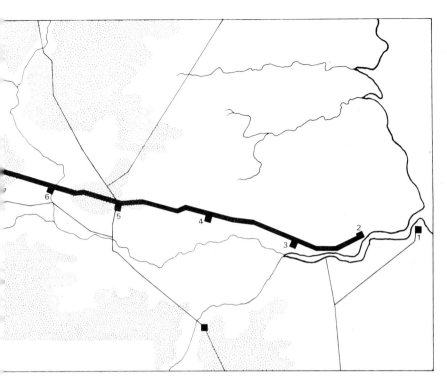

Castle Nick Milecastle (No 39) on Hadrian's Wall (*E. Houlder*)

(1.4–3.8ha) in size, which were to be built of stone on the Stone Wall and turf and timber on the Turf Wall (except Birdoswald, which was stone). They were intended for auxiliary cohorts or *alae*. Nearly all the forts were to be positioned astride the Wall, which meant that gates to the north, east and west opened into the space north of the Wall, while the south and second east and west gates opened into the space behind. It appears that only after several forts had been built in this alignment on the Wall was it realised that in fact they need not have been, and later forts, such as Housesteads, Greatchesters and Carrawburgh were built abutting the Wall at the north side. Likewise, the two Stanegate forts of Carvoran and Castlesteads were rebuilt in stone. The buildings inside were either of stone or of timber, more of stone in the stone forts.

Roman fort design is described on pp 172–82 and the main features of each of the Hadrian's Wall forts are indicated in the Gazetteer, but one or two general points about them may be of interest here. Each was protected by its own ditch and stone wall round the outside. The sites were all carefully chosen so as to be close to natural water supplies: some forts were supplied by aqueducts, like Chesters, and Housesteads got its water by pumping it up from the Knag Burn. The forts were rectangular, with the usual rounded corners (playing-card shape), and most were positioned with the longer sides on the north–south axis, though Housesteads and Greatchesters had their longer sides on the east–west axis. The forts were built over a period from about 124 to the late 130s. Carvoran, just behind the Wall but to be included in the system, was converted to stone in 136 (according to an inscription). Many of the forts later attracted *vici* (settlements) beside them, consisting of retired legionaries and auxiliaries, craftsmen and merchants and perhaps local natives. Some of the forts had an outside bath house of considerable size and complexity, such as at Chesters.

Sometime during Period IA, the Wall system was extended beyond Bowness down the Cumbrian coast, certainly as far as Maryport, twenty-three miles south-west, and probably as far as St Bee's Head, forty miles south-west. At Maryport, a separate fort of 5¾ acres (2.3ha) had already been built for coastal defence, probably early in Hadrian's reign. The order of building along this Cumbrian line is not known thoroughly yet, but a fortlet was located every mile (these are generally referred to as milefortlets), with intervening towers, similar to the original arrangements along the Wall, but here there was no

View of remains of the *vicus* outside the Hadrian's Wall fort at *Vindolanda* (Chesterholm)

wall of stone or turf connecting them. The fort at Maryport was part of the system. On the eastern side of the country, the Wall was extended beyond Wallsend to South Shields on the south side of the Tyne, where a 5 acre (2ha) fort was built to guard the Tyne estuary.

The Wall, with its forts, milecastles and turrets orientated for offensive/defensive roles, commanded the dominant geographical positions across ridge and crag along much of the frontier, providing the army with an almost continuous panorama for observation over the landscape immediately northwards. Today, visitors can see from numerous high points the Wall snaking across the countryside far into the distance, and will readily grasp its value as a strategic frontier. But the Wall was only one edge of the frontier. Behind the Wall, the Romans built a continuous earthwork, from Newcastle to Bowness. This is known as the Vallum, and it was a broad 36m (120ft) barrier consisting in cross-section of a mound of earth 2.5–3m (8–10ft) high and 6m (20ft) wide, an open space (called a berm) 9m (30ft) across, a ditch 6m (20ft) wide and 3m (10ft) deep, with sloping sides and flat bottom, a second berm of 9m (30ft), ending with a second mound of the same dimensions. This remarkable earthwork, which can still be

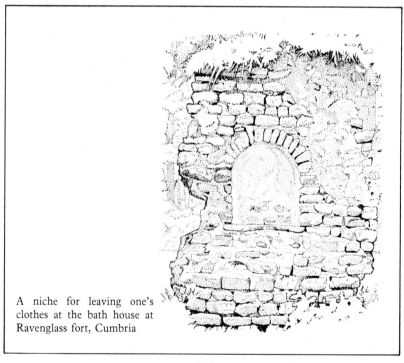

A niche for leaving one's clothes at the bath house at Ravenglass fort, Cumbria

A view of the Vallum (behind Hadrian's Wall) at Sewingshields (*E. Houlder*)

seen for some of its length today (see above), was straight for much of its length, but diverged where it had to skirt round the southern edge of a fort, such as at Birdoswald. The ditch was the central feature and it was protected with care in difficult locations: revetted in stone when it traversed a ravine, embanked if it went across marshland and reinforced wherever the earth was light or sandy. Where it ran close to a fort, it was bridged by a causeway, or later filled in so as to provide a throughway from the fort southwards, in both cases controlled by wooden gates. Before the Vallum was built, there had been a way through the Wall from north to south at every mile point; the Vallum reduced this number to only fourteen or fifteen, the number of forts along the Wall, and this made it easier for the frontier garrisons to control movements. On the other hand, it made legitimate traffic across the frontier more difficult. In a sense, the Vallum was little more than a piece of Roman military red tape.

The Vallum was constructed concomitantly with the fort-building programme. There is still argument as to its purpose, since it was not a defensive work. Rather, it has been suggested that it was simply the southern demarcation line of the frontier which was a military zone, or, as Breeze put it, 'the Roman equivalent of barbed wire'.[10] We have described its original scheme. In the Antonine period, when the whole frontier was advanced northwards into Scotland, the Vallum was tampered with on an extensive scale; causeways across it began to multiply, stretches of the ditch were filled in and chunks of banking were levelled. And it appears that it was never restored when the frontier was later pulled back again to the Wall.

When moving between forts and milecastles the army would use the space between the Wall and the Vallum, or even the berms in the

Vallum complex. Individuals no doubt also used the walk behind the parapet on the Wall. Later, when the Vallum had gone out of use, a Military Way was constructed along it, using either filled-in ditches or laying down road surfaces along levelled stretches of the mounds or on the berms. The Way was about 6m (20ft) across and its surface was metalled. In some parts it is possible to see several layers of roadway (laid over the centuries), notably at the fort at Benwell. The Military Way passed through or beside forts and milecastles, with branches off to the turrets. The frontier itself was served from the principal bases further south by the Old Stanegate which for the most part ran between one and two miles parallel to and south of the Wall.

The last features of the frontier to mention were the outpost forts. These were in the western part where, north of the Wall, the terrain was far less open and less easy to police, being wooded or creased with sharp ridges and valleys. Three forts were built during Hadrian's period in this 'no-man's land' of Cumbria and Southern Scotland: Bewcastle, about six miles north-north-west of Birdoswald and connected to the latter by road; Netherby, on the Esk, eight or nine miles north of Stanwix; and Birrens, about twelve miles almost due west of Netherby. It may be pertinent to add here that the remaining stretch of Turf Wall, from Banks East to Bowness was converted to stone sometime in the 160s.

Hadrian's Wall was a massive work of engineering. Over two million tons of stone and turf were used in its construction. A nineteenth century engineer estimated that ten thousand men using ox-carts and working two hundred days a year would have taken the best part of two years to complete it, without the forts and milecastles. In fact, it took about fifteen years. From inscriptions, it is known that all three legions in Britain, Legio II *Augusta* (Caerleon), Legio VI *Victrix* (York) and Legio XX *Valeria Victrix* (Chester) provided the labour, and contributions were also made by men of the Roman fleet operating in British waters and by auxiliary units. The legions, of course, had their own skilled masons, carpenters, diggers, cement mixers, quarrymen, transport men, as well as surveyors and engineers. Each legion appears to have been allotted a four to five mile stretch, whether Stone or Turf Wall. The milecastles and turrets were built first, following a plan by the surveyors; then the intervening Wall was raised, but it is clear that in some instances, lengths of wall were begun before milecastles were finished. As we have seen, the operations were radically altered when it was decided to add forts to the Wall, which

The Rudge Cup. This was found at Rudge, Wiltshire. It shows part of Hadrian's Wall, with turrets, and round the top are the names of seven forts, including (as seen here) Camboglans, ie Castlesteads. The cup is bronze

involved the destruction of several milecastles and turrets that had only just been built. The forts were planned to be about half a day's legionary march apart, that is, about seven and a half miles, though the distances varied between six and nine miles.

The detail of the construction of the Wall, with its chronology as calculated by inscription, literature and archaeology, is comprehensively and brilliantly described by David Breeze and Brian Dobson, and their work should be read by anyone who has more than a passing interest in Romano-British history.[11]

The Wall was completed by AD 138, the year Hadrian died. Within a year or so, plans were already being made to give up this frontier and advance into Scotland where, from the Firth of Forth to the Firth of Clyde, a new frontier would be built by Hadrian's successor, Antoninus Pius. One may well ask, what was the point of all the effort spent on Hadrian's Wall?

NOTES
1. Dobson, B. 'Agricola's life and career', *Scottish Archaeological Forum* 12 (1981), Paper no 1.
2. Frere, S. S. (1978) p 162, n 5.
3. Breeze, D. J., 'Agricola the builder', *Scottish Archaeological Forum* 12 (1981), Paper no 2.
4. Hobley, B., 'An experimental reconstruction of a Roman military turf rampart', in Applebaum, S. (ed.) *Roman Frontier Studies: Proceedings of the Seventh Limes Congress, Tel Aviv* (1967).
5. Some would argue that these towers were, in part if not entirely, planned and erected by Agricola.
6. In particular Breeze, D. J. (1982) p 69.
7. Among the leading works are: Breeze, D. and Dobson, B. *Hadrian's Wall* (1976); Breeze, D. *The Northern Frontiers of Roman Britain* (1982) and Collingwood,

Bruce J. *Handbook to the Roman Wall*, revised by Daniels, C. M. (1978), and several works by Prof Eric Birley.

8. Readers can keep up to date with this work by consulting annual issues of *Britannia*, *Archaeologia Aeliana* and *Transactions of the Cumberland and Westmorland Antiquarian and Archaeological Society*.

9. It appears that the north wall of the milecastle was generally built with an east and west wing which was later on joined to the Wall as the constructors reached that point in their work; in other words, some, if not all, of the milecastles were being built at the same time as the Wall, or even a little earlier.

10. Breeze, D. (1982) p 92.

11. Breeze, D. and Dobson, B. (1976) pp 64–72.

7
THE ANTONINE WALL

'Though more desirous of peace than of war, he kept the soldiers in training just as if war were imminent' wrote Hadrian's biographer, Spartianus (S. H. A., *De Vita Hadriani* x, 2), and it sums up the emperor's military policy. In a sense it also explains the great Wall, a peace-keeping structure involving large numbers of men who would be constantly occupied building, repairing, furnishing and, when they were not doing that – drilling, patrolling, policing. Clearly, Hadrian intended the Wall to be the permanent frontier in Britain; he may even have enjoined his successor to maintain it so. But Antoninus Pius, whom he made his heir in the last months of his life, soon discovered that the passive attitude towards the Caledonians would have to be abandoned. We do not know what, if any, hostilities broke out in the period immediately after Hadrian's death but Antoninus' biographer, Capitolinus (S. H. A., *Antoninus Pius*, v), is quite explicit that the new emperor waged war against the Britons, ordered the new governor of Britain, Quintus Lollius Urbicus, to drive them back and then to build a second wall further up to contain them. This time it was to be a turf wall and it was to run across the Forth–Clyde isthmus, a distance of almost forty Roman miles (thirty-six and a half English miles). The project has been amply attested by inscriptions and coins as well as in literary references. Britons in this case must mean Caledonians, but what had they done at this time to provoke the emperor to wage war?

One possible reason for the change in policy is that Antoninus was under pressure from the army to go to war – anywhere in the empire. The army had long disliked Hadrian's policy of non-aggression and was champing for a military success. Britain offered a possibility. The Caledonians had evidently not given trouble for some time. They remained in their own territories in the Highlands. But how long would that last? Between them and Hadrian's Wall were the Scottish Lowlands, once held by Rome as part of provincial Britain (from AD79 to about 90), now occupied, presumably with self-governing powers, by the indigenous tribes, the Novantae, the Selgovae, the Votadini and the Damnonii. If the tribes were friendly with Rome, why not absorb them by shifting the frontier northwards to enclose them and also squeeze the Caledonians? If they were not, why not wage war on them and enclose them by force behind a new frontier? Either way, some sort of military success could be scored. As for the frontier itself and the shape it would take, Antoninus will have known all about Hadrian's Wall. At the time of his accession it was still part stone (eastern end) and part turf (western end). He could leave it to Lollius Urbicus to decide whether to build the second frontier wall in turf or in stone.

This, perhaps, was the thinking in military circles at Rome. And in AD139, the fort at Corbridge (*Corstopitum*), just south of Hadrian's Wall, abandoned in the 120s because the Wall superseded it, was reoccupied and modified because it lay on one of the main routes into Scotland, Dere Street.[1] The progress of the army over the next two to three years is shadowy, but in AD142 Antoninus was formally saluted *imperator* for a successful campaign waged by Lollius Urbicus in Britain (*Antoninus Pius*, v). So the Lowlands had been overrun and the barbarians were driven back. Then followed the building of the second wall, begun – though certainly not finished – in Lollius Urbicus' term as governor (AD138/9–43). And while it was being constructed, Hadrian's Wall was gradually abandoned, though not slighted on its principal features. The abandonment was probably not completed before the second wall extended across the whole isthmus (though not yet having all its forts), which is thought to have happened by AD147–8. The abandonment of Hadrian's Wall was limited to lifting the bureaucratic obstacles to getting through it (see p 103), opening the gates of the milecastles (in some cases removing them altogether) and nullifying the defensiveness of the great Vallum with a series of groups of parallel causeways created by 'bulldozing' the ramparts, front and rear, into the ditch, in many stretches as close as 40–45m (45–50yd). Forts were left alone, since they had a military role in providing quarters for troops (auxiliary or legionary). Many of the Hadrian's Wall garrisons, however, were to find themselves not only on service in the Scottish Lowlands but also in the construction of the Antonine Wall itself, which we know was erected by the legionaries of Legio II *Augusta*, Legio VI *Victrix* and Legio XX *Valeria Victrix*.

The campaign of 139–42 was accompanied by the construction of a number of new forts and fortlets in the Lowlands and the reoccupation of earlier forts abandoned after the withdrawal of the late 80s (Flavian period I) and at the turn of the century (Flavian period II, AD90–105). Many of these forts are known, and no doubt more will be discovered. It may help briefly to retrace the building story.

As we have seen (p 88), there were two main routes into Scotland which were opened up by Agricola. The eastern route, Dere Street, began at York, passed beside Corbridge on the Tyne, and from there followed roughly the present A68 road to Dalkeith in the Lothian Region, just south of the Firth of Forth. From Dalkeith it may have continued to Cramond on the southern shore (if the fort there had an Agricolan beginning), or it went on to Inveresk, also on the southern shore, and nearer, where a fort is thought to have been built. Along or very close to Dere Street, key Flavian forts, south to north from Corbridge to the Forth, either Agricolan or of his successors, included Risingham,[2] Blakehope (though this may be Trajanic), High Rochester, Chew Green (fortlet), Cappuck (small fort), Newstead (large fort), Oxton (fortlet), Dalkeith (recently found and also called Elginhaugh) and Cramond or Inveresk. The western route into Scotland, starting from Chester, went via Carlisle across into Annandale and thence to Clydesdale, following approximately the present-day A74, towards the Clyde. Key forts on this line included (south to north) Birrens (small fort), Milton, Crawford (small fort), Castledykes (large fort), Barochan Hill, or the route may have branched to Mollins (small fort) and possibly finished up at Castlecary (later on a fort along the Antonine Wall). Positioned between these two routes were other forts, including (south to north) Broomholm (small fort), Oakwood, Easter Happrew, Castle Greg and, to the west of the western route, a major fort at Dalswinton, a smaller fort at Loudoun Hill, a fortlet at Gatehouse of Fleet, and two so far unproved forts at Glenlochar and Ward Law.[3] Some of these were erected between AD79 and 84, and the remainder soon after Agricola's recall. Forts built north of the Forth–Clyde isthmus were all post Agricolan, as indicated above (p 85). These were in two main lines: on the west the 'glen-blockers' Drumquhassie, Menteith, Bochastle, Dalginross, Fendoch and Cardean (large fort), and the large fort near the east coast of Angus, Stracathro. Between Fendoch and Cardean the great legionary fortress of Inchtuthil was begun but not finished, and on the more easterly side of Scotland, through Strathmore and Strathearn, Camelon (large fort), Ardoch (large fort), Kaims (fortlet), Strageath, probably Bertha (large fort), Cargill and, over on the south shore of the beginning of the Firth of Tay, Carpow.[4]

The great majority of these forts between the Tyne–Solway line and the Highlands were abandoned cAD85–105. A few survived and one or two were reoccupied when Hadrian's Wall was built, such as Birrens. Many more were reoccupied in the Lollius Urbicus campaign, or soon afterwards, but before 158. They were Corbridge, Risingham, High Rochester, Chew Green, Cappuck, Newstead, Oxton, Inveresk, Cramond, Birrens, Milton, Crawford, Glenlochar, Loudoun Hill, Castledykes, Barochan Hill and, north of the Forth–Clyde isthmus, Camelon, Ardoch, Strageath and Bertha. New forts were built in the same period, and (excluding those on the Antonine Wall) they included Carzield, Barburgh Mill (fortlet), Durisdeer (fortlet), Wandel (fortlet), Redshaw Burn (fortlet), Raeburnfoot (small fort), Lyne, Bothwellhaugh and Fairholm (fortlet).

Some of the forts built in northern England in Agricola's time (and before), and which were later abandoned, were now reoccupied in order to accommodate garrisons to watch over the Brigantes who were still a threat to the army in the rear. Likewise, to meet the possibility of trouble among the tribes in Wales, one or two of the first-century Welsh forts were reoccupied, including Forden Gaer and Gelligaer.

The Antonine network of forts in southern Scotland, below the Forth–Clyde isthmus, was linked by a road system. Some of the roads had already been built in the first century and metalled; others had been started and now received metalling, while others were started from scratch. Still more may have been only dirt tracks, to receive surfaces later. The high proportion of fortlets constructed in this period may point to the fact that the total number of forces available to Lollius Urbicus, some thirty-five thousand men (about one-third less than Agricola's total of about fifty thousand), entailed a more economical distribution of resources in a larger number of forts and fortlets than in the Flavian periods. Some authorities believe that the reduced size of the garrisons was balanced by the positioning of watch-towers and/or signal stations between the forts, but not enough traces of such towers have yet been discovered to back up the suggestion. Some men of the fort garrisons were outstationed in nearby fortlets; other forts retained their full garrisons. The arrangement depended upon the dangers and upon the type of fort garrison; for example, an *ala* (or cavalry unit) would not normally expect to be broken up to provide a small detachment for a fortlet.

While the campaign of 139–42 was being waged, Lollius Urbicus began to plan the frontier which the emperor required across the Forth–Clyde isthmus. A number of forts were set out along the projected line: from east to west, Carriden, on the shore of the Forth, Mumrills, Castlecary, Bar Hill, a mile south-west of Kilsyth, Balmuildy and Old Kilpatrick on the north shore of the Clyde. These are generally called the primary forts of the Antonine Wall and they were intended to accommodate one unit of auxiliaries, infantry or cavalry, even though Mumrills at 7¼ acres (3ha), was nearly twice as large as any other Antonine Wall fort. The sites may have been chosen because, apart from Carriden, it has been suggested that each had been occupied in some form during Flavian times. No structural signs have survived to support this, though it is interesting that fragments of Samian and/or coarse pottery of the late first century have been found

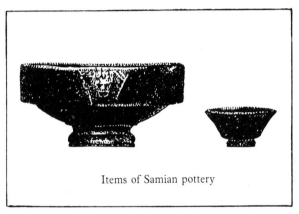

Items of Samian pottery

at each, and coins dating from the late first century have also been found at Balmuildy, Castlecary and Mumrills. If the sites were originally Flavian, it would have been foolish not to use them. If they were not, and the coins and sherds were simply dropped there by Antonine builders, the sites will have been chosen by Lollius Urbicus for reasons of distance to fit into an overall plan for the continuous frontier. From Old Kilpatrick to Balmuildy and from Balmuildy to Bar Hill is nine miles in each case. Then, there are only six miles to Castlecary, but nine miles from Castlecary to Mumrills. The last gap, to Carriden, is seven and a half miles. All the gaps represented less than a day's march for a fully equipped legion or unit of auxiliaries; indeed, more like half a day's march.

In some respects, the frontier that emerged bore resemblance to Hadrian's frontier, with major forts more or less evenly spaced,

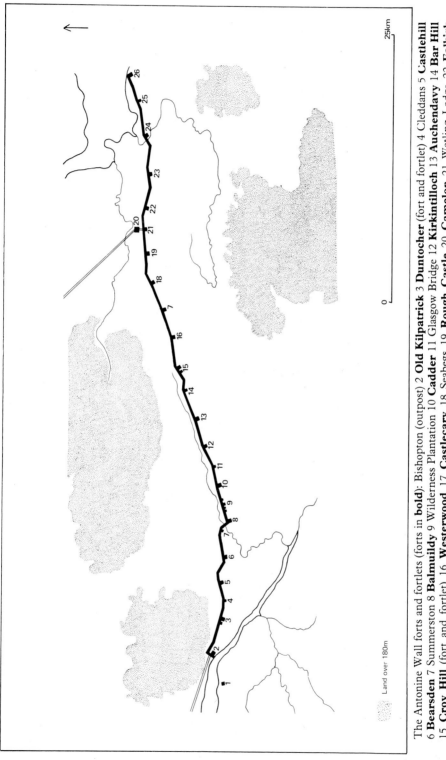

The Antonine Wall forts and fortlets (forts in **bold**): Bishopton (outpost) 2 **Old Kilpatrick** 3 **Duntocher** (fort and fortlet) 4 Cleddans 5 **Castlehill** 6 **Bearsden** 7 Summerston 8 **Balmuildy** 9 Wilderness Plantation 10 **Cadder** 11 Glasgow Bridge 12 **Kirkintilloch** 13 **Auchendavy** 14 **Bar Hill** 15 **Croy Hill** (fort and fortlet) 16 **Westerwood** 17 **Castlecary** 18 Seabegs 19 **Rough Castle** 20 **Camelon** 21 Watling Lodge 22 **Falkirk** 23 **Mumrills** 24 **Inveravon** 25 Kinneil 26 **Carriden**

Land over 180m

0   25km

interspersed with smaller forts and fortlets, linked all along by a continuous barrier structure and fronted northwards by a berm, then a deep, V-shaped ditch and finally a high bank; like Hadrian's Wall, its plan also changed during construction. However, there were substantial differences. The Wall was of turf for its entire length (apart from stone wings of stone forts fed into it). This was probably because turf walling was standard Roman practice for frontiers (there were several examples in Europe), whereas the stone walling of Hadrian was exceptional (we should bear in mind its commemorative function). There was no Vallum to the south, only a Military Way. Only two forts had stonework (Balmuildy and Castlecary). The Turf Wall itself was raised upon a stone base. There were no turrets as on Hadrian's Wall. Thus, the second frontier, though intended to be effective for its purpose and for the duration envisaged, was perhaps not seen as quite so permanent a feature of Roman occupation strategy as Hadrian's Wall had been.

The construction of the Antonine Wall began in the eastern sector, probably in AD 142. The primary forts had already been started, and Balmuildy and Old Kilpatrick finished, before the turf wall reached them. Two inscriptions found at Balmuildy show that it was built in the time of Lollius Urbicus and he left Britain in 143. The construction work was to be divided between the three legions (see p 108) who were allotted about 4½ Roman miles each, ie about 13 Roman miles (12 English miles) together, for each building season. The total length of the frontier was to be almost 40 Roman miles (36½ English miles).

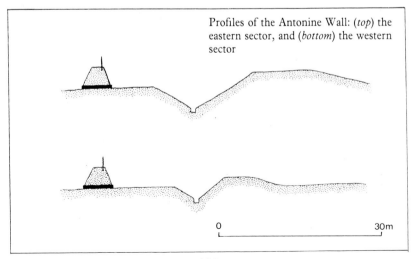

Profiles of the Antonine Wall: (*top*) the eastern sector, and (*bottom*) the western sector

0   30m

Presumably Lollius Urbicus expected that it would be completed by about AD 146.

The basic scheme was a rampart of turf or clay blocks laid upon a cobbled stone base (edged by dressed kerbstones), between 4.5 and 6m (15–20ft) wide, rising to more than 3–3.25m (10–11ft), with a wall-walk fronted by a palisade of wooden planks or, as has been suggested, willow wattle breastwork.[5] Culverts were inserted through the earth-work to drain off the excess water in what the Romans had discovered to be a rain-prone region. The ditch north of the wall was of varying width, from 6 to 12m (20–40ft), and up to 3.5m (13ft) deep, normally V-shaped with a cleaning slot. The profile was not uniform throughout. There was one stretch at Croy Hill where the ground rock was too hard for cutting a ditch. The far side of the ditch was built up from the earth dug out of it to form a high bank.

The location and construction of the forts and fortlets along the Wall have been the subject of extensive investigation and accelerating discussion in recent years, and anything summarised here will doubt-less soon need revision. In addition to the primary forts, it is now the received view that Lollius Urbicus planned to put fortlets in between the six at one-mile intervals along the entire length, making forty structures between Carriden and Old Kilpatrick. Only nine of these fortlets have so far been found, though the possible sitings (or intended sitings) of the remainder have been suggested.[6] The nine are (east to west) Kinneil, Watling Lodge, Seabegs Wood, Croy Hill (very close to the later fort there), Glasgow Bridge, Wilderness Plantation, Summerston (discovered in 1980), Cleddans and Duntocher. Some of the fortlets were begun simultaneously with the primary forts, and this lends weight to the suggested initial plan.

As with Hadrian's Wall, there was a change in the plan during the construction. Several new forts were to be added along the line, some in fresh ground, some beside fortlets already completed or partly built, some to take the place of fortlets. The small-size ³/₅ acre (0.25ha) fort at Duntocher was one early manifestation of the changed plan, and in this case the turf wall had not yet reached the first fortlet there when the fort was raised abutting it.[7] The new fort at Croy Hill was built about 70m (80yd) to the east of the fortlet recently completed. The other forts added during this change of plan, which have so far been discovered, were (east to west) Inveravon, Falkirk, Rough, Westerwood, Auchendavy, Kirkintilloch,[8] Cadder,[9] Bearsden and Castlehill. There may have been a few more which may emerge from

The ditch in front of the
Antonine Wall, Watling Lodge

aerial photography or ground exploration in the future.

Each of the forts and fortlets along the wall was erected with its northerly wall forming an integral part of the wall, except for Carriden which is quite separate from the Wall, and Bar Hill where the fort is about 27m (30yd) south, with its own surrounding ditch. The internal arrangements of all forts were such that they faced northwards, except for those at Cadder which faced eastwards, and this could be taken to indicate a basic difference between the Antonine Wall and Hadrian's Wall, namely, that the Antonine Wall was a more aggressively orientated frontier, designed to provide a linear group of garrisons in post ready to move out into Caledonian territory on the offensive as well as the defensive. Moreover, a shorter frontier was easier to hold. And, of course, forts built north of the wall in earlier times and then abandoned were reoccupied, and among these were Ardoch, Bertha and Strageath. The total garrison (c7,000 men) for the Antonine Wall was only a little less than that (c8,500 men) for Hadrian's Wall which was almost twice as long.[10]

The internal buildings of the forts and fortlets were of stone and/or timber. Stone was generally reserved for the *principia*, the commandant's quarters, the fort granary and, in most forts, the bath house. The interior arrangements varied considerably from fort to fort, and these are indicated in most cases on the plans illustrating the Gazetteer entries. Some forts had an annexe immediately to the east or

115

This is a second-century tombstone found at Croy Hill fort on the Antonine Wall. It shows three legionaries

west side. The shapes and sizes differed; at Bearsden the annexe on the east was the same depth (north to south) as the fort and half the width, and it contained a bath house in the north-east corner; at Rough Castle, the annexe was about the same depth but somewhat wider, and likewise contained the bath house, in the south-west corner. Bath houses are found in the fort itself in several cases, as at Balmuildy (north-west corner), Castlecary (south-east corner) and Cadder (north-east corner).

Linking the forts and fortlets behind the wall was the Military Way. This probably ran the whole length of the frontier, though large sections of it have still to be located. The road was 5–7m (17–20yd) wide. In one or two cases it ran through a fort, forming the *via principalis*, as at Rough (where the Military Way also had a fork bypassing the south of the fort), and Croy Hill; while at Bar Hill it ran north of the fort, between it and the wall. There are traces of the Military Way beyond the most westerly fort of Old Kilpatrick. A prevailing view is that this extension ran to a harbour at or near

Dumbarton on the Clyde. Another Antonine Wall structure of interest, traces of which have been found in at least three locations, is the 'expansion', a squarish platform built as a turf projection on a stone base southwards from the wall itself. Three pairs of these platforms have been identified, two at Rough and one at Croy Hill. Did these support signal towers?

The Antonine Wall ends at the west of Old Kilpatrick, where the rampart suddenly turns sharply down to the Clyde. About three miles to the south-west, on the other side of the river, a fort was built at Whitemoss, near Bishopton, in this period and it may be regarded as an outpost fort. There were two further fortlets in this area, at Lurg Moor and at Outerwards, which overlook the Clyde estuary. At the eastern end of the Wall, the earlier structures at Cramond and Inveresk provided some outpost protection.

The frontier was probably completed in AD148, having taken longer than at first reckoned, because of the changes in plan. The programme of building thirteen mile stretches per season to be split between the three legions was not adhered to.[11] But the army had been fully occupied for several years and doubtless the discontent generated by the long inactivity in Hadrian's time had been pacified.

The Antonine Wall had, however, not long been completed when the province was involved in some serious and protracted trouble. It is difficult to be precise, though a major rebellion among the Brigantes, the tribe supposedly living at peace in the large area bounded by the line of the Trent in the south to the Tyne–Solway, is suggested by a far from helpful source of the second century, the Greek travel writer, Pausanias.[12] If the Brigantes were in revolt, they may possibly have been in collusion with the Caledonians, a combination which would pose a major threat to Rome. Sometime in the early or mid 150s, as the evidence at some forts shows, the Roman forces were indeed in some danger: the Wall was evacuated and several forts were damaged by fire. The buildings at Bearsden were destroyed, the bath house at Balmuildy was dismantled and the ramparts at Mumrills were slighted. These, and no doubt other slightings not yet attested, together with the destruction of the fort at Birrens and the serious assault on the fort at Newstead, seem more or less to coincide with the arrival in the province of a new governor, Gn. Julius Verus, who brought with him, or arranged to follow him soon afterwards, substantial reinforcements for the legions in Britain. This was in AD155. Did Verus order the abandonment of the Antonine Wall and the reoccupation of Hadrian's Wall? There is evidence that parts of the latter were repaired at about this time, in particular by Legio VI, and some of the causeways across the Vallum were removed. Some forts lower down in the province, especially in the Pennines, were reopened. Did Verus intend to abandon the Antonine Wall permanently or did he hope to recover it once the troubles were over?

We should all like to know the answers to these questions, to know what really happened in the decades 150–60 and 160–70, but even the specialists in this period of Romano-British history admit to uncertainty. Soon after the withdrawal to Hadrian's Wall, there is evidence that some of the southern Scottish forts were reoccupied, including Newstead which in excavation revealed signs of quick repairs following the assault above, and Crawford. Verus was succeeded in 158 by a governor whose name is imprecise: Longinus is the preferred name. He was followed in 161 by M. Statius Priscus, a man of high reputation who was almost at once recalled to deal with a more urgent crisis in Cappadocia (AD162). A return to the Antonine Wall was ordered, perhaps by the emperor himself, who would not have wanted to see it permanently deserted. This marks the beginning of what is called the Antonine II period. The overall manning of the frontier was reduced. Balmuildy's garrison was cut; the establishment for a thousand-strong cohort of infantry at Old Kilpatrick was halved; Bearsden fort was not reoccupied at all. Possibly a few fortlets were likewise left empty, though Breeze and Dobson[13] believe that perhaps thirty of the original total of forts and fortlets were regarrisoned. Yet it turned out to be only a brief period. In 161, Antoninus Pius died and was succeeded by his adopted heir, Marcus Antoninus, better known as the philosopher-statesman, Marcus Aurelius. Marcus' biographer, Capitolinus, recorded a number of disasters affecting the empire in the first year of the new reign, among them, troubles in Britain, and that Marcus sent a new governor to Britain, Calpurnius Agricola, presumably with instructions not to overstretch the existing forces in the province, since no reinforcements would be available (*Marcus Antoninus* vii, 9). Calpurnius Agricola arrived in 162–3, and the current view is that during his governorship (162/3–66), the order to withdraw altogether from the Antonine Wall was implemented, and that once more Hadrian's Wall was to be the northern frontier. Clearly the Romans wished to dress up the withdrawal as a redisposition of their forces, for some strategic control was kept in the lowlands; the Antonine Wall fort of Castlecary appears to have been retained, so were Newstead and the chain down Dere Street to Corbridge, plus others in the Dumfries and Galloway region, including rebuilt Birrens. There are also signs that the Romans had started to 'buy off' the Caledonians with silver bullion, attested by hoards found in such parts as the Fife Region which cannot be accounted for by normal trade.

Meanwhile, Hadrian's Wall was extensively renovated. Damaged forts and turrets were repaired, milecastles that had had their gates removed in the 140s now had them refitted. And the last part of the western Turf Wall was now converted to stonework. The Vallum, considerably affected by the succession of changes to the frontier and doubtless ravaged by the weather, was cleaned out. The soil was heaped along the south making a third but smaller mound. This was the time when the Military Way was laid out, some 6m (20ft) wide, between the Wall and the north bank of the Vallum, in places actually running along the top of the bank. The renovations were limited to the east–west frontier, plus a few selected forts and milecastles along the Cumbrian coast scheme which was otherwise to be lightly garrisoned.

Calpurnius Agricola left Britain and the next years are, to say the least, hazy. There is a phrase in the biography of Marcus Aurelius that war threatened in Britain 169–70 (S. H. A., *Marcus Antoninus* xxii, 1) and, according to Dio Cassius, in 175 some five and a half thousand Sarmatian cavalry were sent to the province.[14] These horsemen had formed part of an exchange between the emperor and the ruler of the Sarmatians on the Danube, who had been at war. Beyond this, there is no helpful evidence as to what use the cavalry was put. Archaeological evidence indicates a large-scale refurbishing and reoccupation of forts in northern England, as at Binchester, Ebchester, Lancaster, Manchester, Ribchester and Templeborough. Sarmatians are recorded on inscriptions at Ribchester, not of this date but of the early third century. Were they veterans of the original Sarmatian cavalry?

In 180 Marcus Aurelius died. He had designated his son, Commodus, as his heir. A more worthless successor to the celebrated emperor one cannot imagine. The consensus of ancient opinion is that Commodus was the epitome of evil: cruel, bloodthirsty, debauched, amoral, recklessly extravagant, faithless, sodden with drink, given up to every vice known to man; even if half of it were true, he appears worse than Caligula, Nero and Domitian rolled into one.[15] This disastrous choice was to give the empire one of the most traumatic decades of imperial rule throughout its history. The empire could certainly have done without the major war in Britain in 180 that Dio Cassius reports, 'when the tribes in that island, crossing the wall that separated them from the Roman legions, proceeded to do much mischief and cut down a general together with his troops . . .'[16] Maddeningly, Dio Cassius does not say which wall, but forts along Hadrian's Wall, including those at Haltonchesters, Greatchesters and nearby Corbridge, have revealed signs of destruction at that period. The response to the trouble was to send the 'temperate, frugal, incorruptible but unpleasant' general, Ulpius Marcellus, to Britain as governor.[17] Stern and uncompromising like the worthies of the early Roman republic, Ulpius Marcellus dealt with the tribes with exceptional severity. The victory was commemorated with special coins in 184. Within a year, Ulpius Marcellus was back in Rome standing trial, and the troops in Britain were offering the imperial purple to one of their officers.

We read in Dio Cassius that Ulpius Marcellus was about to be put to death, but was pardoned.[18] He gives no reasons, but we may perhaps speculate that the severity with which he put down the tribes in Britain spilled over on to his own troops whom he blamed for allowing the attacks to take place. This severity provoked a mutiny, in which the troops offered the imperial throne to one Priscus, a unit commander who sensibly declined it. Marcellus returned to Rome, and was no doubt arrested when he made his report. The troops remained restive, however, aggravated by some army administrative changes introduced by Commodus' praetorian prefect, Perennius. They took the unusual step of sending to Rome a huge delegation of some fifteen hundred 'javelin-men', as Dio Cassius described them (which may mean legionaries) to protest. They were met by Commodus himself who weakly gave into their demand for the head of Perennius. The emperor then sent a new governor to Britain: P. Helvius Pertinax, who had served in the island some years earlier and who had been consul twice.

Pertinax tried to pacify the disaffected elements of the army in Britain, but in another outbreak of trouble he was almost killed: 'indeed, he was left among the slain' (Helvius Pertinax, iii–iv). When he recovered he punished the offending legion so severely that the disaffection spread, and he asked Rome if he might be recalled. Commodus consented and Pertinax received a civilian post in Italy. It was AD187. The next few years are obscure in Roman Britain but in 191–2 a new governor arrived, Clodius Albinus.

By 192, Rome had had quite enough of the antics and excesses of Commodus (he had even taken to entering the gladiatorial ring as a combatant) and he was murdered by his mistress, Marcia, with the connivance of palace officials. His death was regretted by few: indeed, in many parts of the empire feeling against him was so high that records of his reign, such as inscriptions and statues, were smashed, which has done much to obscure the closing years of his reign. When the deed was done, the murderers offered the imperial throne to Pertinax, then *praefectus urbi*. Pertinax accepted, though he was an old man for his sixty years, but was himself assassinated less than three months later by the same palace gang. Then an extraordinary thing happened to the imperial office: the praetorian prefect who had been one of the murderers put the office up for sale by auction and a rich senator, Didius Julianus, bought it, promising to give a huge bonus to the army as well. He, too, lasted only a few weeks, and was put to death at the orders of the North African born ex-consul, L. Septimius Severus, perhaps the best army commander then in service, whose troops had begged him to take over the empire and restore order, not without much encouragement from himself.[19]

Severus was to prove one of the greatest of all the Roman emperors. We may date his reign from AD193, though the first four years were absorbed by desperate civil war, as there were two contenders for his imperial office. One was Pescennius Niger, governor and commander-in-chief of the army in the Syrian province, who was proclaimed emperor at Antioch; the other was Clodius Albinus in Britain. The story of the civil war is complex. Severus decided to deal first with Niger, and to that end he sought to neutralise Albinus by offering to make him Caesar. Albinus, confident that the army in Britain would remain loyal to him in any future bid for the supreme power, accepted. This allowed Severus to take swift action against Niger, whom he defeated and put to death, probably in AD195.

NOTES
1. Attested by inscriptions citing Lollius and Legio II *Augusta*.
2. The erection of an Agricolan, or immediately subsequent, fort here is not yet incontestable.
3. These were definitely forts at later dates.
4. It is still possible that Carpow has a Severan beginning (early third century).
5. Breeze, D. J., 'Note on Bearsden fort'. *Britannia* x (1979) p 276.
6. See Keppie, L. J. F. and Walker, J. J., 'Fortlets on the Antonine Wall at Seabegs Wood, Kinneil and Cleddans'. *Britannia* xii (1981) pp 143–62.
7. Nor had the wall reached Cleddans when the fortlet there was built. This was

shown when the fortlet was discovered in January 1980 (see *Britannia* xi (1980) p 353).

8. First-century coins found at this site must leave open the possibility of an earlier foundation.

9. First-century Samian ware was found here, likewise suggesting an earlier foundation.

10. Interestingly, only three forts are known to have accommodated cavalry in any strength, Mumrills (an *ala*), Castlecary (mixed cavalry and infantry) and Bearsden (provided with cavalry quarters). See Breeze, D. J. (1982) p 111.

11. Breeze, D. J. (1982) pp 108–11.

12. Pausanias, *Description of Greece* VIII, xliv, 5.

13. Breeze, D. and Dobson, B. (1976) p 122.

14. Dio Cassius, lxxii, 16.

15. S. H. A., *Commodus Antoninus*, contains a catalogue of criticisms.

16. Dio Cassius, lxxiii, 8.

17. There has been some discussion concerning Ulpius Marcellus, ie when he actually came to Britain, who sent him (Marcus Aurelius or Commodus?), whether he served two separate periods in the province, even whether there was a second Ulpius Marcellus. See notes by Jarrett, M. G. *Britannia* ix (1978) p 291; Brassington, M. *Britannia* xi (1980) pp 314–15; Simpson, C. J. *Britannia* xi (1980) pp 338–9.

18. Dio Cassius, lxxiii, 8.

19. Herodian, *History* II, 9–10.

8
ROMAN BRITAIN
IN THE THIRD CENTURY

The defeat of Niger brought the confrontation between Severus and Albinus a step closer. As Severus left Syria on his way back to Rome, news reached him that Albinus had revolted in Gaul. Albinus had not deserted his province of Britain without thought for its protection, for part of his rebel forces were troops from the British garrisons, and he ensured that town defences were in good order. Presumably, he arranged for this to be done while he made a swift crossing over to Gaul where at Lugdunum (Lyon), the capital of Gaul, he set up his headquarters. If he should lose in Gaul he could carry on the fight in Britain. Severus, meanwhile, changed direction for Gaul and sent word on ahead to the Rhine legions to make for Lugdunum. An engagement was fought in which Albinus defeated the Severan advance forces under Virius Lupus, governor of Lower Germany.[1] Then the two rivals clashed for the deciding battle outside the Gallic capital, which is described by both Herodian and Dio Cassius.[2] After a desperate struggle, in which Severus was knocked off his horse and his troops began to waver because they thought he had been killed, the emperor rallied the men. The timely intervention in his support by one of his generals, Laetus, who had been waiting on the wings to see who was going to win, enabled Severus to turn disaster into victory. Albinus committed suicide or, as Herodian stated, was taken and executed. It was February AD197. Severus was now undisputed master of the Roman world.

Albinus' campaign reduced the strength of the British garrisons, particularly along the northern frontier and perhaps also at forts in the Brigantian lands which were always somewhat unstable. It was clearly necessary to restore the strengths in Britain as soon as possible, and one of Severus' first acts after the Lugdunum victory was to appoint a new governor for the island, Virius Lupus (197–202), and send him over with reinforcements. And not too soon, for the tribes north of the Forth–Clyde isthmus had taken advantage of the depleted Roman forces and invaded the province. They included a hitherto unrecorded tribe, the Maeatae[3] (which may have been a confederacy), whose name is perpetuated in two places in their old territory, namely, Dumyat Hill, near Stirling, where there is a residual hillfort, and Myot Hill, at the east end of the Campsies.

There has been much discussion among Romano-British specialists as to the nature and extent of the invasion. Was it a major disaster, which included the partial destruction of the frontier and a series of penetrating assaults deep into the province, perhaps supported by restive elements of the Brigantes, as far south as the legionary fortress at York, as some have interpreted the archaeological evidence of the period discovered at Hadrianic Wall and other forts? Or was it a less serious matter, in which damage was done, certainly, but in a series of border skirmishes over a longer period? The latter is more probable. Severus made no attempt to come in person to Britain after the collapse of Albinus' revolt: a new governor with fresh troops was considered enough. Moreover, Dio Cassius, who records the fact that Lupus preferred to buy off the Maeatae with a cash payment, but nevertheless took several hostages, makes no mention of any disaster. If the Hadrianic Wall forts had been destroyed, surely this would have been recorded. Nor does Herodian indicate any calamity. Severus' biographer, Spartianus, says that Severus built a wall across Britain from sea to sea to secure the province (*Severus*, xviii), but this must refer to a wider reconstruction programme affecting many forts over the whole northern frontier area, forts which would have required repair work in the normal course of existence. The wooden parts, and these were in the majority in nearly all forts, were bound to have suffered deterioration. Inscriptions referring to building (or rebuilding) works have been found relating to many forts from the Lowlands down to Hadrian's Wall and further south to the Pennine forts and even as far as York, and they cover a longish period, cAD 197 to the end of the first quarter of the third century. The first batch repaired or rebuilt were the Pennine series, including Ilkley, Brough-under-Stainmore and Bowes, in the time of Virius Lupus, to be followed by work on Benwell, Chesters, Birdoswald, High Rochester, Risingham and possibly Corbridge in the governorship of Alfenus Senecio (205–207). Others were attended to later still, under Severus and his successor.

If there was no major disaster in Britain during the period of Albinus' revolt, there was certainly some serious trouble in the north later, in the first decade of the third century. According to Herodian, 'the governor [probably Alfenus Senecio] sent a dispatch to say that the barbarians . . . were in a state of rebellion, laying waste the countryside, carrying off plunder and wrecking almost everything.'[4] The governor asked for reinforcements or for a personal visit of the emperor with an army. Severus responded quickly, for two reasons. For one thing, he is reported to have been concerned that his two youthful sons, Caracalla and Geta, were becoming lazy and corrupted by the soft and vicious life in Roman high society, and he wanted them to get some battle experience. Secondly, Severus himself could not resist, even at the age of 62 years, a chance to go to war again. Dio Cassius says that Severus aimed to conquer the whole of Britain.[5] Perhaps this had been in his mind, but he will have appreciated the need for a large army, major preparations and massive supplies, and until 207 he was preoccupied elsewhere.

In 207, Severus set out with his family, including his wife Julia Domna, and the Praetorian Guard. It was indeed a rare thing for an emperor to embark upon an extensive campaign, taking with him his family and the palace troops: clearly, he was confident of his position, and that all would remain quiet in the capital in his absence. On his way through Gaul he gathered reinforcements. He also took with him an immense amount of money, according to Dio Cassius. This is interesting. Was it because he expected to have to buy off the Caledonians or the Maeatae (as Lupus had in 197)? It cannot have been simply to pay the troops. The answer is linked to the question of how far Severus intended to go in Scotland: Dio says 'the whole of Caledonia'; according to Herodian, he was anxious to win some victories in Britain, to add to the successes he had already won elsewhere. Spartianus reports that in 210, Severus was awarded the title Britannicus, and this is shown on coins and inscriptions of the period. Archaeology does not bear out a complete conquest of Scotland, but many Romano-British specialists are inclined to reckon that he had greater success than the ancient chroniclers admit. Let us look at his progress.

In 208, Severus and his party reached the north and set up headquarters presumably at York, at least on Dere Street. The army was mustered and supply arrangements organised. The fort at South Shields, on the estuary of the Tyne, was converted into a huge depot,

Part of the latrine in the north-west corner of the Roman fort at Cramond, Edinburgh (*Royal Commission on Ancient Monuments, Scotland*)

and some twenty granaries were built, which it is clear were to be kept supplied by sea as well as by land. Corbridge fort received new granaries too, and a new courtyard building (which may have been a forum for the new town).[6] This was to be a second depot. The new building was not finished but its importance on the main road into Scotland was crucial to the campaign. The fort at Newstead may also have been refurbished and reoccupied, and the supply base and its fort at Cramond were definitely repaired and reoccupied.

At the start of the campaigning season of 209 (unless it was at the close of the 208 season), the emperor moved northwards to the Forth–Clyde isthmus and 'after the army had crossed the rivers and fortifications which marked the borders of the empire' (the Antonine Wall, by then abandoned for more than forty years but still a major obstacle), edged into Fife.[7] The campaign was no walkover: the Caledonians and the Maeatae resorted to guerilla tactics ('frequent clashes and light skirmishes . . . the enemy found it easy to escape and hide in the woods and marshes' – Herodian), and wore the Roman army down far more than Severus had reckoned. Once into Fife and through to the Tay, a progress marked by the erection of a series of marching camps, mostly of about 63 acres (25.5ha) (which have been spotted from the air and in some instances excavated), Severus put down a new legionary fortress, at Carpow, of about 24 acres (9.3ha), probably in 210. By this time he had received the title Britannicus. The site has been excavated in great detail and has revealed, among many things, tile fragments stamped with the record that Legio VI *Victrix* had been called *Britannica*. The excavations also indicate that before the fortress was begun, a temporary camp had been built there. The fortress is distinguished by its extensive buildings in stone, and it was built by detachments from Legio VI *Victrix* and Legio II *Augusta*. The conversion of the temporary camp into a fully fledged fortress suggests that Severus changed his strategy once he had overcome the Fife Region, and decided to attempt the conquest of the whole of Scotland. Dio Cassius says he did not desist until he had approached the extremity of the island.[8] The series of marching camps located up the north-east from Carpow to Muiryfold in the Grampian Region is evidence that the region was over-run, but the absence of camps further west or higher up equally indicates that the conquest of the north was not completed. Possibly Severus thought he had reached the top of Scotland when he arrived at the Moray Firth south shore.

Severus tried to draw the tribes into open battle, as Agricola had done, but they would not come, preferring the guerilla warfare which 'made the war considerably longer drawn out' (Herodian). Yet he seems to have forced the tribes to come to terms, for he left the north and made his way back to the legionary base at York. By now, Severus was ailing, with some long-drawn out illness, described by Spartianus

A third-century tile stamped with the inscription LEG· VI· VIC· B·P·F found at Carpow fort, Perthshire. *Legio VI Victrix* was normally stationed at York, but served with Emperor Severus in his Scottish campaigns, 208–11

as a most grievous disease (*morbo gravissimo*), and his difficulties were greatly aggravated by his family, especially his elder son, Caracalla. Unable to wait for his father to die, Caracalla was conspiring to take over the empire and to murder his brother Geta, so that he might become sole Augustus. There is also a suggestion that Julia Domna was also causing him sadness by her continued infidelities. When the Maeatae broke the treaty they had made, Severus was too ill to lead the punitive expedition that was prepared, and Caracalla took command. Again, the Maeatae were joined by the Caledonians. Caracalla appears to have had no stomach for the renewed war, but preferred to spend his time canvassing support in the army for his ambitions. Severus died in February 211 at York, and his two sons were hailed jointly as successors. Caracalla had found no support for his aims. The war in Scotland was closed and the army withdrew, after a second treaty. The royal family then returned to Rome, taking with them the ashes of the dead emperor in an urn, for burial in the imperial mausoleum (Hadrian's tomb, now called Castel S'Angelo).

The pullout from northern and eastern Scotland was probably gradual; there is evidence that building was still going on at Carpow in 212, possibly a year or so later. How far south the army withdrew is not known for certain, but probably to Hadrian's Wall, though Roman units patrolled over wide areas north of the Wall. The expeditions had done much to silence the tribes: there was peace along the frontier and in Brigantia for the best part of the next century and this may be partly due to the further strengthening of the northern frontier. Severus had divided the province into two parts, under separate commands. They were Britannia Inferior, with a provincial capital at York and a garrison of one legion together with auxiliaries, and Britannia Superior, with its capital at London, and two legions, one at Caerleon and the other at Chester. There is doubt about the date of the split: Herodian suggests 197, after the defeat of Albinus, but the prevailing view now is towards the end of Severus' reign, and that it did not take effect until after his death.

This is an appropriate place at which to look briefly at the domestic history of the province during the past century and a half. We have seen that the process of urbanisation in Britain, begun soon after the conquest, was given a sharp boost in Flavian times.[9] By the end of the first century, or soon afterwards, the first *civitas* capitals had been founded and most, if not all, had been given their distinguishing features of *forum* (market place), *basilica* attached or nearby (rectangular hall, with nave and aisles and recess at one end, for court hearings and administrative business), and in some cases the public baths had been started. Also begun was the *curia* (though not always called that), a council chamber which in some towns was part of the *basilica*.

There were, of course, other major buildings and civil engineering works put up in these towns, such as temples, theatres, amphitheatres, *mansiones* (hotels for official travellers), waterworks, sewers and public lavatories. The style and features of these buildings are described in chapter 12. The towns were laid out on a grid system where the two main streets formed an intersection near the centre and the central *forum–basilica* complex occupied one of the corners so formed. The street plan was divided into rectangular blocks, or *insulae*, which contained other public buildings, private houses, perhaps blocks of flats, and shops. One or two towns like Silchester were originally surrounded by a defensive earthwork, but most were, until the end of the second century, without any defence at all. In addition to the towns, the Romans founded two more *coloniae* (towns inhabited by Roman or Latin citizens, usually retired army veterans) at Gloucester (*Glevum*) around AD96 and at Lincoln (*Lindum*) in about AD90, both sites of earlier legionary fortresses.

In the countryside, British agriculture expanded over the period, which was manifest in the growing number of Roman-style farm-steads. These are usually called *villas*, which term will suffice at present (but see chapter 13). A villa was a farming establishment, that is, it was the house and the farm associated with it. The earliest villas began as simple cottage types, one storey high, consisting of a row of rooms without a corridor, but interconnecting, or a few rooms either side of a lobby, sometimes with animal quarters built on somewhere along the structure. Towards the end of the first century AD the villa began to appear more elaborate: the winged corridor type had evolved by about AD100 and this was a development in which the rectangular range of rooms was enlarged by wings at both ends, having a verandah, or a front corridor, along one longer side. The winged corridor villa was either a modification of an earlier cottage type or it was a new villa. Some of the winged corridor types were built in stone.

There was another type emerging at the beginning of the second century, the courtyard villa, built round three sides of a rectangle, approached by an entrance gateway in the fourth side. And one or two versions of an otherwise normally fourth century villa type, the aisled house, started to be built in isolated areas. The aisled house was a rectangular building divided inside by nave and flanking aisles with posts, sectioned with partitions to make rooms. The house was roofed and the light for inner rooms was provided from clerestory openings.

Villas were an integral part of farming, and farming was more productive in Britain in the lowland fields south and east of the line running roughly from Exeter across to the Humber. As towns grew, the demand for farming produce accelerated, so that in the second century it is thought that agriculture enjoyed boom conditions, which in turn generated an expansion in the size of villas. Villa owners were enlarging their farms and taking on more staff, and villas now began to accommodate the family of the owner and the workforce in separate quarters. Yet it has to be remembered that the prosperity of the villa depended to some extent upon the growth of the towns.

It is clear that the second century was a most prosperous period for the province. By the end of it, most of the towns and the *vici* that were

Reassembled painted plaster on a wall found at Blue Boar Lane in Leicester (*Leicestershire Museums, Art Galleries & Records Service*)

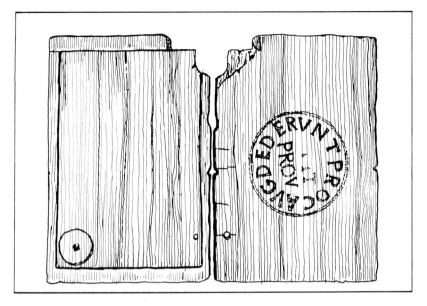

A writing tablet found by the Walbrook in London. It is stamped with a legend which translated means 'issued by the Imperial Procurators of the Province of Britain'

built in the Roman period had been completed or at least reached the fullest extent planned for them; in some cases they had already begun to contract in overall size, though not necessarily in prosperity. They were built in both stone and timber: the widespread remains of burnt timber found in excavations in St Albans have indicated that the town was largely built of timber when it was wrecked by a fire c155. Most of the public buildings in the towns had been completed and were in use. Private houses, commercial premises (factories, shops, banks etc) had been raised in great numbers in all towns. We may look at Leicester (*Ratae Coritanorum*).

Ratae had begun as a fort, as yet not clearly defined but thought to have been built in the late 40s or early 50s. A second fort was raised in the late 50s, or early 60s, nearby to the north-east. Concurrently, a *vicus* was developing beside the two forts. In the 80s the second fort was given up, the land was handed over to the civilian authorities, and the *vicus* was developed into the *civitas* capital of the Coritani.[10] The town was built on the regular grid pattern, and it rose somewhat slowly. But in the time of Hadrian major construction was carried out. A fine new *forum* and *basilica* were raised in the area of the present junction between Vaughan Way and St Nicholas Circle and to the west a new public bath house was built a decade or two later, and this

131

North face of foundations of the north portico of the *forum* at the *civitas* capital *Ratae* (Leicester), located in the early 1960s at Great Central Street (as it was then) (*Leicestershire Museums, Art Galleries & Records Service*)

Part of the Jewry Wall at the *civitas* capital *Ratae* (Leicester), now recognised as part of the *palaestra* of the baths. Taken in 1937 (*National Monuments Record*)

was completed in about AD160. The colonnaded hall of the baths ran north to south opposite the west side of the *forum*. Part of the west wall of the hall survives today to a height of over 11m (36ft), and is known as Jewry Wall. It survived partly because it was later incorporated into a Saxon church. Many houses and shops were also built, mainly in stone, in which several fine wall paintings and mosaics have survived. The scale and grandeur of the public buildings have led to suggestions that *Ratae* had *municipium* status, but this remains to be resolved. By the third century the town had become a major commercial centre.

There is one place that is different from other Roman towns and *vici* in Britain, and that is London, which began to emerge from a pre-Roman settlement probably soon after Julius Caesar's invasions. After the Claudian conquest, London's strategic and commercial position on the Thames dictated that the principal military roads built by the Romans as they consolidated their hold on the south should radiate outwards from it, notably Watling Street and Ermine Street. An early fort was erected in London, which may not have lasted more than a few years, but which led to a *vicus* developing around it.[11] The *vicus* flowered quickly into a busy commercial centre, and in the 50s it is likely that the Romans had decided to base some of their administration there. Almost certainly, the chief office of the financial procurator was at London: Decianus Catus would have been based there in AD61 when he declined to do more than send two hundred troops to the rescue of Colchester during the revolt of Boudica. By the time the great queen was at the outskirts of London, bent on destroying it, there was already much to destroy. Evidence of her activities continues to be revealed in excavations in the capital.

Decianus Catus' successor, Classicianus, rebuilt the burnt *vicus* and began to enlarge it. Among the major structures of this and succeeding procuratorships was a large stone courtyard block, with hall and ranges, that has been deduced as an office block for the procurator or as the first *forum*. Interestingly, this covered the remains of an earlier pre-Boudican stone office building, perhaps for the same official. By the 80s, London was already the biggest urban sprawl in the province and had become the official place of residence of the governor, with a *praetorium* (palace) built beside present-day Cannon Street Station, and a *basilica* and *forum* (later to become the largest in the province) a few hundred yards to the north, at Cornhill. The settlement may have become a *municipium* at this time. In the 120s and 130s a new fort was

Londinium (London) as it might have looked from the air in the early second century AD. Note the fort at top centre. From a painting by the late Alan Sorrell (*Museum of London*)

erected on the north side of the settlement, at present-day Cripplegate, and it may have been intended for the governor's personal guard battalion. The fort was not part of any larger defence system surrounding London, which did not have any outer defences until the end of the century when a two-mile stretch of stone wall, between 2.25 and 2.75m (7–9ft) thick, was raised in an arc from Ludgate Circus (or nearby) via Newgate, Cripplegate (where it joined the fort),

Bishopsgate, Aldgate, to the site of the Tower of London, ending beside the Thames which in that period was wider than today. From Ludgate south the wall probably led down to the water's edge at or near Blackfriar's Bridge.

Along with the major public works, a considerable programme of private residential and commercial building was initiated, seemingly with much assistance from the Roman authorities, so that it has been estimated that London doubled in area, and doubtless in population as well, in the Flavian years, CAD70–120; in other words, the Romans were creating a capital city. And before the end of the second century, it is likely that the now famous temple of Mithras, discovered in 1954, and removed brick by brick to be resited a few hundred yards away in present-day Queen Victoria Street, was built.

The death of Severus in 211 heralded a long period of troubles for the Roman empire. There were protracted spells of inflation, evidenced by cuts in building projects, debasement of the coinage and so forth. The borders of the empire were increasingly under pressure from barbarian movements in Europe, especially in Germany, and pirates ravaged the coasts. Parthia, rejuvenated by a vigorous Persian warrior class led by a new dynasty of kings, the Sassanids, reopened the old conflict with Rome and tied down a sizeable part of the Roman army for much of the century. (In 260, the Parthian king, Sapor I, actually defeated and captured the Roman emperor Valerian.) At Rome itself, in the seventy-three years between Severus' death and the election of Diocletian in 284, no less than forty-two emperors, ruling jointly in pairs or on their own, rose and fell, nearly all of them murdered, and this does not include the handful of so-called 'Gallic emperors' who ruled over Gaul and Britain from 260 to 274. Yet despite these and many other difficulties, there was never any danger that Rome might collapse. The continual changes in leadership do not appear to have affected the basic stability of the imperial system, nor its capacity to deal with the problems. None of the contemporary literary sources gives any suggestion that order in the empire was breaking down. Romans were used to barbarians and knew how to deal with their raids. They understood inflation and learned to live with it. They had encountered piracy many times before and had beaten it. And they did not give up the struggle against the Parthian empire.

In Britain it is clear from the total absence of evidence to the contrary that the province enjoyed a relatively tranquil period in which the principal problem was inflation, although the island did not entirely escape the attention of pirates. The previously held view that recession hit Britain as a result of the revolt of Albinus and the subsequent campaigns in the north under Severus and Caracalla no longer stands unchallenged, for much recent work has shown that, far from being economically stagnant, the economy of Britain continued to flourish for significant periods of the third century. There is evidence of developing trade between Britain and the continent. The home-based pottery industries, particularly those in the Nene Valley, began to come into their own, after generations in which Gallic and German pottery exports had been dominating the market. The countryside continued to prosper, if from time to time at a reduced rate of progress, and this is reflected in the rebuilding and alteration of a wide variety of villas, and in the extension of arable farming into more northerly and westerly areas hitherto noted for the rearing of livestock. Whatever arrangements Caracalla had made on the northern frontier, they appear to have held firm for about three-quarters of a century. As one learned Romano-British work has put it, Britain 'slumbered and her army relaxed while the rest of the empire suffered.'[12]

The strengthening of the northern frontier took the form of rebuilding along the Wall and the refurbishing of at least four forts in front, at Bewcastle and Netherby to the west (original outposts of the Hadrian's Wall scheme) and at High Rochester and Risingham on Dere Street, to the east. Each of these received an enlarged garrison of a *cohors milliaria equitata*, a new military unit of a thousand infantry and cavalry mixed. Taking into account the garrisons along the Wall itself, the total frontier force is thought to have been as high as ten thousand, that is two thousand more than in earlier periods. No one would say that Caracalla could have guessed that this size of defence force would be enough to preserve peace along the frontier forever – he could at most forecast what seemed to be enough in his own time. It is also likely that peace was reinforced with heavy subsidies of Roman grain (a practice already resorted to elsewhere in the empire), and no doubt there were subsidies in the form of bullion, as the Falkirk hoard suggests.[13]

Forts on the Wall to be restored included Birdoswald, Chesters and Chesterholm. And in the early third century it seems that the great Vallum, already subjected to considerable mutilations since Hadrian's time, was finally abandoned as a military zone. In several places, the ditch was filled in and the associated stretches of rampart levelled to allow the building of civilian settlements, houses, shops, amenities or to give room for extensions to existing *vici*, even up to the walls of the forts themselves, as at Housesteads. This may have been the result of the decree of Severus that troops should be allowed to live at home with their wives.[14] The occupation of the Vallum area by civilians also suggests that the army no longer feared a 'stab-in-the-back' from the Brigantes or were confident that they could contain it. That risk had been lessened in any case by the creation of a new *civitas* capital at Carlisle (*Luguvalum Carvetiorum*) which may have been part of the Caracallan settlement or perhaps an even earlier arrangement, and

Part of the coin hoard of nearly 2,000 silver *denarii* found at Falkirk. The coins ranged from first century BC to about AD 230, and almost every emperor from Nero to Alexander Severus was represented (*National Museum of Antiquities of Scotland*)

which certainly went some way to break the unity of these potentially dangerous peoples. It may also be deduced that by the third century the military was getting on better with the native population, which must have been assisted by the decree of Caracalla in 212 that all free men and women in the empire should henceforth be Roman citizens.

The division of Britain into two provinces, effective from Caracalla's time though initiated by his father, may have been the result of Severus' anxiety to avoid a repetition of a governor of all Britain (Albinus) declaring himself emperor with the backing of a fifty-thousand-strong military arm. The approximate dividing line between the two was a right-angled bend from the Wirral down to Staffordshire and then across to the Wash, the northern province, Britannia Inferior, being only half the size of its neighbour. There was considerable building and restoration work on the forts in the north in the earlier part of the third century. Apart from the Wall forts, aqueducts were built at Chester-le-Street and at South Shields, the headquarters building at Lanchester was rebuilt and the bath house and *basilica* at Lancaster. A temple was restored at Ribchester. Other restorations of this time may emerge in future excavations. And the province's own capital, York, was to enjoy a period of expansion and prosperity. It had probably been elevated to *colonia* status by Severus or Caracalla, possibly from earlier *municipium* status, and it had had an imperial palace in the time of Severus. The town was replanned and a start made on the great stone surrounding wall.

As the century proceeds, there is evidence of some decline in the condition of the forts, especially the timber parts, which may be explained by the fact that they were being reduced or partially abandoned because they were not needed, as well as by natural deterioration. This seems to have gone hand-in-hand with growth in the civilian areas, as illustrated by improvements and enlargements in places like Carlisle, Aldborough and Lincoln.

In the southern province, the absence of literary evidence might lead one to suppose that all had been well there for the period, but it was not entirely so. In Wales, while it is no longer believed that the tribes took advantage of the troubles of the Albinian revolt and attacked Roman military establishments, it is clear that Severus had some reason for wanting to make his presence known there, even if only by selected gestures of refortification. The legionary fortress at Caerleon underwent a major overhaul in the early 200s, and repairs were carried out on forts at Castell Collen, Caersws (second), Caerhun and Caernarfon, and also at Gelligaer. And at Leintwardine in Herefordshire, where the first (Jay Lane) fort had been erected in the 50s, another fort of about 12 acres (4.8ha) was built anew in the late second century, on the Roman route from Chester to Caerleon.

In the remainder of the southern province, it looks as if military activity was at a low level throughout the central and western parts, but in the easterly areas, East Anglia, Kent and Sussex, and probably in Hampshire, a new danger to the province's security began to emerge before the end of the second century, which may have affected Lincolnshire and Humberside coastal regions as well. These were pirate raids, assaults on imperial shipping in transit between Britain and the Continent, and perhaps also on the coastal settlements, by German pirate fleets. To deal with this interference, the Romans strengthened one or two coastal and estuarine fort-protected naval and commercial ports, such as Dover, Lympne and Brough-on-Humber,

General view across the site of the town of Caister-on-Sea, Norfolk (*E. Houlder*)

and Caister-by-Yarmouth which may by then have had a fort. One or two new forts were also built, one at Reculver, near Herne Bay on the north Kent coast, to protect the Thames estuary, probably c230, and at much the same time (though possibly in the 240s) another, of 7 acres (2.5ha) at Brancaster, which is in north-west Norfolk and which guarded the approaches to the Wash. There had been a flourishing civilian settlement at Brancaster since the previous century. Both forts used to be bracketed among the well-known, but badly named, forts of the Saxon Shore, but they are both stylistically different from the earliest of the others in that list, and they antedate them by at least thirty years. It is possible that the base at Caister-by-Yarmouth also received attention at this time, and some authorities consider that another fort may have been raised on the Suffolk or Essex coast. These building works were quite extensive just for the purpose of dealing with pirate raiders who might land on the coast after being chased by Roman ships.

Large-scale building in towns had slowed down dramatically by the early part of the third century, but there was still a demand for houses and business premises. Public works were directed to the enclosing of towns with more durable and more impressive walling, ie of stone. The conversion of earth and timber defences to stone appears to have been carried out over a lengthy period, during several decades of the third century. The process had been started in a hurry by Albinus, but his scheme probably did not get beyond the foundations in one or two towns. We have seen that most of London's city wall was raised by the end of the second century. The wall at Silchester was built in the early third century (good stretches of it remain standing today), but Canterbury's was not begun until the 270s and is now mostly buried under the remains of the medieval city wall. Smaller settlements and *vici* also began to acquire stone walling, among which we may mention Dorchester-on-Thames and Godmanchester.

In the middle of the century, the empire suffered a series of major disasters, one after the other in the space of two years. The Alamanni, German barbarians, had been pressing down into Roman Germany, and in 258 had crashed into northern Italy. There they were checked by Roman forces under Gallienus, who was ruling as joint emperor with his father Valerian, but the Romans in Italy, especially in the capital, had had a severe shock. Two years later, Valerian himself, marching eastwards against the Sassanians to check their inroads into the eastern provinces, was defeated, tricked into agreeing to meet in conference with the Sassanid king, Sapor I, and promptly taken prisoner. He was never released. In the same year, Gallienus was worsted on the Rhine. At that moment, one of his trusted commanders, Postumus, seized Gallienus' son and put him to death, and declared himself emperor, not this time of the whole empire, but of a Western breakaway segment of Gaul, the German provinces, Spain and Britain, which came to be called the Empire of the Gallic Provinces (*Imperium Galliarum*). In a sense this was more dangerous to Rome than a usurper claiming the whole empire, for it divided the empire, weakened it and made it easy prey to barbarian onslaughts. Postumus ruled for nine years and there were two, or three, successors: Victorinus, Tetricus I and Tetricus II. Then in about 273 a strong emperor at Rome, Aurelian (270–75), succeeded in re-establishing vital unity under one head.

In Britain the separation period passed quietly. Much work was done to the road system, and some villas were enlarged (such as

The octagonal (?) dining room at Great Witcombe villa, Gloucestershire. It replaced a square room (*Crown Copyright*)

Witcombe), evidence of a steady growth in prosperity. It has been suggested that many businessmen from Gaul emigrated to Britain in these years. But Postumus was unable to hold inflation down, and he allowed the coinage to be debased seriously, which was aggravated by his successors whose coins were imitated in great quantities in illicit mints in Gaul and illegal dies in Britain. These coins are known as barbarian radiates. The Tetricus fakes were not the first copies of official coinage, but they were among the most numerous.

Aurelian restored order to the empire in a series of victories over its enemies; he reformed the monetary problems by issuing new coinage (and thus devaluing the older coins) and began to embark on badly needed reforms, but he was murdered in 275. After a spell of uncertainty, one of his generals, Probus, was chosen emperor and ruled for six years, in which time he introduced army reforms and crushed a serious assault by the Alamanni upon Gaul (in which more than sixty cities are said to have been sacked, few of them having had any protective walls). But Probus, too, was murdered and for the next two years a succession of emperors were raised and toppled, until in 284, C. Aurelianus Diocletianus (Diocletian), an Illyrian by birth and one of Aurelian's officers, was elected by the army in the east. Diocletian's reign was to last twenty-two years, and he retired from it of his own free will. It marked a new and better stage in the fortunes of Rome.

One of the many problems affecting Roman Britain during the uncertain times of the third century was an increase in the attacks along the eastern coast by barbarian (Saxon and Frankish) seafarers from Europe and by other unspecified pirates. To meet these dangers, certain ports on the eastern coast had been partly converted to naval use, and two new special coastal forts had been erected in the second quarter of the third century, at Brancaster (*Branodunum*) in north-west Norfolk to guard the Wash, and Reculver (*Regulbium*) in north Kent to protect the Thames Estuary. Later in the century, perhaps between c270 and c280, more forts were built, first at Burgh Castle (*Gariannonum*), then at Walton Castle, Bradwell (*Othona*), Richborough (*Rutupiae*), Dover (*Dubris*) and Lympne (*Lemanis*), the last three of which were raised on or near sites of earlier bases of the Romano-British fleet (*classis Britannica*, see p 182). Two forts were also built on the European side of the English Channel, at Oldenburg

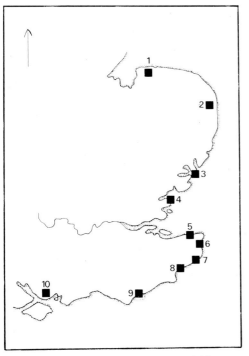

Roman forts of the Saxon Shore:
1 Brancaster
2 Burgh Castle
3 Walton Castle
4 Bradwell
5 Reculver
6 Richborough
7 Dover
8 Lympne
9 Pevensey
10 Portchester

and Boulogne. And in about 285 one more was started on the south coast of Britain, at Portchester (*Portus Adurni*).

The Roman fleet entrusted with the job of policing the Channel used these forts and the harbours they protected as bases for their operations. In 285, the fleet was put under the command of a new admiral, M. Aurelius Mausaeus Carausius, a Menapian Gaul from what is today southern Holland. He was appointed by Maximian, the deputy emperor chosen by Diocletian to manage the western part of the empire (see p 148). Carausius may have begun the fort at Portchester. At first he achieved tremendous success against the raiders. Then, it seems, he fell out with Maximian: either he felt he should have been given higher status or, as is alternatively suggested, he embezzled huge quantities of booty, over and above the 'accepted rake-off', was detected by Maximian and ordered to stand trial. Carausius, confident that his reputation as a commander would win enough support in northern Gaul and Britain, declared himself emperor and crossed with a loyal army into the island where he took over the government, keeping the legions happy with a big cash bonus. It is clear that he was well received. And for the next six or

Gladiators fighting in the arena, on the side of a pottery jar
of the third century

seven years (c286–93) he held sway by means of his undoubted qualities of leadership. One attempt to dislodge him was unsuccessful: Carausius met a fleet of Maximian's at sea and defeated it. He is said to have reformed the economy of Britain by issuing new coinage with a higher silver content and to have stimulated trade by virtually eliminating piracy in the Channel.

Carausius was well served by an able assistant, Allectus, of whom Roman historians say little beyond the fact that he was something of a financial wizard. When Carausius was trapped and defeated at the port of Boulogne by Maximian's Caesar, Constantius Chlorus, in 293, Allectus had his master murdered and declared himself emperor in his place. Two years later, Constantius mounted a two-pronged invasion of Britain, sending one fleet and army under Asclepiodotus to the south where the force sailed behind the Isle of Wight and headed for *Clausentum*, and leading the other himself towards London via the Thames. The London thrust was unsuccessful at first, but Asclepiodotus landed, overcame resistance and marched towards the capital where, somewhere outside, he defeated and killed Allectus. Constantius, meanwhile, had returned to the Thames, this time without mishap, and reached London just as Allectus' retreating troops· were preparing to lay it waste. They were overwhelmed by Constantius and the war was over. Constantius was given a great welcome by the capital. A fascinating medallion commemorating this was found at Arras in 1922. It is a gold medal which bears on its reverse a design depicting Constantius carrying a javelin and mounted on horseback riding towards the city gates outside of which the city's goddess kneels in welcome. Round the top is the legend *Redditor lucis aeturnae* (restorer of eternal light). On the obverse is a head portrait of Constantius. No doubt the feelings of the London populace reflected a much wider sense of relief and gratitude in the province.

NOTES

1. Dio Cassius, lxxvi, 6.
2. Herodian, *History* III, 7.2; Dio Cassius, lxxvi, 6.
3. Dio Cassius, lxxvi, 5.
4. Herodian, *History* III, 14, 1–2.
5. Dio Cassius, lxxvii, 13. Dio also says that Britain was 951 miles long, 308 miles at its greatest width, and 40 miles at its smallest (ie the Forth–Clyde isthmus).
6. *Arch. Aeliana* IV, xxxvii (1959), 12–31.
7. Herodian, *History* III, 14.10.
8. Dio Cassius, lxxvii, 13.
9. To date, there is no better way to study urbanisation in Roman Britain, in all its

facets, than by reference to Wacher, J. *The Towns of Roman Britain* (1975).

10. The tribal name Coritani has recently been reinterpreted as Corieltauvi, from a graffito from Cave's Inn, Warwickshire (*Tripontium*).
11. There is, however, still some argument as to whether a fort was erected in London as early as the Plautian campaigns.
12. Breeze, D. J. and Dobson, B. (1976) p 202.
13. P.S.A.S. (1933–34) p 32.
14. Herodian, *History* III, 8, v.

9
FOURTH-CENTURY ROMAN BRITAIN

Britain had been under the control of rebel emperors for a decade, and this must have called for some reconstruction by the Roman government. Constantius further divided the province into three, and this was later reorganised into four (see p 148); doubtless Constantius made some kind of tour of military installations to reassure garrisons that Roman authority was restored. Work was put in hand to repair some of the forts along the northern frontier. It used to be thought that the Caledonians and others had taken advantage of the Carausius–Allectus breakaway period to mount a major invasion of Britannia Inferior, extensively damaging the Wall and its forts, but it is more likely that they made sporadic and not very destructive raids. Clearly, the position was not serious enough to prevent Constantius returning to Gaul in 297 and remaining there for several years. Repairs done to many of the frontier forts in the last years of the century, such as at Birdoswald, Rudchester, South Shields and Wallsend, appear to have been necessary because of long-term decay and neglect, not destruction. As likely as not, the Caledonians were kept out by diplomacy and hard cash, as they had been in the time of Caracalla. That said, the restoration work on the forts was thorough and several changes in the structures themselves were introduced. Barrack blocks at Birdoswald and Housesteads, for example, were rebuilt (in some instances on changed alignments) with different layouts, to accommodate changes in the organisation of the army. It is also thought that the average garrison along the Wall was reduced in size as a result of the continued stability of the frontier. Repairs and rebuilding were also carried out further south at, for example, the legionary fortresses at Chester and York, and one or two new forts were built, as at Piercebridge and Lancaster.

The emperor Diocletian is rightly remembered for his valiant attempts to reorganise the whole Roman Empire. The empire was divided into four areas of imperial authority, headed by two Augusti (himself and his friend, Maximian), each with one Caesar as deputy, Galerius and Constantius. The system was called the Tetrarchy, or college of four emperors. The two Caesars were heirs-expectant to the Augusti. The various provinces in the empire were broken down into smaller units. As far as Britain was concerned, these were *Britannia Prima, Britannia Secunda, Maxima Caesariensis* and *Flavia Caesariensis* (see p 193). The new Britain was called the diocese of Britain, to be governed by a *vicarius Britanniarum*, which was to be part of the new Praefecture of the Gauls. It seems likely that London (the name of which was changed, then or later, to *Augusta*) was the capital of the diocese: the financial treasurer certainly had his headquarters there. Each of the provinces was governed by a *praeses* and from this time on the governors were civilians, not military commanders: it was part of Diocletian's reforms to separate military and civil power throughout the empire. The military commands in the provinces were put under a new leadership, *duces*. We do not know what date to put on the reorganisation as it affected Britain, but it may be presumed to have begun before Diocletian and Maximian retired from office in 305. Diocletian's reorganisation included major reforms in the army, among which was the deployment of special mobile field armies, in addition to the standing forces along the empire's frontiers. These were not an innovation, but rather a development of an idea conceived by Julius Caesar and employed occasionally by emperors, particularly by Severus. It was perhaps in this guise that Constantius returned to Britain in 306 to wage war against the Caledonians. He had in the previous year become one of the two Augusti (Galerius was the other).

We do not know why Constantius mounted an invasion of Scotland against the Caledonians and others, who are referred to, for the first time, as the Picti (painted men) or Picts. It may be that the Scottish Highland tribes needed a further lesson, in the manner of the campaigns of Severus almost a century before. Indeed, we may note a parallel here, for Constantius, like Severus, was a sick man when he invaded Scotland, and was (also like Severus) accompanied by his son, Flavius Valerius Constantinus (Constantine), a very different young man from the worthless and terrible Caracalla. Constantius advanced into Scotland, across the long-abandoned Antonine Wall and into the north-east where he won a great victory, details of which are unknown. What is probable is that the forces he used were a mix of his own mobile troops brought from Gaul with elements of the north garrisons, and it may be that some of the temporary camps detectable from the air in north-east Scotland date from this campaign. Professor Salway suggests that pottery of the period found at Carpow fort on the Tay could mean that Constantius used a fleet, as both Severus and Agricola had done, as part of a combined operation of land warfare with harassment of the tribes from the sea.[1]

Constantius then returned southwards, presumably having come to satisfactory terms with the Picts for the time being; but when he reached York he died. The troops at once chose his son to succeed him as Augustus, which was not accepted by the other Augustus, Galerius, who had his own candidate, Flavius Severus. But in 308 Constantine was confirmed. He had already proved himself a first-rate military commander. He was popular with the army; he had refused (like his father) to carry out persecutions of Christians ordered throughout the

Milestone of Constantine (when Caesar) at St Hilary Church, Cornwall. The milestone is dated c306–7 (*Janet & Colin Bord*)

empire by Diocletian in the first years of the fourth century, and this had won esteem for his toleration (his Christian mother, Helena, Constantius's first wife, was later canonised). Constantine was soon to display superb gifts of statesmanship as, during the next fifteen years, he undid the Tetrarchy, defeated his rivals in battle and emerged as sole ruler of the empire, by 324. Eleven years earlier at Milan he had issued the Edict of Milan which formally allowed freedom of worship to Christians. And in 324 he laid the foundations of a new capital for the empire at a remote and small fishing port on the Bosphorus where it meets the Black Sea. This was Byzantium. In six years he had turned it into a wonderful new city, the Golden City of Constantinople, which was to become the entrepôt of the Western World for a thousand years.

Constantine probably spent two years in Britain before setting off on his restructuring work. It is impossible in the present state of knowledge to apportion between him and his father the considerable works undertaken in Britain in those first years of the fourth century which were to lead to a generation of peace and prosperity – the last of any length of time in Romano-British history. Hadrian's Wall was repaired, along with some of its forts, and several forts above and behind the frontier were also renovated, including Corbridge Station, but it is important to remember that this work had to be done because of decay and to prepare the forts to resist Caledonian ravages rather than because of ravages themselves. At Birdoswald, for example, an inscription of the time referred to the commandant's house 'having been covered with earth and fallen into ruin'[2] This does not sound like the result of an attack. There is evidence for restoration work at both Chester and York: the former could have been the result of early raids from Ireland, but for York, the capital of the northern province, a different explanation makes sense. York was to receive a major reconstruction. This included overall rebuilding of the walls, especially the south-west front over the river, which was equipped with superb multangular towers. The fortress was to be the headquarters of the new commander of the army in Britain, the *dux Britanniarum*. Whether Constantius or his son did the work, they certainly intended to make the structure impressive, as part of the wall with a multangular tower standing today still testifies. At about the same time, some of the *civitas* capitals acquired fortifications, or had such walls as they possessed supplemented. At Dorchester the walls were converted to stone, and at Lincoln new gates were added to the walls of the town.

And from milestones that have been recovered, it is clear that Constantine put in hand major repairs to the road system. Milestones of his time have been found at Worthing (Sussex), Girton (near Cambridge), Ancaster (Lincolnshire), Llanhamlach (near Brecon, Powys), Brougham (Cumbria), Harraby Bridge (Cumbria), Carvoran (Northumberland) and Crindledykes, to mention a selection.[3]

Constantine could not dally in Britain and he left for Gaul in 307. Little is known of the history of the island for another generation, which lends weight to the belief that they were quiet and – for some people – prosperous times, though the empire's battles against inflation must have been reflected here. The practice of storing up coins as security spread far and wide in these years, if the discoveries of hoards is an indication. Yet many of the great established villas entered their most comfortable days, as witnessed by the verandah, outer courtyard and second bath suite at Chedworth (Gloucestershire), the fine mosaics at Brading (Isle of Wight), the apsidal dining room at Lullingstone (Kent), the tremendous 15sq m (18sq yd) mosaic at Woodchester (Gloucestershire) and the conversion of Bignor (Sussex)

The Deep Room at Lullingstone villa. This was at one time used for cult worship. In the last period, a Christian chapel was built over it (*National Monuments Record*)

The Orpheus mosaic (known also as the Great Pavement) at Woodchester villa, Gloucestershire, when exposed in 1973 (*National Monuments Record*)

to courtyard villa plan. Much rebuilding was done in *civitas* capitals and smaller towns, such as the renovated baths at Silchester, the altered *forum* at Cirencester and rebuilt *forum* at Caistor St Edmund. There is little evidence for major new public works though large private houses were erected at St Albans, Caerwent and Silchester. The toleration of Christianity led in time to the building of chapels at villas, such as at Hinton St Mary (Dorset) and Lullingstone, and public churches at Silchester and Icklingham (a Roman settlement, near Mildenhall in Suffolk). And, curiously, some of the pagan temples of earlier times were refurbished, in particular the Temple of Mithras in London, which for a time in the fourth century was in danger of closure by the Christians. Evidence was revealed in the 1954 excavations that pagan objects had been hurriedly buried under its floor.

The peaceful period was ended in the 340s by some unspecified disturbances, serious enough to bring the new emperor, Constans, with an army into Britain in 343, along with a new army commander, Gratian, who had been commander in Africa. It was on this expedition that Constans created the new British command, the *Comes Litoris*

Saxonici or Count of the Saxon Shore. Was the office so-called because the count commanded the forces stationed in east Britain to deal with Saxon raiders or because the coastal regions of the east had already been settled in places by Saxon immigrants peacefully with Roman consent? The debate is not yet resolved.[4]

Seven years later, Magnentius, a barbarian who had settled in Gaul, declared himself emperor and won over the support of some of the army in Britain. He was defeated and the next emperor, Constantius II, took the sternest reprisals against the island, sending over one Paulus, an official whose job was to root out all 'traitors', who earned the nickname *Catena* (the chain) for the ruthlessness of his investigations. Even the *vicarius* of Britain, Flavius Martinus, was driven to take his own life. In the 360s, the province was progressively demoralised by a series of severe raids on the Welsh coast by Scots from Ireland, on the northern frontier from Picts and from Saxon pirates in the east, and in one cataclysmic year, 367, the three invading peoples formed an alliance to attack from several directions – together. The result was probably the worst disaster to befall Britain since the Boudican revolt. Nectaridus, the Count of the Saxon Shore, was slain; Fullofaudes, the *dux Britanniarum*, was shut up in York and humbled,

Apse of now vanished building at the *civitas* capital *Venta Icenorum* (Caistor St Edmund, Norfolk), found between two structures of the late third century *forum* (*Norfolk Museum Service*)

and the army was defeated on several fronts, not helped by the fact that some of the frontier troops betrayed the province by not sending advance warning to the commanders (it is said they were bribed by the raiders). Virtual anarchy followed, probably for a year, as the discipline of what remained of the army broke down. The emperor Valentinian, son of Gratian, was unable to help as he was bogged down elsewhere in Gaul. Had the invaders stuck together and made a concerted plan, they could have driven Rome out of Britain for good, but they were concerned only with plunder: cattle, gold, goods and slaves. They broke up into small gangs of independent marauders, which were easy to deal with once the emperor succeeded in finding a tough, resolute and imaginative commander to send to Britain. Such a man was Theodosius who, accompanied by his son (also called Theodosius) and an army, landed at Richborough and marched to London, mopping up the gangs along the way.

Some time during 368, Theodosius secured the capital, regarrisoned the forts of the Saxon Shore, and restored order by carefully dividing his forces into select detachments which infiltrated the countryside, catching the raiders by surprise and taking back the plunder. Yet, alarming though the raiders' alliance (*barbarica conspiratio*)[5] had been, there is limited archaeological evidence of serious or widespread damage to towns, forts or villas, despite Ammianus Marcellinus' insistence that great devastation was wrought. Hadrian's Wall was breached but the Picts had simply barged through in one or two places and surged south, leaving the forts alone. That forts were rebuilt in the Theodosian reconstruction seems more likely to have been the result of natural decay, coupled with damage sustained in the 340s and not yet dealt with. The outpost forts above the Wall were given up completely, and Professor Frere suggests that the defence of the northern frontier was entrusted to the Lowland tribes who were offered greater autonomy in return for taking on the buffer role.[6] According to Ammianus Marcellinus, Theodosius restored the cities and strongholds which had been founded to secure a long period of peace, but had endured repeated misfortunes.[7] This suggests an overhaul of towns and forts which had lain neglected for long periods. A programme of modifications in some town defences was initiated, as can be seen from the addition of external towers to the curtain wall at frequent intervals round the perimeter in order to facilitate the deployment of artillery which the raiders were not able to cope with.[8] The fortification of towns is an important factor in the history of the last period of Roman rule in Britain, for it was in them that organised resistance to raids survived the longest, once the Roman army had left Britain altogether.

Theodosius is credited by Ammianus Marcellinus with completely recovering 'a province that had passed into the enemy's hands' and restoring it to its former condition.[9] Allowing for the fact that Ammianus Marcellinus was an unqualified admirer of Theodosius the Younger (emperor Theodosius I, 379–95), there is much circumstantial evidence to support his comment. It has often been thought that the 367 conspiracy spelled the beginning of the end of Roman Britain, that after Theodosius' 'temporary' restoration of order the province went rapidly into decline. This is to overlook several factors. First, there is archaeological evidence for the continued flourishing of villa life in the countryside, right into the middle of the next century, some eighty years later. The villas at Sparsholt (Hampshire), Gadebridge (Hertfordshire) and Brading (Isle of Wight), for example, survived in what is called a sub-Roman phase of occupation, that is, they continued to function in the period cAD410–50 during which time they were occupied by British rather than Romans, or were tenanted or used as offices for big farms. In some cases, immigrants may have taken them over, on lease or through sale. The refortifying of the towns 'enabled them to hold out far into the following century',[10] which means that the towns must also have continued to prosper, as archaeology is beginning to bear out. The fort rebuilding was extensive, and a new element appeared: inhabitants of *vici* outside began to give up their undefended settlements and move into the forts. The troops defending the forts and operating offensively outside were becoming more of a local militia and less of a Roman legionary or auxiliary force. This is illustrated in the changing layout of many forts of the time, which now start to reflect community living, with facilities for civilians, wives and children. There are some parallels here with the fortified burghs of the Anglo-Saxons, hard-pressed by Viking raids in the ninth and tenth centuries. The coasts of Northumbria down to the Humber were equipped with a series of signal stations of stone, built on high cliffs, reaching to perhaps 30m (100ft) tall, with an extensive observation capability out to sea. Protection for other coasts was afforded by such improvements as a new harbour for the fleet at Holyhead, Anglesey, another at *Clausentum* (Bitterne) near Southampton, while forts at Caernarfon, Forden Gaer and Caerhun were restored.

Theodosius returned to Rome probably in 370 and went on to command in Mauretania which was in difficulties with raids by nomadic tribes. Then it appears he was put to death at Carthage, on a trumped up charge. His memory may have lingered in Britain which enjoyed another period of peace until the 380s. In 383, Magnus Maximus, commander of the British armies, who had been born in Spain, rebelled against the imperial authority and declared himself emperor. He had a strong following in Britain (Maxen Wledig he was to become in Welsh folklore) and when he set out for Gaul the army flocked to his standard. The western emperor, Gratian, who had held great promise as a young man but had turned into a second Commodus and was hated by his own troops, fled before Maximus to Italy, where he was murdered. Maximus thereon governed in the West up to the Italian border. Then he tried to cross the Alps in 387, and head for Milan. In the East, Theodosius the Younger, who had become eastern emperor in 379, reacted swiftly to the news and brought both armies and a fleet to the Italian sphere and defeated the pretender by land and sea, finishing him off at Aquileia, putting Maximus to death.

Maximus had held power for five years, with mixed results for Britain. There must have been something in this administration for him to be adopted into Welsh folklore – claimed indeed as the ancestor of a line of rulers – but when he went to Gaul he took with him large numbers of troops from the British garrisons (and many native British, too) and this manpower is thought not to have returned. It used to be thought that the Wall was stripped of its garrisons, but it is now clear that many were left untouched, and that the deficiencies were made up from the co-operating tribes of the Lowlands, the Votadini and the Novantae. Was Maximus among the first to persuade the people of Britain that they would have soon to start fending for themselves, that they could not forever depend upon Roman armies, that Rome itself was doomed before long to bear the brunt of barbarian attack?

The years that followed Maximus' death saw a return of the raiders from Scotland, Ireland and the Saxon coasts, and for a time the heaviest were from the Scots of Ireland who began to arrive and to settle, especially in Dyfed and the Lleyn peninsula. At this time too, the Saxon raiders began to found small settlements in the east. In 395 Theodosius I died. His successor in the West was his ten-year-old son, Honorius, and the empire in Western Europe was effectively managed by Flavius Stilicho for the next thirteen years. Stilicho had been born a

156

Vandal, one of the barbarian groupings that had been the bane of Roman forces in Western Europe for decades. He had risen to the rank of commander in the Roman army (it was Roman policy to employ barbarians to fight other barbarians) and had won the favour of Theodosius and married his niece. Stilicho attempted to bolster the defences of Britain, though we have very little archaeological evidence as to where the work was done. At the turn of the century, the attacks of the Gothic barbarians upon the West had grown so severe that Italy itself was in serious danger. Stilicho defeated the Gothic leader, Alaric, in 403, but two years later a quarter of a million Goths ravaged the peninsula of Italy down as far as Florence. Again, Stilicho checked them, but the unceasing pressure of Goths, Alans, Vandals and others against the slowly disintegrating West forced the emperor to pull out troops from less-pressed provinces, including Britain whose garrisons were drastically reduced. Then, in 406 a pretender to the imperium, Constantine III (as he called himself), gathered up the remnants of the army, crossed into Gaul and fought his way towards Italy, ostensibly to help the beleaguered Romans. Honorius is said even to have recognised the pretender as a co-Augustus. Certainly, Constantine's activities took the pressure off Britain; but while he was out of the island, a concatenation of circumstances, difficult to trace and even more difficult to interpret, drove the British people to rebel once again, at a time when the imperial forces were quite unable to respond. It was the beginning of the end of Roman Britain, the account of which is to be found in chapter 17.

NOTES

1. Salway, P. (1981) p 319.
2. Collingwood, R. G. and Wright, R. P. (1965) 1912 (Birdoswald).
3. Romano-British milestones are catalogued and described in an important paper by Sedgley, J. 'The Roman milestones of Britain'. *British Archaeological Reports* 18 (1975).
4. The various problems connected with the Saxon Shore were discussed at length at a research symposium held at Dean College, Sussex, in 1975. The papers were published in Johnston, D. E. (ed) *The Saxon Shore* (Council for British Archaeology Research Report no 18, 1977). See also Johnson, S. *The Roman Forts of the Saxon Shore* (1979).
5. Ammianus Marcellinus, xxvii, 8, 1.
6. Frere, S. S. (1978) p 392.
7. Ammianus Marcellinus, xxviii, 3, 2.
8. Wacher, J. (1975) pp 75–6.
9. Ammianus Marcellinus, xxviii, 3, 7.
10. Frere, S. S. (1978) p 399.

10
THE ROMAN ARMY
IN BRITAIN

From the Claudian invasion in AD43 down to the last years of the
formal occupation, the Romans kept in Britain an army, of one composition or another, of between forty and fifty thousand troops and
ancillaries. This was about a tenth of the total complement of the
Roman imperial army throughout the empire, which was a substantial
commitment. The role of the army (after initial conquest) was to
maintain control of about two million civilians, and such a commitment required a sophisticated degree of organisation. The army was
one of the fundamental strengths of the Roman imperial system, and
by AD43 it had reached a very high standard in all aspects of military
activity. Although it was not always unbeaten in battle, it was the
greatest army the world had ever seen.

The core of the Roman army was the legion, the mainline force of
professional heavily armoured infantrymen who were recruited
exclusively from Roman citizenship. In the first century AD this meant
from Italy and from Roman colonies in the Mediterranean (but not
provinces), but later the privilege was extended to some provincials,
and after 213, when Caracalla granted citizenship to all in the empire,
almost anyone (provided they were acceptable) could become a
legionary.

The legion was composed of 6,000 or so men, about 5,100 of whom
were actual fighting infantrymen. The fighting complement was
normally made up of 10 cohorts of 6 centuries each. A century
normally consisted of 80 men, which gave a cohort strength of 480,
but the first cohort of a legion was generally 800 men strong in five
double centuries. Added to this figure of 5,120 (probably not always
rigidly followed) was a legionary cavalry arm of 120 per cohort, which
together with the various specialist craftsmen and administrative staff
(see p 162) brought the legion's strength to over 6,000, even 6,400.[1]

Legionaries enlisted for twenty years, and this term was often extended to twenty-five, occasionally even longer, especially if they were in line for promotion. If they retired after twenty-five or more years, they became veterans and were eligible for a gratuity or a land grant and/or a pension, and could either eke out their days on the money or start a small business, farm or market garden. It was a good career – even if one never rose higher than an ordinary legionary – with a chance to see many parts of the world.

In addition to the legions, which were the backbone of the Roman military machine, there were the very important *auxilia* or auxiliary troops, who were not Roman citizens (until 213).[2] Auxiliaries, who were light-armed troops, were raised from provinces and tribes allied to Rome, and their special role was to 'screen the less expendable legions and by operating in advance and on the flanks of the heavily armoured legionaries, take the shock of skirmishes and enemy surprise attacks.'[3] In most engagements they bore the brunt of the fighting and presumably sustained most of the casualties. At Mons Graupius, the legionaries, though ready to be called into the fray, were never sent in by Agricola: the auxiliaries alone succeeded in scattering the forces of Calgacus (see p 82). Auxiliaries were formed into three types of unit: the infantry cohort, the cavalry wing (*ala*) and the infantry cohort with mounted contingent (*cohors equitata*). Each unit was made up of about 500 men, generally known as a *quingenaria*, though there were much larger units, some of 1,000 men (*milliaria*). The *alae* were composed of 16 *turmae* or troops, each 32 strong and led by a decurion (commissioned troop commander), and the cohorts were made up of centuries of 80 men each. The *quingenaria* was commanded by a *praefectus*, the *milliaria* by a *tribunus*, both men being drawn from the *equites* class of Roman citizen. Auxiliary units were often named after the tribal region or province where the original units were raised, or sometimes from where they served, and inscriptions in Britain recording the presence of auxiliaries give us a colourful variety of regional origins, such as the *Ala I Tungrorum* (raised from the Tungrians in northern Gaul), *Ala II Asturum* (from the Astures people in northwest Spain), *Cohors I Nerviorum* (from the Nervii in Gaul, the tribe overcome by Caesar in his Gallic wars)[4] and *Cohors I Alpinorum* (raised in the Alps in the early first century AD).

The auxiliaries were very much part of the Roman army from the time of Augustus though, as we shall see, there were several differences between them and the legionaries. By the second century the practice had begun of raising units among peoples whom the government did not consider suitable for service in the *auxilia*. These were the *numeri* (infantry) and the *cunei* (cavalry). At first they were raised for special tasks or for specific campaigns, then under Hadrian they became part of the army proper, though still in a 'second-class' status. Several *numeri* and *cunei* were stationed in Britain, such as the *Numerus Hnaudifridi* (so called after its German-born commander) and the *Cuneus Sarmatarum*.

The command structure in the Roman imperial army was staffed by a mixture of professional and semi-professional officers (amateur is perhaps too strong a word for those who were given commands following some years as a senator at Rome). The legionary commander, or *legatus legionis*, was nominated by the emperor, would be in his early thirties and would almost always have served as a *praetor*. He will have had some military experience, but not usually of high command. His appointment would normally be for two or three years. The next rank down was the tribune. There were six to the legion: one was the *tribunus laticlavius*, a young man in his early twenties, or even late teens, who would after service go on to become a *quaestor* (a junior magistrate) with a seat in the Senate. This tribune was necessarily inexperienced, yet he was titular second-in-command. It was a splendid opportunity to learn the business of military administration, occasionally the technique of command, for it was not unknown for a young *tribunus laticlavius* to be given independent command of a unit such as a cohort. He would receive training and encouragement from the third officer in line, the *praefectus castrorum* (camp commander) who usually took executive command of a legion in the absence of the *legatus*. The camp commander was a former centurion of at least thirty years' experience of service in the army, and was responsible for all matters relating to the legionary fortress or whatever other base the legion occupied.

There were five other tribunes, all from the equites class (below the senatorial class) and their functions were administrative and judicial. These tribunes were much older than the laticlavian tribune, men in their mid-thirties with several years of magisterial experience and some service as unit commander in auxiliary units. They could be equated with the modern staff officer, and they were liable to be given command of a detachment at short notice, if needed. It will be noted that none of the tribunes was a full-time professional: they served in the army for periods as part of the advancement of their public careers.

It was the centurions who were the mainstay of the legionary leadership. There were sixty in command of the centuries. They were the toughest, boldest and usually the most experienced soldiers in the legion. Most of them had served many years in the ranks and risen to section commands of one kind or another. Some were transferred from the Praetorian Guard (the emperor's personal guard), and a few were recruited from civilian jobs. We have seen that the first of the legion's ten cohorts was nearly twice the size of the other nine, and the first cohort's centurions were always the most senior (*primi ordines*). The top centurion was the *primus pilus*, a highly respected campaigner, generally over fifty, who held the rank for one year. Normally he then retired with a gratuity and was treated with honour, but from time to time the *primus pilus* was given some alternative post at the end of his year, which might not necessarily be a military one. The number two to the *primus pilus* was the *princeps*, whose role was administrative and he received double pay.

The command structure of the *auxilia* was different from that of the legionaries. For one thing, the largest formation of auxiliaries was the thousand-strong cohort (*milliaria*) and most auxiliary units (regiments, as they are sometimes called by specialists) were of five hundred, the *quingenaria*. We have seen that some of the cohorts were infantry and cavalry mixed. The provinces also provided the army with cohorts of archers (notably from Crete and from Syria) and slingers (from the Balearic Islands), and most of the horsemen for the cavalry units in the army were raised from the provinces, among them *alae* from Thrace, northern Spain and Pannonia. The earlier auxiliary cohorts and *alae* generally had their own native leaders, though Roman officers were appointed to command some of the units. Gradually, the cohorts became absorbed into the Roman army proper, and commanders increasingly came from the ranks of Roman citizens, generally from the equites class. The infantry *quingenaria* was commanded by a *praefectus* and the *milliaria* by a tribune. *Alae*, whether of five hundred or a thousand, were headed by a *praefectus*.

In addition to being trained to fight, the Roman legionary was also instructed in several ancillary skills essential to a soldier's art, such as fort-building, ditch and rampart construction for defence and building maintenance, and this meant that he had to be able to quarry and cut stone, fell and shape timber and do the jobs of carpenter, cement mixer, lead moulder and so forth. In the early years of the occupation, the legionaries built not only their own marching and practice camps, and their legionary (and probably vexillation) fortresses, they erected the smaller forts for the auxiliary units. In the mid second century, auxiliaries began to get involved in building forts, possibly contributing to the Hadrian's Wall fort of Carvoran (136–8), and extensively to the Antonine Wall forts.

The legions also had their specialist staff, and it is interesting to see the great variety of crafts, professions and trades that were represented: *librarii* (clerks) for various duties, such as dealing with supplies from the fortress granaries and looking after the legionary savings bank (the bullion was kept in a strong room);[5] *beneficiarii* (orderlies); *architecti* (master builders) and *mensores* (or *metato*) (site surveyors); *hydraularii* (water engineers); *medici ordinarii* (medical officers, but there were other medical grades as well); *haruspices* (priests or, more correctly, soothsayers); *fabri ferrarii* (ironsmiths); *sagittarii* (fletchers); *ballistarii* (catapult makers); *fabri armorum* (armourers); *fabricienses* (workshop technicians); *frumentarii* (corn commissaries).

The legionary was fitted out with a kit of special battle armour. This consisted of a cuirass: a garment of rows of overlapping metal strips and plates strung together with leather thongs but loose enough to make the garment flexible, made to fit the upper part of the body and round the shoulders (*lorica segmentata*). It was worn over a woollen tunic. The lower part of the trunk was covered by a metal-studded leather-strapped sporran. On service in colder parts of the empire, such as Britain, men wore leather trousers down to the calves. On their feet they wore thick-soled sandals with the soles studded with

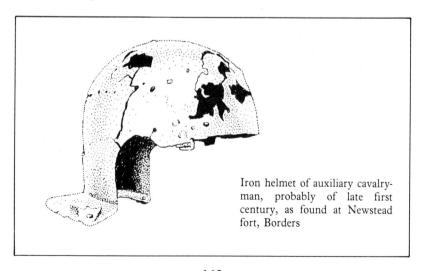

Iron helmet of auxiliary cavalry-man, probably of late first century, as found at Newstead fort, Borders

Reconstruction of a first-century Roman shield whose fragments were found at Doncaster. The shield was 1¼m (4ft) tall and 0.64m (2ft) wide, made of three-ply wood covered with leather and fronted with bronze sheet. It was fitted with a D-shaped handgrip (*Doncaster Metropolitan Borough Museums Arts Services*)

hollow-headed hobnails. Two types of armour were worn by the auxiliaries, chain mail (*lorica hamata*) and scale armour (*lorica squamata*). Chain mail consisted of rows of linked rings on a leather backcloth, providing a very flexible garment from neck to thigh, which would stand sword blows. Scale is best understood from the fine specimen recovered in excavations at Corbridge in 1964, now at the museum. On his head the legionary wore one of several types of helmet (*galea*), the most popular being the hemispherical helmet with a projecting back flap. He carried a rectangular shield (*scutum*), curved to fit round the body, made of leather or wood laminates edged with metal, bearing a centre metal boss that was hollow inside (in which was a handgrip). The shield was slung from the left shoulder by a strap, to give the right arm free movement with the sword or javelin. The auxiliary shield was flatter, oval or hexagonal in shape, and made of wood.

For weapons, the legionary was equipped with a short sword (*gladius*) and a javelin (*pilum*), though he generally carried two of the latter. The sword was for close-quarter fighting and consisted of a short broad blade, about 0.5m (2ft) long, with a double edge and very sharp point. It was a thrusting weapon, not for slashing. Legionaries were often urged by their commanders to aim for the faces of the enemy.[6] He also had a short dagger (*pugio*). The javelins were usually about 2.25m (7ft) long, and had an effective range of 27m (30yd) or so. The javelin had a wooden shaft with a 0.5m (2ft) long iron shank head at the top with a sharp point. The iron of the shank was tempered only for the first few inches of the sharp end. The rest was softer metal, which meant that the whole javelin bent downwards or sideways immediately it struck its target. Lodged in an enemy shield, it rendered the latter a hindrance to the holder who cast it away, thereby leaving his body exposed to an instant follow-through stab from the legionary. The auxiliaries' weapons were sword and spear (*hasta*), the latter was the principal weapon of the cavalryman. The archer carried a medium-length bow of wood reinforced with horn and protected himself with a sharp-bladed axe.

The Roman army set tremendous store on discipline, training and military exercises. As Professor A. Birley has pointed out, it was not accidental that the Latin word for army was *exercitus* and for training, *exercitio*.[7] Ancient sources were at pains to stress the Roman army's devotion to training. Even Rome's one time enemies commented upon it. Josephus, Jewish historian of the Judaean War (AD66–73) between the Jews and the Romans (under Vespasian and his son Titus), wrote that:

> They do not wait for war to begin before handling their arms, nor do they sit idle in peacetime and take action only when the emergency comes – but as if born ready armed they never have a truce from training or wait for war to be declared. Their battle drills are no different from the real thing: every man works as hard at his daily training as if he was on active service . . . victory over men not so trained follows as a matter of course . . . military exercises give the Roman soldiers not only tough bodies but determined spirits, too . . .[8]

Once the legionaries were recruited, they endured (that is the best word) the toughest possible training for the best part of a year. They had to learn to march fully armed and equipped for twenty miles, carrying their impedimenta on their backs and in their hands, armour, stakes for trenches, saws, baskets, spades, axes, cooking pots, a supply of corn, as well as their shield and weapons. The combined weight of all this was over 22.5kg (50lb). They would have to be able to run with this load, and to jump over ditches and scale ramparts. They also spent hours every day on weapon drill, usually on a special parade ground beside the camp or fort. In Britain there are remains of parade grounds at several forts and at the legionary fortress of Caerleon (Gwent). Alternatively, they drilled in amphitheatres attached to forts or fortresses, as at Chester fortress and at the auxiliary fort at Tomen-y-Mur (Gwynedd).

Among the many exercises in the Roman army training programme was practising the building of earthwork and timber fortifications and

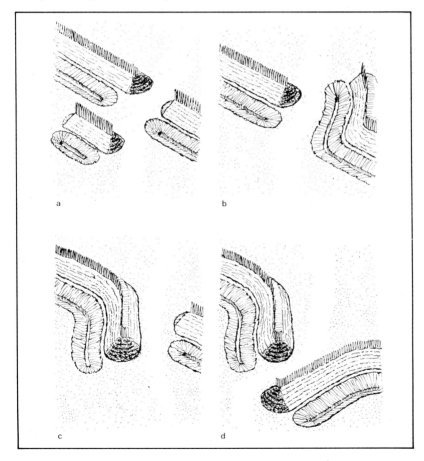

Four types of gates used at marching camps built by the army on campaign in Britain: (a) simple entrance/exit protected by *titulum*; (b) internal *clavicula*; (c) external *clavicula*; (d) Stracathro-type gate

camps. What are called marching or temporary camps were often built by the army while on the march against an enemy, for short-period occupation as a general rule, sometimes only for a night or two. These camps were often of large area: several were as big as 165 acres (67ha), as at Carpow, Newstead (Borders) and Pathhead (Lothian), many were over 100 acres (40.5ha), as at Raedykes (Grampian), Cardean (Tayside) and Ardoch (Tayside), and some at the lower end of the scale, a few acres each. Nearly three hundred camps have been detected from field archaeology or aerial photography. These marching camps were not all the same regular rectangular or square shape; many had to be built quickly at points where the ground dictated lopsided plans, parallelograms, trapezoids and even irregular polygons. Marching camps were simple in layout: an area in which tents could be set out in ordered blocks was surrounded by a quickly dug ditch inside which was a rampart made from the scooped earth and mingled with timber, sometimes rubble if it was easily obtained locally. Camps usually had four gates, one in the centre of each side, though larger camps had a pair along each longer side. Rey Cross (Durham) camp had eleven irregularly placed gates. These gates consisted of entrances in the ramparts flanked outside by a short protecting rampart called a *titulum*, or a special entrance created by a curved extension of the rampart and the ditch inside, outside or both inside and outside the camp. These were called *claviculae*. One type of clavicular gate was the Stracathro gate, where the entrance was protected on one side by an external *clavicula* and on the other by a straight oblique extension of the ditch and rampart outwards. This type was named recently after the first such plan to be discovered, at Stracathro (Tayside), and some ten camps with this type of entrance have been identified in Scotland.[9] The Stracathro gate was introduced in the time of Agricola.

To be able to erect these generally large-area camps very quickly on terrain that was often less than ideal required not only high technical expertise born of plenty of practice but also considerable co-ordination and supervision skills to ensure minimum overlap of duties and waste of time and effort. Legionaries spent many days practising to build marching camps, and in Britain a number of experimental camps have been identified, which are classed as practice camps. They are much smaller than marching camps, since they were needed only for practising techniques. They were about 30m (100ft) square or so and took only a day or two to build. Special attention was paid to practising the

The marching camp at Stracathro (just under 40 acres), seen from the air. Note the double clavicula gates with special Stracathro modifications (see p 166), at top, left and bottom (*Ministry of Defence*)

claviculae and also to making the rounded corners that were a familiar feature of nearly all Roman forts and fortlets. Among practice camps identified are those at Bootham Stray, near York, Llandrindod Common in mid Wales, at Tomen-y-Mur (strictly, at Doldinnas, where the ditch cut in practice looks as if it had been cut wrongly and repacked with earth to get the right shape) and at Haltwhistle, near Hadrian's Wall. Among the three hundred or so earthwork ditch and rampart systems so far discovered and classified as marching and practice camps, some were in fact labour camps to accommodate construction gangs working on more permanent forts.

The skill and the speed with which legionaries built fortifications are frequently highlighted in ancient literature. Caesar noted the efforts of his men in the stupendous earthworks round the Gallic citadel of Alesia, and Josephus says that the legionaries 'erected the outer wall and the buildings inside faster than thought.' On a visit to the North

African frontier defences in 128, emperor Hadrian praised his cavalry: '. . . entrenchments which others take several days to construct, you have completed in a single day . . .'.[10]

Roman forts were intended to be more permanent buildings, whether they were built of stone or of earth and timber. Several types were erected in Britain, all of them more or less constructed along set schemes that prevailed throughout the empire, with modifications according to local conditions or the whim of the army commander (notably Agricola). The largest type was the legionary fortress, usually 50 acres (20ha) or more in size (though some were smaller), built to house a full legion. Ten were constructed in Britain, all of them in turf and timber, and they were (not in any special order): Colchester, Exeter, Gloucester, Usk, Wroxeter, Lincoln, Inchtuthil in Scotland, Caerleon, Chester and York. Only the last three survived to be converted to stone fortresses and had a military life lasting up towards the end of the occupation. Inchtuthil was never finished, and its life was extremely short, about five years (AD85–90). Little of it can be seen today but it has been extensively excavated,[11] and is regarded as a key site in the history of military organisation in the Roman Empire. It is the only legionary fortress in the Roman Empire unencumbered by modern buildings. The other six served their purpose as major bases during the early years of conquest, and then gave way to civilian development over their remains, except Usk which became a smaller fort and then went out of use altogether in the second century.

Smaller than the legionary fortresses were the forts of 20–30 acres (8–12ha), built to much the same plan and in most cases housing a vexillation of a legion or a mixed vexillation of legionaries and auxiliaries. These appear to have been of a less permanent nature and were part of the conquest operations. Fourteen have been identified: Great Chesterford (Essex), Lake (Dorset), Longthorpe (Cambridge-shire which played a role in the Boudican revolt), Clyro (Powys), Leighton (Shropshire), Wall (Staffordshire), Osmanthorpe, Kinvaston (Staffordshire), Rhyn (Shropshire), Newton-on-Trent (Lincolnshire), Rossington (South Yorkshire), Malton (North Yorkshire), Red House at Corbridge (Northumberland) and Carpow in Scotland. Smaller still were the more numerous forts used as permanent bases for auxiliary units of varying size (which determined the fort size). There were a few between 9 and 15 acres (3.5–6ha), but the majority were 9 acres (3.5ha) or less, the greater proportion of these being 4½ acres (1.8ha) down to about 2 acres (0.8ha). Forts of smaller area are more correctly

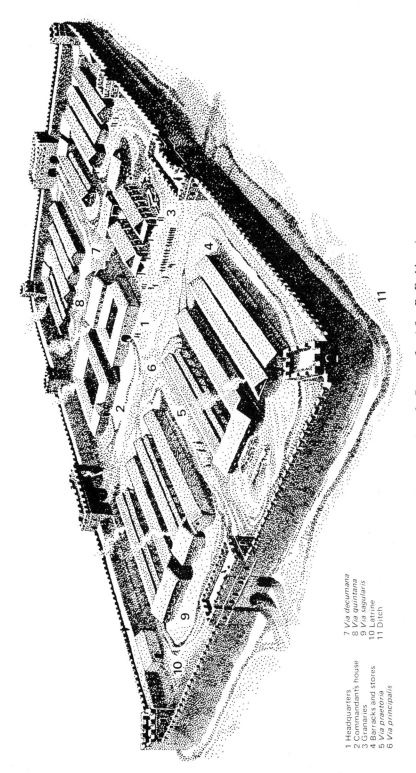

Reconstruction of a Roman fort (after R. Embleton)

1 Headquarters
2 Commandant's house
3 Granaries
4 Barracks and stores
5 *Via praetoria*
6 *Via principalis*
7 *Via decumana*
8 *Via quintana*
9 *Via sagularis*
10 Latrine
11 Ditch

referred to as fortlets, for they were guard posts and were as a rule equipped to hold only small detachments, from about fifty to a hundred and fifty men, and were often sited at vantage points between much larger forts. In generalising here, it must be added that some structures of 2 acres (0.8ha) or less were small forts rather than fortlets (particularly those on Hadrian's Wall and on the Antonine Wall).

The functions of the fort in Britain were to act as a base for troops to police newly conquered areas, to garrison units ready to go into battle against hostile tribes invading conquered territory and to act from time to time as winter quarters for troops. Some forts were occupied for long periods, and underwent several changes, conversion from earth and timber to stone, modifications after first periods in stone and so forth. Some were built in turf and timber and served only for a few years, notably the forts and fortlets on the Antonine Wall (see ch 7), and several in Wales. Some were constructed in stone from the start (as along Hadrian's Wall) and remained in service, with occasional refurbishment, for centuries. In the later third century, a new type of fort appeared, the fort of the Saxon Shore (see p 143), with a specific role to beat off sea raiders along the east and south-east coasts of Britain. These forts were different from their predecessors: they had very tall – 9m (30ft) or so – broad and long walls, with flanking bastions, huge gateways with narrow entrances, and were sited on or very near the coast. In the conquest years, forts were erected in a series of networks, ten to fifteen miles apart, linked by roads (see ch 14). They were built after a successful campaign, mainly to consolidate a hold on the newly won land. One or two were built on the sites of marching camps thrown up on campaign. Some forts were built on the sites of Iron Age Celtic hillforts, as at Hod Hill in Dorset and Ham Hill in Somerset.

Some understanding of the siting, construction, layout and accommodation of forts can be deduced from archaeology, inscriptions and aerial photography. The illustrative panels that spiral up the Column of Trajan in Rome are enormously informative, but there is also much to be learned from ancient literature. We have already mentioned descriptions by Caesar and Josephus. There is more material in Pliny the Elder, Tacitus, Appian and Dio Cassius. The celebrated Roman architect and engineer, Marcus Vitruvius Pollio, discussed many aspects of fortification and devoted large parts of book ten of his great work, *De Architectura*, to machines for war. It is probable that fort builders were able to consult handbooks on fort construction, and this

Building a turf and timber fort, as seen by the craftsmen who decorated the great Column of Trajan in Rome

is suggested by the survival of two treatises which dealt with these matters, namely, *De Metatione Castrorum* by the specialist Hyginus who was writing in the time of Marcus Aurelius (AD161–80), and *Epitoma Rei Militaris* by Flavius Vegetius Renatus (late fourth century). The four books of Vegetius comprise the only surviving manual of Roman military institutions, and are considered to have

171

summarised the contents of a number of works by earlier military writers, which would have included handbooks on camp and fort building.[12] The one time governor of Britain, Sextus Julius Frontinus (AD74–8), was the author of a manual on the art of war, a *de re militari*, which has not survived, but which he mentions in the opening paragraph of his book *Strategemata* (Stratagems) which has survived, and which was probably the sequel to the lost work, for it records many successful examples taken from history that demonstrate the effective application of the rules of military science (see Bibliography).

We cannot go into all the variants of the siting, layout and building processes here, but what follows is a generalisation which should cover most straightforward fort works. Once it had been decided to build in a particular area, the *praefectus castrorum* sent out a team of land surveyors to recommend a suitable spot and, when agreed, the main lines of the defence system of rampart and ditch were marked out with string. Josephus says that the ground was levelled first, but there is very little evidence of this being done in Britain: several forts were built on very uneven ground. Forts were planned to be rectangular with rounded corners, looking on plan like a playing card, or (less often) square with rounded corners. The straight lines were achieved using poles and string, and the right-angle corners were calculated using the *groma*, a special device consisting of a pole on a base, with a horizontal cross at the top (set accurately in four right angles) from which a plumb line was suspended from each arm. Aerial photography has revealed in some instances that the *groma* failed to achieve right angles, resulting in lopsided fort plans, as at Brough-on-Humber, Castleshaw (first) and Ilkley. Some forts were built on uneven ground with the result that they are not symmetrical. At the Baginton fort, the eastern side is markedly serpentine (largely to accommodate in its outward bulge part of the special horse-training ground or *gyrus*), while the western side also curved for part of its length. At Hod Hill, the fort was built into the north-west corner of the Iron Age hillfort, giving it two uneven sides.

Once the site was marked out, legionaries set about preparing the ramparting and ditching. Many rampart remains have been examined in great detail, and the compositions are not all the same. Most were built of an earth or rubble core upon a foundation of broken stone or gravel, but some were stabilised by timber strapping. Their height varied from 2 to 2.25m (6–7ft) from ground to the walkway on the top, to as tall as 3.25–3.5m (11–12ft). Vitruvius recommended walkways to

Ground surface
Timber
Turf
Stone
Earth

Some rampart profiles (after M. J. Jones): (*top*) Wall (Staffordshire), Lincoln; (*second line*) Bowes, St Albans; (*third line*) Strageath, Newstead; (*bottom*) Chester

173

be constructed wide enough to let two men pass one another.[13] They were surfaced with timber slatting, gravel or (as at Chester) stone paving. The outer edge of the walkway was fronted by a palisade of vertical posts of wood, or panels of interlaced vertical and horizontal planks between uprights, the top line of the palisade being crenellated like medieval castle walls. The front of the rampart was either vertical to the ground (as at Lincoln and Bowes) or it sloped steeply (as at Chester and Newstead). The vertical front would be of timber or stone, enclosing the rampart material: the sloping front would be of turf or clay blocks. The rear of the rampart sloped downwards often at a shallow incline, but where it was steep, or on occasions sheer, it would be approached by a short flight of steps at regular intervals. Many turf blocks have been examined and appear to have been of standard sizes, the commonest being about 30×45×15cm (12×18×6in), which weighed about 15–18kg (35–40lb). Clay blocks have also been examined, the average being 30×22.5×10cm (12×9×4in). The turf was obtained from the surface where the ditch was being cut, but it was not enough to cover the rampart slopes, and more turf was obtained from foundation trenches being dug for buildings inside the fort. Where this was not enough, large areas inside

A timber fort gate with two portals

174

Some ditch profiles: (*top*) V-shaped, V-shaped with cleaning slot, W-shaped; (*second line*) Punic ditch, ditch with wide berm; (*third to sixth lines*) various multiple ditch systems used in Roman Britain, some having additional obstacles

the fort were stripped of the top few inches; in some cases the entire inside was stripped.

Along the rampart lines spaces were left for gate towers. These were built round main uprights arranged either in a square (four) or a rectangle (six) or a chevron (six, as at Hod Hill). The six-post gate tower reconstruction at The Lunt was built from prefabricated timbers and took three days to erect, which may be about the time it took to build the gate under actual conditions at the original fort in the early 60s.

While the ramparts were being built, other legionaries were cutting the ditches. These sloped sharply downwards and inwards, and followed a variety of profiles. The simplest and commonest was the V-shape, with or without a small squared-off flat base, variously known as the cleaning slot or the 'ankle-breaker', *pace* Dr G. Webster.

A section of V-shaped military ditch with cleaning slot at the bottom, revealed in recent excavations at Castleford in West Yorkshire

There was the Punic ditch, a 'V' whose outer slope was much steeper than the inner. It was called 'Punic' because its steeper slope was something of an unexpected hazard to attackers attempting to retreat from an assault upon a fort and 'Punic', being the other Latin word for Carthaginian, was regarded as 'treacherous'. And there was the 'W' ditch or, more appropriately, the 'double V' ditch, which may have contained obstacles. Many forts had more than one line of ditching round the perimeter, and these are known as multiple ditch systems. Some had several ditches, as the five at Ardoch (splendidly visible today) and the seven on the south-west side at Whitley Castle.

The internal features of a Roman fort conformed to a standard scheme, and though there were variations at every fort, they do not appear to have been fundamental. The legionary fortress followed much the same scheme, only that it was larger, and several of the standard buildings were erected in greater numbers and larger sizes, such as barrack blocks.

The first forts, up to the beginning of the second century, had timber buildings, some completely wooden, some with timber frames infilled with wattle and daub. Most of the buildings were erected on stone foundations which ensured a somewhat longer life than if the timber went straight into the earth. From the second century, the central range of buildings in the forts was converted to stone or, if new, built in stone from scratch, and ramparts were often revetted in stone.

A fort may be divided into three sections. The front part (facing the enemy, as it were) was the *praetentura* and this contained barrack blocks and, if the fort was garrisoned with cavalry, also stable blocks. Barrack blocks were usually L-shaped, with a small shorter arm. Each block accommodated a century of eighty men, with the short arm housing the centurion and other officers. The men's quarters were provided with ten 'flats', each to house eight men, and each was partitioned into rooms. Barrack blocks were set on stone foundations, and in some cases had stone walls up to about 0.5–1m (2–3ft) thick, thereafter being timber or posts and wattle and daub. The barracks were ranged along either side of a central, or near-central, road leading from the front gate to the central building in the fort, the headquarters building or *principia*. The road was the *via praetoria* and it led to a wider road, the *via principalis*, at right angles separating the

Steps down into the strongroom of the *principia* at Segontium (Caernarfon) fort

177

Part of the courtyard of the commandant's house at the fort at Binchester. This was a fourth-century rebuilding (*Bowes Museum, Barnard Castle*)

Reconstructed timber granary building at The Lunt fort, Baginton, near Coventry. It now houses a museum

Roman stone granary buildings at Ribchester fort, Lancashire (*Janet & Colin Bord*)

Remains of the *valetudinarium* (hospital block) at Housesteads fort on Hadrian's Wall (*E. Houlder*)

praetentura from the central range. The *principia* stood in the middle of the central range. It was a square or nearly square building, which was the administrative block. Built round an open paved courtyard which was flanked by colonnades, it contained at the end furthest from the front of the fort a long, narrow hall with a dais at one end, the *tribunal*, on which the commander stood to address the men. Behind this hall was a row of rooms, stretching from left to right across the width of the building, the middle room of which was a shrine, or *aedes*, which housed a statue of the emperor and other ornaments. The fort's strong room was usually located underneath the *aedes*. It will be noted that the layout of the *principia* resembled that of the civilian forum and basilica block erected in the centre of most towns.

To the left of the *principia* was the fort commandant's quarters, the *praetorium*, another building with a paved courtyard in the centre, which was approached from the *via principalis*. Both buildings were of stone from the second century, with tile or slate roof. Some commandants' houses were equipped with hypocaust central heating, but as a

The bath house outside Chesters fort on Hadrian's Wall, with niches for bathers' clothes in the changing room

The latrine block in the south-east corner of Housesteads fort

rule there was no private bath suite. The commandant bathed with everyone else outside the fort. On the other side of the *principia* were buildings such as fort granaries (*horrea*) – wooden buildings on stilts or stone and wood buildings on stone pillars – and in some forts the unit's hospital block (*valetudinarium*) was placed in this group, as at Pen Llysten. There might also be room for the fort's workshop building.

Behind the central range there was a second transverse road, the *via quintana*, and at right angles, in or near the middle, another road led to the rear gate, the road being the *via decumana*. The rear part of the fort was the *retentura*, and it housed more barrack blocks, stables if needed, stores and more workshops. Inside the fort, between the rampart and the buildings, ran a road skirting the perimeter. This was the *intervallum* or *via sagularis*. The fort bath house was usually erected as a quite separate structure outside the fort, a little distance away (though there were exceptions, especially on the Antonine Wall). From the late first century, bath houses were generally built of stone, though on the Antonine Wall, some were half-stone, half-timber. Legionary fortresses had their bath houses inside, as at Caerleon and Chester.

This is a rough summary of a fort scheme, but we should remember that each fort was slightly – or, in some cases markedly – different from the next, that the degree of stone conversion and the datings, varied from fort to fort, that many forts have exhibited several periods of rebuilding, some of them sharply different from the one(s) that preceded (as, for example, at Housesteads), and that when almost every major fort excavation is completed and written up, it alters in some way the current thinking about fort design and construction in Roman Britain.

The Roman Fleet

The principal role of the army in Britain, once the southern half had been conquered and the process of 'Romanisation' begun, was to police the country and protect it from barbarian attacks from whatever source they came. This was a continuing commitment, and the effectiveness of the army in fulfilling its role is part and parcel of the history of the province. It is easy, however, to overlook the fact that the army was supported on numerous occasions by the Roman navy, which protected the troops and supply transports to and from Gaul and Britain, guarded commercial traffic and stood by in ports along the coast ready to intercept barbarian attacks and, where possible, mount more permanent patrols.

The organisation of the Roman navy is by no means as well documented or understood as its military counterpart, though its role in the campaigns of Caesar in Gaul and Britain are well described, particularly Caesar's personal attention to the building of better ships for his second expedition, in 54BC.[14] The fleet's role is also mentioned by Tacitus, in relation to the Agricolan campaign, and by Dio Cassius for its support of the Claudian invasion.[15] We do know that the empire had fleets based in various districts, several in the Mediterranean (notably those based at Ravenna and at Misenum), along the two main boundary rivers in Europe, the Danube and the Rhine, and possibly the Black Sea. And there was the *classis Britannica* (British fleet) which began as a Roman fleet centred on a naval base at Boulogne. In Britain, the first base was at Richborough, but sometime in the second century a second base was established at Dover (*Dubris*). Evidence was discovered during excavations in the early 1970s in the form of a 2½ acre (1ha) fort which had quarters for seamen, probably a ship's complement for each barrack. Naval installations were also erected at Lympne and Pevensey, perhaps at about the same time as at Dover,

The Roman Painted House at Dover (*Dr Brian Philp*)

and later at Reculver (where barracks of the early third century for naval personnel are attested) and at Brancaster.

The *classis Britannica* assisted in the Claudian invasion, helped in Vespasian's drive to the south-west and certainly played a major part in some of the Agricolan campaigns in Scotland; there is also evidence of naval activity during the Severan campaigns in Scotland of 208–211, where amphibious operations were undertaken across the Tay. Some of the skilled men of the fleet lent a hand in various military construction works, particularly on Hadrian's Wall, including repair work at Benwell fort. In the south-east of the province, the *classis Britannica* controlled a number of iron-producing sites, particularly in the Weald of Kent and East Sussex, witnessed by the discovery of roof-tiles stamped CL. BR, among other evidence at such places as Beauport Park (Sussex), Bardown (Sussex) and Cranbrook (Kent). These industries provided the fleet with its iron needs, supplied the army and perhaps even civilian requirements, and also exported iron to the Continent. Professor Frere has suggested that timber from these and other Weald sites may have been used for shipbuilding.[16]

It is thought that the *classis Britannica* ceased to exist by the mid third century, by which time the fort at Dover had been given up. A fresh fort of a different kind was soon to be erected, part of it over the earlier fort. This was a fort of the Saxon Shore (see p 143). Some of the iron industries in the Weald appear to have been closed at much the same time, eg Beauport Park. Thereafter, naval forces were reorganised and perhaps reallocated to army units, linking up with the Saxon Shore defence system which began to expand soon after the mid third century (Reculver and Brancaster forts had been built earlier in the century, see p 143).[17]

The types of warship used by the *classis Britannica*, their construction and the complements they carried, have escaped the attention of all but a few scholars.[18] It is possible that the standard war vessel was the liburnian, like those used by the Ravenna and Misenum fleets in the Mediterranean, namely, an oared ship 'rowed by two files on each side, either with one man to each oar at two levels or with two men to each oar at one level'.[19] The flagship, or flagships, of the fleet will probably have been triremes, oared ships with three levels of single-manned oars. The average complement of each liburnian is put at about eighty, that is, a century (and so designed), whose commander was not a centurion but a special naval officer, a trierarch. There were ten liburnians in a squadron which was commanded by a nauarch, a

A Roman warship of the late third century, as depicted on the gold medal struck by Constantius to celebrate his recovery of Britain from the usurper Allectus

kind of rear-admiral, who flew his flag in a trireme.

We are less well informed about Roman transport vessels, but the County Hall ship, which was excavated from the south bank of the Thames in 1910, and dated to the end of the third century, may be typical. It was flat-bottomed, with rounded bilge, built of oak and having a shallow keel. Its length was estimated at about 18m (60ft) and its beam at about 5m (16ft).[20]

NOTES

1. There is, of course, room for variation in these figures. The first cohort of a legion, for example, though larger than other cohorts, was not necessarily double their number. This particular problem has been discussed at some length in recent years, see for example, Frere, S. S. 'Hyginus and the first cohort', *Britannia* xi (1980) pp 51–60. A recent and helpful summary of the composition of the legion and of auxiliary regiments may be found in Holder, P. A. *The Roman Army in Britain* (1982).
2. Though sometimes a whole regiment would be granted Roman citizenship for distinguished service.
3. Webster, G. (1973) p 5.
4. 'That day he overcame the Nervii.' (Shakespeare, *Julius Caesar*, Act III, sc 2, I. 177).
5. Two strong rooms of interest are at Chesters and Caernarfon.
6. Florus, *Epitome of Roman History* II, xiii quotes Caesar at Pharsalus (48BC) telling his legionaries to strike the enemy in the face.
7. Birley, A. (1981) p 29.
8. Josephus, *The Jewish War* III, 71ff.
9. See the interesting discussion on marching camps built during the campaigns of Agricola in Scotland, by Maxwell, G. 'Agricola's campaigns: the evidence of the temporary camps', *Scottish Archaeological Forum* 12 (1981) pp 25–54.
10. Caesar, *De Bello Gallico* VII, 69–74; Josephus, *Jewish War* III, 81; inscriptions on a column from Lambaesis.
11. By the late Professor Sir Ian Richmond: detailed reports are in *Journal of Roman Studies* 43 (1953) to 56 (1966).
12. An interesting translation of Vegetius by John Clarke in the eighteenth century can be read in Phillips, T. R. and Lane, J. (eds) *Roots of Strategy* (1943) pp 35–95.
13. Vitruvius, *De Architectura* I, v, 3.
14. Caesar, *De Bello Gallico* III, 9; III, 14; V, 1.
15. Tacitus, *Agricola*, 38; Dio Cassius.
16. Frere, S. S. (1978) p 260.
17. An excellent summary of the *classis Britannica* is included among the papers in Johnston, D. E. (ed) *The Saxon Shore* (Council for British Archaeology Research Report no 18, 1977), notably the paper by Henry Cleere (pp 16–19) and the note on Dover by Brian Philp (pp 20–1).
18. Professor J. S. Morrison, lately President of Wolfson College, Cambridge, and author (with R. T. Williams) of *Greek Oared Ships*, and Dr Sean McGrail, chief archaeologist at the National Maritime Museum, Greenwich.
19. Morrison, J. S. (1980) p 47.
20. McGrail, S. (1981) p 24.

11

GOVERNMENT IN ROMAN BRITAIN

The province of Britannia was governed by Rome for almost four centuries. It cannot have been easy, more than a thousand miles from the centre of imperial power. The detailed history of the administration, most of which conformed to the standard pattern applying to imperial as opposed to senatorial provinces (some of which had to be adjusted to meet day-to-day circumstances peculiar to Britain), is a long and complex one, and is amply covered in several major works (see Bibliography p 546). A summary must suffice here. It may seem astonishing that the Romans were able to maintain the province in what appears from all the evidence to have been reasonable peace and prosperity for the great bulk of the years AD43–410, and that they did so without the availability of such modern facilities as telephones, television, radio, motor cars, railways, aeroplanes and, above all printing, which we take so much for granted. It could not, of course, have been achieved without the voluntary co-operation of the native people, nor without a considerable corps of civil servants and administrators provided by Rome.

Societies crave order, and order is more readily imposed and accepted if there appears to be some consistency in the administration that enforces it. In Roman times, such consistency began to emerge when Julius Caesar put an end to the chaos of the last years of the old Roman republican government, which had broken down as an instrument for both the capital and its empire, and laid the foundations of the imperial system which was to last for centuries (and whose effects are with us still). Whatever else the numerous nations and peoples had or did not have as members of the Roman empire, they always had an emperor and they had the civil service structure that administered the empire. Everyone in it knew who the emperor was, even if they never saw him, because they were informed by coins and inscriptions. Both, but especially coins, were employed for making official announcements – sometimes vaguely, more often directly. The accession (by whatever means) of a new emperor was invariably heralded by the issue of a new coin bearing a good likeness of him. Coins often carried an important message, such as *Concordia Militum* (ie we hope the army will give us their support) or *Libertas Publica* (ie don't forget – everyone in the empire has full rights under the law) or *Victoriae Britannicae* (ie we've just won some great victories in Britain, so don't stir it in the other provinces). Inscriptions more usually recorded the deeds of an emperor or his officials, or commemorated a distinguished or worthy career, or more simply stated that such-and-such a legion built (or repaired) this fort or that milecastle.

It was Roman policy, once a territory had been conquered (or annexed by more peaceful means) to shift the burden of government as far as possible upon the native leaders and their councils, retaining of course overall supervision. The degree of devolution differed in each province, and even from tribe to tribe, kingdom to kingdom. In Britain, Claudius granted formal client kingdom status to three tribes (the Iceni, the Brigantes and the Atrebatic Belgae in Sussex and Hampshire). It is possible that the last tribe was already a client kingdom, for the ruler, Verica, who fled to Claudius in AD42 to ask for help had already been issuing coins marked 'Rex'. The remaining tribes which had been conquered or had submitted (such as the eleven at Colchester, p 38), or which were to be overcome later, were ruled directly. The three client kingdoms lost that status when their rulers died, a normal feature of Roman colonial policy. The Claudian settlement of AD43 also brought the province within the writ of Roman law, and absorbed it into the Roman system of taxation.

As it was an imperial province, Britain was governed, up to the reforms of Diocletian in the early fourth century, by a *legatus Augusti pro praetore*, or emperor's deputy, who was commander-in-chief of the army and also head of the administration. The *legatus*, or governor, was generally an ex-consul who had held important military and pro-consular commands elsewhere: Suetonius had had a long and distinguished career, including the plum job in North Africa; Cerialis had served as brigade commander in Britain, and had gone on to higher things, including commanding a legion in Germany and leading forces that supported Vespasian's successful claim to the imperial purple in AD69. The British command was one of the best appointments in the Roman pro-consular career structure. As a rule, governors were appointed for three years, though two early British governors held the post for six, Trebellius and Agricola. It is not known if their terms were formally extended after the three years were up. The first governor, Aulus Plautius, and his successor, Ostorius Scapula, had their headquarters in Colchester. Probably for the remainder of the first century, this was not permanent: governors would set up their headquarters where they found that they spent the most time. By the end of the century, however, London could be regarded as the province's capital.

The governor was assisted by a staff drawn from the army, whose hierarchy developed over the years. The head of the provincial administration was the *princeps praetorii* (a centurion in military rank), who had several departmental heads beneath him, who in turn had a structure below them, down to the clerical grades who were usually freedmen or in some cases slaves. The province's finances were put under the charge of a special official, the *procurator*, whose rank was a little below that of the *legatus* and whose office was quite independent.

The idea was for one to keep an eye on the other: the *legatus* could check that the *procurator* was not raising taxes by extortionate methods or stealing what he was not entitled to; while the *procurator* was able to advise the governor if this or that action, decree or favour was not fair or legitimate. In the time of Boudica, the governor Suetonius does not appear to have made any effort to check the disgraceful abuses of the *procurator* Decianus Catus, which sparked off the terrible revolt, but the new *procurator* Classicianus certainly objected to Suetonius' severity in dealing with the rebels afterwards, and made a report to Nero about it, which led to Suetonius' recall. The *procurator* had his own staff, and his own headquarters, which was certainly based in London by the time of the Boudican revolt. This is clear from Tacitus and is supported by archaeology.[1] It was the *procurator's* official job to see to the army's pay, to collect taxes from the provincials and to supervise the economics and running of what were called imperial estates, the farms, industries and mines which the state took over in each province, in order that products or revenues from these enterprises would accumulate to the state. The two main forms of tax imposed upon a province were land tax and a tax on personal wealth, or poll tax. There were others, such as the *annona*, a tax on grain specifically raised towards the maintenance of the army, customs duties on imports, tolls at harbours and so forth.

There was a third official, the *legatus iuridicus*, or legal commissioner, a post introduced by Vespasian, who ranked just below the governor. This official does not appear to have been appointed in Britain before about AD80. The job was to take over the administration of justice in the civilian areas, and to handle the legal problems involved in setting up civilian administrations. The office may not have been a permanent feature of the provincial administration, but a post filled as and when required. Two such men were sent in the last quarter of the first century to Britain, and it has been suggested that they may have had their official headquarters at the palace at Fishbourne. The work referred to the *legatus iuridicus* must have got greater with every appointment, as the province expanded to take in all Britain south of Hadrian's Wall. By this time the governor was having to administer justice to 2 million people: the army of 63,000, the population of the *colonia, municipia, vici* and *civitas* capitals of over 200,000, some 50,000 in industries, some 25,000 on the villas and probably 1,500,000 in the rural areas.[2] Moreover, it was not simply a question of one law for the whole province. Those in Britain who were not Roman citizens (the majority, who were known as *peregrini*) were still allowed to have their own Celtic codes where these were not in flat contradiction to Roman law. It is clear that the juridical system in Britain needed a substantial department of its own. Romans could appeal to the emperor in Rome, but *peregrini* had to accept the decision of the governor as the final court of appeal in most matters.

Eastern and Mediterranean civilisations were based upon cities and towns, cohesive structures which facilitated the interchange of ideas and skills and so advanced their societies and cultures. No one grasped this better than the Romans who made their own capital the biggest city in the world (at the time) and whose far flung empire was but an extension of it. The Celts in Britain, quite differently, did not develop towns. The largest units that could in any sense be regarded as urban were their hillforts and their villages of houses and barns surrounded by ramparts and dykes, such as Prae Wood and Camulodunon. The Romans therefore had to introduce the concept of urban life and to get the British to accept it. They began by establishing *coloniae*, towns specifically intended only for Roman citizens, retired army veterans, emigrants from Italy and elsewhere who were Roman citizens, traders and craftsmen. These were to be models. The first in Britain was Colchester, begun cAD48-9, and the next two were Gloucester and Lincoln, at the end of the first century AD. The last was York, developed in the early third century out of an earlier settlement of lesser status, perhaps a *municipium*.

The Romans also created *municipia*, towns for people with Roman or Latin citizenship, usually formed out of existing settlements, such as St Albans and London. These are the only two that we can be sure actually attained this status, though it has been argued that five others, Canterbury, Silchester, Dorchester, Leicester and Wroxeter, also became *municipia*. And for the tribes themselves, the Romans created tribal cities or towns, known as *civitas* capitals, one for each tribe, which were responsible for the whole tribal area.

Each of these town types was governed by a local authority structure which varied little between the three. There was a senate, or *ordo*, with about a hundred *decuriones*, or *curiales*, representatives chosen by the inhabitants and, no doubt, occasionally nominated by the Roman governor or his staff. The electing inhabitants had to have property qualifications, which probably meant that about half the town's population did not have a say. The *decuriones* in turn elected their own magistrates, two seniors or *duoviri*, who alternated as president of the senate and acted as judges in simple law suits and criminal cases, and two juniors, or *aediles*, who looked after the everyday affairs of the town, eg road building and maintenance, public health, public buildings and local taxation. The *civitas* capitals were slightly different from the other two types of town in that the inhabitants remained citizens of their tribes, not of the towns; the inhabitants of *Calleva* (Silchester), for example, were *cives Atrebatum* not *cives Callevae*. And, of course, until Caracalla extended Roman citizenship to everyone in the empire in 212–3, *civitas* inhabitants were not Roman citizens.

Serving in the senate or as a magistrate was expensive and only the wealthy could afford it. Even then, it is evident that some rich men were reluctant to do their share of public service. Magistrates were expected to put on shows, gladiatorial contests and games, miniature versions of the entertainments provided in Rome; and the amphitheatres at many *civitas* capitals, such as those excavated at Carmarthen, Cirencester and Silchester, testify to the importance placed on entertaining the populace. *Decuriones* were obliged to subscribe to (and raise the total cost of) public buildings, or pay for fine statues or water fountains, though having one's name chiselled into an inscription on a building was perhaps not much compensation for the heavy bill at the end of the work! It is generally held that after a while membership of the *ordo* began to be dreaded rather than coveted, and potential candidates often did their utmost to avoid service. Accordingly, an element of compulsion to serve was introduced, which incorporated clauses for exemption. Professor A. Birley notes that in the fourth century some people became Christian priests in order to qualify for exemption.[3]

The *civitas* capitals were not all founded at once. Some tribes had strongly resisted Roman occupation of their territory, and the governor, following normal Roman policy, kept them under direct military rule by means of forts built in the territory during the campaigns or soon afterwards. They would be given permission to have a new capital when they had proved they could be trusted or were ready to be granted autonomy. There is another aspect: the Romans needed to use as many of their armed forces as possible as they spread northwards, and so they worked towards getting those tribes already subdued ready for autonomy as soon as they could, so that they could close down forts and release troops. Exeter legionary fortress, built between AD55 and 60, was run down and evacuated between AD75 and 80 and a *civitas* capital developed over the site for the Dumnonii, to be known as *Isca Dumnoniorum*. The legion (Legio II) was moved to a new fortress at Caerleon in Wales. The Iceni, crushed by the defeat of their queen, Boudica, which must have cost them half to three-quarters of their active menfolk, were regarded by about AD70 as trust-worthy enough to have a *civitas* capital at *Venta Icenorum* (Caistor St Edmund) just south of Norwich, probably near the site of Boudica's own palace.[4] A town with wooden buildings began to go up in the decade AD70-80, and it was converted to stone in the next century.

Several of the *civitas* capitals were not, however, initiated until the second century, and in the reign of Hadrian (117–38) four are known to have been begun, *Venta Silurum* (Caerwent), *Moridunum Demetarum* (Carmarthen), *Isurium Brigantum* (Aldborough) and *Petuaria Parisionum* (Brough-on-Humber).

Apart from the few *coloniae, municipia* and *civitas* capitals, there were many smaller settlements which can be classified as small towns (or large villages) which are called *vici*. The term is not however as straightforward as it seems. A *vicus* could be a settlement that grew up round a fort; there were many of these, particularly those round the Hadrian's Wall forts. It could also be a suburb of a larger town, or a small town that later became a *civitas* capital, eg *Luguvalum* (Carlisle). The *vicus* may be related to the former urban district councils that used to be a feature of English local government structure before 1974. It could be a native settlement of village-type grouped round a

The hot bath (*caldarium*) at Bath

main-road posting station, or a small community that developed beside a special facility, such as the *vicus* beside *Aquae Sulis* (Bath), the principal spa in Britain that was used by both Romans and natives throughout the occupation but which never advanced beyond *vicus* status. *Vici* had their own councils, with fewer magistrates. There was another administrative unit, the smallest in the line, which was the *pagus*, exclusively a rural area (akin to the former rural district councils) and in no sense regarded as a town. At some stage, the *civitates* (tribal territories) were divided into small regions called *pagi*, which in many cases followed the boundaries that had already been made before the conquest, particularly in Belgic territory.

These units functioned pretty much on their own. There was no central parliament or political assembly. The only corporate body in any sense representing all the towns and villages was the *concilium provinciae*, to which *civitates* could send representatives, but which met only once a year and could not make any decisions of policy. Its function was largely connected with the religious cult of the emperor (see p 257), but grievances could be aired at the meetings which might be carried forward to the appropriate quarters. As A. L. F. Rivet has remarked, the council was useful to the Roman government as a sounding board of provincial feeling.[5] The council had clearly not become sufficiently established by the time of the revolt of Boudica, if indeed it was established at all, otherwise the governor, Suetonius, would certainly have gathered something of the seething discontent building up among the tribes in the east.

These local government arrangements do not seem to have changed much throughout the occupation, and they were not materially affected by the reorganisation of the province by Diocletian in the early fourth century. Although the province was divided into four, each under a *praeses*, who was responsible to the *vicarius Britanniarum*, the *ordo* continued to consist of *decuriones* and to govern the *civitas* or *municipium*. Calpurnius, father of St Patrick, was a *decurion* in the last years of the fourth or early years of the fifth century, and the emperor Honorius was still able to write to the *civitates* in Britain in 410 telling them to look to their own defences. Indeed, one of the reasons why the British towns managed to last well into the middle of the fifth century, notwithstanding that the province's ties with Rome had been cut, must be that the *civitas* senates and local organisations (which included defence forces) remained fully operational. It would not be too far fetched to claim that the threads of local government that have been woven into the fabric of British history since early Anglo-Saxon times owe something of their origins to the Romano-British system.

NOTES
1. Brailsford, J. W. (1964) p 48.
2. The estimates of Professor S. S. Frere in *Britannia* (1978) pp 348–50.
3. Birley, A. (1981) p 24.
4. No site for the palace has yet been discovered but, the Thetford site recently excavated by A. K. Gregory notwithstanding (see p 439), I am unmoved in my belief that Boudica had her headquarters near Norwich.
5. Rivet, A. L. F. (1975) p 66.

12

ROMANO-BRITISH TOWNS

In this chapter we shall mainly be looking at the major towns of Roman Britain, the *coloniae*, the *municipia* and the *civitas* capitals (called, by some authorities, cantonal capitals). Smaller urban settlements, such as little towns with no capital status, *vici* and so forth, are dealt with at the end of the chapter. They have been variously grouped, but perhaps the most suitable term for them is minor towns. In discussing towns of any size in Roman Britain, it is important to remember that over the four centuries of Roman occupation none of them remained the same size; by no means all of them increased gradually from a small settlement to a major town and many had several phases of prosperity followed by decline or interrupted by disaster, such as fire or serious depopulation due to plague. As Professor Rivet has said, 'there can be no single acceptable map of Roman Britain: we need at least four maps, one for each century, or, better still, forty maps, one for each decade.'[1]

The building of major towns began soon after the invasion of AD43, and by the year of the Boudican revolt (AD60–1) three had taken shape and were occupied by many thousands of people; and it is possible that one or two more were started, such as Canterbury and possibly Chelmsford. First of the three was Colchester, the first *colonia*, begun in AD48 or 49 as a settlement for army veterans largely, though not exclusively, for men retired from the legions in Britain. The new town was built over the site of the first legionary fortress in Britain, originally erected for Legio XX which had moved to Gloucester in AD48–9, on the hill that overlooked the Celtic *oppidum* of Camulodunon, and the military buildings were modified or dismantled. The *colonia* was provided with most of the principal public buildings erected in Roman towns, namely, *curia*, theatre, temple(s), but not public baths at this stage. The town was built on the street grid system, with east–west and north–south roads crossing each other to form blocks, or *insulae*, amounting in the case of Colchester to some

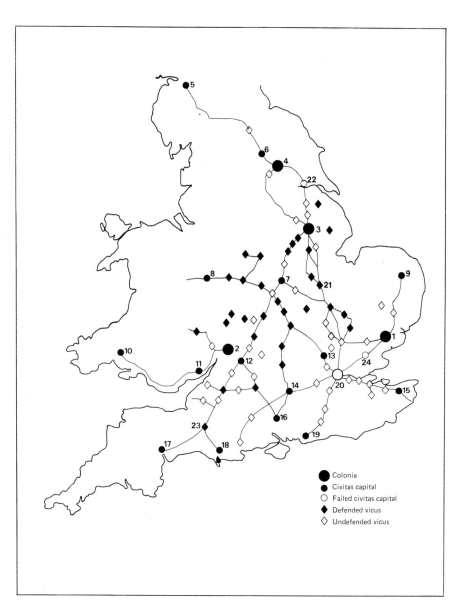

The *civitas* capitals of Roman Britain (after J. S. Wacher), including capitals of much later establishment, 'failed' capitals and principal towns and settlements of lesser status. Also marked are the *coloniae*. 1 Colchester 2 Gloucester 3 Lincoln 4 York 5 Carlisle 6 Aldborough 7 Leicester 8 Wroxeter 9 Caistor St Edmund 10 Carmarthen 11 Caerwent 12 Cirencester 13 St Albans 14 Silchester 15 Canterbury 16 Winchester 17 Exeter 18 Dorchester 19 Chichester 20 London 21 Water Newton 22 Brough-on-Humber 23 Ilchester 24 Chelmsford

A stretch of the wall of the *colonia Camulodunon* (Colchester) as it appeared in the 1920s and as it is still preserved (*National Monuments Record*)

forty blocks. This was the basic plan for all towns, though in each case there was variation in detail. Most Roman town streets were between 4.5 and 7.5m (15–25ft) wide, were surfaced with gravel upon hardcore and were usually cambered. Private houses, shops, public buildings and perhaps factories and warehouses were erected along the streets. The Colchester plan was intended to be a model for the towns that followed, and in principle it was, though, as can be seen from the town plan; each had quite an individual layout.

The second of the three was London, which by AD60 had become a prosperous and well-populated settlement of *vicus* status, described by Tacitus as 'an important centre for businessmen and merchandise'.[2] During the decade AD50–60, London had been chosen as the location for the procurator's headquarters. The choice made sense from a geographical and communication point of view, and the first of the main arterial roads built by the Romans radiated outwards from London, Watling Street. Early London grew up on the north bank of the Thames (in the present City area), but bridges were built across the river, and evidence has been discovered of occupation south of the river.[3] One bridge had been erected by Aulus Plautius in the first months of the invasion, the remains of which may be those recently found (and now reburied) at Pudding Lane, under Fish Hill Street.[4]

The third town was St Albans, which was begun in AD43 or 44 as a military fort beside the west bank of the river Ver, downhill from the Catuvellaunian *oppidum* of *Verlamion* (Prae Wood). The fort was given up in AD48 or 49 and a town built upon its remains, in grid plan and along conventional lines. It was designated as the *civitas* capital of the Catuvellauni and it could have received *municipium* status as early as AD49, though there is an alternative view that this was not accorded until the time of Vespasian (AD69–79). Recent excavations revealed a row of timber-framed shops, near the later theatre (which is still there), that have been dated to about AD50, and which were destroyed during the sack of St Albans by Boudica in AD61. What is more interesting is that St Albans appears to have had stone buildings in these first years, one at least with picture-painted plaster on its walls. All three towns were destroyed by Boudica, by all accounts pretty thoroughly, and

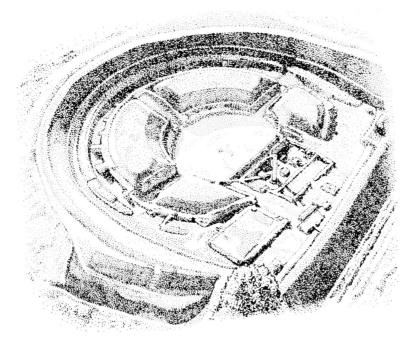

The theatre at *Verulamium* (St Albans)

197

each had to be rebuilt. It is clear that rebuilding took place quickly in London, while St Albans was virtually replanned and its size nearly doubled.

Aside from these three towns, eleven *civitas* capitals and two more *coloniae* were begun in the second half of the first century. One of them, Chelmsford (*Caesaromagus*) has a number of question marks over it, and seems not to have got off the ground as a capital, though it certainly qualified as a town. Another capital, Dorchester (*Durnovaria*), appears later to have had to share its capital status with a second capital for the same *civitas*, the Durotriges, ie Ilchester (*Lindinis*). Some capitals were built over or beside the sites of earlier Roman fortresses (such as Exeter and Wroxeter) or forts (Cirencester and Leicester); others were begun from scratch on or beside sites of Celtic origin, such as Caistor St Edmund. Accurate dating of the beginnings of the new towns is fraught with difficulty, but we may not be far out in assigning date ranges as follows: Canterbury, 50–60; Exeter, 78–80; Dorchester, 80–90; Chichester, 80–90; Silchester, 80–90; Winchester, 80–90; Cirencester, 80–5; Leicester, 80–90; Caistor St Edmund, 70–80; and Wroxeter, 90–100. The two new *coloniae* were Lincoln (*Lindum*) c96 and Gloucester (*Glevum*) c96–8, both built out of legionary fortresses. The fortress at York had a *vicus* that developed on its south side, over the river Ouse, and this became a *colonia* in the reign of Caracalla (211–17).

Each of the *civitas* capitals and the three *coloniae* are described in the Gazetteer. There were four more *civitas* capitals initiated in the reign of Hadrian (117–38), namely Aldborough, Brough-on-Humber, Caerwent and Carmarthen. Three other towns of later date which certainly or probably achieved *civitas* capital status in the third century were Carlisle (possibly during Carcalla's reign), Ilchester and Water Newton. All the sites have been excavated, some more extensively than others, but all of them with skill, imagination – even drama – under brilliant inspiration. Here, we shall summarise the principal characteristics of these major towns, and cite some examples of the particularly interesting features discovered.

The centre of the town was the *forum* and *basilica* complex, and in most cases it was situated in the middle of the town (though not in London or Colchester). It generally lay where two main roads crossed. The ground plans of several *fora* are similar to those of the *principia,* or headquarters building, of a fortress or fort, and this has been taken to mean that military personnel probably helped with the

The street grid of the *civitas* capital *Calleva Atrebatum* (Silchester), seen from the air through the crops and grass (*National Monuments Record*)

construction of this central feature. The *forum* was a quadrangle, three sides of which were given over to shops (back to back), stalls, bars, perhaps warehouses and maybe public facilities, ranged behind colonnaded walkways fronting on to the street outside and on to the courtyard inside, which also contained a variety of market stalls. The three sides also had second-storey accommodation, generally for offices and stores. The courtyard was approached via a *forum* gateway which might be a handsome structure of stone, carrying a splendid inscription of dedication, recording the details of building and the date. The gateway at Silchester was of Purbeck marble and its inscription was in letters graded from 30cm (1ft) tall downwards. The fourth side of the *forum* was taken up by the *basilica*, a great aisled hall, usually with apsidal end, or ends, which was the town hall and civic administration block, with local courtroom and tribunal in the apsidal end(s). Public meetings were held in the main hall, and perhaps the *ordo* also convened here, as the smaller chamber found on the far side

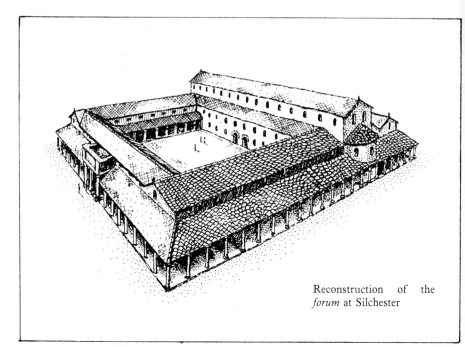

Reconstruction of the *forum* at Silchester

of the *basilica* away from the *forum* in most cases seems to have been too small to accommodate the hundred *decuriones* at one sitting. These *basilicae* were among the largest and most impressive buildings erected in Roman Britain. The hall at Silchester is reckoned to have stood 20m (70ft) tall, while that at London is estimated to have been over 150m (500ft) long. Behind the main hall, away from the *forum*, was an end-to-end row of rooms, probably offices for civic use, for court staff, perhaps even as rooms for hearing some cases 'in chambers'.[5]

Although the *forum* was not the only market place to which traders and farmers could bring their wares, it was the biggest in town. It acted as a meeting place for town and country people who otherwise tended to live separate lives. In some towns, separate market halls (*macellae*) were erected in the central part to provide extra shop and stall areas, as at Leicester and Wroxeter. And in each of the towns individual shops were to be found elsewhere along the streets, chiefly along the main streets that intersected in the centre. Many shops were the front part of a craftsman's workshop, which he used as his retail outlet. Further behind still, or above, would be a flat or rooms for his family. Remains of a tremendous variety of small businesses have been found in excavations: baker's lifting gear in St Albans, butcher's pits in Cirencester, ironmonger's goods at Wroxeter, glassware from a glazier in Leicester, a lamp factory and shop at Colchester, a builder's yard in

Exeter, a carpenter's workshop at Silchester (which has been reconstructed in diorama form at the Reading Museum), a coppersmith's workshop at Carmarthen, and what may be a shoeshop in Walbrook, London. In addition to shops and workshops, other commercial buildings were sited along high streets and side roads, such as banks and moneylenders (even in Roman days the latter charged higher rates than the former), restaurants, taverns, lodging houses and presumably also latrines.

A Romano-British period carpenter's plane, from the Silchester collection at Reading Museum (*Reading Museum & Art Gallery*)

Roman towns were provided with sewerage, drainage and water supply systems. These varied considerably in elaboration and efficiency from the complex underground sewers of Lincoln, into which drains from every street emptied to the simpler wood-lined street drains of Silchester and Cirencester which emptied into pits. Most towns were provided with public water supplies by means of aqueducts, which were generally contour-following channels cut into the ground, bringing the water in from outside. The channels were lined with clay or sometimes wood, and the water was distributed through pipes of clay, wood or lead to water tanks in main streets from where it was channelled to individual premises by means of sluices. Many private houses had their own wells for additional supplies. There are fine remains of underground sewers at York and Lincoln, as well as drains from individual houses into the mains. The principal users of the water system, however, were the patrons of the public bath house, which was a key feature of every major town, not only for health and hygiene but also as a public meeting place. Baths were in

201

The water tank and fountain at Corbridge Roman station

fact the Roman equivalent of clubs, and most Romans were wont to spend a good part of each day there, bathing, exercising, gambling or meeting business contacts.

Roman public baths were immensely impressive buildings. Even in a ruined state today, their grandeur and dominance over other buildings strike one with awe. The shell of the huge baths of Diocletian in Rome is among the greatest of the Eternal City's treasures. Somewhat less imposing, but still notable among Roman remains in Britain, the wall of the exercise room at the baths at Wroxeter still stands at 8m (27ft) and dominates the site. The building of these huge public amenities and the introduction of the habit of bathing in such organised luxury must have taken the Celts aback. This is not to suggest that they were a dirty people, but it was undoubtedly something quite new to them to have access to a series of large bathing pools and steam-heated rooms through which to pass, from cold to hot, to spend an hour or more on what they had been used to doing in a few minutes! Public baths so far found in Roman towns conform to a standard range of service rooms and cubicles, though in each case the arrangements vary: no two plans of baths are alike. At Silchester and Wroxeter, for example, the baths underwent major alterations over their centuries of usage; at Wroxeter, when the first baths (never completed) were rebuilt in the second century, they were actually resited to the other side of the road, and given an outdoor swimming pool as well as a huge *palaestra*, or entrance court-yard, for exercises such as ball games, wrestling and athletics. Public baths were often sited near the town centre, dependent, of course, upon water supply and drainage facilities, though at Silchester they were several blocks to the east, while at Caistor St Edmund they were on the west side and at Aldborough on the north-west.

As a rule, the rooms of the baths were ordered as follows: after going through the doors into the *palaestra*, you went into an *apodyterium* or changing room (sometimes there were two or three) to undress and leave your clothing in a locker or niche. Then you went through a series of rooms of different temperatures, (in order) the *frigidarium*, or cold room, the *tepidarium*, or warm room, and the *caldarium*, or hot room, which produced a very considerable heat like a modern Turkish bath. Generally, this was the time to take up a *strigil*, a metal skin scraper, with which to scoop off the dirt and natural oils that were being helped out of the skin pores by the heat. You could then plunge

The 'Old Work' at the *civitas* capital *Viroconium* (Wroxeter). It contains the entrance into the *palaestra* of the town baths (*E. Houlder*)

into a special hot bath in a side cubicle. If you wanted, you could increase the cleaning process by having yourself rubbed over with fresh oil by an attendant, to help make up the natural greases, and perhaps have a massage as well. In some establishments there was an extra sweating room where the heat was intense and dry, not moist, like the sauna bath of today. This was the *laconicum* and was variously sited, generally with access from the outside for those who did not wish to go through all the other rooms first. At Silchester the *laconicum* was off the *tepidarium*; at Wroxeter there were two and they were exclusive chambers off the *apodyteria*, but when the baths were demolished and later rebuilt, they disappeared.

When you were clean, or felt you had had enough, you returned the way you had come, finishing up with a cold plunge beside the *frigidarium*, which closed the pores and helped to prevent your catching cold when you emerged outside the baths. Out in the *palaestra* you could play games or, preferably perhaps, sit under a colonnaded covered walkway and sip drinks with a friend. Mixed bathing appears to have been discouraged in Roman Britain and, as in present-day Turkish or sauna baths, the mornings were set aside for one sex, the afternoons for the other.

The manner in which the water and steam heat were produced was as follows: water was heated by furnaces situated next to the *caldarium*. Under the floors of the *caldarium* and *tepidarium* (and their adjoining off-cubicles, *laconica* etc) were rows of squat pillars of tile or stone supporting the floors, round which the furnaces circulated hot air to heat the floors. This underfloor area was the hypocaust, a word often used to embrace the system. Hot air was also drawn up through special box-shaped flue tiles into the walls of the rooms above, for extra and sustained heat. The lower temperature of the *tepidarium* was arrived at because the room was further away from the furnace.

Among the other main public buildings, we should note the theatres, amphitheatres, temples (see chapter 16) and *mansiones*. Public shows and spectacles played an important part in the life of the urban Roman, whether in Rome or in the provincial towns. There were three main showplaces: the theatre, amphitheatre and circus. So far no remains of a circus have been discovered in Britain, but it is most unlikely that none was built, as the circus, the arena for the tremendously popular chariot races, was among the basic entertainments. It is possible that some races might have been held in amphitheatres, but the dimensions of those so far excavated in Britain are

Remains of the amphitheatre outside the south gate of the *civitas* capital *Durnovaria* (Dorchester) (*Reece Winstone*)

Amphitheatre at Caerleon legionary fortress, Gwent (*Wales Tourist Board*)

against it. Amphitheatres in Britain were erected on the edge of, or outside, the town, though that at Caerwent, added late in the town's history, was within the urban area. None of them ever approached the scale and splendour of the great stone examples at Nîmes in France or Pula in Yugoslavia or the tremendous Colosseum in Rome itself, and they appear to have been built chiefly of timber or stone-revetted earth banks. Several have been excavated, including those at Carmarthen, Caerwent, Cirencester, Chichester, Dorchester and Silchester, and one or two at Roman forts and fortresses (cf Caerleon). The amphitheatre was the arena for gladiatorial contests, wild beast shows and other bloodthirsty sports for which the Romans were famous. Usually the building was oval in plan, with rising tiers of seats all round, punctuated by gangways. None so far examined seems to have been more than about 105m (350ft) across the greater overall diameter: Dorchester, at 103m (345ft) across and whose arena was about 58×52m (196×176ft) does not seem large enough for chariot racing.

The third showplace was the theatre, erected to provide less bestial, more intellectual entertainment, such as plays, mimes, verse readings, ballet and, in some places such as Gosbecks and St Albans, religious gatherings or functions, since both were situated close to temples. So far, only the two named and Canterbury (found in 1950 under St Margaret's Street) have been excavated. Both St Albans' and Canterbury's theatres appear to have been rebuilt. Theatres were generally D-shaped and were open to the elements. The seats were

The theatre at the *civitas* capital *Verulamium* (St Albans) (*E. Houlder*)

A fine cropmark showing the *mansio* at Lower Wanborough, near Swindon (see *Britannia*, viii) (*B. Hill*)

arranged in semi-circular tiers rising towards the back. St Albans' theatre was a complicated building of several periods of modification, which ended up as the local rubbish dump. The main auditorium and stage were arranged in three-quarters of a circle.

Mansiones were official hotels or large inns for government or military personnel, couriers, members of the imperial post service (*cursus publicus*) and important visitors. They appear to have been luxuriously appointed, were built in towns, in or beside forts, and here and there as part of key staging posts on main roads. In a town the *mansio* generally comprised a courtyard building with two dozen or more rooms or suites, with a bath house and a variety of public rooms, and with stabling for horses outside. The Silchester two-storey *mansio* was sited near the south gate, 90m (100yd) or so from the road that led out towards Winchester, and it was a substantial building, nearly as large as the *forum*. The large house near the south gate at Caerwent is likely to have been a *mansio*.

Mosaic from the town house in the north west of the *civitas* capital *Durnovaria* (Dorchester) (*Reece Winstone*)

Private houses formed by far the greatest number of buildings in Roman towns, and were considerably more numerous than shops, many of which were owned by people who did not live above or behind them, or indeed in the town at all. Houses were of many kinds. The wealthy man's house, owned by a businessman or professional man who had become a Roman citizen, or a non-Roman who was a decurion in his *civitas* capital, was either a rough L-shaped house, with corridors on both sides of both arms, to give rooms privacy, or an even larger property with three or four wings round a courtyard. Large houses of these kinds excavated have revealed many rooms (more than two dozen at one in Wroxeter). They were often single-storeyed, with gable roof covered with clay pantiles and accommodation for the family and the servants (in segregated quarters). The earlier houses were built with timber frames, whose walls were coated with wattle and daub and set in stone foundations. Heating was by open fire or brazier, since the chimney had not been invented. Then, as building techniques advanced, more and more houses were constructed of stone and brick, and this enabled owners to have central heating by hypocaust installed. These heating systems were similar (but smaller) to the public bath house system. Some private houses had their own bath suites, but this was rare; the public baths were preferred for their social as much as their hygiene function.

From quite early on, larger houses in Britain were tastefully and often elaborately decorated. Wall plaster was widely used, and among the ruins of many excavated properties fragments of plaster have been found bearing parts of an overall wall painting. Some houses had the luxury of decorated friezes round the top of the walls; equally early, house-owners commissioned mosaic floors to be laid in principal rooms, particularly the dining-room which in Roman times served also as a drawing-room. House-owners could actually choose mosaics for their floors from pattern samples: as the generations went by, several schools of mosaic artists developed individual ranges of designs based upon expanding varieties of themes. (Mosaic decoration is discussed more fully on pp 222–4.)

If the larger houses were single-storeyed, they were often well sited in the town, within sizeable gardens which flanked two or three sides, as at Silchester and St Albans. Most houses had one side fronting on to a main street. Smaller houses for lesser folk were frequently of the barn-type, a long rectangular building with pitched roof, the gable end facing the street. These were erected on small, narrow building plots, and in many instances there was little room for lateral development, and so extra space was obtained by building upwards or to the rear. Excavations have shown that many single-storey small houses could be as long as 30m (100ft). They were retail shop, workshop or warehouse, and accommodation area in line. Where the houses were of two storeys, the living rooms were generally upstairs, and there is evidence that some of these houses had first-floor balconies.

Small Towns

The status and development of smaller towns in Roman Britain have been the subject of much investigation and discussion in recent years, especially since the problems were so succinctly set out by Professor Malcolm Todd in his excellent paper, 'Small towns of Roman Britain', printed in *Britannia* i (1970). A key conference on the subject was held at Oxford in 1975, and the papers were published later in the year as

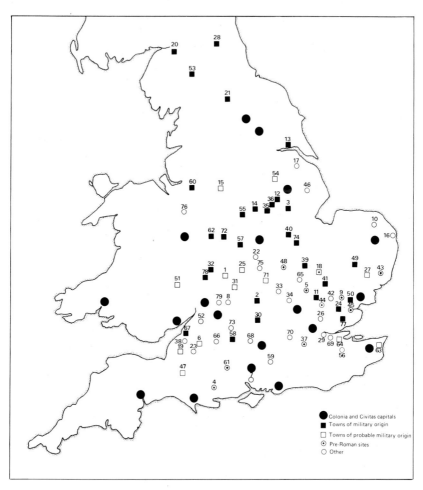

Small Towns: 1 Alcester 2 Alchester 3 Ancaster 4 Badbury 5 Baldock 6 Bath 7 Bitterne 8 Bourton-on-the-Water 9 Braintree 10 Brampton 11 Braughing 12 Brough 13 Brough-on-Humber 14 Broxtowe 15 Buxton 16 Caister on Sea 17 Caistor (Lincs) 18 Cambridge 19 Camerton 20 Carlisle 21 Catterick 22 Caves Inn 23 Charterhouse 24 Chelmsford 25 Chesterton-on-Fosse 26 Chigwell 27 Coddenham 28 Corbridge 29 Crayford 30 Dorchester-on-Thames 31 Dorn 32 Droitwich 33 Dropshort 34 Dunstable 35 East Bridgford 36 East Stoke 37 Ewell 38 Gatcombe 39 Godman-chester 40 Great Casterton 41 Great Chesterford 42 Great Dunmow 43 Hacheston 44 Harlow 45 Heybridge 46 Horncastle 47 Ilchester 48 Irchester 49 Ixworth 50 Kelvedon 51 Kenchester 52 Kingscote 53 Kirkby Thore 54 Littleborough 55 Littlechester 56 Maidstone 57 Mancetter 58 Mildenhall 59 Neatham 60 Northwich 61 Old Sarum 62 Penkridge 63 Richborough 64 Rochester 65 Sandy 66 Sandy Lane 67 Sea Mills 68 Speen 69 Springhead 70 Staines 71 Towcester 72 Wall 73 Wanborough 74 Water Newton 75 Whilton Lodge 76 Whitchurch 77 Wickford 78 Worcester 79 Wycomb

Brough-on-Humber, Carlisle and Ilchester were also *civitas* capitals at some time. Chelmsford was a 'failed' *civitas* capital and Water Newton was a possible *civitas* capital (adapted from Rodwell, W. and Rowley, T. [Eds], p 2)

British Archaeological Report no 15, edited by W. Rodwell and T. Rowley. The phrase 'small town' was not easy to define – and still is not – but the conference limited itself to considering settlements outside *colonia, municipia* and *civitas* capitals at one end of the scale and at the other end, farmsteads, villas and villages, and on the whole covered settlements that occupied between about 25 and 125 acres (10–50ha). It may generally be agreed that a small town differs from a large town not simply in the matter of size (indeed, one or two small towns were much the same size as one or two *civitas* capitals), but more in the fact that the layout was not planned so much as haphazard. If there was a grid of streets, it developed rather than was laid down, and grew both sides of one longish main street. There were grids of a sort at Catterick and Alchester, for example, but the *civitas* grids were in a different class. There were other differences.

The conference had before it a tentative list of some 79 minor towns, and this covered towns of military origin, possible military origin and towns developing from pre-Roman sites. The military origin is important in the light of Professor S. S. Frere's fundamental point, explained in his contribution to the conference, 'The origin of small towns', pp 4–7, namely, that towns sprang up where military commanders put forts.

The list has been enlarged since 1975, but although the total is now nearer 80, there is still argument over some of the new candidates, and also over some of the originals, and for these reasons the 1975 list is deemed appropriate for this work.

NOTES
1. Rivet, A. L. F., 'The classification of minor towns and related settlements', in Rodwell, W. and Rowley, T. (eds) *The Small Towns of Roman Britain* (British Archaeological Reports no 15, 1975).
2. Tacitus, *Annals* xiv, 33.
3. *Britannia* ix (1978) pp 453–5; x (1979) p 318; xi (1980) pp 381–2; xii (1981) pp 353–4.
4. *Britannia* xiii (1982) pp 271–6.
5. Wacher, J. (1975) p 45.

13
THE COUNTRYSIDE

Towns were centres of population in Roman Britain, but the majority of the people in the province lived and worked in the countryside. Most were engaged in some form of farming activity. This was the position throughout the four hundred or so years of Roman occupation. During that time there were several developments in farming techniques and equipment, and marketing methods were greatly improved, but we shall look in vain for dramatic advances comparable with, say, those of the agrarian revolution of the eighteenth century. The farmers of the late Iron Age were not the humble and disorganised earth-scratchers they are so often said to have been (see pp 12–13). Where the 'Romanisation' of Britain, however, undoubtedly made major contributions was in better organisation of agriculture, the introduction of some new crops, new growing patterns, the expansion of livestock farming, innovations in corn-drying, threshing and grain storage, the introduction of horticulture and gardening, and the building and development of villas and their associated structures. If it were necessary to summarise in a sentence what Rome did for British agriculture, it could be said that it converted it from a haphazard spread of individual farms geared to providing enough for the owner and his dependants to live on into an industry which created a surplus, which fed the province, including the army of occupation, which produced profits and enriched the countryside dweller and his environment, and which afforded a significant source of revenue for the empire.

The villa was as a rule more than just a simple farmhouse; it was the whole farm with all the buildings associated with it. Although this may be an unsatisfactory definition, it remains the best we have. Numerous works have been written about the villa, for it was the principal structure or cluster of structures in the countryside, and at least a thousand of one kind or another were erected during the Roman occupation of Britain (see Bibliography p 546). This has not

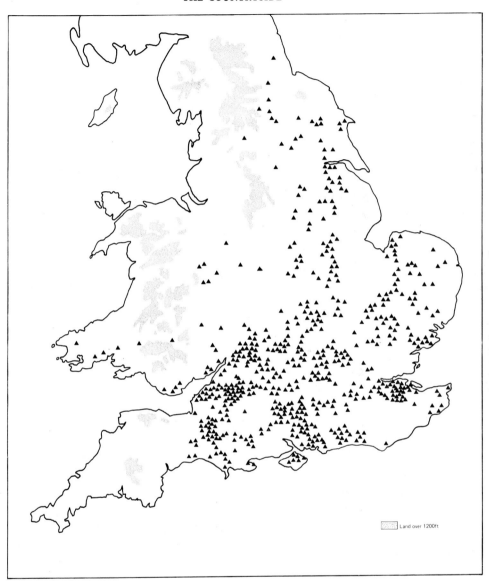

Land over 1200ft

Distribution of villas

unnaturally led to attempts to classify villa buildings and types, an exercise in which specialists have found much room for disagreement, not helped by the growing number of archaeological excavations and re-examinations of villa sites that has been taking place in Britain in the past decade or so. In this discussion, however, the four basic types of farmhouse enumerated a generation ago by Collingwood and Richmond will suffice: the cottage house, the corridor house, the courtyard house and the aisled house.[1] Each type has many variations and the building works are not necessarily limited to one period or even one century of construction. For example, many villa houses began as a timber-framed cottage on stone foundations, like Lockleys, near Welwyn in Hertfordshire, and Hambleden in Buckinghamshire, both of the first century, and were later enlarged into corridor houses built largely of stone, Lockleys in three and Hambleden in two further stages. Some, like Little Milton in Oxfordshire and Bazeley Copse, Micheldever, in Hampshire, began and remained cottage house types. The villa house at Iwerne in Dorset had started as a timber-framed cottage house of the first century and was rebuilt in stone in the fourth century on much the same plan, without corridor and yet with fine painted plaster walls and flagstone floors (one of the rooms was photographed during excavations at the end of the nineteenth century and a print can be seen at the Dorset County Museum in Dorchester). At Park Street, near St Albans, a first-century cottage house, with an off-centre front-to-back passage and a cellar at one end, was built over an earlier and simpler Belgic farmhouse, from whose remains an iron slave gang chain was recovered.[2] Park Street was enlarged into a winged corridor house in the second century, and further improved in the fourth.

The drawback of the cottage house, if such it was in early Roman Britain, was that the rooms were interconnecting and so there was little privacy. This has been taken to suggest that the house was occupied by a family plus perhaps a worker or two, all on equal terms. Other cottage houses were at Cox Green, near Maidenhead in Berkshire (later enlarged), Bignor Villa, West Sussex, which began as a stone cottage house in the early third century upon the foundations of an earlier timber house and which was converted to a corridor house later in that century and extended further into a sumptuous courtyard house in the fourth century, and Brixworth in Northamptonshire (which, like Lockleys, received a verandah very early on).

Villas were sited in areas where the arable land was known to be

Aerial photograph of site of large winged corridor villa at Reach, near Cambridge. The villa was of more than one period. Its overall length was about 46m (151ft). Each wing had a broad projection with a semi-circular bay in front. Some rooms had tessellated pavements (*Cambridge University Collection*)

good; many were built upon the sites of earlier Iron Age farms, widely demonstrated by the remains of circular houses or other buildings beneath or very close to villa remains, revealed by excavation (as at Park Street and Lockleys) or by air photography (as at Bazeley Copse, and Great Doddington in Northamptonshire). In the present state of knowledge, most of the villa houses built in the first century were the cottage house type. Exceptions included Fishbourne (a palace and not a farm residence), Eccles, Angmering and Southwick.

Towards the end of the first century, or maybe at the start of the second, the corridor type of villa house began to appear, either in the form of a modification of the cottage house or as a new building. Some of the cottage houses had in the first century been given a verandah which served as a corridor (as at Lockleys and Brixworth), but the walled corridor proper is more usually ascribed to a second-century development. It was a significant improvement, for it cut out the interconnecting feature between rooms. Many villa houses falling into this category were provided with rooms or sets of rooms projecting from each end of the central rectangular block, which were served by the corridor along the centre part. This type is called the winged corridor house, and the styles and modifications varied widely, with one corridor along one long side, or one on each long side, and the arrangement of rooms and their openings differed in almost every instance. A good example of a simple winged corridor house is Great Staughton (fourth century) in Cambridgeshire, which in its earlier phases had consisted of a rectangular range of three rooms (the central room much larger than the end rooms) fronted by a corridor and with one projecting room at each end of the corridor. The villa house built at Ditchley in Oxfordshire in the early second century (first works) was a rectangular block of seven rooms, with two large rooms projecting at each end, the end wall continuous with the central block end, that is, E-shaped without the centre bar. Ditchley was later equipped with a corridor along the length of the back (and in the fourth century it was rebuilt and enlarged). In the later half of the second century Park Street had been converted into an H-plan, and Hambleden (which was turned round to face the other way) became an H-plan in the fourth century after an intermediate phase of having a small bath suite added to the southern end of the original rectangular block. The final phase included corridors along two long sides and an extra bath suite at the end of the east corridor.

The third type of villa house is the courtyard house (already described on p 129), a basically quadrangular structure of two or three (or less often, four) sides of rooms arranged in residential blocks of one design or another, with corridors, baths, halls, etc.[3] The courtyard house in Britain evolved from earlier and simpler buildings or groups of buildings, and the evolution was different in every case. Interesting examples, the phases of which have been traced and of which significant remains can be seen today, include North Leigh, near Witney in Oxfordshire which has an irregular quadrangle courtyard surrounded on three sides by ranges of rooms flanked by a continuous corridor; the fourth side is a further continuation of the corridor with an entrance plus a keeper's quarters, which grew out of a simple corridor house with detached bath suite begun in the second century. Chedworth, near Cirencester in Gloucestershire is another example. A double-courtyard house, also of second-century origins, but not reaching its magnificence until the late fourth century, it is regarded as the best-preserved villa site in Britain. Bignor, near Chichester in West Sussex is another double-courtyard house, begun in the third century; its fourth-century mosaics are among the best in Britain. Many courtyard villa houses are of irregular plan like these three, and this has been taken to suggest that they were lived in by more than one family, or perhaps more than one branch of a family, in separate blocks.

The fourth type of villa is the aisled building, sometimes described as a basilican building since it had a nave flanked by two aisles. These buildings fall into three functional categories, itemised by Pat Morris[4] as (a) main residential building on the farm, (b) subsidiary building where the main building was a courtyard or a winged corridor house and (c) subsidiary building whose use is wholly or mainly agricultural. As residential buildings, they were used by the farm owner and his family, with or without his workforce, and sometimes with space allotted for stock, or as separate housing for the workforce and their families, or as agricultural buildings proper, in which there were cattle byres, corn-drying kilns, metal-working hearths, even granaries, with living accommodation squashed in at one end. Any of these features might be found in aisled buildings erected principally as residential places. Where the aisled building was predominantly residential is generally indicated by traces of partitioning to form rooms or compartments of an obvious living nature, by the presence of tessellated flooring, mosaics, painted wall plaster, bath suites (as at Brading, Isle of Wight, and Mansfield Woodhouse, Nottinghamshire), hypocausts,

An aisled building

217

hearths and ovens (though some hearths might indicate metal-working areas). Examples of aisled buildings having a mainly residential function are at North Warnborough (Hampshire) Sparsholt (Hampshire) (first phase), Great Casterton (Leicestershire), Clanville (Hampshire), Denton (Lincolnshire), and Shakenoak (third phase). Morris believes that most of the aisled houses that had begun as main residential buildings had become subsidiary by the third or fourth centuries.

It is difficult to generalise about the plan of aisled buildings used as main residences, but the entrance was usually in one of the longer walls, was often wide enough to admit a cart and was often placed in or near the centre of the wall. There are examples, however, of the entrance being in one of the shorter end walls. It was the same for aisled buildings used as subsidiary residences, and examples include Norton Disney (Lincolnshire, doorway in end wall), Apethorpe (Northamptonshire) and West Dean (Hampshire). The partitioning of aisled buildings for residential purposes entailed some attempt to provide lighting and ventilation. There is still some discussion as to how this problem was solved, but some aisled buildings were roofed over the nave, the long walls of which were fitted with windows under the roof eaves, that is, given a clerestory, with a half-gabled roof over each aisle lower down. Windows were also put in at the shorter ends. It is also thought that dormer windows and/or ventilators were put in the nave roof in some instances, as is said to have occurred at Park Street (second-century phase) central residential block.

The layout of rooms in villa houses is clear in numerous excavated sites, but we cannot always be sure to what use each was put, except of course that the bath suites leave us in no doubt. The principal room may have been a drawing-room/dining-room, the *triclinium*, and it was often the largest room in the building. Frequently it was decorated with a mosaic or a tessellated floor, and it was often also used as a bedroom under a variety of circumstances. In some houses the *triclinium* had underfloor heating, produced by hypocaust and box-flue tiles in the thickness of the wall. The hypocaust was either of the pillared kind where the hot air circulated round a network of squat brick or stone columns supporting the floor or by means of underfloor

Part of the central heating system under the floor of one of the living rooms at King's Weston villa, near Bristol (*Reece Winstone*)

218

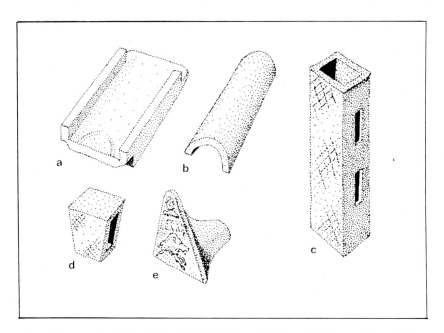

Some Roman tiles (after N. A. Griffiths): (a) *tegula* (flat with flanges, for roofing); (b) *imbrex* for covering the flanges of *tegulae*; (c) box flue, for wall central heating; (d) voussoir flue for heating and also for weight reduction in arches; (e) *antefix* for capping *imbrices* at eaves and elsewhere

channels. The heat was generated in a furnace attached to the outside wall of the room with the hypocaust, which was fed via a stokehole. In others, the heat was provided by an open fire or hearth in the centre. Large villa houses had more than one main room, particularly where the house was occupied by two or more families or other groups of people. A good example of a hypocaust-heated *triclinium* using box-flue tiles is at Chedworth villa where, in addition, the next-door bedroom was likewise warmed. The decoration of the *triclinium* would often be the best in the house, and there have been many finds of artistically painted wall plaster fragments from such walls, often in dark red, olive-green and rich brown shades, and in some cases there were panels and pilasters of marble, and occasionally fine ceiling paintings. The *triclinium* was generally square or rectangular in plan, but some exceptions have been discovered, like the rounded apsidal dining extension to the square drawing-room at Lullingstone, with its remarkable mosaic flooring.

Two other major appointments in the villa house were the bath suite and the kitchen. Bath suites were invariably sited at an extremity because of the fire risk from the furnaces, and in some instances they were erected in detached buildings, as at the earliest phases of North Leigh in Oxfordshire, at Frocester Court in Gloucestershire and at Stroud in Hampshire, or in an annexe-like arrangement as at Lullingstone. Most villa houses had bath suites at some time in their history, later rather than sooner, and in many instances they were quite elaborate, reproducing in miniature, as it were, the public baths in the *civitas* capitals, which is what they were designed to do. At Chedworth there were two separate bath suites, one providing a dry sauna-type bath, the other the more popular moist Turkish variety, with hot and cold plunge baths. Both can be seen today. Several other sites have interesting baths remains, such as at Dicket Mead villa, near Welwyn in Hertfordshire (now preserved in a concrete vault underneath the A1 (M) motorway), at Newport, Isle of Wight (a four-room suite with hypocausts, associated with a second-century corridor villa house), at Lydney in Gloucestershire and at Lullingstone. The earliest baths probably did not appear until the second century. If you had no

A *caldarium* with hot plunge, at Chedworth villa

View of hypocaust in Room 8, central range of rooms, at Boxmoor villa, Hertfordshire. The hypocaust is early fourth century (*Verulamium Museum*)

private baths at your villa, you went to the public baths in the nearest *civitas* capital or small town, or perhaps visited a neighbour who had a suite. Today, it would be a sign of almost abject poverty not to have your own bath suite, but in Roman times it was not so; public baths were the place at which to gather and meet one's friends or business contacts (see p 201). By the end of the second century, however, it had become standard practice to install baths in villas. It was also usual to decorate the suite with mosaic or tessellated flooring. The *frigidarium* at Low Ham in Somerset had a fine series of scenes from Virgil's tale of Dido of Carthage (in *The Aeneid*) depicted in mosaic, and this is now in the Taunton County Museum.

The decorating of house floors with mosaic is seen as a status symbol in Roman Britain. By the fourth century there were several schools (*officinae*) of mosaicists who produced their own individual pattern books for clients, and whose distinctive styles are beginning to be understood and recognised (and, of course, classified). Mosaic art is attracting a growing amount of study. It has even been held to be evidence for the degree of 'Romanisation' of the province. Basically, mosaic art consists of putting together geometric or figured designs using coloured tesserae or cubes of stone, tile or glass. The various colours were obtained as follows: yellows and browns from sandstones and limestones; blues from shales, slate and Lias; reds and oranges from chopped brick or tile or Old Red Sandstone (especially in the West Country); purples and greys from Pennant sandstone; greens from Greensand or Purbeck marble; whites and creams from flint, chalk or oolitic limestones; browns from ironstones; blacks from shale and slate and perhaps the dark part of flint. Glass tesserae, used for the eyes of animals or people in figure designs, or for highlighting certain features, were made out of bottles, vessels and perhaps glass-blowing spoil.

There were three ways of laying the tesserae on to the base, prepared as a series of layers of crushed gravel, concrete, *opus signinum* (a paste of crushed brick or tile mixed with mortar) and a running mortar, often in that order. One method was to press the tesserae one by one according to the design into the fresh bed. A second method entailed glueing the top side of the tesserae already laid out in the required pattern and fixing over it a sheet of cloth, enclosing the tesserae within a frame, smothering the bottom ends of the tesserae with cement and then pressing the frame top end up into the bed. A third method was a more elaborate version of the second, in which the design was sketched out in reverse on a sheet and the tesserae glued down on to the design.

Mosaic of Bellerophon slaying the Chimaera, the centre panel in the Reception Room at Lullingstone villa, Kent (*Crown Copyright*)

There was a huge variety of designs, especially in the figured mosaics, embracing a range of mythological subjects, historical allusions, religious symbols (the Chi-Rho christogram appears in several, as at Hinton St Mary in Dorset), and in almost every case the figures were quite individual, very rarely repeated anywhere else. There is also an easily detectable variety of quality in the artistic design and execution of the pictures. The geometric designs, incorporating borders or panels of guilloches, interlaced polygons, chequers etc, are understandably found repeated widely. Very occasionally a mosaic picture is accompanied by an inscription set in tesserae, which might be an apposite line from a Latin author such as Horace or Vergil, as in the Lullingstone *triclinium* apse mosaic depicting the abduction of Europa by the king of the gods, Jupiter, disguised as a bull.

Numerous floors were covered with tesserae set in a much simpler style, in rows with some colour variations, or in monochrome, or perhaps in a huge black and white chequer-board pattern, and these are called tessellated floors or pavements to differentiate them from more artistic mosaic work. It was less usual to lay mosaics on kitchen floors in villa houses, though such floors are found, and the diorama of the kitchen from Roman times at the London Museum has a handsome reproduction of one. The occasional mosaic has also been found in what was clearly a bedroom or study, as at Clanville, and mosaics and tessellated pavements frequently feature in anterooms and in passage-ways. There has even been mosaic decoration in servants' quarters, as at Great Weldon in Northamptonshire.

Granary

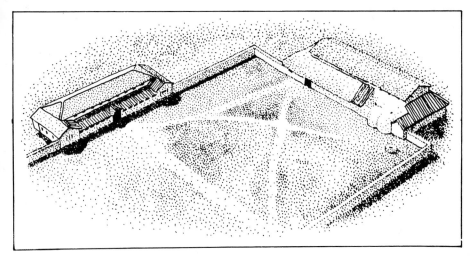

Reconstruction of Sparsholt villa: the main house is at left and the aisled building, with bath house, is at right

Outside the villa house there were other farm buildings, sometimes arranged round the sides of a quadrangle, or more haphazardly located, such as granaries, corn-drying kilns, animal stalls and byres and threshing floors. Granaries were needed for storing seed corn for the next harvest, for grain to be used by the household and for corn for consumption by the animals. Many Roman granaries were of the military type, ie their floors were raised on stilts, pillars or stone walls pierced to let air circulate underneath. If they were stone-walled, the higher courses were often buttressed outside to support both the tiled roof and the weight of the grain pressing on the wall interiors. Floors were often constructed of stone slabs resting on pillars or of timber planks on stout posts or resting on transverse beams lying along the ground. There were several variations within the basic design ideas. On the whole, granaries were rectangular in plan, as at Shakenoak, Winterton, Iwerne, Stroud and Lullingstone, but some square-plan granaries have been excavated, as at Ditchley (late in its history) and at Whitton. As a rule, military-type granaries were positioned on the north or east side of the farm, with their windows and/or louvred ventilators opening north or east, to avoid the wetter winds from the south and west. Some traces have also been found of what appear to have been silo-type granaries, as at Gadebridge in Hertfordshire and Iwerne in Dorset.

Iron Age farmers used to dry corn and hay in simple ovens, made generally of cob. In Roman times, these were replaced by the construction of special kilns, and in many cases special drying floors (as at Park Street). One type of drying kiln consisted of a two-chambered (one over the other) structure which was heated by a furnace underneath: the hot air circulated in the lower chamber by means of vents and this produced a gentler heat in the chamber above. There were other styles, one with a single floor and with warm air escaping at the end of cross flues. There were several shapes of furnace for corn-drying kilns, and these have been classified in great detail by Pat Morris.[5] The commonest appear to have been the T-shape, the bowl and the H-shape.

Corndrier

Livestock, notably horses, cattle, sheep and pigs, were kept on most villas, and a variety of byres, stalls and enclosures were built for them. Not many traces have survived, since they do not appear to have been built of durable materials, and were largely of timber. Surviving sites show that they were provided with drains. Some had stone foundations for both exterior walls and internal partitions and stalls. Morris suggests, however, that the majority of the cattle breeds of the time, hardier than the cross-breeds of today, were quite used to spending the winter outside.

The other structure present at some villa sites is the threshing floor which was cut into the ground and given a surface of stone, *opus signinum* or packed rubble, surrounded by turf blocks or kerbstones and covered by a timber roof or roof of shingles. Threshing floors were round or oval, as at Winterton, Barnsley Park and Ditchley, or rectilinear, as at Godmanchester and Catsgore. These floors, too, are dealt with in detail by Morris.[6]

These are the main components of the villa in relation to its predominantly food-producing role. There were other industrial activities going on at many villas, such as tanning and leather production (largely for the army), pottery and tile production (many villas were

A bronze candlestick discovered at Branston, Lincolnshire, 1974 (*Recreational Services: Lincoln City and County Museum*)

associated with important kilns and tileworks), metal working (pre-dominantly iron, bronze and copper work), wool production (where sheep raising was part of the farm's concerns), timber growing and felling, cloth manufacture and, in the third and fourth centuries, viti-culture and wine-making (though not on any great scale for most wines continued to be imported from Europe). The picture emerges of hundreds of villas scattered about Roman Britain, chiefly to the east and south of the Jurassic Ridge, each having an independent existence as a producing and servicing unit but together making up some form of rural economic structure that played a key role in the economy of the province – and a not inconsiderable one in the economy of the empire.

Villas were owned for the most part by 'Romanised' Britons. The earliest units built in the first century were probably occupied in the main by leading men of pre-Roman society who co-operated with the first governors and who kept out of the Boudican revolt (notably Cogidubnus, see p 72). When the *civitas* capitals began to emerge as the new Roman towns, the magistrates and other leading men doubtless built themselves villas and ran them as profitable farms. Some villas were owned by the imperial family in Rome, or by wealthy landowners in Italy or other provinces, and these were managed by official agents or 'crown' tenants in the case of imperial estates, contract tenants in the case of private owners. There is still a vast amount to be discovered and studied about the role of the villa and about rural society in general. Pointers as to what may emerge over the next decade may be studied in several major works and key papers listed in the Bibliography.

We have said that no dramatic agrarian advances were made as a result of the Roman occupation of Britain, and that the principal benefits of 'Romanisation' to agriculture lay in the opening up of greater areas for cultivation and stock-rearing and in the superior Roman organisation of production and marketing. Villas were an improvement upon Iron Age farms inasmuch as they brought together 'under one roof' all the different agricultural features that the Celtic farmers already enjoyed in a more haphazard layout. There were also benefits to be had from the road system, built primarily to link up the military forts and stations but to which villas were connected in many instances by spur roads or trackways. The Romans introduced some new crops, such as oats (grown widely in highland areas) and one or two new types of wheat, and they stimulated native fruit growing (hitherto mainly apple and pear trees) by introducing cherry trees and the grape vine.

NOTES
1. Collingwood, R. G. and Richmond, I. A. (1969 edition) p 134.
2. Lending weight to the belief that the Belgic Celts had a slave class.
3. Walthew, C. V. 'The town house and the villa house in Roman Britain', *Britannia* vi (1975), argues that town houses were influenced by houses built in the countryside.
4. Morris, P., 'Agricultural buildings in Roman Britain', *British Archaeological Reports* 70 (1979) pp 55–66.
5. Morris, P. (1979) chapter 1.
6. Morris, P. (1979) pp 23–8, 108–11.

14

THE ROMAN ROAD SYSTEM
IN BRITAIN

Roman roads are the main surviving visible evidence of the Roman occupation of Britain. Although the best stretches of Roman road do not have the same dramatic impact as, say, the Old Work at Wroxeter, the town wall at Silchester, the pharos at Dover or the forts at Chesters or Housesteads on Hadrian's Wall, the road network as a whole is the most impressive testimony to Roman practical genius and organisation in Britain. More than six thousand miles of main road built during the occupation (the majority in the first century or so) have been traced, and thousands more miles of secondary road between the main routes are also known. Much of this mileage is to be found underneath more recent roads or beside them.[1] Motorists today have cause to be grateful for long stretches of straight Roman highway that carved their way across country, which have simply been improved upon and are still main routes, such as great lengths of Watling Street (which began at Dover and ended at Wroxeter), the Fosse Way (Topsham, near Exeter, to Lincolnshire) and Ermine Street (London to York via Lincolnshire), which were three of the earliest arterial roads in Roman Britain.

The achievement of an integrated network of probably over 22,000 miles of well-built roadway during the occupation is all the more remarkable when it is recalled that Roman engineers had none of the sophisticated equipment available to civil engineers today, nor did they have binoculars, telescopes, compasses or maps as we know them (though they must have had something resembling maps). Yet we would be mistaken if we assumed that when they came to Britain they found it roadless. There were many trackways, some of them dozens of miles long and in use for a thousand, perhaps two thousand years, such as the ridgeways along high ground, or the famous Icknield Way that appears to have begun near Salisbury, stretched across the chalky

229

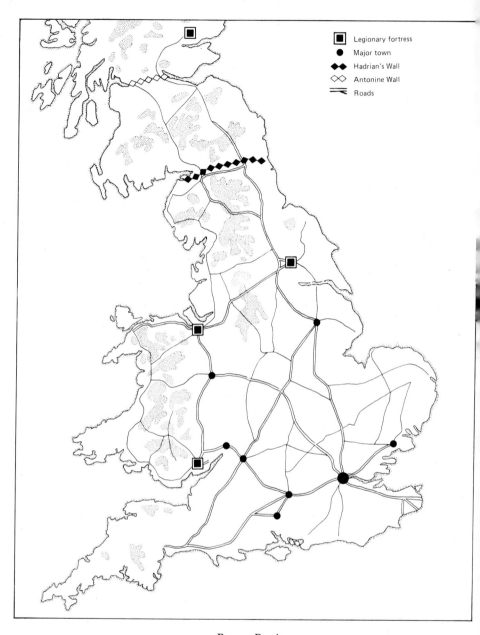

Legionary fortress
Major town
Hadrian's Wall
Antonine Wall
Roads

Roman Roads

plains into Berkshire and thence into the south Midlands and on into the western part of East Anglia where it ended beside the Wash in west Norfolk. The Romans were to develop stretches of the Icknield Way for their own use and for British traders, especially in Buckinghamshire and Norfolk, but they were not part of a main arterial route. Some of the trackways in Britain ran between the Celtic *oppida,* and the Roman army used these in the early campaigns until they had had time to survey the land and see whether a better road might be built.

The simplified map of the road system in Roman Britain (see p 230) at once shows its straight-line, grid-like nature. If we are tempted to think that it was a better network than ours today, we should remember that the Roman system was constructed as a concomitant of conquest and occupation. Straight roads between forts, military stations or settlements made it easier to get from one to another; they were simpler to build, less difficult to widen (as happened with many Roman roads) and were easier to police. Troops could be moved quickly about the countryside wherever they were needed. There is no evidence that the Roman army kept the main roads to themselves and compelled the provincial people to use only the secondary roads or their own ancient tracks, but R. W. Davies has drawn attention to a body of troops, the governor's *beneficiarii,* having among their duties the job of keeping watch on key points in the road system,[2] which certainly suggests that road users other than the army, civilian officials, bona fide residents or accredited traders, and those with special permits used the roads with caution.

Roman road building in Britain began as a purely military need in the execution of invasion and conquest. It was geared to linking the close networks of forts about ten to fifteen miles apart, that is, half to three-quarters of a day's march, that were being erected upon the area over-run.[3] Each area of advance was surveyed and a road system planned for it, taking into account existing roads and tracks, neighbouring villages and settlements considered worth developing, and noting additional countryside sites that might later be strategically valuable for military or civilian purposes. Some of the early roads were native tracks that the army engineers improved by widening, straightening and gravelling. Others were roads planned and built from scratch in the usual Roman manner, on straight alignments, though this does not mean they were always rigidly straight so much as that the intention was to link one place to the next in the straightest

Travelling in the Roman Empire, from a bas-relief at Trier

practicable route. If it were deemed desirable to take a road along a river valley or a ridge, the road followed the course even if it was sinuous, though it did so in a series of short straights. Roads were often built on higher rather than lower ground because more could be seen from them. it was easier to protect travellers and it was easier to drain the roads. Mountains and high hills were not regarded as insoluble problems: the road simply followed its course as far and as high as possible, but instead of going over the top it more often skirted round the summit and returned to the line on the other side. A good example of a highway that began as a military route and which obeys these demands is the great Fosse Way, begun probably in AD46 before Aulus Plautius' term of office as governor ended, which eventually ran for over two hundred miles from Topsham, near Exeter, to Lincoln and beyond to the Humber, never deviating more than six miles from a straight line.

The earliest roads built by the Romans were of course in Kent, and almost certainly the very first was the stretch from Richborough (where the main forces of Aulus Plautius landed in AD43) to Canterbury where branches were begun soon afterwards into south Kent (especially to Dover), to Sussex and north to Reculver where a small fort was built not long after the landings. From Canterbury the main road went west to Rochester, to Crayford and then to the Thames in London; the actual point is still debated but it was probably in the City near London Bridge. This first road is the lower section of the long arterial highway called Watling Street.

Although the first roads were built for military purposes, other factors played their part. From the beginning, it was Roman policy to make the province flourish commercially, and good roads facilitated the marketing of agricultural and industrial products. Roads were also constructed between important mining centres and the nearest towns, en route for harbours and ports. An early road was built between the lead mines in the Mendips near Charterhouse in Somerset down to Old Sarum, to Winchester (*Venta Belgarum*) and thence to the estuary of the Test near modern Southampton. When the Cornish tin mines were reopened in the third century, new roads were built, along which to convey the ore for export to the Continent; probably in the first generation of the occupation the branch roads off the London to Chichester, London to Brighton and London to Pevensey roads into the iron ore areas of the Sussex Weald were laid down, though native trackways were also used. With the emergence of villas and the

Stretch of Roman road at Blackpool Bridge in the Forest of Dean (*Reece Winstone*)

The Roman Road (Margary 81b) at Wheeldale Moor, N. Yorkshire

development of farming, attention was also paid to making road links between farms and main roads leading to capitals and smaller towns, and there are examples of major villas being linked to each other by special roads, such as the road between Ditchley and North Leigh, in Oxfordshire, both villas lying near to the main St Albans to Cirencester road, part of Akeman Street.

The road system was planned on a major scale, or series of scales, and never on the basis of one jump at a time. The surveyors and engineers were skilled men well used to networking huge areas of conquered land, and the speed and efficiency with which they worked must have made a great impression upon the native people. Normally, the army provided the road gangs, for the Roman legionary was always far more than just a soldier trained to march, pitch tent, dig ditches and fight. If the army could not spare enough men, which was probably quite frequently, local labour was employed, with or without pay, according no doubt to the 'co-operativeness' of the conscripts. It is clear that during the long periods of relative inactivity endured by the troops along Hadrian's Wall, road-building, maintenance and repair work were sometimes organised to occupy the men.

234

We have a vast reservoir of excavated evidence of the manner in which roads were built in Britain. They were almost always surfaced with rammed gravel and not, as is sometimes believed, paved with huge stone slabs, which was exceptional. Local materials were used wherever possible, such as iron slag, crushed chalk and flint. The crazy-paving appearance on the surface of the road across Wheeldale Moor, just off the Whitby–Malton road (A169), made up from a jumble of broken slabs, is not the original surface at all but is the remains of the slabs that formed the road foundation. The gravel surface has long since been washed away. Very few slab-paved stretches of Roman road have so far been found in Britain; there is a short piece of paved road at a ford near Benenden in Kent (the paving of roads is usually of the late Roman period). If gravel was not used, alternative surfaces found have included iron slag, flint stones and conglomerations of other small stones and pebbles; there are also examples of cobblestone.

Roman roads were often built over a specially raised embankment known as an *agger* (which in a different context also means rampart).

A stretch of Ermine Street north of Lincoln, showing the road resting upon an *agger*, with the ditch at left.

This was to provide proper drainage for the layers supporting the road surface. The *agger* was usually created by the spoil taken from a ditch cut along each side of the intended stretch. Sometimes it was a simple bank of earth: in other cases it was more robustly prepared by mixing earth with rubble, stones, sand, chippings and clay in any combination. The road foundation of slabs or large stones was laid upon the *agger* and the top then dressed with the surface. The width of the road varied from about 4m (14ft) to about 9m (30ft), more or less according to the grade of road. The *agger* was generally 2–3.5m (6–12ft) wider on each side; it varied considerably in height and sometimes its flanking ditches were 4.5m (15ft) or more deep. Many roads were built across the countryside without being raised high by an *agger*, and these are less easy to trace as the edges have often become blurred.

One important feature of the Roman road system in Britain is that the roads appear to have been regularly repaired or maintained. Numerous excavations have exposed parts of road showing several different periods of building or maintenance activity, and there is also evidence in the form of milestones. A milestone found at Bitterne (one of several found built into later stone walls there) carried an inscription that includes the words '. . . in the eighteenth year of his tribunician power [he] restored the roads which had fallen into ruin through age . . .'. This is believed to refer to work ordered in the time of Severus or his son Caracalla. Some milestones of the time of Constantine's period as Caesar (305–6) suggest road repairs following the restoration of order by his father Constantius, and a stone found at Chesterton, near Water Newton, points to repairs ordered under the 'Gallic' emperor Victorinus in c270. Both these examples are listed by J. Sedgley.[4]

One important use to which some of the main roads of Britain were put was as a facility for the *cursus publicus*, the imperial communications service introduced by Augustus throughout the empire. This was operated by means of carriages and gigs drawn by horses, or individual riders with fast horses, on a relay basis up and down some sixteen of the principal arterial routes. Along each road used by the *cursus publicus* were posting stations where horses could be changed and mail and goods deposited and collected for despatch. These stations were called *mutationes* and were sited in towns or *vici*, or near forts, or more generally along the roads. They were meant to be spaced at intervals from ten to fifteen miles apart. Larger stations which incorporated accommodation or meal facilities as well as horse

A short section of the Roman road (Margary 28b) at Thorpe Audlin, near Wentbridge, West Yorkshire, where horse hoof prints were revealed in recent excavations (*E. Houlder*).

Reconstruction from fragments of a second-century wheel found at Newstead fort, Borders. The wheel was from a cart or waggon (*National Museum of Antiquities of Scotland*)

changes, (in some cases with facilities for baths and games too) were built on average about thirty miles apart, and these were the *mansiones* which we have met before. They, too, were built in towns or along the road. Some *mansiones* later on grew into small towns, with shops, workshops and houses, on one or both sides of the road, particularly where the *mansio* had been at or near a crossroads.

Many roads had to be taken over narrow streams and across wide rivers, and some interesting remains have been revealed that show how Roman engineers tackled these problems. At Tomen-y-Mur in Wales, site of an Agricolan fort of earth and timber beside a stream, which was subsequently rebuilt partly in stone, some of the earthwork support is visible for the timber bridge across the stream, which carried the road from the fort to Caer Gai fort. At Piercebridge fort, near Scotch Corner in Yorkshire, parts of the stone and timber bridge over the Tees were discovered recently under much silt, during some dramatic excavations. The parts included stone piers that had supported the bridge. Equally interesting was the discovery of foundations and part of the superstructure of a first-century bridge at Aldwincle near Thrapston in Northamptonshire, on the Godmanchester–Leicester road (Margary 57a), which spanned the Nene river. The remains indicated that wooden piles had been shod in iron. Two subsequent bridges were raised on the first structure, one of them supported by sloping buttresses.

The extent of the known network of Roman roads in Britain is the result of generations of painstaking research by numerous enthusiasts, professional and amateur, and is a field of study which continues unabated. The work has been helped tremendously by a handful of ancient sources, which should be mentioned here. Chief among these are the *Antonine Itinerary*, the *Peutinger Table* and the *Ravenna Cosmography*. The *Antonine Itinerary (Itinerarium Provinciarum Antonini Augusti)* is a kind of gazetteer of some 225 routes in the empire, giving the distances between the stopping places on them. It is thought to date from the reign of Caracalla (211–17), with later additions and alterations. It includes a section on Britain; and the itinerary has been copied in several manuscripts over the centuries.

The *Peutinger Table (Tabula Peutingeriana)*, a guide book and map of the empire, which is said originally to have been produced in the fourth century and which today survives in a twelfth-century copy, was obtained in 1508 by Konrad Peutinger, and it lies in the Hofbibliothek in Vienna. The places, routes and mileages are inscribed upon a map of the empire squashed into a roll 6.8m (23ft) long by 34cm (14in) wide. Much of the map relating to Britain is regrettably missing, but the eastern part from north Norfolk down to Kent and along the south as far as Exeter have survived, with some sixteen names that can be matched with names in the *Antonine Itinerary*: they include Colchester, Dover and Canterbury (in Latin). The *Ravenna Cosmography (Ravennatis Anonymi Cosmographia)* is a gazetteer of countries, towns and rivers of the world as known to the compiler, and it was produced in about AD700 by a cleric at Ravenna, who drew upon earlier gazetteers and maps including, probably, the other two already mentioned. The compiler added many place names and the routes on which they lay. All these and other sources are discussed in the most comprehensive and up-to-date detail by Professor A. L. F. Rivet and Dr Colin Smith.[5]

NOTES

1. Detailed studies of Roman roads in Britain continue all the time; new discoveries are made every year, and some previously supposed routes are shown to have been misplaced. The greatest work on the subject to date is the masterly survey by Margary, I. *Roman Roads in Britain* (3rd ed, 1973). Some corrections to his routes have been made in the past decade, and for the most part these are detailed in issues of *Britannia*, county archaeological journals and reports from the Council for British Archaeology; from *Archaeology in Wales* and from *Discovery and Excavation in Scotland* (annual reports).
2. Davies, R. W. 'Singulares and Roman Britain', *Britannia* vii (1976) p 134.
3. See chapter 10 for the strategic policy of fort siting.
4. Sedgley, J. P. 'The Roman milestones of Britain', *British Archaeological Reports* 18 (1975) pp 21, 25.
5. Rivet, A. L. F. and Smith, C. (1979) pp 3–234.

15

INDUSTRY
IN ROMAN BRITAIN

There was considerable industrial and commercial activity in Iron Age Britain, and traders from Europe had long been visiting the islands. Caesar recorded something of the vigorous agriculture of the British tribes, particularly those of more recent immigration who occupied the south and east, and he refers to tin production in the Midlands and iron production in the 'maritime' counties (such as Sussex and Kent).[1] Plenty of evidence has been accumulated of Iron Age pottery industries, of leather production and, of course, of tin mining in Cornwall over several centuries.

The Roman occupation, however, stimulated the economy of Britain, its industries and its agriculture, but in saying this we have to remember that the over-riding interest of the Roman government in Britain was what it could get out of the province – what it could exploit in both natural and manufactured resources – to help keep the imperial treasury filled. To pay for the privilege of 'Romanisation', the province had to feed the occupying army, to surrender huge areas of land for the government to award to retiring veterans from the army, to allow investment in land, farms and industries by private business-men in Italy and elsewhere, and in some areas of industry to provide slaves or convicts, such as in the Dolaucothi gold mines in Wales. It is beyond the scope of this work to try to present an economic picture of Britain during four hundred years of occupation, but it can be said that the economy of the province was healthier in the later than in the earlier centuries, and that on balance Rome probably benefited more than it lost despite a protracted and costly occupation.

We may begin with a look at the extractive industries: metal and stone. The Roman government monopolised metal working to begin with, using the army, but appears as soon as possible to have farmed it out to private concessionaires, or *conductores*, some of whom worked

240

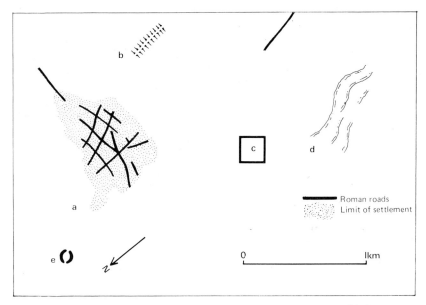

Plan of the Charterhouse-in-Mendip lead mining site: (a) small town (b) dam across River Blackmoor (c) forts (d) trenching (e) amphitheatre

individually, while others formed companies (*societates*). The army continued to guard sites in which the government was interested directly or indirectly. The fort recently discovered at Pumpsaint in west Wales was probably built for troops to protect the gold mines at nearby Dolaucothi. The army also provided transport for products to distribution points at home and to ports for export, using both road and river transport.

One of the earliest metal workings of the conquest period was the lead mine area in the Mendip Hills in Somerset. Traces of the settlement that grew up around the mines have survived at Charterhouse-in-Mendip, near Shepton Mallet. Some very early ingots of lead from this area have been found, one of which, discovered near Blagdon in the 1850s, is in the British Museum and is dated to AD49–50. The Mendip mines are thought to have been partly hived off to imperial agents by about the year AD60. An ingot from the area of that date has been found bearing the name of one Nipius Ascanius, whose name interestingly is found on further ingots of later date, only this time from north Wales where he may by then have become a *conductor* though still under government supervision.[2] Lead mines were worked in many parts of Britain, notably Shropshire, Cheshire, West Yorkshire, Derbyshire and Northumberland. In Derbyshire, a lead mine of some importance seems to have flourished for some time: it

241

Lead seal for labelling goods consignments, found at the *civitas* capital *Ratae* (Leicester), and inscribed for *Legio XX Valeria Victrix*. This is one of several found (*Leicestershire Museums, Art Galleries & Records Service*)

was operated by the Lutudarum Company, which stamped its ingots 'Socio Lut Br' or similarly, though the actual site of these works has not so far been located. Two suggestions are Carsington, near Wirksworth,[3] and a site near Matlock. Evidence of lead working has also been found at Ffrith, on the Clwyd–Cheshire border, at Pen-y-Crogbren in Powys, Melandra Castle in Derbyshire (the fort at Melandra may have played a guardianship role) and at Machen in Powys.

Lead working was controlled more strictly than other metal working (except for the gold mines at Dolaucothi) because the Romans extracted silver from silver and lead alloys produced by smelting the combined ores. Silver was required for imperial coinage and for exchange bullion. Control appears to have been relaxed later during the occupation, and the mining given over more freely to private enterprise, although the government retained an interest by claiming up to half of the production. Lead was also required in its own state for a variety of military and civilian uses, such as water pipes (of which many examples have survived and can be seen in most museums with Roman collections), water tanks, coffins (a fine example was found at Holborough in Kent and is now in Maidstone Museum) and, after the beginning of the third century, for mixing with tin to make a new alloy, pewter, which leapt into popularity for domestic utensils, plates and vessels as a substitute for silverware and for fine pottery. One centre of pewter manufacture was at Camerton, about seven miles south-west of Bath, which probably received its tin from Cornwall.

The importance of gold to the Roman government does not need to be stressed. So far as we know there was only one source of the precious metal in Britain, at Dolaucothi. Tacitus described Britain as having gold, silver and other metals, that made it worth conquering the island.[4] The extracted metal, however, was worked at many places, and sites of jewellers' workshops where gold was used have been found at St Albans, Cirencester, at Norton near Malton in Yorkshire, and under the later site of Government House in London, near the Thames, about 135m (150yd) east of the Walbrook.

Copper was much in demand in Britain, chiefly to make bronze, but apart from mines in Anglesey (notably Parys Mountain), on the north Wales mainland coast and on the Shropshire–Powys border, especially at Llanymynech, Britain had to obtain copper from abroad, as Caesar noted[5]. On and near to Parys Mountain, interesting copper ingots in the shape of buns have been found, some bearing official stamps. Coppersmiths' establishments have been discovered at Catterick and at St Albans. Bronze works occur in many areas, including Dinorben (Clwyd), Heronbridge, near Chester, Baldock (Hertfordshire) and Silchester. Bronze working was a major industry in Roman Britain and a wide variety of utensils and decorative objects was turned out, such as skillets, bowls, cups, buckles, furniture fittings, statuettes, ornaments, brooches, bracelets, pins and rings.

There seems to have been relatively little demand for tin in the early occupation period. It was not used on a wide scale by the Romans (or

A fine *patera* (skillet) of bronze, of the first century, found at Dowalton Loch, Dumfries & Galloway (*National Museum of Antiquities of Scotland*)

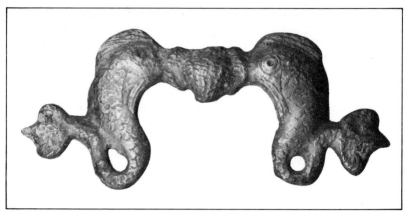

A bronze dolphin carrying handle found at Brampton, Norfolk (*Dr Keith Knowles*)

by the native British) and the Cornish stream processes probably supplied the bulk of the needs for bronze alloying. Nor does tin appear to have been exported on any great scale, for the Spanish tin mines supplied most of what was needed in Europe. But in the third century, the introduction of pewter manufacture generated a fresh demand for tin, and this appears to have coincided with a sharp decline in the output of tin from Spain. The government began to take a new interest in the Cornish mines, and constructed new roads to facilitate movement of the extracted metal. A milestone of the reign of Gordian III (238–44) was found at Gwennap in 1940, which indicated a rebuilt Roman road in mining territory,[6] while an ingot of tin bearing a possible, but disputed, imperial stamp has been found of this and of later periods in Cornwall.

The most widespread metal-working industry, however, was iron, and here the Romans developed the already extensive iron-working areas which they had found when they first came to Britain, the Weald of Kent and Sussex areas, the district round the Forest of Dean and more scattered areas on the Jurassic Ridge, particularly those in Northamptonshire and Lincolnshire. In the Weald and Forest of Dean areas, it is becoming clear that the government was directly involved, through agents and lessees, maintaining a close interest in production not only because of the need for iron in the programme of public works initiated by Agricola and those continued by successors, but also for strict military needs, notably the Hadrianic and Antonine fortifications. H. Cleere states that by the end of the first century, Britain was self-supporting in iron production and was also exporting.[7]

There were iron workings all over the country. Many villas were to have their own smiths' forges, as at Rockbourne (Hampshire), Brading (Isle of Wight), Frocester (Gloucestershire) to mention a few. Many of the forts had their own metal workshops – those that did not obtain their supplies from smiths in the *vici* growing up beside them. The army exploited iron deposits in several districts, including the Northumberland and Cumbrian hills where the great Hadrian's Wall weaved its way. But on the whole, iron making was largely in the hands of the native people to whom the presence of many thousand Roman troops, officials and citizens and immigrants from Europe in search of trade and business represented a healthy and continuing source of work and income. To give an idea of how widespread the industry was, a few examples of sites where iron working took place in Roman times are as follows: Blackpool Bridge in the Forest of Dean, Brampton in Norfolk, Din Lligwy in Anglesey, Great Chesterford in Essex, Kettering in Northamptonshire, Kenchester in Herefordshire, Lydney in Gloucestershire, Melandra in Derbyshire, Piddington in Northamptonshire, Romsey in Hampshire (extensively in the fourth

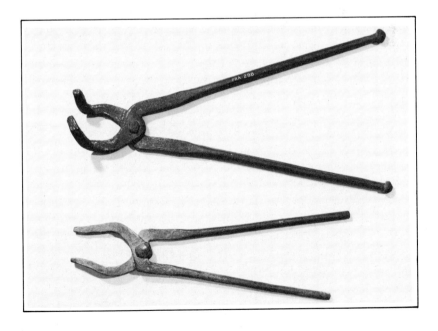

Two pairs of Roman blacksmith's tongs. Newstead fort, Borders (*National Museum of Antiquities of Scotland*)

Fourth-century iron shaft-furnaces recently excavated beside the Roman road (Margary 28b) at Thorpe Audlin near Wentbridge, West Yorkshire (*E. Houlder*)

century), Scunthorpe in Lincolnshire, Silchester, St Albans and in London. Where possible, iron workings are mentioned as appropriate in the Gazetteer.

There was little that the Romans could teach the British about iron-making, though in the period of occupation there were two useful innovations: the shaft furnace (as opposed to the bowl furnace) and the process of carburisation and quenching to produce better quality tool edges. The shaft furnace was up to 2m (6ft) tall, created a far better draught for the fire at the bottom and enabled larger amounts of iron ore to be smelted at a time. Some furnaces were more than 0.5m (2ft) across.

Moving from metal to stone, the Romans were quick to search out sources for building stone. It is difficult to indicate which are the earliest stone remains of Roman Britain, but Colchester and London had stone buildings before the Boudican revolt. The temple of

Claudius at Colchester had a stone podium and probably much of its superstructure completed before AD60. Two inscribed tombstones predating the sack of the town have been found, one of stone from Northamptonshire, the other of Bath stone. By the end of the first century, stone was being quarried in some quantity from Purbeck in Dorset, the Bath region, Kentish rag from the Maidstone region, limestone from Lincolnshire and Northamptonshire, local greensand from many parts, septaria from London clay. The Romans moved stone about the country on a large scale, using waterways and also carting it by road. They also imported it from Gaul, and sometimes from further afield, such as alabaster and porphyry from Egypt. Stonemasons set up their workshops either near the quarries or beside the site where the stone was needed. There are remains of several quarries used by the Romans, including the quarry of local red sandstone used for the legionary fort at Chester, and there are traces of stone-splitting activities to make the blocks for Hadrian's Wall at Limestone Corner and at Black Carts. There are quarries beside the river Gelt (with names carved in the rock face, one called the Written Rock of Gelt) at Old Brampton, a mason's yard exists under the palace at Fishbourne and there are chalk quarries at Canterbury. Local stone was available in many districts, though it was not easy to find it in the Kent and Sussex area, or in East Anglia, where builders had recourse to flint. The Pharos at Dover was built from local flint rubble but was faced with ashlar (dressed stone) brought in from elsewhere.

Various kinds of stone were used for decorative purposes or in the making of utensils. Kimmeridge shale from Dorset was employed in jewellery-making, for bowls (turned on lathes) and now and again for parts of furniture, such as chair legs (though these are rare). Kimmeridge artefacts have been found all over Britain. Black jet had long been a popular material for jewels and ornaments in Iron Age Britain, much of it originating from the Whitby district, and in Roman times the industry continued, with a well-attested export business to Roman settlements in the Rhineland in Germany.

Although it is not strictly an extractive industry, mention should be made of the cultivation, felling and use of trees for timber. The Roman army used vast quantities of wood: all its early forts (with their various components), military stations, signal stations, docks, *mansiones, mutationes* and the civilian buildings for which the army was responsible were made of timber, while the great majority of private houses, shops and workshops going up in the early *civitas*

Remains of some drinking glasses of the Roman period, with (above) reconstructions of their original shapes. The fragments were found at Woodchester Villa, Gloucestershire (*National Monuments Record*)

capitals and smaller towns were at least half-timbered. That so many timber buildings were in fact put up (which we know from excavation) during the Roman period suggests that there was a plentiful and readily available supply of wood, but we should marvel at the hard work and ingenuity involved. Clearly, the government will have needed to maintain control over at least some of the forest regions and to have embarked upon planned programmes of reafforestation. There is evidence also for the re-use of timber when short-lived forts were dismantled, such as the huge legionary fortress at Inchtuthil in Scotland.

Timber was also used in great quantities for open fires and hearths, for blast furnaces for metal industries and for pottery kilns, and for the hypocausts in bath houses, suites and central heating systems. In the north and west, there were several districts were coal could be quarried on outcrops, and excavations at several forts on Hadrian's Wall have revealed residues of coal heaps, notably the store at Housesteads, and also along the Antonine Wall. Coal was also quarried in the Bath–Bristol region, and some of the villas in the westerly Cotswolds used coal as well as wood for their fires and hypocausts. There does not appear to have been any deep mining of coal, but a few shafts about 3–4.5m (10–15ft) deep have been found, including shafts at Benwell on Hadrian's Wall.

The other main building materials needed all over the province were bricks and tiles. These were sometimes manufactured by potteries which had special facilities, but it is probable that the majority of brick and tile works were separate organisations. Many were set up by the army for its requirements, and for the earlier *civitas* capitals. There was a major tilery at Silchester run by the *procurator's* department. There was a substantial 20 acre (8ha) site at Holt, a few miles south of Chester, beside the Dee, which supplied Legio XX in the legionary fortress at Chester. There was a tilery run by auxiliary forces at Pen-y-Stryd, near the fort at Tomen-y-Mur in Wales, and another at Muncaster, near the fort at Ravenglass in Cumbria. There were tileries at Colchester, Canterbury, Lincoln, a major one at the priory of St Oswald, outside the north-western corner of Gloucester,[8] and another at Minety, near Cricklade in Wiltshire. Possibly there were tileries in or beside all the *civitas* capitals, and there was a government brick and tile works at London, which was also run by the *procurator's* department. Tiles are often found bearing stamps of the production company or even individual craftsmen. Occasionally they contained a graffito message or warning. The Gloucester tilery products were stamped RPG (*Rei Publicae Glevensium*). Tiles were made in a variety of shapes and sizes, the most common probably being the pantile. Tileries also produced the well-known box-flue tiles used as a wall lining for channelling warm air from hypocausts into other parts of the building.

Among the other industries of Roman Britain, we may mention salt, wine, leather, weaving and textiles and, with the greatest number of remains, pottery. Salt was produced in pre-Roman times by evaporating sea water in cauldrons, a process which must have taken enormous effort for very little end product. It was produced at coastal sites and at certain inland areas, such as the salt marshes of Fenland which were then more water-logged than they are today. The Romans accelerated production by working the salt centres on the Essex, Sussex and Lincoln coasts, up the Severn Estuary, and by developing works at salt-laden springs at places like Droitwich in Worcestershire and Middlewich and Northwich in Cheshire. Salt was often collected by evaporating brine in ceramic pans, an equally long process.

Wine was generally imported into Britain but in the third century British wine growers were allowed, sometimes encouraged, to produce for the home market. Remains of vine plants have been found near Boxmoor in Hertfordshire (but it is disputed whether they are Celtic or Roman), and at Silchester and Gloucester.

Leather was required by the army for tents, uniforms, shields, purses, shoes and boots, buckets, belts, aprons for blacksmiths, armourers and other workmen, and by the civilian community for items of clothing, shoes and a variety of utensils. Evidence of tanneries has been uncovered in some areas, though so far those found all relate to military sites, as at Catterick, Chesterholm and Silchester. There was a leather-working centre in London which was supplied with hides from cattle reared in the south-east and, it is suggested, also from cattle from Ireland. There was a leather works at Alcester, and what is thought to have been a tannery was found under a mosaic floor in a second century courtyard house north of the forum at Leicester. Shoes were marketed in shops: one has been found at Cirencester.

Textiles do not generally survive from ancient times, and if a fragment does emerge in excavation, it arouses great interest. At Carpow fort some scale armour was discovered in 1979, which still had part of its textile backing; it was a two-over-one linen twill.[9] British woollen goods are listed in the Edict of Maximum Prices issued by Diocletian in 301. One was the *byrrus Britannicus*, a kind of duffel coat and the other, the *tapete Britannicum*, a thick rug. Weaving mills were established in Roman Britain in the fourth century by the government, and weaving equipment has been found at several places, including Great Chesterford and Caistor St Edmund.

The pottery industry in Roman Britain has left us with more evidence of its history and development than any other industry. Every site of Roman occupation so far excavated has yielded fragments of pottery, which are generally called sherds (or shards). These have been studied in the greatest detail for over a century, and a huge corpus of details, drawings and photographs has been built up, which is expanding all the time. Sherds have for a long time been used as one of the principal means of establishing the approximate date or

A number of leather shoes, late-first to second century, found at Newstead fort, Borders (*National Museum of Antiquities of Scotland*)

dates of sites where they are found. Sometimes this method acts as a corroboration in the presence of coins, or when dating is given in ancient texts or inscriptions, but there are many instances where the origin and type of pottery found are the only available evidence on which to estimate dates. Pottery was manufactured in numerous areas, sometimes over long periods, in an extensive range of materials and in an ever-changing variety of shapes and sizes. Some forty sizeable potteries are known in Britain, and evidence of over a hundred pottery kilns or groups of kilns has been recovered. Some of the pottery was of high quality, which is often classified as 'fine ware'; rather more was of lesser quality, known as 'coarse ware'. Pottery made in one area was often sold and used in other areas. Some was stamped by the firms or the individuals that made it (which have been and are being classified all the time for reference purposes) and many of the individual styles are distinctive enough to be quickly recognised by specialists, even if they are only in fragmentary form. The whole subject is too extensive – and in several respects too controversial – to be gone into here, but we can mention a few points about which there is general agreement.

When the Romans came to Britain they found many pottery industries already well established. The potter's wheel had been introduced by the Belgic Celts, probably in the late second century BC, and much fine ware was being produced, particularly in the south-east and in Dorset. Pottery was also imported in some quantities by the Belgae (and doubtless by other non-Belgic British) from Gaul and even from northern Italy. One of the most widely used items was the Italian made amphora, or flagon, which was shipped to Britain primarily as a container for wine, less often for oil, which was later used as a domestic storage vessel. The Romans therefore had not so much to instruct the natives in pottery techniques but rather to introduce them to new types and to more effective production and marketing methods. It is generally accepted that the army brought its own pottery specialists, but encouraged civilians later on to come to Britain to set up businesses to supply the considerable needs of the army establishment. These specialists in turn encouraged native craftsmen at or near military sites. A number of kilns have been found around the early fortress at Longthorpe, probably dating to the 50s, and kilns of the later decades of the first century have been located at Gloucester, Caerleon, Wroxeter, Usk and Holt, near Chester. In the first century, the native craftsmen copied the styles brought over by the Romans almost slavishly.

By the end of the first century the army was no longer producing pottery on any scale, and it was depending upon the civilian sector, with whom it had major contracts. There are several areas that have revealed intense pottery activity during these decades, suggesting arrangements to supply the army on a contract basis, notably in Dorset, in the Savernake area of Wiltshire, in the Nene Valley and in north-east Norfolk (particularly Brampton, near Aylsham).

252

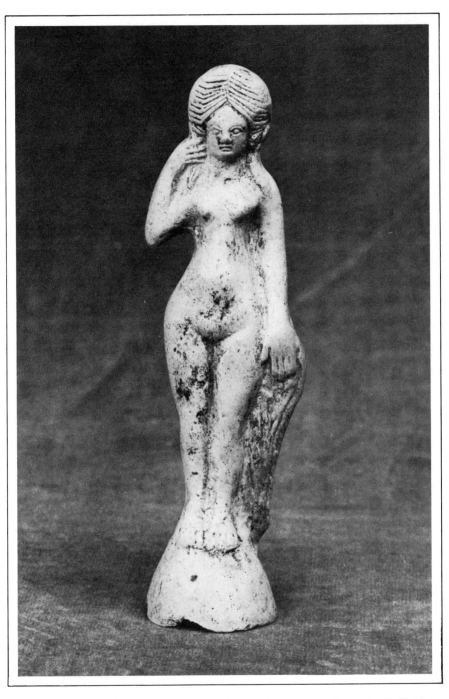

A pipe-clay figurine of Venus (7¼in tall), found at Brampton small town by Dr Keith Knowles (*Dr Keith Knowles*)

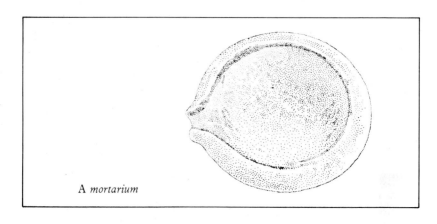

A *mortarium*

When the army arrived in Britain in the 40s, it introduced the celebrated Samian pottery, a fine, glossy redware manufactured in potteries in southern Gaul, and the items included cups and bowls, plates, jars, dishes, *mortaria*, even inkwells.[10] Much of the ware was distinctive for its relief decoration. Many of the potteries making Samian ware stamped their pieces, which has helped specialists in the task of type classification. Samian ware more or less dominated the British market in the first and second centuries. Several attempts were made in Britain to imitate it, not necessarily in its colour but in its shape and design motifs, as at factories at Colchester, West Stow in Suffolk and at Gloucester, but it was neither successful nor long lasting. By the end of the second century, native pottery styles were taking the market over from imported wares, and Samian was disappearing. Among the best known of the British wares – and in some respects the most attractive – were the Castor wares from the Nene Valley, Oxford wares, Crambeck wares from Yorkshire, New Forest pottery, and Severn and Black Burnished wares.

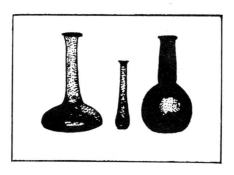

Glass bottles of the Roman period

NOTES

1. Caesar, *De Bello Gallico*, V, 12.
2. One found at Carmel in Clwyd is now in the National Museum of Wales.
3. *Current Archaeology* 75 (1981) pp 125–6.
4. Tacitus, *Agricola*, 12.
5. Caesar, *De Bello Gallico* V, 12.
6. Sedgley, J. 'The Roman milestones of Britain', *British Archaeological Reports* 18 (1975) pp 6, 23.
7. Quoted by Salway, P. (1981) from (then) unpublished material by Cleere.
8. The tilery was excavated and examined in great detail in 1975–6 in advance of development, and is written up by Heighway, C. M. and Parker, A. J. 'The Roman tilery at St Oswald's Priory, Gloucester', *Britannia* xiii (1982) pp 25–77, who describe it as the public tilery for the *colonia* at *Glevum* and estimate that its operating period was from the end of the first century to the third century.
9. Wild, J. P. 'A find of Roman scale armour from Carpow', *Britannia* xii (1981) pp 305–6.
10. A *mortarium* was a mixing bowl, usually with gritted inner surface to facilitate mixing, with a heavy gripping rim. Almost every soldier needed one, as well as every civilian family. See Swan, V. *Pottery in Roman Britain* (1980) which is an excellent booklet giving a masterly summary of the pottery industry in Roman Britain, which will steer the serious student to deeper studies.

16

RELIGION

People in the Roman world were a great deal more superstitious than we are today, and their religious beliefs played a major role in their lives. The ordinary Roman believed that his destiny was in the hands of a number of spirit gods, or *numina*, who controlled all aspects of life. There were gods of the household, who could bring good luck and ward off evil, indoors or outside, in the fields, on the farm, in the factory or the shop; there were gods who watched over the departed souls of the family and ancestors. In most Roman houses, special areas were set aside to provide shrines for the making of offerings to the gods or spirits, which was part of the bargain with them for their protection. These offerings were made according to well-defined rituals. Beyond the household gods, there were those who looked after the public life of Rome and the empire, headed by Jupiter, king of the gods, and his wife Juno, and including Minerva, goddess of wisdom; Mars, god of war (also worshipped as a god of healing in Roman Britain); Mercury, the messenger of the gods who was also worshipped as the god of commerce and of travellers; Vulcan, the god of fire and the protector of metalsmiths; Apollo, the Sun god; Diana, goddess of hunting, and many more in a well-known pantheon. The army was especially superstitious – understandably, since the men risked their lives so often in the pursuance of their careers – and worshipped among others Jupiter, Minerva and Mars. Numerous examples of their devotion to Jupiter Optimus Maximus (Best and Greatest) have been found in Britain. In some quarters it was customary to dedicate altars to him on a regular basis. Altars have been found at Maryport fort in Cumbria and Housesteads on Hadrian's Wall, and a statue to Jupiter was discovered at Colchester. Over the centuries the Romans added to their growing catalogue of deities, taking on gods from lands outside their empire, most notably the cult of the Persian god, Mithras. And as the empire expanded, the army was supplemented by the recruitment of troops from new races, who had their own native deities.

When the Roman army came to Britain it encountered new mythologies among the British tribes who also had deities watching over all aspects of life. In time, many of the Roman and the Celtic gods became linked. Among the best-known examples are the coupling of the Celt goddess Sul (or Sulis) of the hot springs at Bath with Minerva, the identification of Brigantia, patroness of the Brigantes tribe, with Minerva and various linkings between Mars and British deities, such as Mars Medocius (identified on a bronze tablet found at one of the several temples at Colchester). In addition, the Romans introduced their own cult of emperor worship, a vital unifying force in the empire. It had begun when the great Julius Caesar was deified following his senseless and catastrophic murder in 44BC. His grandnephew Augustus, first emperor of Rome, did not let himself be deified at Rome in his own time, but he allowed it in the provinces where he was generally bracketed with the goddess Roma (patroness of Rome), and altars began to be dedicated to *Roma et Augustus*. Emperor worship continued after his death, depending upon the popularity of the actual incumbent. Claudius, Vespasian and Titus were the first-century emperors who were accorded deification.

The Roman government was generally tolerant of the religious beliefs and rituals of the peoples it administered following conquest or annexation, but there were two sects to which it took strong exception: druidism and Christianity (nor indeed did they like Judaism). Druidism was first encountered directly by the Romans in the campaigns of Caesar in Gaul (59–50BC), though it is likely that it had been known about for some time in educated circles at the capital. How far it influenced politics among the Celtic tribes, or to what extent it acted as a unifying force among them, particularly in their wars against Rome, has long been debated. Some see druidism as the core of national resistance to Rome, in Gaul and in Britain; others write druidism off as an esoteric cult that had once wielded influence but was already on the way out by the time Augustus forbade Roman citizens from embracing it. Caesar devoted two lengthy paragraphs to the role of the druids in Celtic society, pointing out that druidism had originated in Britain, but nowhere does he suggest that druids played any part at all in the counsels of his enemies in Gaul.[1] He mentions the druidic practice of human sacrifice but does not labour the point because it was not long since the Romans themselves had given the practice up. It is unlikely that Roman opposition to the druids was motivated either by humanitarian or political reasons. The druids were wont to publicise gloomy prophecies: if these reached the ears of the troops or officials of the occupying forces, they could affect morale. For that alone druidism would be marked down for prohibition, as Pliny the Elder suggested.[2]

The early attitudes of the Romans to Christianity are not hard to understand. The core of Christian belief was the existence of only one god which precluded Christians from worshipping any of the Roman pantheon and, more importantly, meant they would not acknowledge the divinity of the emperor. By refusing to worship at the altar of Rome and the emperor, Christians were breaking the law. They also met in secret, and the government was suspicious of secret societies. Christians criticised the whole concept of slavery – much of Rome's prosperity rested upon the work of slaves – and they objected to the gladiatorial shows. Most Romans saw Christians as eccentrics, but the authorities regarded them as trouble-makers. It was not hard for a superstitious people to blame the Christians for a variety of disasters that afflicted the empire, and quite early on they became scapegoats. Severe persecution began under Nero (AD54–68), during whose reign both St Peter and St Paul travelled to Rome to encourage the early clandestine Christian community there, and were caught and martyred. When the great capital city was engulfed in the appalling fire of AD64, Christians were blamed and numbers of them were arrested, tortured and put to death, some being thrown to the wild beasts in the arena. Thereafter, Christians were extremely vulnerable for over two centuries. In some reigns there was a measure of leniency (the term is used relatively), notably under Trajan, but in others savage persecutions were conducted, as under Domitian, Commodus and Diocletian.[3] It was Constantine who granted Christianity official toleration throughout the empire, by the Edict of Milan in 313. This does not mean Constantine himself embraced Christianity; indeed, it becomes less and less likely that this was so.

Before the Edict of Milan there had been a small Christian organisation in Britain, working under cover, which might have begun as early as the late second century. St Alban appears to have been the first martyr in Britain. He was a Roman soldier who became a convert at the beginning of the third century, while on duty at *Verulamium* or nearby. He was executed in 209. Beyond that, there is little evidence for Christian activity in Britain before the end of the third century.

The physical remains of the various religions in Roman Britain are

The shrine of Nemesis at the amphitheatre at Chester

relatively scant, considering the importance of religion in Romano-British life. There are inscriptions with dedications to various gods of the Roman pantheon, such as that to Mercury (patron of travellers) found at Lincoln, the stone to Jupiter Best and Greatest at Chichester and the dedication to the imperial genius at Colchester. There are also altars such as the seventeen found at Maryport fort (see p 400), the altar to Mars at Wallsend fort, and there are statues to Mercury at Gosbecks and Mars at Fossdyke, Jupiter at Ranksborough in Leicestershire and Venus at Colchester. The cult of Mithras, the god of Persian origin who represented the victory of the spirit over death, the mediator between God and man, was a major religion in the army almost from the beginning of the occupation and continued after the establishment of Christianity as the official religion, yet there are relatively few remnants of it. There are a handful of *mithraea* (temples to Mithras), as at London, Leicester, Housesteads, Carrawburgh, and a possible one at Colchester, and other relics at Caerleon, York and Chester. Mithras was credited with having captured and slain a wild bull, and is sometimes depicted with a bull, and sometimes as a sun god (as at Carrawburgh). The *mithraea* were smallish buildings,

erected partly or completely below ground level to lend weight to the secrecy that cloaked the mithraic rites. The *mithraeum* in London (which was discovered in 1954 on the site of the present Bucklersbury House and dismantled, brick by brick, for re-erection some 54m (60yd) away) has yielded some fine sculptures that are now in the Museum of London. *Mithraea* were designed in basilican style, oblong with benching set down each longer side, behind a row of aisle columns, with apse or recess at one end to contain the 'high' altar, on or behind which was the altarpiece representing Mithras, with bull or as sun god or as himself rising from rocks. The *mithraeum* at Carrawburgh fort on Hadrian's Wall, which was built towards the end of the second century, is some 8m (26ft) long and 5.5m (18ft) wide, with evidence of side benching and an altar platform. There is evidence of later enlargement of the building, with a narthex and an apse.

Temples were built for other deities, and these were generally small buildings. There was a temple to Isis in London, one to Sulis Minerva in Bath, a temple to Serapis in York, a temple to Antenociticus at Benwell on Hadrian's Wall and, of course, the temple to the Emperor and Rome at Colchester. There were several other temples in Colchester, most of them less than 12m (40ft) along the greater dimension. The circular enclosure at Frilford in Oxfordshire was 11m (36ft) in diameter. Religious rites and celebrations involving large numbers of people would probably have been held either outside the temple or in a nearby theatre or amphitheatre. A few Romano-British temples have been found sited close to theatres, in particular at Gosbecks (near Colchester), St Albans, Woodeaton (Oxfordshire) and Catterick in Yorkshire.

Temples were built in a variety of styles. The Claudian building at Colchester and the temple to Sulis Minerva at Bath were classical in style, with columns, podium and pediment. Both were similar to the fine temple that has survived at Nîmes in southern France. Rather more temples were built on the Romano-Celtic model, so-called because they were erected to house statues and other dedications to the joint gods. The plan was an inner square or rectangular *cella*, or shrine, enclosed by a square plan outer wall or portico, like those at St Albans, Silchester, Richborough, Caistor St Edmund, Harlow, Great

The Temple of Mithras at the Hadrian's Wall fort at Carrawburgh (*E. Houlder*)

Remains of the small temple to the god Antenociticus, outside the Hadrian's Wall fort of Benwell (now visible in Broombridge Avenue) (*Author*)

Roman-Celtic temple at Farley Heath, near Guildford (*Janet & Colin Bord*)

Reconstruction of the small fourth-century Christian church at Silchester

Chesterford, Maiden Castle (Dorset) and Caerwent. A few were built on a round or polygonal plan, also with a surrounding wall, as at Brigstock (Hampshire): polygonal; Weycock (Berkshire): octagonal; Pagan's Hill: octagonal; Frilford: round; and Silchester: round.

So far as Christian churches are concerned, very few remains indeed have so far been discovered of new buildings raised for the new religion. The best known, perhaps, is the church at Silchester, with its rounded apse and mosaic pavement, and with narthex at the eastern end. There was a wooden church of the fourth century (or perhaps early fifth century) at Richborough, and at Lullingstone villa a special chapel was built whose wall plaster incorporated the Chi-Rho monogram (the plaster is now in the British Museum). At Hinton St Mary in Dorset, a mosaic of Christ with the monogram over his head was found in the villa and is now also in the British Museum. Some of the earlier pagan temples may have been converted to Christian use, but it is important to note that the Christians often destroyed pagan buildings, especially Mithraic temples. Mithraic objects in the London temple were hidden presumably to escape detection during the Christian era.

Silver strainer, with handle at the end of which is the Chi-Rho monogram. Total length, 202mm (8in). This is one of the items found at Water Newton in 1975 (see page 264) (*British Museum*)

263

One recent archaeological find of Christian importance is the hoard of silverware at Water Newton, which included three wine mixing bowls, two flagons, a chalice, a strainer and several triangular plaques, some with the Chi-Rho monogram. They were found in 1975. Present opinion is that the silverware is the earliest from the whole empire, that it dates from the early fourth century, or perhaps even the late third century. This hoard is now in the British Museum, where there is an interesting range of Christian artefacts, such as the lead tanks with Chi-Rho monogram found at Icklingham in Suffolk, one of which may have been a font.

NOTES
1. Caesar, *De Bello Gallico* VI, 13–14.
2. Pliny the Elder, *Natural History* XXX, iv, 13.
3. Trajan's attitude was summed up in a letter to Pliny the Younger: '. . . Do not go out of your way to hound these people: if they are brought before you, punish them, but only after giving them the opportunity to recant and to revert to the worship of our gods . . .' (*Letters* x, 97).

17

THE END OF
ROMAN BRITAIN

When the self-styled Constantine III crossed from Britain into Gaul in 406–7, he took with him the bulk of the island's active military forces. For a time he had some success in Gaul against the barbarians, and even made headway in Spain, but when he attempted to move into Italy, possibly in an aggressive capacity against Honorius, his army disintegrated. The cause of the break-up is not completely clear, but it began when one of his commanders in Spain, the British-born Gerontius (Geraint in Welsh) pulled the Spanish contingents away, at much the same time that the recently pacified barbarians in Gaul rose in revolt, perhaps at Gerontius' instigation. Constantine was stranded. At this point, the Britain he had deserted was again attacked by barbarians, in this case probably in several waves, including Saxon commandos, and there were no imperial forces available to beat them off. Constantine certainly could not help, even if he had wanted to.

The British cities therefore took it on themselves to organise their own resistance, and they also decided to get rid of Constantine's Roman government personnel who were ordered to leave the country. As the late fifth-century historian Zozimus put it '. . . they revolted from Roman rule and lived by themselves, no longer obeying Roman laws . . .'.[1] It was the end of direct Roman rule in Britain, and the situation was emphasised by the famous letter written in 410 to the *civitas* capital authorities throughout the province by the emperor Honorius, to the effect that the cities must look to themselves. This is known as the rescript of Honorius, which is generally taken to be a reply by him to an appeal by the cities for military help. Direct rule ceased but it was not the end of Roman Britain. That was to be a gradual process, lasting well into the middle of the century. The whole subject of the end of Roman Britain, the transition from Roman rule to Celtic and Germanic autonomy, has loomed increasingly large in recent years among historians and archaeologists.[2] Overall, there seem to be as many question marks as ever. What J. N. L. Myres could in

1936 describe as 'a great gulf' between Roman Britain and Saxon England, 'a void of confusion whose obscurity remains a standing challenge to historical enquiry . . .' has struck some scholars as still true today.[3] The most that can be said even now is that we are better informed, as a result of fresh archaeological and historical data, about certain aspects of the state of Britain between about 410 when central Roman government gave way to makeshift local indigenous policies and the 450s when Jutes, Angles and Saxons had begun to construct autonomous communities in southern and eastern Britain.

It is clear from excavation at some of the *civitas* capitals, notably at Cirencester, St Albans and Silchester, that urban life continued for several decades after 410, while at Canterbury Saxons appear to have been in control by the 450s after a period under Romano-British local government. In Cirencester and St Albans, new buildings were erected in this period. That these towns did survive was due in some measure to the fact that they had stone wall defences, which inhibited attacks by barbarians who were not familiar with sophisticated siege warfare. Barbarians here must include Germanic Jutes, Angles and Saxons. How far the societies within the cities resembled the ordered structure of Roman times is not clear, though the inhabitants presumably elected their own leaders.

In the countryside, there is interesting evidence of the continued occupation of villas by people under Roman influence during the earlier decades of the fifth century. Villa studies have also shown that here and there Anglo-Saxons took over villas and continued to run the estates and industries for themselves. One example was the villa at Barton Court Farm at Abingdon, excavated between 1972 and 1976, which revealed Anglo-Saxon pottery of mid fifth century style in the Romano-British ditching.[4] Meanwhile, there is evidence for post-Roman occupation at many villas, such as at Chedworth, Latimer, Barnsley Park, Frocester and Gadebridge Park, for the first two to three decades of the century.

In coinage and pottery manufacture, however, the separation from the empire seems to have had swifter and deeper results. Gold and silver coinage circulation in Britain dropped sharply from the very beginning of the fifth century, and by about 430 had gone out of use, with no apparent substitutes produced in Britain. This suggests a breakdown in the economic life of the country, but it may be too early to write off post-Roman society as incapable of devising a currency structure of its own. Pottery manufacture appears also to have declined from about the end of the fourth century, with few Roman factories producing anything in the first years of the fifth century.[5] Yet we learn from Gildas that the years after the break with Rome were years of prosperity, which is perhaps explained by the fact that the separation would immediately have ended the taxes paid by the province to the imperial treasury, both in cash and kind. It is probably safe to assume that, although law and order were seriously endangered for a prolonged period, there was no concomitant period of economic poverty.

What was the leadership position in a Britain without Roman government? The province had become accustomed to imperial rule transmitted through governors, *duces Britanniarum, vicarii* and so forth, but Honorius sent his rescript to the *civitas* capitals because there were no Roman officials left. For a time, each *civitas* operated as an autonomous regional authority, probably raising and equipping individual defence forces, but which were not co-ordinated on a national basis. But before long, leaders began to emerge, probably in the decade 420–30. The historian Procopius, writing a century later, observed that after 410 the Romans never succeeded in recovering Britain, which was thereafter ruled by usurpers.[6] One such 'usurper' – the word may be deliberate since whoever ruled in Britain after the 410 severance was doing so *in loco Augusti* (in the emperor's place) – was Vortigern, a shadowy figure whose name was in fact a title, High King. This ruler probably rose to power c425 and was to govern at least part of southern Britain for about three decades. This is the Vortigern of the *Anglo-Saxon Chronicle* (he appears first in the entry for 449), the 'superbus tyrannus' of the British historian Gildas (sixth century)[7] and the Vortigern of Nennius (ninth century).[8] Vortigern sought the aid of Germanic tribes to help him beat off the Picts rampaging down from the north. It is probable also that he wanted their help to discourage attempts by Rome to recover Britain. Nennius notes that Vortigern was driven by fear of Roman attack. We do not know how far Vortigern's sway extended, but he evidently had the authority to offer lands in Kent and East Anglia to the Germanic tribes as payment for their military assistance. The sequel to his appeal to Hengist and Horsa, the Germanic Jutish leaders, was (as in most cases where barbarians are enlisted to beat off other barbarians) that they turned on their employer.

Vortigern was not the only leader in those decades. One of his contemporaries, and an adversary, was Ambrosius Aurelianus, a pro-

Roman military commander who desired the return of imperial government and who is recorded in Bede's *Ecclesiastical History of the English Nation* (I, xvi) as having led the resistance of the British against the Germanic invaders in the mid fifth century, which means he was anti-Vortigern too. Ambrosius was a 'Romanised' Briton of whom Vortigern was afraid (Nennius).

Nor should we overlook the Gallic bishop Germanus (c380–448) who in 429 travelled to Britain on a mission to combat the Pelagian heresy. He visited St Albans (which he found to be a well-ordered urban community with a military garrison) and then formed an army of Christian Britons which he led into battle against Picts fighting alongside Saxons at a site in hilly countryside, perhaps the Chilterns or further west in the Cotswolds. Although he was appointed (directly or indirectly) by the Pope to carry out the religious mission, to have commanded Britons in war would have entailed appointment by British authorities or by local election. The army defeated its enemies, and Germanus returned to Gaul. In the 440s he came a second time to Britain, again to combat Pelagianism, and then returned to Gaul in 447 or 448.

Vortigern's policy of using barbarians to combat barbarians now began to recoil on him. In the late 450s he was defeated by Hengist and Horsa at Aylesford in Kent and his Britons (possibly under him again) were defeated a second time the next year, at Crayford. Further British defeats followed in the south and east and the Britons were gradually displaced.[9] In the last quarter or so of the century Britons further west resisted the Germanic invaders, with some success, notably a major victory at the Battle of Mount Badon, sometime between about 490 and 516, which stopped the Anglo-Saxon advance for some years. The site of the victory is still unproved, but seems likely to have been in Wiltshire, Gloucestershire or Somerset. It was to be another century before the British were driven out of what is now England altogether.

The story of the years from the mid fifth century to the early seventh century are not the concern of this work, but it may be pertinent to note that among the Britons fighting to hold on to their territories there lingered many traditions of Romano-British times, much of the language and culture, stronger in some places than in others (especially strong in parts of Wales where the native people were fortified by the evangelism of St David and others). It is also becoming more clear that the Germanic tribes, far from discarding everything

Roman that they found on their paths of conquest in southern Britain, as was once believed, in fact adopted much that was left of Roman civilisation. To put it another way, whatever form the 'end of Roman Britain' took, it does not appear to have been followed by any sort of Dark Age.

NOTES

1. Zozimus vi, 5.
2. Enough to generate material for a major conference held at Durham University in March 1978, at which a remarkable range of papers was presented. See Casey, P. J. (ed) 'The end of Roman Britain', *British Archaeological Reports* 79 (1979).
3. Collingwood, R. G. and Myres, J. N. L. *Roman Britain and the English Settlements* (1937); Haselgrove, S. 'Romano Saxon attitudes' in Casey, P. J. (ed) *British Archaeological Reports* 79 (1979).
4. Excavations by Oxfordshire Archaeological Unit and the Department of the Environment.
5. The Alice Holt/Farnham pottery on the Surrey–Hampshire border produced new wares at the beginning of the century, see *Current Archaeology* 54 (1976) pp 212-13.
6. Procopius, *De Bello Vandalico*, l, ii, 38.
7. Gildas, *De Excidio Britanniae*.
8. Nennius, *Historia Brittonum*, 33.
9. *Anglo-Saxon Chronicle* for the years 455, 456, 465, 473.

GAZETTEER

INTRODUCTION
TO GAZETTEER

There are over a thousand entries in this gazetteer. They represent the great bulk (though not all) of the Roman sites in England, Wales and Scotland, including almost all of those of which there are remains visible. This is probably the most extensive gazetteer of Roman sites in Britain ever assembled in one volume. More than half can no longer be seen, and to some readers this may be disappointing. But what is important is that, though not visible, either the sites are still there, and we know exactly where they are, underneath newer buildings or below heavily ploughed fields, or if now destroyed, the destruction is of relatively recent date. Either way, they have all been excavated at some time, some cursorily, far more of them extensively, and the results have been written down, the layout, or parts of the layout, drawn and/or photographed. The entries in the gazetteer summarise the finds. Some of the now vanished sites are not included, though they are known about.

We therefore know something about every site so far discovered, and this information, a corpus of material that is added to almost every day, enables us to comprehend something of the nature and extent of the occupation that took up over a fifth of the recorded history of Britain. Recent standard gazetteers have been strong on visible remains and have more than proved their great value, but they have eschewed the sites that do not at present reveal anything to the visitor. I believe that by leavening the tally of sites having visible remains with descriptions of several hundred sites that cannot now be seen, the serious enthusiast should be able to get a broader picture of the 'Romanisation' of Britain, by which is meant, how far the occupation forces and civilian personnel implanted their organisation upon the British tribes and their countryside, and to what extent they mixed and worked together, shared their leisure, crafts, beliefs, industries and day-to-day living during those four centuries.

The gazetteer is arranged alphabetically by country (England, Wales and Scotland). There is also a county-by-county alphabetical list of sites after the gazetteer. Four-figure grid references are given for the larger sites, roughly from a square kilometre upwards; otherwise, the six-figure grid references should help to locate smaller sites. Additionally, there are more than a hundred site plans, many of which are drawn from plans made at the time of excavation (the latest excavations where there have been more than one) or soon afterwards. With regard to the major sites such as the *civitas* capitals and some small towns, industrial sites and larger military establishments, knowledge of these is continually advancing and changing in the light of fresh excavation or the re-examination of existing evidence, and from time to time plans will need to be revised.

At the end of the county-by-county catalogue of sites, there is a list of selected references relating to individual sites. These include completed excavation reports, progress reports of current and interrupted excavations, comments and interpretations by leading Romano-British specialists in books, journals, articles and guides, and other sources. The abbreviations used in these references, as in the footnotes to the main text, are elaborated in the bibliography. There is also an index to the book.

ENGLAND

Abbey Gills Wood see **Milecastle 54**

ABBOTSBURY Dorset
SY 544866 *Signal station*
A signal station was thought to have been placed in the south-west corner of Abbotsbury Iron Age hillfort, but close examination of the square plan earthwork of about 1 acre (0.4ha) in the corner of the fort failed to produce supportive evidence. Pottery of the second century was found, but more work needs to be carried out.

ACTON SCOTT Shropshire
SO 468898 *Villa*
Villas are rare in the west Midlands, and the discovery of an aisled residential building here was of considerable interest. The building was about 34m (112ft) long; it had a cross-wall, a verandah and a bath suite. Fragments of painted plaster were found, and the outer walls were of sandstone. It is conjectured that the villa was associated with the army's control of the lead-mining operations at nearby Linley.

ALCESTER Warwickshire
SP 088572 *Small town*
The Roman small town here has been investigated during a programme spread over many years, particularly since the late 1960s. Much of it lies under later development, medieval and industrial, which has made the assessments very difficult. It was long suspected that it was preceded by a fort of the first century, and recent finds of military equipment now seem to confirm this. Civilian remains located include stone buildings, with painted plaster, of more than one period. Some traces of timber structures

(a few of the late first century) have also been seen, as well as iron-working evidence.

ALCHESTER Oxfordshire
SP 573203 *Small town*
Some remains of the earthworks that enclosed this small town can still be seen today. It was an early foundation of the late first century, probably built over the site of a Conquest period fort. The plan was almost square, with a regular street grid, and the town received a stone wall (more of a gravel bank with rubble facing) in the late third century, which enclosed an area of about 26 acres (10.5ha). Several stone buildings have been traced, including a large courtyard house that was probably a public building, a kind of miniature *forum*. There was a temple outside the wall.

ALDBOROUGH North Yorkshire
SE 4066 Civitas *capital of the Brigantes:*
Roman name Isurium Brigantum
Aldborough lay on the route to York at a crossing of the river Ure in a seemingly

Aldborough. The centre panel of a mosaic from a town house

274

Short stretch of the south wall of the civitas capital *Isurium Brigantum* (Aldborough, Yorkshire) (*Author*)

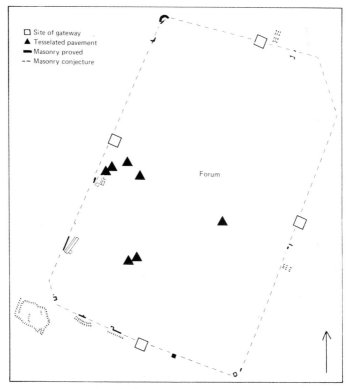

□ Site of gateway
▲ Tesselated pavement
■ Masonry proved
-- Masonry conjecture

Forum

Aldborough

unattractive position for settlement and without a good view of the surrounding countryside. This may be why no early fort has been found here. Yet there must have been some military settlement, at least for a short time, to give the impetus for the *vicus* on which the development of Aldborough was based. Certainly, late first-century stonework from the east gate area indicates that the *vicus* was already well established before the settlement was given the status of *civitas* capital. By the second half of the second century the town area of 55 acres (22ha) was enclosed by an earth rampart and ditch.

Little is known of the interior of the town since much of the excavation of the site was carried out in the eighteenth and nineteenth centuries. Of the finds of these excavations, two are notable. A large structure of about 82m (270ft) was traced in the eighteenth century which could have been a public building, perhaps a wing of the *forum*. A mosaic in perfect condition, dating from the fourth century, was found in the nineteenth century. It has a geometric design, and another from the same house depicts a lion. The most famous mosaic, showing Romulus and Remus with the she-wolf, is displayed in Leeds City Museum. The presence of mosaics of this quality suggests that Aldborough had its share of wealthy inhabitants.

Other buildings traced in these early excavations include a set of baths to the south of the west gate and two houses of substantial size with walls bearing painted designs. One had two wings and a hypocaust, as well as mosaics. The dating of these buildings is difficult, since the early excavators made little attempt to establish the structural history of the site. It is possible, however, from coin evidence, to date the conversion of the defences to stone to the mid third century. An angle tower of the fortifications has been excavated, and has been shown to be contemporary with the first stone curtain wall. The final phase of development of the fortifications came in the mid-to-late fourth century, when bastions (probably rectangular and external) were added to the wall. These bastions could relate to the Theodosian programme of defence improvements of this period (see p 154).

Before the end of the fourth century, Aldborough seems to have come to a non-violent end. Coin finds include a large number of Valentinian I, which are usually considered to be rare. It has been suggested that this could point to a military occupation of the town during the barbarian conspiracy of AD367. The final fate of Aldborough remains obscure – the fortifications seem literally to have crumbled away.

ALDEBY Norfolk
TM 452938 *?Temple*
Traces of what may have been a Gallo-Roman temple were found inside a ditched enclosure in the Waveney valley. The *cella* was about 18m (20yd) across.

ALDERMASTON Berkshire
SU 605681 *Agricultural site*
An agricultural site with an extensive field system of the later Roman period has been examined at Aldermaston, uphill from the nearby known Bronze Age and Iron Age site. A simple bath house of about 12×4m (40×13ft), adjacent to a second structure, was excavated in the mid 1970s. A well was discovered. The bath house and well were inside an enclosure, and the bath house was part of a larger building complex which has disappeared in quarrying.

ALDWINCLE Northamptonshire
TL 002805 *Bridge*
A dramatic discovery was made at Aldwincle during excavation of a gravel pit in 1967–8. It was the remains of a Roman bridge that had carried the Godmanchester to Leicester road (Margary 57a) across the Nene. The principal feature of interest was the discovery of the remnants of the timber superstructure. Excavations continued into the mid 1970s, and in 1976 the head of the team, D. A. Jackson, published a full report in *Britannia* vii (1976) pp 39–72.

There were three structural periods, shown by the discovery of three adjacent rows of vertical piles near the bridge abutment, and by three layers of road metalling. The first period was late first or early second

century, at the end of which period the bridge apparently collapsed. It was rebuilt during the time of Hadrian, and continued in use throughout the rest of the second century, collapsing a second time at the end of that century. It was rebuilt again. The evidence suggests that while the first bridge was a substantial structure, the second and third were rather makeshift, erected upon the remains of the first.

ALFOLDEAN West Sussex
TQ 1133 *Posting station*
A Roman road station was excavated in the 1920s by S. E. Winbolt. It was on the Chichester to London (Stane Street) road. The site comprised a *mansio*, covering about 105×93m (350×310ft), which had a headquarters building and a restaurant, as well as other structures. Part of the defending earthworks has survived. The *mansio* attracted a civilian settlement outside its defences, to the south. The *mansio* was probably built in about AD70, and the site seems to have been occupied until the fourth century, with a short interval in the early third century.

Side view of the abutment of the bridge at Aldwincle (*D. A. Jackson*)

ALICE HOLT Hampshire
SU 810402 *Potteries*
A collection of mounds in the southern part of the forest here, about 4½ miles south of Farnham, represents the remains of the one-time prosperous Alice Holt potteries. These had been founded in the first century as a local industry, but eventually grew into a major works distributing grey wares, some with white slip and combing decoration, to many parts of Britain in the third and fourth centuries. Products included flagons, dishes, bowls, jars and cooking pots. Much has been done to classify these products, attesting their wide circulation in the province. Recent excavations uncovered a rubbish dump for wasters of early production runs. Also found were traces of a large building with several rooms, including a drying room, which may have been a factory.

Allolee see **Milecastle 44**

277

ALRESFORD Essex
TM 061199 *Villa*
A number of villas were built during the Roman period along the estuary of the river Colne, south-east of Colchester. The main villa building at Alresford was a winged corridor-type with a long and narrow central range which, with its wings, extended to some 65m (70yd). The villa consisted of at least two houses, one with a bath suite.

ALREWAS Staffordshire
SK 183147 *Settlement*
Traces of a settlement of about 5 acres (2ha), south of Ryknild Street, were seen from the air, and afterwards examined on the ground. Some timber buildings were indicated from post holes. Pottery found was of the second and third centuries.

ALTON Hampshire
SU 7139 *Settlement*
A recently discovered Romano-British site of as yet undetermined origin or purpose has yielded sherds of Alice Holt wares.

AMBERWOOD INCLOSURE
Hampshire SU 205136
Pottery kilns
A number of kilns, which in the late third and in the fourth centuries produced New Forest wares, were found in excavations of the late 1960s at this location, about 4 miles east of Fordingbridge. Sherds indicated bowls with elaborate rims, flagons in grey sandy fabric, *mortaria* and, in one kiln, painted ware. The kilns had floors supported on pilasters.

AMBLESIDE Cumbria
NY 372034 *Fort: Roman name* Galava
The fort at Ambleside, at the head of Lake Windermere, was of two phases. A 1¾ acre (0.7ha) fort of earth and timber was erected during the Flavian period, though not before about AD90, with a double-ditch and a 3.6m (12ft) rampart. The plan was an irregular quadrilateral to take in a small rocky knoll in the north-west corner. This fort had two sets of gates, one of which had guardrooms. There were wooden towers on the corners. This fort was demolished in the second

century, probably in the first quarter; the rampart was levelled and a platform of earth constructed over it. On this, a second fort, of 2½ acres (1ha), was built with a clay rampart, the outside of which was revetted with stonework. The inside contained stone central buildings, such as the *praetorium*, *principia* and granaries with buttresses, but the barrack blocks were of timber. The *porta praetoria* was double and had guardrooms. Outside the gate was a paved parade ground. The fort continued to be occupied up to the late fourth century, by which time some of it had been turned over to different uses, such as metal working (carried on in the *principia*).

ANCASTER Lincolnshire
SK 9843 *Fort and small town*
Ancaster is famous for its stone: it was considered fine building stone in both medieval and Roman times. It is about 18 miles south of Lincoln, on the old Ermine Street. A fort was erected here in the early Claudian period, perhaps in AD47–8, on an Iron Age settlement. It had double-ditching, and was occupied until the AD80s. A marching camp of 8 acres (3ha) nearby was recently spotted from the air. A civilian settlement grew up round the fort, but little of its earlier story is known.

By the mid third century, a small town of some 9 acres (3.6ha) had become consolidated, straddling Ermine Street. It was surrounded by a stone wall some 2.25m (7½ft) thick at the base, which was later given corner turrets. Outside the wall was some impressive ditching. Not much is known of the buildings inside the town. The settlement, however, spread over a much greater area, of some 60 acres (24ha), and it incorporated a variety of industries such as potteries and stoneworks (where sculptors in stone worked). An aisled building of 15×8.5m (50×28ft) was found in excavations; it had two corn driers.

ANGMERING West Sussex
TQ 0504 *Villa*
This is the site of one of the very first villas built in Britain. It was begun probably in the AD70s, and was fitted with a bath house before the end of the century, as well as

several mosaic and tessellated floors. In its decoration it incorporated limestone setts brought from north Italy. The villa had a short existence.

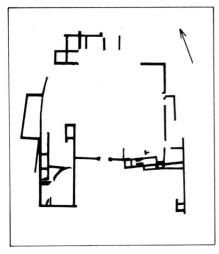

Apethorpe villa

APETHORPE Northamptonshire
TL 0294 *Villa*
This was a Nene valley villa of courtyard-type. Basically, a winged corridor house on the north stood at right angles to an aisled building on the west, forming two sides of the yard, with walling and outbuildings making up the rest of the rectangle. The north building was the main dwelling house, but the west building was also residential. There was a bath house in the south-east corner in a building group of two, perhaps three, units.

APPLEFORD Oxfordshire
SU 522935 *Settlement*
A settlement ½ mile south of the Thames has been investigated in advance of gravel digging, and evidence of Iron Age and Roman occupation detected.

ARNE Dorset
SY 933867 *Pottery factory*
There was a pottery industry at Arne, near Wareham, producing black burnished ware

of type I which originated among the Durotriges. This ware was made on an extensive scale, and the factory probably had a contract to supply the army along Hadrian's Wall. Much debris of this ware has been found, and evidence of factory buildings emerged in recent excavations. No kiln has been found, which suggests alternative methods of firing.

ASH Kent
TQ 608650 *Villa*
The remains of a villa, about 30 × 16m (100 × 54ft), were discovered in 1914–15, and a number of rooms at one end were defined. The site lay covered and neglected for half a century. Then, when the site was threatened with development, a swift re-examination was carried out at each end of the building, and traces of further buildings were found, attached to the outside of the villa.

ASHLEY Northamptonshire
SP 790916 *Villa*
A third-century villa site was excavated here in the 1960s. Occupation continued to the fourth century.

ASHTEAD Surrey
TQ 1760 *Villa*
There was a villa at Ashtead Common, near the Roman tilery. It was begun in the late first century. Excavation in the late 1920s yielded several interesting marble and stone fragments, including a fine carved slab of sandstone.

ASHTON Northamptonshire
TL 048890 *Minor settlement*
A small settlement of some 65 acres (26ha) beside the Nene river has been the subject of excavation throughout the 1970s and early 1980s. The remains of several industrial buildings have emerged, including metal works. In 1976, examination of a well yielded a cylindrical tank made of lead, which bore the Constantinian Chi-Rho symbol. The occupation of the site reached back to pre-Roman times (attested by a coin of Tasciovanus, see p 28), and it lasted almost throughout the Roman period.

Lead tank with Chi-Rho monogram at Ashton (*Nene Valley Research Committee*)

ASHWELL END Hertfordshire
TL 259404 *Villa*
The remains of a courtyard villa consisting of several buildings were found in examination of debris here, and its positioning was exposed by ploughing. The site is about 30m (100yd) north of Ashwell church.

ASTBURY Cheshire
SJ 837620 *Fortress*
A large fortified enclosure, of parallelogram shape and about 60 acres (24ha) in area, originally identified as a fort in the eighteenth century, was re-examined in the late 1960s. Parts of V-shaped ditching were exposed, and also what may have been the base of a rampart. Evidence was found of timber structures inside the enclosure, suggesting that the enclosure was more than a marching camp, and may have been a fortress, from its large area. No dating is as yet possible. The defences are visible in places.

ASTON BLANK Gloucestershire
SP 1418 *Settlement*
A settlement along both sides of the Fosse Way at Aston Blank was examined in 1970, and two hoards of coins were found. One, which had been in a bag, contained 2749 coins.

ASTON SOMERVILLE Hereford & Worcester SP 037378
Villa
A courtyard villa was spotted from the air in the mid 1970s, and investigation on the ground produced pottery of the third and fourth centuries.

ATWORTH Wiltshire
ST 856665 *Villa*
The villa at Atworth, near Melksham, was basically an L-plan, with a continuous corridor along both insides of the L. It had begun as a residential establishment with heated rooms and a bath suite, but the evidence of excavation suggests that later in its history some of the dwelling areas were abandoned and altered to agricultural uses; for example, corn driers were inserted into quarters such as the bath suite.

AUGILL BRIDGE Cumbria
NY 819147 *Signal station*
The site of a signal station at Augill Bridge was examined in 1975. Post holes suggest

the position of the wooden tower, which was enclosed inside two concentric ditches and a rampart.

AYLESBURY Buckinghamshire
SP 819139 *Roman remains*
During recent major building schemes in Aylesbury, one or two Roman features have been discovered. About 18m (20yd) of ditch cut into the limestone rock were found filled, containing sherds of the first and second centuries. A V-shaped ditch was traced running west on the site of The Bull's Head development at SP 820138.

BADBURY Wiltshire
SU 194809 *Villa*
The remains of a courtyard villa (previously examined in the 1950s) were further examined during road building works just north of Badbury, near Chiseldon, in the late 1960s and early 1970s. Much of the villa was destroyed by the roadworks. In 1969–70, the bath house was discovered on the east side of Ermine Street. It contained four rooms, two of which were hot baths. Some of the hypocaust *pilae* survived to a height of about 1.8m (6ft). The pottery finds suggest third- and fourth-century occupation.

BAGRAW Northumberland
NY 850965 *Temporary camp*
About 1 mile south of High Rochester are the remains of Bagraw marching camp, where Dere Street crosses the A68. The camp was about 20 acres (8ha) in size and was trapezoid in shape. It was later divided in half by a ditch and rampart.

BALDOCK Hertfordshire
TL 253340 *?Small town*
Baldock is generally classified as a small Roman town, but a series of excavations has failed to uncover any substantial private houses or grand public buildings. Certainly, there was a sizeable settlement at Baldock throughout the Roman period, but it seems to have been a native settlement that simply carried on under Roman occupation, taking on such aspects of Roman life as the inhabitants desired. Excavations have revealed evidence of bronze manufacturing,

pottery and agricultural activity (eg corn driers). Some streets have been identified, but a very few buildings have emerged. In 1980–1 a rectangular building, about 6 × 2.5m (20 × 8ft), with a flint floor, was uncovered on Upper Walls Common, south of a burial enclosure of La Tène origins.

BANCROFT Buckinghamshire
SP 826404 *Villa*
Considerable excavations have been undertaken at Bancroft villa, Bradwell, Wolverton, in the 1970s and in the present decade, and what has emerged is a villa consisting of a main winged corridor structure, with rear extension, an adjoining octagonal structure and several outbuildings to the north. The winged corridor building had a front porch on the east; it contained mosaics and channelled hypocausts, and was equipped with two bath suites.

Banks Burn see **Milecastle 53**
Banks East see **Turret 52a**
Bankshead see **Milecastle 52**

BANWELL Avon
ST 398593 *Villa*
A hypocausted room, about 6m (20ft) square, with an apsidal end, was discovered at the bath house of this site in 1968. The floor had a mosaic pavement.

BARBURY CASTLE Wiltshire
SU 147768 *?Marching camp*
What may have been a marching camp, with a single entrance with *clavicula* gates, was noted near the Iron Age hillfort at Barbury, near Wroughton.

BARDOWN East Sussex
TQ 663294 *Settlement*
Bardown, near Ticehurst, was one of the settlements in the Weald iron-working area. Excavations of the late 1960s exposed two timber-framed buildings, dated to the late second or early third century.

BARHAM DOWNS Kent
TR 212505 *?Cemetery*
A possible Roman enclosure surrounded by double-ditching, adjacent to Watling Street,

was noted in 1933 and re-examined in the late 1960s. It may have been a Romano-British cemetery.

BARHOLM Lincolnshire
TF 095114 *Villa*
An aisled building nearly 30m (100ft) long, within an enclosure at the north-east of the present village, served as a residence and was probably the main structure of a farmstead.

BARKSORE Kent
TQ 8768 *Pottery kiln*
A pottery kiln was found during reclamation work in Upchurch marshes, Barksore, near Lower Halstow. It has been dated to the first century.

BARNACK Cambridgeshire
TF 080066 *Villa*
Two aisled buildings have been noted from

Barnsley Park. Masonry buildings of the villa. Bath house is towards top right

aerial photography and part-confirmed in ground investigation at the known villa site at Barnack. One was a barn erected in the mid third century which was almost 40m (130ft) long. It had had stone side walls. This was demolished at the end of the century, and a second barn was built on the site. The latter building was about 6m (20ft) shorter. The second aisled building noted was about 200m (220yd) to the east.

BARNETBY TOP Lincolnshire
TA 050110 *Pottery kilns*
Two pottery kilns were discovered during road works here in 1975. Some of the sherds were Dales ware (grey, coarse, shell-gritted utensils).

BARNSLEY PARK Gloucestershire
SP 083067 *Villa*
An interesting villa of more than one period was excavated in great detail over the years 1961–79. The first building was a rectangular house about 26m (86ft) long, which

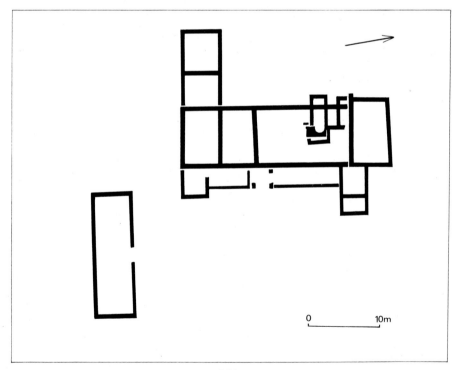

0   10m

received a bath suite in the north-west corner at a later phase. This bath suite was subsequently demolished and the space given over to other uses. The site appears to have been occupied from the second to the end of the fourth century, and it was associated with an extensive farm of arable fields, stone-walled stockyards and paddocks. There was also evidence of iron working.

BARNWELL Northamptonshire
TL 0585 *Villa*
The fourth-century villa site at Barnwell was examined in the early 1970s, and a bath suite investigated.

BARTLOW Cambridgeshire
TL 5844 *Burial mounds*
A group of Romano-British burial mounds can be seen at Bartlow, near Linton, under the Bartlow Hills. One mound is the largest of its kind so far identified, and is nearly 15m (50ft) high. It was examined internally in the 1830s.

BARTON COURT Oxfordshire
SU 514978 *Villa*
A simple farmhouse-type villa was raised at Barton Court, Abingdon, upon an earlier Iron Age site. The house was a strip-type with one wing and a single corridor on the east side. This had tessellated flooring. Other buildings associated with the house have been located, including a smith's forge and a corn drier to the south-east. The site also revealed much evidence of early Saxon occupation, including a wattle-lined well and traces of Anglo-Saxon houses built largely over the remains of some of the Roman parts. Nearby, fragments of colour-coated pottery from Oxfordshire kilns were gathered.

BASING Hampshire
SU 650513 *Settlement*
A settlement was excavated near Common Plantation, during construction of the M3 motorway in the late 1960s. It had been an enclosure surrounded by ditching. A rectangular timber building was traced. The occupation period extended from about the mid first to the fourth century.

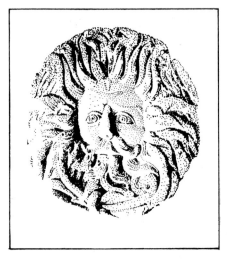

The head of the Gorgon, from the temple of Sulis Minerva at Bath

BATH Avon
ST 7565 *Spa town of obscure status: Roman name* Aquae Sulis
Bath was an exceptional town in Roman Britain and indeed in the north-west provinces as a whole, being apparently established to serve almost solely as a recreational and curative centre. The spa was developed possibly after the establishment of a fort to the north of the springs, although no firm evidence has yet been found. The site lies where the Fosse Way crosses the river Avon. The first monumental buildings were laid out at the end of the first century, although the hot springs had probably attracted people to the site before, a fact attested by the presence of military tombstones of men of different regions.

The early buildings displayed the simple grandeur of the Flavian period. From then on the 'town' (to date Bath does not fall into either category of proper town or small town) flourished and prospered, enabling the buildings to be extended and improved. The range of bathing and curative facilities was enormous – from 'Turkish' baths to all sorts of plunges and pools. Apart from the baths, one public building, the Temple of Sulis Minerva, serves to remind us that Bath was also an important religious centre. Great

The Great Bath at Bath (*Reece Winstone*)

controversy surrounds the dating of this temple, but the most likely period of construction is the reign of Nero. The building underwent many changes. The most important point about it, however, is the degree of 'Romanisation' of the whole province which it appears to reflect, even at this early date. The temple was tetrastyle with a porch and two rows of columns, standing on a podium measuring 20×10m (67×33ft) above a colonnaded courtyard. It had a pediment and façade, the pediment incorporating the famous disc portraying a gorgon's head. This fine piece of sculpture possibly dates from the third century, although with provincial work it is often difficult to tell. Immediately to the south of the temple, in isolation, stood the altar, the carved corners of which have survived. In the south-east precinct of the temple lay the sacred spring and reservoir,

entered through a façade on the south side with an ornamental pediment; on the north side was the façade of the four seasons (now preserved in Bath Roman Museum).

The baths went through several periods of development: the first massive and plain construction held the Great Bath, 20×9m (72×29ft) and fed by the hot spring, which lay in an aisled hall. Other features included a large hall, *caldarium, tepidarium,* two *natationes* and a smaller (the Lucas) bath. Soon after the original construction, another range of hot/warm rooms was added at the east end, a cold circular bath to the south and a *laconicum* to the west. In the late second or early third century re-roofing occurred with barrel vaulting, and later in the third century a huge new *caldarium* and a similar *tepidarium* were added.

Of the rest of the 'town' much less is known. In the second half of the second century, defences were provided in the form

284

of a rampart and ditch. The area they enclosed was not large; Bath is in fact somewhat smaller than the average Roman market town. A domestic building of the third century has been excavated in Abbeygate Street, which does not appear to have been particularly rich or elegant. The collapse of the house in the fourth century, suggesting abandonment or demolition, coincides with the decline of the baths in the same period. The water table appears to have started rising in the third century and attempts were made to combat the processes of silting and flooding. Eventually in the fourth century even the financial resources of Bath seem not to have been able to cope with the wiles of nature. Abandonment and decay followed, and the site reverted to marshland.

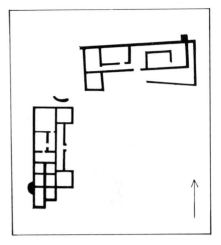

Beadlam. The north and west houses

BAUNTON Gloucestershire
SP 011048 *Undetermined site*
Samian and other pottery, brooches, part of a quern, a Constantinian coin and other artefacts were found here, near Ermine Street, in 1980.

BAWBURGH Norfolk
TG 155092 *Cemetery*
A cemetery of early Roman date has been examined here, revealing several burials, some in wooden coffins.

BAWDRIP Somerset
ST 326404 *Settlement*
Many sites of the Roman period were uncovered during the construction of the M5 motorway as it passed through Gloucestershire, Avon and Somerset. One was a settlement at Bawdrip, on the south side of the present road from Crandon Bridge to Puriton. Some ten buildings of stone were located, including workshops, storage huts and a latrine. Finds suggest occupation from the first to the fourth centuries.

BEADLAM North Yorkshire
SE 634842 *Villa*
A recently discovered courtyard villa at Beadlam, near Ryedale, is among the most northerly of Roman villas in Britain. It was probably begun in the Antonine period, and appears to have enjoyed long prosperity.

Mosaic pavements have been found, including one over a hypocaust. The villa site is to be opened to the public following major excavations over several years beginning in the late 1960s.

BEAUFRONT RED HOUSE
Northumberland NY 971651
Fort
The series of forts at the *Corstopitum* (Corbridge) site were long thought to have begun with an Agricolan fort of c79–80, hitherto not located but believed to be under the later structures. Then in 1974 C. M. Daniels, J. P. Gillam and W. S. Hanson discovered the real Agricolan army base of that period about a mile west at Beaufront Red House, during work on the Corbridge bypass. The base, of 25 acres (10ha), was a substantial establishment, with fifteen timber buildings in line within a ditched enclosure. These included a barrack block, workshops, a possible *valetudinarium*, stables and stores sheds. Excavations showed that the buildings had been dismantled, probably during the pullout from Scotland soon after Agricola's recall. The bath house to the east of Beaufront Red House, discovered in 1955, was properly seen as part of the original base. Beaufront Red House was built as a depot for Agricola's army on its advance into Scotland. (See p 329 for plan.)

285

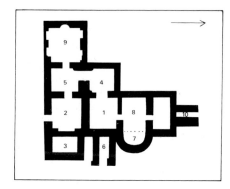

A confusing order of rooms at Beauport Park bath house began with the entrance at (2), progress through (5) to changing room (9). Then back to hot rooms (4) and (1) which were heated by furnace (6), or to alternative hot room (8) and plunge (7), heated by (10). Cold plunge obtained by working back through several rooms to (3). (after G. Brodribb)

BEAUPORT PARK East Sussex

TQ 786140 *Iron works*

A major iron-working area flourished at Beauport Park over the first two centuries of Roman occupation. In the 1870s a huge slagheap of Roman origin was broken up during Victorian railway building, but a considerable amount remains, and specialists think the site produced over 50,000 tons of iron at its peak. The site was administered by the *classis Britannica* (see p 185) and this has been attested by excavations at a nearby bath house where over 1200 tiles of one kind and another were found, bearing the CL BR monogram. The bath house was built in the second century, enlarged later and then abandoned in the third century. The bath house may be set out for public viewing.

BELLSHIEL Northumberland

NY 818999 *Marching camp*

On the edge of the Sills valley, beside the road from High Rochester to Cappuck, are the remains of a 40 acre (16ha) temporary camp which may be associated with the Agricolan campaigns or with the mid second century. It had both *titulum* and *clavicula* entrances.

BENWELL Tyne & Wear

NZ 214647 *Fort on Hadrian's Wall: Roman name* Condercum

Benwell is the third fort from the east end of Hadrian's Wall. Little can be seen today, for its northern section lies under a reservoir and the remainder is swamped by a housing estate. The fort was excavated, however, some time ago and was a standard wall fort with some variations. Standing on high ground with a good view, it occupied 5½ acres (2ha), and was built for a cavalry *ala*, which it remained for most of its long history into the fourth century. The fort was raised, possibly on the site of an earlier fort, in the governorship of Platorius Nepos (122–4), which is attested by an inscription relating to granaries built there in his time by engineers from the *classis Britannica*, who built them on impressive foundations. The *principia* had an underground strongroom, cut into the rock, and its walls were plastered.

The Vallum skirted the south end of the fort. Where the ditch faced the fort's southern entrance, a causeway was erected across it, which had a stone gateway that controlled passage to and from the Military Zone between the Wall and the Vallum. This causeway and some Vallum ditching on either side are well preserved, and are the only surviving example of this type of zone control along the Wall.

A *vicus* grew up round the fort, which eventually obscured the Vallum. Two interesting buildings have left visible remains: a *mansio* for travellers, just south of the Vallum causeway, and a temple, 4.8×3m (16×10ft) internally, with rounded apse, which can still be seen in Broomridge Avenue (see p 261). An inscription shows that it was dedicated to the god Antenociticus in the governorship of Ulpius Marcellus, c180. Some 270m (300yd) southwest of the fort, the bath house was excavated but has since been obliterated. There is a model of the fort at the Museum of Antiquities in Newcastle upon Tyne.

BERWICK DOWN Wiltshire

ST 941197 *Farmstead*

A small enclosed farmstead probably

founded by the Durotriges, and featuring a circular house, appears to have continued in occupation in Roman times.

BEWCASTLE Cumbria
NY 565747 *Fort: Roman name* ?Fanum Cocidii
This was an outpost fort on the Hadrian's Wall scheme. The remains, such as they are, lie alongside the remains of the medieval castle, which was built over the fort's north-east corner. The site is the summit of a hummock. Details of the first fort are scanty: even its shape is not known, but remains of an internal bath house of Hadrian's time were found, and it is deduced that the bath house continued to be used into the fourth century.

In the Severan period, or that of his son Caracalla, the fort was rebuilt: this time it was of hexagonal plan so as to enclose the whole of the hummock. It faced east, had a *principia* 22×30m (72×100ft), a *praetorium* 26×23m (88×78ft) and incorporated the original bath house. It also contained a stable block, indicating the presence at some time of a mixed garrison. The general view is that Bewcastle accommodated a large force for most of its long life, probably a thousand strong. An inscription in sandstone, referring to a vexillation, was found in 1977 and is in the Carlisle Museum. The fort was badly damaged in the late third century and was partly renovated by Constantius.

BICESTER Oxfordshire
SP 573227 *?Villa*
A settlement at King's End Farm was investigated before building works in the area. Part of the surrounding wall of a villa was identified, together with roof tile fragments.

BIERTON Buckinghamshire
SP 836152 *Settlement*
A settlement of Iron Age origin, which was later developed in Roman times, was examined in the late 1970s. Buildings of stone and timber were located, and tesserae, painted wall plaster and pottery were uncovered.

BIGBURY Kent
TR 116576 *Hillfort*
An Iron Age hillfort close to Pilgrim's Way, near Harbledown, Canterbury, consists of an enclosure of some 25 acres (10ha) thickly covered with trees for most of its area. Traces of its bank and ditching are clear, reinforced in parts by counter-scarping. Entrances can be seen on both west and east sides of the enclosure. On the north side are traces of an additional smaller enclosure, protected by its ditch and bank, which may have been for livestock. Excavations here yielded a quantity of Iron Age matter: implements, chariot tackle and a gang chain some 5.5m (18ft) long, with slave collars (another of these chains was found at Llyn Cerrig in Anglesey, see p 22). Bigbury is undoubtedly the hillfort which Caesar and his troops besieged and overran in the early days of his second invasion of Britain.

Biglands see **Milefortlet 1**

BIGNOR PARK West Sussex
SU 988147 *Villa*
Bignor Park, near Pulborough, was a large courtyard villa that grew on the site of an earlier settlement positioned on the south slope of a sandstone bank slightly to the north of the Downs. Stane Street, an important communications route, ran to the east of the villa. The buildings that formed the courtyard developed slowly. Suggestions of a Romano-British farm of the late first century have been found. A timber house of about 190–200 has been traced and the first stone building, simple and rectangular, dates to c225. This building probably had low stone walls with a half-timbered elevation. A portico and a channelled hypocaust probably for drying corn were added soon afterwards. In the third century, a corridor and small wings were added to the villa, and in the second half of the century the first mosaics were laid.

It was, however, in the fourth century that the villa reached the height of its prosperity. The rectangular courtyard measured 60×34m (200×114ft). The interior of the villa was luxuriously appointed, with hypocausted rooms and very fine mosaics, notably the famous Ganymede mosaic which dates from the first half of the fourth century. The bath suite was elaborate and hypocausted, with an arrangement of rooms into *caldarium, tepidarium* and *frigidarium* with a cold plunge. The positioning of the baths in the east of the south wing, with the main domestic rooms remaining in the west wing, suggests that the villa was a single domestic unit, and not fragmented as other villas of this type appear to be. An outer court with an enclosing wall contained outbuildings, including a barn and what were probably slaves' quarters and stables. By the end of the century, however, the villa had fallen into decay and was badly robbed for building materials. Although it shows no signs of destruction by fire, Bignor Park villa was probably abandoned by the early fifth century.

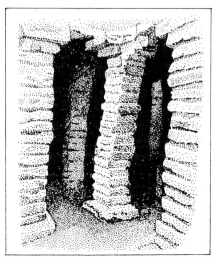

Fourth-century hypocaust at Binchester fort

BINCHESTER *Durham*
NZ 2131 *Fort and* vicus: *Roman name* Vinovia

Binchester was originally excavated in the nineteenth century when a general idea of its layout was gained. A remarkable hypocaust was discovered. Recent work has now established the chronology of the site's different periods. The fort, which is believed to have housed a cavalry unit at first, lay on the strategically important Dere Street on top of a hill which allowed good visibility of the surrounding terrain.

Excavations in the fort south-east of the bath suite have revealed that the first fort was Agricolan. Signs have been found of timber buildings, their positions indicated by stake and post holes. A floor of burned clay and cobbles also dates to this period. The remains of these buildings were sealed with dumped material in the late first to early second century, indicating a period of disuse. The next period is known as the industrial phase, since the remains of a large, half-timbered building with industrial associations have been found, incorporating an oven. Archaeomagnetic techniques have dated this as being no later than AD140.

Traces of a stone building, possibly the *praetorium*, were first thought to be Severan, but this structure has now been dated to the years between 270 and 290. The final developments occurred no earlier than about 340. The first stone building was partly demolished to make room for a free-standing bath suite. This had a courtyard and a triple-arched entrance, and must have been imposing. Two new rooms and a new drainage system were added at a later period, and later still two of the three arched entrances were blocked up.

Binchester boasts one of the finest fourth-century hypocausts in Britain, which has been excellently preserved. It is believed to be the heating system for the commanding officer's bath suite. The floor of one room and wall flues for the escape of heat are still visible. Under the floor are 88 *pilae* of tiles, and two arches in perfect condition which allowed the heat to pass underneath to heat the next room.

The last phase of fourth-century occupation is represented by a house with a possible cobbled courtyard, *opus signinum* floors and plastered walls. The last dates gained from coin evidence put the end of Roman occupation at Binchester in the first half of the fourth century. Pottery evidence, however, suggests that Roman life continued until c367.

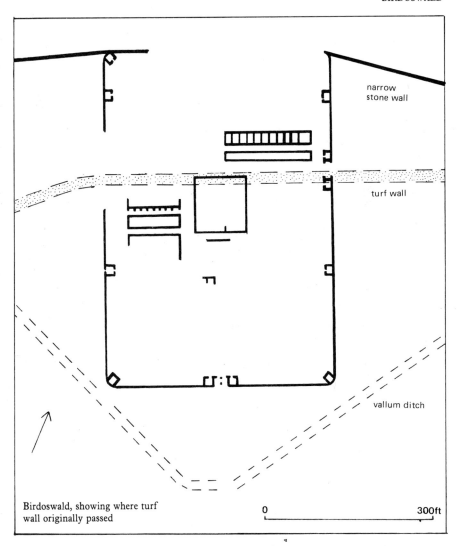

narrow
stone wall

turf wall

vallum ditch

Birdoswald, showing where turf
wall originally passed

0   300ft

BINCOMBE Dorset
SY 690839 *?Settlement*
What may have been an Iron Age and then a
Romano-British settlement has been tested,
and some shale floors found.

BIRDHOPE Northumberland
NY 826988 *Temporary camp*
A 25 acre (10ha) marching camp with
claviculae was built in Flavian times; its
outline is easily seen today.

BIRDOSWALD Cumbria
NY 6166 *Fort on Hadrian's Wall: Roman
name* Banna
This fort occupied a spectacular position,
with a steep scarp to its south, on Hadrian's
Wall. It commanded an important north-
south route and a crossing of the river
Irthing. Whilst knowledge of the interior
layout is limited, the defences are in a good
state of preservation, particularly in the
south-west area.
Before the main Hadrianic fort was con-

structed, there was possibly a small military post at the site, suggested by early second-century pottery. The Turf Wall and Vallum that preceded the stone wall were in position before the fort was built. Excavation has shown that their lines pass below the site. Thus, the fort was originally built projecting through the line of the wall with three gates to the north of it. Perhaps the intention was to house cavalry at Birdoswald, the positioning of the gates favouring cavalry sorties to the north. The fort was, however, garrisoned with infantry, so that when the Stone Wall was built it was brought up to meet the fort at its north corners. This ensured that three of the gateways lay behind the wall's fortifications. The Vallum was diverted round the back of the fort to the south, with a causeway left for access to the south gateway.

Inside the 5¼ acre (2ha) fort a few buildings have been investigated. In the *praetentura* barrack blocks have been found. One has been dated to the early second century by a hoard of thirty Hadrianic *denarii*. The barracks seem to have been rebuilt and extended in a later period. A centrally situated *principia* has been identified, and a hypocausted room near the eastern postern could have belonged to the bath suite of the commandant's house. Most impressive of the remains of the interior buildings are the walls of the buttressed and ventilated granaries to the west of the *principia*, parts of which stand to a height of 2.5m (8ft).

The fort must have been left vacant and allowed to decay for some time, since a gateway inscription of 219 indicates a general refurbishing in the third century. The masonry gateways had portals and guardchambers, the main east gateway having been excavated. Parallel to the 1.5m (5ft) thick fort wall were external interval towers. One on the east has been studied; it measured 4×3m (13½×10ft). The early fourth century, according to another inscription found at the site, saw more restoration: the rebuilding of the *praetorium, principia* and baths. From the period before the fort was finally abandoned, signs of strengthening of the defences have been observed, notably the blocking of the north portal of the main east gate in the fourth century.

Birdoswald see also **Turret 49b**

BISHOPSTONE DOWNS Wiltshire
SU 260815 *Villa*
A known villa site was examined in the early 1970s and two buildings traced, one of which had mosaic fragments and some remains of a hypocaust.

BITTERNE Hampshire
SU 433133 *Fortified town: Roman name* Clausentum
This was a small fortified town, also serving as a port, in a bend on the river Itchen. It covered a triangular site, edged by a ditch to the landward side. A stone wall enclosed the north and east sides, had bastions and was about 3–3.25m (10–11ft) thick, with earth backing. The wall was erected in the period c365–80, though the settlement and port had developed in the first century. The Mendip lead industry (based at Charterhouse) used *Clausentum* as an embarkation point for lead ingot supplies to Europe. Remains of a small bath house were found, which appeared to date from the second century and which was later demolished.

Black Carts see **Turret 29a**

BLACKDOWN Dorset
SY 603881 *Signal station*
Remains of a signal station were examined in the early 1970s, about 2 miles south of Winterbourne Steepleton. It was about ¼ acre (0.1ha), surrounded by a V-shaped ditch with bank, its entrance being to the east. The station may date to the mid first century.

BLACKPOOL BRIDGE Gloucestershire
SO 653087 *Road*
At Blackpool Bridge in the Forest of Dean, beside the present road, is a short stretch of old Roman Dean Road (Margary 614), manifest in a strip of broken paving stones edged with kerb stones. The road surface is worn in two parallel lines, which suggests regular wheeled traffic, probably carrying iron products from nearby iron workings.

BLACKWARDINE Hereford & Worcester
SO 535565 *Settlement*
Investigation in the mid 1970s at the Blackwardine settlement exposed a stone hypocaust as part of a range of five rooms, with a courtyard. Fragments of painted plaster were found, and also coins of the second, third and fourth centuries.

BLAKEHOPE Northumberland
NY 859945 *Fort and camp*
This was a Flavian fort, Agricolan or post-Agricolan, beside Dere Street, which guarded a crossing of the river Rede. It was 3¾ acres (1.5ha) in area, with timber buildings, surrounded by a rampart with gates in the north and west sides, and outside was a single-ditch system. Ditch and rampart can be seen today at the site, which is close to the A68, near Dargues. The fort had an annexe to the south, and the whole structure was erected inside the area of an earlier 15½ acre (6.3ha) temporary camp.

BLAXHALL Suffolk
TM 373576 *Pottery kiln*
A pottery kiln, which had produced grey wares, was found severely damaged during drainage operations at Blaxhall in 1972.

BLETSOE Bedfordshire
TL 018586 *Cemetery*
A Romano-British cemetery was discovered close to Bletsoe church. More than forty skeletons were found, some in stone cists.

BLUNTS GREEN Warwickshire
SP 138688 *Settlement*
A settlement was examined at Blunts Green, near Ullenhall, in the 1970s, and traces were found of timber buildings, one of which appeared to have been polygonal in shape, which suggests (though does not prove) a possible temple or shrine.

BOOTHAM STRAY North Yorkshire
SE 5954 *Practice camps*
The Roman army built several practice camps at Bootham Stray, which is about 2 miles north of the legionary fortress at York. The camps were probably built as practice for fort construction.

BOSCOMBE DOWN Wiltshire
SU 206383 *Settlement and villa*
There was a large settlement on Boscombe Down, near Allington, in the late Iron Age, and this continued into the Roman period, though to what extent is not known. In the late third century, a corridor villa was built, simple in style with three rooms and a corridor. This was later enlarged at one end with two extra rooms and a lengthening of the corridor. The extension was subsequently rebuilt on slightly wider dimensions.

BOSHAM West Sussex
SU 8105 *Church*
Some of the western wall in the nave of the church at Bosham, near Broadbridge, is of Roman origin.

BOUGHSPRING Gloucestershire
SO 559973 *Villa*
A simple villa building was located among trees at Boughspring, near Tidenham, in 1972, from scattered tesserae and hypocaust fragments. It was confirmed in further examinations of the late 1970s. The villa building measured 30×16m (100×53ft); it had one floor of *opus signinum* and some walls were faced with painted plaster. Pottery finds were from the second to the fourth century.

BOURTON ON THE WATER
Gloucestershire SP 159208 *Small town*
There was an unwalled town, the buildings of which spread along both sides of the Fosse Way, chiefly in the region of the crossing over the Windrush. The town spread several hundred yards eastwards towards the earlier Iron Age site at Salmonsbury. Building remains recovered included a winged villa with portico, first seen in the nineteenth century, several workshops, a stone-faced circular shrine and a bakery next door to what may have been a restaurant! The town appears still to have been in occupation in the fifth century.

BOW BRICKHILL Buckinghamshire
SP 890336 *Small town: Roman name*
Magiovinium
There was a small Romano-British settle-

ment, perhaps a town, at Dropshort, Bow Brickhill. The area has been excavated over the past fifteen years or so in advance of road development. The sequence is not entirely clear. Streets, ditching, traces of timber buildings and evidence of industrial activity, including iron smithies and pottery kilns, have all been traced. There is a suggestion that an early fort preceded the settlement: some military-type ditching was examined in the mid 1970s, and pottery of the mid first century was recovered. Nearby, at Caldecotte (SP 8935) an oval enclosure seen from the air was trial trenched, and pottery from Bow Brickhill found.

BOWES Durham
NZ 993135 *Fort: Roman name* Lavatris
Bowes fort was begun by Agricola. The rampart was built (unusually) of river boulders set in clay between a front lacing of timber and a rear face of turf. Several periods of building were revealed in excavations in the 1970s. It was rebuilt in the early second century, and again under the governor Virius Lupus (c197–8), who restored the bath house. In the third century, more works were carried out. The site of the fort was used by Henry II (1154–89) in which to build a rectangular great tower castle in the 1170s.

BOWES MOOR Durham
NY 930126 *Signal station*
Some rampart and ditching of this signal station can be seen beside the A66 road. There was a wooden tower within the enclosure.

BOWNESS-ON-SOLWAY Cumbria
NY 221626 *Hadrian's Wall fort: Roman name:* Maia
This was the most westerly fort on the main Hadrian's Wall frontier. It began as a rectangular timber and earth fort of the early 120s, on an east–west axis. It stands on a clifftop overlooking the sea, and does not project ahead of the Wall. The Vallum began at the east end on its course across the Solway–Tyne isthmus. The fort comprised 7 acres (2.8ha). Phase II, perhaps of the mid, or more probably of the late, Hadrianic period, was marked by conversion to stone. There were two further phases, of the third and fourth centuries. Remains of a number of timber buildings have been found, as well as stone traces. The fort may have accommodated a mixed garrison of cavalry and infantry. South of the fort was a substantial *vicus*, one of the main roads of which led south-eastwards towards Kirkbride. Traces of the external bath house were found in the *vicus*, east of the Kirkbride road.

BOX Wiltshire
ST 823685 *Villa*
North of the church, a courtyard villa was found in the early nineteenth century, and it has been examined several times. The most detailed work was probably done at the beginning of this century. The villa was large; it appears to have had at least forty rooms, including bath suites and a possible indoor fountain. Walls were decorated with painted plaster, some in the form of coloured panelling. The roofing was of hexagonal tiles or red flanged *tegulae*. Some mosaics and some tessellated flooring have survived. There was evidence of destruction in the fourth century.

BOXMOOR Hertfordshire
TL 038056 *Villa*
Boxmoor, near Hemel Hempstead, was one of the early villas in Hertfordshire, and it was begun probably in about AD75 as a seven-roomed timber house with corridors. The house was burnt down and a new house built, largely of cob, with ten rooms. This second house was renovated in the second century, again in cob, with additional wing rooms, making it a winged corridor villa house. The new structure had painted wall plaster and mosaic flooring, and a bath suite was added. In the third century the villa was again altered, as a result, it seems, of a decline in the prosperity of the associated farm business, and the new villa was smaller, with only eight rooms, and with a return to timber building in some parts. The final stage of Boxmoor in the fourth century was a shadow of the villa's former splendour. In the second half of the century it had become little more than a group of farm cottages.

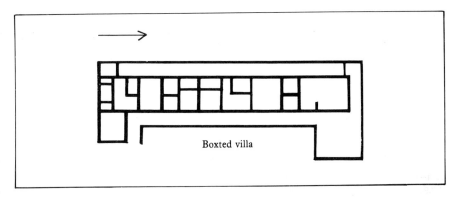

Boxted villa

BOXTED Kent
TQ 852662 *Villa*
A long winged corridor villa at Boxted, near Upchurch, was first excavated in the 1880s. It was about 66m (218ft) in length and had corridors on both long sides, between which were three units of rooms (one centre room flanked by smaller rooms on both sides). Each unit was probably for a family. Some of the side rooms were subdivided. Excavations about 270m (300yd) south-west of the main block, carried out in the late 1960s and early 1970s, exposed remains of a Romano-Celtic temple, built of flint, the *cella* of which was about 6.5m (21ft) square, surrounded by an ambulatory. The temple was probably, though not certainly, associated with the villa block (see Titsey Park).

BRACKLEY Northamptonshire
SP 592373 *?Villa*
What may be a villa site of the late Roman period was located in investigations of the early 1970s.

BRADFIELD Berkshire
SU 602738 *Pottery kiln*
During road construction associated with the M4 motorway in the late 1960s, a pottery kiln was located about ½ mile north of Bradfield village. It may be associated with the nearby site of Maidenhatch.

BRADING Isle of Wight
SZ 599862 *Villa*
The site at Brading is particularly suitable for a villa, sheltered from the north by

Brading Down and having a well-protected harbour nearby. Little is known of the history of this winged corridor villa, and since most of the excavation was carried out in the nineteenth century, what information there is is difficult to interpret. The site was occupied from the first century onwards, but the villa itself was possibly a second-century foundation. The west wing seems to have been built first, with the later north and south wings making up the villa complex and forming a three-sided courtyard – possibly a garden. The west wing was the main domestic area and had painted plaster on some walls and mosaics with many different classical scenes, including the Bacchus mosaic. One room had a hypocaust. The north wing measured 40×15m (135×50ft) and was possibly built as an aisled hall or barn with the west end later being divided into domestic rooms, one with a hypocaust. The south wing was a large, open barn with three rooms at the west end, possibly workshops or workers' quarters. The period of maximum prosperity was during the third and early fourth century. However, even in this period the villa appears to have lacked a bath suite, although there were bathing facilities in a separate aisled farmhouse. Later, in the fourth century, standards seem to have declined; a corn-drying oven, for example, was cut through one of the mosaics in a corridor of the west wing. This is probably just one example of a more general decline as the villa fell into disrepair.

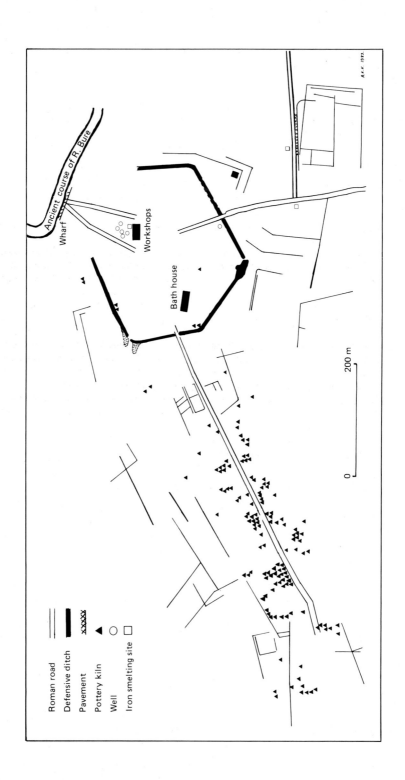

Roman road

Defensive ditch

Pavement

Pottery kiln

Well

Iron smelting site

Ancient course of R. Bure

Wharf

Workshops

Bath house

0   200 m

BRADLEY HILL Somerset
ST 480303 *Agricultural settlement*
An interesting agricultural settlement was
excavated at Bradley Hill, near Somerton, in
the late 1960s and early 1970s. It appears to
have been largely of fourth-century occupation, on or beside a much earlier and quite
different kind of site. There were three main
buildings, two of which were dwelling
houses (each with three rooms) and a long
stockbuilding attached to one house, as an
annexe. The stockbuilding was open at one
end, and may have been used for storing
farm carts. There is evidence of metal
working, and a large number of burials
suggests that the settlement had its own
cemetery. It was still in occupation in the
fifth century.

BRADWELL-ON-SEA Essex
TM 031082 *Fort of the Saxon shore: Roman
name Othona*
The fort at Bradwell-on-Sea comprised at
least 5 acres (2ha). Three sides of its irregular
quadrilateral shape survive, but the east (sea-
ward) side has vanished. The fort walls have
almost disappeared as well, but they have
been traced and seem to have been up to
4.25m (14ft) thick. There was a wide ditch
outside, surrounding the fort. On the west
side, traces have been seen of several horseshoe-plan bastions, especially on the north-
west and south-west corners. The present
ruin of St Peter's chapel (of seventh-century
Saxon origin) lies across the area where the
west gate stood. Bradwell was built in the
period c276–85.

BRAINTREE Essex
TL 755240 *Small town*
The Roman road from Braughing in Hertfordshire to Colchester is known as the Stane
Street (Margary 32). It skirted the north of a
small Roman town at Braintree. Excavations
in the 1970s unearthed remains of timber
buildings, some belonging to the second
century. There is some evidence that before
the Romans developed the town it had been
an Iron Age *oppidum*.

Plan of Brampton

BRAMDEAN Hampshire
SU 6228 *Villa*
To the north-east of Woodcote Manor, a
villa was partially investigated in the 1830s.
The main building appears to have been a
courtyard villa, the principal range of which
had seven rooms in line, with a corridor.
The floors were tessellated, but there were
also mosaics.

BRAMPTON Norfolk
TG 2223 *Small town with extensive potteries*
Brampton, near Aylsham, is classified as a
small town site beside the river Bure. It is
distinguished for its extensive pottery
industries, which flourished over a long
period, from the late first to the mid fourth
century. Over 150 kilns have been found, the
great majority lying in an industrial sector on
the western end of the town. There is also
evidence of iron working and bronze
working, and of buildings associated with
these skills. In the early 1970s a small bath
house was found in the town centre, which
had painted plaster walls, and it is clear that
the structure was a free-standing facility not
associated with any private house or public
building. (Could it have been for the workers
in the potteries?) Remains of a wharf, which
once flanked the river (whose course
originally ran closer to the town than it does
today) and which was served by a road from
the town, have also been found. It is thought
that the pottery items, of which vast quantities must have been manufactured, were
loaded on to vessels at the wharf for distribution by sea to many parts of Britain including, the excavators believed, the army at
various depots and forts. *Mortaria* stamped
by the second-century potter *Aesuminus* who
worked at Brampton have turned up in
several places, such as Lincoln and
Corbridge. The excavations have been a
triumph of skill, patience and ingenuity
under the astute leadership of Dr Keith
Knowles.

BRAMPTON OLD CHURCH Cumbria
NY 510615 *Fort*
Some cobble base and core of part of the
rampart at the 3½ acre (1.4ha) Brampton fort
were examined in 1982. The fort was a short-

Bath house at Brampton Roman town, Norfolk
(*Dr Keith Knowles*)

life establishment of Trajan's reign, built to
fill the gap between Carlisle and Nether
Denton forts on the Stanegate frontier (see
p 88). An inscription in the rockface of a
nearby quarry indicates legionary building
work in the neighbourhood in about 107,
which could bear out the dating of the fort. It
had associated pottery kilns worked by

auxiliaries during their occupation of the
fort.

BRANCASTER Norfolk
TF 781441 *Fort of the Saxon Shore: Roman
name:* Branodunum
The fort at Brancaster was built c240–50:
almost square in plan, with rounded corners,
the corners having towers, with four gates
(one on each side) and a surrounding stone
wall about 3m (10ft) thick. The wall was

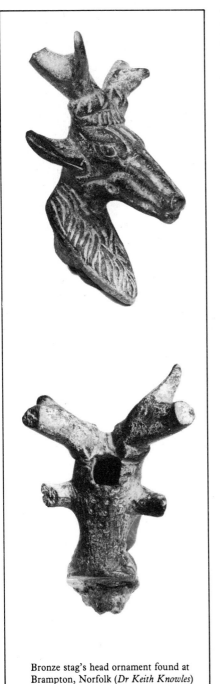

Bronze stag's head ornament found at Brampton, Norfolk (*Dr Keith Knowles*)

backed by a rampart and protected outside by a wide ditch. The fort occupied about 6½ acres (2.6ha). It was built over a levelled part of the site of earlier enclosures which represented an extensive settlement of the late second and early third centuries. The site today is about a mile from the sea, though in the Roman era it lay beside an estuary. It was close to Peddars Way Roman road. The civilian settlement declined and by the fourth century the fort was on its own. By that time it had become part of the Saxon Shore fort system (later third century).

BRANTINGHAM Humberside
SE 9328 *Villa*
Little is known of the villa at Brantingham which lay 1 mile north-north-west of Brough-on-Humber (*Petuaria*). Two excavations have taken place in the area. The more recent one in the early 1960s uncovered several rooms of a courtyard building, which obviously belonged to a prosperous owner. The largest room can be dated by pottery and coin evidence from under the floor surface to after 330. The south-east corner of the masonry of this room was the only stone architecture noted, and the room measured 11 × 8m (36½ × 25½ft). The main feature of the room was a mosaic pavement which had a central panel of the head of a goddess, with other figures surrounding. The mosaic is preserved in Hull City Museum. Part of the floor had collapsed into the hypocaust flues under the pavement. On top of the mosaic were fragments of painted plaster which reveal that the walls were decorated with female figures. A long corridor, also with a mosaic, and another room with collapsed hypocaust *pilae* and a fragmented mosaic, were also found. Although Brantingham villa has revealed little about its history and development, the richness of its interior decoration suggests that it was a more ambitious building project than most other villas in this part of the country (cf Rudston, Langton).

BRAUGHING Hertfordshire
TL 391243 *Small town*
Recent excavations at this previously neglected site which lay on a chalk ridge

above a flat-bottomed valley at the crossing of two important routes, Ermine Street and Stane Street, have revealed more information about its development. A native settlement preceded the establishment of the Roman town, the status of which is not known. The extent of the town is unknown partly because of an apparent lack of defences. The natural barriers of marsh, river and forest around the settlement possibly meant that none was needed, although fortifications may yet be discovered. The nucleus of the settlement seems to have been at the north end of the ridge. A rudimentary street pattern of Claudian/Flavian date has been traced at Skeleton Green, along with signs of early timber buildings. Aerial photography has revealed that the buildings and streets are not always aligned, suggesting different phases of development. The only masonry building uncovered is a bath house with a hypocausted, apsed *caldarium* which still had plaster on its walls when excavated. The bath house had two main phases of building, with a room being added to the *frigidarium* in the second period. The baths seem to have been abandoned, probably in the third century. The buildings fronting onto streets in the Ermine Street area seem to have changed in function from trading establishments to manufacturing areas during the third century, suggesting a possible switch in the economic base of the town. Evidence for later periods is unfortunately limited.

BRAY Berkshire
SU 913781 *Industrial site*
A small industrial site was excavated in the late 1960s and early 1970s beside a gravel quarry. Traces of fourth-century timber buildings were located, with some evidence of metal working in the fifth century, which suggests Romano-Saxon occupation at that time. The site is close to the river Thames, and work in 1971 exposed evidence of a timber building over the water's edge, which may have been a mole.

BREAGE Cornwall
SW 618285 *Milestone*
A rectangular pillar, about 1.5m (5ft) tall, was used as a gatepost for a long time near Breage Church, about 4 miles west of Helston. Then, in 1920, it was noticed that the pillar, which is of granite, carried part of an inscription. The pillar has been dated to about AD260, and is considered to be a milestone of the time of Postumus.

BRENLEY CORNER Kent
TR 0359 *Settlement*
There was a Roman roadside settlement beside Watling Street, about a mile or so west of Boughton Street. This was investigated in the early 1970s and evidence of iron working was found. What may have been a temple or shrine was also excavated a little to the west.

BRIDGEWORTH Somerset
ST 392574 and 391517 *Salt-manufacturing sites*
The sites of two salt-manufacturing works were seen in rescue operations of the mid 1970s at Bridgeworth, near Weare.

BRIGHTLINGSEA Essex
TM 084172, 077187 and 059187 *Villas*
Three villas have been located at Brightlingsea, quite close to each other. One, at TM 084172, consisted of two buildings; the second TM 077187 has not been defined beyond noting that its remains are under the present parish church, and the third TM 059187 appears to have been a substantial structure, though no plan has yet been defined.

BRIGSTOCK Northamptonshire
SP 961858 *Shrines*
An unusual group of Celtic shrines has been uncovered here over recent years, circular and polygonal in plan. Among the finds were bronze statuettes, and Roman coins of the first to the fourth centuries.

BRISLINGTON Avon
ST 6170 *Villa*
A corridor villa stood here, overlooking the Avon. It had several mosaic and tessellated floors. The villa may have been pillaged and burnt in the great conjoint invasion of southern Britain in 367. Examination in recent years has shown bodies pushed into

the villa well and much violent destruction. A number of artefacts have been recovered, including several pewter flagons and cups and an iron-bound chest.

BRISTOL Avon
ST 587743 *Building*
Investigations in a demolished church in Upper Maudlin Street in the mid 1970s exposed the foundations of a stone wall of Roman origin which may have supported a timber barn.

BRIXWORTH Northamptonshire
SP 747719 *Villa*
Brixworth villa was excavated in the later 1960s. It had begun as an Iron Age site, with a circular house. Early in the Roman period, probably between about AD70 and 100, five rooms with painted plaster walls were erected, four in line, the third divided into two. It was fronted by a verandah. In the second century, the northern half was reconstructed, with extra rooms being added. A corridor was built on the east side, and also a south wing. This work may have been of the early fourth century. The villa lay next to ironstone deposits.

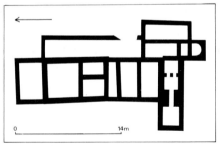

Brixworth villa. The original five-room house was in the central range

BROADFIELDS East Sussex
TQ 258353 *Iron-working site*
One of the larger Roman iron-working sites in the Wealden iron area, Broadfields was excavated in some detail in the 1970s. Numerous furnaces were found, as well as slagheaps, puddling pits, forges and ovens, over a wide area of some 30 acres (12ha). Activities were attested over nearly four centuries.

BROCKWORTH Gloucestershire
SO 891168 *Settlement*
A settlement about 4 miles south-east of Gloucester and close to Ermine Street was investigated before house building. A rectangular ditched enclosure was located, about 72×36m (238×118ft).

BROMHAM Bedfordshire
TL 027523 *Pottery*
This was a pottery where Clapham Shelly ware began to be produced before the Conquest. In the late first or early second century a rectangular enclosure was erected. Inside were several buildings, including a granary and a T-shaped corn drier of the mid second century which continued to be used in the third. The corn drier was located inside a wooden building with a tiled roof. The clay floor of the drier may have been supported on iron bars. The site was excavated in advance of gravel quarrying.

BROMHAM Wiltshire
ST 9765 *Villa*
There was a corridor villa at Bromham, which has been investigated several times and some mosaic paving found.

BROMLEY HALL FARM Hertfordshire
TL 418216 *Potteries*
This is the site of considerable pottery manufacture from the Much Hadham pottery industries of the third and fourth centuries, which included some of the Romano-Saxon wares. Excavations of the late 1960s uncovered several pottery kilns and also tile kilns.

BROUGH Cumbria
NY 796139 *Fort: Roman name* Verteris
The first fort at Brough, by Brough Castle, was built in about AD80, and was occupied on and off over the next century until c197 when it was rebuilt. In the third century, the fort was a centre for the collection and distribution of a variety of military stores, including raw materials such as lead ingots. This was attested by the discovery of numerous stamped seals bearing the names of units forwarding goods to one another and to government-controlled centres. A *vicus* developed

nearby, which was flourishing by the second century. The medieval castle, of which the great tower remains standing, was erected within the fort's area and across some of its ditch and rampart.

BROUGH BY BAINBRIDGE North Yorkshire SD 937902

Fort

The first fort was built on this site probably after the departure of Agricola. It was of parallelogram plan, had clay ramparts and covered 2½ acres (1ha). Foundation trenches for Flavian or Trajanic timber buildings were found in the late 1960s. The fort was abandoned, then reoccupied later in the Antonine period, during which time the rampart was revetted with stone and a *principia* of unusual design was erected (the forecourt led not to a large hall but to a range of small rooms). The fort was rebuilt again in the third century, and included a new *principia* of the more usual style and this was

not altered for a century and a half. Further works were carried out at the beginning of the fourth century. After the 360s the role of the fort underwent some changes, for the *principia* was destroyed and a number of industrial buildings were erected, including metal workshops and a lime kiln.

BROUGH-ON-HUMBER Humberside SE 9327 *Probable* civitas *capital of the Parisi and early fort: Roman name* Petuaria

Brough raises problems in that it does not conform in many ways to the pattern of development experienced by most *civitas* capitals, although it is mentioned as one in an inscription. It also lacks the usual street pattern and amenities of a capital. This has led to much speculation as to its nature and function. The site lay at a strategic point, where Ermine Street crosses the Humber, and the Romans chose a spot already occupied by a native settlement.

The first sign of Roman occupation dates from about AD70 when a temporary camp which was also a stores base was established.

Sketch plan of Brough-on-Humber

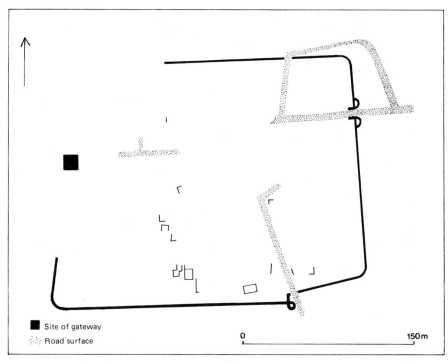

■ Site of gateway

⠂⠂⠂ Road surface

0   150m

Between AD70 and 80 a more permanent fort of 4½ acres (1.8ha) developed. The *porta decumana* and three streets have been traced. In c80 a general evacuation of the fort occurred, but the bank and ditch defences were left intact and the storehouses were maintained. A brief reoccupation of the fort appears to have occurred in about 125, by which time the *vicus* had already begun to develop. A slow process of expansion continued until about 200, but the military flavour of the site remained. It was still defended by a bank and ditch, and no attempt appears to have been made to level these for the purpose of expansion. The settlement seems never to have exceeded about 12 acres (4.9ha).

At the end of the second century or the beginning of the third, there was a spate of fresh internal construction and a refurbishment of the defences. An inscription suggests that there was a theatre, and from this other public buildings associated with a *civitas* capital might reasonably be expected. But where are they? The theatre was certainly in ruins by the late third century, since the inscription we have mentioned was incorporated in a new building of this period. In about 270 the fortifications were converted to stone in stages, with some parts being left unfinished. After a lapse of about twenty years, the fortifications were finished off with the addition of bastions, gate towers and new buildings inside the fort.

There was a naval base attached to the Brough site, the presence of which could explain the preponderance of military architecture. It was abandoned in about 360 and the occupants could have moved inside the fortified area. The disuse of a guardroom on the fortifications points to a lack of manning after the beginning of the fourth century.

All in all, Brough is a mysterious site. Its military nature and its continual use as a store depot cannot be explained fully by the fact that it was related to a naval base. The lack of public buildings could be misleading. Was Brough a 'failed' *civitas* capital (like Chelmsford) or perhaps the civilian settlement was elsewhere? Whatever the true position, our understanding will only be furthered by more excavation.

BROUGH-ON-NOE Derbyshire
SK 181827 *Fort: Roman name* Navio

There were two successive forts on this strategic site overlooking the river Noe. The first, of about 3 acres (1.2ha), was built in the Flavian period. Some of the buildings were identified in the 1960s, including the timber *praetorium*. The fort was abandoned in the early second century. Then, in the later Antonine period, the old works were levelled and a new, smaller fort, with stone and timber buildings and a stone wall, was erected by the first cohort of Aquitanian mixed cavalry and infantry, in the period AD155–8. A possible stable block has been identified. The fort was surrounded by a triple-ditch system. Refurbishing was carried out in the Severan period. The fort seems to have been occupied into the fourth century. It was used to protect the neighbouring lead ore deposits, and may also have acted as a depot for lead supplies.

BROUGHAM Cumbria
NY 5328 *Fort: Roman name* Brocavum

A first-century (possibly Agricolan) fort was erected by the junction between the rivers Eamont and Lowther, and some outline can still be seen. Little excavation has been carried out, but a variety of inscriptions have been found over the years, including one that refers to the *civitas* capital of the Carvetii, that is, Carlisle, established in the third century. The fort is south of the remains of the Norman castle.

BROXTOWE Nottinghamshire
SK 5242 *Fort*

This fort was discovered during building works for a council estate just outside Nottingham in the late 1930s. It had been erected on the hillside in the middle of the first century, perhaps before AD50. A number of military objects were discovered on the site, including a scabbard mount. The size of the fort is not established.

Brunton see Turrets 26a & b

BUCKNOWLE FARM Dorset
SY 954815 *Villa*

A villa was revealed at Bucknowle Farm, Corfe, in excavations that began in the 1970s

301

(which are still in progress), following the discovery of a tessellated pavement near Corfe Castle. The villa seems to have been a courtyard type, the main block having been a corridor-type house with many rooms. The bath house was a separate structure on the east side, reached by a corridor or verandah. The villa rose upon an earlier Iron Age site and appears to date from the third century.

BURGH Suffolk
TM 225523 *Settlement*
A settlement surrounded by ditch and rampart was located here in the mid 1970s.

BURGH CASTLE Norfolk
TG 475046 *Fort of the Saxon Shore: Roman name* Gariannonum
One of the early batch of Saxon Shore forts built in the period c276-85, Burgh stands beside a tributary of the Yare, about 4 miles inland and with no direct view of the sea. Three of the fort's four walls, up to 3m (10ft) thick, built of split flint interlaced with tiles round a concrete core, are still standing. In some parts they are up to 4.5m (15ft) tall. The west wall has disappeared. The plan was trapezoid, with flanking horseshoe-plan bastions, some protecting a postern, some gates and corners. Excavations revealed traces of timber buildings in the north-east corner, including a barrack block. In the south-west corner a motte castle was later raised by the Normans. Burgh was occupied well into the fourth century.

BURGH BY SANDS Cumbria
NY 3258 *Hadrian's Wall Fort*
The 5 acre (2ha) fort, Burgh by Sands II, was built upon Hadrian's Wall as part of the frontier scheme, and it projected over the Wall to the north. The fort had an external bath house to the east, and a *vicus* developed outside. A second fort was recently discovered (Burgh by Sands I) about ½ mile to the south, and this appears to have been an earlier structure, probably of Trajan's reign and therefore part of the Stanegate system.

BURGHWALLIS South Yorkshire
SE 519120 *Fort*
A fort was recently identified by aerial photo-

graphy near Burghwallis village, about 1½ miles off the A1. It has not been fully excavated, but a few finds suggest occupation between the Antonine period (Samian pottery) and the unsettled decades of the mid to late third century (coins of Tetricus and Carausius).

BURNHAM ON CROUCH Essex
TQ 944967 *Settlement*
Some kind of settlement has been detected at the north-west of the village during construction of an industrial estate. It has been dated to between the first and third centuries.

BURROW-IN-LONSDALE Lancashire
SD 617761 *Fort*
A fort of undetermined size was built on the east of the Lune river in the Flavian period. It was abandoned, and a second fort erected on a different alignment, probably in the second century. Fragments of second-century Samian ware were found.

BURWELL Cambridgeshire
TL 584675 *Undetermined site*
A quantity of bronze vessels of the fourth century was found to the west of the village in 1969. These are now in the Museum of Archaeology and Ethnology in Cambridge. Eight years later, a cylindrical lead tank with a capacity of 200 litres (44 gallons), of similar period, was found as a result of metal detection, lying amid pottery and other fragments.

BUTCOMBE Somerset
ST 508629 *Farmstead*
A small rural settlement was excavated here. It consisted of a farmhouse with outbuildings, including a stockbuilding of about 14×8m (46×26ft) which had had a flagged floor, and a wide centre door on one long side. The period of the settlement was about mid to late third century until the mid fourth century. It had been raised on an earlier Iron Age site. The buildings stood in the centre of a complex of stone-wall enclosures, probably cattle pens, and were associated with surrounding arable fields, which showed up well on aerial photographs.

BUTLEIGH Somerset
ST 506317 *?Marching camp*
Traces of the rounded north and east corners of a possible marching camp were seen in 1975.

BUXTON Derbyshire
SK 0673 *Spa and fort: Roman name* Aquae Arnemetiae
Buxton was the site of one of two health resorts in Roman Britain centred on natural warm water springs (the other was Bath). Little has been found of the resort; one of the baths was discovered in the seventeenth century and a second, about 9 × 4.5m (30 × 15ft) was found in the 1780s. The natural springs were probably discovered by the Romans when they built a fort at Buxton in the later first century, probably the AD 70s. This fort lay underneath Bath Street at the south end of the present town. The Roman road from Manchester to Littlechester (and Derby) crossed the road from Brough-on-Noe going south-west (Margary 710a and 713).

CAERMOTE Cumbria
NY 202368 *Fort*
A 3¾ acre (1.5ha) fort with a 6m (20ft) wide rampart was erected here in the Flavian period. Two entrances have been found, and in the north-east corner a quantity of timber post holes that may belong to a tower. A second, smaller fort was built much later in the north-west corner.

CAISTER-ON-SEA Norfolk
TG 5212 *Small town*
A small town was built here in the early second century at what was then the mouth of the Yare (the landscape has changed since Roman times). It began as a seaport from which the *civitas* capital of the Iceni, *Venta Icenorum* (Caistor St Edmund, just south of Norwich) was supplied. Sometime in the third century, Caister was surrounded by a stone wall, enclosing in a trapezoid plan some 9 acres (3.6ha). The wall was about 3m (10ft) thick, and sets of gates were inserted at intervals, including a south gateway flanked by two towers which had guardchambers. A military role, perhaps as a fort of the Saxon Shore, has been suggested for the town by some authorities, but investigations have so far failed to find evidence of military buildings inside the walled area. One building, however, was identified as a possible brothel.

CAISTOR Lincolnshire
TA 1101 *Small town*
Caistor was a small Roman town which was enclosed within a stone wall of the early fourth century. Bastions were added, fragments of one of which can still be seen today in Chapel Street. There has been some discussion about the role of the town: whether it was fortified as part of the defence of the coast against Saxon and Frankish raids in the third and fourth centuries or whether it was fortified because it was a centre for tax collection. Traces of the wall can still be seen.

CAISTOR ST EDMUND Norfolk
TG 2303 Civitas *capital of the Iceni: Roman name* Venta Icenorum
The foundation of this *civitas* capital is set against the stormy background of the Boudican revolt, a factor which may have played a part in the settlement's later development. It is at least possible that the site had been the headquarters, or near the headquarters, of the Icenian queen at the time of her revolt (cf Gallows Hill, Thetford).

The grid-like street plan was laid out c70, and aerial photographs suggest that the town was originally planned to be bigger than it actually grew to be. This, coupled with the apparent lack of public buildings from the earliest period of settlement, could be a reflection of the impoverished state of the *Iceni* after the Boudican rebellion and the severe retribution of Suetonius Paullinus upon the defeated tribe (see p 67). Timber buildings only have been found from this early period.

The first large-scale building programme was undertaken in the Antonine period. A *forum* with a colonnaded piazza measuring 30 × 30m (100 × 100ft) was built, with a *basilica* raised above the open area on the west side. The main hall measured 9 × 53m

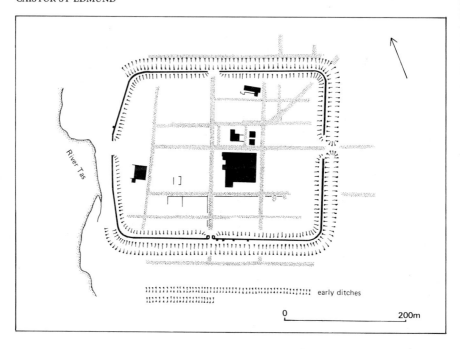

early ditches

0   200m

Caistor St Edmund showing the forum block in black (centre)

(30 × 177ft) and the plan of the building was fairly typical of a *basilica* of a *civitas* capital, although it lacked the usual range of offices at the rear. Another important public building, the baths, was also built in this period. The east end of the complex has been excavated, revealing the *frigidarium*, hypocausted *tepidarium* and a partly covered *palaestra*. The baths infer the existence of a sewerage system and water supply, indications of which have been observed in aerial photographs. The remains of two Romano-Celtic temples and a possible set of early earth defences date from the second century.

Sometime in the late second or early third century, the baths and the *forum* were destroyed by fire, and they were left derelict until the end of the third century. The rebuilding programme for the *forum* changed its plan, the east wing comprising a hall-like structure, and the north and south wings having two rooms projecting back centrally from the piazza. The fortifications were rebuilt in flint and brick during the course of the third century, and enclosed some 35 acres (14ha), which was smaller than the original area. The wall was banked up behind and ditched in front and carried two types of bastion, alternating between rectangular and semi-cylindical shapes. The south gate has been excavated, revealing an opening created by an in-turn in the curtain wall with a single tower flanked by two separate guardrooms.

The domestic buildings of the third century were comparatively simple, being largely wattle and daub structures. These seem to have been remarkably durable. One large house of wattle and daub with a bath suite appears to have remained unaltered right into the fifth century. This also shows the stability of the settlement, and the length of time that Roman life lingered on at Caistor. The end of Roman occupation is shrouded with controversy. A suggestion, based upon a group of skeletons found in one house, that a massacre brought about the demise of the capital is dubious. Certainly this group of people met violent deaths, but it is dangerous to extrapolate from this the fate of the entire population, especially since occupation carried on well into the fifth century.

CAMBRIDGE Cambridgeshire
TL 443592 *Small town*
A Claudian fort built soon after the conquest is postulated for the foundation of Cambridge as a Roman settlement, although this is not yet proved. Later in the first century a large rectangular enclosure, 60 × 30m (198 × 99ft), was constructed at the junction of the Sandy and Godmanchester roads. This was most probably a military installation, guarding the Cam valley and Icknield Way. The site would have been of strategic importance considering the presence of a river crossing as well as the road as a line of communication. No internal features have been recognised, but by AD70 rectangular wooden huts were spreading over the fort site. Two parallel streets about 30m (100ft) apart have been traced, but no masonry buildings or public works, except one possible shrine. Parts of a sepulchral monument and other religious monumental fragments, however, show that a number of large or public buildings did exist. Other evidence for the period 100–300 comes from pits, rubbish dumps, ditches and roads. There is also evidence of iron working and a local pottery industry. However, very little sign of the status of the town has been found. At the beginning of the fourth century Cambridge was fortified with a ditch, wall and bank complex enclosing a polygonal area of about 25 acres (10ha). The west gate has been located, but no bastions have been found. Settlement in the town intensified, but no really richly appointed buildings have been excavated. No trace of burning or destruction has been discovered, so Cambridge probably fell into decay or was abandoned towards the end of the fourth century.

CAMERTON Somerset
ST 6856 *Small town*
A small industrial town, which was not provided with a surrounding wall, flourished at Camerton in the third and fourth centuries. Traces of various buildings have been located, including small houses, a substantial villa house, a shrine and various factory buildings. Furnaces were discovered, some of them associated with iron and bronze work, and there was much evidence of pewter manufacture in the fourth century. It is clear that the town developed along a regular street grid. One interesting find was a kiln that may have been used for malting barley. There is also a hint that the site began as a military one.

CANTERBURY Kent
TR 1457 Civitas *capital of the Cantiaci:
Roman name* Durovernum Cantiacorum
Canterbury, the capital of the Cantiaci, stood at a meeting point of several important routes and commanded the best crossing point on the river Stour. A grid-based street pattern was laid out upon an Iron Age site soon after the invasions by Aulus Plautius, but timber buildings do not appear to have been replaced until the end of the first century. The most interesting feature revealed about the early settlement is that there were no earth ramparts. In fact, there were no defences at Canterbury at all until the flint and mortar walls of the late third century were constructed. The lack of fortifications perhaps points to the peaceful nature of the area and its comparatively easy 'Romanisation'.

The line of the walls has now almost certainly been proved to have been the same as the medieval fortifications. Some parts of Roman wall can be seen embedded in the medieval stonework. The width of the wall was up to 2.25m (7ft 6in) in parts, and it was banked with earth on the inside, with an exterior ditch. Some remains of internal and external interval towers have been traced, the latter being either bonded into the curtain wall or added later. All the gates, with the exception of the Riding Gate, seem to have been single, narrow-arched openings in the wall, the London Gate being only 2.5m (8ft) wide. The Riding Gate was a more substantial affair with a double carriageway and flanking towers.

These walls enclosed an area of 130 acres (53ha), in which excavations have revealed the existence of an affluent, well-organised

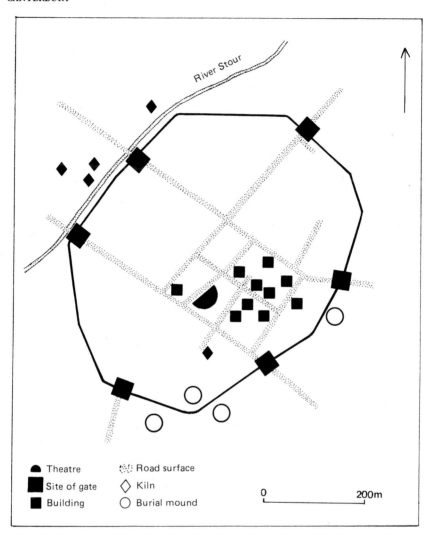

Theatre

Site of gate

Building

Road surface

Kiln

Burial mound

0   200m

Canterbury

community. Building operations earlier this century brought to light the piazza of the *forum* and a richly marbled public building. Two sets of baths have been discovered, the larger ones, now under St Margaret's Street, perhaps being a public complex. The domestic buildings excavated have been, on the whole, large and well equipped, some with courtyards and gardens and others with flint and mortar hypocausts. Particularly fine

mosaics and tessellated floors have been unearthed, for example those that can be seen at the Roman Pavement in Butchery Lane.

The most prominent of all Canterbury's public buildings was the theatre. Although fragmentary and difficult to interpret, the foundations show that a large, stone structure was built in the late second to early third century on the site of an original earth and timber building of the 80s. Neither of the theatres was aligned with the grid pattern of the streets, perhaps indicating that they were built on the site of an earlier structure (a temple or pre-Roman gathering place?).

The end of Roman Canterbury has aroused some debate. It is now thought that an abrupt but non-violent abandonment occurred towards the end of the fifth century. Recent excavations have shown that there was a general decline in standards in this period with the sewers silting up and buildings falling into disrepair. By the end of the sixth century evidence shows a repopulation, with Saxon dwellings being built in the open areas of the ruined Roman town.

CARDURNOCK Cumbria
NY 172595 *Military sites*
The most southerly military sites of the Cumbrian extension of Hadrian's Wall, north of Moricambe Bay, are Tower 4b, west of Cardurnock village, near Bowness on Solway, which had three phases of building (first in timber, then in stone), and Milefortlet 5, which is due south of the village. The milefortlet was almost obliterated during the Second World War to make room for an airfield. The milefortlet was about 53×43m (178×142ft), nearly three times larger than most of the other milefortlets along the extension scheme, and it was presumably built for special purposes, perhaps to accommodate a much larger unit, say, a century. The milefortlet was occupied over the second, third and fourth centuries, with some intervals, and in the fourth century was reduced in overall size.

CARISBROOKE Isle of Wight
SZ 485882 *Villa*
Part of a villa site, having mosaic and tesellated pavements, was discovered in the gardens of the vicarage in the late 1850s. It had been a walled courtyard villa, with an aisled farmhouse main dwelling of the third century, which had begun as a simple barn. This building had had *opus signinum* flooring. The building was enlarged and made more residential by the addition of a bath suite in the south-west corner. The decoration inside included interesting painted dado, and mosaic and tessellated flooring.

CARKIN MOOR North Yorkshire
NZ 1608 *Fort*
A 2 acre (0.8ha) auxiliary fort was located on Stainmore by aerial observation.

CARLISLE Cumbria
NY 3955 *Fort and probable* civitas *capital of the Carvetii:* Roman name Luguvalium Carvetiorum
Carlisle stood at the west end of the Stanegate road, commanding a major route into Scotland and a crossing point of the river Caldew. Positioned on a low hill, with the river running round its west and south-west sides, the site was well situated in terms of communications and control over the surrounding area.

The first Roman occupation of the site probably dates to around AD75. A fort with some sort of legionary garrison is suggested by the presence of tiles stamped with the monogram LEG IX. Recent excavations have traced the existence of two separate forts. A timber platform of 11sq m (40sq ft) was probably the base for a rampart: pottery evidence suggests a Flavian date. Other features identified in work on the north-west edge of the Roman town include a ditch with what appears to have been a plank bridge across it. Nearby was a wattle and timber wall. This does not appear to have been part of a rampart for it would have blocked passage from the bridge. Possibly it was part of an industrial area in a supply depot. Numerous fragments of worked leather from the same level support this industrial interpretation. The south gate of the timber fort has also been excavated. The towers projected behind the turf and timber rampart and were carried on six posts. The excavated tower had a guardroom with wattle walls.

Little evidence of the later probable *civitas* capital of the Carvetii has been discovered. A stone building of about AD200, with a hypocaust in one room, has been identified. A tombstone and a milestone mention Carlisle as *civitas* capital and these date it to no earlier than about 260. The town was of considerable size – up to 70 acres (28ha). There appear to have been no defences on the north side and the lines of others are in doubt, although St Cuthbert in the seventh century noted the walls as still being massive. A street grid is indicated and some stone bases and columns suggest the presence of public buildings. Remains of a hypocausted building, possibly a bath suite, were found in the eighteenth century. Inscriptions help with evidence for religious life in Roman Carlisle, including dedications to Hercules, Mars Ocelus and a Romano-Celtic combination of deities. Apart from these meagre suggestions, the later development of the *civitas* capital remains shrouded in doubt.

Carraw see **Milecastle 32**

CARRAWBURGH Northumberland
NY 859711 *Fort on Hadrian's Wall: Roman name* Brocolitia
In the well of a shrine excavated at Carrawburgh fort 13,487 coins, including gold and silver varieties, were found in the 1870s. Dedicated to the worship of a water goddess,

The *mithraeum* at Carrawburgh

Coventina, the shrine remains about 75m (250ft) from the south-west edge of the fort, beside the southern rampart of the Vallum. (Many of the coins were stolen, but the remainder are in the museum at Chesters fort.) And 45m (150ft) or so due south of the fort lies the substantial carcass of a temple of Mithras built in the early third century, modified several times before destruction in the fourth century. A model of the temple in its full glory is at the Museum of Antiquities at Newcastle upon Tyne.

Those are the main relics of Carrawburgh fort, itself an unusual structure in that it was built in the 130s over the Vallum which was levelled and filled in to accommodate it. Curiously, the stretches of Vallum leading to each side of the fort are among the best along the whole of Hadrian's Wall. The fort is smaller than most in the Hadrianic scheme, 3½ acres (1.4ha) for an *ala* of cavalry. Little remains today beyond its platform and the ditch and rampart, though the positions of the fort gates are clear. Recent excavations revealed parts of the *principia*, barrack blocks

running east to west and traces of granaries. An earlier excavation had unearthed the bath house.

Carrawburgh was built to 'plug the gap between Chesters and Housesteads', which explains why it was raised over an already completed Vallum. The Wall itself had been finished some time before and the fort was let into its structure.

CARSINGTON Derbyshire
SK 250524 *Settlement*

A small settlement of roughly second- to fourth-century occupation was identified here very recently, centred on what is Shiningfield Farm. Finds included traces of timber buildings, some belonging to the early second century, with evidence of lead working, and stone buildings from the end of the second century. Further south, at SK 249516, an interesting rectangular rural building, with a central room flanked by rooms at each end, was identified. The main room had two hearths; the room at the north showed signs of having been heated via stone-lined channels. The date of this building is not yet established, but was probably later than the settlement.

CARVORAN Northumberland
NY 665657 *Fort: Roman name* Magna

Carvoran fort is part of the Hadrian's Wall frontier, but it was not actually built into the Wall. It lies about 225m (250yd) south. The first fort was probably erected in Agricola's time. The famous Carvoran *modius*, or bronze measure for official testing, found on the site in 1915, bore the name of Emperor Domitian (later erased after the emperor's assassination). This is now in the Museum at Chesters fort. The fort lies on the Stanegate and there was certainly a fort as part of that system, of Trajanic period, though no remains have been found of the period. The site was reoccupied as part of the Hadrianic scheme, when it was given stone walls and covered some 3½ acres (1.4ha). The fort was garrisoned by the first cohort of Hamian archers (from Syria) for a time, who built the walling. There is not a great deal to see today, though many individual relics of its

occupation have been found, such as building stones, inscriptions, artefacts, altars, tombstones and a most interesting slab containing a metrical hymn dedicated to the Virgin of the Zodiac. The fort was still in occupation in the third century.

Carvoran see also **Milecastle 46**

CASTLE DYKES North Yorkshire
SE 2975 *Villa*

One of the most northerly of villas, Castle Dykes, near North Stainly, was inside a ditched enclosure (hence, perhaps, its name). The plan has not been fully discovered, but appears to have been one building divided into accommodation for two families. Two bath suites have been noted and fragments of wall painting were recovered.

CASTLEFORD West Yorkshire
SE 427256 *Fort* and vicus: *Roman name* Lagentium

A fort has been suspected at Castleford for a long time, and during excavations in the 1970s led by Philip Mayes (of Sandal Castle fame) defences were discovered, in some places very close to the present-day surface. These were shown to relate not to the fort but to what must have been annexes to the fort, including one that contained the bath house (which has been excavated). Among the quantities of debris were tiles with stamps of Legio IX and one of Cohors IV *Breucorum* (which served in several parts of the north of Britain in the first and second centuries). Several buildings were excavated in what seems to have been the *vicus* outside the (as-yet-undiscovered) fort. Among these buildings were an iron workshop, some retail shops, an inn and a glass-blower's workshop.

Castle Nick see **Milecastle 39**

CASTLESHAW Greater Manchester
SD 9909 *Fort*

An Agricolan fort of just over 3 acres (1.2ha) here had a natural water course in front of the north-east rampart, obviating the need for a ditch. A smaller fortlet, of about ³/₅ acre (0.2ha), was built inside in the Trajanic or Hadrianic period. Part of the road from the fort towards the fort at Slack (Margary 712) was identified in 1970. A hypocaust was found at the site in the 1920s.

CASTLESTEADS Cumbria
NY 5163 *Fort on Hadrian's Wall: Roman name* Camboglanna

Castlesteads began as an earth and timber structure in the original Hadrianic scheme. It was later converted to stone. It covered 3¾ acres (1.5ha). There are some traces of fort ditching. The outside bath house was located in the eighteenth century. The fort was not actually on the Wall itself but about 200m (220yd) or so behind, on a knoll, so that the Vallum to the south had to be deflected. Castlesteads housed infantry for a time, and at a later date is recorded as accommodating cavalry units. The fort is one of the names on the famous Rudge Cup (see p 105).

CASTOR Cambridgeshire
TL 1297 *Pottery centre*

The Castor area was the centre of an extensive and well-organised pottery industry sprawling over the Nene valley (which now gives its name to the productions from the area) around Peterborough. Some of the products were coarse ware, and the industry began to develop on a large scale in the later second century, lasting for almost two centuries. Products included flagons, bag-shaped beakers, Castor boxes (with round lids), in white to grey-white fabric, and a range of goods in colour-coated ware, the shades spanning orange to brown. During this period the Nene valley industries also produced some imitation Samian ware. Excavations in the region have revealed kilns, factory buildings, hearths and so forth, suggestive of intense industry – one might say, a Roman 'Black Country'.

At TL 125985, beneath modern Castor village, an interesting villa has long been known. It was generally called the *praetorium*, but was more civilian in layout than the name suggests. Ranges of buildings, some detached, formed three sides of a large square which was a courtyard. The north side contained a variant of a winged corridor building with many rooms, some heated, some with mosaics, some with painted

plaster. There was a bath house on the south-west side. The villa probably began in the mid third century.

CATSGORE Somerset
ST 506265 *Settlement*

Catsgore, near Somerton, is about 3 miles north-west of the late period second *civitas* capital of the Durotriges, *Lindinis* (Ilchester). There, an agricultural settlement developed in the late first century alongside the Roman road (Margary 51), and its first buildings were rectangular and circular timber structures. The settlement grew, and in the second century the first stone buildings appeared, and this was followed by more building in the third century. Structures included cattle byres, farm buildings with corn driers, a building with an apsidal end, and residential houses, some with tessellated flooring. The area of the settlement was about 10 acres (4ha). It was systematically excavated during the 1970s and the evidence is that the settlement declined rapidly after the combined barbarian assault on southern Britain of 367. About ½ mile from the settlement was a villa which is not yet fully understood.

CATTERICK North Yorkshire
SE 2299 *Fort and later town: Roman name* Cataractonium

Like Corbridge in its later phases, Catterick did not follow the pattern of development nor display the elements usually associated with a Roman town, in its strictest sense. Excellently positioned on a spur above the river Swale, Catterick commanded not only the river crossing, but also the important route north through Swaledale.

The first signs of Roman occupation are those of an Agricolan fort of about AD78–80. The remains of an outer defence ditch, a bath house and possibly a military tannery have been traced. This site appears to have been evacuated c120, and it is presumed that any associated *vicus* would have also been abandoned. Curiously, after the evacuation, a *mansio* with a portico was established in the area of the bath house. The baths were altered and enlarged to serve the *mansio*. An inscribed stone implies that the fort was built for, or at least by, legionaries.

In about AD160 the site was reoccupied and the *mansio* was demolished at the end of the second century. The *vicus* developed to the south of the site. Catterick is notable for the apparent lack of destruction associated with the troubles of 196. Although soon after this date the fort was again evacuated, the *vicus* continued to be occupied into the third century, by which time a start had been made on the renovation of the bath house. The town had no defences or street pattern, however, until the beginning of the fourth century. The planning included very regular *insulae*, an unusually late development for this type of settlement. The defences comprised a ditch and stone wall, about 2.25m (7½ft) thick, and had no rampart or bastions. They appear to be a hotch-potch of several

ideas of how to fortify: the fourth-century style was in the process of being developed. An area of 15½ acres (6.3ha) was enclosed.

The fourth century saw major rebuilding. In c370 the nature of the buildings and their alignments changed. One *insula* of shops was blocked on its street side, whilst two large buildings with courtyards were created by amalgamating several houses into one unit. One of these had a gate with an archway of 2.75m (9ft), as well as a new hypocausted room. It has been suggested that these changes could be attributable to a military reoccupation of Catterick during Theodosius' reorganisation of defences. Were the two courtyard buildings a *principia*

Restored, decorated second-century Roman wall plaster at Catterick (*The Yorkshire Museum*)

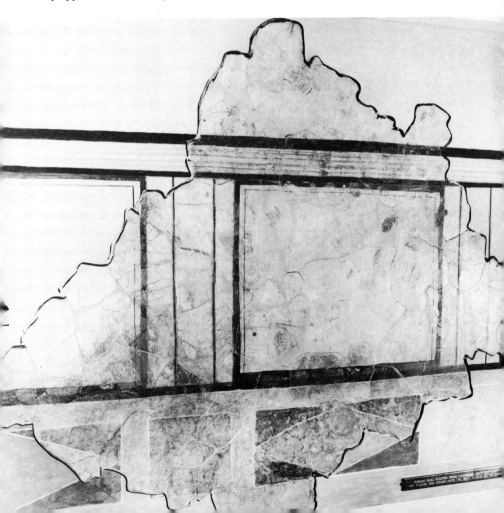

and *praetorium*? The blocked-in *insula* may, if this is the case, have been a conversion to a barrack building. Certainly a military presence is indicated by the finds of weaponry dating from after 370.

CATTLE HILL Somerset
ST 667298 *Villa*
An examination of the villa at Cattle Hill, Bratton Seymour, has revealed a number of building phases, all between the third and fourth centuries. Buildings were positioned on two or three sides of a cobbled courtyard. Some walls were wattle and daub.

CATTYBROOK Avon
ST 593834 *Settlement*
A small agricultural and domestic settlement was excavated in advance of quarrying at Cattybrook, near Almondsbury, in the mid 1970s. There seem to have been two phases of occupation: the last quarter of the first century and the first half of the third century. The remains of several buildings were investigated, including rectangular workshops and barns and a T-shaped corn drier.

CAVE'S INN Warwickshire
SP 535795 *Settlement: Roman name* Tripontium
Cave's Inn, near Churchover, lay beside Watling Street. The site has been heavily quarried, and it has not been easy for excavating teams to assess it. Evidence of military presence (perhaps a fort) in the first century lay beneath and beside a later civilian settlement which may have become a small town. Remains of what is considered a *mansio* have been found, and a third-century bath house was also located.

Cawfields see **Milecastle 42**

CAWTHORN North Yorkshire
SE 7890 *Practice camps*
Cawthorn is the site of at least four practice camps, or similar structures, put up by the Romans as part of peacetime exercises. Two of the four were practice forts, generally known as Cawthorn A and Cawthorn D. A is a long structure, with a roughly semi-

hexagonal north end. This had a ditch, rampart, palisade and four gates. Excavations inside exposed ovens and water tanks. Cawthorn D was almost square, lay next to Cawthorn A (and its south-east corner cut across the west side of A) and had double-ditching all round, with gates at the west, south and east. Cawthorn A is thought to have been erected at the end of the first century and D sometime during the reign of Trajan. Both were built by vexillations of Legio IX stationed at the legionary fortress in York. The other two structures are thought to have been temporary labour camps used by the men building the A and D forts.

CHALK Kent
TQ 678730 *Villa*
On what is now Readers Estate at Chalk, near Gravesend, there was a villa consisting of one large hall-type building with cellars, and a bath house about 40m (45yd) to the west. The bath house was excavated in the early 1970s in advance of development of the site. Fragments of painted plaster and window glass were found.

CHANCTONBURY RING West Sussex
TQ 139121 *Hillfort*
Chanctonbury Ring is famous as the site of an early Iron Age hillfort. The hillfort was taken over by the Romans, probably during the first years of occupation (c43–50), and they built there a temple. Excavations at Chanctonbury in the late 1970s showed that the temple had been in use for most of the occupation. The shrine was of polygonal plan. The Iron Age defences marked the *temenos* boundary.

Chapel House see **Milecastle 9**

Chapelhouse see **Milecastle 47**

CHARLBURY Oxfordshire
SP 3119 *Villa*
Investigations over a wide area in the Charlbury region in the early 1980s located a courtyard villa. It is hoped that more information may emerge in the next years.

CHARLTON KINGS Gloucestershire
SO 973186 *Settlement*
Remains of a number of buildings on a natural platform of about ½ acre (0.2ha) in area at Vineyard's Farm were examined in 1979–80. The site was occupied from the second to the fourth centuries. Finds included a corn drier, cobbled surfacing and part of a limestone column.

CHARTERHOUSE Somerset
ST 507564 *Industrial site and small town*
Charterhouse-on-Mendip, near Cheddar, is an interesting site that was associated with lead mining from the earliest days of the Roman occupation. By about AD50, lead was being produced and transported across country to ports (especially Bitterne) for shipment to Europe. The mining operations were controlled by the army, at first with Legio II (lead pigs inscribed LEG II have been found). A fort was built near the mining area, probably in the Claudian period, and it appears to have been about 3 acres (1.2ha). It remained occupied for about a century. Near the fort, a civilian settlement grew up, which eventually became a town with a street grid and with various civic facilities including, to the west, an amphitheatre, the banking of which can still be seen. Sometime in the later second century the mining operations were handed over to private contractors or, equally probably, to local government operation and control.

CHEDDAR Somerset
ST 460530 *Metal-working settlement*
A settlement associated with metal working has been investigated here. It appears to have been in use at the end of the first and beginning of the second centuries. The settlement was fortified by ditching and scarping.

CHEDWORTH Gloucestershire
SP 052134 *Villa*
Chedworth villa is one of the best preserved of Britain's excavated Roman monuments. It lies beside a spring and was only 3 miles from the Fosse Way. The villa was originally built in the mid second century, but underwent a series of alterations which made it an exceptionally well-appointed building with various unusual refinements. The villa buildings consisted of three main ranges set round a courtyard which was divided into inner and outer parts by a wall. The north and south wings projected beyond this wall to flank the outer courtyard. The main set of rooms was in the west wing and included a magnificent *triclinium* (dining room) with an anteroom that had heated flooring, painted plastered walls and a fine mosaic of Bacchus and the four seasons. Also in the west wing was a set of Turkish-style baths with a dressing room, *tepidarium, caldarium,* where the hypocaust *pilae* are still visible, and a *frigidarium* with a cold bath 1.25m (4ft) deep and lined with *opus signinum.* Contemporary with the early building period was another set of Turkish-style baths in the north-west corner of the north wing. These were later remodelled and finally rebuilt entirely as a sauna-type bath with a *laconicum* where bathers underwent subjection to intense dry heat before plunging into a cold bath in a nearby room. This room actually contained three cold baths, two for slow immersion and one acting as a plunge bath.

The north wing also contained several heated principal rooms. The south wing appears to have been a range of service rooms, with a kitchen in which the base of a large circular oven is still visible, a latrine with an elaborate sewer system, and what is thought to have been the steward's office. The east end of the south wing is unexcavated, but probably contained storerooms and servants' quarters. Finally, in the fourth century a large new dining suite was added to the east end of the north wing. This included a kitchen and a very large dining room heated by a hypocaust which incorporated channels as well as *pilae.* To the north-west of the villa complex a *nymphaeum* housed a spring. This small shrine had an octagonal central pool which can still be seen. Chi-Rho symbols on flagstones from the *nymphaeum* suggest that the shrine was ultimately 'Christianised'.

CHELMSFORD Essex
TL 7006 *Town, perhaps failed* civitas *capital: Roman name* Caesaromagus
Excavations at Chelmsford have been neces-

313

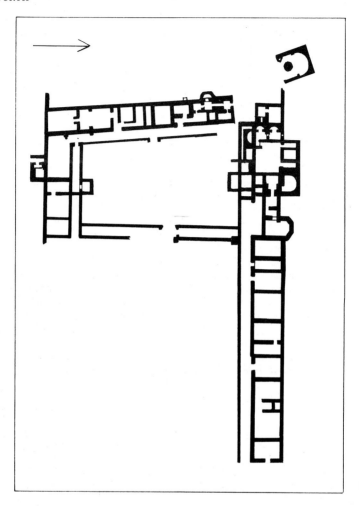

Chedworth. Plan of the villa: damp heat baths at top centre, dry heat baths at top right

sarily fragmentary owing to the built-up nature of the areas thought once to have been occupied by the Roman town, south of the river Chelmer under the modern suburbs. What has been discovered, however, points to an unusual pattern of development. It has been suggested that the town was originally intended as a *civitas* capital for the Trinovantes, but that it failed to establish itself owing to economic competition from the *colonia* at Colchester and from London.

An early fort is indicated at Chelmsford by the presence of Claudian coins, pottery and military equipment, but since occupation was probably only for a short period the foundation of an associated *vicus* is unlikely. Sometime after the Boudican revolt (AD61), a second, Flavian fort was established a little to the south of the first settlement. From this period remains of a baths complex survive, probably rebuilt on the site of those of the first fort. The first phase of construction was of timber between AD65 and 75. This construction could have been associated with a building programme designed to establish

314

Chelmsford as a *civitas* capital. The baths were later converted to stone in the mid second century, and at this stage could have been part of a *mansio*. They measured 64×65m (214×217ft) and had a central courtyard.

Levels of domestic occupation have been recorded from the first to the fifth century in the Moulsham Street area, and there is evidence of destruction by fire at the end of the second century, followed by a slow recovery. A recent rescue excavation has revealed that building methods remained fairly static, with rectangular huts of wattle and daub being built as late as the third century. No stone fortifications have been found (although they may yet be discovered) and even the sections of clay rampart fronted by a 3m (10ft) deep ditch that have been found were soon levelled after their construction in the late second century. Occupation seems to have continued into the fifth century: signs have been found in both domestic contexts and in the temple north of Rochford Road. This was built c325, was octagonal, apsidal and had a portico with a porch on the south-east side. Whatever the status of Chelmsford, Roman life was well established and continued to a relatively late date.

CHESTER Cheshire
SJ 4066 *Legionary fortress and* vicus: *Roman name* Deva
Recent excavation has added considerably to our knowledge of the internal layout and structural history of Chester. Standing on the tidal estuary of the river Dee, at a crossing point, the legionary fortress, together with that at Caerleon, formed the hub of the Roman command in Wales.

We now know that there were three phases of timber construction at Chester. The first was a fort, probably built in the late 50s. From the 70s, when the fort was enlarged into a legionary fortress, the site was occupied by Legio II *Adiutrix*. The remains of a timber colonnaded *principia* have been dated to this phase. The final timber phase dates to the late 80s. There is evidence for a second timber *principia* and barracks, which

Part of the amphitheatre at Chester, just outside the fortress on the south-east corner (*Graham Sumner*)

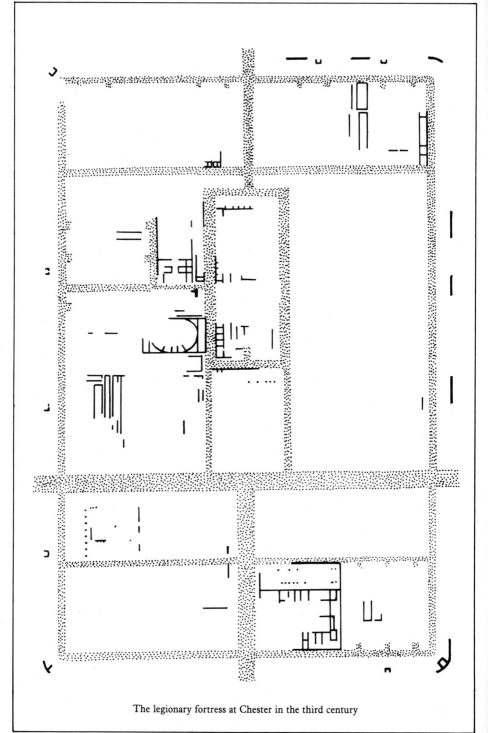

The legionary fortress at Chester in the third century

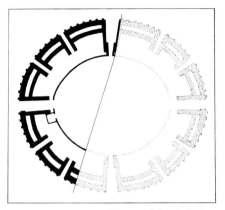

The amphitheatre at Chester. The dark line represents exposed remains

have traces of preserved plaster and daub. The defences during this early period were of turf and timber with ditch and rampart. They enclosed an area of about 60 acres (24ha).

One surprising discovery was the unusually early use of stonework in the construction of the fortress. The *praetorium*, north of the *principia*, appears to have had no timber predecessor, and was laid out in stone in the Flavian period. The earliest attempt to build appears to have been unsuccessful, but problems were solved, and a courtyard building 64m (212ft) from east to west with a hypocausted room and an anteroom with an *opus signinum* floor have been found. Two Greek inscriptions by doctors have led to speculation about whether this structure was in fact a hospital. Its position and form, however, make it seem more likely to have been the administrative area of the *praetorium*.

Other early stone buildings include a bath complex with covered exercise hall inside the fort's defences dating from c79, according to a marble inscription, and a *principia* over 90m (300ft) long with an *aedes* and strongroom probably of the early second century. The defences were altered with the addition of a stone wall at the turn of the first to second century.

Later periods saw much alteration and redevelopment of the stone fortress. There appears to have been widespread rebuilding in the first two decades of the second

century. Later, c200, the defences were refurbished and internal structures rebuilt. It is thought that the garrison was at full strength in this period, probably in response to the troubles of AD166–7. Towards the end of the third century, there is evidence of intentional demolition and overpaving at the fortress. The reason why remains a mystery, especially since the fortification wall was rebuilt in the late third and early fourth centuries. Unusually, no bastions were added to the fortifications during the fourth century. The *praetorium* and *principia* were occupied at this time and new buildings of timber erected (eg one at Goss Street dated to 340–50).

Comparatively little is known about the extramural settlement at Chester. Excavations have been carried out in specific areas so it is difficult to interpret the site as a whole. Certainly early structures were of timber, later replaced with stone in the case of conjectured 'official' buildings such as the *mansio*. The impressive amphitheatre to the south-east of the fort (substantial remains can be seen today) was also originally of timber. This must have been a temporary measure, however, for a coin of Vespasian puts the date of the stone construction at AD80. It was of sandstone and measured 104×86m (345×286ft) on its long and short axes. More excavation is vital for conclusions to be made about the structural history of the *vicus*.

CHESTERFIELD Derbyshire
SK 384711 *Fort and industrial site*
Two successive forts were located in excavations at Chesterfield in the mid 1970s. The sequence now seems to have been as follows. An early Claudian fort, one or two buildings and some ditching of which were found, was replaced by Agricola with a second fort of different dimensions on a different alignment. Annexes appear to have been added. The second fort was abandoned in about 120–30, and there is evidence of some industrial activity subsequently on the site.

CHESTERHOLM Northumberland
NY 7766 *Fort and* vicus: *Roman name* Vindolanda
The fort at Chesterholm lay close to the

317

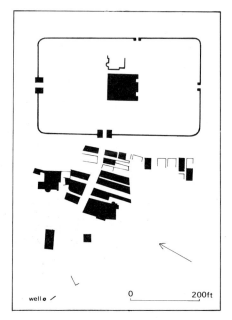

Chesterholm: fort and vicus

well o ╱

0   200ft

strategically important road, the Stanegate, on a plateau overlooking the confluence of two burns. Extensive excavations at this remarkably well-preserved site have established a sequence of stages of development of the fort and its associated *vicus*.

The first fort was identified by chance in the 1971–72 excavations, under the remains of the *vicus*. The fort dates to the early AD80s. It had an earth rampart and ditch and covered 3½ acres (1.4ha). There then followed a series of larger timber-built forts, all of about 8 acres (3.2ha). A workshop has been traced, but the layout of the forts and even the direction in which they faced are uncertain. The difference in size from the first fort could reflect an enlargement of the garrison – perhaps a change to cavalry? These forts span the years c90–125, the last fort being the one which formed part of the Hadrianic Wall scheme.

A period of abandonment of the fort ended c163 when a new stone fort was established. Associated with this fort was a *vicus*. Interesting features of the first *vicus* include a corridor house previously unknown on the

frontier in which was found, mysteriously buried, a fine bronze military standard. Four large structures were traced, unusually surrounded by a clay rampart. Three of the buildings were probably married quarters. The fourth is thought to have been a *mansio* and was comfortably appointed, with a small bath suite, a servants' block, stables, a kitchen, a dining room and a latrine. Also outside the fort, and dating originally from this period, is the well-preserved military bath house. Situated about 22.5m (25yd) outside the fort, its main features, including the hypocaust and hot plunge bath, are still visible. Its west wall stands to a height of 2.25m (7ft) in some parts.

Another period of abandonment followed between the years 245 and 270. Then, a second stone fort was established c270 and a second *vicus* developed outside the rectangular enclosure. The buildings, with the exception of one, did not follow the lines of the first *vicus*. The settlement was a jumble of small rectangular structures clustered around roads and tracks. A few roughly rectangular strip houses to the south of the baths belong to this *vicus*.

The fourth-century *principia* was a very fine building and is remarkably well

Chesterholm. The Vindolanda standard

318

preserved. It had a small courtyard, a large cross-hall, armouries, an *aedes* (where the regimental standards were kept) and a sunken pit for the safekeeping of cash. All these features are still visible. After about 367, major alterations were carried out. A latrine was added to the *principia* and a heated office inserted into one of the administrative rooms. The north and west gates of the fourth century have been investigated and shown to have had single carriageways and projecting guardrooms. By about 370 the second *vicus* was virtually abandoned, but the military presence is attested up to about 400.

CHESTER-LE-STREET Durham

NZ 276514 *Fort: Roman name* Concangium
The 6 acre (2.4ha) fort here may have begun as a first-century timber and earth structure. Early defences were discovered in the 1970s. The site was reoccupied in the Antonine period, but it was in the early third century that a major conversion to stone was carried out. This included a stone defence wall, a bath house which received some improvements soon after the first works, and an aqueduct to bring water into the fort. The *praetorium*, also built of stone, was later altered. Very much later still, probably mid fourth century, part of the *praetorium* was changed into use as metal workshops.

CHESTERS Northumberland

NY 912702 *Fort on Hadrian's Wall: Roman name* Cilurnum
The fort at Chesters held a very important strategic position, guarding the western approach to the North Tyne bridge. The fort lay 5½ miles from that at Haltonchesters, and was joined into the fabric of the Wall on two sides. About a third of the fort projected beyond the north side of the Wall. The fort was built after the original phase of construction of the Wall, and the ditch fronting the Wall had to be filled in to level the site for further development. Chesters was probably initially built for cavalry, although later, under Commodus, the second *ala* of Asturians was stationed there. The fort covered a rectangular area of 5¾ acres (2.3ha), which was surrounded by a wall about 1.5m (5ft) thick. Of the defences, two interval towers and an angle tower remain exposed, and several of the six gateways have been investigated. The east gate is

The strong room in the *principia* at Chesters

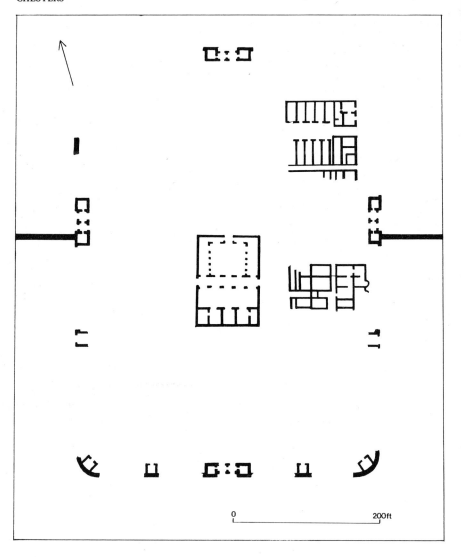

Chesters. Plan of fort: *principia* in centre, and at right of it, commandant's house, with its bath suite. Buildings in north-east are barrack blocks

particularly well preserved, with walls of its guardchambers standing up to twelve courses high.

Inside the defences a centrally positioned *principia* has been located. This had a courtyard with a portico and a *basilica* with a monumental doorway. A raised dais stood at the west end of the *basilica*. Other rooms identified adjoining the *basilica* include the *aedes* (or regimental chapel) where the standards were kept, a pay room and under this a subterranean strongroom. To the east of the *principia* lay three blocks of buildings, one of which was probably the commanding officer's house. This building had hypocausts added after its initial construction. The easternmost block was probably the commanding officer's bath house, built over

320

The stoke hole for the hot dry room (*laconicum*) at the bath house at Chesters fort on Hadrian's Wall (*Author*)

The latrine at the bath house at Chesters fort on Hadrian's Wall (*Author*)

the site of an earlier set of baths. The suite included a pair of cold baths as well as a *tepidarium* and a *caldarium* with an apse. To the north of the central buildings lay a street with barrack blocks to its east and west. The blocks were divided into rooms fronted by verandahs and probably housed sixty-four men apiece. Larger rooms at the ends of the blocks nearest the ramparts were probably designed as living quarters for the decurions.

Outside the fort, the remains of the legionary bath house have been excavated. This had a large dressing room, 13.5×9m (45×30ft), with seven niches at one end, probably used as lockers for bathers' clothes. A latrine adjoined the dressing room. In the *frigidarium* a base of a laver used for cold water douching is visible, as well as two cold baths, the larger being the earlier. The baths were complex, with a *laconicum* (a room with dry heat rather than steam) as well as two *tepidaria* and a *caldarium* with two hot baths. Near the bath house the foundations of the western abutment of the Tyne bridge can be seen. Also found were the remains of a large *vicus* associated with the fort. The later history of the fort is vague, but there are some traces of civilian occupation from the fourth century onwards.

Chesters see also **Turret 27a**

CHESTERTON Staffordshire
ST 832489 *Fort*
An early fort was built at Chesterton in Staffordshire (not to be confused with Chesterton in Warwickshire), about 1½ miles north-west of Newcastle-under-Lyme. It was between 3 and 4 acres (1.2–1.6ha), and had a double-ditch system, the inner ditch cut into bed rock. The rampart was of sandstone core, revetted with turf and laced with timber. The inner ditch was later filled. The fort was probably built in the early 70s.

CHESTERTON-ON-FOSSE
Warwickshire SP 3459
Small town
Chesterton was a small, walled Roman town. Not much is known of the site, but excavations have suggested a straggling settlement rather than a planned, compact town. It was less than 10 acres (4ha) in area.

CHEW GREEN Northumberland
NT 787084 *Temporary camps and fort*
A complex and impressive group of temporary camps and a fort are situated on the slope of Chew Green as it leads down into

the river Coquet, beside Dere Street. There are three camps: I, probably Agricolan, almost square, 19 acres (7.7ha); II, a rectangular camp lying across the west end of I, with six entrances protected by *titula*, probably of Antonine origin; and III, a rhomboid camp with four entrances protected by internal *claviculae*, erected inside the old camp I. On the north-east wall of the original camp I a small fortlet with a triple-ditch was built, with two annexes opening on to Dere Street. It is not so rare to find such complexes in Roman Britain, but the Chew Green site is remarkable for the preservation of the ramparting, and its complexity is heightened by remnants of medieval earthworks squashed in between and cutting across the site.

CHICHESTER West Sussex

SU 8604 Civitas *capital of the Regnenses: Roman name* Noviomagus Regnensium
Chichester was a new foundation, as its name *Noviomagus* suggests, and it did not have a native settlement as its predecessor. It became the centre of government for the client king, Cogidubnus, and later the *civitas* capital of the Regnenses. Recent excavations have revealed that the earliest Roman occupation was military. Timber buildings have been traced, but this had come to an end by AD47. Expansion then occurred and a slow process of 'Romanisation' began, culminating in the elevation of Chichester to the status of *civitas* capital between AD75 and 85, after the death of Cogidubnus. Before this, there is an indication that a street plan had been established and the centre had been levelled and gravelled in readiness for public buildings. A dedication to Nero (54–68) implies that at least one public building or statue was already in existence.

In the last years of the first century the street grid was firmly established and the *forum, basilica*, public baths and amphitheatre installed. Shops and houses of the first and second centuries were mainly built of timber and clay, but information about the interior is scanty, even for the masonry buildings. The *forum* probably lay at the intersection of two of the main streets. A fragment of wall 2m (6ft) high could be part of the early *basilica*. A black and white mosaic floor was possibly part of the decoration of the bath complex. The amphitheatre stood outside the south-east gate and was built between AD70 and 90.

At the end of the second century, defences

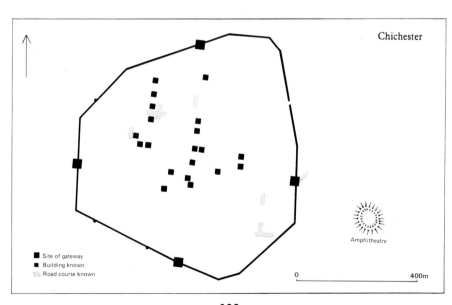

Chichester

Amphitheatre

■ Site of gateway
■ Building known
꙳ Road course known

0   400m

were built round Chichester, comprising an earth rampart and two ditches. The four main gates were probably of masonry. Early in the third century the rampart was cut back to receive a masonry wall of coursed flints, 2.5m (8ft) wide at the base. The apparent lack of urgency in the building of the fortifications suggests that civic pride was a greater motivation than defence against enemies. The gates were probably flanked with towers at this time.

The prosperity of the third and fourth centuries is demonstrated by apparent alterations to the public buildings and the indication from a 1m (3ft) inscribed base that a column to Jupiter was erected in the *forum*. Knowledge of the domestic buildings in this period is unfortunately fragmentary, although one courtyard house with a tessellated floor was occupied until the end of the fourth century. There is also evidence of industrial activity in the form of a lined pit with a deposit of fuller's earth, indicating a fuller's establishment, and from an earlier, second-century context, crucibles and unfinished brooches pointing to a bronzesmith's. Towards the end of the fourth century, possibly in the wake of Theodosius' reorganisation (see p 154), external bastions were added to the fortifications. The ditches were recut at the same time, to put them in the firing line from the tops of the bastions.

The final fate of Roman Chichester remains a mystery. The defensive ditches became clogged with rubbish and scatters of sherds suggest that occupation lingered well into the fifth century.

CHIGNALL ST JAMES Essex
TL 6610 *Villa*
An interesting courtyard villa was identified from the air in the mid 1970s. The overall area of the rectangle occupied by three sides of buildings was about 47 × 57m (155 × 188ft). There is some suggestion that the villa consisted of more than one residence. To the west of the west wing of the main structure, a building was found which may have been a bath house. Other buildings also located, together with traces of a strip field system, indicate an important agricultural settlement centred on the villa.

CHILGROVE West Sussex
SU 8211 *Villa*
A villa at Cross Roads Field, Brick Kiln Farm, has been investigated in recent years, notably between 1969 and 1976. It consisted of a courtyard flanked on three sides, with associated farm buildings including a military-type granary and a third- to fourth-century aisled stockbuilding, about 30 × 15m (100 × 50ft). The aisled building had extra rooms added to the south.

CHILSWELL Berkshire
SP 4903 *Building*
A building was discovered during field surveying at Chilswell, near Cumnor. It had an *opus signinum* floor and some painted plaster walls; remains of box-flue tiles indicated some heating. The excavators have dated the structure to the second to third centuries.

CHILVERS COTON Warwickshire
SP 342893 *Pottery kilns*
A tile and pottery kiln site of several kilns was examined in the late 1960s at Chilvers Coton, Arbury, to the south-west of Nuneaton.

CHURCHILL HOSPITAL Oxfordshire
SP 5405 *Extensive potteries*
Among the better known types of pottery manufactured in Roman Britain were the Oxfordshire wares. They were produced on the outskirts of the present city of Oxford, on an increasingly extensive scale so that examples of them are found in many parts of Roman Britain. By the fourth century, these wares had become one of the major wares in the province. A number of kiln sites are known. Several kilns and associated structures have been excavated in the grounds of Churchill Hospital, at New Headington, to the south of Oxford. These kilns had produced *mortaria* in both the second and third centuries, some in an orange fabric, and also flagons and beakers in fine, hard cream fabric. The site also produced parchment ware, so called from its white powdery fabric with pink core and red or brown paint decor. The workshops were of two shapes: circular and rectangular. The

potteries were still producing in the early fifth century.

CIRENCESTER Gloucestershire
SP 0201 Civitas *capital of the Dobunni: Roman name* Corinium Dobunnorum

Roman Cirencester lay at a meeting point of two great roads, Ermine Street and the Fosse Way. The army arrived in the area by about AD44 and an earth and timber fort of 30 acres (12ha) was erected at Cirencester by about AD50. This fort was soon evacuated and a second fort erected nearby in about 60, which was abandoned by the late 70s when the settlement was raised to the status of *civitas* capital of the Dobunni. A grid pattern of streets was laid over the site of the early *vicus*.

Although only a *civitas* capital rather than a *colonia*, the excavations at Cirencester have revealed it to have been remarkably wealthy in terms of public buildings. It also had a very high standard of domestic architecture. The *forum* and *basilica* were the largest outside London, excavation revealing the area of the *forum* to have been 168×104m (185×114yd). The apsidal *basilica* was marbled, and possessed a large aisled hall. There are signs of rebuilding during the

second century.

Domestic buildings excavated so far have shown a remarkable degree of advancement. Very early use of stone in domestic structures has been established as, for example, in one *insula* where stonework dating from the first decade of the second century has been found. As early as the Flavian period, painted wall plaster was being used to decorate some houses. There are many splendid mosaics of the late second and early third centuries, for example those found below Dyer Street, including the remarkable Actaeon mosaic, which along with other fine examples can be viewed in the Corinium Museum. Mosaics are a good indicator of the wealth and status of the occupants of a Roman settlement. Those at Cirencester are of a unique style and quality. This has led D. J. Smith to believe that a mosaic industry flourished in and around the *civitas* capital. He has traced the recurrence of certain designs and patterns in many mosaics in Cirencester itself and in neighbouring settlements. Hypocausted fourth-century houses and the discovery of fourth-century shops indicate the endurance of the vigorous domestic and commercial life of Cirencester.

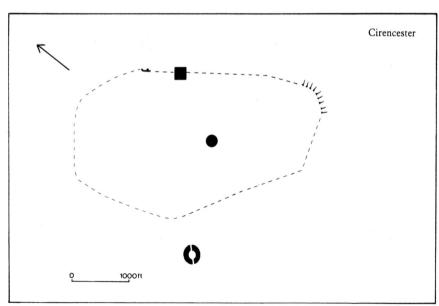

Cirencester

0   1000ft

South-west of the centre of the town lay a large amphitheatre (beside Cotswold Avenue), which has survived to the present. It appears that this was originally built of turf and timber, but was converted during the early second century to stonework. The arena was elliptical and measured 49×41m (162×135ft). Rebuilding in the late second century added small chambers, possibly for holding prisoners or wild beasts for the shows.

Interpretation of the defences at Cirencester is problematic. Numerous excavations have revealed a complex series of building periods. The town certainly had fortifications by the end of the second century. Sections of stone walling seem to have been interspersed with earthen ramparts. Both internal and external interval towers have been traced. Work on the fortifications appears to have been continuous for about two hundred years. The defences stood until the early fifth century and continual clearance of the *forum* piazza suggests that commercial life continued until the mid fifth century.

CLANVILLE Hampshire
SU 3148 *Villa*
Clanville was a courtyard villa with structures on three sides. The west building began as an aisled structure with a door in the long east side. This was burned down, and replaced on the same alignment by a slightly larger stone aisled building with stone partitions. Living rooms were in the northern part. There were tessellated floors and hypocausts, and a bath house. This was the principal house of the villa. The northern rectangular building was an out-building.

CLAXBY-BY-LINCOLN Lincolnshire
TF 100961 *Pottery kilns*
Pottery kilns were found during investigations at Claxby in the early 1970s.

CLAYDON PIKE Gloucestershire
SU 190996 *Settlement and possible taxation depot*
Excavations at Claydon Pike are still underway, so any conclusions made upon existing finds may have to be altered if new evidence emerges. The settlement stood in the valley of the river Coln halfway between modern Lechlade and Fairford. The first signs of Roman occupation date to c70, preceded by an Iron Age settlement. The main street of the Roman settlement was a road 5m (16½ft) wide and ditched on either side. Parts of this road were metalled. The area of occupation covered about 15 acres (6ha), although only one area has produced signs of domestic use – that to the east of the settlement's nucleus. The rest of the area has yielded paddocks, yards, a large aisled barn and a large rectangular enclosure to the south of the central crossroads. It has been suggested that this could have served as a shrine area. It had a cobbled space at the rear and a large pit, not as yet excavated, but a nearby pit has yielded a limestone pillar and animal skeletons. These and other finds suggest a possible religious function. Also from c70 are military finds, for example a cavalry decoration and an inscribed sherd bearing the letters LEG II A. Was Claydon Pike a veteran colony? Or, as has been recently mooted, was it an imperial estate acting as a tax collection and administration centre for the area? More evidence from the excavation will help to answer these questions.

Clear Cupboard see **Farmington**

CLIFFORD Hereford & Worcester
SO 2446 *Fort*
A 14 acre (5.7ha) fort with double-ditching was seen from the air at Clifford.

COBHAM Surrey
TQ 089594 *Bath house*
A bath house excavated by S. S. Frere in 1942 at Chatley Farm was re-excavated in 1979 by Surrey County Council Archaeological Unit. Roof tiles and pottery of the later Roman period were found, but no building remains.

COBHAM PARK Kent
TQ 683693 *Villa*
A simple villa house with masonry foundations was begun in the mid to late first century, and corridors were added before the

325

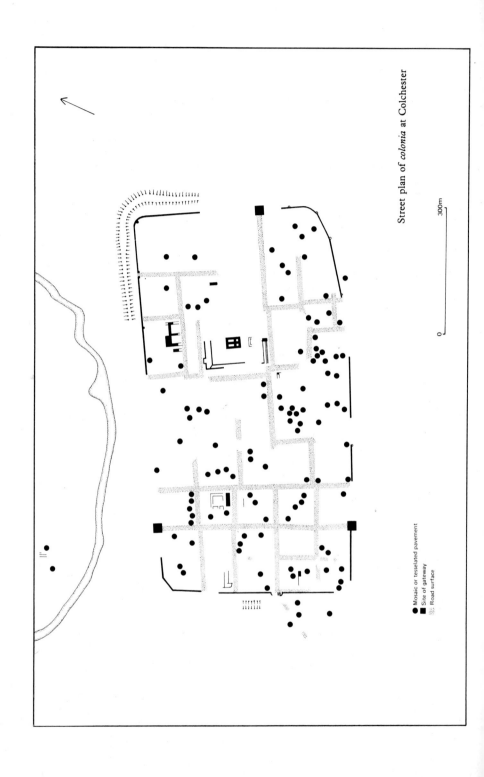

Street plan of *colonia* at Colchester

● Mosaic or tesselated pavement
■ Site of gateway
▨ Road surface

0   300m

end of the century. Some of the rooms had tessellated floors and painted plaster on the walls. The site had originally been that of a Belgic farmstead. A rectangular building, about 13.5m (45ft) long, was erected as a byre in the second century. This was examined in the late 1950s.

CODDENHAM Suffolk

TM 118528 *Settlement and fort: Roman name* Combretovium

There was a Roman settlement near Baylham House, Coddenham. It had been preceded by an Iron Age settlement. The site was on the main route from Caistor St Edmund (*Venta Icenorum*), known as Pye Road (Margary 3d). The road continued southwards to Colchester (*Camulodunum*) (Margary 3c). The Roman aspects of the site began as a fort put down after the Boudican revolt, as part of Suetonius Paullinus' crushing of the Iceni (see also Ixworth). The small town that grew up on the fort site has been examined, though little beyond some rectangular buildings of timber, with evidence of industrial use, and some burials, has been found. The fort has not been properly located, so its size is not yet known, but some military ditching was noted in the mid 1970s from air observation, which suggests two forts, one following the other.

Coesike see **Turret 33b**

COLCHESTER Essex

TL 9925 *Colonia: Roman name* Camulodunum

Roman Colchester was situated in an attractive position on a gravel ridge above the river Colne, 5 miles from the sea. The site had originally been that of a pre-Roman *oppidum*. It was chosen for the construction of a fortress in AD43 or 44 and founded as a *colonia* for veterans in AD49. Little is known of the pre-Boudican town, which was so thoroughly sacked in AD61, though some remains have been found. In the North Hill area an early timber building has been identified with associated military equipment. An area of early street planning has also been traced, although the position of the *forum* and *basilica* is in doubt, if indeed they

had been built at all.

Controversy surrounds the early Temple of Claudius. This was certainly a magnificent building and possibly the earliest stone and mortar construction in Roman Britain. It stood on a podium 32×24m (105×80ft) and probably had a portico at the front. An open-air sacrificial altar stood 27m (90ft) from the façade of the temple. The foundations were later incorporated into those of the Norman great tower castle. A date of AD54 or earlier has been given for the temple, although it seems unlikely that it was dedicated in Claudius' lifetime, if indeed it was dedicated to him at all. Another possibility is that it was voted after his death.

The temple and other buildings were destroyed by fire in the Boudican revolt of AD60–1, but a recovery was made in the Flavian period with an expansion of the town eastwards. Unusually, in the early second century, a free-standing wall was built, with a street running behind it rather than the more usual rampart. This fortification attempt was left unfinished, although the external double-portal Balkerne Gate was probably built at the time. Other information about second-century Colchester is scanty. Three houses, originally timber-framed, were rebuilt in masonry in the Middleborough area. The largest had a courtyard and stretched back 45m (150ft) from the road. It had a mosaic and tessellated floors. About fifty mosaics of restrained geometric style have been found in Colchester, indicating the prosperity of the owners of the larger private houses.

A circuit wall was built in the late second century and a rampart behind it added during the third century. The wall had a width of 2m (6ft), and there were rectangular internal towers bonded in with its fabric. The north-east gate has been excavated, and found to have had a single portal and tower. The third century saw continuing prosperity, borne out by the building of the fortifications and the possibility of a mint in the town. If the 'C' mintmark on some coins of the late third century does refer to Colchester, it could point to the administrative centrality of the town.

Colchester. Reconstruction of Balkerne Gate on west side of *colonia*

Outside Colchester, a possible *mithraeum* has been found measuring 22×13m (74×42ft). A spring was incorporated in the building, leading to other suggestions about the building's use – possibly a spa or even (more prosaically) a latrine. At Gosbecks, 3 miles south-west of Colchester, a walled enclosure held a temple and a theatre (dismantled in the third century). The area round Warren Field appears to have been a centre for industry, where traces of the manufacture of pottery, bricks and tiles and glass were found.

Evidence for the end of Roman Colchester is slim. Gradual decay was probably the pattern during the fourth century and by the fifth century Saxon burials were taking place.

COLERNE Wiltshire
ST 8171 *Villa*
The villa at Colerne was on a hillside. There was a main residential block which revealed at least eleven rooms during excavation, some of which had had mosaic floors. One mosaic was of a sporting scene, with a charioteer and four horses pulling a chariot. Further down the hill, as part of the complex, an aisled building was found, which had an exterior drain.

COLESHILL Warwickshire
SP 195905 *Settlement with temple complex*
A settlement was detected during recent development in the area to provide industrial sites. Various buildings were traced, and water tanks, fragments of painted plaster and roof tiles found. One interesting discovery in the late 1970s was a Romano-Celtic temple, with a square *cella* of stone surrounded by a square ambulatory, both erected over an earlier timber temple. The temple was

328

enclosed by a *temenos*, and inside this were at least six other structures, including a small square shrine and four circular structures, with a quantity of debris including sherds, loom weights and querns. Outside the temple complex to the south, a small sandstone block bath house was discovered and examined. A cold plunge was located.

COMB END Gloucestershire
SO 984110 *Villa*
The remains of a corridor villa were examined in the eighteenth century at Comb End, Colesbourne. An interesting feature comprised long stretches of wall, about 39m (130ft) in all, which still had the bottom edge of wall paintings, depicting the extremities of human figures. Some of these were copied by the nineteenth-century antiquary, S. Lysons (who had also copied some of the paintings at Bignor villa). One of the Comb End buildings excavated in the late eighteenth century had had a corn drier in the north end.

COMBE HAY Somerset
ST 729612 *Industrial site*
An industrial site was excavated here in the late 1960s and early 1970s. Traces of coal-fired iron furnaces of the second century were seen, which were superseded in the third century by new industries of glass and pottery. The site is beside a modern fuller's earth quarry.

COMBLEY Isle of Wight
SZ 538878 *Villa*
A villa has been partly excavated at Combley, near Arretor, though it seems probable that more remains are to be found, or else it may have disappeared through destruction. It was probably a walled court-yard-type. A bath house, with mosaic and tessellated flooring, stoke-holes and plunge baths, was found, adjacent and linked by a corridor to an aisled building, also with mosaics. The aisled building was a farm-house with partitioning at the west end for residential quarters, the east end remaining open-aisled, presumably for agricultural purposes.

COOKHAM Berkshire
SU 885841 *Pottery oven*
A gravel pit at Strand Castle, Cookham Rise, was examined in 1968 and a pottery drying oven of flint and clay walls was found. This was associated with sherds of the second, third and fourth centuries.

CORBRIDGE Northumberland
NY 9864 *Forts and* vicus *(*cum *supply station): Roman name* Corstopitum
Corbridge is a unique site in Britain since its function changed significantly over a period of time. It is also the only site of its type yet found from the period of the Roman occupation. Fortunately, it has been well excavated and buildings which gave it its unique functions are visible. Roman Corbridge stood on a river terrace near to a crossing of the Tyne in the vicinity of Hadrian's Wall. The first period of Roman occupation dates to no earlier than c87. The settlement lay at Beaufront Red House, about 1 mile west of the later site.

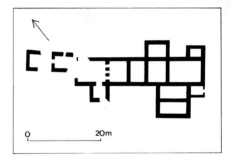

The bath house at Beaufront Red House

The first fort at Corbridge probably housed the *Ala Petriana*, and had turf and timber fortifications. Little is known about this phase of development other than that it was destroyed c105, probably by enemy action. Equally little is known about the second, Trajanic fort, which was a Stanegate post, and the third fort, in which the central range of buildings appears to have been rebuilt, with an *aedes* added to the *principia*.

The first period for which sound information is provided by the remains is that of the

329

mid second century. Inscriptions date the fourth stone and timber fort to c139–40. It probably housed a mixed cavalry and infantry garrison, and the *principia, praetorium* and what may be a hospital have been identified. There were major alterations c163. First, the barracks were demolished and replaced with stone structures and later a similar operation was carried out on the *principia* and the *praetorium*. Also in this period a stone courtyard was constructed, which could well be interpreted as the projected site for a *forum* and *basilica* complex. Other suggestions are that it represents an unfinished *principia* for a projected legionary fortress (Birley) or a building for a major grainstore. The fort period comes to an end c180 when building stopped. The turf and timber defences on the west side were levelled out and a period of stagnation set in.

Corbridge saw a new spate of building and development c208 under Severus. It is after this date that the site took on its unusual role. It appears to have been a prosperous little market town, but with a difference. Corbridge is most likely to have been a supply and maintenance station. The granaries were rebuilt and the area of the *forum* of the preceding period was converted to accommodate shops. Two military work compounds, separate at first, and later united, have also been identified from this period. The whole settlement covered an area of perhaps 40 acres (16ha). Corbridge may have been a local collecting point for the compulsory 'corn levy'. Sculpture and dedications show that Roman, Celtic and exotic deities were worshipped by this apparently cosmopolitan community.

The last period of Roman occupation in the late third century saw alterations to some buildings and the demolition of others. Roman life seems to have lingered on until the end of the fourth century. The many interesting remains at Corbridge include a

(opposite above) One of the main drains at Corbridge Roman station *(Author)*

(opposite below) The Corbridge lion. A sculpture by a local craftsman

considerable aqueduct and some splendid water tanks at the bottom end of it.

COSGROVE Northamptonshire
SP 795421 *Villa*
The first stage of the villa at Cosgrove began in the early second century. It was a corridor villa with passages at front and back. A bath house was erected in the mid second century. Additional buildings were raised beside the main house to form a courtyard sometime in the third century. In the early years of the fourth century, a small rectangular temple with a central post was erected on the site of earlier buildings.

COW ROAST Hertfordshire
SP 955102 *Settlement*
There was a settlement between the line of Akeman Street and the present A41 road, which may have had some links with the villa site at nearby Northchurch, a mile to the south-east. Excavations at Cow Roast exposed extensive indications of occupation, including buildings associated with iron working and iron tools and slag. One interesting find was a coin of Tasciovanus (son or grandson of Cassivellaunus) and this confirmed Iron Age association. Military items were also found, such as a javelin head, a sword grip and pieces of a *lorica*.

COX GREEN Berkshire
SU 8779 *Villa*
A simple oblong house of one long and one short room, 27m (90ft) in overall length, was erected in the second century. It was converted later into a winged corridor villa, with a bath house at one end.

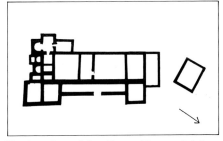

The first phase of Cox Green villa occupied the central block. Bath house at left

CRACKENTHORPE Cumbria
NY 650237 *Marching camp*
A 20 acre (8ha) marching camp of square plan, with titular gates, was erected here in the early Flavian period, perhaps before the governorship of Agricola.

CRANE GODREVY Cornwall
SW 589426 *Enclosure*
A late Iron Age enclosure continued to be occupied for much of the Roman period. It was enclosed by a stone-faced bank.

CROMHALL Gloucestershire
ST 6889 *Villa*
The villa plan at Cromhall was of two adjacent sides of a courtyard, the longer side on the north-north-west, the shorter on the west. The west range was the main residential block, and may have been a separate farmhouse that was later joined to the longer northern range which itself composed two distinct houses. On the southern side of the courtyard was an east-west aligned granary, or large barn, with raised flooring.

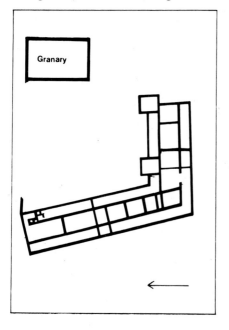

Cromhall villa

CROSBY-ON-EDEN Cumbria
NY 445605 *Stretch of Hadrian's Wall*
A stretch of Hadrian's Wall was examined here in 1980–1, and revealed traces of the later Stone Wall laid down upon the earlier Turf Wall which had been levelled.

CROWBOROUGH East Sussex
TQ 515313 *Iron-working area*
More than three hundred iron slagheaps have been noted in the Crowborough iron-producing region. A sample was examined, and ten proved to be of Roman origin. Pottery of the first and second centuries was found.

CURBRIDGE Oxfordshire
SP 337089 *Settlement*
A small settlement beside the Witney bypass at Curbridge was investigated, and traces of timber buildings located. The site appears to have been occupied from the first to the fourth centuries.

DALTON PARLOURS West Yorkshire
SE 402445 *Villa complex*
A winged corridor-type villa, with a separate bath house, together with a long aisled building (with its own bath suite) and two other ranges, comprise the main finds on this villa site, near Collingham, Wetherby, excavated in the later 1970s. The site was occupied from the second to the fourth centuries, though the majority of finds were later rather than earlier in date. One of the (aisled) buildings contained a T-shaped corn drier. There were also some mosaic pavements.

DANEBURY Hampshire
SU 323376 *Hillfort*
An Iron Age hillfort, which superseded a Bronze Age site, on Danebury hill was run down and abandoned in the first century BC. Then, at the time of the Roman campaigns in the south in the AD40s, the fort was reoccupied and strengthened by a new ditch and a renovated rampart. Early Romano-British finds suggest that there may have been a settlement here after the south was pacified.

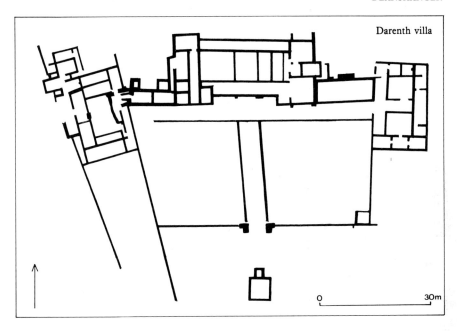

Darenth villa

0   30m

DANESHILL Hampshire
SU 657541 *Farmstead*
A Romano-British farmstead was located at Daneshill, near Basingstoke, in the early 1980s. It had been occupied throughout most of the Roman period. Evidence of iron working was found in one corner of the plot which had been enclosed by a ditch.

DARENTH Kent
TQ 564706 *Villa*
If the plan derived from a variety of recent excavations is anything to go by, the villa complex at Darenth was in its time almost palatial. It consisted of a long central winged corridor villa, about 48m (160ft), with major extensions flanking both ends, set out in fan style (looking at the villa from the south), which surrounded an extensive courtyard. This courtyard was probably given over to gardens for some of its time, at least. Dividing the courtyard down the middle, from central block towards a monumental gateway at the south, was a long hall-like structure with walls of tile-faced flint. This may at some time have been a pool, and evidence has been found of decorative water-

spouts (eg a lion's head) and a semi-circular basin with inflow and outflow channels. At least three suites of baths have been found, as well as two substantial aisled buildings, one of which had living accommodation.

DARGUES Northumberland
NY 860937 *Temporary camp*
Dargues marching camp was built in Flavian times. It was about 16 acres (6.5ha), with *claviculae* at the gates. Some of the eastern rampart is visible.

DARTFORD Kent
TQ 540740 *Romano-British settlement*
Part of a Romano-British settlement was discovered and examined during building development work at the junction of Spital Street and Lowfield Street in the early 1970s. Sections of first- and second-century ditching were traced, as were timber buildings of the later Roman period.

DEANSHANGER Northamptonshire
SP 770396 *Villa*
A corridor-type villa was excavated at this site in the late 1950s. About 67m (75yd) to

the north-west, further excavation of the site, in the early 1970s, revealed several other buildings, including circular houses of timber of second- and third-century date and a third-century barn which had stone foundations and which measured about 13×22m (42×72ft). This had a square shed added to one long side. A T-shaped corn drier was also found.

DENTON Lincolnshire
SK 8730 *Villa*
A complex site which was largely destroyed in the 1950s by open-cast mining, Denton appears to have been a winged corridor villa with associated aisled buildings. Probably in the late fourth century one of the aisled buildings was residential, shared by the owner, workforce and animals, as is clear from the partitioning (cf Exning). The residential part had mosaic flooring, and there was a separate bath suite outside.

DENTON Tyne & Wear
NZ 195657–NZ 214649
Section of Hadrian's Wall
Where the A69 runs out of Benwell, west of Newcastle upon Tyne, the road passes the sites of Turrets 6b (opposite the road to Howgate), Milecastle 7 and Turret 7a (opposite the crematorium). Then in the grounds of a Methodist chapel is a stretch of Hadrian's Wall, about 2.75m (9ft) thick. A few hundred yards on is Turret 7b, south of the road, 3.9×4m (13×13¾ft). A further few hundred yards on is another stretch of Wall.

DERBY Derbyshire
SK 3637 *Civilian and industrial settlement after fort*
Considerable excavations have been undertaken at sites by the west bank of the river Derwent, on the other side of which is the military site of Littlechester. The discoveries have not yet formed a definitive picture, but at Strutt's Park (SK 349373), for example, there is evidence of mid first century military occupation, perhaps a fort that preceded the more permanent fort at Littlechester. This evidence includes traces of barrack buildings, a water tank and early coins. At

the site of the racecourse, SK 361376, investigations revealed timber and stone building traces, beginning probably in the mid second century, and some pottery kilns, hearths and iron-working furnaces. The finds confirm an industrial site associated with civilian occupation.

DEWLISH Dorset
SY 768972 *Villa*
The remains of Dewlish villa were discovered by accident in the 1740s when a tree was blown down and a mosaic revealed. The latest series of excavations began in 1969 and continued through most of the 1970s. The main dwelling house was a corridor type with about thirty rooms, many of which had mosaic or tessellated flooring. The villa had a bath suite in which one room had a semi-hexagonal apse and a channelled hypocaust. Next to this room were two plunge baths. An extension at the north-west was used as a workshop. In the debris on the site were found numerous coins, some as late as Honorius (suggesting occupation into the early fifth century) and an interesting stone roof finial. There were also outbuildings and livestock yards.

DICKET MEAD Hertfordshire
TL 236161 *Villa*
On high ground on the north-east of the Mimram river valley is the site of Lockleys villa. A few hundred metres south-west, just over the river, on the other bank, is another villa, Dicket Mead, begun probably in the third century. It was a large walled enclosure consisting of two main buildings, about 60m (200ft) apart, linked on the north-west side by the wall. The more northerly building has been described as a glorified cricket pavilion, with a wide raised verandah fronted by a colonnade. The centre range does not appear to have been partitioned, but it was flanked by a corridor, and the range had a hypocaust at one end. The range was later destroyed as a deliberate act. The second building was in some particulars similar, with flanking corridors. At its southern end, there was a bath suite with two plunge baths. A substantial height of the suite was discovered, the stoke-hole part reaching over 3m (10ft).

This bath suite has been excavated and preserved for the public to see, in a special display area under a new section of the M1 motorway.

DITCHLEY Oxfordshire
SP 399200 *Villa*
The plan of Ditchley is a symmetrical winged corridor house. It had begun as a timber house and was converted to stone at the beginning of the second century. The house lay within a rectangular walled enclosure and was protected by a ditch. No baths have been found but it does seem unlikely that there was none. In the fourth century, the house was adorned by a colonnaded front. There were some extra buildings, including a large granary of the early fourth century which appears to have been built over the site of an abandoned block of farmworkers' apartments. There were also two large circular threshing floors. In the fourth century, and possibly before, the villa seems to have been the centre of a prosperous farming complex which embraced perhaps 1000 acres (405ha) or more, on which several small subsidiary farms were operated by tenant farmers.

DODDERHILL Hereford & Worcester
SO 902636 *Fort*
An early fort was built at Dodderhill, near Droitwich, probably between AD50 and 60, and it remained in occupation until the early second century. The fort was about 10 acres (4ha) in size.

DONCASTER South Yorkshire
SE 5703 *Fort: Roman name* Danum
The Roman army built a fort here in about AD71–2. It was about 6 acres (2.4ha) in size and was constructed of earth and timber. In the early second century, the fort wall was strengthened with stone revetment. In the Antonine period the defences were repaired. Some evidence of this work was found in excavations in advance of roadworks in 1969. There was further renovation in the Severan period, but the fort appears to have been given up soon afterwards and remained unoccupied for most of the third century. By this time a *vicus* had developed to the south, and it was enclosed by a triple-ditch system. In the fourth century, the fort was reoccupied and new timber buildings were erected. Road surfaces were remetalled.

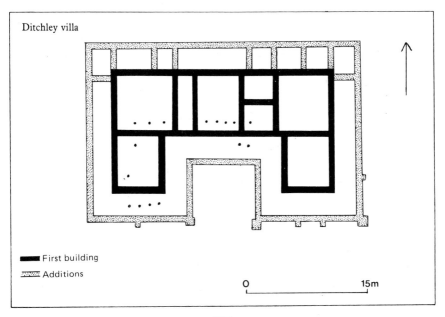

Ditchley villa

■■ First building
▨▨ Additions

0   15m

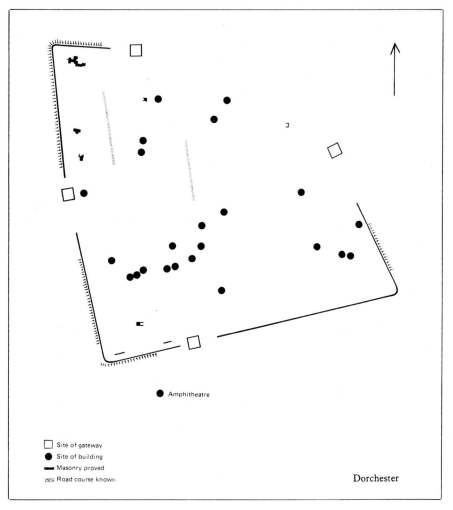

● Amphitheatre

☐ Site of gateway
● Site of building
━ Masonry proved
〰 Road course known

Dorchester

DORCHESTER Dorset

SY 6990 Civitas *capital of the Durotriges: Roman name* Durnovaria

The *civitas* capital, Dorchester, was positioned on a chalk promontory above the river Frome. As yet no remains have been found of an early fort here, but pre-Flavian coins, Samian ware and military equipment show that some sort of settlement was present. At the end of the first century Dorchester was raised to the status of *civitas* capital of the Durotriges.

The earliest buildings of the town were timber-framed and some traces of these have been found. The position of the *forum* is uncertain. A large bath complex has recently

been found, which could have been the public facility. It was built c75–100, had a circular *laconicum* (dry heat room) and other heated rooms, and it underwent considerable alterations until it fell into disuse in the mid fourth century. Also from the late first century, and probably associated with the provision of baths, are the remains of an aqueduct, 2m (6ft) wide and 1.25m (4ft) deep, that carried water from over 11 miles away. Why this was needed remains a mystery since wells could easily have provided water for the town.

The defences at Dorchester were built at the end of the second century; a rampart and ditch arrangement enclosed an area of about

336

70–80 acres (28–32ha). The rampart was fronted by a masonry wall probably towards the end of the third century. The position of the gates can be inferred from the road alignments, but although an internal grid plan of streets seems apparent, little is known of the full town layout. Outside its defences Dorchester had its own amphitheatre, a conversion of an originally Neolithic earthwork called Maumbury Ring. Because of its origin the amphitheatre was of unusual form, being circular and having only one entrance, at the north. The banks stand as an impressive monument to this day.

Dorchester seems to have reached the height of its prosperity in the fourth century. One house in the Colliton Park area had mosaics in all the rooms of its main range. Hypocausts and mosaic floors along with enlargements of existing buildings point to a flourishing period for the wealthy sector of society at this time. The number of mosaics from Dorchester and their consistency of style has led to suggestions that a mosaic industry was based in the town during the fourth century. (This 'school' of mosaic-making appears to have provided works for outlying areas – some at a considerable distance, notably one at Withington villa in Gloucestershire.)

This period of opulence was short lived, however, and towards the end of the fourth century the town began to be abandoned, though occupation lingered on into the fifth century.

DORCHESTER-ON-THAMES
Oxfordshire SU 5741
Small town
Under the present town, to the west of the great abbey, are the remains of a small Roman town. It was walled in the third century, having been surrounded by a ditch and rampart in the second. The town developed upon the site of an Iron Age settlement. Several timber buildings of the Roman period have been located. The town appears to have been occupied well into the fifth century. Then, as Roman occupation died out, Saxon settlers moved in and put up houses among the Romano-British ruins. The Roman town may have grown out of a

vicus of a fort whose location has not been confirmed.

DORKING Surrey
TQ 165493 *Settlement*
The first evidence of Roman occupation in Dorking was found in the mid 1970s during excavations in advance of redevelopment in the north of the High Street. Ditching with discarded pottery of the late first century was found. The Chichester to London road (Margary 15), known as Stane Street, passed through Dorking, and excavation on the line of the road in the early 1980s exposed a section of V-shaped ditching, as well as signs of workshops of the second century.

DOVER Kent
TR 3141 *Forts and* vicus: *Roman name* Dubris
Situated admirably for the protection of the Kentish peninsula, Dover appears to have provided a focal point for commercial and military activity on the south-east coast over a considerable period of time. Two major stages of development can be identified, with a fort associated with each. The first signs of Roman occupation on this site, overshadowed by hills on the west bank of the Dour estuary, can be dated to the last years of the first century.

The first fort appears to have been constructed on a north-south axis in the middle of the second century. Traces of chalk masonry show that the fort was of rectangular shape with rounded corners, the walls being a substantial 1.2m (4ft) thick. Barrack rooms and a large military bath house of this period have been found, perhaps indicating the size of and importance of the garrison. There now seems to be no doubt that Dover was one of the great naval forts of the *classis Britannica*. A number of tiles with the monogram CL BR bear this out. A timber jetty and quay on the Dour estuary have been excavated, showing the use of the settlement as a harbour from the late first century. The magnificent second-century *pharos* (a Roman lighthouse), in the castle precincts above the town, indicates the importance and frequency of use of the harbour.

337

The *vicus* around the first fort appears to have been extensive and prosperous. Most notable is the Painted House in the area outside the north gate of the first fort, excavated during the 1970s. This is a fine hypocausted building of c200, with well-preserved painted plaster decoration on the inside walls.

The second major period of development was the late third century, when Dover became prominent as one of the forts of the Saxon Shore (see p 143). In c275 the army enclosed 5 acres (2ha) of land with carefully built walls, banked with earth on the interior, and with external towers added at 25m (83ft) intervals. The buildings of the earlier *vicus* appear to have been ignored in this operation with, for example, one of the D-shaped projecting towers being constructed on top of the Painted House. Parts of the south and west walls have been located, along with traces of a fort ditch 5m (16½ft) wide. Pot sherds of the fourth century reveal that the site was occupied well into the late Roman period.

DOWNTON Wiltshire
SU 182213 *Villa*
Downton villa was a simple corridor-type, the main range divided into two units of two rooms flanking a narrow passage, with a large central hall sandwiched between and shared by the units. The south unit had its own corridor and porch. On the south-east end another corridor led to the bath suite. The house had several mosaic and tessellated floors. What appears to have been a water shrine was located in one of the porches.

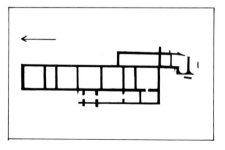

Downton villa

DRAGONBY Humberside
SE 905138 *Settlement*
A settlement at Dragonby, near Scunthorpe, originating in the first century had early pottery works making Rustic ware, from the Flavian period to the time of Hadrian. Kilns have been found, as well as timber buildings, ovens and metal furnaces.

DROITWICH Hereford & Worcester
SO 898639 *Small town: Roman name* Salinae
Droitwich has natural salt springs. These were worked in Iron Age times, and they were taken over by the Romans. Excavations in the area of Bays Meadow revealed evidence of brine pans, storage pits, timber buildings and so forth. A settlement developed here, which has been classed as a small town. A fourth-century town villa of winged corridor plan, evidently of some splendour, has been investigated. It had painted plaster walls and hypocausts, and a double T-shaped furnace. Evidence of other residential buildings has also been found, and in 1972 part of an aisled building of the fourth century was unearthed. It had been built on foundations of large dressed sandstone blocks.

DRUMBURGH Cumbria
NY 266598 *Fort: Roman name* Congavata
The first fort at Drumburgh, near Bowness, was a small earth and timber structure of 2 acres (0.8ha), with a clay rampart. It was built into the original Turf Wall of Hadrian's Wall. Later, a stone fort was erected within the area of the first fort, when that part of the Wall was converted to stone.

Dubmill Point see **Milefortlet 17**

DUCKLINGTON Oxfordshire
SP 363072 *Villa*
What seems to have been a large villa on the line of the bypass at Ducklington was excavated in the mid 1970s. Some pottery was found, as well as post holes of buildings, and a stone-lined well; however, the excavations were not completed.

DUNCOT Shropshire
SJ 576117 *Fortified site*
An elongated rectangular site, fortified by

V-shaped double-ditching, was erected in the mid first century near Wroxeter in advance of the legionary fortress that later rose at Wroxeter about 1½ miles to the south.

DUNSTABLE Bedfordshire
TL 019217 *Small town: Roman name* Durocobrivae
The small town of *Durocobrivae* lay in the *civitas* of the Catuvellauni. It is still not fully understood. Excavations in the late 1960s uncovered traces of a huge timber building in Friary Field, near Watling Street (the old A5). This was over 30m (100ft) long and was probably one of a pair. Later excavations uncovered numerous burials of late Roman period.

DURRINGTON WALLS Wiltshire
SU 150437 *Agricultural settlement*
This is the site of an important Neolithic henge monument. During excavations in the late 1960s, the Romano-British agricultural settlement established south-west of the henge was examined. The principal find was a corn drier, with a T-shaped furnace, in a rectangular building, probably of the fourth century. The semi-circular vault over the fireplace was found partly intact.

DUSTON Northamptonshire
SP 730605 *Major settlement*
Excavations of the mid 1970s at the major settlement at Duston, sponsored by Northampton Development Corporation's Archaeological Unit, revealed traces of a timber building of undetermined date, and also of a stone building of the third or fourth century. The latter contained a stoking pit lined with stone, part of a corn drier.

Dykesfield see **Milecastle 73**

DYMOCK Gloucestershire
SO 705311 *Iron works*
A small iron-working area beside a Roman road (probably Margary 610) was examined in the early 1970s. The site was occupied between the mid second and the fourth centuries. A number of bowl furnaces were found.

EARITH Cambridgeshire
TL 392760 *Settlement*
Part of a settlement here was examined before quarrying, and traces were found of a first-century circular house, several pits dating from c100 to the fourth century and a timber aisled building of AD290–300, about 15 × 9m (50 × 30ft). This has two corn driers.

EAST ANTON Hampshire
SU 371475 *?Road station: Roman name* ?Leucomagus
A Romano-British site named *Leucomagus* appears in the Ravenna Cosmography list (see p 239), but it has not been definitely identified. Recent consideration has suggested a spot in the region of Andover, where the Winchester to Cirencester Roman road (Margary 43) crossed the Silchester to Old Sarum Roman road (Margary 4b). This crossing has been located at East Anton, about 2 miles north-north-east of Andover, and foundations of some buildings have been found nearby, including a flint-based structure which had two ovens. This is suggested as the probable location of *Leucomagus*, which may have been a road station.

EAST BRIDGFORD Nottinghamshire
SK 700415 *Fort and town: Roman name* Margidunum
Margidunum was a small Roman walled town, the remains of which are in the area of Castle Hill, East Bridgford. It had begun as a fort on the Fosse Way, south-east of the Trent; its first phase was about AD50. Among the finds in excavations of the late 1960s were pieces of military gear. The later town occupied some 10 acres (4ha), and various building remains have been traced, including that of a villa to the south-west. Part of the defences on the eastern side can still be seen.

EAST COKER Somerset
ST 5413 *Villa*
About 1¼ miles south of Yeovil, a villa was discovered in the 1750s. Not much is known of the plan, but several rooms were located, some with mosaics, including one picture of the birth of Bacchus. The villa flourished in the fourth century.

EAST GRIMSTEAD Wiltshire
SU 2327 *Villa*
The villa here contained an aisled building about 43m (140ft) long which was modified over its lifetime. It served as a residential farmhouse, with a bath suite and hypocausts; fragments of tile indicate a tiled roof.

EAST HOLME Dorset
SY 896859 *Pottery*
Evidence that black burnished ware was manufactured at East Holme, near Wareham, during the second century was found during excavations in the early 1970s. This was one of several factories producing the ware in the Poole district. Some of the wares were supplied to the army on Hadrian's Wall and, it is suggested, also to forces along the Antonine Wall.

EASTON Cumbria
NY 274579 *Watchtower*
There was a six-post watchtower at Easton which is established as having been part of the Stanegate frontier. It was enclosed by a circular V-ditched enclosure, with a rampart.

EATON-BY-TARPORLEY Cheshire
SJ 571634 *Villa*
A discovery of some importance occurred recently at Eaton when the remains of a winged corridor-type villa complex were excavated. A hypocaust was found. It was part of a bath suite. Some of the floors were paved with *opus signinum*. The villa appears to have been occupied for a long period, and is thought to be the first discovered in Cheshire.

EBCHESTER Durham
NZ 104554 *Fort: Roman name* Vindomora
A small (2½ acre/1ha) fort of Agricolan origin, which was occupied at various times until the late fourth century, Ebchester was converted to stone in the later Antonine period, or perhaps a little later. The rampart, which was very wide, was originally of clay blocks and received stone facing. There were several rebuildings. In one phase, stone structures (including a suite of heated rooms)

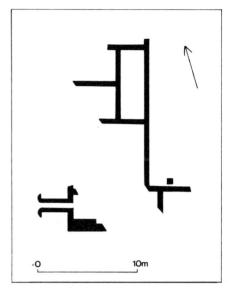

Eaton-by-Tarporley. Buildings so far found of a winged corridor villa (1981)

were erected across part of the fort's roadway. In the late third century, or early in the fourth, chalet-type buildings were put up, some of which were not residential but appear to have been used as metal workshops. There are a few remains, including the hypocaust of what was probably the bath house of the *praetorium*.

ECCLES Kent
TQ 722605 *Villa*
The substantial villa at Eccles, near Aylesford, raised on an earlier Iron Age site, was one of the first built in Britain. It was probably begun in about AD60–5, and remained more or less continuously occupied throughout the Roman period. It was enlarged and modified, had some of the first mosaics in Roman Britain and sported in front of its main house a long, narrow pool.

Eccles was a palatial winged corridor villa that was discovered in the 1960s. It has been well excavated. It received its first bath house in the first century, perhaps in the first building phase, which is unusual. The original structure was a long range, about 112m (123yd) from north to south, divided into several rooms, and this was added to over the centuries, converting it into a major winged corridor house that had among its facilities a water fountain, and a long, slim, fishpond in the front garden (as it were); it also had agricultural buildings including a granary and corn driers. The early mosaic found in the cold room of the first bath house (of the 60s–70s) contained a centre square panel with a picture of two gladiators fighting.

EDLINGTON WOOD West Yorkshire
SK 550978 *Earthworks*
Excavation in the early 1970s in advance of quarrying revealed three building periods at this site of complex earthworks which were occupied from the Flavian period to the early fourth century. Traces of stone walling, and of buildings with tiled roofs, were found at the site.

ELLINGHAM Norfolk
TM 378015 *Pottery kiln*
An interesting pottery kiln was discovered during building work at Ellingham in 1977. It had a tiled floor on pedestal and on pilasters along the walls. Pottery fragments were of the second century.

ELSLACK North Yorkshire
SD 924494 *Fort*
Two successive forts were built at Elslack, near Skipton. The first was a 3½ acre (1.4ha) earth and timber structure of the Agricolan period. Its rampart had a limestone boulder and squared sandstone block base, and the wall itself was of clay revetted with turf. The fort was enclosed by two ditches. The second fort was built very much later, though there is still argument as to the dating. Most authorities opt for Constantius (early fourth century). For some of its life it accommodated an *ala* of cavalry.

ELSTED West Sussex
SU 812190 *Farmstead*
A Romano-British farmstead which was enclosed by a ditch was examined in the mid 1970s. Several phases of post holes and pits were discovered, of the second and third centuries. To the north, a stone building was located by aerial photography, but this has yet to be excavated.

The oven floor of a pottery kiln discovered at Ellingham, Norfolk, in 1976 (*D. A. Edwards, Norfolk Archaeological Unit*)

ELTON Cambridgeshire
TL 121941 *Villa*
Trial excavations were carried out on the known villa site about 2 miles east of Elton. Traces of a stone building, about 12m (40ft) long, were found.

EMPINGHAM Leicestershire
SK 944077 *Farmstead*
A farmstead was investigated here in the late 1960s and early 1970s, in advance of reservoir works. Several buildings were identified, including an aisled agricultural building of the third century and a residential block with a hypocaust.

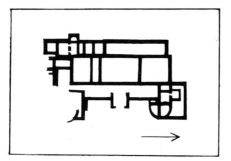

Engleton villa: bath suite at top left corner

ENGLETON Staffordshire
SJ 8910 *Villa*
A winged corridor villa, whose central range had three rooms in line, with a passage separating two of them, and which had a bath suite attached to the south-west corner, was built in the second century. It had two bow-fronted winged projections. In renovations of the fourth century, these were completely replaced by larger rectangular projections.

Errington Arms see **Milecastle 22**

EXETER Devon
SX 9192 Civitas *capital of the Dumnonii: Roman name* Isca Dumnoniorum
Roman Exeter was sited on a hill overlooking a crossing of the Exe estuary. An auxiliary fort at the site preceded the late Claudian legionary fortress. Parts of four barrack blocks have been excavated, as well

as a well-preserved military bath house, the hypocaust *pilae* of which survive. There is also evidence for a *fabrica* in the fortress. The occupying force was probably Legio II *Augusta*. The fortress was abandoned in the 70s and parts of it were demolished between AD75 and 80.

In c80 the *civitas* capital of the Dumnonii was established at Exeter, possibly growing out of the *vicus* that had evolved around the fortress. The new town adopted the street plan and part of the defence system of the fortress site, and the legionary baths appear to have been converted for later use. A Flavian *forum* and *basilica* were built. The *basilica* lay on the south-east side of the *forum* and had a 10m (33ft) long nave. Water pipes found in the *forum* suggest there had been a public fountain. The public baths lay to the south-east of the *forum* and were provided with a colonnade and a sandstone block pavement. There was an impressively large (16m/52ft) cold plunge bath in the complex. The street plan was regular, and the town was divided into about 25 *insulae*, about 75×90m (250×300ft) each.

Evidence for domestic life is scanty. One Antonine house, which was timber-framed and had two *opus signinum* floors, has been found. The remains of a bag of *tesserae* imply that a mosaic was intended for one of its rooms. Walls, tessellated floors and hypocausts from other houses have been noted.

The permanent defences were constructed after AD100 with an earth rampart measuring 7.5m (25ft) at the base. The south gate has been investigated and proved to have been of masonry, although constructed at the same time as the earthworks. It had either a single or dual carriageway. The defences were modified in the third century, when a stone wall was inserted in front of the rampart. The enclosed area was of 32½ acres (13ha). The wall still stands to 4.25m (14ft) in some places.

In the late third to early fourth century the *forum* and *basilica* underwent alterations, but other public buildings were beginning to fall into disrepair. By about 380, grass and weeds were growing in the *palaestra* of the baths and, despite further alterations to the

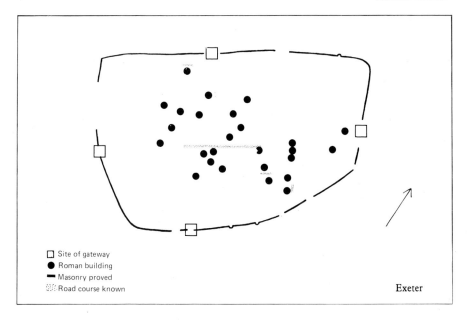

Site of gateway
● Roman building
▬ Masonry proved
Road course known

Exeter

forum complex in the mid fourth century, Roman civic life appears to have gradually died out. Colonisations by Welsh and Irish settlers during the late fourth to fifth centuries have been suggested.

EXNING Suffolk
TL 6167 *Villa*
The villa at Exning, often referred to as Landwade, was originally an aisled house of timber, and it was raised in the second century. At this time it is probable that the owner and workers shared the building, though in separate quarters, and space was also allowed for livestock, as at Denton

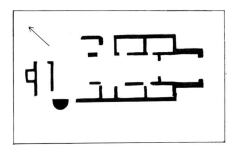

Exning: the aisled house with apartments. Bath suite at bottom left corner

(Lincolnshire) and elsewhere. In the third century the building was reconstructed in stone, with a large room at the western end, which was paved with mosaic. Several smaller rooms filled the rest of the house. A bath suite was installed on the west corner, and fragments of painted plaster have been found.

Fallowfield see **Turret 25b**

FAR COTTON Northamptonshire
SP 735584 *Pottery kilns*
A number of pottery kilns were found at Far Cotton, Camp Hill, during recent excavations. Products included first- and second-century wares.

FARLEY HEATH Surrey
TQ 052449 *Temple*
A Romano-Celtic temple was first located and excavated in the 1840s. It was re-excavated at the beginning of the Second World War. A range of religious objects was discovered which are now in the British Museum and the Guildford Museum. The temple was a square *cella* within a *temenos* with polygonal plan walling. It appears to have had two phases. The temple and

343

temenos were raised in the later first century and, at a subsequent date, an inner wall was built to the north of the *cella*. The structure was destroyed in the fifth century.

FARMINGTON Gloucestershire
SP 132158 *Villa*
Farmington, also known as Clear Cupboard, began as a simple rectangular house, about 28 × 10m (92 × 33ft), with only two rooms. The larger room comprised about three-quarters of the whole building, and it had a rough floor and hearths and was probably the kitchen. The smaller room was the bedroom-cum-sitting room, and had *opus signinum* flooring. Later in the fourth century, the simple house was substantially enlarged by conversion to a winged corridor house. The wings projected forwards and outwards. One wing was equipped with hypocaust heating. The bath suite was put into the original kitchen. Later still, one of the rooms was altered to accommodate livestock.

FARMOOR Berkshire
SP 443055 *Settlement*
A Romano-British settlement succeeded Iron Age occupation of this site at Farmoor, near Cumnor, which is now partly obscured by a new reservoir. Excavation of the mid 1970s revealed a circular house, a stone-lined well, corn driers and some evidence of field systems.

FARNHAM Suffolk
TM 3758 *Substantial building*
In the early 1970s, remains of a major building of the Roman period were found at Farnham. The building was rectangular, about 5 × 27m (16½ × 90ft), with projections, and contained hypocausts.

FARNINGHAM Kent
TQ 555675 *Villa*
Known as Franks villa, this consisted of two rectangular blocks in an L-plan, with a third undetermined structure in the re-entrant. One block appeared to have separate housing

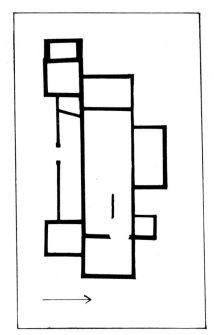

Farmington. The original house occupied most of the central (east–west) range

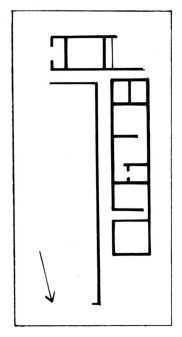

Phase I of Farningham villa

units for different families. The villa complex is of various periods. Some of the walling has been dated to the Flavian period, and this was discovered in the late 1940s. It had painted plaster, some of it in a trellis-work motif.

FEATHERWOOD EAST
Northumberland NT 8105
Marching camp
A marching camp of about 135 acres (55ha), with *titula*, was erected here.

FEATHERWOOD WEST
Northumberland NT 815059
Marching camp
A trapezoid plan marching camp was erected here, with five *titula*, about ½ mile from the marching camp at Featherwood East (see above).

FENCOTT Oxfordshire
SP 572168 *Bridge over river*
A most interesting recent discovery at Fencott has been some of the piles for the bridge carrying the Dorchester to Alchester road (Margary 160b) over the river Ray. Examination of some of the piles has shown that one row of three was cut from one oak tree; the tree ring count gave the date for felling as cAD95–110. What may have been abutments to support the bridge were also seen.

FINCHAMPSTEAD Berkshire
SU 782639 *Stretches of road*
Excavations in Finchampstead in the 1970s were undertaken to locate parts of the London to Silchester Roman Road (Margary 4a). Several stretches were identified, and in 1977 the alignment of the road was checked at Wick Hill Lodge Paddock (SU 804641). The alignment was found to be on a straight line between the north-west corner of Heath Road and the spot in Six Acres Field where in 1841 a Roman milestone had been found on the 4a road. This milestone was later moved to Banister's Farm, at SU 782639.

FINGLAND Cumbria
NY 269575 *Fort*
An auxiliary fort was noted on a ridge by

aerial observation in 1979. It was probably, though not certainly, a Trajanic fort of the western Stanegate system.

FINGRINGHOE Essex
TM 0319 *Military supply base*
Legio XX, stationed at Colchester soon after the first phase of Aulus Plautius' conquest, AD43–4, may have been supplied from a military base at Fingringhoe on the Colne estuary. Some military equipment has been found, as well as fragments of buildings, but the site was unfortunately destroyed by gravel workings before proper recording of finds could be carried out.

FISHBOURNE West Sussex
SU 839046 *Palace*
The palace at Fishbourne is unique among the remains of Roman Britain in its complexity and size at such an early point in the history of the province. Lying on a promontory of gravelly clay with streams running to either side, the palace was well positioned, and had access to deep water anchorage in a sheltered harbour. Of pre-Roman occupation there is very little evidence, and the first post-Conquest occupation was a military installation built of timber, dating to soon after AD43. After being abandoned by the army, the site was altered for civilian use with wattle-and-daub buildings being constructed sometimes re-using the timbers of the original military settlement. Between 65 and 75, major rebuilding and renovation took place, the timber work being replaced by masonry in some areas. An unusual Neronian building consisting of a range of rooms sandwiched by corridors with an elaborate bath suite and colonnaded garden was constructed. This has been labelled the 'Proto-Palace'.

In c75 the site was levelled and the four-sided Flavian palace with its formal, laid-out gardens was constructed. The possible owner of the palace was Cogidubnus, client king of the Regnenses, the local tribe who were on the whole pro-Roman. The palace was of considerable size, with a luxuriously decorated interior. Most floors had mosaics, painted plaster decorated many walls and different coloured marbles were

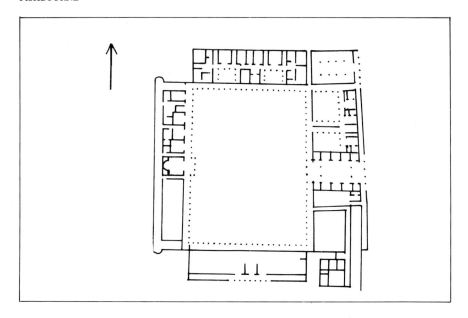

Fishbourne palace had building ranges on all four sides of the courtyard and gardens

used to frame doorways. Some rooms had moulded stucco friezes, an unusual feature for a Romano-British building.

The four wings of the palace surrounded a garden which was laid out with hedges forming patterns, and which probably had a series of decorative fountains. The west wing consisted of a set of rooms which opened onto a colonnaded verandah. This verandah ran round the entire length of the interior of each of the palace wings. The centrepiece of the west wing was an audience chamber which had an apse that once had a fine mosaic. All but four of the wing's rooms had mosaic floors, with black and white geometric designs. The north wing was an E-shaped range of rooms set round two colonnaded courtyards. The east wing was in this period the most sumptuous part of the building. At the north end stood a large aisled hall, with four pairs of piers supporting the roof, the bases of which survive. Immediately to the south of the hall were two colonnaded courtyards flanked by a range of eleven rooms. Centrally in the wing

stood an entrance hall, which was probably colonnaded and pedimented at both its east and west ends. At the west end was an ornamental pool with a fountain. The southern end of the east wing was taken up with the rooms of the Neronian structure that was incorporated into the Flavian complex. It was linked to the east wing by a courtyard backed by a set of rooms. The south wing of the palace is an unknown since it lies buried beneath modern houses and gardens.

Among alterations that took place in the early second century was the reroofing of the aisled hall. This may have become the exercise area for an adjoining new set of baths built in the north wing. This bath suite had rooms of graded temperature with a hypocaust heating system. The most far-reaching alterations to the palace took place in the mid second century when a substantial part of the north wing, including the new bath suite, was demolished. Two rooms of the remaining part of the wing were provided with hypocausts, whilst other rooms received new mosaics, one of which was a very fine piece depicting a cupid astride a dolphin. A new bath suite was fitted in the east wing to replace the demolished set. Only minor works were carried out in the early third century, but some rooms and the north and east sides of the verandah were refloored.

Towards the end of the third century, Fishbourne palace was destroyed by fire. The east wing escaped, but the building was abandoned and no rebuilding took place. Soon after the fire the ruins of the palace were substantially robbed for building materials.

FISHTOFT Lincolnshire
TF 371409 *Agricultural site*
An agricultural site of the Roman period was located at Fishtoft, near Nunn's Bridge, and excavated in the mid 1970s. Coins give occupation as the third and fourth centuries.

FLITWICK Bedfordshire
TL 026350 *Enclosure*
A rectilinear crop mark seen from the air on an intended housing estate at Manor Way proved to be part of a ditched enclosure that

yielded pottery of the second to fourth centuries. A T-shaped furnace with sandstone fireplace was situated in a circular drying chamber, the roof of which had been supported on a central post; the walls were of wattle and daub.

FLORE Northamptonshire
SP 642617 *Settlement*
A site known to have been occupied in Roman times, Flore, near Weedon, was examined in the late 1970s, and quantities of limestone fragments, broken tiles and associated pottery were found. Some pottery sherds were of Samian ware.

FOLKESTONE Kent
TR 2437 *Villa*
Folkestone villa seems to have been a residence of some importance, and it was splendidly positioned upon the cliff edge overlooking the sea. Some of the cliff has since fallen away, taking with it some of the villa remains. It began as a winged corridor

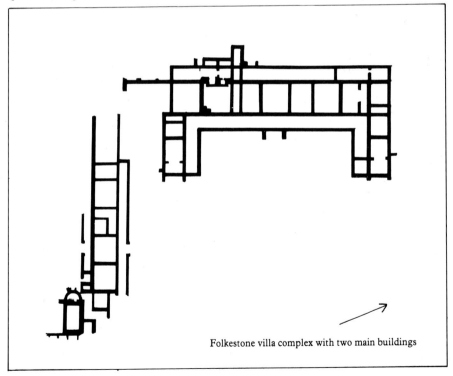

Folkestone villa complex with two main buildings

347

villa (corridors front and back), probably of the second century, with bow-fronted wings (as at Engleton in Staffordshire). Later, the wings (and perhaps other parts of the main block) were rebuilt and enlarged. A bath suite was erected at the south-west end of the back corridor. The wings were rebuilt square. The central dining room had a mosaic floor. There was also a second building, at right angles, on a north-west to south-east alignment, and this consisted of a central range with corridors front and back, each with a porch. At the extreme south-east end of the second block there was a second bath suite. The villa may have been associated with the high command of the British Fleet (*classis Britannica*), for several tiles and bricks with the monogram CL BR were found in the ruins.

FORDHAM Cambridgeshire
TL 635684 *Villa*
The villa just south of Fordham was excavated in the early 1970s. A hypocaust was found (in 1971), and a quantity of painted wall plaster. Pottery was of the third century.

FOTHERINGAY Northamptonshire
TL 079944 *Villa*
A villa, with associated aisled barn on low stone walls, was examined in 1970 in advance of development.

FOXHOLES FARM Hertfordshire
TL 338125 *Industrial site*
Excavations in a gravel pit over the Lea valley at Foxholes Farm, near Hertford, during the later 1970s exposed industrial and agricultural activities of both Iron Age and Roman periods. The Roman works were metal and pottery industries and appear to have been in operation in the third and fourth centuries. A number of furnaces were revealed, as well as corn driers, including one in almost perfect condition (which is now in Hertford Museum).

FRAMPTON Dorset
SY 6195 *Villa*
Frampton villa was L-plan, and appears to have been an impressive structure. Excava-

tions have revealed a rich variety of mosaics, including a remarkable pavement consisting of a rectangle and a square with classical scenes in segments and an aspidal projection at one end of the square, containing the Chi-Rho monogram. Acting as borders to two sides are two sets of Latin couplets, which are rare in Romano-British villas. Among the artefacts uncovered were fragments of chairs and tables made of Kimmeridge shale.

FRILFORD Oxfordshire
SU 4297, 4396, 4496 *Small town*
The area round the village of Frilford has yielded several interesting Roman remains, including a temple complex (at SU 4396) investigated in the 1930s, a building with a bath house close by, a villa (SU 4297) and an amphitheatre (some 65m [213ft] in diameter) near Noah's Ark Inn at Frilford (SU 4496). These and other remains suggest the existence of a small town, which lay astride a road junction. This is probably another example of a temple being associated with an amphitheatre as a major religious centre, like Gosbecks, near Colchester, and Catterick, St Albans and Richborough. The villa at Frilford was a simple corridor-type house with one wing on the south-east, containing a hypocaust.

FRING Norfolk
TF 735343 *Enclosure*
A rectangular enclosure, partly defended by double-ditching, partly by single-ditching, was spotted during aerial reconnaissance near Peddars Way. The enclosure appeared to be divided into three sectors, the middle of which showed building traces. Ground checks unearthed pottery of the third and fourth centuries.

FROCESTER COURT Gloucestershire
SO 785029 *Villa*
Frocester Court villa began as a simple cottage house. This was enlarged into a winged corridor house, one corridor of which was later given a mosaic pavement. A bath suite was added on the north-west wing in the mid fourth century, by which time the villa had a walled courtyard. Frocester has been excavated in detail, and found to have

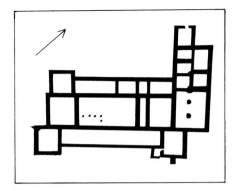

Frocester Court villa. The original simple house occupied part of the central range

been associated with extensive enclosures around its courtyard, which were devoted to farming and also to what may have been market gardening. There was also evidence of more formal gardens.

FULLERTON Hampshire
SU 3740 *Villa*
The villa at Fullerton was on winged corridor plan. It lay near a stream which was harnessed to operate the villa's mill. So far, no traces of granary or other farm buildings have been located, and the mill may have serviced other villas and farms in the neighbourhood. The villa had mosaic floors: some were lifted in the nineteenth century and relaid in Fullerton Manor, only to be covered by building work by vandals in the twentieth.

GADEBRIDGE PARK Hertfordshire
SP 051086 *Villa*
The villa was built on the east bank of the river Gade about 5 miles from *Verulamium* (St Albans). No previous occupation is known from the site before the Roman foundation which probably dates to c75. Little is known of the early years of occupation, apart from the fact that the site probably consisted of buildings slightly to the east of the later villa. The first building was probably of timber on a masonry base, and had a separate three-roomed bath house. During the second century, redevelopment occurred on a large scale. The villa was built as a winged corridor-type and, at 42m (140ft)

wide, was larger than other nearby villas. The building was symmetrically laid out with a central range and two projecting wings. A cellar was included in the building and the bath house was enlarged and refurbished. Although large, the villa was not apparently very luxuriously decorated: not many traces of painted plaster have been found. Of the two wings, the east was joined onto the body of the villa whilst the west was separate, the two being united by a boundary wall to the south.

During the third century, as at Gorhambury, there seems to have been a period of neglect, although there is no evidence of abandonment. The fourth century saw a large rebuilding project, with rooms being added to the main body on the north side and one – if not both – of the original wings being demolished. Thus the villa was turned back-to-front with the new courtyard on the north side. In c325 a large, new, heated hall, 20m (66ft) long, was added and a vast new pool constructed, 12 × 20.5m (40 × 68½ft), almost as large as the Great Bath at Bath. This points to the complex being used by large numbers of people. The villa was destroyed at some point before 353, but there are signs of some occupation up to the end of the fourth century and probably into the fifth century, with cattle stockades built amongst the ruins.

GARDEN HILL East Sussex
TQ 444319 *Iron-working settlement*
An iron-working settlement of Roman times was established upon an earlier Iron Age hillfort at Garden Hill, Hartfield. It was discovered in 1968 and excavated in the mid 1970s. The hillfort had been hastily defended by the British against the advancing Roman army of conquest of AD43–4. Then it fell, and was taken over. Excavations exposed timber buildings, ore roasting and smelting furnaces and a forging hearth, all of the first century. Residential buildings of the first century were also located. In the second century, a large timber-framed building on a stone platform, with an attached bath house, was erected. The settlement has been described as a base from which several local iron-smelting industries were operated.

349

GARTON SLACK Humberside
SE 953601 *Settlement*
A small settlement of Iron Age origin continued to flourish in the Roman period. Roman pottery fragments covering the second and third centuries were found in excavations of the late 1960s and early 1970s. A well was excavated down to a depth of 18m (60ft) or so.

GATCOMBE Avon
ST 526699 *?Private estate*
Gatcombe, Long Ashton, has presented archaeologists with problems of interpretation. It does not resemble other villa sites in towns of its size and in the existence of defences, and yet it does not seem to resemble any other small town settlement yet found. Of the different suggestions made so far, a private estate appears the most likely interpretation. The earliest pottery from the site is of the second half of the first century. A timber building of the second century with stone foundations could be the focus of a small farmstead. If this is so, the site appears to have been run down or abandoned for a period between c200 and the last quarter of the third century. A sudden change occurred c280–90, when defences and a number of stone buildings were erected at the site. The walls probably stood to 3–4m (10–13ft) high and enclosed a trapezoidal area of 17½ acres (7ha). No trace of ditch fronting the wall has been found. The parts of the interior buildings excavated are enigmatic. None can

be confidently described as domestic, but they do not appear to have been used for agricultural purposes. One has been found to have had ovens, probably for baking, and another with large quantities of butchered bones of cattle was possibly a slaughterhouse. The buildings were plain in terms of interior decoration, with no plaster, decorative floorings or hypocausts. There are, however, some clues to the existence of a nearby villa in the form of hypocaust flues and a mosaic panel from near the site.

Whatever form the site took, it was apparently abandoned abruptly c380, suggesting a marked change in the fortunes of the occupants. This would point to the existence of a private estate at Gatcombe, rather than a small settlement of individual owner-occupiers. Later occupation of ruined houses and rebuilding suggests the site ended as it started, as a small farmstead.

GAYHURST Buckinghamshire
SP 853464 *Villa*
An interesting villa site was examined in the late 1960s. It had traces of two circular timber buildings on stone foundations, dated to the second century. Sometime in the third century, these buildings were replaced by a single rectangular villa, about 15m (50ft) long, erected in the space between the houses. The villa house had a tessellated floor in the corridor, and its walls were wattle and daub. The house was abandoned in the fourth century.

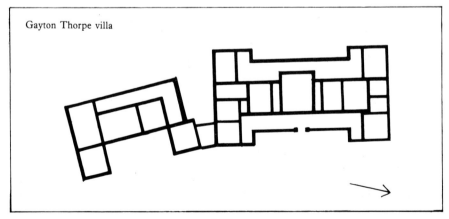

Gayton Thorpe villa

350

GAYTON THORPE Norfolk
TF 7318 *Villa*
Gayton Thorpe complex is regarded by villa specialists as unusual, since it began as two independent houses situated close together, both of them residential. The larger house, facing east, had corridors along east and west sides of the centre range, with symmetrical wings, producing an H-plan. Two mosaic pavements were found. The second structure at the south end, a few metres away, also had corridors and had two symmetrical wings. The two houses were eventually linked by a small passage block to convert them to a single substantial house which may, nevertheless, still have been occupied by more than one family. One find was a tile stamped LEG VI VICT.

GILLALEES Cumbria
NY 591718 *Signal station*
A signal station which guarded the Roman road from Birdoswald fort to Bewcastle fort stood near the top of Gillalees Beacon, out of sight of any intruders from the north but in good view from Birdoswald and other points along Hadrian's Wall.

GLASSHOUSE WOOD Warwickshire
SP 311719 *Settlement*
A building with stone foundations was found in excavations on a settlement near the Kenilworth bypass. It had been erected over an earlier timber structure and across part of a ditch from which first-century pottery fragments were lifted. A number of walled pens had been erected along the building's north side. Fragments of stamped tiles were also discovered.

GLOUCESTER Gloucestershire
SO 8318 *Legionary fortress and* colonia:
Roman name: Glevum
A legionary fortress of some 43 acres (17ha) dating from about AD67 preceded the founding of the *colonia* of Gloucester at a strategic crossing point of the river Severn. The settlement owes its position to the proximity of the navigable reaches of the river, although this advantage does not appear to have made Gloucester as great a trading centre as its fellow *colonia* at Lincoln. The

colonia was founded in emperor Nerva's short reign between AD96 and 98 for veterans of the Roman army.

The planning of the *colonia* owed much to that of the legionary fortress. The *forum*, now under Eastgate Street, was in an equivalent position to the fortress *principia* and the wall followed the line of the original fortifications. Hurst's recent excavations have established that the *colonia* buildings were erected immediately after the demolition of those of the fortress. The first colonial domestic accommodation seems to have followed the pattern of the old barrack blocks, and to have been of wattle and daub built on low stone foundations. Also associated with this phase is a narrow circuit wall following the earthen ramparts of the fortress. Later, at the end of the second century, a stone wall was built with rectangular stone towers. The positions of the gates are believed to have been similar to those of the medieval period.

The original Trajanic *forum* was gravelled and provided with half-timbered ranges. The piazza was later paved with flagstones and the buildings replaced with stone constructions. A *basilica* stood to the south-west of the *forum*, with dimensions of 97.5 × 68.5m (108 × 75ft). Another large, possibly public, building in the Westgate Street area had massive foundations and a colonnade. The scale of the public buildings suggests a population with civic pride, wealth and an interest in conforming to the Roman 'model' of a *colonia*. A uniformity of taste can be detected in the wealthier domestic buildings that have been uncovered, where there were many mosaics of similar designs.

Little evidence has, as yet, emerged about the industrial activities of this apparently prosperous colony. The large number of bricks and tiles with a municipal stamp suggests industries producing these. There is equally little evidence for the religious life of the *colonia*. Only small fragments provide information, for example a piece from an altar dedicated to Mars from the Kingsholm area.

The decline of the Roman city in the fourth century may have been helped by possible flooding of the central area. There is no evidence for use of the *forum* from the beginning of the fifth century. A deposit of untainted grey loam spread over the *forum* area could be attributable to waterlogged conditions.

GODMANCHESTER Cambridgeshire
TL 2470 *?Fort and small town: Roman name*
Durovigutum
Godmanchester is one of a number of sites that are difficult to classify as a particular type. Lying in the valley of the Great Ouse at a point where it was crossed by the major route to the north, Ermine Street, Godmanchester was strategically well positioned as the site for a fort.

This fort, which was Claudian, had two ditches measuring 2–3m (7–10ft) wide and a rampart; a four-post interval tower has also been traced, as has a grid of post holes suggesting a granary. Traces of a possible extramural settlement have also been found. The fort was apparently burnt down c60–1, probably during the Boudican uprising. The *vicus* was then laid out and rapid expansion followed during the Flavian period, particularly in the form of 'ribbon' development along Ermine Street. The style of building retained a pre-Roman flavour with both Iron Age-style round huts and rectangular cottages being built.

The most impressive building of the second century to have been found was the *mansio*. The building was probably half-timbered above the ground floor which had walls of masonry. It dates from after 120, was 95m (105yd) long, had a courtyard and two tower granaries. Its associated bath house had a hypocaust and plunge baths, substantial enough to have been open to the public. Also dating from the second century were timber-framed cottages and workshops and a shrine.

Early in the third century the *vicus* provided itself with a single-aisled *basilica* measuring 24×13m (79×43ft). Defences of the late third century enclosed an irregular hexagonal plan area with a stone wall nearly 3m (10ft) thick, backed with a clay rampart nearly 10m (33ft) wide. Two gateways, the south and part of the north, have been explored. Both appear to have had a central

carriageway with flanking footways and gate towers. At the end of the third century a disaster occurred when the *mansio* and baths were burnt down. A slight revival of the town occurred c369 when bastions were added to the fortification walls. This could be a result of Count Theodorius' plan to refortify the towns of the province. The bath house was also rebuilt and continued in use until the end of the Roman period. The *mansio*, however, never recovered and its site was built over with timber buildings. These, along with their associated scatters of Saxon pottery, probably represent the pattern of reoccupation of the whole site after the end of the Roman period.

GOLDSBOROUGH North Yorkshire
NZ 836151 *Signal station*
One of the chain of fortified outward searching signal stations built along the Yorkshire coast in the later fourth century to guard the coast against pirate raids (others included Huntcliff, Ravenscar and Scarborough), Goldsborough's remains lie under a mound. The stone tower had been about 15m (50ft) square, with 2.5m (8ft) thick walls. The height may have been as much as 27 or 30m (90 or 100ft). The tower stood inside a square plan stone wall enclosure, with rounded angle turrets (or bastions) on the corners. It was probably built c370 and appears to have functioned until the end of the fourth century, when it looks as if it was overwhelmed in a surprise attack. The skeleton of one of the garrison was found slumped over a fire bed, his skull severely damaged.

GOLTHO Lincolnshire
TF 116774 *Homestead*
A series of Saxon manor houses in the deserted medieval village here was recently excavated, and traces of a Romano-British homestead were detected underneath. The building seems to have been occupied between about AD50 and AD200. The homestead had been surrounded by a timber wall.

GORHAMBURY Hertfordshire
TL 117079 *Villa*
Gorhambury villa lay on a spur sloping east

into the valley of the river Ver and only about ½ mile north-west of *Verulamium* (St Albans). The villa was constructed on the site of a pre-Conquest settlement; traces of the timber buildings of this early settlement have been found. The first Roman occupation dates from the first century and seems to have consisted of a timber building, although this was replaced early in the second century by a fine masonry structure with five rooms, a single corridor and a wing room on the north-east side. Small but luxurious, Gorhambury had a cellar with a polygonal apse, on the walls of which were stuccos showing half life-sized figures. Also from this period, unusually early for a British villa, are fragments of mosaics. At this time the villa was ahead of the town of *Verulamium* in terms of architectural achievement and interior decoration.

In the later second century, the villa was rebuilt further to the west and comprised a set of rooms with double corridor and a small bath suite on the south-west side. The orientation of the villa was changed from that of the earlier structure with the frontage reversed, turning the villa back-to-front. The baths were altered and modernised slightly later, but on the whole the villa seems to have been neglected in the third century, although not abandoned. An unusual rectangular outbuilding was constructed during the period with a ramp-like entrance. Early in the fourth century, minor repairs were made to the villa and the bath suite, but decline followed shortly after this and there is no sign of the 'fourth-century revival' found in so many other places. The last absolute date for the villa is 348.

GOSBECKS Essex
TL 9622 *Romano-Celtic site*
The site at Gosbecks, near Colchester, was excavated in some detail during the 1960s and 1970s and has been the subject of much aerial observation, though little can be seen at ground level today. A number of interesting features have been located. It was originally an Iron Age sanctuary surrounded by a sizeable ditch. In the Roman period, the religious importance was enhanced by the building of a Romano-Celtic style temple

within its own porticoed court. This was in the second century. The whole site of some 30 acres (12ha) appears to have been enclosed partly, if not entirely, by walling, within which were also built, about 120m (130yd) south of the temple, a south-facing theatre of masonry and timber, in half-moon plan (not unlike that at St Albans), a bath house and other structures. The area, or part of it, was used as a fairground. The theatre does not seem to have been built for stage performances, but for gatherings to watch religious rites, and as a meeting place at festival occasions connected perhaps with the temple.

About 500m (550yd) north-west of the fairground site, a fort was noted by aerial observation and confirmed, which was a nearly square parallelogram. It covered over 5 acres (2ha) and traces were found of the *principia* and two gates. Dating the fort poses problems. Gosbecks is close to Colchester. Did the fort come before the legionary fortress at Colchester, begun in AD44, or was it raised after the Boudican revolt, when Colchester was burnt?

GRAMBLA Cornwall
SW 693283 *Defended enclosure*
An Iron Age enclosure of almost square plan at Grambla, near Wendron, was occupied in the Roman period. It was enclosed by a V-shaped ditch. There was one entrance. Two buildings of dry-stone walling were excavated in the early 1970s. It is clear that the enclosure continued to be occupied well into the fifth century.

GRASSINGTON North Yorkshire
SE 0065 *Agricultural site*
Some well-preserved Celtic fields at Grassington, the dividing banks of which are visible, have been confidently claimed as arable fields worked under Roman influence, and this was attested by pottery finds.

GRAYS Essex
TQ 625787 *Pottery kilns*
Several pottery kilns have been investigated in and near the playing fields of Palmer's School, dating to the second and third centuries. Evidence of products included

fragments of jars, pedestal urns and flagons (the last in red with cream slip).

GREAT CASTERTON Leicestershire
TF 0009 *Small town*

Positioned on Ermine Street near a crossing point of the river Gwash, the settlement at Great Casterton appears to have first taken the form of a rectangular round-cornered fort with permanent defences and timber buildings. The fort probably dates from soon after the Conquest. To the south-west of the fort a *vicus* developed near the river crossing. In the late second century, Great Casterton, which had presumably grown in size and importance as a town after its military function had ceased, was provided with defences. These consisted of a stone wall backed with earth and fronted by a ditch. On the north side, which was particularly vulnerable, three ditches have been traced. The area enclosed was polygonal and occupied 18 acres (7ha). Little is known of the interior of the town, which appears to have lacked a regular street pattern. Traces of timber buildings and of a stone structure,

The temple at Great Chesterford

probably a *mansio*, have been found. In the mid fourth century, the defences were rebuilt with rectangular bastions 6×3m (20×10ft) added to the wall. Although the nearby villa was burnt at the end of the fourth century, life probably continued within the town's defences for some time.

GREAT CHESTERFORD Essex
TL 503430 *Small town*

A large fort of about 35–7 acres (14–15ha) was erected at Great Chesterford, probably by Suetonius Paullinus in AD61 as part of his measures against the peoples of the area following the defeat of Boudica. It may have been built to house a vexillation of legionaries along with auxiliary units. Tacitus refers to 2000 legionaries, eight auxiliary infantry units and 1000 cavalry being transferred from Germany to Britain after the revolt, and to their being stationed in new winter quarters (*History* xiv, 38). A *vicus* developed outside the fort, on the east side of the Cam. This grew into a walled town of 40 acres (16ha) or so, and this has been excavated. Some stone buildings, including a large rectangular storehouse, have been detected. Also located was a

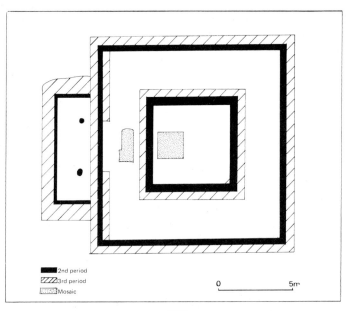

2nd period
3rd period
Mosaic

0   5m

Romano-Celtic temple, about 1 mile east of the town, which had a mosaic-floored *cella*, wall plaster and an ambulatory (TL 514436). A number of artefacts were found and they are now in the Museum of Archaeology and Anthropology at Cambridge.

GREATCHESTERS Northumberland
NY 706672 *Fort on Hadrian's Wall: Roman name* Aesica
Greatchesters fort was built into the scheme of Hadrian's Wall later than many of the forts, and it replaced a milecastle after a change in the overall plan. The fort therefore does not project north of the Wall and its north wall lies along the Wall. The fort occupies about 3 acres (1.2ha); it was begun not earlier than AD 128 and it accommodated, to begin with, an infantry cohort of auxiliaries. The arrangement of the fort was that it faced east. Today, all that remain are extensive earthworks, notably four ditches and ramparts protecting the west side. The gate in the west side is of interest because its history can be seen in surviving remains: a normal entrance with a turret on each side and with two portals, which were reduced later to a single portal and later still closed off altogether. Some of the fort's interior buildings were uncovered in investigations of the nineteenth century and early years of this century. Outside the fort, to the south and east, was the *vicus* and, to the south, the bath house, first discovered in 1897.

One of the interesting features of Greatchesters is the 6 mile long winding water channel, 1–1.25m (3–4ft) deep, from the Caw Burn to a point outside the fort, which provided a constant stream of water for flushing the latrines as well as supplying the fort's water requirements. The fort's granary was rebuilt in about 225. In the late third century, a number of chalet-type barrack blocks were built, traces of which have been found. Some chalets had flagstone flooring.

GREAT DUNMOW Essex
TL 626219 *Small town*
A small Roman town just north of Stane Street (Margary 32) has been investigated in recent years by Essex Archaeological Society. Finds include the remains of timber buildings, a 6.5m (22ft) deep oak-lined well, several burials and a variety of artefacts and coins, ranging over nearly four centuries of occupation. One find of special interest was a timber shrine, the inner chamber of which had been about 5×3m (16.5×10ft) and was subsequently rebuilt.

GREAT MONGEHAM Kent
TQ 347513 *Farmstead*
A native Belgic farmstead, which continued to be worked in the early Roman period, was examined in the late 1970s and early 1980s. Considerable quantities of sherds of both Belgic and early Roman pottery were found.

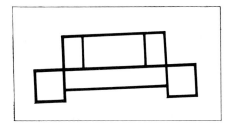

Great Staughton winged corridor villa

GREAT STAUGHTON Cambridgeshire
TL 1363 *Villa*
One of the villa buildings at Great Staughton, raised in the early fourth century, was a very simple but symmetrical small corridor house about 32m (105ft) from east to west, with two square projecting wings. There were mosaics in both wings and in the corridor, and painted plaster walls. Fragments of cut glass are said to have been found among the debris in excavations of the late 1950s. There was a second building with a corridor nearby, about 60m (200ft) south. These two buildings succeeded an earlier villa, probably of the second century. One of the surviving mosaics, a complex geometric design, was particularly fine.

GREAT TEW Oxfordshire
SP 4027 *Villa*
The villa here was excavated nearly two centuries ago, and it has been re-examined since. The bath house was located, and two fragments of mosaic paving were found.

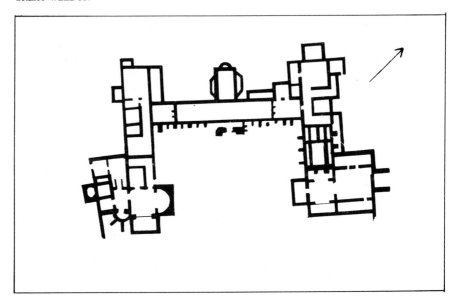

Great Witcombe villa: plan incorporating all additions. Note the first rectangular dining room at top centre, which was later replaced by polygonal room

GREAT WELDON Northamptonshire
SP 929899 *Villa*
A corridor villa of the late first to early second century was examined in the early 1950s before the whole site was destroyed in mining operations. It had been a relatively prosperous establishment to judge from the mosaics and the interesting wall painting (which included imitation marble patterns on some panels). A courtyard wall jutted out from the villa front. There was a rectangular building in the complex, the history of which is uncertain but which was at some time used for metal working.

GREAT WITCOMBE Gloucestershire
SO 907143 *Villa*
The villa at Great Witcombe has a very fine situation lying on the slopes of Cooper's Hill, 1 mile south of Brockworth, near Gloucester. The villa probably dates from the first century AD and was occupied continuously until its eventual abandonment in the fourth century. A series of alterations and additions took place during the villa's occupation. The interior decoration was of a quite high standard, eight of the rooms having mosaic floors and the walls being covered with painted plaster. Pots which once contained the paint for this decoration have been found. The first of the mosaic pavements is probably the work of local craftsmen and has an unusual design of an underwater scene showing fishes and other sea creatures. Most of the building remains are still buried, but one area is on display – a set of baths with an adjoining room which contained a basin and niches along one wall. A religious function has been ascribed to this particular room.

GREEN ORE Somerset
ST 5850 *Lead-working settlement*
The owner of Rookery Farm, Green Ore, Chewton Mendip, renamed his farm Vespasian Farm following the discovery in 1956 of four lead pigs of Vespasianic date on his land. These were stamped with the pro-cessor's name, Triferna, who may be the same Triferna that had worked at *Lutudarum* in Derbyshire. Remains of a lead-working settlement were uncovered at Green Ore, including lead-smelting furnaces, and nearby

on the road from Charterhouse to Fosse Way a cupelling hearth was located.

GREENSFORGE Staffordshire
SO 864886 *Fort*
This is the site of one of the earliest Roman forts in Britain. Built by Ostorius in about AD50, it covered about 4 acres (1.6ha). Nearby are traces of two marching camps. The fort was later reduced in size. There is still much to be learned from the site, but it appears to have been occupied in the fourth century, though whether continuously from the 50s to that time is not established.

GREETWELL Lincolnshire
SK 9971 *Villa*
A small 'suburban' villa house outside the *colonia* of *Lindum* (Lincoln) was excavated in the 1890s. It had had painted plaster walls.

GRENDON Northamptonshire
TL 8661 *Pottery kiln*
During excavation of the prehistoric enclosures here, an early Roman pottery kiln was located.

GRETA BRIDGE Durham
NZ 085132 *Fort: Roman name* Maglona
The fort at Greta Bridge has left some visible remains, notably its southern ditch and rampart (the ditching was a double system). The fort was built in Agricola's time and was occupied periodically into the third century. There was a *vicus* nearby with timber buildings, which first developed in the Trajanic period. There was some renovation to the fort in the Severan period.

GRIMSBY Humberside
TA 275075 *Pottery*
An enclosure of Iron Age origin was examined in excavations at Weelsby Avenue, in the late 1970s, and some Roman pottery was found.

Grindon see **Milecastle 34**

GUN HILL Essex
TQ 655778 *Pottery kilns*
Pottery kilns were found in a ditched enclosure of the first century.

GWENNAP Cornwall
SW 720419 *Milestone*
A rectangular pillar of granite, about 1m (3½ft) high, was found in 1940 near Gwennap Pit, near Redruth, and it has been re-erected in Mynheer Farm. The inscription dates the milestone to the emperor Gordian III (238–44). This is the milestone that marked the rebuilding of the road to and from Gwennap tin production site, which was re-activated in the mid third century (see p 244).

HACHESTON Suffolk
TM 3157 *Industrial settlement*
An industrial settlement about 1¼ miles south of the village was excavated in the 1970s. Remains of residential and workshop buildings, including metal workshops and pottery kilns producing grey ware, were discovered, the site being mainly of the third and fourth centuries. One interesting discovery was a timber-lined well about 5m (17ft) deep, from which some of the oak boards were recovered. The well appears to have been of the second century.

HADLEIGH Suffolk
TM 024437 *Settlement*
A rectangular enclosure surrounded by a U-shaped ditch was examined in the late 1970s. A rectangular corn drier which had collapsed was found to contain sherds of fourth-century pottery. Elsewhere, pottery finds stretched back to the second century.

HALSTOCK Dorset
ST 533076 *Villa*
Halstock villa has been extensively excavated on a continuous programme since the late 1960s. Though not completed, the works have revealed a large and complex courtyard villa of several main structures with extensive corridors, bath suites, several mosaic pavements and a number of agricultural buildings. One of the latter was an aisled building on the north side of the courtyard, which had corn driers, and another is a second aisled building, on the south side, with a single aisle, whose purpose is not yet established. There is also clear evidence of several phases of building.

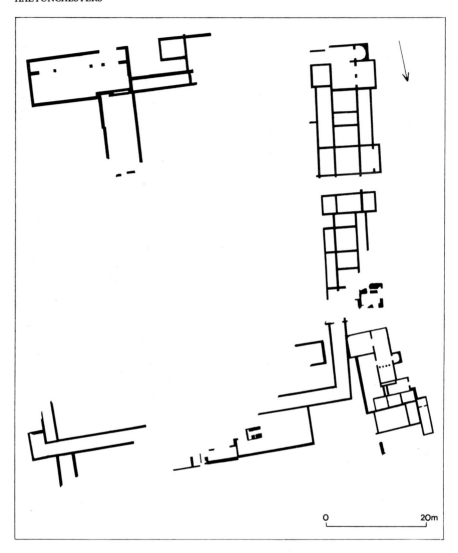

General plan of Halstock villa as excavated so far

HALTONCHESTERS Northumberland
NY 997685 *Fort on Hadrian's Wall: Roman name* Onnum
The fort at Haltonchesters lay on the east bank of Fence Burn, 7 miles west of Rudchester. The original Hadrianic fort was joined into the fabric of the Wall at the south towers of its main east and west gates. It was probably built by c126 over the original Wall defences, necessitating the filling of the ditch that fronted the Wall in the area the fort covered. The fort occupied an area of 4.3 acres (1.7ha) and was of the usual rectangular shape. The first fort had gates with strong masonry foundations, twin portals and towers with guardrooms. Buildings included barrack blocks, stables, a granary and a courtyard house beside the *principia*. The first fort appears to have been destroyed

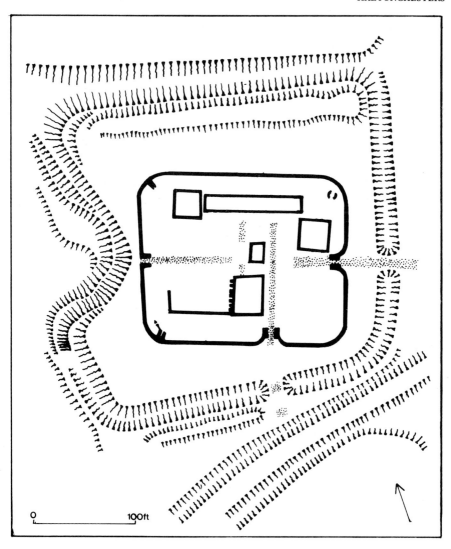

under Commodus c180.

During the third century, Haltonchesters fell into disrepair, although it does not seem to have been abandoned entirely: a unit of cavalry was stationed at the fort for a considerable period of time, from the beginning of the third century to the end of the fourth century. In c369 there was a sudden burst of activity, with large scale rebuilding and refurbishing. By this time the fort had been enlarged by the addition of an extension on

Haltwhistle Burn fortlet (see p 360)

the west side, increasing the area of the fort to 4.8 acres (1.9ha). The focus of the fort at this time was a monumental hall 48m (160ft) long which lay in front of the *principia*. Also dated to the fourth-century building programme is a bath house of elaborate design situated, unusually, inside the fort. Thus the final building phase at Haltonchesters,

359

although occurring a little later than at other forts, was on a fairly large scale.

Haltonshields see Milecastle 20

HALTWHISTLE BURN Northumberland
NY 694655–NY 725660 *Camps and fortlet on Hadrian's Wall/Stanegate*
This is a collection of sites to be visited, which are better described together. Here, the old Stanegate frontier of Trajan's time has survived in one or two stretches of road, running parallel to Hadrian's Wall, and ½–1 mile south of it. From east to west, the principal features are as follows. (a) The remains of a large camp (ditch and rampart to the south), NY 725660. (b) A fortlet of ¾ acre (0.3ha) of Trajan's time, with stone-faced ramparts, three gates and the remains of several buildings, which may have been for a vexillation. The fortlet was superseded in the Hadrianic scheme by the fort at Great-chesters and was dismantled. (c) A series of temporary camps, some with clear remains, the most westerly at Fell End lying across Stanegate and erected probably before the Stanegate road and so was perhaps the camp used by the road builders. A milestone of the time of Emperor Aurelian (273–5) was found nearby and is now in the Museum of Antiquities at Newcastle upon Tyne. There are several stretches of Stanegate west of the camp, leading to the site of the Hadrianic fort of Carvoran.

HAMBLEDEN Buckinghamshire
SU 785855 *Villa*
Hambleden villa was a courtyard-type with its main residential building on the west side, and with a variety of detached buildings on the north and south, at least two of them aisled buildings. The residential block began as a cottage. It was enlarged by a room at the north end and a small bath house at the south. Then, corridors with wing rooms each side were added front and back, with porches, and one rear wing room was a second bath suite. The aisled buildings, both of them 8m (26ft) or so long, contained corn driers. One of the buildings was modified with a projecting wing room which had a hypocaust. There were several more corn

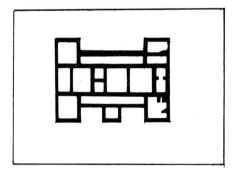

Hambleden winged corridor villa. Bath suite at top right

driers in the villa precinct, and the site is believed to have accommodated the largest number of corn driers in any villa so far excavated. This may be related to the fact that the villa was used as a base at which to collect the *annona militaris* tax, an impost paid by the province to feed the army, often paid in kind, such as in grain.

HAM HILL Somerset
ST 484164 *Fort and settlement*
A considerable Iron Age hillfort, about 200 acres (80ha) in area, may have been used by the Romans as a site for a fort, early in the occupation period. The only evidence so far to support this interesting proposition by Dr Graham Webster is the discovery in 1975 of a V-shaped ditch on the site and some finds much earlier in the century of military items. But it is a perfectly sound proposition, made by perhaps the leading specialist on the military aspects of the Roman occupation of Britain. There is quite separate evidence for Roman occupation of the site and area during the Romano-British period. The quarry appears to have been worked and the Hamdon Hill stone used in various places. There are some villas in the immediate neighbourhood. A hoard of coins was found in the hillfort precinct, the latest being issues of the mid third century.

HAMWORTHY Dorset
SZ 0090 *Supply base*
There was a supply base at Hamworthy, near Poole, for the army (probably Legio II

under Vespasian) in the Hampshire–Wiltshire–Dorset region during the early Conquest period. It was linked by road later on to Badbury Rings (Margary 4d) and thence to Bath. Badbury was the site of an Iron Age hillfort. Hamworthy was also linked to Lake Farm vexillation fortress.

HARDHAM West Sussex
TQ 030175 *Posting station*
There was a Roman posting station at Hardham. It was severely damaged by railway works in the nineteenth century and, more recently, by gravel quarrying. It is sited on Stane Street, the Chichester to London Roman road. The station consisted of a *mansio* enclosed by a ditch and rampart. Inside the enclosure there were other buildings, some of them built of brick and tile.

The fort at Hardknott, Cumbria. West gate in foreground, East gate in background. Behind the East gate is the parade ground (*Graham Sumner*)

HARDKNOTT Cumbria
NY 218015 *Fort: Roman name* Mediobogdum
This fort was built in the early second century, probably while Trajan was still emperor. The remains are almost as dramatic as the site: perched on a commanding rock spur over the Esk valley, the 3 acre (1.2ha) site still has much of its stone surrounding wall which at one time was backed by an earth rampart. The plan is almost square. The site is such that the ground falls aways sharply at most points, and so it was not necessary to cut ditching all round. What was cut, however, was in rock and in some parts was double. The fort had angle towers without entrances at ground level: they were reached through doors accessible only from the wall walk. Among the remains are the *principia*, part of the commandant's house and a pair of granaries (once a simple building, later turned into two). Outside is the simple in-line bath house, which had a circular Spartan room on the north-east of

The north gate at Hardknott fort

the range. To the east, outside, a special parade ground was prepared by levelling the rock, some 3 acres (1.2ha) in area, with a tribunal.

Hare Hill see **Turret 53a**

HARLOW Essex
TL 4712 *Small town*
There have been considerable finds in excavations of the Roman town at Harlow, which was developed on a Belgic settlement site. Four buildings, one with mosaic floor and hypocaust, were uncovered at Holbrooks. Structures at Stafford House included a farmstead of two periods, which contained an aisled building and nearby a timber-lined well, and northwards over the river Stort further buildings point to the town having spread over both sides of the river. The most interesting discovery, however, was the Romano-Celtic temple on a hillock beside the river, which was enclosed inside a *temenos*. The temple

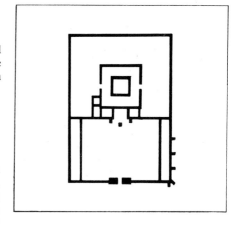

The Romano-Celtic temple at Harlow

appears to have been erected in the first century, and was still in use in the fourth, being demolished probably during Constantine's reign. The temple was of stone, had wings added to the front and had tessellated flooring. There were several associated buildings within the temple precinct.

362

HARPHAM Humberside
TA 0863 *Villa*
A modest corridor villa discovered in the 1920s and re-examined in the 1950s, Harpham was found to have some mosaic flooring, including a chessboard panel, and also fragments of some very good quality wall painting.

HARRINGWORTH Northamptonshire
SP 934980 *Agricultural site*
An agricultural site excavated in advance of ironstone quarrying in the early 1970s yielded remains of a barn which had internal partitions and a stone floor. Corn driers were found. Later excavations nearby exposed an iron-smelting furnace of pre-Conquest times.

HARROLD Bedfordshire
SP 933553 *Pottery*
There was a Roman production centre at Harrold for shelly calcite gritted pottery (pottery in which particles of shell, limestone grit and calcium compounds were incorporated in the clay and used largely for cooking utensils). It was excavated in the late 1960s and early 1970s. Several kilns were found. One was made of limestone set in clay, with opposite stoke-holes leading to a rectilinear firing box.

Harrow's Scar see **Milecastle 49**

HARTLIP Kent
TQ 8263 *Villa*
Hartlip villa consisted of several buildings scattered round a 3 acre (1.2ha) site, about ½ mile south-west of the present parish church. Among the buildings was a barn, or barn-house, which may have been aisled and had a bath suite on its north corner. About 60m (200ft) away was a residential block, in which two underground rooms were recently discovered and are said to have been wine cellars (cf Chalk villa).

HASHOLME HALL Humberside
SE 822327 *Settlement*
There was a settlement in the area of Hasholme Hall, about 4 miles south of Holme-on-Spalding-Moor. Excavations revealed several pottery kilns of third and fourth century date, though the settlement had developed much earlier. Pottery fragments showed that some of the kiln products were similar to the wares made at the nearby Throwlam pottery.

HAVERHILL Suffolk
TL 683449 *Settlement*
Some building materials, including roof tiles and floor *tesserae*, were found in drainage works in the mid 1970s. A coin of Antoninus Pius perhaps suggests mid second-century occupation.

HAYLING ISLAND Hampshire
SU 724030 *Temple*
At the beginning of the present century, remains of a building of Iron Age origin on which was superimposed a Roman structure were found on Hayling Island, but they were not fully understood. Aerial photographs of the mid 1970s located the structure again and revealed a circular building within an enclosure with a portico, thought at first to be a mausoleum or shrine. The site has been investigated over the years since the aerial reconnaissance and it has emerged as that of a Romano-Celtic temple with circular *cella* (central shrine) with a rectangular porch on the east side. This is enclosed in an almost

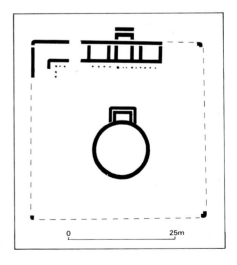

The circular *cella* is the main feature of the Romano-Celtic temple at Hayling Island

363

square *temenos* (enclosure) surrounded by an ambulatory which also has a porch on the east. The Romano-Celtic temple was begun in the mid first century; the ambulatory walls were erected in the Flavian period and the porches were enlarged in the early second century, along with other changes. It seems that the temple was abandoned in about AD200. Underneath the temple, traces of an Iron Age temple of similar size and plan have been found, which probably date to the first century BC.

HAYTON Humberside
SE 818456 *Fort*
A 4 acre (1.6ha) fort of the Flavian period was spotted by aerial photography in 1974 at Hayton, near Pocklington, and excavated soon afterwards. It had double-ditching. The rampart was not visible but its position could be identified by post holes for the uprights of the fort gate towers. The fort was occupied for a short period and then levelled when it was abandoned, probably before AD100.

Haytongate see **Turret 53b**

HECKINGTON Lincolnshire
TF 1444 *Settlements*
There appear to have been two settlements at Heckington. Investigations of the late 1970s unearthed building stone fragments, broken tiles, *tesserae* and sherds.

HECKINGTON FEN Lincolnshire
TF 171452 *Pottery and tile kilns*
Pottery and tile kilns have been found at the Heckington Fen pottery site, south of Holme House, a mile or so north-east of Heckington village. One kiln located in 1970 has been dated to c200.

HEDDON-ON-THE-WALL
Northumberland NZ 1267
Hadrian's Wall features
There is a stretch of Hadrian's Wall, about 90m (300ft) long, just south of the main road, by the hamlet of Heddon-on-the-Wall (NZ 136669), near Rudchester, well preserved up to seven courses, about 3m (9½ft) wide. It has been restored by the Department of the Environment. Then, a little

further west is some ditching of the Vallum, and outside the hamlet the site of Milecastle 12, but no remains. Continuing along the main road, a short stretch of Vallum is encountered, beside which is the site of Turret 12a (Heddon West), and further on along the B6318, Turret 12b (North Lodge), site only, also beside a stretch of Vallum. On the other side of the road is a stretch of Wall ditch, between Turrets 12a and 12b. Then, a few hundred yards on is the platform of Milecastle 13 (NZ 122673), which is 18 × 15m (59 × 50ft) interior measurement.

Heddon West see **Turret 12a**

HEIGHINGTON Lincolnshire
TF 053696 *Tile and brick kiln*
Some 200m (220yd) south of Car Dyke, at Heighington, an interesting tile and brick kiln was uncovered during excavations in the mid 1970s. It had a main flue with six cross-flues. Various fragments were found, including green tile, waste tile, flue tile, bonding tile and quarter-round tile. There was some pottery among the debris, most of it of the fourth century.

HELPSTON Cambridgeshire
TF 123042 *Villa*
Helpston was a large villa of two blocks set at right angles. Both buildings had tessellated flooring, and appear to have been occupied from late second to the fourth century.

HEMBURY Devon
ST 1103 *Hillfort*
The Iron Age hillfort of Hembury, near Honiton, which had been built over a much older Neolithic site, was taken over by Roman troops in the AD50s. Recent excavations have uncovered signs of timber buildings (including a barrack block of between c50 and c70), most of which were in the middle of the hillfort. One building seemed to have had a verandah.

HEMSWORTH Dorset
ST 9605 *Villa*
Hemsworth villa was discovered in the 1830s, but the great part of the remains which had included a bath suite have since

been eroded by continuous ploughing. Some mosaic flooring was found, including a portrait of Venus, and a fragment of wall painting showed part of a column of what was perhaps a temple. This fragment is in the British Museum. Among the building remains were fragments of hypocaust associated with the bath suite.

HENLEY WOOD Avon
ST 441652 *Temple*
A Romano-Celtic temple has been investigated at Henley Wood, near Yatton. It had several phases, beginning as an Iron Age shrine of Belgae origin. The last phase comprised a 7.5m (25ft) square *cella* surrounded by an ambulatory. It was probably built in the mid third century and survived into the fifth.

HERONBRIDGE Cheshire
SJ 4163 *Major settlement*
Coal deposits were found at the settlement early in the second century, and coal was extracted and shipped to the legionary fortress at Chester, and also to the military tileworks at Holt, using barges which berthed in the dock built by the Romans at Heronbridge.

HEYBRIDGE Essex
TL 850082 *?Industrial site*
A possible industrial site of the Roman period was examined here in the early 1970s.

HIBALDSTOW Humberside
SE 958032 *Settlement*
There was a settlement at Staniwells Farm, Hibaldstow, spread along both sides of Ermine Street. Major excavations in advance of road works in the mid 1970s exposed various buildings, notably – and unexpectedly in the centre of a settlement – a large villa-type structure, with outbuildings. This appears to have been a winged corridor villa (erected over an earlier aisled building). It was of the fourth century and was set back from the main road. A number of other buildings also fronted on to Ermine Street, and it seems the site sprawled for about ½ mile along the arterial route.

HIGH CROSS Leicestershire
SP 473886 *Minor settlement: Roman name Venonae*
During road widening here, near the present crossing of the A5 (Watling Street) and the A46 (Fosse Way), some traces of Roman occupation were seen, but there were no signs of the junction of the original Roman highways, which have yet to be found. The search for a fort, or posting station, at this point was also fruitless. It was at High Cross that Suetonius Paullinus had expected to meet reinforcements from Legio II for his approaching confrontation with Boudica (see p 60).

High House see **Milecastle 50**

HIGH ROCHESTER Northumberland
NY 833987 *Fort: Roman name* Bremenium
High Rochester, situated on Dere Street, was first built as a 4 acre (1.6ha) fort in Flavian times, in turf and timber. A second fort was superimposed on the first soon afterwards. Then it was abandoned for a long time, receiving no attention, it seems, in the Hadrianic period. In the first Antonine period, however, the site was reoccupied and converted to stonework. An inscription records Lollius Urbicus, the governor from 139 to 142, as commissioning the fort for a cavalry unit, erected to police the Lowlands while the Antonine Wall was being built further north. High Rochester appears to have remained occupied after the pullback to Hadrian's Wall in the 160s. It was improved by Severus and was occupied for much of the third century, during which time gun platforms were installed behind the ramparts, perhaps for one-armed stone-throwers, though this is argued. The gun platforms are attested in a surviving inscription, now at the Museum of Antiquities in Newcastle upon Tyne.

New barracks and other buildings were raised in the fourth century, but the fort may have been fired by Picts in raids and it was abandoned sometime in the mid fourth century. Among interesting features found in excavations were substantial remains of the west gate, with a single portal which had moulding, and in the *principia* a sunken

The Hinton St Mary mosaic pavement, now in the British Museum (*National Monuments Record*)

strongroom with a sliding stone door still with its iron wheels *in situ*. Inscriptions and sculptured panels were also found and have been put into the museum at Newcastle and at Durham Cathedral. The fort still has stone remains to be seen, including stretches of wall.

HIGHSTEAD Kent
TR 215660 *Enclosure*
A double-ditched enclosure that contained timber buildings, associated with Roman field systems, has been investigated here. The site also revealed evidence of earlier Iron Age occupation, and Bronze Age activity before that. A structure with hypocausts was also found.

HIGH WYCOMBE Buckinghamshire
SU 890931 *Villa*
The villa at High Wycombe was built in the mid second century and was a winged corridor-type, with corridors at front and rear, the corridors turning outwards at the ends. The building was of masonry. It stood in a walled enclosure, with a gatehouse. A separate bath house was erected just off one end. Several mosaic floors were found in excavation. Some interesting *tesserae* were identified as Samian pottery pieces. There was also evidence of wall painting and of hypocaust heating. The villa was first investigated in the eighteenth century and the bulk of the remains were destroyed in the mid 1950s by development.

HINCASTER Cumbria
SD 512854 *?Military site*
Finds of some Samian ware and of coarse pottery here during work on a motorway have been taken to suggest a small military site.

HINTON ST MARY Dorset
ST 780160 *Villa*
Hinton St Mary villa was a courtyard-type, with buildings on three sides, the fourth side being a ditch. Little survives of the structures, but the part with the most remains is the wing on the north-east range which housed the famous Hinton St Mary mosaic pavement which consisted of a head

of Christ, a Chi-Rho monogram and scenes of paradise in panels surrounding. The mosaic is now in the British Museum. There has, however, been some argument in recent years as to whether the portrait was not that of Christ but of the emperor Constantine. The villa dates roughly from about AD270 to the end of the fourth century.

HOD HILL Dorset
ST 8510 *Iron Age hillfort and Roman fort*
This Iron Age hillfort of the Durotriges tribe was captured by Vespasian in his campaign in southern Britain, AD43–6. It was then converted (in its north-west corner) into a fresh Roman fort of some 7 acres (2.8ha), using the Iron Age north and west defences and constructing a double-ditch system with gates on the remaining sides, the gates protected by *titula*. The interior plan of the fort had the *principia* in the centre and not forwards, and there was no rear gate or *via decumana*. The fort may have been garrisoned by a mix of legionaries and auxiliaries, for a time the legionary contribution being from Legio II *Augusta*. P. A. Holder (*The Roman Army in Britain*, 1982) suggests there could have been cavalry and that they practised jumps and manoeuvres up and down the ditches and ramparts of the old hillfort.

HOLBEANWOOD East Sussex
TQ 664305 *Iron-working site*
Holbeanwood, near Ticehurst, was one of the Sussex Wealden iron-working sites, and in excavations of the late 1960s hearths of smelting shaft-furnaces were found. The site was associated with that at Bardown, of which it may have been an offshoot.

HOLCOMBE Devon
SY 315928 *Villa*
Holcombe villa near Uplyme, was discovered in the 1870s, when ruins of an octagonal bath house (not unlike that at Keynsham) were found. Excavations in the late 1960s and early 1970s have revealed an unusually long range of two (or possibly three) linear houses with corridors, the most southerly corridor leading to the bath house. The complex had begun as a simple rect-

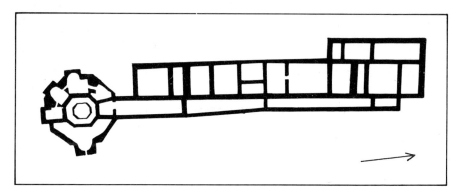

Holcombe villa, showing at left the south octagonal bath suite of the fourth century

angular Iron Age farmhouse, which was converted into an aisled farmhouse. Over at least three more phases, it was enlarged into a corridor villa. The bath house was fourth century. A series of chambers radiated off an ambulatory round the centre octagonal plunge bath. A fine Celtic bronze mirror was discovered in an oven from the early farmhouse.

HOLME HOUSE North Yorkshire
NZ 221152 *Villa*
A civilian settlement about a mile north of Manfield, to the east of Dere Street, near Piercebridge fort but on the south side of the river Tees, was seen from the air and excavated between 1969 and 1973. One of the structures was a villa-type building, with a bath house having tessellated floors, originating from the second century. Among other buildings was a circular Iron Age-type house, in the floor of which was found a coin of Trajan. The relationship of this villa and its surroundings to the Piercebridge fort and *vicus* is being investigated.

HOLTYE East Sussex
TQ 448382 *Iron-working site*
An iron-working site spread over about 3½ acres (1.4ha) was noted at Holtye, near Hammerwood, in 1970. It was close to the Lewes to London Roman road (Margary 14) which served as a trunk route for the iron industry in the Kent and Sussex Weald.

HOLWAY TEN ACRES Somerset
ST 246232 *Settlement*
During the construction of the M5 motorway, remains of an agricultural settlement were found at Holway, near Stoke St Mary. Traces of timber buildings of the third and fourth centuries were found, as well as an earlier corn drier.

HOOK Hampshire
SU 742533 *Tile kiln*
Excavations at Scotland Farm, about a mile or so south-east of Hook, in the late 1960s, exposed a tile kiln of rectangular shape, part of which had survived to about 45cm (1ft 6in). The kiln is thought to have been of the fourth century to judge from a coin now in the Farnham Museum.

HORKSTOW Humberside
SE 9819 *Villa*
The villa, found at the end of the eighteenth century and since then excavated, had some very interesting mosaics, with mythological pictures, including a round Orpheus panel. One mosaic was of a chariot race, showing one competitor having shed a chariot wheel. The mosaics are thought to have been executed by local mosaicists from Brough-on-Humber, known to specialists as the Petuarian school.

HORNCASTLE Lincolnshire
TF 259695 *Small town*
Horncastle was the site of a small Roman town, surrounded by a stone wall which was backed on one side by earth ramparting. The

town plan was approximately rectangular, with rounded corners, occupying about 7 acres (2.8ha), and the shape has led to suggestions that the site was military. There are several stretches of wall to be seen, some of it as high as 2m (6ft). Evidence of settlement outside the walled area to the south during the Roman period has been found.

HORSTEAD Norfolk
TG 278193 *?Marching camp*
A rectangular enclosure surrounded by a single ditch was spotted during aerial observation in 1974, and again in 1978. The enclosure was about 24 acres (9.7ha), and is thought to have been a marching camp.

HORTON KIRBY Kent
TQ 560685 *Villa*
The villa site at Horton Kirby was explored in the early 1970s as a result of a rescue operation in advance of a sewer scheme, near the village football field, by the river Darent. Excavations exposed a large Roman granary with stone foundations, about 18×30m (60×100ft), which appears to have had a range of rooms round the outside. These were perhaps accommodation for workers. The granary was of military-type, and it had standing space for carts at one end. The building was erected in the second century. To the south-east of the granary was the main villa house, of which a few traces have been found, though not enough to indicate its shape, size or history.

HOUSESTEADS Northumberland
NY 7968 *Fort and* vicus *on Hadrian's Wall: Roman name* Vercovicium
Housesteads was founded on the site of a fort of earth and timber before Hadrian's Wall, begun in AD122, had actually reached that point. The most completely exposed fort along the Wall, it overlooks Knag Burn Gap, and is strategically positioned on a north-south route.

The fort is joined to the Wall on its north side, and covers an area of 5 acres (2ha). It is of the usual rectangular shape with rounded corners. The walls of the fort are about 1.5m (5ft) thick and would have been banked with earth behind, for extra protection. The more

vulnerable areas, for example the northern parts of the east and west walls, are protected by short lengths of ditch. There are four massive stone gates which are towered on either side of the passage. Angle towers on the corners, and interval towers between, completed the defences. The fort was, however, considerably altered and reconstructed during its period of use. Three main phases of rebuilding can be traced, each following the sackings of the fort, in about 196, 296 and 367.

The original grid pattern of streets within the fort was preserved, but during each reconstruction alterations were made. Soon after about AD200 the first (Severan) rebuilding included the construction of a new *principia* over the Hadrianic original. In the early fourth century, after the second destruction, the barracks were enlarged and modernised. The most comprehensive alterations occurred after the 367 disaster, when a preoccupation with possible further attack is shown by the blocking of some of the passageways in the gates. The *vicus* associated with the fort appears to have been abandoned after 367, the inhabitants possibly moving into the fort for safety. Women's trinkets of this period have been found in the barrack rooms.

The *vicus* had been most highly developed in the third and fourth centuries. A group of civilian buildings outside the south gate have massive foundations, showing how well established the civilian settlement had become. Also outside the fort were a number of religious buildings. The most notable and well preserved of these is south of the *vicus*, on Chapel Hill, a semi-underground *mithraeum* of the early third century.

Occupation seems to have come to an end after about 383. The abandonment appears to have been abrupt, suggested, for example, by the discovery in the smithy of a hoard of freshly made arrowheads.

Housesteads see also **Milecastle 37**

HUCCLECOTE Gloucestershire
SO 8717 *Villa*
A small winged corridor villa was excavated in 1909–10. It had mosaics in several rooms.

Plan of Housesteads fort

One lay over a coin of emperor Theodosius I (379–95), which suggests that the villa was still occupied in the last years of the Roman presence. It may have belonged to a wealthy family with interests in *Glevum* (Gloucester).

HUNSBURY Northamptonshire
SP 737582 *Villa*

Hunsbury villa began as a rectangular stone block of rooms, probably of the second century. It was rebuilt in much the same style but on a different alignment, and a corridor was added at the front. There was a separate bath house, with *frigidarium*, *tepidarium* and *caldarium* and a cold plunge. This corridor block later became the east wing of a larger structure, which also incorporated the bath house.

HUNSDON Hertfordshire
TL 406126 *?Villa*

What may have been part of a villa was uncovered at Olive's Farm, about a mile south-west of Hunsdon in 1970. It was a hypocausted chamber with apsidal end.

HUNTCLIFF Cleveland
NZ 6821 *Signal station*

One of the fortified signal stations on the north-east coast (cf Goldsborough) of the late fourth century, Huntcliff's corner bastions on the square plan stone wall enclosure were D-ended, with smaller rectangular extensions on the inside face, added later. Huntcliff appears to have come to a sudden and violent end: the skeletons of fourteen people were found in the well, the skulls detached from the bodies.

HUNTSHAM Hereford & Worcester
SO 565175 *Villa*

The villa at Huntsham was a simple rectangular cottage-type, with a corridor between the two end rooms. The house was later improved by adding a second corridor fronting the whole rectangle. The cottage was part of a farmstead on which a major aisled building had been erected, which contained three water tanks (perhaps for wool-washing) and which had been roofed with stone slabs.

HUTTONS AMBO North Yorkshire
SE 744676 *Industrial site*

An industrial site has been examined, and finds which included sherds, a kiln dome and a T-shaped drying oven of the fourth century suggest a pottery which was producing Crambeck ware or copying it. This ware flourished in the fourth century, especially in the military establishments in northern England.

ICKHAM Kent
TR 231591 *Industrial site*

A site that had something for several different kinds of interest in Roman Britain was found during excavations in the mid 1970s north of Ickham, in an area endangered by gravel quarrying. Two possible Roman water-driven mills which operated in a channel of the river Stour were examined. Areas of river bank were discovered to have been lined with timber. Fragments of millstones were found, and remains of a timber sluice were uncovered. The area appeared to have had industrial associations, including pewter-making in the late third century. Also found were the bones of what may be the earliest known donkey to have been traced in the British Isles.

ICKLETON Cambridgeshire
TL 494435 *Villa*

The villa here comprised a main residential house and, some 22.5m (75ft) away, an aisled barn that does not seem to have been used domestically. The barn had been partitioned and it yielded painted plaster, one fragment of which displayed a picture of a woman's foot, perhaps of a dancer who was depicted fully on the whole panel before it was smashed.

ICKLINGHAM Suffolk
TL 782721 *Settlement*

A settlement at Icklingham has been investigated and finds included the remains of buildings, one of which was a large residential block, perhaps part of a villa. In the mid 1940s a cylindrical lead tank, bearing the Chi-Rho monogram and Alpha and Omega symbols, was found (and is now in the British Museum). In 1971, a second lead tank, or cistern, also with the Chi-Rho monogram, was found at Weatherill Farm. Excavations of the mid 1970s exposed an apsed structure that may have been a very early Christian chapel.

IDEN GREEN Kent
TQ 8032 *Paved ford*
This is an interesting example of a Roman paved ford over a stream, said to be the only one of its kind in Roman Britain. Excavations of the 1920s uncovered squared stone blocks, the bed of the ford as it crossed the stream. The position of the present stream is several feet below the part of the bank where the paving lies. It was part of the Rochester–Maidstone–Hastings Roman road (Margary 13).

ILCHESTER Somerset
ST 5222 *Town and ?second* civitas *capital of the Durotriges: Roman name* Lindinis
Ilchester is another of the more problematic town sites of Roman Britain. Its precise status is not known, although it is thought to have been promoted from *pagus* to *civitas* capital during the Severan period. If this is so, then it would seem that the Durotriges territory had been split in two, with Ilchester as the capital of the north-west part.

Little information about the structural history of Ilchester has been gathered. There were three main phases in the development of its fortifications. A simple clay bank enclosing 35 acres (14ha) was constructed in the late second to early third century. Sometime later, a timber revetment was added to the rampart with tie beams attached at right angles to upright posts. During the fourth century a stone wall replaced the timber fortifications at the front of the bank. The position of the south gate has been established by excavation.

Of the interior even less is known. The main development appears to have been in the third and fourth centuries, although little has been found of the streets and public buildings. Only further excavation will tell whether Ilchester was lacking in public amenities, as has been suggested.

ILCHESTER MEAD Somerset
ST 512222 *Villa*
The Roman town of Ilchester (*Lindinis*, see above), which is suggested as a later *civitas* capital for the northern half of the Durotrigian *civitas*, was surrounded (as it is today) by attractive countryside, and a number of prosperous villas grew up in the neighbourhood. One was Ilchester Mead. It became a courtyard villa. One building in the south of the yard was a long hall which was later divided into rooms. Another block found in excavations of the early 1970s was the west range of the villa. The villa went through several changes. A great variety of debris has been recovered, including window glass, painted plaster, tiles, mosaic and *tesserae*.

ILKLEY West Yorkshire
SE 116478 *Fort: Roman name* Olicana
The fort at Ilkley was built during Agricola's governorship, and appears to have been occupied until about AD120, when it was evacuated. It was reoccupied in the later Antonine period by a part-mounted regiment, when refurbishing included stabling in the *praetentura* for the regiment's horses. Further development took place under Severus, when the ramparts were converted to stone walls, with stone gateways which had guardchambers. In the early fourth century, parts of the fort were levelled and new buildings raised, including another *praetorium* and a granary. At this time, or perhaps a little later, workshop buildings were erected over some abandoned barrack blocks, suggesting civilian occupation.

ILLOGAN Cornwall
SW 6342 *Villa*
Illogan villa was built probably between the later second century and mid third century. It is clear that although it was raised during the Roman occupation, it was essentially a native British house. It was a simple winged corridor villa, but it does not seem to have had any bath facilities or central heating, and the highest pretension to fashion was some tessellation in the corridors. The house was over 30m (100ft) long, and the walls were of local slate.

INWORTH Essex
TL 883182 *Pottery kiln*
A pottery kiln of the later Roman period was found in the early 1970s, with associated debris in pits nearby.

IPING West Sussex
SU 8426 *Settlement*
A small settlement here is known to have flanked the Roman station, but little of it has been found. Remains of enclosing ditch and rampart can be seen.

IRCHESTER Northamptonshire
SP 917667 *Small town*
A small town which probably grew out of the *vicus* to a fort (not yet identified), Irchester was almost rectangular, covered about 20 acres (8ha) within the walls and had a stone wall built round it, probably in the third century. The site has been examined several times, most recently in the early 1980s. A rough grid of streets has been traced but this does not look as if it were planned in advance. There is evidence of two temples, one of which was octagonal in plan. Various religious artefacts have been found, including a torso in stone of the god Mercury, now in the Northamptonshire Museum. The town spread outside its surrounding wall and some traces have been detected.

ITCHEN ABBAS Hampshire
SU 5234 *Villa*
The villa at Itchen Abbas was partially explored in the late 1870s, and five rooms were examined. The largest was heated by a hypocaust. There were three good quality mosaics. Among the remains were fragments of painted plaster and some Samian ware. Coins of Constantine I were found.

IVY CHIMNEYS Essex
TL 811136 *Settlement*
A small settlement at Ivy Chimneys, near Witham, has recently been excavated. It began as an Iron Age settlement, and was 'Romanised'. Various timber buildings were located, including a Romano-Celtic rectangular temple with a double entrance at the east end. This was close to a rectangular pond, also excavated, which was found to

have had a cobbled bed and had been provided with running water from nearby springs. It is conjectured that the pond held freshwater fish. An octagonal plan font was found nearby, dating to the late fourth century.

IWERNE Dorset
ST 8513 *Villa*
Iwerne villa yielded some remarkable remains of wall painting in what is known as 'the painted room' during excavations of the late 1890s. The villa was a simple cottage-type, long and on an east-to-west alignment. It consisted of an entrance, a very long room which appears to have been shared by humans and animals, though partitioned, a paved kitchen, and an end residential bed-sitting room (this was the painted room). Projecting from the north side was a short rectangular granary (it may have been a tower granary). There was a paved corridor along part of the south side of the house. In addition to the main building was an aisled farmhouse building, which had partitions and a verandah. This had been an earlier building and may have been completely abandoned before the cottage next door was raised.

IXWORTH Suffolk
TL 9369 *Fort*
Aerial photography located part of the first-century fort at Ixworth. The photographs revealed the playing-card shape of one corner very clearly, showing the triple-ditch and rampart configuration. The fort has not been excavated, though some artefacts have been found. It was probably erected immediately after the Boudican Revolt, as part of the suppression of the area by Suetonius Paullinus.

JORDON HILL Dorset
SY 7082 *Temple*
A Romano-Celtic temple was built on Jordon Hill in the early fourth century, and may have survived in use until the mid fifth century. The outer wall has not survived, but the portico floor was uncovered, along with a well in the south-east corner of the *cella*. The temple appears to have been about

373

76m (250ft) square, with walls over 1m (3.3ft) thick.

KELVEDON Essex
TL 865190 *Fort and small town: Roman name* Canonium

There was a small Roman town at Kelvedon (*Canonium* in the *Antonine Itinerary*), which lay on the Roman road from Colchester to Chelmsford. It rose on the site of an early fort. Excavations have been carried out in Kelvedon throughout the 1970s and are still in progress. These have revealed clear traces of earlier Iron Age settlement before the Roman fort was established there, probably in the Claudian or Neronian periods. Some military finds have established the fort's existence, including pieces of scale armour, and traces of timber military buildings. Parts of the V-shaped ditching were also found. The fort was given up and part of its area was later used as a cemetery. The small town developed upon the eastern edge of the fort. Several pottery kilns were found beside a stretch of the military ditch. What may have been a timber mausoleum of the second century was also located.

KENCHESTER Hereford & Worcester
SO 440428 *Small town: Roman name* Magnis

It was once believed that a fort preceded the small town and that the town developed from the fort's *vicus*, but excavations in the late 1970s, while enlarging knowledge of the civilian buildings and town layout, have not confirmed any military origins. At best, we have to regard Kenchester as a small town that had fortifications. Among the finds have bee: some early second-century timber buildings, late second-century stone buildings, including two houses of some size set back from the main road, some buildings with hypocausts and some street drains. A number of interesting mosaics have been uncovered, some of which are now in the Hereford Museum. Also found was a suspected Romano-Celtic temple and some evidence of iron working.

KENILWORTH Warwickshire
SP 315724 *Enclosure*

A rectangular enclosure surrounded by a palisade, near Crewe Farm, contained a circular building and a rectilinear timber building which followed the former.

KESTON Greater London
TQ 415634 *Villa*

A large Iron Age, then Romano-British, settlement has been excavated several times at Keston, near Bromley. In the late 1960s, the settlement's cemetery was examined and three substantial tombs were uncovered. They may have been associated with occupation of the villa in the settlement, further down the hill, which was itself excavated in 1969. The area between the cemetery and the villa was investigated in the 1970s, and a number of buildings found, including a timber-framed possibly two-storeyed aisled structure, about 20 × 30m (66 × 100ft), which contained in its west end three large corn driers. There were also several stock enclosures near the villa house.

KETTERING Northamptonshire
SP 886781 *Settlement*

The settlement at Kettering was a mix of agricultural and industrial activities. It was close to ironstone deposits. Excavations of the late 1960s and early 1970s uncovered many features, notably a Y-shaped corn drier of third-century origin, some pottery kilns including an early second-century type, which had thin sheets of limestone for fire bars, and much evidence of iron working.

KEYNSHAM Avon
ST 645693 *Villa*

A substantial courtyard villa was built as a new structure on a virgin site in the fourth century. Very little can be seen today beyond a few fragments of the north wing. It was a corridored complex of at least fifty rooms round three sides of a yard. Many rooms had fine mosaics, a few of which have been rescued and can be seen in Somerdale and elsewhere. When examined, one of the larger rooms in the villa was found to have been burned in the mid fourth century, and an occupant's skeleton was found in the collapsed wall debris. The north wing had a most interesting hexagonal room with pro-jecting square rooms off. To the east of the

The hexagonal room in the north wing at Keynsham villa

site, at ST 656690, a small rectangular structure with six rooms was discovered in 1922. It was uprooted and moved about 270m (300yd) to where it is today, opposite the entrance to Fry's chocolate factory. The house contained a bath suite and living rooms.

KIMMERIDGE Dorset
SY 931776 *Stone production site*
One of the natural stones used in Roman times for decorative objects, utensils, furniture (including some surviving table legs), was the soft, soapy shale quarried at Kimmeridge. Excavations near Rope Lake, by the coast, in the mid 1970s revealed fresh Kimmeridge shale sites, and located a settlement nearby, presumably for the management and workforce operating the quarries. Remains of a third-century building were found, along with examples of products. There was also some evidence that salt was being produced from sea water.

KIMPTON Hampshire
SU 289473 *Granary*
What may have been a granary on chalk footings was investigated in the late 1970s. The building is on a site that had been enclosed by ditching, in which pottery of the third and fourth centuries was found.

KINGSCOTE Gloucestershire
ST 806960 *Settlement*
A substantial Roman settlement, with an emphasis on agricultural activities, has been excavated in some detail in the years 1975–82. It was a settlement of some 200 acres (80ha) – a sizeable area in Roman terms. There were three phases of occupation. In the second century, a limestone quarry was flanked by timber buildings, including a residence (perhaps for the quarry supervisor). At the beginning of the third century, the quarry pits were filled in and stone buildings were raised over the sites. Whatever these buildings were for, they seem to have had a short life, and were demolished by the fourth century to make way for a villa house inside an enclosure.

KINGSHOLM Gloucestershire
SO 8318 *Fort*
In AD48–9, Legio XX moved out of the fortress at Colchester and proceeded westwards to a new temporary base in the Westcountry. The site was probably Kingsholm, just over ½ mile north of Gloucester, where excavations have attested military presence, probably a Claudian fort. Finds include traces of timber buildings, one with wall plaster (which is not very usual and could point to an original intention that the fort should be permanent) and a cheekpiece of a cavalryman's bronze helmet. The fort, the size of which is not known, was abandoned in the mid 60s when the new and larger legionary fortress of about 43 acres (17ha) was built just a mile south at Gloucester, and Legio XX moved there.

KING'S LANGLEY Hertfordshire
TL 078022 *Villa*
The existence of a winged corridor villa was known for some years, but in some emergency excavations in 1980 and 1981 the rough layout of the villa was defined. It had two wings, evidently added at a later stage to the original house. Traces of a bath house were found outside the main building.

KINGS STANLEY Gloucestershire
SO 809041 *Villa*
A villa courtyard was known in the grounds

of Stanley House. The first building was a timber cottage-type residence. This was succeeded by a stone structure. Excavations of the mid and late 1970s exposed evidence of an iron works.

KING'S WESTON Avon
ST 5377 *Villa*
King's Weston appears to have been built in the later third century. It was a winged corridor villa with (probably) a front corridor only. The wing rooms were large. There was a bath suite on the western side. Some rooms had mosaic floors of mediocre quality. The corridor was backed by an arcade that overlooked a central space said to have been an internal (and presumably open) courtyard or, alternatively, a long covered hall, in either case with rooms opening off on all sides. There is evidence that the villa was burnt in the late 360s, perhaps during the disaster of 367. It was reoccupied afterwards, and hearths were built in the debris. The site is open to view, by application, and some remains are visible, notably of the bath suite.

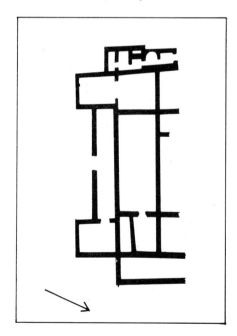

The villa at King's Weston: bath suite at top

KINGSWORTHY Hampshire
SU 4833 *Villa*
The villa at Kingsworthy, which included two residential blocks on two sides of a yard, was built over an earlier Iron Age farmstead. Fragments of a carved stone top for a large item of furniture were found and are in the Winchester Museum.

KINVASTON Staffordshire
SJ 9011 *Fort*
There were two forts at Kinvaston, near Penkridge. The first, of about AD50, and some 26 acres (10.5ha) in area, was enclosed by double-ditching. It was built for a vexillation of Legio XIV during the Ostorian campaign against Caratacus in Wales. The fort was later reduced in size to about 18 acres (7.3ha), probably in the late 60s. The reduction was achieved by shortening the eastern end and cutting a new double-ditch system. Traces of buildings from both phases have been detected.

KIRKBRIDE Cumbria
NY 231573 *Fort*
Between 4 and 5 miles south of Bowness, Kirkbride military site stands on the south bank of the river, and it marks the extreme western end of the Stanegate system. A 5 acre (2ha) fort was built there, though little remains to be seen. The fort may have been started before the end of the first century. A road leading from it towards Carlisle was located in the late 1970s.

KIRKBY THORE Cumbria
NY 626252 *Fort and marching camp: Roman name* Bravoniacum
There was a fort here in the Flavian period, and the marching camp of 12 acres (4.8ha) (in which the fort builders may have stayed) was recently identified from the air. The fort was rebuilt probably in Hadrian's time, and could have lasted until the third century. Nearby, a civilian settlement grew up, which became extensive enough to be classed as a town.

KIRKHAM Lancashire
SD 4331 *Fort*
Remains of a long suspected fort at Kirkham

were found in excavations in the east end of the town. The fort had begun as an earth and timber structure, probably of the late first century. In the second century, the rampart was faced with red sandstone. No buildings have been found.

KIRK SINK North Yorkshire
SD 939536 *Villa*
In the late 1960s, excavations at Kirk Sink, near Gargrave, where some Celtic field systems were known, located two large buildings which had heated rooms and some mosaics. The site was explored and a sequence of occupation established. A British settlement with circular and rectangular houses and barns, of the first and second centuries, was followed by a stone-built winged corridor house with a porch and with a bath suite in a west extension, and by a second adjacent building, both of the mid second century. In the third century, another block was added to the west end, and by the fourth century both newer buildings had been renovated. The first house was then abandoned and the second house appears to have become the main residential part. Occupation continued to the end of the fourth century.

KIRMOND-LE-MIRE Lincolnshire
TF 1893 *Villa*
A 9 acre (3.6ha) villa site was excavated in the mid 1970s. Finds included pottery of the second to the fourth centuries, some fragments of wall plaster and a mosaic paving about 6×3m (20×10ft), in geometric pattern, which was part of a corridor floor.

KNAG BURN Northumberland
NY 792689 *Section of Hadrian's Wall*
Hadrian's Wall crossed over a part of the Knag Burn, near Housesteads fort, and this was illustrated when sections were cut across the Wall in the 1970s. The burn was the water supply for the fort.

KNOWL HILL Berkshire
SU 7878 *?Villa*
Remains of an aisled building, probably a barn, were examined in the early 1930s. It had had two rows of post colonnades which

supported the roof. It has been dated to the end of the first century and appears to have been occupied throughout the second century. The barn was about 18m (60ft) long and the lower stone courses were of sandstone. It may have been part of a larger and as yet undiscovered villa.

LAKE FARM Dorset
SY 997990 *Fortress*
An early vexillation fortress, for part of Legio II *Augusta* when on campaign in southern Britain in the AD40s, was erected at Lake, near Corfe Mullen. It has been examined in the years since the late 1960s. The fortress covered 29 acres (11.7ha), was surrounded by a V-shaped ditch and appears to have been in use for only a few years. Traces of timber buildings were found. There were several phases of construction within the short period of its existence.

LAMYATT BEACON Somerset
ST 669363 *Temple*
There was a Romano-Celtic temple on the summit of the beacon which superseded a shrine of the Durotriges tribe. The temple has left few traceable remains. In the early 1970s an annexe was located, and also an underground chamber to the south of the temple, which was reached by steps. Some fragments of statuary were found, as well as a large hoard of coins of late third to mid fourth century date. The finds are now in the Bristol Museum.

LANCASTER Lancashire
SD 474620 *Fort and* vicus
The fort site at Lancaster (Castle Hill and St Mary's Church) had a long history. It began as an earth and timber fort of the early Flavian period. Nothing was known of this structure until the 1970s, when ditching and ramparting were found. In the early second century, some modifications were carried out, including building in stone. There is evidence of a serious fire at the fort in the mid second century, which may have been the result of the revolt of the Brigantes in the mid 150s. The fort was rebuilt soon after this, and a bath suite was erected outside. The bath suite has been uncovered, and

there is evidence that the baths were rebuilt in the third century.

The fort was abandoned by the end of the third century, but in the 320s another fort was built on the site. This later structure is known as the Wery Wall, from the surviving 2.5m (8ft) tall stretch of walling. It is thought to have been built as part of the coastal defences which were being developed as an extension of the Saxon Shore system. Lancaster fort had thick stone walling, with bastions, similar to some of the south-eastern coast forts. There was a *vicus* outside the fort. This has been investigated, and buildings of various periods have been noted, including a courtyard house next to the old fort bath house.

LANCHESTER Durham
NZ 159469 *Fort: Roman name* Longovicium
Lanchester fort was first built in the earlier Antonine period, comprising 5½ acres (2.2ha), to accommodate a cohort of 1000 men, part infantry, part cavalry. It was repaired in the 170s and abandoned at the end of the century. A fine inscription (now in Durham Cathedral) found at the site records that the fort was refurbished in the reign of Gordian III (238–44). Some of the remains visible today are of this period, including stretches of stone wall (which overlay earlier walling). The fort baths were rebuilt as well. It appears that the fort was abandoned in the 360s.

LANCING DOWN West Sussex
TQ 1706 *Temple*
A Romano-Celtic temple was built in an Iron Age cemetery on the side of the hill, on the summit of which is Lancing Ring hillfort. The temple was of square plan, with two concentric 1m (3ft) thick walls. It stood inside an oval *temenos* surrounded by a ditch. The temple was probably erected at the end of the first century.

Landwade see **Exning**

LANGTON North Yorkshire
SE 8167 *Villa*
The villa at Langton began as a native British farmstead, perhaps of the Parisi tribe,

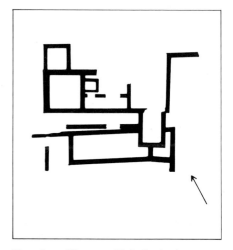

First phase of Langton villa is the simple range at bottom

in the second century. In the third century Roman influences began to emerge in some new stone buildings in the enclosure. The process was a gradual one. In the fourth century the farmstead consisted of a group of several free-standing buildings. The only residential farmhouse was replaced with a slightly bigger house a few metres north, which had square wing rooms with hypocausts attached at each end, forming a kind of winged corridor structure. Later in the century this became a proper winged corridor villa, and it was occupied until the end of the fourth century. Other buildings included a rectangular granary and a rectangular threshing floor.

LATIMER Buckinghamshire
SU 998985 *Villa*
A large corridor villa which eventually held over thirty rooms, Latimer began as a simple timber house of the early second century, which was replaced in stone later in the century. The villa appears to have been abandoned for a time in the third century but was reoccupied and renovated in the fourth. A number of mosaics were found. Associated with the villa were farm buildings, including a threshing floor, of the third century.

Leahill see **Turret 51b**

378

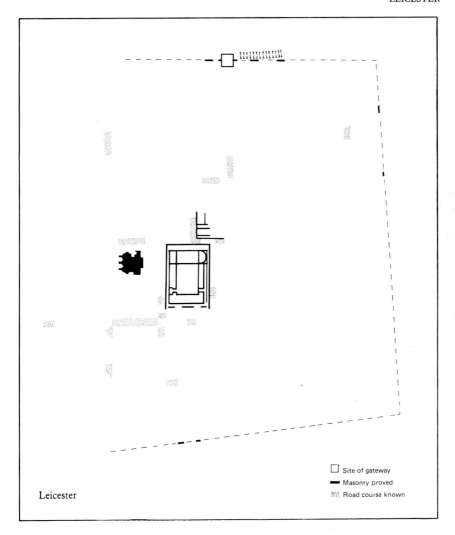

Site of gateway

■ Masonry proved

Road course known

Leicester

LEASE RIGG North Yorkshire
NZ 814042 *Fort*
A small fort of about 2½ acres (1ha) was
excavated at Lease Rigg, near Grosmont, in
the late 1970s. Pottery finds have been dated
to between c70 and c120, suggesting that the
fort was begun in the governorship of
Petillius Cerialis (71–4) or perhaps Agricola.
Remains were found of the *principia,*
praetorium, barrack blocks, granary and a
possible cookhouse.

LEICESTER Leicestershire
SK 583045 Civitas *capital of the Coritani:*
Roman name Ratae Coritanorum
Leicester attained the status of *civitas* capital
after having first developed as a *vicus*
associated with a fort. The site was already a
tribal centre before the Roman arrival, and
so Leicester followed a pattern of development traceable in a number of other
Romano-British settlements.
Scanty evidence remains of the fort which

379

represented the first phase of Roman occupation. Part of a fortification ditch and a series of Neronian timber buildings have been found. There is also a possibility that in the *vicus* outside the fort an early street layout was planned, though more evidence is needed. After c80, the army withdrew and the street plan for the *civitas* capital was laid out. A modest start to the town's development was made with the building of wattle-and-daub houses during the Flavian period, with an open space probably being reserved for the *forum*.

During the early second century, several more spacious domestic buildings were established, for example one which was built of clay blocks on stone foundations around a courtyard. The *forum* and *basilica* were late Hadrianic constructions. The *forum* had a portico and was 130m (433ft) long with a conventionally planned *basilica* at the north end. To the west of this complex

Columns and plinth from the east colonnade of the *forum* at Leicester, now re-erected near Jewry Wall

was an imposing bath house, the well-preserved remains of which can still be seen, with the Jewry Wall of the *palaestra* to a height of about 9m (30ft). The building was begun c145–50 and altered about ten years later. The *palaestra* was enclosed by porticoes on the north and south sides. The complex included *tepidaria* and *caldaria*, plunge baths and an elaborate drainage system and running water supply.

To the north of the *basilica*, remains of houses, built in the early second century and converted a generation later, have been found. These lavish houses had very fine frescoes decorated with birds and human figures, which can be seen in the city museum. They also had mosaics, which incidentally provide a clue to the end of one house's occupation in the late second century. It was apparently ruined by this period and the mosaics were taken up. The area was probably converted to industrial use. The mosaics from Leicester attest its wealth. They were numerous, and mostly of very high quality. A good example is the famous Peacock mosaic.

At the end of the second century to the beginning of the third century, the area north of the *basilica* was levelled and a large market hall was built. This measured 54×29m (180×96ft) and had columns. It provided more space for offices and shops, and shows the continuing prosperity of the town. Some of the shops and offices had painted plaster ceilings. The third century also saw the building of fortifications, comprising a ditch and stone wall backed by an earth bank. The wall's foundation was 3m (10ft) thick. No positive identification has been made of the sites of the gates. A possibly third-century temple has also been found to the south of the baths, which could have been a *mithraeum*; it had a nave 15m (50ft) long, and sculptured pieces along with incense burners have been found inside.

Despite signs of continued prosperity in the early fourth century, with the rebuilding of some shops in stone, by the end of the century the town had gone into decline. Sometime in the last few years there was a fire in the centre of the town and many buildings collapsed. No attempt was made to rebuild them.

LEIGH PARK Hampshire
SU 727091 *Villa*
A small villa of the third century, with five rooms and a lobby on one side of a walled courtyard, was investigated in the late 1960s at Leigh Park, Havant. There was also an aisled building to the north, probably a barn.

LEIGHTON Shropshire
SJ 600050 *Fortress*
What appears to have been a vexillation fortress of about 20 acres (8ha) was erected at Leighton, near Wroxeter, probably in the early AD50s, in support of the campaign against Caratacus. It was noted in aerial reconnaissance in the early 1970s but has not been fully excavated. Some preliminary investigation has confirmed a triple-ditch system.

LEINTWARDINE Hereford & Worcester
SO 4074 *Forts*
Many Roman forts were sited so as to guard important river junctions and crossings. The two forts at Leintwardine protected the confluence of the Clun and the Teme. The first fort was at Jay Lane, north-west of the confluence. Here, an almost square 4¾ acre (2ha) fort was built in about AD50 as part of the campaign against Caratacus. This fort had corner and interval towers of timber. It seems the fort went out of use in the 70s. About 80 years later, in the Antonine II period, a second and larger fort (11¼ acres/ 4.5ha) was built about 450m (500yd) to the south-east of Jay Lane and almost exactly at the point where the rivers meet. The rampart was laced with timber, and in the early third century a stone wall was raised along the top. Excavations have shown various alterations during the occupation of the fort, between the Antonine construction and the third century. It appears the fort was then abandoned for most of the century, reoccupied in the early fourth century when the bath house was altered, and finally given up and burnt in the late fourth century. Very little is visible today.

LENHAM Kent
TQ 873512 *Farmstead*
A Romano-British farmstead, which included a small iron-working industry, was examined at Runhams Farm, Lenham, in the early 1980s. Remains of a timber building were located, and among the debris were window glass fragments and quantities of iron slag.

LEXDEN Essex
TL 983264 *?Tile kiln*
A probable Roman tile kiln was discovered on the north side of the Colne river, in 1970, about a mile north-east of Lexden. The pottery appears to be mid first century. Was this supplying tiles for buildings in the new *colonia* at Colchester?

LIDGATE Suffolk
TL 731571 *Villa*
About ½ mile south of the village a winged corridor villa was spotted from the air in 1970. The site was examined and flint building footings unearthed, along with *opus signinum* fragments. The villa had been rebuilt.

Inside the north tower of the east gate at the *colonia* of Lindum (Lincoln) (*Author*)

Limestone Corner see **Milecastle 30**

LINCOLN Lincolnshire
SK 9771 *Legionary fortress and later* colonia: *Roman name* Lindum
The first Roman settlement at Lincoln was a legionary fortress sited at the south end of a ridge 180m (200ft) above the valley floor of the river Witham. The Fosse Way and Ermine Street provided excellent communications for the site, which was ideally situated for a military post, though unusually located for a large town.

The fortress was founded to house Legio IX *Hispana* in about AD61–2, and until recently very little was known of this early period of Lincoln's history. Recent excavations have, however, revealed that there were several phases of building in timber, including a building with post pits indicating an aisled hall of considerable size. This has been tentatively described as the cross-hall of the early *principia* at the site. In 69 or 70 the fortress was taken over by Legio II *Adiutrix*, which later on moved to Chester (c76–9). Following the withdrawal of the garrison, Lincoln was founded as a *colonia* for veterans by Domitian in the 90s. The original defences of the fortress, enclosing an area of about 41 acres (16.5ha) were left in position, strengthened by the addition of a stone curtain wall 1.25m (4ft) thick and stone cladding at the gateways. Internal interval towers of masonry were also provided. The layout of the interior of the *colonia* is not well known, but recently signs of an early second-century, possibly Trajanic, building with a porticoed courtyard and an east range of rooms have been found.

The *colonia* appears to have retained the

382

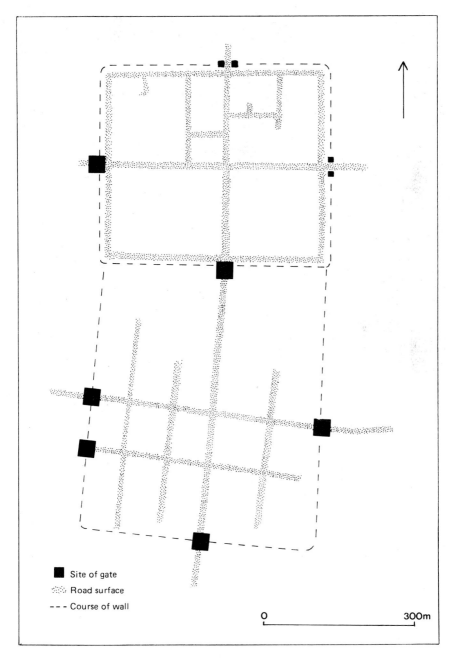

The fortress and *colonia* of Lincoln

The Newport Arch at the *colonia* Lindum (Lincoln). This was part of the north gate (*Author*)

fortress street plan and, although not many indications of its public buildings have come to light, a possible site for the *forum* has been suggested. Recent discoveries in the Bailgate area of the city, originally thought to be the frontage of three unified buildings, may now prove to be one of the ranges of the *forum*. The complex includes a room with a mosaic and a courtyard associated with a colonnade. Another building could have been a bath house, since flues, stoke-holes and hypocausts have been found. The same building had painted plaster walls and tessellated pavements. Temples of Apollo and Mercury can be inferred from inscriptions, as can a shrine of the Imperial cult attested by an inscription from Bordeaux. The level of 'Romanisation' at Lincoln appears to have been high.

In c210–30 the main gates were probably rebuilt on a monumental scale. The east gate had two semi-circular towers flanking a dual carriageway. The substantial excavated remains of this gateway can still be seen.

Also on view to this day is the Newport Arch, the only surviving arch from the Roman period in Britain. This entrance was part of the north gate and comprised a single carriageway flanked by foot passages and solid external towers. These towers were either built in the third century, when the defences were modified, or were additions to the gates in the early fourth century.

Lincoln also possessed a very advanced drainage system. The main sewer was 1.5m (5ft) high and 1.25m (4ft) wide. The system would have been capable of carrying a very large volume of water and effluent – an indication of the substantial size of the town. There is also evidence of an aqueduct with earthenware pipes, sections of which have been found. All in all, the evidence points to an efficiently organised administrative centre. The breakdown of organisation which accompanied the end of Roman life in many British towns is not well attested in Lincoln. Our knowledge of the last Roman period is hazy, and the evidence for Anglo-Saxon intrusion not good. This could be attributable to the fact that most Saxon settlement in Lincolnshire seems to have been in the south of the county.

LINLEY Shropshire
SO 347927 *Lead-working site*
Evidence of Roman lead working has been found on the slopes of the hill between Linley and Norbury.

LINWOOD Hampshire
SU 192101 *Pottery kilns*
Pottery kilns producing grey coarse New Forest ware have been re-excavated at Linwood, near Ellingham. The products included jugs, colanders and storage jars. This excavation was a rescue exercise by Vivien Swan, the Roman pottery specialist, partly occasioned by growing damage being done by local badgers.

LITTLEBOROUGH Nottinghamshire
SK 824825 *Small town: Roman name* Segelocum
There was a small town on the west side of the Trent at Littleborough. The site was explored in the late 1960s and early 1970s. Kilns, pottery and timber buildings that had had tiled roofs of mid to late first century were found under later layers. It was once thought that a Fosse Way frontier system fort had been erected here in the time of Ostorius Scapula or soon after, but that fort now appears to have been built on the other side of the Trent, at Marton (SK 8383).

LITTLECHESTER Derbyshire
SK 353375 *Small town: Roman name* Derventio
Littlechester began as a military site, and a succession of forts were built there, from Flavian times to the later Antonine period. Traces of these military works were found in excavations of the 1960s and 1970s, including a stone gateway situated across a street in the west side, near the river Derwent, and evidence of timber barrack blocks. The military works were built within a 9 acre (3.5ha) area that later on was enclosed by a stone wall. That wall was built, however, after the military occupation had ended and a small town had developed over the site. The town included industrial areas of pottery and iron working. The wall was erected late in the third century.

LITTLECOTE PARK Berkshire
SU 301705 *Villa*
Littlecote Park villa, near Hungerford, is of the winged corridor-type and grew on the site of a late first-century building. This structure of the first phase was possibly a timber building with a chalk floor. A masonry structure of the late second century has been excavated, which had an iron smelting hearth. Painted plaster and *tesserae* associated with the building of this period suggest that there was a large, well-appointed building nearby. In c300 a bath suite with a corn drier was attached to the villa. The main room seems to have been converted to an open paved court c360 and the baths enlarged with the addition of a *frigidarium* with cold plunge. Also dating to c360 is an apsidal hall of unusual shape which was floored with the magnificent Orpheus mosaic, first uncovered in 1730, but now unfortunately largely destroyed. The shape of the mosaic reveals that the building had three apses. This part of the building was converted c380–90, probably coinciding with the demolition of the main house. Excavations are continuing and will no doubt reveal more information about this important site, so much of which has been damaged by post-medieval activity.

LITTLE MILTON Oxfordshire
SP 624003 *Villa*
Little Milton began as it remained, a cottage-type villa, with front and rear row of rooms and passages and, nearby, a separate bath house building. The farmhouse was enclosed in a walled yard, surrounded by a ditch.

LITTLE MUNDEN Hertfordshire
TL 139014 *Pottery kiln*
An early Roman kiln was excavated at Little Munden, Bricket Wood, in 1973. It consisted of a chamber with a floor on pillars built up from tiles. Fragments of flagons and *mortaria* were found.

LITTLE OAKLEY Northamptonshire
SP 782592 *?Villa*
Excavations at the rural farmstead site at Little Oakley in the late 1970s indicated the possibility of a villa. Among the finds were

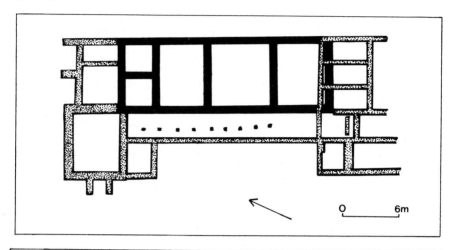

(*above*) Lockleys villa: the original strip house is in black; (*below*) Lockleys in the fourth century (after H. C. Lander)

debris of tiles, fragments of *opus signinum*, blue-green slate pieces and other building material.

LOCKLEYS Hertfordshire
TL 238162 *Villa*
Lockleys was a Belgic farmstead site in which the dwelling house had been a circular hut. In the later first century, a Roman-style strip house of timber was erected over the earlier site. The first plan had five rooms, four in line and the north-west end room divided in two, and with a simple verandah. Sometime in the late third century the house was converted to stone, on the same plan, and wings were added with a corridor in front. As the ground on the north-west sloped downwards, the end room was elevated to first floor level, with a room underneath. The house was burnt in the early fourth century and it was rebuilt. The villa was very close to Dicket Mead villa.

LONDON

Roman name Londinium Augusta

The Roman remains in London are extremely difficult to interpret, since much of what could help our understanding is inaccessibly buried, while that which does come to light is often swiftly destroyed by modern building projects. Thus, knowledge of Roman London is fragmentary. Recent suggestions have been made that the Roman settlement does not date to soon after the invasion in AD43, as was once believed. Very little pottery dating from before AD60 has been found, and what evidence there is suggests a scantily populated civilian settlement of scattered dwellings confined to the southern bridgehead from about AD50. In the Boudican revolt, London was destroyed by fire. After this, a rebuilding programme took place which established London as the

most important town of the whole province. Owing to the extensive nature of the remains found, it is best to consider a few important buildings in detail within the framework of a basic outline of the town's development.

The position of London on the river Thames accelerated its growth as an important port. Recent excavations have revealed signs of a first-century timber quay. Between about AD70 and 100, London expanded and achieved higher status, which is attested by the early presence of a *forum, basilica* and two sets of public baths. By the early second century, the town was probably the official capital of *Britannia*, and a new *forum* and *basilica* complex was built, along with a huge

Sketch plan of London

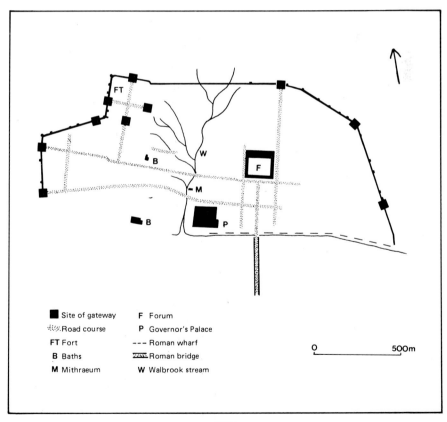

■ Site of gateway	**F** Forum
⠿Road course	**P** Governor's Palace
FT Fort	− − − Roman wharf
B Baths	▨▨ Roman bridge
M Mithraeum	**W** Walbrook stream

0   500m

1 State rooms
2 Gardens
3 Pool
4 Gardens

O   30m

The Governor's Palace at London

set of baths. Also belonging to this period was the governor's palace. This has been identified by the sheer size of the construction and the monumental style of the architecture. Lying just to the east of modern Cannon Street, the palace stood on three levels, terraces being cut back into the sloping ground. In the main range was a hall 13×24.5m (50×80ft), and in front of this a large garden equipped with an ornamental pool. Such luxurious dimensions and appointments make this a highly probable candidate for the governor's palace.

The Cripplegate fort, which was built shortly after AD100, is thought to have accommodated the governor's military body-

Part of the Roman wall at London Wall (*Janet & Colin Bord*)

The *mithraeum* in London, discovered in 1954 while the foundations for a new office block (Bucklersbury House) were being dug. The temple was dismantled and moved to a new site about 60m to the north-west, in Queen Victoria Street (*Graham Sumner*)

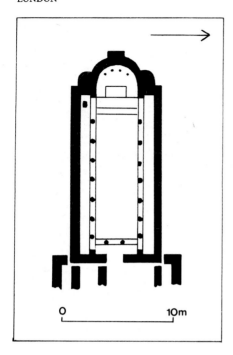

Plan of the *mithraeum* in London

of a shrine for the worship of Mithras. Situated beside the Walbrook, the temple consisted of a sunken aisled nave reached by a flight of steps. The building measured nearly 18m (60ft) long by nearly 8m (26ft) wide, and had an anteroom 11m (36ft) wide at its east end where double doors led into the nave. At the western end was an apse in which one may presume stood a statue to Mithras. The temple was 'lifted' and moved a few hundred yards away for resiting in recent building works.

One major discovery dating to the fourth century is the riverside wall, which defended the town along the north bank of the Thames. The foundations of this wall were brilliantly conceived, consisting of timber piles in rows on the unstable ground supporting a chalk raft. The wall incorporated pieces of a monumental arch which had probably stood 8–9m (26–30ft) tall. This wall reflects a growing preoccupation with security and defence. At the same time, external bastions were added to the landward wall for extra fortification.

During the fifth century, London, like many other Roman towns in Britain, appears to have declined markedly, and this would

guard. Covering about 11 acres (4.5ha) and enclosed by a stone wall, the fort was a major military installation, but yet not large enough to have been a legionary fortress.

London was damaged by a second fire, this time in about 125–30, but the town continued to develop. In about 200, the main landward defensive wall was built to protect the major part of the town that lay to the north of the river. This wall was of ragstone with brick coursing, was about 2 miles long, 6m (20ft) tall and about 2.5m (8ft) thick. The defences enclosed what was swiftly becoming a wealthy and cosmopolitan city.

There was one building in London that has attracted special interest ever since it was excavated in the early 1950s. This is the *mithraeum*, so far the only temple devoted to a 'mystery' religion that has been found in London. Inscriptions suggest the presence of other centres for foreign cults (including those of Cybele and of Isis), but the *mithraeum* points to a wealthy community that was ready to subsidize the construction

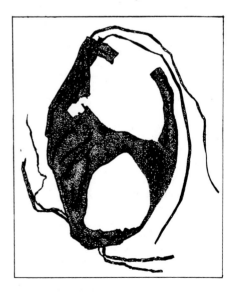

A pair of leather briefs found in recent London excavations

A timber-lined water tank with wooden outflow pipe, as it was excavated in 1974 at the bathhouse found at Lower Thames Street in London (*Museum of London*)

have been hastened by depopulation in the wake of the invaders from north-west Europe.

LONG BENNINGTON Lincolnshire
SK 829741 *Building*
Remains of a rectangular stone building were uncovered here in the mid 1970s. It seems to have been occupied between the second and fourth centuries, and it was rebuilt at one stage, the newer building being smaller.

LONGSHAWS Northumberland
NZ 135885 *Fortlet*
Stretches of rampart up to about 1.25m (4ft) tall can be seen at the site of this fortlet.

LONGTHORPE Cambridgeshire
TL 1597 *Vexillation fortress*
The fortress at Longthorpe was identified through aerial observation in 1961. It lies 2 miles west of Peterborough on a terrace between the river Nene and one of its tributaries. The site has increased our

knowledge of this type of military station, of which there are now 14 examples known in Britain. The most probable use to which these fortresses were put was that of providing winter quarters for mixed groups of legionaries and auxiliaries. They are known as vexillation fortresses. Longthorpe would have been in a position to control the movements of the Iceni and neighbouring tribes to the north-west.

There were two forts at Longthorpe, one being a contraction of the original construction. The first, and larger fortress, Longthorpe I, was unusually irregularly laid out. This suggests that initially it was regarded as a short-term campaign fortress, and it dates from between AD44 and 48, probably nearer the later date. The irregularly cut ditches, up to 3m (10ft) apart enclosed a rectangular area of 27 acres (11ha). The fortifications were

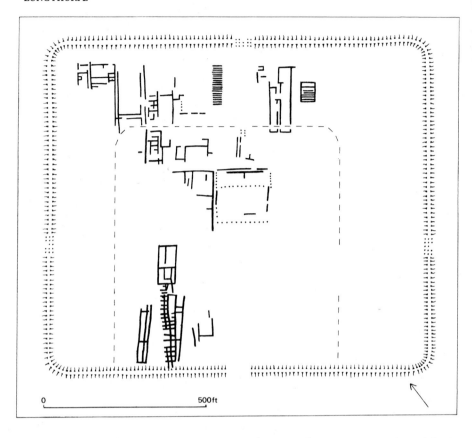

0 _____ 500ft

Longthorpe fortress: broken line indicates ditch of second, smaller fort

about 360×300m (396×330ft) and would have included an earth rampart, but this has been ploughed out.

Continuous ploughing has created difficulties in the dating of structures within the fortress, since the stratification inside buildings has been destroyed. The timber buildings, however, can be traced by the identification of post holes, although even these are often ill defined. The north and east gates have been excavated, and have been shown to have had dual carriageways, separated by a *spina* of two posts and flanked by towers with six posts, which projected out from the line of the defences. Buildings located in the fortress include a rectangular *principia* of 53.5×48.5m (176×160ft), store houses with

rock-cut trenches to support an elevated floor framework and sets of barracks. The length of the barrack blocks in the *praetentura* and the presence of an adjacent centurion's block almost certainly identifies them as legionary quarters.

The second fort (Longthorpe II) was superimposed directly on the plan of Longthorpe I. The buildings within the new fort appear to have been kept without alteration. The ramparts of Longthorpe II used the original defences to the south and a single-ditch was constructed to form the other three sides of the smaller rectangle. The second fort covered an area of 11 acres (4.5ha). The gate was a simple affair with five posts, probably supporting a tower. The construction of Longthorpe II occurred in about AD60. The reason for the change remains a mystery, although a link with the decimation of the vexillation of Legio IX by Boudica's forces under Cerialis in AD60-1 has been suggested. Evidence from Samian pottery shows that the Longthorpe site was not occupied for long after AD60, and coins point to a complete evacuation before 64–5.

LONG WITTENHAM Oxfordshire
SU 5595 *Agricultural settlement*
An agricultural settlement with an extensive field system, occupied from the late first to the third centuries, was excavated in the late 1960s, on the south bank of the Thames. One or two buildings had already been noted at the site in the nineteenth century.

LOW BORROWBRIDGE Cumbria
NY 610012 *Fort*
The fort at Low Borrowbridge on the main Roman road from Ribchester to Carlisle (Margary 7c) was first erected in the Flavian period. Little is known of it. The site is a commanding one, with steep slopes overlooking the Borrow. Another fort was built on the first site in the second century, about 3 acres (1.2ha) in size, which was repaired during the Severan campaigns in the north. The fort is thought to have still been in occupation in the fourth century.

Low Brunton see **Milecastle 27**

LOW HAM Somerset
ST 436288 *Villa*
A considerable villa complex, with outbuildings, was probably begun in the third century here, near some stone quarries. A cluster of buildings around one corner of the yard included a winged corridor house, with bath house, and to the north-east there were at least two other major buildings. Excavations revealed a number of very good quality mosaics, including a mosaic depicting scenes from Vergil's epic poem *The Aeneid* (now in the Taunton Museum). This may have been copied from a drawing in an illuminated manuscript of the poem of about 400 (now in the Vatican Library). This mosaic was in a plunge pool in the bath house. The villa continued to be occupied well into the fifth century.

Low Mire see **Milefortlet 20**

LUFTON Somerset
ST 5117 *Villa*
Lufton villa was distinctive in its time for its bath house, an impressive structure whose central feature was an octagonal pavilion in which was a plunge bath surrounded by an ambulatory. The whole bath house has been likened to a baptistery. It was in stark contrast to the rest of the villa, a relatively

Reconstruction of the bath house at Lufton villa

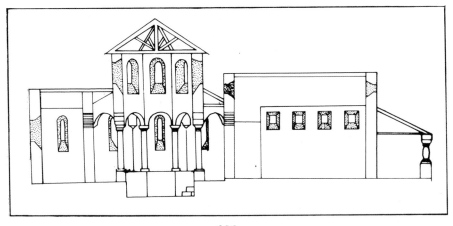

simple house of several rooms, a few with mosaics.

LUGWARDINE Hereford & Worcester
SO 561400 *Settlement*
The site of a settlement, probably begun in the second century, was examined and some tile fragments and sherds of coarse pottery were found.

LULLINGSTONE Kent
TQ 530650 *Villa*
Positioned on the west bank of the river Darent, near Sevenoaks, on a low terrace cut back into a hillside, Lullingstone villa is very well preserved, with parts of the walls still standing to a height of up to 2.5m (8ft). The first house, built c80–90, was sited on the remains of a pre-Roman settlement, and consisted of a range of rooms with a back corridor and a front verandah. A wooden staircase led down to the Deep Room, a cellar which was used for storage. During the second century a circular temple was built on a terrace behind the house of flint

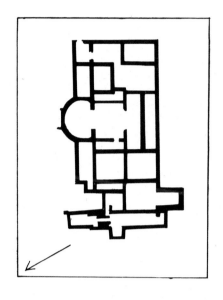

Plan of Lullingstone villa in the fourth century

The mosaic depicting Bellerophon slaying the Chimaera, at Lullingstone villa

and mortar construction, 4.5m (15ft) in diameter. Red and white plaster decorated the walls, and red and yellow *tesserae* the concrete floor. The latter part of the second century saw an enlargement of the house, with a bath suite being added to the south end. A 'cult' room was added at the north end, and the Deep Room was remodelled. The 'cult' room had a crushed brick floor into which was set a circular receptacle. Painted plaster covered the walls, and a kind of ambulatory corridor surrounded the room, which strongly suggests religious usage. The Deep Room had a square pit sunk in its floor and a niche added which contained a fresco of nymphs. The bath suite had a hypocausted hot room with *caldarium* and a deep cold plunge pool. These features, along with finds of portrait busts in Greek marble of eastern Mediterranean style, suggests a high level of 'Romanisation' among the occupants.

In c200, the villa appears to have been abandoned, with valuable objects being left behind in the process. Early in the third century the kitchens were converted to a tannery, and later in the century the villa was

Alan Sorrell's impression of Lullingstone villa as it may have been in the mid-fourth century (*Crown Copyright*)

reoccupied and renovated. The baths were refloored and a large granary was built to the north of the main building. In the fourth century the villa became, once more, luxuriously decorated with fine mosaics dating to the early part of the century, and an apsidal dining room was added to the west side. A temple – mausoleum was built on a terrace behind the house as a tomb for a young man and woman. Later in the fourth century the baths were abandoned and filled in, and the granary was dismantled. Among these signs of decline, however, a unique Christian chapel was established in the room above the Deep Room. Remarkable figured and painted plaster and a Chi-Rho symbol were found in this chapel. The villa was destroyed by fire in the early fifth century.

LUNDY ISLAND Devon
ST 628252 *?Roman settlement*
Huts on Lundy Island date from both Bronze and Iron Ages. A cemetery on

395

Beacon Hill was examined and some circular houses were found, associated with pottery of the Roman period.

Lunt, The see **The Lunt**

LYDIARD TREGOZE Wiltshire
SU 117843 *Pottery kilns*
A Romano-British pottery of second- and third-century operation was discovered at Whitehill Farm in the early 1970s. Remains of several kilns were examined.

LYDNEY PARK Gloucestershire
SO 6102 *Temple complex*
An interesting temple complex that lay within the boundaries of an Iron Age hillfort was excavated and found to contain a temple,

built in the 360s and dedicated to the healing god, Nodens, and along side it a bath house, a courtyard house and a long, narrow building which might have been a kind of hospital ward for sick people coming to pray for relief. These buildings were enclosed in a protective stone *temenos* which had a gateway. The temple had been built over the remains of a pre-Roman structure. The temple was about 18 × 24m (60 × 80ft), with a front entrance at the south-east and two rear doors. The *cella* was originally formed by six piers round which was an ambulatory with chapels, and with a three-shrine sanctuary at one end. Later, the *cella* was modified by the provision of a continuous wall. It contained a mosaic. Several religious finds of some interest have been preserved and are at

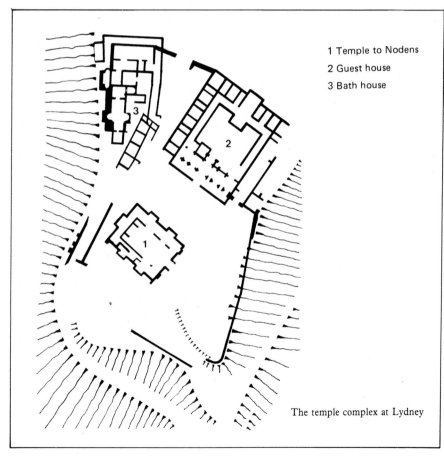

1 Temple to Nodens

2 Guest house

3 Bath house

The temple complex at Lydney

Lydney, in the Bristol Museum or in the British Museum. Before the temple complex arose, the site had been occupied by a British community which mined iron ore. One of the mines can still be seen.

LYMPNE Kent
TR 119342 *Fort of the Saxon Shore: Roman name* Lemannis
The fort at Lympne (known as Stutfall Castle) was a fort of the Saxon Shore, and was erected during the last decades of the third century. It lies on sloping ground below the remains of Lympne medieval castle, and in Roman times it edged the estuary of the Rother. Not much is to be seen today. The walls are fragmentary. There were flanking bastions, probably taller than the walls, of which several remain. There was a twin-towered gateway on the east, which has been examined. Inside the fort, the only structures so far found have been the remains of a stone *principia* and an internal bath house. The fort was erected on the believed site of an earlier base for the Roman fleet, and excavations in the south and east may reveal useful information when carried out and completed. As it is, fragments of tiles with the fleet's monogram (CL BR) have been found at the later fort site.

MAIDEN CASTLE Cumbria
NY 871132 *Fortlet*
A mountain pass fortlet at the head of Stainmore Pass was erected, probably in the mid second century. There are traces of stone-faced rampart.

MAIDEN CASTLE Dorset
SY 6688 *Hillfort*
This is the famous Iron Age hillfort of several phases, erected on an earlier Neolithic site, which was brilliantly and dramatically excavated by Mortimer Wheeler in the 1930s. Our interest lies in the fact that the fort was heavily defended by the British against the forces of Vespasian in AD44 during his conquest of south-western Britain. The Roman force attacked the fort on the east side, broke through the complicated gate system and beat the occupants into surrender. Once defeated, the occupants

were permitted to continue living in the fort, and traces of wooden buildings of the mid first century have been found.

Three centuries later, in about 367, a small Romano-Celtic concentric square plan temple was built in the northern sector of the hillfort. The *cella* is about 6m (20ft) square. The inner walls had been plastered and painted, and the floors tessellated. Today, the walls of both *cella* and verandah are visible for about 0.5m (2ft). North of the temple are the remains of a two-roomed house.

MAIDENHATCH Berkshire
SU 619739 *Villa*
Along the route of the M4 motorway, in the Pangbourne–Bradfield district, a variety of sites was examined in the late 1960s and early 1970s and a villa complex was investigated in and around Maidenhatch Farm. A fourth-century building of six rooms around a yard was examined, which had been erected over the remains of an earlier rectangular building. The later building contained corn driers. A huge hoard of nearly six thousand coins of the fourth century was discovered. About 30m (100ft) to the west of the six-room structure was another block, this one of seven rooms and a corridor, covering about 30 x 15m (100 x 50ft). Five rooms had had *tesserae* floors. The building had been put up in the third century over an earlier structure containing a pottery kiln.

MAIDSTONE Kent
TQ 756563 *Villa*
A winged corridor villa, about 50m (165ft) long, which lay at the Mount, beside the right bank of the Medway, has been excavated, the first time about 140 years ago. The villa was unusual for having octagonal and apsidal terminations to the wings. Mosaics were found. Works on the inner relief road in Maidstone in the early 1970s demonstrated more than one period of building at the villa site.

MAINS RIGG TOWER Cumbria
NY 613651 *Watchtower*
A watchtower (or signal station) at Upper Denton near the Stanegate frontier, about ¾ mile south of Birdoswald fort has been

excavated, and found to have been about 6.5m (21ft) square, with stone walls about 1m (3ft) thick, on a platform surrounded by a ditch. The tower would have been readily visible from Birdoswald.

MALDON Essex
TL 887075 *Salt-producing centre*
There was a salt-producing industry here during the Roman period. Excavations in the early 1970s exposed two groups of evaporating tanks, waste products and some fragments of salt kilns.

MALHAM MOOR North Yorkshire
SO 913655 *Marching camp*
There are traces of what is seen as a marching camp here.

MALTON North Yorkshire
SE 7171 *Fort and* vicus: *Roman name* Derventio
The earliest military installation at Malton appears to have been a large campaigning fortress of about 30 acres (12ha), built in about AD71–2. The garrison was then probably transferred to a more permanent base at York, leaving Malton occupied as an auxiliary fort from c79 to the end of the fourth century. The size of the enclosed area was contracted considerably, to about 8½ acres (3.5ha). Little is known of the interior, but two phases of building in stone have been identified, the first in the Trajanic period, the second in the late third century.
More is known about the *vicus*, which lay to the south-east of the fort, and parts of which have been excavated. Building in masonry began as early as the second century. Occupation of the *vicus* continued throughout the third century and there appears to have been a period of increased prosperity in the first part of the fourth century. Remains of large and luxurious houses of this date have been found, including one with a portico façade. The *vicus* appears to have been destroyed violently, however, in the mid fourth century, after which additional emergency defences including a ditch were built. The *vicus* was finally abandoned, and the civilian popula-

tion possibly withdrew into the comparative safety of the fort.

MANCETTER Warwickshire
SP 326967 *Fort and town: Roman name* Manduessedum
Mancetter is the site of an early Neronian period fort erected on the south-west of the river Anker, which may have been associated with the final confrontation between Suetonius Paullinus and Boudica in AD61. It is also the site, nearby but just over the river, of the later small town that spread over Watling Street. The fort lies underneath the present village, and evidence of it emerged in excavations of the mid 1950s, including its defences.

MANCHESTER Greater Manchester
SJ 8397 *Fort and* vicus: *Roman name* Mamucium
Three main phases of development have been identified at Manchester, and it is now thought that the *vicus* that grew in association with the fort became, in later periods, a more important focus of activity than the military site that gave it its initial impetus. The first fort was founded c79. The defences of the square-shaped fort consisted of an earth and timber rampart fronted by a double-ditch system on three sides. The natural steep slope to the river Medlock to the south provided enough defence to make a

A fragment of an amphora found at Manchester in 1978. It bears part of the famous word square (thought by some to have Christian significance) ROTAS OPERA TENET AREPO SATOR. Another example of the square was found at Cirencester

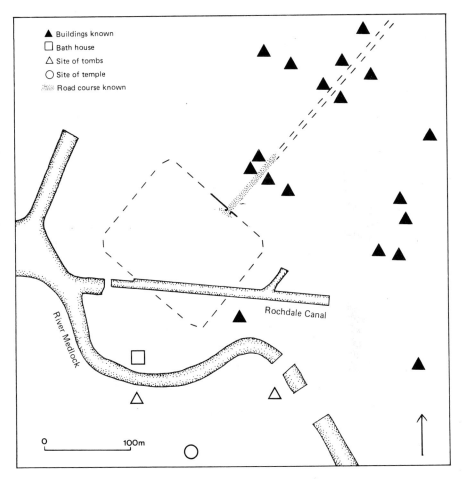

Buildings known

☐ Bath house

△ Site of tombs

○ Site of temple

⬗ Road course known

Rochdale Canal

River Medlock

100m

General plan of Roman Manchester

ditch system unnecessary on the south side. The north gate, which has been investigated, had a pair of timber towers with a single portal between them. The *vicus* was already establishing itself in this first period. The fort seems to have been deliberately destroyed and abandoned in the early second century. The *vicus*, however, was sufficiently well established to continue as a centre of settlement after the garrison left.

In about AD 160, the fort was rebuilt in the more familiar rectangular shape with rounded corners (period II). The new size suggests a garrison of either 800 infantrymen or 500 mixed cavalry and infantrymen. The *vicus* continued to prosper, and metal working grew in importance as an industrial

activity. In the final period of the fort's development, the turf and timber defences of the period II fort were replaced by masonry fortifications. This occurred in the late second century to early third century, with a stone wall 2.5m (8¼ft) thick replacing the clay rampart and the timber north gate giving way to a double-portalled stone tower. The buildings inside the fort appear also to have been rebuilt in stone. The fort was probably occupied continuously until the beginning of the fifth century, during which time many alterations were made to the fortifications. The *vicus*, which had become an important industrial centre in the earlier periods,

Reconstruction of north gate (after drawing by Greater Manchester Archaeological Unit)

appears to have reverted during the final period to a more domestically based settlement. This can probably be explained by the more permanent nature of the fort and the resulting influx of soldiers' dependents to the area for long-term occupation. How Roman settlement at Manchester came to an end is uncertain. Further excavation will no doubt throw further light on this question.

MANSFIELD WOODHOUSE
Nottinghamshire SK 5264
Villa
The villa at Mansfield Woodhouse was L-shaped. The west building was a corridor villa house, with a range of five rooms flanked by wing rooms, fronted by a corridor or verandah, with an outbuilding connected by another corridor. The centre room of the range was the dining-room and it had a mosaic floor. The second building was an aisled farmhouse, along the north side of the courtyard. It was partitioned for quarters for workers; it had hypocausts and a bath suite at the south-east.

March Burn see **Milecastle 14**

MARTINHOE Devon
SS 6649 *Fortlet*
Martinhoe was a fortlet and signal station of

the early Roman period situated on the south shore of the Bristol Channel and occupying about 600sq m (700sq yd). The fortlet was probably built in about AD55 and was occupied until the 70s. It contained three barrack blocks which included quarters for officers, and it may have been garrisoned by a century. The fortlet acted as an observation post in conjunction with the Roman fleet operating against the Silures from Wales in the Bristol Channel.

MARYPORT Cumbria
NY 0337 *Fort: Roman name* Alauna
Maryport was built on a spur overlooking the sea, as a fort to guard the Solway coast, during the Hadrianic period. It is thought that the fort, of which little remains except some fort ditching and the parade ground outside, was erected over an earlier fort perhaps of Agricola's campaigns. The later fort occupied 6½ acres (2.5ha). The rampart was faced with a stone wall about 2m (7ft) thick. Outside were three ditch systems, though not all necessarily used at the same time. Excavations in earlier years have revealed some buildings, including barrack blocks which had been rebuilt, stables and a number of stone altars buried just outside the north-east of the fort where, later, a *vicus* developed.

Matfen Piers see **Milecastle 19**

Mawbray see **Milefortlet 16**

MEDBOURNE Leicestershire
SP 792933 *Villa and minor settlement*
Little is known of the villa at Medbourne, which was excavated several times during the nineteenth century and in the process so badly damaged that there are now only fragmentary remains. One important find was a fine mosaic thought to have come from the villa's small internal court or *atrium*.

MELANDRA CASTLE Derbyshire
SK 010950 *Fort and* vicus
The fort here was sited on a fine spur with commanding views, and it can be visited today. There are a few remains, notably some rampart with stone revetting, about 2m

400

(6ft) tall, and some stonework of the south-east corner of the fort. Inside lie the remains of the *principia*, set out, and there are also some remains of the fort's bath house outside to the north. The bath house appears to have been modified twice after the original work. The fort began as a 3 acre (1.2ha) rectangular earth and timber structure, probably raised by Agricola, certainly in the early Flavian period. In the time of Trajan, the earth rampart was revetted with a 1.5m (5ft) thick stone wall. This may have been the occasion when the *principia* was built. The fort was abandoned altogether in the 140s. A *vicus* developed outside, and evidence has been found of iron smithing, lead smelting and glass making. The *vicus* was given up at much the same time as the fort.

Melkridge see **Turrets 40a & b**

MENTLEY FARM Hertfordshire
TL 382241 *?Villa*
Remains of an extensive stone building were examined at Mentley Farm, Standon, near the small Roman town of Braughing. Fourteen rooms were defined, three of which had red tessellated flooring and one a mosaic pavement. The building was probably a villa, and is dated to the third and fourth centuries.

METCHLEY West Midlands
SP 043836 *Fort*
The first fort at Metchley was erected by Ostorius Scapula in about AD48. It comprised about 10½ acres (4.25ha) and was enclosed by a timber-stake and earth rampart and double-ditching. Traces of barrack blocks and granaries have been found. Some time after the first work, an annexe of about 4 acres (1.5ha) was added on the north side. Then, both fort and annexe were levelled. In the late Flavian period, a second fort was built within the area of the older fort, now surrounded by a single-ditch. This newer fort occupied 6½ acres (2.5ha). Some internal timber buildings have been located, as well as traces of the *via decumana*. The second series of buildings were burned down early in the second century, and the fort's life came to an end. Some of the northern corner

of the fort has been reconstructed and can be seen in the grounds of Birmingham University Medical School.

MIDDLE FARM Berkshire
SU 301828 *Settlement*
A Romano-British settlement at Middle Farm, which included a villa and farmyard, was investigated in 1981–2 and further results are expected.

MIDDLETON Cumbria
SD 622858 *Milestone*
An interesting cylindrical milestone was found about 4 miles north of Kirkby Lonsdale in 1836. It was re-erected a few hundred yards from its discovery point. It had stood on the road from Ribchester to Low Borrowbridge (Margary 7c). The stone is inscribed LIII – 53 Roman miles measured from Carlisle.

MIDDLETON STONEY Oxfordshire
SP 534233 *Buildings*
The twelfth-century motte castle at Middleton was excavated in the 1970s, and traces of a second-century agricultural building, 8×13m (26×43ft), were found in the bailey. The building may have been a farmhouse and was demolished in the third century.

MIDDLEWICH Cheshire
SJ 705665 *Salt-producing centre: Roman name* Salinae
Located at Kinderton, this site was one of the handful of natural inland salt springs so far shown to have been used by the Romans. Excavations in the 1960s and early 1970s have revealed brine kilns, iron-working furnaces and a variety of timber strip houses and shops. The evidence suggests a long period of occupation, from the late first to the third century at least.

MILDENHALL Wiltshire
SU 216695 *Small town: Roman name* Cunetio
A small walled town on the Speen (Berkshire) to Bath Roman road (Margary 53), Mildenhall lies by the Kennet river. There had been pre-Roman settlement there,

and probably in the first century AD a Roman fort of some kind was erected. Eventually, a small town evolved, the defences of which have been detected from the air and part examined at ground. They consisted of two main circuits, one of them of stone, the latter raised in the fourth century. The stone circuit was reinforced with semi-circular bastions. Remains of residential and working buildings inside and outside the wall have been found. The walled area was about 19 acres (8ha). The plan of the town was rectangular, with rounded corners like the conventional Roman fort, but it is not agreed among specialists whether in fact the fort-style plan seen from the air relates to a fort that there may have been at Mildenhall in the early period.

MILECASTLES (Hadrian's Wall)
7 see **Denton** Tyne & Wear

9 Chapel House Northumberland
NZ 178662
Milecastle 9 has been excavated. It was about 15 × 18m (49 × 60ft). Its north gate was uncovered in the 1950s. The milecastle was in use up to the late fourth century.

10 Walbottle Dene Northumberland
NZ 165667
This has been excavated and was about 17m (58ft) east–west and 14m (47ft) north–south. Both gates were found.

12 see **Heddon-on-the-Wall**
Northumberland

13 Rudchester Northumberland
NZ 122673
The outlines of Milecastle 13 can be seen near Rudchester Burn. It has been investigated and was nearly 18m (59ft) east–west by about 15m (50ft) north–south. Two centuries ago, a large hoard of first- and second-century coins (up to the 160s) was found.

14 March Burn Northumberland
NZ 107677
This is now a low platform at March Burn on the Wall line.

15 Whitchester Northumberland
NZ 094678
A platform marks the remains of this milecastle. There are also traces of the Vallum to the south.

17 Welton Northumberland
NZ 063682
Milecastle 17 was excavated in 1931 and found to be about 17m (58ft) east–west by about 15m (49ft) north–south. It may have been built by Legio II. The site is visible as a low mound.

18 Wallhouses East Northumberland
NZ 048683
The milecastle here was excavated in 1931, was about 16m (54ft) east–west and about 18m (60ft) north–south, with walls nearly 2.5m (8ft) thick.

19 Matfen Piers Northumberland
NZ 033685
It is probable that there was a temple to the Mother-goddesses near this milecastle. An inscription of dedication to them by a cavalry cohort of Vardullians was found here in 1931. The milecastle was about 16m (53ft) east–west by about 17m (56ft) north–south.

20 Haltonshields Northumberland
NZ 019686
Milecastle 20 was about 16m (54ft) east–west by about 18m (59ft) north–south.

22 Errington Arms Northumberland
NY 989687
This milecastle was sited near the point where Dere Street crossed the Wall. It was examined in 1930. The north gate had been blocked up, probably in the modifications of the 180s.

23 Stanley Northumberland
NY 975689
This was excavated in 1930. It was 15m (49ft) east–west and some of its surrounding ditch is visible.

24 Wall Fell Northumberland
NY 961693
This was about 15m (50ft) east–west. Its site is marked by a prominent platform.

27 Low Brunton Northumberland
NY 917700
This was about 18m (59ft) east–west by about 14.5m (48ft) north–south. It appears to have been abandoned at the time of the modifications to the Wall scheme in the 180s.

29 Tower Tye Northumberland
NY 889711
Marked by trenching where the stonework has been dismantled, this milecastle has traces of its surrounding ditch.

30 Limestone Corner Northumberland
NY 876716
At the top of the hill at Limestone Corner was Milecastle 30. It was here that attempts were made by the Romans to cut ditching into the rock and the results of their efforts can be seen. The ditching by the milecastle was not completed, but the position of the fortlet was such that it would have been almost impossible to attack it by surprise.

32 Carraw Northumberland
NY 846710
Less than a mile west of Carrawburgh fort is the platform of Milecastle 32, which lies between two long stretches of Vallum and just behind a stretch of Wall. The milecastle was excavated in the 1970s and the south gateway had been stripped. Pottery finds suggest that the fortlet was still in use in the fourth century.

33 Shield on the Wall Northumberland
NY 831707
The northern wall and the gateway of Milecastle 33 can be seen just off the main road, to the north.

34 Grindon Northumberland
NY 817705
A small copse today marks the position of Milecastle 34, near Sewingshields.

35 see **Sewingshields**

37 Housesteads Northumberland
NY 785687
About ¼ mile west of Housesteads fort is

Milecastle 37, about 17m (58ft) east–west by about 15m (50ft) north–south, which is an interesting site. Inscriptions have shown that it was built by Legio II, in the time of Hadrian's governor of Britain, Platorius Nepos. The Wall is broad along the north side of the milecastle but narrows immediately at both ends. The north gateway is in good condition. It was reduced in span in the Severan period. Inside the milecastle are remains of a stone barrack block and traces of one of timber have been found. The milecastle was occupied up to the late fourth century. This is one of the best surviving milecastles visible today on the Wall.

38 Milking Gap Northumberland
NY 773682
This milecastle is near Hotbank Farm. It was examined in 1935 and is about 19m (62ft) east–west by about 15m (50ft) north–south. It was occupied up to the mid fourth century. The milecastle yielded interesting inscriptions (now in Newcastle Museum), showing that it had been built by Legio II during the governorship of Platorius Nepos.

39 Castle Nick Northumberland
NY 761677
Milecastle 39 is slightly wedged-shaped and longer than broad, about 19×14.5–15.25m (62×49–51ft). Much of the walling is in good condition. There are remains of an internal structure. The south gate was partially blocked in its later years. The fort was built by Legio XX.

40 Winshields Northumberland
NY 745676
Winshields is like Milecastle 39, longer than broad. On the top of Winshields Hill, it is the highest part of the whole Wall scheme, nearly 369m (1230ft). The gates were remodelled in the modifications of the 180s, and the milecastle was occupied into the fourth century. The remains are overgrown. A fine view of the Solway can be enjoyed on a clear day.

42 Cawfields Northumberland
NY 716667
This is one of the best preserved milecastles

403

Milecastle 42 at Cawfields, on Hadrian's Wall

on the Wall. The walling is complete up to several courses high, and both north and south gates have substantial remains, the south gate up to 2m (6ft) of masonry. Cawfields is situated just where the Wall bends south-westwards on the western side towards Greatchesters. The milecastle was built by Legio II.

44 Allolee Northumberland
NY 689669
Allolee milecastle can be seen in outline. It is close to good stretches of repaired Wall.

46 Carvoran Northumberland
NY 665660
The position of this milecastle is about 250m (275yd) north of the Stanegate fort of Carvoran.

47 Chapelhouse Northumberland
NY 649670
Chapelhouse was excavated in the mid 1930s. It was a large milecastle, some 21m (70ft) north–south by about 18m (60ft) east–west. Remains were found of two barrack blocks. Also found was an important

inscription of Hadrian's time indicating that Legio XX built the milecastle.

48 Poltross Burn Northumberland
NY 634662
Poltross Burn is one of the best preserved milecastles along the Wall. It was erected by Legio VI, is about 21m (70ft) north–south by about 18m (61ft) east–west, and is larger than most of the milecastles on the original stonepart of the Wall scheme. Finds in excavations show that it remained in use into the late fourth century. The milecastle has one of its original ovens, in the north-west corner, and the foundations of both stone barrack blocks can be seen, together with a few steps of the flight that once went up to the walk along the rampart.

49 Harrow's Scar Cumbria
NY 620664
The first milecastle on the narrow Wall, Harrow's Scar was 22.5m (75ft) north–south by about 19.5m (65ft) east–west. The walls are visible, and also parts of the gates.

50 High House (Turf Wall) Cumbria
NY 607658
High House on the Turf Wall had timber

buildings. A fragment of wood was recently found bearing a small amount of lettering that enabled the milecastle to be attributed to the governorship of Platorius Nepos. A causeway leading out of the north side is thought to have led to a road which went on to Bewcastle fort. The milecastle was occupied only for a few years. Then it was demolished, and Milecastle 50 on the Stone Wall was built to take its place (see below).

50 High House (Stone Wall) Cumbria
NY 607660
This replaced the first Turf Wall milecastle at High House (see above). It was about 23m (76ft) north–south by about 18m (60ft) east–west. The earliest buildings inside were timber, and these were replaced by stone buildings.

51 Wall Bowers Cumbria
NY 593655
Wall Bowers is at the point where the original stretch of Turf Wall westwards of Willowford and the stone-converted Wall also westwards of Willowford meet. The milecastle is surrounded by ditching, and there are traces of two barrack blocks. The south gate was rebuilt in the fourth century.

52 Bankshead Cumbria
NY 579649
Bankshead is near Lanercost Priory, and two altars of the Roman period from the milecastle are now to be seen at the Priory. The milecastle was nearly 23m (77ft) north–south and over 27m (90ft) east–west, making it one of the biggest milecastles on the Wall. The north gate was blocked up in the fourth century. The south gate was remodelled, perhaps at the same time. Nearby is the site of Pike Hill Roman signal tower.

53 Banks Burn Cumbria
NY 565646
Banks Burn was examined in 1932. Very little remains. It was almost square in plan.

Hadrian's Wall at Wall Town crag looking west (*J. S. Buck*)

54 Abbey Gills Wood Cumbria
NY 551644
Abbey Gills Wood was examined in 1934 and found to be nearly 23m (78ft) north–south by about 19.5m (65ft) east–west. The westerly barrack block was investigated. It had consisted of two rooms. One was lined with stone benches which may have served as bed bases. It was still in use in the fourth century.

59 Old Wall Cumbria
NY 486617
The site of Milecastle 59 is at Chapel Flat Farm.

65 Tarraby Lane Cumbria
NY 405576
Milecastle 65 on Hadrian's Wall, ½ mile north-east of the fort at Stanwix, was located in 1976. It was built as part of the original Turf Wall in about AD124, early in the Wall scheme. Part of the Vallum ditch was observed during Post Office digging at NY 412580.

71 Wormanby Cumbria
NY 338592
Wormanby milecastle was located in 1960.

73 Dykesfield Cumbria
NY 310594
Dykesfield has been investigated and found to be almost square in plan, about 18m (61ft) east–west by about 18.5m (62ft) north–south.

79 Solway House Cumbria
NY 236622
Solway House, Bowness Marsh, is the last milecastle on the Wall scheme before the endmost fort of the original scheme, that is, Bowness-on-Solway. It has been excavated, and it was discovered that the stonework walling was built round the outside of the original turf walling of the first fortlet. The stone fortlet was about 17m (57ft) square. South and north gateways were discovered, as were several hearths and the base of a flight of steps that led to the rampart, situated in the south-east corner. The stonework conversion is thought to have been not in Hadrian's time but in that of his successor, Antoninus Pius.

MILEFORTLETS (Cumbrian coast)

1 Biglands Cumbria
NY 208618
Biglands was a Hadrianic fortlet on the Cumbrian coast. It was about 35 × 29m (115 × 95ft), surrounded by a V-shaped ditch and contained timber buildings including a six-post north gate with a tower. The fortlet seems to have had three phases, all of the second century, and it was abandoned after the Antonine II period.

11 Silloth Cumbria
NY 1054
Milefortlet 11 has been located at Silloth, but little was recovered because the site has been severely eroded.

16 Mawbray Cumbria
NY 082470
Milefortlet 16, Mawbray, was noted some time ago, and examined in the early 1970s. Post holes of the gatetower were found.

17 Dubmill Point Cumbria
NY 077456
Aerial photography showed up what may be the outline of Milefortlet 17. The area was 45sq m (50sq yd) and the ditch was broad.

20 Low Mire Cumbria
NY 076412
Milefortlet 20, Low Mire, was found in the 1960s and examined in the late 1970s. It began as a Hadrianic fortlet, occupied 15 × 18m (48 × 60ft), contained timber buildings and was rebuilt at least twice. It probably went out of use, but appears to have been recommissioned during the fourth century.

26 Rise How Bank Cumbria
NY 026352
Milefortlet 26 is on Rise How Bank, to the south-west of Maryport fort. Recent excavations revealed part of the main road and the enclosing ditch, with some pottery of the Hadrianic period.

Milking Gap see **Milecastle 38**

MILTON COMMON Oxfordshire
SP 645037 *Settlement*
A small settlement near Great Milton was examined in the early 1970s. Evidence of iron smelting was found. Building remains were of the third and fourth centuries.

MORESBY Cumbria
NX 982210 *Fort*
The 3½ acre (1.5ha) fort for part-mounted auxiliaries at Moresby was built between about 128 and 138 as an addition to the original scheme for Hadrian's Wall and its forts and milecastles to help guard the Cumbrian coast. It was built by Legio XX *Valeria Victrix*, according to an inscription now in the British Museum. The only visible remains are the fort platform, but walls and building foundations of stone have been examined in earlier excavations. The fort appears to have been in occupation until the fourth century. South of the fort, remains of the neighbouring *vicus* were found.

MOUNT BURES Essex
TL 912322 *Tile kiln*
A tile kiln of the early Roman period has been found here at Fen Farm.

MOUNT WOOD Buckinghamshire
TQ 025988 *Roman remains*
About ¾ mile north of Chenies, remains of a timber building with tiled roof, situated on the river bank, were found beside a corn drier, part of which remains.

Mucklebank see **Turret 44b**

NANSTALLON Cornwall
SX 034670 *Fort*
Nanstallon fort, near Bodmin, was about 2 acres (0.8ha) in size, with a turf rampart and 2.5m (8ft) wide ditch. Evidence was found of timber corner towers and double gates. The fort was probably built in about AD55 and may have been occupied for about a quarter

The fort at Nanstallon

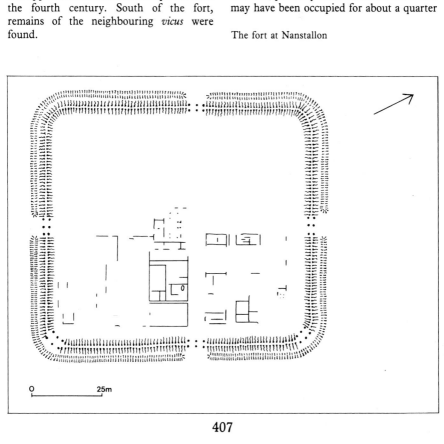

0   25m

of a century. Some barrack buildings were found in excavations of the late 1960s and early 1970s (an excellent report of which appears in *Britannia* iii (1972) pp 56–111). The *principia* and the commandant's house were also located.

NEATHAM Hampshire
SU 742412 *Small town*
A small town developed about 2 miles north-east of Alton along the Chichester to Silchester Roman road (Margary 155). Excavations throughout the 1970s exposed traces of timber buildings, one of which was an aisled workshop which had wood-lined tanks. Near the grouping of buildings was a bath house of flint walling, which had been demolished after a century of use (third to fourth century). One graffito found scratched on a tile was a drawing of a woman.

NETHER DENTON Cumbria
NY 596645 *Fort*
A fort site of about 8 acres (3.25ha), which had an associated *vicus* to the south-west, Nether Denton was excavated in the nineteenth century, and again in the 1930s when only part of the structure was noted. The excavator of the 1930s calculated an area of 3 acres (1.2ha). Aerial photography of 1976, however, revealed that in its first (Flavian) stage the fort had been much larger (about 8 acres/3.25ha) and the smaller area was a Trajanic reduction of size. The Trajanic work incorporated the fort into the Stanegate frontier, and included conversion of much of it to stone.

NETHERTON West Midlands
SO 991422 *Settlement*
A settlement was detected from the air near Chapel Farm.

NETHERWILD FARM Hertfordshire
TL 142011 *Villa*
A villa site at Netherwild Farm, about a mile north-west of Radlett, was excavated in the 1960s. Remains include a buttressed barn that was aisled, approx. 38 × 11m (42 × 12yd), several tile kilns and two bath houses linked by a corridor.

NEWCASTLE UPON TYNE
Tyne & Wear NZ 251641
Fort: Roman name Pons Aelius
Hadrian's Wall was originally planned to start on its westwards course at Newcastle. The first length was in broad wall, about 3m (10ft) wide at this point. A new bridge of stone piers with timber superstructure, carrying a road about 5.5m (18ft) wide, was built early in the Wall scheme, and was known as *Pons Aelius*, after Hadrian. This later came to be the name of the stone fort erected in Newcastle, not at the time of the Wall scheme but probably towards the end of the second century. Very little is known of the fort since excavation has not yet succeeded in establishing beyond question its location, though remains of a stone military granary, found under the arched railway line in 1978–9, may provide a clue. There is some reason to believe the fort may lie under the present cathedral.

We do know about some of the units stationed at *Pons Aelius*. One was the First Cohort of Cornovians, almost the only unit raised entirely from a single British tribe, and this may have been raised in Hadrian's time. An inscription found in the Tyne records the reinforcement of the army along the Wall by troops from the army in Germany, in the years 155–8, and these will presumably have occupied a simple earth and timber fort at Newcastle before the building of the stone fort.

The bridge crossed the Tyne at approximately the point where the present Swing Bridge now crosses it. The first bridge is said to have survived for more than a thousand years, with occasional repairs, to the mid thirteenth century when a new bridge was erected on the old piers.

NEWHAVEN East Sussex
TQ 445013 *Enclosure*
An enclosure of Iron Age beginnings, taken over in early Roman times, has been excavated as a series of rescue operations in advance of the new ring road. Traces of various timber structures were seen, including a military-style granary of the first century, and an aisled building of the second century. Also seen were traces of a stone

building which had painted plaster walls and window glass, box-flue tiles and *opus signinum* flooring. The building appears to have been pulled down at the end of the second century.

NEWINGTON Kent
TR 178373 *Farmstead*
Traces of a Romano-British farmstead, occupied between the first and third centuries, were found during road building on the M20.

NEWNHAM Bedfordshire
TL 074494 *Villa*
The site of a villa at Newnham, near Bedford, was investigated in the early 1970s. It was of courtyard type, there were several buildings, some of them with hypocausts and channels, and finds established that it was in occupation from the second to the fourth century.

NEWPORT Isle of Wight
SZ 500880 *Villa*
A small corridor villa here began as a timber-framed building of the second century. The

corridor house that developed in the third century received a bath suite at one end, remains of which have been exposed and preserved for viewing. The *frigidarium* has a mosaic pavement. The water cistern supplying the bath suite was also found.

NEWTON ON TRENT Lincolnshire
SK 8273 *Vexillation fortress*
A vexillation fortress with double-ditching and covering about 25 acres (10ha) was detected from the air in the 1960s. Although it has not been excavated, it is estimated to have had an early structure, probably of Claudian origin, and it may have accommodated part of Legio IX *Hispana*.

NEWTON ST LOE Avon
ST 7165 *Villa*
Two large residential blocks were set at an obtuse angle. One block was a simple winged corridor building, the other a more complex corridor house of many rooms, several with mosaics, fronted by a long corridor that faced east. The two houses were self-sufficient and could have been occupied by two or three families.

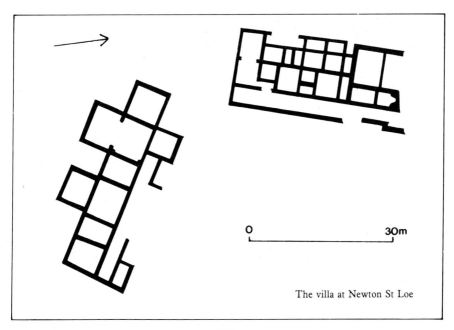

The villa at Newton St Loe

409

NORDEN Dorset
SY 9582 *Industrial settlement*
An industrial settlement at Norden, near
Corfe, was examined in the late 1960s and
early 1970s. Evidence of iron-smelting
furnaces, and also stone production (including *mortaria*) was found. Dating of the site
ranges from the second to the fourth
centuries.

NORTHCHURCH Hertfordshire
SP 973095 *Villa*
The villa at Northchurch, Berkhamsted, lay
near the river Bulbourne. It had started as a
simple timber house in the late first century.
Early in the second century it was rebuilt in
stone as a corridor villa. There is some
evidence of an early isolated bath house.
Sometime later in the century the villa was
enlarged, with wing rooms and an upper
storey. The villa appears to have been
flooded in the third century and then
evacuated, but it also seems to have been
reoccupied later on, and the roof repaired.

NORTHFLEET Kent
TQ 616741 *Villa*
Northflleet villa was excavated in the late
1970s and early 1980s. The site had been
badly damaged in earlier years by tramway
works and by industrial exploitation. Chief
among the interesting finds were remains of
a bath house with hot room, and a warm
room which had modifications. Some of the
bath house had been decorated with mosaics.
A clay-lined tank connected to a wooden pipe
in a trench was also seen. The villa
flourished between the second and fourth
centuries.

NORTH LEIGH Oxfordshire
SP 397155 *Villa*
Several miles to the north and west of
Oxford there is a group of villas, including
that at North Leigh, which lies close to the
villa at Shakenoak, and three miles north-east
of modern Witney. North Leigh was a courtyard villa. During the second century it consisted of a small main house with a detached
bath house and other buildings to the south-
west. Short wings were added to the main
house and these were later extended. Two-

coloured mosaics were already being laid in
the second century, suggesting a growth in
the wealth of the owner. The baths were
later joined into the main fabric of the villa
and remodelled, with better mosaics being
added.

By the fourth century, North Leigh had
reached the height of its prosperity. The
main domestic apartments were in the north
wing and had a channelled hypocaust
heating system. The buildings were now
ranged around a central courtyard with a
corridor running round the inside of all four
wings. The main gate was on the south side
of the court. The west wing was possibly
used for servants' quarters, whilst two more
sets of baths were added, one cramped in the
south corner and another more spaciously set
in the east corner. The size of the building
complex and the duplication of amenities
could point to dual occupancy of the villa.
The mosaics of the early fourth century,
along with the perfectly preserved hypocaust
pilae in the main heated room, make North
Leigh a site well worth a visit.

North Lodge see **Turret 12b**

NORTH TAWTON Devon
SX 6699 *Fort*
A 6 acre (2.4ha) fort was seen from the air at
North Tawton, and ground examination
revealed pottery of the first century. The site
has not been fully excavated, but some ramparting is visible. A practice camp has also
been identified nearby.

NORTH WARNBOROUGH Hampshire
SU 7352 *Villa*
An aisled farmhouse, about 45 × 10.75m
(50 × 12yd). was excavated and found to have
been partitioned into rooms in the south-
west corner, and also in the west and east
ends. The building appeared to have been
altered to look like a winged corridor house.
There was a granary of dwarf wall-type in
the south aisle. Some painted plaster was
found.

NORTHWICH Cheshire
SJ 656737 *Fort and town: Roman name*
Condate
Northwich was a small town that grew out of

an early fort. The fort had been of two phases. Phase I, of early Flavian time, had an earth rampart and ditch defences, with wooden stakes in the outer lip of the ditch. Phase II was probably early second century, and was marked by the ditch being re-cut and the rampart faced with stone. In 1969, the remains of an auxiliary infantryman's iron helmet were found and are now in Liverpool Museum. The town beside the fort has also been investigated, and several industrial features uncovered, notably iron-reducing furnaces and pottery kilns.

NORTH WRAXALL Wiltshire
ST 8376 *Villa*

A hall-type villa consisting of two houses flourished in the fourth century. The main block was a rectangular hall with additional quarters off the west wall. At the south end was an integral bath suite. Close by was a second building, this one aisled. Excavators discovered mid fourth-century coins in the mortar under some stone flagging in the courtyard, which may date the original building period.

NORTON North Yorkshire
SE 7970 *Settlement*

This was a small settlement near the fort at Malton. Investigations showed that pottery was manufactured here, and an inscription described a goldsmith's premises which may have been run by a slave on behalf of his owner.

NORTON DISNEY Lincolnshire
SK 8560 *Villa*

This was a fortified villa, L-plan in layout, consisting of a winged corridor structure with three main rooms in the centre range and an aisled building as the other arm of the 'L'. The two buildings were separate at first, but later joined by a small block containing a bath suite. There were mosaic floors. The villa was protected by ditching.

ODELL Bedfordshire
SP 956568 *Agricultural settlement*

There was an agricultural settlement at Odell throughout the Roman period. Excavations in the mid 1970s exposed traces

of circular houses, and displayed a number of changing field systems marked by re-cut boundaries.

OKEHAMPTON Devon
SX 598948 *Fort*

A 2½ acre (1ha) fort of the period c50–80 was spotted from the air, and in 1976–7 it was excavated. The dig confirmed a fort, and exposed some V-shaped ditch with cleaning slot, clay rampart about 6m (20ft) wide at the base and pottery that included Samian ware.

OLD BURROW Devon
SS 7849 *Fortlet*

Old Burrow was a temporary fortlet and signal station on the north Devon coast, built to watch over the Bristol Channel. It was erected probably before AD 50 and had a short life. No traces of permanent buildings have been found. The gateway was a simple four-post type. It is thought that the fortlet was given up in the mid 50s in favour of the nearby, more permanent Martinhoe, though the life span of the latter was not a long one, either.

OLD CARLISLE Cumbria
NY 259465 *Fort*

Old Carlisle, near Wigton, was a cavalry fort, some of whose history is recorded on inscriptions. It was garrisoned by the crack cavalry regiment, *Ala Augusta*, from about 185 to the 240s, and was renovated in the time of Caracalla (211–17). A substantial *vicus* developed beside the fort in the third century, partly as a settlement for veterans. The fort had begun in the early second century. The ditches and much of the rampart (some of which was faced with stone) are visible.

OLDCROFT Gloucestershire
SO 6406 *Coin hoard*

A hoard of some 3150 bronze coins was discovered near the Roman road from Mitcheldean to Lydney (Margary 614) in 1971.

OLD DURHAM Durham
NZ 2841 *Villa*

Probably the most northerly villa in Roman

Britain, Old Durham was part of an agricultural settlement. The building shapes and the site layout are not fully known, but excavations yielded two circular structures, one of them between 10 and 10.5m (33 and 35ft) in diameter. They had been eroded by continual quarrying. The buildings are thought to have been threshing floors. Some fragments of a farmstead were found nearby, and the pottery sherds spread over the period from Hadrian to the mid fourth century. Traces of a fourth-century bath house, with hypocaust, were also located.

OLD PENRITH Cumbria
NY 4938 *Fort: Roman name* Voreda
A 3 acre (1.2ha) fort of possible Agricolan construction, but also argued for Trajan's reign (98–117), Old Penrith, Plumpton Wall, may have been abandoned in Hadrian's reign. In the mid second century, however, the fort was reoccupied, and a *vicus* developed outside, some building remains of which were found in recent excavations (including striphouses, hypocausts etc). The fort accommodated a regiment of mixed Gallic cavalry and infantry. It was repaired in the third century (suggested by an inscription of the time of Caracalla), but abandoned towards the end of the century. There is evidence that the fort was occupied again in the last years of the fourth century, but the *vicus* appears to have been deserted by then.

OLD SARUM Wiltshire
SU 1332 *Settlement/road junction: Roman name* Sorviodunum
This was a road junction quite early in the occupation period. The presence of building remains and other ruins suggests at least a posting station, and quite probably a minor settlement. Webster (1980) has suggested a fort of the early period.

OLD STRATFORD Warwickshire
SP 178538 *Settlement*
Pottery of the second, third and fourth centuries was recovered during examination of crop marks here, on the north side of the Avon. It included buff-orange Severn ware.

Old Wall see Milecastle 59

OLNEY Buckinghamshire
SP 892526 *Settlement*
There was a settlement at Olney. Investigated in the mid 1970s, quantities of limestone rubble were uncovered, which may have come from a building. Four Roman ditches were traced.

ORPINGTON Greater London
TQ 4565 *Villa*
A simple villa building was excavated in Poverest Road at Fordcroft in the late 1970s. The principal find was a bath suite, of which some remains can be seen.

OTFORD Kent
TQ 5359 *Villa*
A small villa which was associated with a walled enclosure for stock, Otford may have been begun in the late first century. Several mosaics were located in the residential building, and interesting fragments of wall painting were found, including some of a scene from Vergil's *Aeneid* and some lettering presumed to be from quotations from the appropriate parts of the text. There was an aisled building nearby, which had a cobbled floor, which may have housed animals. The roof of the building is thought to have been thatched.

OVERMOIGNE Dorset
SY 772857 *?Villa*
Excavations at a Tudor house, Moigne Court, exposed evidence of a possible Roman villa of the third century. Some painted wall plaster, roof tiles and building rubble were noted.

OVERSTONE Northamptonshire
SP 804646 *Farmstead*
Traces of a Romano-British farmstead were found near South Lodge Farm. Building remains included those of a circular house with cobbled floor, some timber buildings and a later stone house, also circular.

PAGAN'S HILL Avon
ST 557626 *Temple*
A Romano-Celtic rural temple, consisting of an octagonal *cella* inside a second octagonal wall with a portico and buttressed outside,

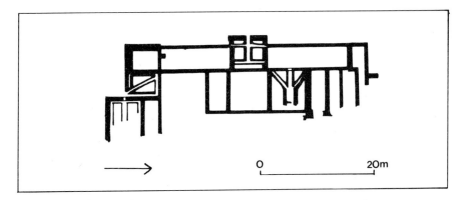

→

0   20m

was excavated in the late 1940s and early 1950s at Pagan's Hill, Chew Stoke. Evidence was found of decoration on wall surfaces. An outbuilding was also traced, which may have been a resting place for priests. The temple appears to have been used from the third to the fifth century, during which time it was rebuilt.

PAPCASTLE Cumbria
NY 110315 *Fort*
There were two forts at Papcastle, the first a timber structure of the early second century and the second, a stone fort superimposed on the first, much later in the fourth century. It is thought that the first, of which some traces of timber structures have been excavated, was given up for at least the whole of the third century. The rebuild in stone may have been as late as c370. Stone building remains have been found, including part of the bath house attached to the *praetorium*. The defences were renewed at this time. Some scale armour was also found.

PARK STREET Hertfordshire
TL 147032 *Villa*
Park Street had been an Iron Age homestead, and was probably destroyed during or immediately after the Boudican revolt. It was then rebuilt as a simple oblong cottage of stone, with six rooms, the most northerly having under it a cellar (for wine storage?). The house was fronted by a verandah, and had a separate bath house. In the second century two wings were added forming an H plan, giving the house eleven rooms, and it

Park Street villa: the earliest oblong cottage occupied the shorter central range

was also embellished with a corridor. In the fourth century, Park Street was again altered, and this time it received additional rooms that were heated by stone channelled hypocausts.

PENTREHYLING Shropshire
SO 2493 *Fort*
A military installation at Pentrehyling, near Brompton, which was seen from the air, has been investigated. Pottery dates to the first and second centuries.

PETERBOROUGH Cambridgeshire
TL 1899–2198 *Various settlements*
There have been several excavations of Roman remains in the Peterborough area throughout the 1970s, and they are still in progress. The sequence of occupations and their features are not yet fully determined. Evidence has been found of salt boiling, farming, stock rearing, pottery industries and of many civilian residential buildings, all of the Roman period. At Cat's Water, excavations revealed an earlier Iron Age settlement beneath later Roman enclosures.

PEVENSEY East Sussex
TQ 6404 *Fort of the Saxon Shore: Roman name* Anderida
One of the Roman forts of the Saxon Shore, Pevensey was the last to be built and the largest in area. It was also the most irregular in shape. It is roughly oval. The enclosing

413

West gate at the Roman fort of the Saxon Shore at Pevensey (*National Monuments Record*)

wall was erected on firm chalk and flint foundations laced with timber, and rose about 3m (11ft) or so thick to nearly 7.5m (25ft) high, with battlements on top. Eleven bastions, roughly U-shaped, now flank the enclosure as part of the wall, some 5m (16½ft) in diameter, though there used to be more. There were three gates, the west one between strong bastions, 10m (33ft) apart. The interior buildings of the fort are hardly known, though it may be presumed that they were for the most part timber, as was the case with most other Saxon Shore forts. Some hearths were found in excavations. Pevensey was built between 330 and 340. For a time, a detachment of the Roman fleet was based in the estuary which in those times came alongside the fort.

PIDDINGTON Northamptonshire
SP 796540 *Villa*
A substantial Roman villa of corridor-type has been uncovered in excavations for the Upper Nene Archaeological Society, which

began in 1979. The first building was an Antonine villa with long corridor at the front but no wings. This was destroyed by fire probably in the early third century, and was afterwards rebuilt, with additional rooms (some of them hypocaust heated). The floor of the corridor was paved with two-colour herring-bone tiling on a limestone base. Many of the rooms behind the corridor had tessellated floors. In the fourth century, the villa's residential role gave way to industrial use, as part was turned over to workshop accommodation.

PIERCEBRIDGE Durham
NZ 211156 *Fort and* vicus
Seven miles north of Scotch Corner on a crossing of the river Tees and strategically positioned on Dere Street lay the fort of Piercebridge. To the east of the fort of the main period lay another fort of Hadrianic or Antonine date. The main phase of development came c270 with a totally new foundation at Piercebridge. The fort was surrounded by a stone wall 3m (10ft) thick and backed by an earthen rampart. The area enclosed was about 11 acres (4.5ha). Part of a

414

large courtyard building, well appointed, with hypocausts, wall plaster and a private bath suite, has been found and was most probably the commandant's house. Recent excavation of the south-east corner of the fort and the east defences have revealed the eastern gate, which was double-portalled with a dual carriageway. This dates to the same period as the defences, c270, but c350 the south portal was blocked. This blocking reflects a reoccupation of the fort in the mid fourth century following an apparent abandonment in about 300–10. The remains of piers, the south abutment and paving on the river bed attest the presence of a timber bridge across the Tees at Piercebridge. Aerial photography has revealed the position of the *vicus* that grew up in association with the fort. It seems to have had an irregular street system with strip buildings along the routeways.

Piper Sike see **Turret 51a**

PITNEY Somerset
ST 4530 *Villa*
An interesting courtyard villa which incorporated a sizeable farm, Pitney was a large rectangular site that was arranged as follows. On the shorter west side was a corridor villa house which had some mosaic paving, and a walled garden to the extreme west. Along the longer north side was, first, a narrow pigsty block, and at the other end a group of structures filling the east corner and extending down the east side: a grain store, a cattle byre and a second pigsty. Further down the east was a barn and beside it a buttressed granary tower. The south side was open for much of its length, and then came a bath house followed by a narrow block of quarters for the workforce. The mosaics were of good quality. One was a continuous mosaic of two different patterns designed to fit into two adjoining rooms linked by a wide interconnecting doorway.

PLUMPTON HEAD Cumbria
NY 500354 *Marching camp*
A Flavian marching camp of about 25 acres (10ha), in irregular trapezoid plan, at Plumpton Head, near Penrith, was excavated after aerial observation in the early 1970s. There are stretches of rampart still visible.

Poltross Burn see **Milecastle 48**

PORTCHESTER Hampshire
SU 624046 *Fort of the Saxon Shore: Roman name* ?Portus Adurni
Portchester is probably (though not yet indisputably) the Roman fort of the Saxon Shore labelled *Portus Adurni* in the *Notitia Dignitatum* (see p 239). It stands on the north shore of Portsmouth Harbour, and was built in the mid 280s, quite probably by Carausius, the rebel 'emperor' whose career is outlined on p 144. The fort has been more extensively excavated than any other Saxon Shore fort, notably by Professor Barry Cunliffe in a series of brilliant investigations between 1961 and 1972. At least six phases of building were found. The fort may have been abandoned for a while after the collapse of Carausius' regime and the end of Allectus, say, from about 295, and was reoccupied in the early fourth century. At this period, it is clear that the fort was occupied not only by the military but also by women and children (perhaps, the troops' families, unless a civilian nucleus was permitted to live there). There is also evidence of repairs in the later 330s to early 340s, which were concurrent with the building of the Saxon Shore fort at Pevensey.

Portchester was regular in plan, almost square, about 8½ acres (3.5ha), which is larger than the other Saxon Shore forts. Its wall was about 3.6–4m (12–13ft) thick and was flanked all round and equidistantly by U-shaped towers (most of which remain today). The towers look as if they were repaired in medieval times when a Norman castle, erected in the fort's north-west corner, was in use.

PORTISHEAD Avon
ST 461758 *Settlement*
Hut circles in which some huts were of centre post construction, with turf walling, were located in work on a building site at St Mary's Park. A reap hook was found, along with pottery ranging from the first to the fourth centuries.

POUNDBURY Dorset
SY 685911 *Cemetery*
A Roman cemetery on the hillside, near to the Iron Age hillfort of Poundbury Camp, near Dorchester, has been examined from time to time since the late 1960s. Nearby, there are remains of a Roman aqueduct which brought water to the *civitas* capital of Dorchester from the river Frome at Notton Mill. These remains are visible as terracing, beside the north edge of Poundbury Camp.

PRESTON Dorset
SY 7082 *Villa*
A simple cottage-type villa building, aligned east–west, was excavated in the 1920s beside Jordan Brook. Fragments included pieces of mosaic and some broken bits of Kimmeridge shale chairs and tables. A furnace in one of the rooms was not connected with water or room heating.

PRIDDY Somerset
ST 531514 *Lead-working site*
Lead-working operations flourished at a settlement at Priddy, about ¼ mile west of the present St Cuthbert's lead works. Excavations of the early 1970s exposed smelting hearths.

PUCKERIDGE Hertfordshire
TL 388288 *Settlement*
A suburb of Braughing small town, the settlement at Puckeridge was excavated in the early 1970s. An Iron Age village had been expanded into a Romano-British settlement near Wickham Hill which straddled the new Roman Ermine Street. Timber buildings were put up on each side. In the third century many of the roadside buildings were workshops.

PUNCHBOWL INN Cumbria
NY 829148 *Signal station*
One of the signal stations in the Stainmore Pass (another was Augill Bridge), Punchbowl Inn has rock-cut ditching. The station consisted of a centre earth mound (which supported the tower) surrounded by two concentric ditches.

PURBROOK Hampshire
SU 686074, 691072 *Agricultural and industrial settlement*
An agricultural site, with industrial associations, beside the road from Chichester to Bitterne (*Noviomagus* to *Clausentum*, Margery 421), was examined again in the mid 1970s in advance of development. Among remains were an aisled building of the second to third century outside of which was a T-shaped drying furnace, and to the north a tile kiln in which fragments were found of box tiles, *tegulae* and plain tiles. The site is close to a villa site first identified in 1926.

PURITON Somerset
ST 315415 *Settlement*
An agricultural settlement, probably of Iron Age origin, was developed in the Roman period at Cricket Field. Remains of buildings have been excavated.

QUERNMORE Lancashire
SD 523622 *Pottery and tile works*
This was a pottery works that was operated by craftsmen employed by the garrison at the fort at Lancaster. Products were supplied from the late first century well into the third. Some of the kilns have been excavated.

QUINTON Northamptonshire
SP 775535 *Agricultural and industrial settlement*
An agricultural and industrial settlement, with circular houses, Quinton developed before the Conquest and continued in Roman times up to the fourth century. Several Roman features have been excavated, including an aisled building with a verandah, an ironsmith's workshop, a cobbler's premises and some pottery kilns.

RADFORD SEMELE Warwickshire
SP 342624 *Villa*
The courtyard villa at Radford Semele was excavated in the mid 1970s. The site appeared to have been occupied between the mid second and late fourth century, and traces of both stone and timber buildings were found. Pottery sherds included some Samian ware, and colour-coated ware of the fourth century. Part of the road from the

villa to the Fosse Way, about 1½ miles away, was found. ·

RADWELL Bedfordshire
TL 010575 *Farmstead*
A late Roman farmstead has recently been located at Radwell, near Felmersham. Excavations of the early 1970s revealed remains of a large timber building and quantities of roof tiles that came from the building and perhaps from others nearby. Some coins found were of late third and early fourth centuries. A villa site was seen from the air.

RAMSDEN Oxfordshire
SP 339152 *?Villa*
The site of a possible villa appears to be confirmed by a recent survey, and a bronze figure of a bird was found.

RANSCOMBE HILL East Sussex
TQ 432089 *Farmstead*
A Romano-British farmstead of the second and third centuries was excavated in the mid 1970s at Ranscombe Hill, South Malling. Finds included a corn drier, part of a hearth and some sections of enclosing ditch.

RAPSLEY Surrey
TQ 080415 *Villa*
A villa complex at Rapsley Farm, Ewhurst, dating originally from the second century and at one time associated with nearby pottery kilns, had several buildings including two separate blocks and a free-standing bath house. One block was an aisled building of the third century, about 22.5m (25yd) long, in which evidence was found of lead working.

RATHAM MILL West Sussex
SU 8006 *Temple*
Two miles south-west of the Fishbourne Palace complex, aerial photographs located a Romano-Celtic temple site at Ratham Mill, Funtington. The temple appeared to be of three concentric squares. It dates from the late first century.

RAVENGLASS Cumbria
NY 087961 *Fort: Roman name* Glannaventa
Ravenglass fort was part of the Cumbrian

coastal defence system extending from Hadrian's Wall. It began as a small fortlet probably of the end of the first or the second century. In Hadrian's time, the fortlet was levelled and a 4 acre (1.5ha) fort built over it, with a turf rampart later faced with stone, and a single, V-shaped 6m (20ft) wide ditch system in front. This fort has been eroded by the sea and also by railway works. The bath house, part of which is still 3.5m (12ft) high, lay to the north-east of the fort. Excavations of the mid 1970s revealed traces of timber buildings, including two fourth-century barrack blocks.

RAVENSBURGH Bedfordshire
TL 099295 *Hillfort*
A rectangular Iron Age hillfort has been known at Ravensburgh, near Barton, for some time. It was excavated by J. F. Dyer in 1964, and again in 1970–2. There were two main construction periods, the first probably in the fifth century BC, the second a reinforcement of the mid first century BC. Post holes and evidence of heavy fortification by timber lacing of the ramparts of this date were revealed. There is evidence of the destruction of the rampart on one side (east) which could attest an assault by Roman forces under Caesar in 54BC (see p 25). If this is so, Ravensburgh can be considered strong candidate for having been the *oppidum* of Cassivelaunus.

RAVENSTONE Leicestershire
SK 402117 *Rural settlement*
A recently excavated site of a rural settlement (the work is not completed) contained pottery kilns which had produced grey ware, and also a tile kiln. The settlement appears to be chiefly of the third and fourth centuries. Nearby, on a site stripped for open-cast mining, most interesting remains *of a circular stone building were located, about 10.5m (12yd) across, with a coin of Tetricus in the foundations.

RECULVER Kent
TR 227694 *Fort of the Saxon Shore: Roman name* Regulbium
The Roman fort of the Saxon Shore at Reculver is marked today by the presence of

ruins of a twelfth-century church inside what is left of the fort's walling. Gateways on the east and south of the walling survive. This fort had been nearly square, with the usual rounded corners but without bastions, since it was built somewhat earlier than the other Saxon Shore forts. Excavations inside the fort revealed the stone *praetorium* just south of the church, the *principia* and an internal bath house. Half of the original fort has disappeared beneath the sea which now comes up almost to the church.

The fort was built probably in the first half of the third century, about forty years before some of the other Saxon Shore forts and a century before Pevensey. This has been taken to show that the Saxon Shore fort scheme was not a hastily conceived programme in reaction to sudden danger but rather a 'gradual process in response to a build up of Saxon pressure' as Stephen Johnson put it. The fort's early date may possibly, though by no means certainly, be linked with the Severan and Caracallan campaigns in the north of Britain, when the *classis Britannica* may have been moved northwards, leaving it necessary to install the army in fresh forts to protect the south-east coasts.

RED HILL Shropshire
SJ 726110 *?Fort*
There were two fortified enclosures at Red Hill, Oakengates. The first, of some 2½ acres (1ha), was probably of mid first century construction. Inside the first enclosure a second, smaller fortified site was erected later on, with double-ditching, of about 1½ acres (0.6ha). Evidence of timber buildings in the later fort was found in excavations of the early 1970s. The second fort appears to have been renovated in the late third century.

REY CROSS Durham
NY 900125 *Marching camp*
The 20 acre (12ha) marching camp at Rey Cross stands on the summit of the Stainmore Pass, beside the Roman road from York to Carlisle (Margary 82). It is often cited as the best preserved camp in Britain: certainly, it is in good condition after so many centuries. The rampart was built 6m (20ft) wide and up

to 2m (6ft) or so high because the camp is on rock and ditching could not be cut. The camp has been dated to the governorship of Petillius Cerialis (71–4). It had eleven gates, protected by *titula*, of which nine survive.

RHYN Shropshire
SJ 305370 *Fortress*
Aerial photography in the mid 1970s showed up two forts at Rhyn, near St Martins, one overlapping the other. The smaller, of 15 acres (6ha), was probably a temporary camp. The larger, about 46 acres (19ha), which preceded the smaller, has been described as a vexillation fortress. It had double-ditching round three sides, with four gates protected by *titula*, an indication that the fortress was not intended to be permanent. Pottery fragments were similar to some wares used at Wroxeter. The fortress is possibly one built by Ostorius Scapula during his campaign against the Deceangli of north Wales or it could date from similar campaigning later on under Suetonius Paullinus (59–60). The smaller fort, or camp, was perhaps an earth and timber structure connected with the campaigns of Frontinus in the mid 70s.

RIBCHESTER Lancashire
SD 6535 *Forts and* vicus: *Roman name* Bremetennacum
The first excavations at Ribchester, situated on the north bank of the river Ribble, 12 miles from the sea, established the outline of the defences, but did not reveal a sequence of development. The job of piecing together Ribchester's history is rendered difficult by the fact that the Ribble has washed away the south-east corner of the site.

Originally an Agricolan structure of about AD78, the fort covered 5¾ acres (2ha) and was the usual rectangular shape. This was probably an auxiliary fort, as recent excavations of the barrack buildings have attested. There were two phases of Flavian timber building at Ribchester and the early layout of structures appears to have been different from that of later periods. The defences of the first fort comprised a turf and timber rampart with double-ditching.

The second fort at the site was Trajanic in date. The defences were modified in this period, with a stone wall being set in front of the rampart, and a new palisaded ditch being cut. The wall was nearly 2m (6ft) thick. The north gate of these fortifications has been excavated and found to have been 8.5m (28½ft) wide with a guardchamber of about 4×3m (13×10ft). The earliest timber buildings were replaced by new barrack blocks, two of which have been traced. Other evidence from inside the fort is scanty, but what is thought to be the *principia* has been traced, which had an eight-pillared portico and a courtyard with two wells. Remains of two third-century granaries have also been found, the north one measuring 32×7m (105×23ft). Both seem to have had raised floors to encourage cool and dry conditions. Charred grain indicates that they perished by fire. In the early fourth century, the final phase of rebuilding occurred in the second fort. The barrack blocks were renovated and another ditch was cut to add to the fortifications.

Recent excavation has increased our knowledge of the *vicus*. In the late first century and early second century, there appear to have been two phases of timber buildings to the north-west of the fort. In the mid to late second century, cobbles were laid over the area. The *vicus* seems to have been enclosed in the Antonine period by the construction of a palisaded rampart and a ditch.

RICHBOROUGH Kent

TR 3260 *Fort and later fort of the Saxon Shore: Roman name* Rutupiae

The earliest visible signs of the Roman Conquest of Britain can be seen at Richborough where two parallel north–south ditches were dug as defences soon after the invasion began in AD43. These defended the military beach-head, since at the time Richborough lay on a small promontory of the mainland. Apart from the causewayed ditch system, only two hearths show signs of occupation in the period. Soon after the establishment of the beach-head, Richborough lost its military importance and the site became a supply base, the ditches being filled in and timber buildings being constructed. Towards the end of the first century, Richborough had become the

chief port of Roman Britain, and in AD85 a marble-faced monument, with a four-way arch 27m (90ft) high, was erected as a sign of the commercial importance of the settlement. This position was lost, however, as Dover increased in importance, and by the mid third century Richborough had declined to the extent that the monument was stripped of its facings and used as a signal tower. At this time a small fort of about 1 acre (0.4ha) and surrounded by triple-ditches and a rampart occupied the site. The ditches are designed to avoid a second-century stone *mansio* on the north-east side of the fort. The Saxon Shore fort seems to date to the decade immediately before 285, and it is the remains of this fort's defences that can be seen, impressively well preserved, today.

The three ditches of the earlier fort were filled with material from their own banks and from the monument, which was now mostly demolished. The new rectangular fort was surrounded by walls 3.3m (11ft) thick constructed with small ashlar and double-tile courses, some of which still stand to a height of 8m (26ft). External interval towers stood midway between the gates and at the corners of the fort. The whole was surrounded by a double-ditch system, with one point on the west side defended by three ditches. Of the interior of the fort comparatively little is known. A small bath house in the north-east corner stood on the site of the second-century *mansio*, and two other buildings of an official or public nature have been found – possibly temples or guildhalls. The base of the monument was used as a foundation for a rectangular building, possibly the *principia*. There is also a little evidence of timber barrack blocks. Richborough was a centre for settlement well into the fifth century and in the north-west corner a timber Christian church has been found.

Rise How Bank see **Milefortlet 26**

RISINGHAM Northumberland

NY 890862 *Fort: Roman name* Habitancum

Doubt still hovers over the foundation date of this 4 acre (1.6ha) fort, near Woodburn, that overlooks the Rede. Its ditching is still visible along with the platform and some stonework, especially of the west gate of the fourth century. The received view is that Lollius Urbicus (governor from 139 to 142) built the fort while the Antonine Wall was being constructed further north. The fort was garrisoned with cavalry, and at a later date with a detachment of army scouts (*exploratores Habitancenses*) for special patrolling in the Lowlands. Unlike many other forts abandoned after the pullback to Hadrian's Wall in the 160s, Risingham appears to have remained occupied, certainly until the 180s, possibly through to the first decade of the third century when (c205-8) it was rebuilt by the governor Alfenus Senecio in the time of Severus, attested by an interesting inscription in medallion shape, now at the Newcastle Museum. The fort was occupied through the third century and into the fourth, and was modified, the modifications being the main parts to be seen today, such as parts of the west gate and the eastern corner. Excavations in the nineteenth century and in the present century exposed walling of good quality sandstone ashlar blocks, angle towers, a gate in the south which had two projecting turrets with seven sides each, *principia*, bath house in the southeast corner and barracks which had been renewed in the fourth century. There is a large inscription from the fort, about 5×3m (18×9ft), which was dedicated to Caracalla,

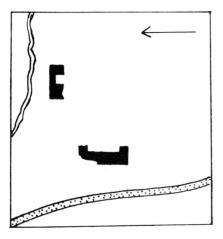

The Flavian period buildings at Rivenhall villa

and it is now in the Museum of Antiquities at Newcastle.

RIVENHALL Essex
TL 828178 *Villa*
The villa at Rivenhall had very early beginnings. Situated in Trinovantian territory, there is more than a hint that it began as a house of a Trinovantian noble or merchant during the first Roman period. A bronze mirror of Celtic manufacture was found under the floor of the first Roman building of the Flavian period (there were two buildings of this period) which may still have been erected by a Trinovantian under Roman encouragement. The villa developed during the second century into a courtyard-type, and included an aisled building on the west side, about 48m (53ft) long. One of the earlier buildings appears to have been destroyed by fire in the late second century.

ROCESTER Staffordshire
SK 1139 *Fort and later settlement*
A Roman settlement developed from an early fort, on the west side of the river Dove. The fort may have been early Flavian.

ROCHESTER Kent
TQ 7468 *Small town: Roman name* Durobrivae
Rochester was the location of a small town which developed from an Iron Age settlement. It may have been the place where the army of Aulus Plautius crossed the Medway and engaged with British forces in AD43 (see p 37). The Romans may have built a fort at Rochester after the battle. Traces of a timber bridge across the river have been found. The town grew slowly, and it was not walled in stone until the third century. Lengths of this walling survive today, especially in Eagle Court garden. Part of the wall on the north side was examined in the mid 1970s and what appears to have been a simple archway was probably the north gate, for the river estuary came up to the wall at this point in the Roman period.

ROCK Isle of Wight
SZ 424841 *Villa*
A corridor villa site, first discovered in the

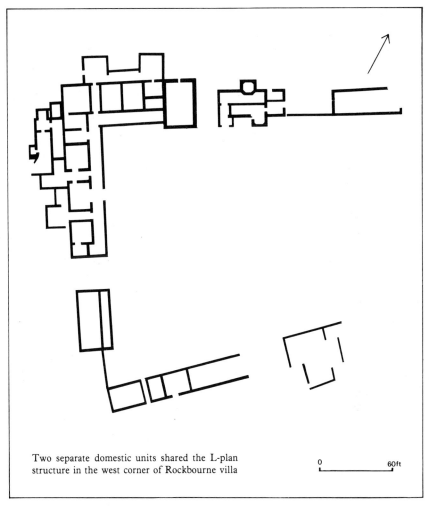

Two separate domestic units shared the L-plan
structure in the west corner of Rockbourne villa

0 _____ 60ft

1830s, was investigated in the mid 1970s at
Rock, Brightstone. It was enclosed on three
sides by a U-shaped ditch. Some of the north
wall stood to nearly 1.5m (5ft) and some
inside wall had painted plaster. A wing
appeared to have been built on to the south-
east corner, in front of the corridor, though
how long the wing was is not clear. Finds
suggested that the villa had been built in the
late third century. Sometime in the late
fourth century, a T-shaped corn drier with
stone-lined flue was built inside the house, in
the central room. By then, perhaps, the villa
had been turned over to industrial use.

ROCKBOURNE Hampshire
SU 120170 *Villa*
Rockbourne was a courtyard villa of some
sophistication. The north-west corner was a
substantial L-plan double block of residential
accommodation, containing separate houses
for two families, each block having its own
bath suite. The period of occupation appears
to have begun in the third century and continued to the mid fourth, though there were
traces of earlier, simpler accommodation of
perhaps the late first century. The south-
west and south-east corners of the yard comprised a work-hall with its own verandah,

421

and separated from it, an agricultural range including an aisled building which had corn driers, a possible granary and an iron forge. The dwelling parts contained more than seventy rooms, a few with mosaics, and several with hypocausts. There is also evidence of private formal gardens.

ROCKBOURNE DOWN Hampshire
SU 1019 *Ranch*
A large ditched and stockaded ranch of nearly 100 acres (40ha) flourished during the third and fourth centuries, not far from Rockbourne villa. A number of corn driers found on the site (including a double T-shaped drier with the flues arched by stone slabs) were of earlier date, suggesting that a corn-drying business associated with well-cultivated fields had been in occupation previously.

RODMARTON Gloucestershire
ST 9498 *Villa*
Rodmarton villa was a winged corridor-type, which had a small inner courtyard or *atrium*.

ROMSEY Hampshire
SU 435211 *Industrial settlement*
Remains of first- and second-century timber buildings were traced during works at Narrow Lane in Romsey. There was some evidence of iron working. The site seemed to be a mix of late Iron Age of first century AD and earlier Roman.

ROPER CASTLE Cumbria
NY 8811 *Signal station*
The mound of a signal station is visible here.

ROSSINGTON BRIDGE South Yorkshire
SK 6399 *Vexillation fortress*
This 20 acre (8ha) vexillation fortress of the first century, near Doncaster, was first identified from the air in the late 1960s, though its existence had been calculated for some time. It has not been excavated. Later in the Roman period, probably in the late second century, black burnished pottery of Type I (originating in the Durotriges *civitas*) was made in an offshoot industry nearby, which supplied items to the army.

ROTHERLEY Wiltshire
ST 948196 *Farmstead*
Not far from the settlement at Berwick Down, a similar Iron Age farmstead that continued into Romano-British times was examined in the nineteenth century. It has been examined again, the last time in the late 1960s. The farmstead appears to have been abandoned in the third century. Traces of T-shaped corn driers were found.

ROWLANDS CASTLE Hampshire
SU 735106 *Pottery*
The pottery industry identified at Rowlands Castle produced a local ware chiefly in the second and third centuries. Aerial photographs identified workshops, two of which appear to have been aisled. The site was enclosed.

RUDCHESTER Northumberland
NZ 112675 *Fort on Hadrian's Wall: Roman name* Vindovala
Rudchester, near Heddon-on-the-Wall, is the third fort on Hadrian's Wall going west from Wallsend. Its 4½ acres (2ha), projects about 36m (120ft) north of the Wall and has three gates north of the Wall and three to the south. The fort has been excavated, but not much found. In 1972 remains were found of a stone barrack block for cavalry, of Hadrian's time, which had subsequently been burned down (probably in a raid) and then replaced. The fort deteriorated in the third century and by the 290s was ruinous. In the fourth century, new timber buildings were erected on the debris of the older stone ones. There was a *vicus* south of the Wall, to the west of the fort, and some 120m (400ft) south-west of the fort was a *mithraeum* of the third century, which was renovated before final demolition in the fourth century. The original shape of the *mithraeum* was a *basilica*, some 13×7m (43×22ft), with an apse at the western end.

Rudchester see also **Milecastle 13, Turret 13a**

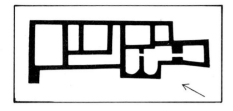

The villa at Rudston: bath suite at south-east end

RUDSTON Humberside
TA 088667 *Villa*
Rudston was a small and rather poorly built villa that had a relatively short life. Although built long after the arrival of the Romans, the villa showed few signs of Roman influence. The mosaics were primitive, the Venus picture in particular is gross, and even the lettering of the captioning for the surrounding scenes is illiterate. The villa consisted of a group of free-standing structures, the main one being a simple farmhouse with projecting bath suite at the south-east end, with one corridor.

RUSHDEN Northamptonshire
SP 943660 *Pottery kilns*
A group of pottery kilns producing late Belgic ware during the first years of the Roman occupation was located during investigations of the 1960s at a 15 acre (6ha) site that was about to be levelled to make new playing fields at Boundary Road. The site had been taken over by the Romans and began to produce quite different wares, some of them unusual, decorated and in some cases exotic in form. The whole site appeared to be a large industrial area of Romano-British times. The period of better quality production was short, and was followed by a relapse into simpler styles. A number of artefacts were found, some of them more or less whole, others capable of repair, and many are housed for public view.

SACREWELL Cambridgeshire
TF 077005 *Villa*
The villa site at Sacrewell, Thornhaugh, was examined in the mid 1970s and a number of buildings were located, some with *opus*

signinum flooring and with painted wall plaster. There was much evidence of iron manufacture, including a shaft furnace and a rectangular room that may have been used for ore washing. The iron workings appear to have been after the occupation of the villa.

ST ALBANS Hertfordshire
TL 1307 Civitas *capital of Catuvellauni:*
Roman name Verulamium
St Albans, which became the third largest town of Roman Britain, was originally developed by the Romans near the site of the native Belgic settlement of *Verlamion* at Prae Wood. The site lay at a crossing of the river Ver and commanded several important routes including Watling Street. The first Roman occupation was likely to have been a military post, established to keep watch over the strategically well positioned *oppidum*. This conjectured fort was quickly evacuated, however, when the *civitas* capital was founded, probably c50 (see p 46).

Very early earthwork defences of c61 enclosed an area of 119 acres (48ha). The earliest settlement consisted of timber buildings, some of which were of the native type. This foundation was severely burnt in the sack of the town by the hosts of Boudica, in 61, and traces of the fire were found in excavations, including burnt shop buildings. By the end of the Flavian period, however, the town had recovered and a *forum* and *basilica* had been built. An inscription dates the *forum* to 79. Other public buildings include one, and possibly two, other stone temples. The first half of the second century saw expansion and alteration at St Albans. Domestic buildings were on the whole half-timbered, some having *opus signinum* floors and being decorated with painted plaster. A devastating fire c155 destroyed about 50 acres (20ha) including parts of the *forum*. No signs of contemporary burning in other towns of the area suggest that this was accidental, not deliberate.

The mid second century public buildings were impressive. The *forum* and *basilica* complex measured 160×115m (530×385ft). The *basilica* was second only to London's in size, being 115×36m (385×120ft). The *forum* piazza was surrounded by a

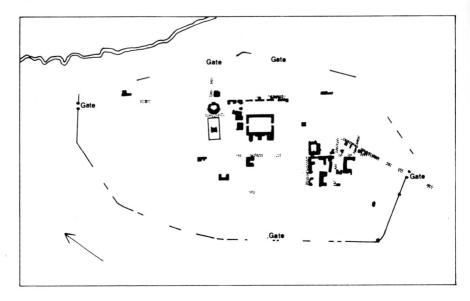

Plan of St Albans: the *forum* and theatre are in the centre

colonnaded ambulatory. Unique to St Albans' *forum* complex was a *curia* and magistrates' building separate from the *basilica*. The theatre, of which substantial remains can be seen, had at first an almost circular orchestra nearly 24m (80ft) in diameter. Later, the stage was modified which cut the orchestra into a semi-circle, and a Corinthian *proscenium* was installed, making the form more classically Roman.

After the fire, the remains were cleared and new buildings erected with an increase in the use of masonry in domestic structures. By 160–70 expansion was such that the original ditch defences were levelled to allow for extension of the town area. This expansion continued into the third century despite economic crises in the empire, with continued building activity creating larger scale shops and houses. The defences were rebuilt with stone walling following a different course to the original earthwork and enclosing 200 acres (60ha).

The end of Roman St Albans is now thought to have followed the familiar pattern of slow decline in the late fourth century. The last structural alterations were made to the theatre in the period 345–60, and it was possibly not disused until as late as the 380s, from which time it was used as a rubbish dump. The running water supply seems to have been in use in the fifth century, and a reasonable level of population maintained until c450–70, suggesting that the inhabitants of St Albans seem to have been unwilling to give up the Roman way of life.

ST HILARY Cornwall
SW 550313 *Milestone*
A rectangular milestone, about 1.25m (4ft) tall, dated by inscription to the period when Constantine I was in Britain as Caesar, 306–7, was found built into the chancel of St Hilary's church, near Marazion. It was later moved to the south aisle.

ST MARTINS Isles of Scilly
SV 944147 *Settlement*
An open settlement with two circular houses and other features has been examined at St Martins. There is evidence of some occupation during the Roman period.

SANDWICH Kent
TR 319573 *Villa*
A small, simple winged corridor villa has been excavated at Sandwich in recent years,

following its discovery during roadworks in 1978. It was about 28m (93ft) long, with a narrow central room fronted by a verandah, and at each end a wing room. Outside were found three ovens, and some ditching. Pottery finds included Samian ware. Occupation appears to have been from the late first century into the third century.

SANSOM'S PLATT Oxfordshire
SP 452188 *Villa*
In the early 1970s remains of a villa were discovered about 180m (200yd) south of Akeman Street, near Tackley village. Three rooms of the main building were identified, one having had painted plaster walls. There was also an outbuilding on the east side. The villa was begun in the first century, in timber work with wattle and daub, but by the mid third century it had been partly converted to stone.

SAPPERTON Lincolnshire
TF 018330 *Settlement*
A long known site of a small Romano-British settlement, Sapperton was excavated again in the 1970s. The site may have been a posting station. It covered some 5 acres (2ha) on the Bourne to Ancaster road (Margary 26). There were signs of furnaces and hearths used for the production of iron tools, in an aisled building of stone which had had painted wall plaster at the back, suggesting domestic accommodation for the metalsmith. A second aisled building of the fourth century to the south had a T-shaped corn drier. The settlement was occupied between the mid second and the early fifth century. There were other stone buildings, some built on the same alignment as earlier levelled structures underneath.

SAUNDERTON Buckinghamshire
SP 8003 *Villa*
The villa at Saunderton was seen from the air in the early 1970s. It was at the north-east corner of a trapezoid enclosure surrounded by ditching. The plan started as a simple rectangular house which in the second century received a corridor round three sides and wings with several rooms, forming an H-plan. The villa was later divided into self-

contained residential units. A suite of baths was found at the southern end. The villa declined probably during the third century, followed by a revival in the fourth century. A corn drier was found near the main central room.

SAWLEY Derbyshire
SK 474313 *?Practice camp*
A ditched rectangular enclosure of about 1½ acres (0.6ha) here was examined in 1975. Evidence of a *titulum* was noted on the west, but no gate has been found. It may have been a practice camp.

SCALESCEUGH Cumbria
NY 449495 *Tilery*
A military and civilian tileworks was recently discovered at Scalesceugh, near Scalesceugh Hall. Quantities of pottery from the first to the fourth century were uncovered. Stamped tiles discovered attest a period when the factory was worked on behalf of Legio IX Hispana, early in the second century.

SCAMPTON Lincolnshire
SK 954785 *Villa*
The site of Scampton villa has been known for well over two centuries. A fine mosaic pavement from a corridor was found in 1795 and drawn by W. Fowler in Cayley Illingworth's *Topographical Account of the Parish of Scampton, 1808*. The site was examined again in the early 1970s.

SCARBOROUGH North Yorkshire
TA 0589 *Signal station*
This is one of the Yorkshire coastal signal

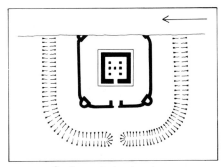

Scarborough signal station

stations of late fourth century (cf Goldsborough). The station consisted of a ditched enclosure inside which stood a square-plan tower with rounded angles, whose walls rose from foundations discovered to be somewhat wider than the walls themselves. There is evidence of external buttressing of the walls. Today, the outline of the station is indicated in concrete.

SCARCLIFFE PARK Derbyshire
SK 512710 *Settlement*
A number of native sites of occupation were examined in the late 1960s, and a variety of houses of timber-framed construction were found. They emerged in several shapes (oval, round, rectangular, square). They were associated with coarse pottery of the second and third centuries. There was also evidence of iron and lead working.

SCOLE Norfolk
TM 147786 *?Fort*
It has long been held that a fort was built at Scole during the first decades of the Roman occupation. Was it built before or after the Boudican revolt? Excavations of the early 1970s, by the old Roman road (Pye road, Margary 3d, Caistor to Baylham) which crossed the Waveney not far west of the present bridge at Scole, revealed traces of defences and a late first-century timber building. But it is too early to say if the fort was pre- or post-rebellion. Remains were also found of a small settlement, dating from the second to the fourth centuries.

SCOWLES Gloucestershire
SO 5708 *Iron mine*
An open cast iron mine is known to have been worked here during the Roman period.

SEA MILLS Avon
ST 558137 *Small town: Roman name* Abonae
This is the site of some kind of supply base, probably for detachments of the Roman Fleet (*classis Britannica*) operating in the Bristol Channel, and perhaps associated in some way with the naval station recently discovered at Glan-y-Mor, Cold Knap, near Barry, in south Wales. A settlement has been excavated at Sea Mills (*Abonae* in the

Antonine Itinerary) overlooking the harbour on the river Avon where it meets the river Trym. The earliest finds were of military character, which indicate the presence of a garrison, though no fort defences have yet been found. The first buildings were of timber, but stone structures of the second, third and fourth centuries have been located, including houses and shops.

SEATON Devon
SY 237909 *Villa*
This is a villa associated with a group of buildings, including outbuildings, an aisled structure (on stone foundations of about AD100) and a bath house (discovered in 1969 and still visible), all in an area of about 12 acres (4.8ha). The site is known as Honeyditches. It was occupied over at least four centuries, beginning as a small Iron Age farmstead of the Durotriges tribe, and being developed into a Roman villa complex from the end of the first century AD. The site has been examined in some detail, and the most comprehensive report is in *Britannia* viii (1977) pp 107–48. A lotus flower motif mosaic was discovered. This type of large villa estate was fairly common in the south-east of the province, but was exceedingly rare in the south-west.

SEWINGSHIELDS Northumberland
NY 813704 to NY 803705 *Section of Hadrian's Wall*
Near Sewingshields Castle, Turret 34a survives as a ruin. A javelin head was found among the remains in the 1971 excavations. Several hundred metres west, under Sewingshields Farmhouse, lies Turret 34b, many stones of which were used to build the farmhouse. Milecastle 35 at Sewingshields is also fragmentary. It was 15 × 18m (50 × 60ft). Part of the Wall has recently been uncovered on either side of the milecastle, to about five courses tall, the foundations being about 3.5m (12ft) wide. A little further west, Turret 35a is thought to have been abandoned by the end of the second century.

SHAKENOAK Oxfordshire
SP 374138 *Villa*
The winged corridor villa at Shakenoak lay

in the Wilcott valley in an abandoned meander of the river Windrush. A spring lay half a mile away and a stream ran nearby which divided the buildings of the site in two. Shakenoak was probably occupied all through the Roman period, from the first century onwards, and the investigation of three main buildings has shown the history and development of the site as a whole.

The first dwelling house on the north side of the stream was a simple Flavian building 20 × 13m (65 × 42ft), with ten rooms and projecting wings. At the beginning of the second century, the house was enlarged and a corridor built round the east, west and north sides. At this time an aisled barn was also built, to the south of the stream. By the mid second century, the house north of the stream had reached its maximum size of 41 × 14m (137 × 47ft), with a verandah added to the south side. In the late second century the aisled barn was replaced by a larger agricultural building.

Third-century alterations to the winged corridor part of the villa included the insertion of a channelled hypocaust in the west corridor, but by the middle of the century two-thirds of the building had been demolished, leaving only four western rooms and the corridor. Another building to the south of the stream then appears to have become the central focus of the site, changing from functioning as a working area to a domestic one. In the later third century, baths were added on the west side, and the mid fourth century saw the peak of the settlement's prosperity when the baths were remodelled and a stone-channelled hypocaust was added. This building was occupied at least until about 430, but by the end of the fifth century had been abandoned. Although a difficult site to interpret, Shakenoak villa shows a remarkable picture of continuous development.

SHAPWICK Dorset
ST 948028 *Fort*
Discovered from the air in 1975, Shapwick fort was of mid first-century origin, and it covered 6 acres (2.5ha). It was surrounded by triple-ditching on three sides and double on the fourth. From the air it appeared to be astride the Old Sarum to Dorchester road, but this road was in fact of later date than the fort.

Shield on the Wall see **Milecastle 33**

SHORTLANESEND Cornwall
SW 805475 *Enclosure*
An enclosure was examined at Shortlanesend, near Truro, in the late 1970s. It had a U-shaped ditch surround. Pottery of the Roman period was found.

SHOTTLEGATE Derbyshire
SK 319471 *Pottery kilns*
Pottery kilns have been excavated at Shottle Hall, near Hazelwood. Products were Derbyshire wares (pimply fabric texture, especially on jars). It has been suggested that these kilns supplied the fort at Littlechester.

SHREWLEY COMMON Warwickshire
SP 213672 *Settlement*
A rescue dig on a building site exposed a cobbled surface in which were several post holes and pits containing sherds, broken tiles, nails. The pottery was chiefly third and fourth century, and included Severn valley ware, black burnished and grey ware.

SILCHESTER Hampshire
SU 6462 Civitas *capital of Atrebates: Roman name* Calleva Atrebatum
Silchester is one of the best known sites of Roman Britain, since it has been left unencumbered by the buildings of succeeding generations. Despite this, the defences are almost the only remains visible to the modern visitor. Built on the site of a native settlement, Silchester probably saw a short military occupation before power was handed over to Cogidubnus, king of the Regnenses. The first earthworks were built c43–4, but were soon levelled, and the second earthworks replaced them c61–5. Towards the end of the first century the street grid was laid out, and at the same time a *mansio* was planned in the south. The *forum*, baths and temples appear to have been on a different alignment from the street grid, suggesting that they predate the plan and possibly belong to an earlier one.

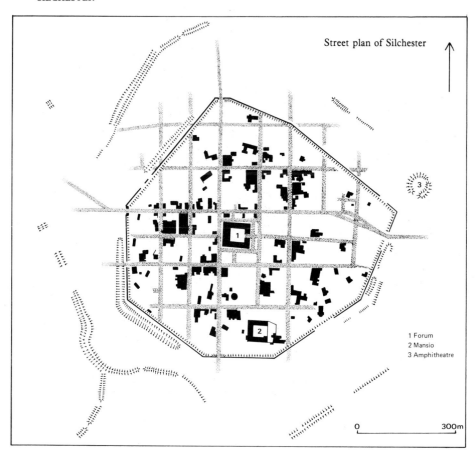

Street plan of Silchester

1 Forum
2 Mansio
3 Amphitheatre

0   300m

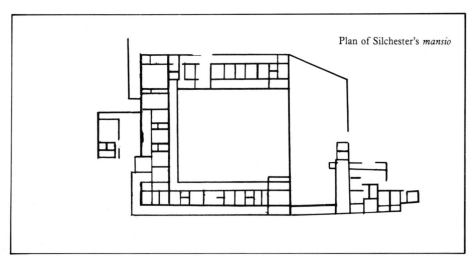

Plan of Silchester's *mansio*

The *forum* had a porticoed piazza measuring 43 × 39m (142 × 130ft). The entrance was probably in the form of a triumphal arch with an inscription. The *basilica* had a hall of 70 × 17m (234 × 58ft) with Corinthian columns. An early alteration to the building replaced the apse with three administrative rooms. The baths, probably one of the earliest public buildings, lay to the south-east of the *forum* and possessed a series of rooms of graded temperature with hypocausts and a courtyard *palaestra*. The temples of this

A stretch of the wall of Calleva Atrebatum (Silchester) showing the North Gate before the walls were cleared of vegetation (*L. Grinsell, Winchester City Museums*)

period were of simple design, the best example being a shrine with a portico.

Another public facility, outside the town's defences on the north-east, was the amphitheatre. The arena was 54 × 36m (180 × 120ft) across its axes, and the seating was of timber. The capacity was about 4000 – possibly relating to the population of the town?

The early domestic buildings were timber-framed, wattle and daub structures, although after the mid second century masonry began to be used in construction. The early second-century *mansio* had three ranges of rooms with a central courtyard and a private bath suite. One of the interesting features of Silchester's private houses is that a number appear to have had gardens or orchards. The presence of frescoes on their walls, hypocausts and excellent mosaics indicates the level of wealth of the higher levels of Silchester's society. Thirty houses have been traced that had mosaics, some with excellent hunting scenes, others with floral and geometric designs.

In the late second century, new earthworks were built to strengthen the defences. These

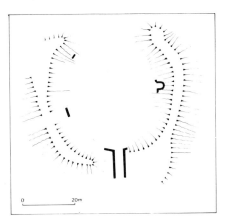

Plan of Silchester's amphitheatre

429

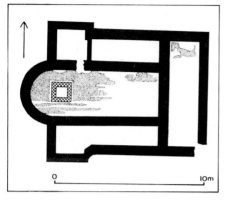

Plan of the Christian church at Silchester

enclosed an area smaller than the street planners had originally envisaged. Probably contemporary with these fortifications were masonry gates. The south gate had a single archway and tower, whilst there is evidence that the east and west gates had a dual carriageway with flanking guardchambers. In the early third century a stone wall was added to the fortifications, which was 2.25m (7½ft) thick and of bonded stone with flint. Parts still stand to a height of 4.5m (15ft). Soon after the stone defences were constructed, Silchester appears to have been sacked.

The reinforcement of this town was obviously in vain. The *basilica* shows signs of having been burnt at the end of the third century, although it was reconstructed with arches replacing the original columns. The most interesting feature of the remains of the fourth century town is the possible Christian church to the south-east of the *forum*. Dating from the middle of the century, this aisled building had an east–west orientation and a decorative mosaic. Its alignment and position in the town plan suggest strongly that this building was a church. If this is so it is a fine indicator of the change in the fabric of society in the empire at this time. Other evidence of the fourth century points to relative prosperity and self-reliance. There is an indication that Roman life continued in Silchester into the fifth century, although it is difficult to tell whether standards declined. Certainly, there is no sign of widespread

destruction so it is more likely that slow depopulation led to the eventual end of the Roman town.

SILLOANS Northumberland
NT 822007 *Temporary camp*
The 44 acre (18ha) camp at Silloans appears to have been built facing north, and to have been used only for a short period. Soon afterwards, the main road from Corbridge into the Lowlands, Dere Street, was pushed through the site via its south and north gates. The camp should therefore have been Agricolan.

Silloth see **Milefortlet 11**

SILLSBURN NORTH Northumberland
NY 8299 *Marching camp*
North of High Rochester fort, near Sillsburn South camp, is a small, square marching camp. Much of its rampart survives.

SILLSBURN SOUTH Northumberland
NY 8299 *Marching camp*
A rectangular camp with *claviculae* at its entrances lies beside Dere Street by the Sills Burn, north of the fort at High Rochester.

SLACK West Yorkshire
SE 084176 *Fort and* vicus
A 2¾ acre (1ha) fort of almost square shape was built at Slack by Agricola in AD79 or 80. It was occupied for about seventy or eighty years, and no alterations were made. The ditching was cut into hard rock, being single in some places and double at others. Remains of a timber tower, nearly 3m (10ft) square, on four wooden posts, were located at the north-east. Examination of the fort gates showed they were in different styles. There was a paved parade ground outside, and nearby a tilery that was operated by the garrison. Excavations in the area of the fort revealed remains of the *vicus*, including timber buildings, a granary, ovens and kilns, and also a cemetery. The *vicus* was abandoned soon after the giving up of the fort.

SNOWFORD BRIDGE Warwickshire
SP 397670 *Villa*
A villa-type complex has been known at

Snowford Bridge, Long Itchington, for some time, and it was confirmed by aerial photography in 1978. The main house was of the winged corridor-type, with a courtyard on the south. There were other buildings to the west and south-east, and the complex seems to have been enclosed by walling. It was begun in the second century.

SOBERTON Hampshire
SU 592135 *Iron works*
There were Roman-British iron workings in the region of Upperford Copse.

SOLDIER'S RING Hampshire
SU 0817 *Cattle enclosure*
Not far from Rockbourne Down ranch was another stock-rearing enclosure, known today as Soldier's Ring. It is pentagonal in plan, one of the sides being curved. It was a cattle enclosure and may have been linked with the Rockbourne complex.

Solway House see **Milecastle 79**

SOMERTON Suffolk
TL 8152 *Pottery kilns*
A group of kilns was found at Somerton in the late 1970s. Fragments of pottery suggest the kilns were in use in second and third centuries.

SOUTH CADBURY Somerset
ST 628252 *Hillfort*
An Iron Age hillfort appears to have been occupied by the British for some time after the Roman conquest of the west in the mid AD40s. In about AD60 it was attacked by Roman forces and captured, and this may have been as a result of disturbances arising from the Boudican revolt. The inhabitants may have threatened to join the revolt and were dealt with by the Romans, or the assault on the fort could have been part of Suetonius Paullinus' punishment of the tribes afterwards. Some Roman military equipment was found in excavations of the late 1960s.

SOUTHORPE Cambridgeshire
TF 0703 *Settlement*
Occupation of an area beside Ermine Street was identified in the late 1970s as a result of

surveys. Building stone and colour-coated pottery fragments were found.

SOUTH SHIELDS Tyne & Wear
NZ 366679 *Fort: Roman name* Arbeia
This fort was part of the Hadrianic frontier scheme, though it is not certain exactly when it was built. Most probably it was erected in phase II, when the forts on the Stanegate were moved to the Wall line. The fort occupied 5 acres (2ha), and its first buildings were of timber, inside a stonework enclosure. It was built for a cavalry wing of 500 men. The fort was drastically altered internally in the time of Severus, who decided to convert it to a major supply base for his campaigns in Scotland. A complete new set of granary buildings was erected, 22 of which have been excavated and 10 of which can still be seen. These must have housed grain supplies for a substantial army. Some authorities believe Severus intended to occupy Scotland. There is also evidence that the fort produced its own tiles and much of its pottery needs. A number of lead seals of Severus' time were also found.

The Severan granaries did not remain in use for long, however, and there are signs that some were converted later into barrack blocks. The fort was neglected for a lengthy period in the later third century, but was refurbished in the fourth century. Among the considerable remains discovered in excavations over the past thirty years or so are a good stretch of the base of the fort wall where it curves along the south-east corner, a latrine block nearby, the fort's parade ground and some of the gates and corner turrets.

SOUTHWICK West Sussex
TQ 244056 *Villa*
A well-planned courtyard villa was built at Southwick in the early second century. Excavations in advance of development have shown that the villa was occupied for a relatively short period, perhaps only half a century. Tile, *tesserae* and bronze fragments were found.

SPARSHOLT Hampshire
SU 415301 *Villa*
Sparsholt was excavated in detail in the early

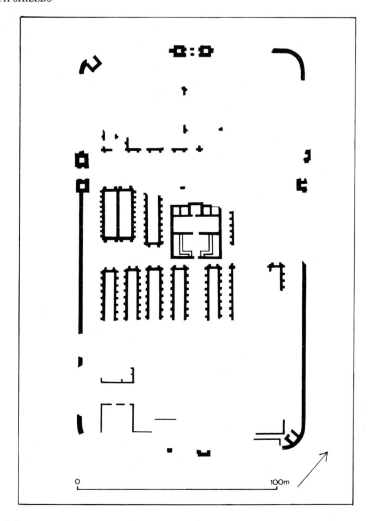

South Shields fort. In the centre are the ten granary buildings, around the *principia*

1970s. Its development is interesting. It began in the second century as a simple aisled farmhouse, with a bath suite on the north side of the site, which adjoined and encroached upon an earlier Iron Age settlement. This house was pulled down and a new aisled farmhouse superimposed more or less over the earlier site, but on a slightly different axis, and this also had a bath suite at almost the same position. Then, in the fourth century, a new symmetrical winged corridor house was erected at right angles – but separated from – the aisled building, and the two were later made to form part of a courtyard by the erection of four walls along an approximately parallelogram plan. A long, thin rectangular structure was also raised, on the south side of the yard, and this may have been a barn. There were mosaics and tessellated pavements in the aisled house and in the corridor house, but there appears to have been no bath suite in the latter. The villa was abandoned in the mid fourth century.

432

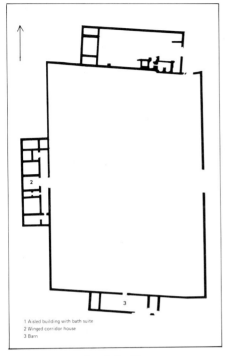

1 Aisled building with bath suite
2 Winged corridor house
3 Barn

Sparsholt villa

SPONG HILL Norfolk
TF 981195 *Pottery kiln*
Recent excavations at Spong Hill, North Elmham, exposed an early Roman kiln, and traces of a ditch of perhaps the late first century.

SPOONLEY WOOD Gloucestershire
SP 0425 *Villa*
A large, complex walled courtyard villa here began as a winged corridor house on the north-east side. The south-east side and the south-west sides were also filled with winged corridor residences, with a bath suite in the latter, and there were hypocausts and mosaics in both. The three dwelling houses were linked.

SPRINGHEAD Kent
TQ 617725 *Small town: Roman name ?Vagniacis*
A sizeable Roman settlement grew up at Springhead beside Watling Street, in which industrial remains and traces of religious buildings have been the major excavation finds to date. The religious buildings were temples or associated structures like shrines, of Romano-Celtic origin, some in sequence (one built upon or beside the remains of others). Among the industrial buildings were iron smithies and bronze workshops. The period of occupation is judged to have begun in the AD60s and lasted into the third century. The settlement does not appear to have been defended.

STAINES Surrey
TQ 0371 *Small town: Roman name* Pontibus
There was a Roman settlement (regarded by some specialists as a small town) at the crossing of the Thames. Excavations in the years 1974–82 have exposed various timber buildings, some with painted plaster walls, some stone buildings with tessellated floors and, perhaps most interesting of all, the remains of foundations, piles and other parts of the Roman bridge across the river. The bridge appears to have been a wooden raft situated on piles, which supported a sandstone superstructure. It was reached by a road, also supported on a wooden raft surmounted by chalk and concrete. There were traces of a wharf beside the bridge. Staines was occupied from the mid first century into the fifth century.

STANFORD-IN-THE-VALE Oxfordshire
SU 325951 *?Villa*
A possible villa was identified in ground surveying in 1976. Among remains were building rafts, walling and some pottery fragments of the second, third and fourth centuries.

Stanley see **Milecastle 23**

STANTONBURY Buckinghamshire
SP 844413 *Farmstead*
A Romano-British farmstead was excavated in the late 1970s, in advance of construction work associated with the new city of Milton Keynes. Among the building remains was a farmhouse of several rooms, with bath suite containing two plunge baths, one of them heated.

433

STANTON CHAIR Suffolk
TL 9574 *Villa*
The site at Stanton Chair (Chare) was excavated in the 1930s and found to be an extensive rural estate consisting of a villa and a number of associated cottages and outbuildings. The settlement was near Peddars Way. Among the buildings were a major villa of the winged corridor-type, with a bath house to the north of one wing. The bath house had hot, tepid and cold rooms plus plunge bath and a separate latrine. Several small rooms, some of which may have been dressing cubicles, were located round the cold room. Finds included Samian ware, Castor ware and also pottery from nearby potteries at Wattisfield.

STANTON FITZWARREN Wiltshire
SU 174901 *Villa*
There was a villa at Stanton Fitzwarren, which was occupied in the third and fourth centuries. An investigation in 1969–70 revealed part of the bath house.

STANWICK North Yorkshire
NZ 1812 *Fort of the Brigantes tribe*
Stanwick is not a Roman site but is briefly mentioned here because it was the *oppidum* of the Brigantes, which was stormed and eventually taken by the Roman army under Cerialis in AD72 or 73. British resistance was led by Venutius, erstwhile husband of Queen Cartimandua (see p 71). Major excavations were carried out at Stanwick over a wide area under Mortimer Wheeler, but some of his conclusions have since been argued after subsequent re-examination. The sequence of building was an Iron Age hillfort of about 17 acres (7ha) which was run down by the early first century AD. There followed a new fortified area of about 130 acres (53ha) which was defended by ditching and rampart, the centre of which had by about AD50 become a flourishing *oppidum*.

STANWIX Cumbria
NY 402572 *Fort on Hadrian's Wall: Roman name* Petriana
Stanwix fort on Hadrian's Wall, near Carlisle, was over 9 acres (3.6ha) in area, big enough to accommodate 1000 men, and in fact did house a crack cavalry unit of 1000 Gallic horsemen for a time. The fort, called *Petriana* in the *Notitia Dignitatum*, was begun by Platorius Nepos and was probably the headquarters of the senior officer of the whole Wall command. There is little to see today as it has been almost entirely obscured by subsequent building, but a series of excavations in the present century exposed a variety of features, including traces of the *principia*, which faced eastwards, some barrack blocks and a large granary. The site is in the area of the present Stanwix church on the north side of the Eden.

STAUNTON-IN-THE-VALE
Nottinghamshire SK 802448
Agricultural settlement
In a rescue excavation in 1970, several circular houses of timber, of the mid third to late fourth centuries, were found. The houses and associated structures were part of a 4 acre (1.6ha) site that was probably an agricultural settlement, only marginally affected by 'Romanisation'.

STIBBINGTON Cambridgeshire
TL 085986 *Industrial site*
A small industrial site near Church Lane, examined in the late 1960s, included pottery kilns which produced mortaria with reeded rims in Nene valley pottery style, and also jars and dishes in grey ware. There was a workshop that had four stone-lined tanks along the inside of one wall. The site was about 180m (200yd) north-west of a similar complex excavated in the nineteenth century, and also close to other complexes of the same kind seen in the 1950s.

STOKE BRUERNE Northamptonshire
SP 755501 *Villa*
In the late 1960s a small corridor villa, with farm buildings, was detected from aerial reconnaissance and then investigated on the ground. Finds included tessellated floor pieces.

STOKE GIFFORD Avon
ST 616800 *Rural settlement*
A small rural settlement was discovered here during house building works. Several

434

structures were seen, including a byre and four circular buildings of stone. There was evidence of workshops.

STOKE HILL Devon
SX 923954 *Signal station*
A signal station was built at Stoke Hill, near Exeter, in the early Roman period. Very little is known of this first period here. It was enclosed by a double-ditch and rampart. The site appears to have been reused in the late third century, which may be the period when the outer rampart was revetted in stone. The station was excavated in advance of building work.

STONEA GRANGE Wimblington, Cambridgeshire TL 4937
Roman administrative centre (?)
A most interesting and what seems so far a unique site in Roman Britain is currently being excavated and studied at Stonea Grange, in the heart of the Cambridgeshire Fens. A few hundred metres north of the Iron Age hill fort of Stonea Camp, which may have been the site of the siege by Ostorius Scapula in 47/48 (see page 42), a team has uncovered what is suggested as having been a major administrative centre, with a massive central 'office' complex from which the surrounding farms and lands were directly administered on behalf of the Emperor. Basically, the complex consisted of a rectangular building some 17×20m

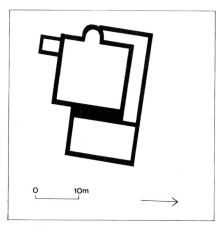

o ____ 10m

Plan of large tower at Stonea Grange

(56×66ft), with an apse on the west side and a portico on the east. This building may have been a huge tower, perhaps four storeys tall, with windows all round, gabled roof, and part surrounded by a wall enclosing a courtyard and incorporating a hall. On the south-west corner was found a sizeable furnace which points to the tower being heated by underfloor heating. The tower was built of stone which appears to have been brought from the Peterborough district, at least 30 miles away. If the tower was as large as suggested, it may have resembled a similar structure near Anguillara a few miles north of Rome. Both buildings appear to have been erected at much the same time, that is, second quarter of the second century AD, probably started if not completed in the reign of Hadrian.

The Stonea tower, whatever its purpose, did not last very long: by the end of the century it had been carefully dismantled. Much remains to be dug and examined at the site, but it is undoubtedly a most promising discovery and developments are eagerly awaited.

STONE-BY-FAVERSHAM Kent
TQ 9961 *Settlement: Roman name* Durolevum
The Roman settlement of *Durolevum*, mentioned in the *Antonine Itinerary*, is thought to have been at or close to Stone-by-Faversham, about ½ mile from Ospringe. Burials of the Roman period have been found in the neighbourhood. An early Roman fort of Aulus Plautius may have been erected here.

STOWMARKET Suffolk
TM 054589 *Pottery kiln*
Pottery of the first century, in Belgic forms, was found in a kiln discovered during building works in the late 1970s. The kiln was circular and its floor was supported on pedestals.

STRATFORD SUB CASTLE Wiltshire
SU 134318 *Settlement*
A settlement, which may have had military associations, was examined in the late 1960s at Stratford sub Castle, New Sarum. Remains of both timber and stone buildings

435

were found. Pottery finds ranged over the first to fourth centuries. The settlement was beside the road from Badbury Rings, and part of the road was found to be about 6m (20ft) wide.

STRETTON MILL Staffordshire
SJ 8911 *Fort*
A fort of some 3½ acres (1.5ha) beside the west bank of the river Penk near Penkridge was located by aerial reconnaissance. The fort overlooked the river, had double-ditching and may have been erected during the campaign of Ostorius against Caratacus, or perhaps later in the 50s.

STRETTON ON FOSSE Warwickshire
SP 218383 *Settlement*
A settlement of Iron Age beginnings was occupied also in Romano-British times. The site was re-examined during quarry work in the mid 1970s. A variety of finds came to light, including traces of buildings, some roof tiles and second- and third-century pottery.

STROUD Hampshire
SU 7223 *Villa*
The villa at Stroud was a walled courtyard villa, with buildings on three sides. The main dwelling house on the north side was an aisled farmhouse of some size, about 42×16m (140×52ft), which had had two rows of timber columns. Later, residential quarters consisting of several rooms were formed at the west end by partitioning, and most of the rooms had tessellated flooring. Two projecting wing rooms were added at the south-west and south-east corners. The south aisle was used as a corridor. Next to the south-east projecting wing was a curious octagonal plan structure which is thought to have been a shrine. On the west side of the courtyard was an extensive bath house, with several hypocausts. There was also a square-plan granary on the east side next to and part of a large rectangular structure given over to stalls for animals. The size of the bath house has led to suggestions that it served a number of families who probably lived in small farmhouses in the neighbourhood,

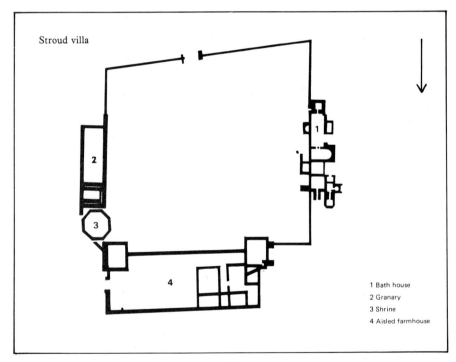

Stroud villa

1 Bath house
2 Granary
3 Shrine
4 Aisled farmhouse

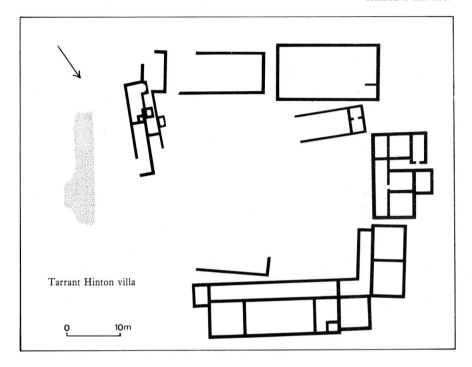

Tarrant Hinton villa

0   10m

indicating that Stroud was the focus of a large estate.

Stutfall Castle see **Lympne**

SULEHAY Northamptonshire
TL 060991 *Pottery kiln*
A pottery kiln was found, severely damaged by quarrying south of Wansford.

SUNNY RIGG Northumberland
NY 695667 *Marching camp*
A small camp, sandwiched between the Stanegate and the modern road beneath, Sunny Rigg is rectangular, with no ditch and only slight ramparting. It may have been a construction camp.

SUTTON COURTENAY Oxfordshire
SU 497596 *Settlement*
A second-century settlement was investigated in advance of gravel quarrying. Some ditching and a well were found.

SWINDON Wiltshire
SU 158836 *Settlement*
Traces of a Roman settlement were found in the grounds of the demolished Swindon House. Stonework of two buildings was dated to the second century.

SWINE HILL Northumberland
NY 9082 *Temporary camp*
Swine Hill camp is about 90m (100yd) west of the A68, is square in plan, occupies about 6 acres (2.5ha) and has internal *claviculae*. Much ramparting is still in good repair.

Tarraby Lane see **Milecastle 65**

TARRANT HINTON Dorset
ST 927118 *Villa*
This was a courtyard villa of some size and importance, and it may have been the centre of an estate consisting of several associated farms. There were several buildings round three sides of the yard. One was an aisled structure, nearly 19m (63ft) long. There was a separate bath house, a workshop and an

L-plan corridored house on the north-west corner. This house had hypocausts, and it was roofed with Purbeck stone tiles. The residential accommodation appeared to have been occupied, at some time, by three separated families.

TATTERSHALL THORPE Lincolnshire
TF 208595 *Pottery kilns*
Traces of kilns, with sherds of the third and fourth centuries, have been found on this known pottery site.

TEMPLEBOROUGH South Yorkshire
SK 4191 *Fort*
A fort of about 6 acres (2.5ha) was erected at Templeborough, on the south bank of the Don, perhaps in the mid AD50s. Professor Frere (*Britannia*, p 101) suggests it may have accommodated troops sent by the governor, Didius Gallus, to help Cartimandua, queen of the Brigantes, in her campaigns against her anti-Roman husband Venutius (see p 71) in the mid to late 50s. Tile stamps of Legio IX have been found there, which at the time was based at Longthorpe and Newton on Trent, and this could support the suggestion. The fort was later rebuilt in stone, probably in Trajan's reign, when it was reduced from 6 to 5 acres (2.5 to 2ha). Then it was abandoned for at least a century, perhaps much longer. It was reoccupied at the end of the third century and refurbished. A new stone wall was built, but not on the remains of the first one of Trajan but along the line of the first-century ramparting. There was a *vicus* nearby which appears to have been in continuous occupation.

TEMPLE SOWERBY Cumbria
NY 619264 *Milestone*
A cylindrical milestone stands in its original position about ½ mile south-east of Temple Sowerby, beside the road to Brougham, on the same axis as the Roman road (Margary 82) from Kirkby Thore.

TEVERSHAM Cambridgeshire
TL 500575 *Settlement*
A settlement is being excavated at Teversham, near Cambridge (1980–1) and among finds so far has been a pottery kiln.

THE LUNT (Baginton) West Midlands
SP 344752 *Fort*
One of the most instructive forts of the Roman occupation is The Lunt, Baginton, near Coventry. First excavated in the 1930s, and again in the early 1960s, it was made the subject of a special excavation-cum-reconstruction scheme in 1966, which is not completed. Enough has been investigated, however, to enable an extremely valuable simulation to be made of what a Roman fort looked like. The Lunt ought therefore to be at or near the top of the visiting list of anyone interested in Roman Britain. What cannot be seen on the ground is compensated for in the well-planned display set out in the reconstructed granary.

The first fort was raised in the period immediately before or after the Boudican revolt (AD61). The defences of this fort have been detected on the east. It is possible that the fort was used during the revolt as a depot for Suetonius' forces in preparation for the final confrontation that took place in the neighbourhood (Mancetter or High Cross, whichever may be preferred). A few years later, the fort was altered, and it was altered yet again in the late 70s when it was reduced in size. This may have been an Agricolan enterprise. It was abandoned in about 80, but nearly two centuries later the site was once more used for military purposes, and some of the ditching of this last fort has been found.

Today, several of the period II structures have been copied and built anew, notably a fine granary, a stretch of rampart with ditch surmounted by a timber wall (built in the same manner as it would have been in the first century, see p 172), the east gateway, where the timbers have been put into original post holes, and the *gyrus*, a structure so far not found anywhere else in Britain. The *gyrus* was a cavalry training ring. It was over 30m (100ft) across. It may have been used by the Romans to break and train horses captured from Boudica's host after the battle. Other features at the fort include the floor layout of the *principia* marked out in concrete, and evidence for locations of the *praetorium*, barracks and a workshop.

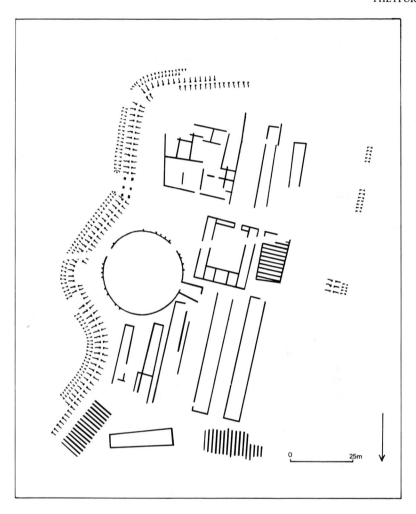

The fort at The Lunt, Baginton. Note the *gyrus* on the east and the rampart beside, shaped to accommodate it

THENFORD Northamptonshire
SP 525415 *Villa*
Thenford villa was a third- and fourth-century group of buildings of courtyard-type which arose on the site of a long-established settlement that had begun in the Iron Age. Excavations of the early 1970s exposed a mosaic pavement in the main residential block. This had a bath suite which was modified twice during the later fourth century. The villa appears to have been pulled down at around the turn of the fifth century.

THETFORD Norfolk
TL 8684 *?Icenian palace*
Early in 1981, acting upon an aerial photograph of what appeared to be the site of a rectangular Roman camp, on the undeveloped part of the Fison Way Industrial Estate on Gallows Hill in north-east Thetford, a team of the Norfolk Archaeological Unit led by A. K. Gregory, assisted

Aerial view of the Gallows Hill, Thetford, a site excavated under the direction of Tony Gregory, 1980-2. It was a ditched enclosure that had several round houses (traces visible), and which appears not to have been used after AD61 (D. A. Edwards, Norfolk Archaeological Unit)

by the Department of the Environment and employing young people on a Manpower Services Commission Youth Opportunities Project, stripped some 6 acres (2.5ha) inside a larger 11 acre (4.5ha) defended site. The site had two separate occupations. To the north there was Iron Age occupation, probably mid first century BC to early first century AD. A mould for Iron Age Belgic coins was found and three silver Icenian coins.

Beside the Iron Age area – and overlapping part of it – was an early, strongly defended,

Romano-British rectangular site, described by the excavation leader, Tony Gregory, as of 'noble, even royal significance', sherds from which put its occupation approximately between AD47 and 60, that is, before the Boudican revolt. The site consisted of: an outer ditch about 4m (12ft) wide, 1.5m (5ft) deep (backfilled probably after 60-1); within the outer ditch, a second (middle) ditch, 6.5m (22ft) wide, 2m (7ft) deep (backfilled); and within that an inner enclosure surrounded by a ditch 2.5m (8ft) wide, 1.25m (4ft) deep (backfilled). The space between the outer and middle ditches was about 30m (100ft) wide. The inner enclosure covered about 1 acre (0.4ha), with a gateway in its eastern side.

The rectangular 'ring' between outer and middle ditches was filled with timber slots, about 15cm (6in) square, set about 30cm (1ft) apart, in rows about 3m (10ft) apart. These were for timber stakes, positioned obliquely. About 10,000 stakes had been raised in the 'ring'. This was a major engineering work requiring substantial labour. The massive system of obstacles had been erected as much to impress, to emphasise status, as to defend.

The inner enclosure appeared to have contained in a row three circular plan buildings, round houses of about 12m (40ft) in diameter, each having the doorway facing east. This was confirmed by post holes and by subsequent aerial photography (see p 440). Gregory believed these to have been 'royal' apartments.

The question arises, was this the palace of Prasutagus, built for him (as sole chief of the Iceni) with Roman help after the AD47 rebellion of the Iceni put down by Ostorius Scapula, in which Prasutagus had played no part and had consequently been rewarded? If so, it suggests that the hosting of the tribes after Boudica's call to arms in 61 could have taken place in the plains east of Thetford, and the march towards Colchester could have proceeded eastwards along the Thetford to Bunwell road (Margary 37) to Roudham Heath where Peddars Way crossed. There, the march would have turned southwards to Coney Weston in Suffolk and then to Ixworth, forked left to Bildeston and made its way for the last 15 or so miles across country to Colchester (so far, no road of the period between Bildeston and Colchester has been found). Alternatively, the host could have taken Margary 37 all the way to Bunwell and from there to join Pye Road (Caistor St Edmund to Colchester, Margary 3d and 3c) at or near Tasburgh, and swung south along Pye road via Scole (allowing the host to clash with the Roman fort garrison at Scole) and thence directly to Colchester. This does seem a difficult route for a host of 100,000 plus, though the other route is hardly less so. (The stretch from Bunwell to Tasburgh is still an inferred and not a certain route.)

The Gallows Hill site excavation was one of the most dramatic archaeological finds in Britain in recent years. It cogently argues for Prasutagus and Boudica having ruled from

the Thetford area (which is much the same as saying from Breckland district, a long-held tradition), although I am still inclined to prefer the hosting to have taken place near Caistor St Edmund, near a (?second) Boudican palace as yet undiscovered.

THEYDON GARNON Essex
TL 478014 *Tilery*
In 1975 a tile-producing area was investigated during road building on the M11, and quantities of debris were found. The site was close to a second area where a third-century pottery was uncovered.

THISTLETON DYER Leicestershire
SK 9117 *Settlement*
A rambling site that has been systematically eroded by quarrying, so much so that there is a major amount of the site missing. It comprised several buildings, including residential blocks, more than one temple and some outbuildings. One residence was a winged corridor house, about 23m (76ft) long by about 15m (50ft) wide, with an entrance porch with columns. The house had hypocausts and mosaic pavements. Farm buildings were attached to three sides of the house, and these were of later date than the house which was early fourth century. Evidence has also been found of much earlier timber structures on the site, some from the first century. There is evidence that the farm operations at the site were mixed, crops and livestock.

THORNBOROUGH Buckinghamshire
SP 729332 *Settlement with temple*
A settlement here is marked by a pair of Romano-British burial tumuli (which were examined in the nineteenth century and several artefacts including bronze jugs and glassware found). Nearby, close to the river Twin, by a bridge to the east of Buckingham, a rectangular Romano-Celtic timber temple on solid footings was identified, associated with a nearby *basilica*, also of timber.

THORPE AUDLIN West Yorkshire
SE 475166 *Industrial site*
A small industrial site of the Roman period

441

was discovered at Thorpe Audlin, near Pontefract, and excavated in 1982, during sectioning of the Roman road (Margary 28b) from Doncaster to Tadcaster, known as the Roman Ridge. Finds included an ore-roasting hearth (there was local iron ore available), footings of a stone building and an iron pan. One interesting discovery was a stretch of roadside along which were clear Romano-British horse hoof prints. More detail is available from an excellent short report from the Pontefract and District Archaeological Society. The excavation was directed by Eric Houlder.

THORPE-BY-NEWARK
Nottinghamshire SK 760504
Fort and later small town: Roman name Ad Pontem
This site, near East Stoke, almost defies summary. It is a complex story of what probably began as a fort close to the river Trent to guard an important crossing, and this may have been the time when a bridge was built there, which would explain the name. No bridge, however, has been found yet. A further complication is that the Fosse Way cuts across the site. Did the road come first? The site, seen from the air, has two ditch systems, separated by an unusually wide gap of about 20m (70ft) or so. Does this mean one fort succeeding another? There was also a *vicus*, which has been proved, but its extent is not fully known. There followed, at some period, a small town which eventually became enclosed by a stone wall.

Throckley see **Turret 10a**

THROP Northumberland
NY 6365 *Fortlet*
When the first scheme of the Hadrianic frontier was built in the early 120s, a new fortlet was erected on the Stanegate as part of the scheme, at Throp, about 2 miles from Carvoran. This fortlet was a little under 1 acre (0.4ha) in size, and was almost square in plan, with a turf rampart on stone founda-tions, surrounded by a single-ditch. The interior buildings were of timber. There were two timber gates, at the north-east and south-east, on either side of one of the fortlet's corners.

TINTAGEL Cornwall
SX 076891 *Milestone*
A rectangular blue-grey siltstone milestone, about 1.5m (5ft) tall, was found in a stile in the churchyard at Tintagel in 1889. It was moved into the south transept. It is dated to emperor Licinius (308–24).

TITSEY PARK Surrey
TQ 404545 *Villa*
The villa at Titsey Park, near Limpsfield, was first seen in the 1840s and investigated in the 1860s. Some of it is still visible. The villa was a double corridor-type with a central suite of rooms and smaller rooms at each end. It was built in the later second century, but it was not occupied as a residence for long. Evidence has been found of later industrial use. Nearby, a Romano-Celtic temple was built beside the Roman road from London to Lewes, and it consisted of a square *cella* within a square portico surround. Titsey is claimed as one of the very few sites at which a villa was associated with a temple in Roman Britain.

TOPSHAM Devon
SX 957890 *?Port*
What is thought to have been the site of a port and supply base at Topsham, near Exeter, on the estuary of the Exe, has been examined in recent years, though the finds have been on the whole disappointing. Work on a new bridge to take the M5 over the Exe north of Topsham village exposed some first-century remains, including a simple cottage villa of three rooms with verandah, other structures and some V-shaped ditch.

TOTTERNHOE Bedfordshire
SP 9920 *Villa*
A courtyard villa, roughly 60 × 72m (200 × 240ft) in area, with buildings on north, east and west sides and on the south-east corner, was investigated in the 1950s. Remains of hypocausts in the east building and several tesselated floors were found.

TOWCESTER Northamptonshire
SP 6948 *Small town: Roman name* Lactodorum
Well sited on Watling Street, Towcester was

a small town which in the early third century was enclosed by a substantial earth rampart wall. One or two stretches of this can still be seen. The site has been examined, particularly in the mid 1970s when part of the road to Alchester (Margary 160a) was explored. On either side of the road several workshop buildings have been found, circular and rectangular in plan, including some lead works of the fourth century.

Tower Tye see **Milecastle 29**

TREBARVETH Cornwall
SW 796193 *Salt industry*
A salt-production centre was examined in the late 1960s. Ovens, a kiln and other finds bolstered the belief that salt was manufactured here from seawater.

TRENT VALE Staffordshire
SJ 868433 *Fort*
What was probably a 30 acre fort of the AD50s or early 60s was examined in a rescue dig in the early 1970s on this site, on the right bank of the Trent, about a mile southeast of Stoke on Trent town centre. A pottery kiln of Neronian date was discovered.

TRETHURGY Cornwall
SX 034555 *Settlement*
A large enclosure, surrounded by a stone-revetted bank, containing a number of oval, one square and one D-shaped buildings (some of them residences), was occupied from the second to sixth centuries. The buildings were ranged round the inside of the wall. The site was excavated in the early 1970s in advance of china clay detritus depositing. Among finds were shreds of Mediterranean pottery of the sixth century. The pottery may have been imported directly by sea.

TREVETHY Cornwall
SX 051884 *Milestone*
A rectangular milestone of the mid third century, of granite, was for a time used as a gatepost on the site of what is believed to have been the monastery of St Piran. The stone is now beside the house there, which is named Pirans.

TROUTBECK Cumbria
NY 3827 *Fort and marching camps*
Three marching camps, one of 10 acres (4ha), have been known at Troutbeck for some time. Two of them had clavicular entrances. Both were of Flavian I period, perhaps Agricolan. In 1972, a fort of the Flavian period was discovered, about 3 acres (1.2ha) in size, some of the ramparts of which are still visible (NY 382272). The fort straddles the modern road. There is evidence that the fort was later reduced in size. Timber buildings were indicated by post holes. The rampart was built of clay blocks.

TURRETS (Hadrian's Wall)

6b, 7a, 7b see **Denton**

10a Throckley Northumberland
NZ 160669
Turret 10a, Throckley, lies in Callerton Road. It was examined in 1979 and found to be of usual turret size, with an eastern gate. Some wall survives to three courses. A section of Vallum was located nearby.

12a Heddon West Northumberland
NZ 131671
Turret 12a was part of the original Wall scheme. It has been investigated and appears to have been occupied into the third century (see also Heddon-on-the-Wall).

12b North Lodge Northumberland
NZ 126672
This was excavated in 1930. Investigations were carried out immediately to the west of the turret in the mid 1970s, when some Wall was found, up to four or five courses high (see also Heddon-on-the-Wall).

13a Rudchester Northumberland
NZ 116674
Turret 13a was excavated in the early 1930s.

18a Wallhouses East Northumberland
NZ 043684
Turret 18a has been excavated and is in an interesting state of preservation. Several stone steps which led up to the second-storey ladder platform are in position.

443

18b Wallhouses West Northumberland
NZ 038685

This turret was beneath an eighteenth-century tollhouse until, in 1959, it was examined and some building debris of the Roman period found.

25b Fallowfield Northumberland
NY 935694

This was examined in 1959. Some arrowheads were found at the site in the mid 1970s. The turret is near Fallowfield where a local stone quarry was worked by the legions. Here, a soldier cut his name into the rock face, (P)ETRA FLAVI CARANTINI (the rock of Flavius Carantinus). The piece concerned was later chipped out and taken to the museum at Chesters fort.

Brunton Turret (Turret 26b) on Hadrian's Wall, with two recently discovered altars (*E. Houlder*)

26a & b Brunton Northumberland
NY 9269

Between Milecastle 26, near Brunton Bank, and Milecastle 27, near Chesters fort, were Turrets 26a (opposite High Brunton House) and 26b (in the park of Brunton House). The remains of 26a were examined but are now covered, though a stretch of Wall can be seen beside. Turret 26b, however, can be seen recessed into a good stretch of Wall, its west wing joining with broad wall and its east wing with narrow wall. Turret 26b was erected by Legio XX.

27a Chesters fort Northumberland
NY 913703

This turret, part of the original Wall scheme, was found during excavations in the mid 1940s under the site of Chesters fort. It had been demolished to make way for the fort. The turret site was just next to the north-east corner of the *principia*.

29a Black Carts Northumberland
NY 884713
Some good masonry stretches of the Wall can be seen at this site, and the turret itself has been excavated and preserved. It is about 3m (11ft) square inside. An inscription was found by the site in the early 1970s.

33b Coesike Northumberland
NY 821705
Several courses of the walling of Turret 33b at Coesike, near Şewingshields, remain. The turret has been excavated in recent years, and the stonework tidied up for display. It had been erected in the Hadrianic scheme, with an east gate, and allowed to decay. It was renovated in the 150s return to the Wall, abandoned again soon afterwards and then dismantled in the early third century. There are some good stretches of the Wall ditch running north of the turret. An inscription found records that building work was done by Legio VI *Victrix*, although it is often ascribed to Legio XX. This could mean that Legio VI undertook repairs in the 150s.

34a & b, 35a see **Sewingshields**

40a & b Melkridge Northumberland
NY 3367
Remains of both turrets are visible. Turret 40a has its door on the east side.

44b Mucklebank Northumberland
NY 682667
Mucklebank Turret was excavated in the 1890s. It was erected in an angle of the Wall, which provided its north and west sides. The turret is in a high position, over 260m (860ft) above sea level. It remained in use after the abandonment of several other turrets in the 180s, probably because of its high position and its value as a possible signal station.

45a Walltown Crags Northumberland
NY 674664
There had been a Stanegate signal tower at the site of this turret. When the Wall scheme reached the site, the tower was taken into the Wall as Turret 45a. Several hundred metres of Wall on either side of the turret have survived in excellent condition.

48a & b Willowford Northumberland
NY 6266
Turret 48a, of which several courses of all four sides are still standing, and Turret 48b, of which there are also some remains, are the last before the point where the Wall slopes down the valley of the river Irthing towards the bridge across the river. The Broad Wall part of the scheme ended at the Irthing and the Turf Wall began, which was later converted to stonework but in narrower gauge. These turrets were still in use in the fourth century.

49b Birdoswald Cumbria
NY 612662
Turret 49b on the stone part of the Wall here, west of Birdoswald fort, was examined in 1911. It was still in use in the fourth century.

51a Piper Sike Cumbria
NY 588653
Turret 51a on Hadrian's Wall, Piper Sike, near Waterhead, was excavated in 1970. The poor quality of building may be an example of Roman jerry-building. Some remains are visible on the north verge of the road.

51b Leahill Cumbria
NY 584652
Leahill, which had an east door instead of the more usual south door, was re-examined in the late 1950s. It appears to have been given up in the mid second century, but remained more or less intact for about two centuries. Then it was reoccupied after about 369. The reoccupation, however, consisted of a small possible lean-to hut built of some of the blocks from other parts of the turret.

52a Banks East Cumbria
NY 575647
Turret 52a at Banks East is an impressive ruin, and a good example of a Turf Wall turret. The Narrow Wall abutted it on both sides. Some of the Wall still stands at about fourteen courses high. Traces of the garrison's hearths have been found. The turret was occupied at least into the third century.

445

53a Hare Hill Cumbria NY 562647
53b Haytongate Cumbria NY 555646
Turrets 53a and 53b are interesting. The former projected very slightly northwards of the Wall. It was constructed of stones of a smaller size than the Wall nearby. The latter is fragmentary but its stonework was red sandstone instead of the buff stone hitherto encountered (eastwards to westwards).

72b Watch Hill Cumbria
NY 314593
Turret 72b, an original Turf Wall turret, projected about a metre north of the Wall.

Turrets (Cumbrian Coast) 16a Cote How, 16b Dubmill Cumbria
NY 078461
Between Milefortlet 16, by Mawbray Road, which has been partly obscured by quarrying, and Dubmill Milefortlet (17) are the remains of two intermediate turrets, 16a (Cote How) and 16b (Dubmill). Dubmill was re-examined in 1953–5, and the turret of the Hadrianic period was found to have been levelled and the site covered with stone and clay as a foundation for a new turret, possibly of the late fourth century.

TWYFORD Hampshire
SU 4824 *Villa*
Remains of a courtyard villa were discovered in the late nineteenth century, and the site was re-examined in the late 1950s. A bath suite was investigated and a mosaic fragment found. The villa was probably begun at the end of the first century on the site of an Iron Age settlement, but at that stage would have been almost certainly a simple cottage-type, perhaps with a corridor.

ULEY Gloucestershire
ST 789996 *Temple complex*
A Romano-Celtic temple complex of more than one period overlay an earlier Iron Age enclosure at West Hill, Uley. The temple was the familiar square-plan type, with inner *cella* and ambulatory, and was built in stone and timber in the fourth century. Several other stone foundations were located in excavations of the late 1970s, including those of domestic premises, some with tessellated pavements, *opus signinum* flooring and painted wall plaster.

UPCHURCH MARSHES Kent
TQ 847696 *Building*
A timber building was traced during reclamation at Upchurch marshes in 1970.

UPPER RAWCLIFFE Lancashire
SD 441428 *Farmstead*
A farmstead of the Roman period, circular in plan and surrounded by a ditch, was seen from the air in 1978. Test digging unearthed coarse pottery of the late first to early second century.

UPTON ST LEONARDS Gloucestershire
SO 859151 *Agricultural settlement*
An agricultural settlement was examined in the late 1970s in advance of building works, near Portway. A T-shaped corn drier with a 1.25m (4ft) flue, associated with third- and fourth-century pottery, was found. Inside the corn drier were samples of cereal and what are said to have been some thirty-five species of weeds of Roman times.

WADDON HILL Dorset
ST 450015 *Fort*
The fort at Waddon Hill, Stoke Abbot, was of irregular plan, dictated largely by the hill-top site on which it was built. It was raised in the Claudian period, perhaps after about AD50. The ditching was complex, and on the east side it was threefold, with one ditch being of 'Punic' profile. The fort was about 2½ acres (1ha), and may have been occupied by detachments of Legio II *Augusta* when that legion was stationed at Exeter.

WADFIELD Gloucestershire
SP 0226 *Villa*
On the Andoversford to Winchcombe road, near Belas Knap prehistoric barrow, are the remains of Wadfield villa, among trees and scrub, which was uncovered in the 1860s. There is some stone walling. One wing of the courtyard villa contained the bath suite. A room containing part of a geometric mosaic is enclosed in a wooden shed.

WAKERLEY Northamptonshire
SP 940983 *Agricultural and industrial settlement*
This was an agricultural and industrial settlement occupied throughout the Roman period. Excavations, particularly those of the mid 1970s, discovered several buildings, including two second-century aisled buildings, one of them 30×14m (100×46ft), which appears to have had partitions plastered and decorated with painting. A variety of corn driers were also found, including T-shaped keyhole and bowl furnace types. There were also several iron-smelting furnaces of both Iron Age and Roman beginnings, and pottery kilns of the third century. Evidence was also found of watchtowers.

Walbottle Dene see **Milecastle 10**

WALESBY Lincolnshire
TF 146927 *?Villa*
A possible villa has been located at Walesby.

WALL Staffordshire
SK 0906 *Forts and later town: Roman name* Letocetum
There appear to have been two forts at Wall, and a sprawling town which developed in the extramural area. As yet, excavation has revealed disappointingly little about the nature and extent of the settlements, but at least it now seems that a chronology can be established for the site.

The first fort was probably founded between AD50 and 58. There were two phases of timber building in this period. A possible Neronian granary has been traced as well as a large Flavian wattle-and-daub building which had plastered walls. The south-east defences of the early fort have been identified and lie within the area of the second. The first fort was probably destroyed by fire – burnt timbers were found in the Neronian granary. A coin from the destruction levels dates the disaster to the reign of Domitian.

The second fort was built over the ruins of the first, and dates to cAD110–20. Over the remains of the large wattle-and-daub Flavian building was constructed a stone building with a colonnade facing on to Watling Street, which ran through the site. In the foundations of this building were crudely carved sandstone blocks with representations of human figures – a curious find and probably representing the reuse of material from an earlier demolished building. The second century also saw the development of the bath house which is the finest building at the site. This was probably based on the military baths, and had a buttressed and vaulted roof.

The bath-house at Letocetum (Wall, Staffordshire) (*Janet & Colin Bord*)

The *pilae* of the hypocausted *tepidarium* and *caldarium* are still in position, and can be seen by visitors to the site. During the third century an undressing room and a cold plunge were added. Fourth-century alterations included the addition of a small hot bath and a large exercise court (*palaestra*).

Another fourth-century feature of the site are the defences. These were built unusually late for this type of military-based town. Another odd point about them is that, once constructed, they did not enclose the area of the baths – surely one of the later foci of the town's life. Much more needs to be known about the development of Wall before explanations for these problems can be given.

Wallsend fort on Hadrian's Wall

Wall Bowers see **Milecastle 51**
Wall Fell see **Milecastle 24**
Wallhouses East see **Milecastle 18, Turret 18a**
Wallhouses West see **Turret 18b**

WALLSEND Northumberland
NZ 3066 *Fort and* vicus: *Roman name* Segedunum
Its position at the eastern end of Hadrian's Wall at the mouth of the river Tyne made Wallsend an important military centre. The fort here would have commanded a good view of two reaches of the river, and any attempt to cross would have been noticed. The modern town has almost completely obliterated the Roman site, but recent excavations have established the outline of the fortifications and revealed more about

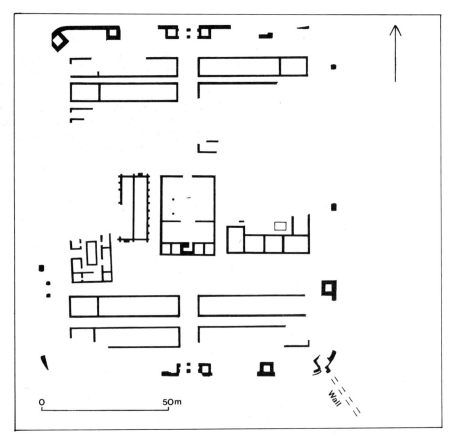

the development of the settlement.

Traces of pre-Hadrianic timber buildings have shown that the fort was built on an existing site. The date of the establishment of the fort is about 126. The walls of the fort are bonded in, on the north-west, with the second phase of the building of Hadrian's Wall, the so-called Narrow Wall. The wall runs down from the fort to the river to prevent passage through the gap. The rectangular fort enclosed an area of just over 4 acres (1.6ha). Within the walls was a grid pattern of streets, and excavations of the northern portion of the area in 1975 revealed four barrack blocks and other buildings of the Hadrianic period. After about 180, there seem to have been alterations to existing buildings and reconstruction of others.

At the end of the third century the fort underwent considerable change, with the demolition of buildings and a change of street pattern. One example is the alteration of the commandant's house, a rectangular courtyard building of 34sq m (40sq yd) in the south-west area of the fort. One wing of this opulent house was demolished and overlaid by a new road. The new street pattern is associated with the construction of more smaller, detached buildings. An unusual feature of this period is the lack of blocking in the north gate of the fortifications, usually a standard alteration in this uneasy time. Traces of the *vicus* have been found which suggest that the civilian settlement was on the north bank of the river, with buildings extending on the slope between the south rampart and the river. Another part of the *vicus* has been identified south-west of the fort. A large civilian bath house was discovered in the nineteenth century, but was destroyed during rebuilding. Pottery evidence suggests that Roman occupation continued until between 370–400.

WALLTOWN Shropshire
SO 6978 *Fort*
There was an early fort here, which has not been satisfactorily dated yet, but could be early Flavian. A second fort was built at the site in the mid to late second century, possibly connected with the insurrection of Welsh tribes c170.

Walltown Crags see **Turret 45a**

WALTHAM ABBEY Essex
TL 382005 *Settlement*
There was a Roman settlement here alongside a north to south road. Recent excavations in the area of the present market place yielded late third- and fourth-century pottery, including wares from the major factory at Much Hadham.

WALTON Cambridgeshire
TF 165023 *Farmstead*
A Romano-British farmstead, occupied from the second to the fourth centuries, was excavated in advance of development in the early 1970s. Traces of an agricultural building, probably used for hand threshing, about 16 × 8m (53 × 26ft), had a paved double entrance. There were many finds of ashlar blocks, hypocaust tiles and *tesserae*, that may have come from a nearby residential structure. The site ceased to be occupied by Romano-British towards the end of the fourth century, but there are signs of a take-over by Saxons.

WALTON Suffolk
TM 3235 *Fort of the Saxon Shore*
Washed now by the sea, fragments of one of the Roman forts of the Saxon Shore can sometimes be seen at Walton, near Felixstowe, at very low tide, about 100m (300yd) or so out. The fort was probably built at about the same time as that at Bradwell, that is, about 270–80. Cunliffe (CBA Report no 18, pp 5–6) has suggested that it was built immediately after serious attacks by barbarians in Gaul in 276, a threat dealt with by emperor Probus. The only clue as to shape is in some local drawings of the seventeenth century, and it appears to have been a long, narrow rectangular plan, the longer sides north-east to south-west, with rounded bastions on the corners but with no intermediate turrets.

WALTON-LE-DALE Lancashire
SD 551282 *Settlement*
A settlement consisting of residential buildings and factories and workshops existed here for a period not yet determined.

The settlement's main north-south road was resurfaced more than once. Rectangular buildings were ranged along either side. The site may have been a supply base for the authorities.

WANBOROUGH Wiltshire
SU 195852 *Small town: Roman name Durocornovium*
A small town of mid to late first-century beginnings, but which flourished much later, Wanborough was not walled. It has been excavated, and among finds were remains of two small town courtyard houses, shops, some stretches of Ermine Street and some evidence of iron working.

WARE Hertfordshire
TL 352143 *Settlement*
A settlement on either side of Ermine Street, by Ware Lock, has been excavated in recent years, particularly in the premises of Allen & Hanbury's factory. Finds confirm a concentration of industrial buildings. Some were erected on specially made chalk base rafts in the marshy ground near the river Lea, and traces of piles and timber frameworks have been found along what was seen to have been the course of the river in Roman times. In some quarters, the Ware site is mentioned as being a small town, but it is too early to confirm this.

WASHINGWELLS Tyne & Wear
NZ 219602 *Fort*
Aerial photographs in 1970 located a fort just south of Washingwells, on the south bank of the Tyne, which has yet to be properly excavated. It is thought it may be part of a possible eastwards extension of the Stanegate frontier, from Corbridge. The ditching configuration suggests two phases on the same site.

WASPERTON Warwickshire
SP 262582 *Field systems*
Very recent excavations at Wasperton exposed Iron Age and Romano-British field systems.

Watch Hill see **Turret 72b**

WATERBEACH Cambridgeshire
TL 485664 *Part of Car Dyke*
A stretch of the Roman Car Dyke drain in Cambridgeshire can be seen beside the A10 Cambridge to Ely road by Waterbeach airfield.

WATERCROOK Cumbria
SD 515917 *Fort and* vicus: *Roman name Alauna*
There is very little to see of the fort and *vicus* at Watercrook. It began as a fort in the late Flavian period (c90–100) and was almost rectangular in plan, about 2½ acres (1ha), surrounded on three sides by water. It was enclosed by a rampart and double-ditch system. In excavations, signs have been found of renovation of the Antonine period, which may be the date when the stone revetting of the rampart was carried out. The fort was given another face lift in the 270s after about half a century's neglect. Evidence has been found of iron working in the associated *vicus* which had both stone buildings and timber strip housing. The *vicus* flourished in the second and third centuries.

One of the votive plaques, with the Chi-Rho monogram, found with the hoard discovered at Water Newton

WATER NEWTON Cambridgeshire
TL 1296 *Town, ? later* civitas *capital: Roman name* Durobrivae

The Water Newton (Chesterton) area is a complex of Romano-British activity. It began as a fort on the west side of Billing Brook, ½ mile south of the Nene, with double- and triple-ditching, covering 5 acres (2ha). The date is not known but can probably be put at the 50s or after the Boudican revolt. The fort was given up and just south of it there evolved, first, a *vicus* and then a town, for the area was crossed by Ermine Street. The street pattern of the town appears, unlike most other towns, not to have been decided in advance but to have developed to meet needs. Some streets were closely built up. The middle of the town, an area of some 40 acres (16ha) or more, was walled, perhaps early in the third century, though the town continued to expand outside to a total of nearly 250 acres (100ha). There is little to see today.

Excavations and aerial photography have

The site of the town (or possible *civitas* capital) of *Durobrivae* (Chesterton/Water Newton, Cambridgeshire), showing the broad line of Ermine Street and some irregular plan side streets (*National Monuments Record*)

revealed buildings with stone foundations, substantial timber structures and in the middle, just south of Ermine Street, a large courtyard structure with blocks of rooms all round. This has been described as a *mansio*, but it is also possible it was a late period *forum*, which has helped to foster the idea that *Durobrivae* did become a late *civitas* capital, a question that is still argued.

Outside the town, a considerable industrial area sprawled along the banks of the Nene, much of it devoted to potteries making what are generally grouped as Nene valley wares. In the mid 1970s a major hoard of gold and silver Christian artefacts was found in a building which may have been a chapel. These included Chi-Rho monogrammed plaques and a chalice, bowls and flagons.

451

WATTISFIELD Suffolk
TM 0174 *Pottery kilns*
Excavations in the 1930s and in the later 1950s located more than twenty pottery kilns of the Roman period at Foxledge Common and beside Caulke Wood at Wattisfield, with further kilns at nearby Hinderclay Wood and Rickinghall village, substantiating the existence of a sizeable pottery industry in the Wattisfield area. The present Wattisfield pottery is sited several hundred metres to the west of the Roman working area, but one kiln has been moved there and can be seen by visitors to the present pottery.

WEEKLEY Northamptonshire
SP 8881 *Pottery and lime kilns*
Three enclosures surrounded by ditching were spotted here during aerial reconnaissance, in an area where a number of mosaic pavements were known to have been found two centuries ago, about ½ mile north and north-west of Weekley church. Two were pre-Roman, but the third was of mid first-century Roman origin, with a V-shaped ditch which suggests military association. The Roman site occupied about 2 acres (10.8ha). Pottery kilns were located here, and a well-preserved lime kiln, which is the subject of a key monograph by D. A. Jackson in *Britannia* iv (1973). The lime kiln is probably second century.

WEETING Norfolk
TL 778878 *Substantial building*
In 1974, a considerable hoard of bronze vessels was found at Weeting. Trial excavations in the area of the find revealed traces of a rectangular building of mortared flint, dated to the fourth century, which had had *opus signinum* flooring and was heated by hypocausts via box-flue tiles.

WELLINGBOROUGH Northamptonshire
SP 8767 *Industrial settlement*
Excavations at Hardwick Park, Wellingborough, in the late 1960s and early 1970s in advance of new housing exposed the remains of major pottery and lime burning industries. The potteries appear to have begun in the mid second century. Several complete kilns were examined, and remains

of mortaria, jars, roof and floor tiles were found. Other kilns were located. A lime kiln and other lime-burning apparatus were found. The site has since been largely built over, though its details have been photographed, drawn and described by the Wellingborough Archaeological Society.

WELLOW Avon
ST 7258 *Villa*
A prosperous courtyard villa in the Bath area, Wellow's main block on the north had corridors on both sides, with mosaic pavements. The villa had partial central heating, bath suites, and the west range, a narrow building, probably comprised servants' quarters. A number of hexagonal stone roof tiles were found. The villa appears to have been excavated several times, the first occasion during the seventeenth century.

WELLS Somerset
ST 552459 *Mausoleum*
Excavations in the south-west of the Cathedral Close, near the cloister, in the late 1970s exposed a sequence of Anglo-Saxon church buildings that were superseded in the twelfth and thirteenth centuries by the fine Gothic cathedral now dominating the city. Under the Anglo-Saxon structures was found a late Roman mausoleum, with a burial chamber of about 2×3m (7×10ft) that was once covered by a timber-posted canopy. This was the first recorded evidence of Roman occupation in Wells. The mausoleum was later demolished and part of it covered by an Anglo-Saxon burial chapel which itself was later incorporated into the east end of an Anglo-Saxon church, St Mary's; this in turn later became part of the Anglo-Saxon cathedral.

Welton see **Milecastle 17**

WELTON WOLD Humberside
SE 974279 *Villa*
A corridor villa, with additional aisled buildings, flourished at Welton between the later second and the end of the fourth century. These were the central structures of an agricultural complex of stock enclosures, industrial premises, corn driers and circular

houses, spread over an area of more than 20 acres (8ha). The area was protected by a double-ditch system. The site had previously been an Iron Age settlement. Considerable excavation has been carried out over the 1970s, and this has included practical experiments with firing corn driers.

WENDENS AMBO Essex
TL 507360 *Agricultural settlement*
A villa associated with an agricultural settlement was excavated at Wendens Ambo in the nineteenth century and again in the early 1970s. The house was a substantial building. The settlement had several buildings, including a rectangular barn with doors at both ends, later subdivided into sections, which contained corn driers. This was rebuilt and a hypocaust inserted into one room. Traces were also found of a granary. The settlement had been developed over an earlier Iron Age farmstead.

WEST BLATCHINGTON West Sussex
TQ 275074 *Villa*
This was an aisled farmhouse, about 35m (115ft) long, the northern half of which was partitioned for residential purposes. A pair

The Roman mausoleum found underneath the Anglo-Saxon building remains in the Cathedral Close at Wells (*Western Archaeological Trust*)

of rooms had *opus signinum* floors and were flanked by a corridor on each side. The house was built in the second century.

WEST DEAN Hampshire/Wiltshire
SU 257271 *Villa*
This villa sprawled across what is now the county border between Hampshire and Wiltshire. It had two main buildings inside an enclosure. One was an aisled farmhouse, whose internal divisions suggest domestic use. The other building had porticoes and a bath suite. Excavations yielded Samian ware, hexagonal roof tiles, painted plaster fragments and window glass pieces. There were also some outbuildings.

WESTLAND GREEN Hertfordshire
TL 425224 *Tile kilns*
Several tile kilns were detected in the early 1970s at Westland Green, near Little Hadham. They may have been associated with the pottery and tile works at Bromley Hall Farm.

WEST MEON Hampshire
SU 6324 *Villa*
A small villa was excavated here at the beginning of the present century. It had some tessellated floors and two mosaics. A small bath house was also found, at the west corner.

WEST MERSEA Essex
TM 009025 *Villa*
On a hill at West Mersea, overlooking the Blackwater estuary and the sea, a villa was built probably in the last part of the first century. The main block is closer to the sea, and though not properly excavated and so not definable in shape, it had mosaics. Behind was a second, smaller building. To the east of the villa was a remarkable mausoleum, remains of which can be seen. It was a circular ring of tiles and mortar on rag-stone foundations, some 20m (65ft) in diameter, with six equidistantly radiating internal walls springing from a central hexagonal chamber. The circular wall was supported by twelve equidistantly placed buttresses. It is the largest mausoleum so far found in Britain.

WEST STOW Suffolk
TL 797714 *Settlement*
The Anglo-Saxon village at West Stow, near Bury St Edmunds, some of which has been reconstructed after prolonged and careful excavations, appears to have been built on or beside the site of an earlier Romano-British settlement, which featured several pottery kilns. The fragments of wares found included examples of imitation Samian ware.

WHARRAM PERCY Humberside
SE 858646 *Villa buildings*
Two villa buildings, about 1 mile apart, and other structures associated with them, have been located in a series of recent excavations at Wharram. The work is continuing. Both villa sites, seen first from the air, have so far yielded mosaic flooring, box-flue tiles and so forth, and at the site known as Wharram Grange villa, a bath house and a stone-lined drain have been investigated.

WHEELDALE MOOR North Yorkshire
SE 796945 to 802963 *Road*
The Roman road between Malton and Whitby (Margary 81b) contains a splendid stretch over Wheeldale Moor for over a mile, which still has the slabs that lay underneath the gravelly surface. Some of the kerbstones remain along both edges, and some drainage culverts with cover stones are also visible. The road stretch can be walked today by turning off the A169 Whitby to Pickering road, near Goathland.

WHILTON LODGE Northamptonshire
SP 613646 *Small town: Roman name* Bannaventa
A small, walled town that was spotted from the air in 1970, Whilton Lodge was surrounded by a stone wall that was erected upon a filled-in ditch of earlier date. The area of the town was about 12 acres (5ha). A new ditch system was cut round the outside of the stone wall. The town plan was an irregular rhomboid, with curved corners. The site was cut across by Watling Street. Some timber building remains have been located. The town may have been a fortified station for military use in the fourth century.

Whitchester see **Milecastle 15**

WHITCHURCH Shropshire
SJ 544409 *Fort and later small town: Roman name* Mediolanum
The small town at Whitchurch has been explored. Excavations of the mid 1970s revealed timber buildings and a rampart of the second century. The town was preceded by a fort of two phases. The first was in the early 60s, and this fort was refurbished with new defences in the mid 70s. The fort remained in occupation until the second century.

WHITLEY CASTLE Cumbria
NY 6948 *Fort*
An early second-century fort built on rhomboid plan (was the *groma* askew?), Whitley was surrounded by an interesting five-ditch and five-rampart system (seven on the south-west side). The system is splendidly clear today. The *principia* lay on

454

the area of uneven ground in the middle of the fort. There is some evidence of rebuilding in the early third century by a vexillation of Legio XX. For a time the fort was garrisoned by a cohort of infantry of the Nervii. Part of the fort's role was to protect the military-controlled lead mines on Alston Moor nearby. It was probably abandoned in the mid fourth century.

WHITMINSTER Gloucestershire
SO 779066 *Villa*
A villa associated with an agricultural settlement of about 2 acres (0.8ha) has been excavated, though not completely, at Whitminster, near Eastington. The settlement began in the second century and lasted into the fifth. Among remains are a T-shaped kiln and scattered *tesserae*.

WHITTINGTON COURT
Gloucestershire SP 010200 *Villa*
A villa here was rebuilt in the fourth century. Excavations exposed eight geometric mosaic floors. There was also evidence that part of the villa buildings were converted from residential to agricultural use and corn driers were inserted. Some traces of destruction were found (burnt rafters, heaps of broken tile etc), perhaps of the late 360s, but there were also signs of more natural deterioration – from neglect. Coins of Honorius show that the site was still occupied at the end of the fourth century.

WHITWELL Leicestershire
SK 928075 *Settlement*
An early Romano-British settlement of about 5 acres (2ha), which followed upon an Iron Age community on the same site, was examined in the mid 1970s. The pottery included good quality Samian ware. Later, in the third century, a single-range villa of four rooms was erected, which was given an extension at one end. Later still, the villa was altered to accommodate an aisled hall. There was also evidence of iron works, and traces of a shaft furnace were found.

WICKFORD Essex
TQ 762937 *Farmstead*
A Romano-British farmstead occupied

throughout most of the Roman period yielded interesting remains during excavations of the late 1960s and early 1970s. These include a military-style 21m (23ft) long granary with *pilae*, which contained a corn drier. This building appears to have been erected and burnt down within the fourth century. Also found were a clay-lined pit with wickerwork for grain storage, a blacksmith's hearth and an interesting well of the third century which was timber lined, well preserved and contained in the rubbish thrown into it a wooden bucket, some shoes of leather and a pewter dish which bears a graffito. A number of timber-lined tanks had been used to store oysters.

WICKHAM BUSHES Berkshire
SU 865648 *Settlement*
A settlement at Wickham Bushes, Easthampstead, about ¼ mile north of the Devil's Highway has been known for some time. Limited excavation in one area in the early 1970s exposed remains of a timber structure about 20m (22ft) long, which had stone foundations. This seems to have been rebuilt several times, the last time in the second century. In the late 1970s, further excavation located traces of a rounded corner of an enclosure with a ditch and bank, which may have been of military origin.

WIDFORD Oxfordshire
SP 2712 *Mosaic*
Fragments of a Roman mosaic pavement have been inserted into the floor of Widford church. Their origin is not yet established.

WIGGINTON Oxfordshire
SP 3933 *Villa*
About 160 years ago a small section of a Roman house was discovered near Wigginton parish church. Two rooms were identified, one with a semi-hexagonal apse, which was heated by channelled hypocaust. The site was further examined in the mid 1960s, and it was confirmed as a third-century foundation that had been rebuilt in the fourth century. Some fifteen rooms were exposed, and there was evidence of at least ten tessellated floors. There were also remains of geometric pattern mosaics.

Mosaic specialists consider that these were designed and executed by the Corinian School at Cirencester.

WIGSTON PARVA Leicestershire
SP 464894 *Fort*
A small fort of about 2 acres (0.8ha) was identified by aerial photography in the 1960s, under Watling Street, near to High Cross (*Venonae*). Three gates, a V-shaped ditch and traces of a barrack block were found in confirmatory excavations. The fort was Claudian, and Watling street was built across the site, in the AD50s.

WILDERSPOOL Lancashire/Cheshire
SJ 611865 *Major settlement*
There was an important industrial site at Wilderspool, near Warrington, containing several timber built factories and workshops, principally connected with metal working. Furnaces were found for the production of hard bronzes and brass, some of which were fired using coal. A glass furnace was also identified. The industrial site appears to have flourished for much of the occupation. Excavations in the mid 1970s revealed fragments of sandstone columns.

Willowford see **Turrets 48a & b**

WILMINGTON Kent
TQ 540728 *Building*
A Roman building of unknown function was first noted a century ago at Wilmington. The site was re-examined in 1975 and walling uncovered. Debris included pottery and tile sherds.

WILSTROP North Yorkshire
SE 479549 *?Settlement*
During field drain works, a hypocaust in part of a building was found. Further work may establish whether the site was once a settlement.

WINCHESTER Hampshire
SU 4829 Civitas *capital of the* Belgae: *Roman name* Venta Belgarum
Winchester, situated on the bank of the river Itchen, was originally a native settlement, although it had been unoccupied for about a century before the Romans arrived in Britain. Traces of timber buildings have been found, which date from the earliest occupation period, but it is not possible to tell whether these were civil or military structures. An earthwork, consisting of a bank of clay with flints and chalk with flints, which dates from the late Neronian/early Flavian period has also been found. The extent of and reason for these early fortifications are in doubt.

On the death of Cogidubnus, Winchester became *civitas* capital of the Belgae. Little is known of the early town, although the Flavian street grid has been traced. The courses of the main streets north-south and east-west have been established. There are signs of a central public building complex which was probably the site of the *forum* and *basilica*, although lack of evidence makes interpretation of the remains dangerous. A house from the first half of the second century has been excavated in the Wolvesey Palace area. This was timber-framed and had painted plaster on the walls. Also from the second century comes a Romano-Celtic temple. Only known in plan, it measured 13.5 × 12m (45 × 38ft).

New fortifications were given to the town at the end of the second century. The bank was probably re-erected with turves. In the early third century the modifications were completed, and a masonry wall was erected in front of the existing bank. The wall was of courses of flint in mortar and was 2.75–3m (9–10ft) thick. The rampart was widened, making it 12–18m (40–60ft) at the base. There was also probably a ditch cut before the whole, although the medieval ditch has destroyed traces. Of the gates not much is known: a mass of masonry could be the site of one.

Domestic buildings have often been indicated by the presence of mosaics alone. The best of these, with human figures and dolphin motifs is in the town museum. A house of the early fourth century on Lower Brook Street has been more fully excavated, revealing a corridor with rooms leading off, a porch and a courtyard to the south. In one room was a raised hearth, a trough and two ovens. Cakes of bronze were found in association, suggesting industrial activity, but no tools or slag were found. Evidence of dense occupation at Winchester during the fourth century indicates that it flourished as a centre at this time. Improvements of domestic buildings were still being made at the end of the century; one house at Wolvesey Palace from this period has a tessellated floor. The fortifications were also modified in the fourth century with the addition of bastions. A semi-circular tower, 5m (17ft) to the east of the south gate, has been identified.

Very little is known of the end of Roman Winchester. Some graves at the Larkhills cemetery site contained late military equipment, animal snaps, buckles and belt tags which could suggest a military presence. The breakdown of civil discipline is indicated by the construction of houses over the lines of streets. However, occupation of the site appears to have continued.

WINDMILL HILL Buckinghamshire
SP 844338 *Agricultural site*
Work on a new golf course on Windmill Hill, Bletchley, in the early 1970s exposed ditching and nearby remains of three T-shaped corn driers all dated to the fourth century. Other finds suggest that occupation of the site started in the second century.

WINGHAM Kent
TR 2457 *Villa*
Wingham was an early villa, built probably in the Flavian period. The ruins were discovered a century ago and have been re-examined. The villa consisted of a main residential block with a bath suite which had walls decorated with mosaic. Associated with the house was an aisled building of the second century, which was partitioned.

Winshields see **Milecastle 40**

WINTERTON Humberside
SE 911182 *Villa*
The villa at Winterton expanded gradually on a site about 4 miles south of the Humber, just to the east of Ermine Street. The earliest

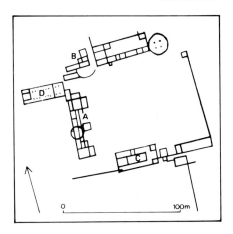

Winterton villa: (a) winged villa; (b) bath house; (c) aisled building; (d) aisled building used as a work place

buildings were circular and probably performed some function associated with farming, and date to the early second century. Before 180 a radical change had occurred, with the circular structures being demolished and a long rectangular building with sets of rooms at each end being built in their place. The villa was very advanced in its interior decoration, and was one of the few villas so far found in Britain to have had mosaics as early as the second century. Also dating from the later second century are two buildings probably used for stock housing. Recent work in the courtyard area has revealed more signs of late second-century activity, in the form of ovens, drains, rubbish pits and traces of metalled roads. A detached bath house with cold plunge and a furnace has been found which dates to this period.

Early in the third century, one of the stockbuildings was incorporated in the construction of a new aisled building, and another building was added opposite across the courtyard. This building had domestic apartments at the western end, with some figured mosaic floors and a hypocausted heating system. The rest of the building was given over to a barn-like area which had corn driers set into its floor. Recent work outside the villa to the south and west has revealed two aisled outbuildings.

What happened to the Winterton villa at the end of the Roman occupation is uncertain, but a gradual decline seems likely, backed up by the fact that the detached bath building was demolished in the mid fourth century, despite indications of refurbishing of other parts of the villa in the early part of the century.

WITHINGTON Gloucestershire
SP 0314 *Villa*
Interesting mosaics were found at Withington, including a portrait of Neptune and an Orpheus panel. These are said by mosaic specialists to have been executed by the Durnovarian School and the Corinian School.

WIVELISCOMBE Somerset
ST 0927 *Fort*
What is generally accepted as an early Roman fort has been examined here. It was double-ditched, covered about 3½ acres (1.5ha), and had a timber-strapped rampart about 5.5m (18ft) wide at the base. The ditches had cleaning slots.

WOLLASTON Northamptonshire
SP 913624 *Villa*
Remains of a small corridor house beside the river Nene, north of Wollaston, were found , in the early 1970s.

WOOD BURCOTE Northamptonshire
SP 6946 *Villa*
Investigations were carried out on the site of a known villa at Wood Burcote, south of Towcester. Some quantities of broken stone moulding and painted plaster fragments, tesserae and miscellaneous pottery ranging from the first to fourth centuries were gathered. Two stone buildings were identified, one of them an end-building on the main villa structure, with corn driers, and the other, a separate structure. The earliest pottery is dated to the mid first century.

WOODCHESTER Gloucestershire
ST 838032 *Villa*
Woodchester, near Stroud, was a large and sumptuous villa which today is not normally visible at all. From time to time, its principal mosaic is uncovered for public viewing. Otherwise, the extensive site is under earth. It was a double courtyard villa, with residential accommodation ranged round one courtyard and a grouping of agricultural buildings round an adjoining second yard. The site was excavated in the 1790s and considerable remains found and recorded. Among these was evidence of sixty-four rooms, twenty mosaics (made probably by craftsmen from the Corinian *officina* (see p 222). The principal mosaic was the Orpheus pavement, as it is known, which has a central octagon in which it is believed there was a fountain. The pavement, which is in the main great dining room in the residential courtyard, was covered by a roof supported by four corner pillars. Hypocaust channelling was found underneath the pavement, stone-walled with roof tile covering. In the second courtyard, one wing was formed by a long aisled building divided into rooms and containing a granary and a kiln.

The late eighteenth-century excavator, S. Lysons, noted that the outside of some of the villa buildings was dressed with red plaster, and the same coloured material was also present in some interiors. The site was examined again in the 1970s, but clearly there is much left to be discovered at Woodchester.

WOODEATON Oxfordshire
SP 533123 *Temple*
A Romano-Celtic temple, probably built in the 60s and rebuilt in the second century, was in use right into the fifth century. The *cella* was enclosed by a *temenos*. The temple was later surrounded by a wall with a gateway. The location of the temple indicates that it was a rural shrine, and quantities of coins were found, along with a number of votive objects, statuettes, axe heads, etc, which are now in the Ashmolean Museum in Oxford.

WORCESTER Hereford & Worcester
SO 851545 *?Fort and* vicus
There may have been an early fort at Worcester in the area of the cathedral

precinct. If so, it would have been of the mid first century. Excavations have confirmed little of the belief beyond a V-shaped ditch. There was more evidence of civilian occupation, however, and timber buildings of the third and fourth centuries, iron works' slag and pottery of the second and third centuries have been uncovered. But it is pertinent to remember the comment of Professor Frere (in Rodwell, W. and Rowley, T. (1975) p 4) that *vici* sprang up where military commanders put down forts, and a military establishment may well be found at Worcester.

Wormanby see **Milecastle 71**

WORSHAM Oxfordshire
SP 3011 *Villa*
Remains of a villa building survive on the edge of a wood at Worsham Bottom. Traces of one floor with red tesserae can be seen, and there are a few fragments of stone wall, covered with scrub.

WORTH Kent
TR 335558 *Temple*
A Romano-Celtic temple of uncertain origin was excavated here in 1926-7. It is on rising ground. The building work was in at least two phases, the second of the late fourth century AD. It was built over an earlier Iron Age shrine, traces of the timberwork of which were discovered, as well as Belgic pottery of the first century BC. There is a strong possibility that Caesar's base camp for his second invasion in 54 BC, erected as soon as his legions landed on the Kent shore nearby, was close to this site. Some of the pottery finds of the first century BC are now in the Ashmolean Museum at Oxford.

WORTHY DOWN Hampshire
SU 458357 *Settlement*
During the early stage of road building on the A34 bypass round Sutton Scotney, the Iron Age hilltop settlement on Worthy Down was examined before destruction. Post holes were found, and also traces of a road from east to west, both of which were suggestive of some Roman association.

WOUGHTON ON THE GREEN
Buckinghamshire SP 862374
Settlement
Excavations in advance of road building involving a roundabout exposed a group of ditches belonging to enclosures, probably of the late first or early second century. Traces of timber buildings of Roman construction were seen. Circular houses were also observed, and these were dated to pre-Conquest times.

WROXETER Shropshire
SJ 5608 Civitas *capital of the Cornovii:*
Roman name Viroconium Cornoviorum
Its position on the river Severn and Watling Street gave Wroxeter control of the Severn valley and of routes into Wales, thus enabling it to become a wealthy border town after it had been given the status of *civitas* capital and eventually the fourth largest town of Roman Britain. The military phase of its occupation has now been divided into three distinct phases of timber construction. This period spanned the years between c58 and 90, during which time a legionary fortress housing first Legio XIV and later Legio XX developed. Legio XX was moved to Chester leaving the site in a state of flux with the bath house unfinished.

Soon after the military withdrawal the town was raised to the status of *civitas* capital and the street grid was laid out in the last years of the first century. On the site of the unfinished military bath house the *forum* was built with a very large porticoed piazza measuring 73×68m (242×225ft). A *basilica* with a nave 11.5m (38ft) wide was constructed at the western end of the *forum*. This complex dates to c120, as does the public baths complex at the east of the *forum*, although it appears to have taken about thirty years to complete. The baths had a covered *palaestra* measuring 73×20m (80×22yd) and an external portico on the north side. The main range of rooms was on the east side, the *frigidarium* being decorated with mosaic on the wall. Part of the *palaestra* wall, known as the Old Work still stands to an impressive height. A fire damaged the *forum* in the late second century, and the remains of stalls indicate that a market was

Plan of Wroxeter

0   300m

operating at the time. The *forum* was later rebuilt and modified.

At the end of the second century, defences were provided for the town, which consisted of an earth rampart with two ditches and timber interval towers. During the third century, the addition of a stone wall completed the fortifications, although there is some evidence that external towers and a ditch were added still later. The wall ran along the top of the earth rampart rather than in the more usual position in front of it.

About twelve large houses have been traced, along with many private shops indicating the independent wealth of a considerable proportion of the population. One

460

very large house of 90m (100yd) in length is reminiscent of a winged corridor villa in plan. Could this be an indication of town-based agriculture? If so, it could explain the existence of an empty area crossed by ditches in the north of the enclosed area.

Towards the end of the third century there was limited demolition of the *forum, basilica* and baths. These public buildings were never rebuilt, but there is no reason to believe that Roman life did not continue in Wroxeter for longer. By about 400 timber buildings were constructed over the ruins of the *basilica*, and the hall attached to the bath complex was still in use. In the final years of occupation, however, life appears to have been fairly squalid, with bodies left unburied in the streets and traces of fires and meat bones littering the shell of the *basilica*.

WYCOMB Gloucestershire
SP 025197 *Settlement*
A small settlement at Wycomb was investigated during road works in the late 1960s and early 1970s.

The Old Work at Wroxeter, as seen before recent major excavation and restoration work. Pillar in *palaestra* doorway has been removed (*National Monuments Record*)

WYE Kent
TR 049475 *Iron-working site*
An iron-working site which functioned between the first and third centuries was noted in excavations about ½ mile north-west of Wye village.

WYMBUSH Buckinghamshire
SP 829389 *Farmstead*
A farmstead at Wymbush, near Loughton, which has been excavated in recent years, had two stone buildings of two phases, third and fourth century. The larger, rectangular building, 22 × 11m (73 × 36ft), had begun as a three-room structure, one of which had *opus signinum* flooring. This was later enlarged by the addition of two more rooms and a corridor. The other building was a barn of 13 × 6m (43 × 20ft), with an open front. A fragment of tile was found, with a graffito greeting to the tile maker.

YARCHESTER Shropshire
SJ 6000 *Villa*
A corridor villa here was partially excavated in the late 1950s. A range of rooms was located, one of which ended in an apse.

YARDHOPE Northumberland
NT 909009 *Temporary camp*
A small temporary camp of about 5 acres (2ha) was discovered in 1976, about 45m (50yd) north of the road from High Rochester to Devil's Causeway. Much of the turf rampart survives, some to a height of 1m (3ft) and over 3m (10ft) at the base. There were three gates protected by *titula*.

YEOVIL Somerset
ST 548157 *Villa*
Westlands, at Yeovil, seems to have been a considerable complex, beginning as a simple winged corridor plan and evolving into a substantial courtyard villa with several associated outbuildings. Several of the rooms excavated had mosaic or tessellated floors. Two groups of buildings were located in excavations of the late 1970s.

YORK North Yorkshire
SE 6052 *Legionary fortress and later* colonia:
Roman name Eboracum
By the late first century, York had taken over from nearby Malton as an important military post. The original legionary fortress of 50 acres (20ha), built on a slightly elevated spur, 15m (50ft) above sea level, gave the occupants control of the basin of the river Ouse and routes to the west and south-west. Thus, Legio IX, and later Legio VI *Victrix*, were able to observe the movements of the Brigantes tribe.

The defences of York seem to have developed in three phases. A gate inscription of 107–8 reveals that the original fortifications were renovated and rebuilt under Trajan. A second period of rebuilding occurred in about 197 when the walls had to be reconstructed after devastation. Finally, they were extensively altered c300. Although dating evidence for the fortifications is meagre, there is no doubt that they were of a monumental nature, reflecting York's importance as a *colonia*, its military and

commercial status and its probable position as headquarters of the *Dux Britanniarum* in the fourth century.

It was the civil settlement which grew up on the opposite bank of the river from the legionary fortress that gave York the commercial backing that allowed it to be elevated to the status of *colonia*. The first reference to York as a *colonia* comes from an altar inscription from Bordeaux dated to 237. Certainly, extensive replanning occurred during the third century, which makes it seem unlikely that the town was given colonial status before the early 200s. The emperor Severus lived at York for three years, and the Emperor Constantius I and Constantine I (when Caesar) spent time there. It seems likely that an imperial palace was built, and one is mentioned in Severus' biography, although no certain remains have been found. Other domestic buildings excavated have revealed that York had wealthy occupants. One house, now below Toft Green, was discovered to have had three mosaics. An extremely large set of baths, now under the old railway station, with a *caldarium* measuring 9 × 10.5m (28 × 35ft) is

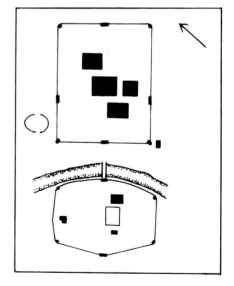

York: sketch plan of the legionary fortress (top) and the *colonia* south-west of the Ouse, about AD 300

The famous multangular tower on the western corner of the legionary fortress at York. Most of the masonry is Roman, patched here and there in later times. The top courses, which incorporate the arrow loops, are medieval (*Graham Sumner*)

one of the most impressive bath houses found in Britain. A colonnaded building, with two rows of columns 12m (40ft) apart, has been described as a possible *basilica*. If this is so, then perhaps the site of the *forum* can be conjectured.

The most interesting feature about the remains of the large and public buildings in York is that their orientation lies on a different axis from that of the grid pattern imposed on the town during the third-century developments. This suggests that they predate the replanning and illustrate how highly developed York had become when still a provincial capital. No temples have been found, however, although inscriptions provide evidence of religious practice. A dedication to Hercules has been found in High Ousegate, for example. Much information about the population has been gleaned from the remains found in the extensive cemeteries. These date from 140 to the end of the fourth century and are the largest yet discovered from Roman Britain. One cemetery yielded 350 skeletons. Standards of living appear to have been maintained until the fourth century. The decline of York as a Roman centre can possibly be attributed to a general change of sea level, which led to the destruction of the river defences and harbour area.

WALES

ABERFFRAW Gwynedd
SH 355690 *Fort*
After defeating the Ordovices in Anglesey in
AD60, the Roman governor of Britain,
Suetonius Paullinus, garrisoned the island.
So wrote Tacitus (*Annals* xiv, 30), and it is
possible that the Roman fort discovered after
excavation at Aberffraw in 1973 and 1978
was part of this military work. The earliest
phase of the fort's history has been put at
AD60, though it may have been later
(AD78-9) during the time of Agricola's
campaign in north Wales. The remains of
the fort were found beneath the present
village, and included part of the north and
west ditches, showing a clear stretch of
cleaning slot at the bottom of the first ditch,
2m (6ft) deep. One of the fort's functions
may have been to protect workings in the
Parys Mountain copper mines.

ABERGAVENNY Gwent
SO 299140 *Fort: Roman name* Gobannium
The fort at Abergavenny was built in two
phases, the first by Didius Gallus in the early
50s BC, though it has been argued that it
might even be an establishment of Ostorius
Scapula during his campaign against
Caratacus and the Silures. Remains of the
rampart were found in excavations near the
medieval town wall, in 1971-3, showing that
it had been built of clay and gravel, with a
turf front and with some timber lacing,
though it is not clear whether the rampart
belongs to the first or second phase. Some
parts of two successive ditches have also
been found, the later one being twice as wide
as the first. The second phase was probably
raised in Frontinus' time (74-8). Roof tiles of
Legio II *Augusta* (then based at Caerleon)
were found in the excavation.

ARDLEEN Powys
SJ 260159 *?Marching camp*
Rescue excavation here in advance of road
building revealed pottery and scorched
debris in the inner ditch of a double-ditched
enclosure which was perhaps a marching
camp.

AROSFA GAREG Dyfed
SN 8026 *Marching camp*
On the south side of the Brecon to
Llandovery Roman road (Margary 62c) not
far from Y Pigwn, is a 45 acre (18ha)
marching camp, probably of Frontinus'
period (mid 70s), of which most of the
rampart outline can still be seen. The camp
was large enough to accommodate two
legions temporarily quartered in tents.

BEULAH Powys
SN 923502 *Fort*
A 4 acre (1.6ha) rectangular fort on a slope
beside the old road from Llandovery to
Castell Collen (Margary 623) was erected in
the Flavian period, probably before AD80.
During Trajan's reign (98-117) the fort was
altered, and appears to have been abandoned
in the middle of the second century. Built of
timber and turf, no stonework additions have
been found. Just above the fort are the earth
remains of a practice camp. Little can be
seen today of Beulah (also called Caerau),
though there are good stretches of rampart.

BIGLIS South Glamorgan
ST 140694 *Farmstead*
An interesting Romano-British farmstead
was recently excavated at Biglis, Cadoxton,
in advance of a new road to the Barry docks.
The farmstead was begun in the second
century, with a circular house some 7m

464

(23ft) in diameter, associated with two circular corn driers. Later, the farm was expanded and surrounded by a double palisade. Stock pens were erected against the inside. The palisade was replaced in the third century by a rampart of clay and rubble which had an east entrance. Through this a road was laid across the farm. There was some dry stone walling on the southern side, and traces of timber buildings have been found.

BLAEN-CWM-BACH West Glamorgan
SS 793986 *Marching camp*
Scanty remains of a 61 acre (25ha) marching camp, perhaps of the Frontinus period (mid 70s), lie near Neath, not far from the Neath to Brecon road, on the east side of the river Neath. The most prominent traces of rampart are on the west side. The camp was big enough for three legions, though it is not likely it was intended ever to accommodate so large a force.

BRECON GAER Powys
SO 004296 *Fort*
Brecon Gaer was a centrally placed 7¾ acre (3ha) fort in the Brecon Beacon region, controlling the meeting points of six major Roman roads: to Caerleon (Margary 62b, 62a), to Cardiff (Margary 621 south), to Neath (Margary 622), to Llandovery (Margary 62c), to Castell Collen (Margary 621 north) and to Clyro (Margary 62c). It was built in c75 as part of Frontinus' campaigns and consolidations thereafter. The fort began as an earth and timber structure, with ramparts on a cobble base, and with double-ditching. There were four gates, centrally along east and west. By the end of the century the fort had become the base of an *ala* of Vettonian auxiliary cavalry (from Spain).
In the Hadrianic period (117–38) the buildings inside were converted to stone, a bath house was built inside the north-west corner, suggesting that the garrison strength was reduced, and the gates were also built in stone. This new work was rebuilt in the early third century, probably following a major attack on the fort; scorching was found at some of the gates and the fort's well was

filled with debris of the period. The guard-rooms on the west gate projected in front of the fort's stone wall, an unusual feature for Roman forts of the earlier periods, though it does occur at Caerleon. Excavations have also revealed the remains of an indoor training area for horses and cavalrymen, attached to one side of the *principia*.
Brecon Gaer was abandoned early in the third century and then reoccupied towards the end of the century, when the south gate was repaired. Today, remains of the south, west and east gates, walling – some of it to about 3m (10ft) in height – and two angle turrets can be seen. It is near Y Gaer Farm in the village of Aberyscir, 2½ miles from Brecon.

BRITHDIR Gwynedd
SH 773187 *Fort and industrial site*
This is a complex site near Dolgellau. A Flavian auxiliary cohort fort, of c75, was built with double-ditches, and with a bath house and a *fabrica* outside. The fort was sited by the old Roman route to Caer Gai (Margary 66b). It appears to have been raised beside an earlier Iron Age small four-post building. The fort was later dismantled and replaced by a smaller fortlet on a different alignment, probably in the period 110–20. Associated with the fortlet was a small industrial site, with lead-working furnaces, a tannery with a stone-lined tanning pit, and the original *fabrica* was rebuilt in stone. These are thought to have been features of an army ordnance depot. Occupation of the whole site came to an end in the 120s. It has been largely built over.

BRYN GLAS Gwynedd
SH 502634 *Signal station*
This was a signal station or policing post, 270m (300yd) or so north of a presumed stretch of road between Caernarfon and Caerhun. Some of the earthworks remain. Excavation revealed part of a U-shaped ditch. The station may be Flavian in origin.

BRYN-Y-CASTELL Gwynedd
SH 728429 *Hillfort*
Remnants of the defences of the hillfort at Bryn-y-Castell, Ffestiniog, are in the form of

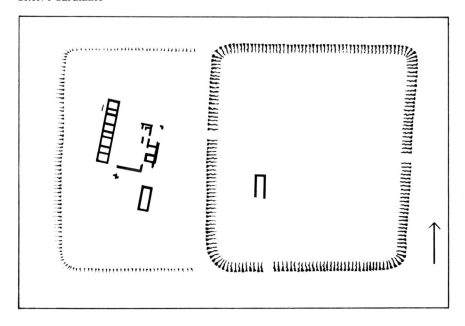

The fort at Bryn-y-Gefeiliau, showing the *mansio* in the west annexe

a drystone wall, about 1.5m (5ft) wide and up to 1m (3ft) tall. The area of the fort was about 40×25m (130×80ft). The entrance was a single space in the wall, about a metre wide. Work is continuing, in particular upon an oval structure inside the entrance. Glass bangles similar to some found at Traprain Law in Scotland have been found, and these suggest habitation during the Roman period.

BRYN-Y-GEFEILIAU Gwynedd
SH 746572 *Fort and* mansio
A fort, nearly 4 acres (1.6ha) in area, was built here in c90, perhaps as part of a programme of strengthening the hold on Wales following the withdrawal of Roman forces from Scotland. Bryn-y-Gefeiliau (also called Caer Llugwy) lies along the route between the forts at Caerhun and Tomen-y-Mur. Today, only traces of the fort can be seen, though there are some other remains in what was the annexe on the west side of the fort. The first rampart of the fort was built of clay on a rubble base, with a stone kerb. It was surrounded by a double-ditch system,

the inner ditch being 4m (13ft) wide and 2m (6½ft) deep, and the outer 3.25m (11ft) wide and 1.25m (4ft) deep. The stone remains in the annexe appear to be those of a later *mansio*.

CAE GAER Powys
SN 824819 *Fortlet*
What is thought to be a late Roman fortlet, parallelogram in plan, was excavated in 1913. The fort had been protected by a rampart 5m (16½ft) wide. The ramparting is well preserved. The fortlet was probably a police post. It is on Forestry Commission land.

Caerau see **Beulah**

CAER GAI Gwynedd
SH 877315 *Fort*
A square fort on a spur overlooking the Dyfrdwy, near the A494 by Lake Bala, Caer Gai was built in the Flavian period. Excavation has shown that part of the rampart was later revetted with stone, and two sides are well preserved. An inscription found in a shrine to Hercules, and now in the National Museum of Wales, indicates that for a time

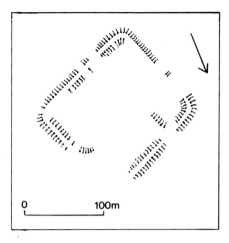

Caer Gai fort

the fort was the base for the first cohort of Nervian auxiliary cavalry (a regiment from northern Gaul). The fort was occupied for about half a century.

CAER GYBI Gwynedd
SH 247826 *Fort*
Caer Gybi, near Holyhead, Anglesey, is a small, quadrilateral fort, built much to the same pattern as the larger Roman forts of the Saxon Shore in eastern and southern England but much later. About 75×52.5m (250×175ft), with cylindrical turrets on the corners, it stands on a low cliff. Much of the

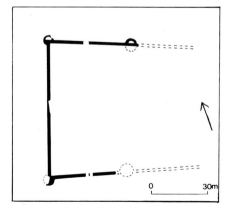

Caer Gybi fort

walling has survived in quite good condition to a height of about 4.25m (14ft) or so on the north and west sides. The walls are a little over 1.5m (5ft) thick and constructed of mortared rubble fronted with coursed stone, some of the courses being set in herring-bone style. The north-east cylindrical turret rises to nearly 8.5m (28ft), but the bulk of the stonework is restoration of much later date, possibly eighteenth century. Some of the rampart walk has been preserved. The north-west to south-east wall at one time continued beyond the north-east turret down to the beach, and it is suggested that in Roman days the enclosure protected a harbour whose waters came up to the walls.

The fort was built in the fourth century, probably to protect the Parys Mountain copper mines from barbarian assault, but it may also have been to protect shipping in the Irish Sea or traders with Ireland. It resembles naval fortifications on the Rhine of the late fourth century. Inside the enclosure the church of St Gybi was built in the sixth century.

CAERHUN Gwynedd
SH 777705 *Fort and* vicus: *Roman name* Kanovium
Some 4½ miles south of Conwy, just off the B5106, lies the now covered fort of *Kanovium*, beside the river Conwy. This began as a timber and earth construction of the AD70s (by Frontinus or Agricola), just under 5 acres (2ha) in size. Outside the fort on the east was a bath house, and to the south a jetty and docks, accessible to medium-sized vessels. The fort was converted to stone in the early Antonine period (140s), and among the new buildings was a double granary. The fort was destroyed at the end of the second century, was rebuilt later and occupied from time to time in the fourth century. Its strategic position on the river Conwy, and on the east–west road from the Chester area along the top of north Wales to Caernarfon (Margary, roads 67b and 67c), was clearly important. It is situated beside the present-day churchyard.

Caerhun was excavated in 1926–9. It has been examined again since, notably from the air in 1974, revealing substantial traces of

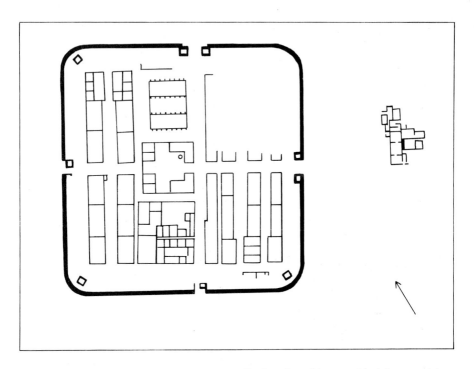

Caerhun fort, with external bath house at right

Milestone erected in Hadrian's reign at Llanfair-fechan, some eight Roman miles from Caerhun (*Kanovium*)

the *vicus* developed outside the fort. Part of the fort rampart is visible as are some building remains. The fort is named on a milestone found about 7 miles from the site in the 1880s, now in the British Museum. The cylindrical stone reads A KANOVIO M P VIII (8 miles from *Kanovium*), and is said to date from c120.

CAER LEB Gwynedd
SH 473674 *Enclosure*
Caer Leb, near Llanidan, Anglesey, is a third-century pentagonal enclosure defended by double-banks and ditches which drew water from the marshy ground in which it was situated. The banks were faced with stone. Some of the outer bank has been flattened but most of it remains to a metre or so in height. Inside the enclosure, traces of a small circular hut, about 2m (6ft) in diameter, and of a larger, rectangular structure, were found in excavations over a century ago.

468

Caer Llugwy see **Bryn-y-Gefeiliau**

CAERLEON Gwent

ST 3390 *Legionary fortress and* vicus: *Roman name* Isca

Caerleon was an important link in the chain of defences that formed the bulwark of Roman military power in the west of Britain. It was tactically well positioned on the navigable estuary of the river Usk, at the east end of a coastal plain and adjacent to the mountains, thus commanding routes into the interior. The fortress housed Legio II *Augusta*, which set up and occupied it in CAD75.

The first phase of development consisted of the construction of a set of banked and ditched earth and wooden ramparts, timbers of which have been traced in excavation. The rampart was reinforced in about AD100 by a stone wall about 1.5m (5ft) thick. Interval towers were built along the walls at 45m (50yd) spacings. There were four gateways into the fortress, one of which, the south-west entrance, when excavated was shown to have had two arched passageways with flanking towers. The walls here were 2.25m

Plan of legionary fortress at Caerleon, with the amphitheatre outside on the south-west

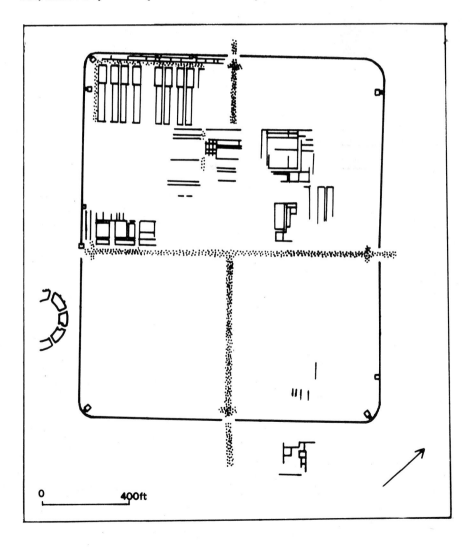

0 ____ 400ft

(7ft) thick. Inside the 50 acre (20ha) rectangular area that the walls enclosed was a typically designed Roman grid pattern of streets and buildings. A number of excavations within the fort area have revealed the paved courtyard of the *principia*, pairs of barrack blocks and a mid second century square, and stone cook-houses. The barrack blocks are fine examples of the layout of Roman military accommodation, rectangular buildings about 75m (250ft) long divided into twelve cubicles, one for every eight soldiers.

In the early part of the second century, signs of decay and disuse of some buildings – for example the barrack blocks in the *praetentura* – suggest a reduction in the size of the garrison. This period of decline can also be traced in other excavated buildings, as in the amphitheatre, which suffered a partial collapse c125. The amphitheatre, situated outside the fortress in association with the *vicus*, is the largest in Britain. It is oval, built of stone and had eight vaulted entrances. It held up to 6,000 spectators. Other buildings outside the fortress include an exterior bath complex of two or three buildings which underwent three periods of improvement and alteration.

The early third century saw the renovation of many of the buildings, associated with the renewal of military activity in the area. The amphitheatre was, for example, given a complete overhaul in the period between 212 and 222, and some barrack blocks were reoccupied. By the end of the third century, however, it appears that Caerleon was no longer playing such an important military role, as the coastal Welsh strongholds were reinforced. The administrative buildings were occupied up to the middle of the fourth century, while other areas fell into disuse. An interesting fact discovered in the 1980 excavations is that one set of barracks was rebuilt and occupied for about twenty years in the second quarter of the fourth century. After this there is no evidence, as yet, of further Roman reoccupation.

CAERNARFON Gwynedd
SH 485624 *Fort: Roman name* Segontium
An important fort in the Welsh network, Caernarfon began as an earth and timber structure put up by Agricola c77–8, covering over 5 acres (2ha), with four gates, and enclosed by two W-shaped ditches. It was constructed for a military cohort. The fort was renovated in the Antonine period with stonework, again under Severus at the end of the second century and subsequently in the 360s, when some of the fort wall was rebuilt in stone for the first time. The work of the Antonine period is interesting, for it was built in red sandstone brought all the way from the quarries around Chester, site of the legionary fortress. Among the restoration works of Severus was the aqueduct.

The remains include stretches of wall, foundations of the barrack blocks, a granary, the fort's *fabrica* or workshop block (which may have replaced a workshop area built outside the fort in about 90–100 and which was used only for a generation or so) and the *praetorium* which had been built of the Chester red sandstone but which was later rebuilt, using some of the red stone along with local stone.

The remains of the *principia* include the strongroom of the third century, reached by a short steep flight of steps. There are also remains of two bath houses, both inside the fort's enclosure, the smaller bath house being the earlier (mid second century). There are also remains of gates on the south-west, north-west and north-east. A *vicus* grew up outside the fort and among the remains so far discovered have been a *mithraeum*, about 14×6m (48×21ft).

CAERPHILLY Mid Glamorgan
ST 154873 *Fort*
On the north-west corner of the site of Caerphilly Castle, earthworks were raised during the Civil War, and it may be from these that the great medieval concentric castle (built by the de Clares in the late thirteenth century) was bombarded. These earthworks were excavated in the early 1960s and traces of a 3–4 acre (1.2–1.6ha) Roman fort of almost square plan were found. The fort has been dated to Frontinus's governorship (AD74–8), and it lies just east of the Roman route from Gelligaer in the hills to Cardiff. It also lies near the Roman lead mines at Cefn-pwll-dhu which it protected.

The rampart had been built on cobble foundations and was about 6m (20ft) wide. In front were two V-shaped ditches cut in the clay. Very little trace remains today, but the site can be seen by visiting the great medieval castle.

CAERSWS Powys
SO 050922 *Forts*
There were two forts at Caersws. The first, built by Suetonius Paullinus in AD59 or 60, was just over 9 acres (3.6ha), with a complex ditch system, and was situated to the north-east of the present town on rising ground overlooking the Severn. The second fort was constructed in Flavian times, probably by Frontinus, about half a mile south-west, near where the Severn and the Carno meet. This later fort was 7½ acres (3ha), large for an auxiliary fort, but necessary for the control of the intersection of at least four Roman roads, the east–west Margary 64, the road to Carno (Margary 643) and the Margary 642 going north. There appear to have been several phases of occupation, with modifications to ditch and rampart arrangements, and some renovations in Severus' reign

(193–211). These included stone buildings, such as three heated rooms next to the *praetorium*, and some of the timber barracks were demolished and not replaced. Gradually, a civilian *vicus* was developed in the space between the two forts, and this included a bridge across the Severn about 200m (220yd) south-east of the second fort, traces of which have been found.

CAERWENT Gwent
ST 4690 Civitas *capital of the Silures: Roman name:* Venta Silurum
Early confusion about the foundation of Caerwent, capital of the Silures, has at last been cleared up by the fact that it is now thought to have originally been the site of a fort with an associated *vicus*. This roughly rectangular site covered an area of about 44 acres (18ha). It was probably enclosed at the end of the second century by an earth rampart and ditch.

Although Caerwent has undergone a great deal of excavation, much of it occurred before the establishment of modern archaeo-

Part of town wall at Caerwent

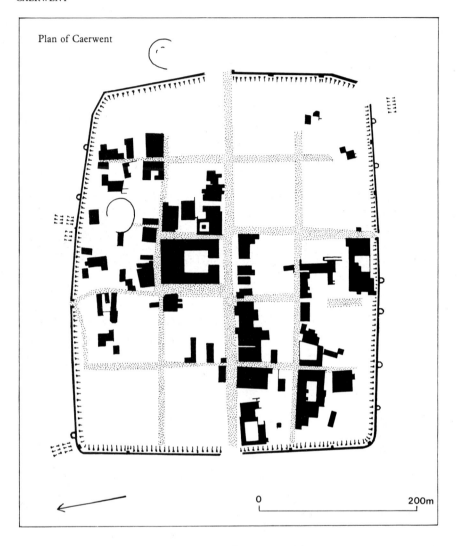

Plan of Caerwent

0 ——————— 200m

logical techniques. The interpretation of building sequences is therefore difficult. It seems likely that the *forum*, the baths and the grid pattern of streets belong to the first period of development. The *forum* had a piazza measuring only 31×33m (100×110ft). It was colonnaded and had ranges of shops. A coin of Nerva (AD96–8) discovered here gives a clue to the date of construction. The baths were also of modest dimensions for a *civitas* capital. The suite had a covered hall rather than an open peristyle, which measured 34×12m (112×40ft). Another public building was the ornamented *basilica*, raised up at the north end of the *forum*. This was a fairly simple structure by comparison with corresponding buildings in other *civitas* capitals.

The dimensions of the *insulae* suggest small, closely packed dwellings. There are about sixteen larger houses, presumably belonging to the wealthier classes. These are often equipped with a courtyard or garden. One has been found to have had a tessellated

(*above*) Roman walling at the *civitas* capital *Venta Silurum* (Caerwent); (*below*) Remains of some shops at the *civitas* capital *Venta Silurum* (Caerwent)

floor surrounding the open area of a peristyle. Others had mosaics. A very large domestic structure, with a mosaic and hypocausted rooms, has been described as a *mansio*.

Caerwent is rich in remains which reflect religious activity. What is believed to have been a temple has been found in an *insula* east of the *forum*. It is an apsidal Romano-Celtic structure. Two other probable religious sites have been identified: one a hall with a large podium on the west wing of the *forum* and the other an octagonal structure outside the east wall.

Stone fortifications were built round Caerwent, probably in the mid third century, to replace the original bank and ditch. Parts of these walls are still in existence, reaching to a height of 5.25m (17ft) in some places. The walls are of limestone and are 2.75–3m (9–10ft) thick. A series of 'counterforts' of dubious function were placed at regular intervals round the perimeter. They are thought to be contemporary with the walls and are bonded into their fabric. Bastions were added c340, and are spaced irregularly round the exterior of the fortifications. This strengthening of defences reflects the growing instability of the Roman position in the fourth century. This is also borne out by the blocking of the north and south gates. Roman life, of a sort, lingered on into the fifth century, the *forum* remaining in use longer than the *basilica*. Somewhat surprisingly, the drainage system was refurbished in this period, suggesting that the bath house was possibly still in use. The *basilica*, along with some shops and houses, was destroyed by fire during the century, but there was probably limited occupation thereafter.

CAE SUMMERHOUSE South Glamorgan
SS 864779 *Farmstead*
A native ditch-enclosed farmstead at Cae Summerhouse, Tythegston, begun probably in the late first century, continued in existence with modifications into the fourth. Among finds were Roman corn driers, a barn and several four- and six-post buildings. One corn drier was heated by a T-shaped furnace, the flue being lined with limestone slabs.

CALDICOT Gwent
ST 473893 *Settlement linked with Caerwent*
An extensive Iron Age settlement that gradually developed into a Romano-British settlement here, about half a mile south-east of Caerwent, was enclosed by palisading and ditching. Excavations in recent years have exposed remains of various buildings, including circular structures and pottery kilns, which may indicate a sizeable coarse pottery industry. The pottery fragments covered a wide period, the earliest being a Samian bowl of Flavian date. Pottery of the third and fourth centuries was also found. Excavations in the later 1970s were directed by Glamorgan–Gwent Archaeological Trust.

CAMNANT West Glamorgan
SN 862102 *Marching camp*
Traces of a marching camp have been found at Camnant, near Coelbren Gaer. Parts of the western and eastern rampart and ditching are visible.

CAPEL EITHIN Gwynedd
SH 489727 *?Small temple*
This is a curious archaeological site near Gaerwen, Anglesey – bleak, exposed, with the Snowdon mountains far away to the south. Finds spread across the centuries, from the Bronze Age to the Viking period. The site is known as the Chapel of the Gorse from the name of the field. The Roman interest is a small square-plan building, about 5sq m (6sq yd) in size, one of whose corners overlay a pit which was found to contain among the debris a sherd of Samian ware dated about the reign of Hadrian (117–38). The alignment of the building is exactly east–west, which is taken to indicate that the remains are of a small temple or chapel.

CARDIFF South Glamorgan
ST 1876 *Forts and* vicus
It now seems that there were four successive forts at Cardiff, as well as a *vicus* associated with the second fort. Cardiff lies at the head of the Taff estuary, an obvious strategic position to protect anchorages in the river for ships of the Roman fleet, to dominate the southern approaches to the Vale of

Glamorgan, to guard approaches to the Severn estuary and to ward off assaults upon south Wales from the sea. The first fort, traces of which were only confirmed in recent years, was built sometime between AD55 and 60, and was out of use by about AD90. It was about 30 acres (12ha) in size. A second fort was built over part of the site of the first, in Domitian's or Trajan's time, but did not last long. Around it a *vicus* developed.

In the late third century a major stone-walled coastal fort was erected, with flanking turrets at corners and mid-wall, and with massive twin-towered gates, along the lines of the stone forts of the Saxon Shore on the east and south-east coasts of England (see p 143). This structure is of more than one phase of building and was in use to the 360s.

The ruins of the Roman fort were chosen by the Normans as a site on which to build a motte castle, in the 1080s, the wooden tower of which was later transformed into a polygonal stone shell keep, in the mid twelfth century. This involved some renovating of the old Roman fort walls. Towards the end of the nineteenth century, during the great building schemes of the Marquess of Bute, the stone walls were renovated again, this time on three sides, and the twin-towered north gate was completely refurbished. It is still possible to see stretches of original third- and fourth-century Roman stonework along the lowest courses, now chiefly at basement level, indicated by a course of reddish stone. Considerable excavation and examination have been carried out under the direction of Mr and Mrs P. Webster for the Department of Extra-Mural Studies, University Collage, Cardiff, in the 1970s and early 1980s.

CARMARTHEN Dyfed
SN 4120 Civitas *capital of the Demetae: Roman name* Moridunum
Carmarthen was the *civitas* capital of the Demetae in west Wales. It began as a fort of the Flavian period (under Frontinus or Agricola), the remains of which are to the south-west of the present town near the river Towy. For a long time, preoccupation with the fort obscured the possibility that

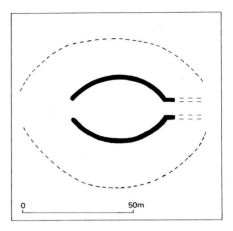

Sketch plan of the amphitheatre at Carmarthen

Carmarthen was a town. It is clear that the Demetae gave the Romans little trouble and accepted dominion readily. As a result, a *vicus* quickly grew up round the fort, which in the mid second century (or a little earlier) became a *civitas* capital. This town grew over the years, and by the fourth century (or earlier) it occupied about 30 acres (12ha), and was surrounded by an earth wall revetted in stone.

Excavations in Carmarthen have been going on since the early 1960s, and among numerous finds have been remains of buildings in timber and stone, some with tessellated floors, with evidence of hypocausts. Many buildings were ranged along streets set out in grid pattern. Buildings were both residential and industrial. Outside the town, to the east (signposted off the A40) are some traces of an elliptical amphitheatre, with some of the elaborate drainage system. The amphitheatre had been spotted in 1936, but the recent works have produced a much more detailed layout. It had been cut into the hillside and fitted with timber-supported terraces of seats. Its dimensions amounted to 1½ acres (0.6ha), much larger than the estimated population of Carmarthen of the time would have needed: was the amphitheatre built as a meeting place for the whole tribe?

The fort appears to have been built between present-day Spillman Street and

475

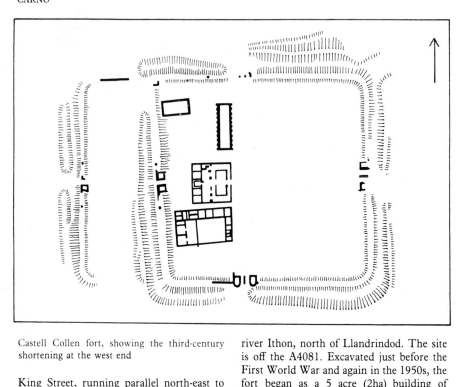

Castell Collen fort, showing the third-century shortening at the west end

King Street, running parallel north-east to south-west to the river Towy. The position of the town at the head of the Towy estuary would have allowed the capital at some time to have accommodated a naval base, perhaps later in the occupation period. The town Museum is well worth a visit for its Roman period collection and displays.

CARNO Powys
SN 962966 *Fort*
This is a 2½ acre (1ha) fort (or possibly fortlet), much of which is very faint in outline. Excavation has revealed a section of rampart about 4.25m (14ft) wide and a V-shaped ditch. Known locally as Caer Noddfa, the fort has not been incontestably proved to be of Roman origin, but the site does lie beside the Roman road to Caersws.

CASTELL COLLEN Powys
SO 055628 *Fort*
The first fort at Castell Collen, near Llandrindod Wells, was built c75 by Frontinus on a knoll beside an S-bend in the

river Ithon, north of Llandrindod. The site is off the A4081. Excavated just before the First World War and again in the 1950s, the fort began as a 5 acre (2ha) building of timber and turf, for a detachment of a thousand auxiliaries. Much of the ditch was cut into boulder clay which would have held water from rain or from flooding of the river. The ditch was W-shaped. The fort was refurbished in Trajan's time, was abandoned in about AD120 for a while, but was re-occupied in the later Antonine period, when the rampart was faced with stone and the gates were reinforced with semi-cylindrical gate towers. The fort was abandoned again, and then reoccupied once more in the third century, this time being reduced to about 3½ acres (1.5ha), which was achieved by removing the western end. The original western ditch stands on its own today.

Parts of the *principia* stonework have survived, and also part of a rectangular granary adjacent to the *principia*, built in about AD200. There are also remains of the bath house outside the south wall. Near the fort are many traces of practice camps, including the large group at Llandrindod Common.

476

CEFN GRAEANOG Gwynedd
SH 455489 *Settlement*
A native settlement of three phases of stone building at Cefn Graeanog, Clynnog, was excavated in 1976-7 by R. B. White and a team for the Gwynedd Archaeological Trust. Phase I (a round house) is put at the beginning of the first century BC. Phase II, first to second centuries, consisted of another round house. Phase III was more extensive, a quadrilateral stone enclosure, some 30sq m (35sq yd) with round houses in north-west, north-east and south-east corners, rectangular buildings on the inner side of the north and east walls, one aisled and one a byre, and at the south end, on either side of the enclosure entrance, a pair of barns on the outside wall. This phase seems to be of the later Roman period. Finds include some black burnished ware jars and saddle and rotary querns.

CHEPSTOW Gwent
ST 536939 *?Temple*
Some Roman remains from cremations have been found under the vestigial medieval barn at the priory in Chepstow. These may relate to a temple of Roman times that is attributed to this site.

CLYRO Powys
SO 227435 *Fort*
When Ostorius Scapula had defeated Caratacus in AD50-1, he left troops behind in Silurian territory to build forts. Some of these men were ambushed by the Silures and some senior staff were killed. A potential disaster was only averted when the governor returned in person to take command (Tacitus, *Annals* xii, 38). The fort at Clyro, near Hay-on-Wye, may have been one of these forts; if not, then it was begun a few years later either by the next governor, Didius Gallus, or his successor, Veranius. It was a 26 acre (10.5ha) vexillation fortress, overlooking the west bank of the Wye. It was rectangular in plan, and there is evidence of the periods of building, taken by some to indicate two forts of slightly differing dimensions, one built shortly afterwards over the other. Clyro was abandoned by about AD75. There is scope for further excavation, since

to date no internal buildings have been found.

COED-Y-CAERAU Gwent
ST 379917 *Fortlet*
A small earth fortlet of about 2 acres (0.8ha) protected by ditching, little is known of Coed-y-Caerau but it has been suggested that because of its high position towering over several miles of the Usk valley, it was an observation post for the great legionary fortress at Caerleon (*Isca*) about 3 miles down the Usk.

COELBREN GAER West Glamorgan
SN 859108 *Fort*
Coelbren Gaer was a late first-century timber and earth fort, about 5.2 acres (2ha) in area. First laid out probably in the AD70s as a small fort by the road from Brecon Gaer to Neath (Margary 622) for up to a thousand infantry or about five hundred cavalry, it was surrounded by a rampart of clay and turf reinforced with brushwood, or with logs at the corners, some of the rampart being upon a base of rough stones. There was a ditch on either side of the rampart. The fort was abandoned in the middle of the second century. Some of the rampart is still visible. The fort was excavated at the beginning of the century and the principal finds are now in Swansea Museum. The site has been re-examined, the last time in 1960-1.

COLLFRYN Powys
SJ 222173 *Camp*
Some evidence of the rampart and ditching of a camp at Collfryn, Llansantffraid Deytheur, has been found in very recent excavation work. Roman pottery fragments of the second to fourth centuries were uncovered.

COWBRIDGE South Glamorgan
SS 994748 *Building*
Recent excavations in Cowbridge (especially in High Street and behind The Bear Hotel) by the Glamorgan-Gwent Archaeological Trust, uncovered remains of a thirteen-roomed building of the first to second centuries. The foundations indicate a structure of limestone and sandstone blocks,

roofed with tiles some of which bore the inscription LEG.II.AUG. There was a small furnace room in the early phase, which was later replaced by a much larger furnace room. The structure appears to have been abandoned by the close of the second century, due to flooding, and the site was then farmed. The nature of the building is not yet determined, but may have been an administrative block.

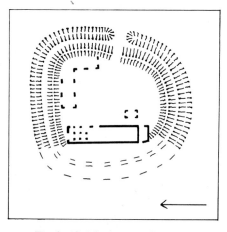

The fortified farmstead at Cwmbrwyn

CWMBRWYN Dyfed
SN 256123 *Farmstead*
This is the site of a Roman farm. In 1906, a narrow rectangular building, about 30m (100ft) long, surrounded by ditched earthworks, was discovered and stated to be a military structure because of its position inside a fortified enclosure. The enclosure was thought to be a fortlet, but recent opinion, following excavations of the late 1960s, is that it was a farm building inside a protective enclosure which also featured a small smithy, a furnace and some pits. There was evidence of iron clinker and charcoal. The building may have contained a corn drier. Several querns were found on the site.

DERWYDD-BACH Gwynedd
SH 477454 *Marching camp*
Remains of a 15 acre (6ha) marching camp have been found at Derwydd-bach. Parts of a rampart about 3m (10ft) wide, in front of

which was a ditch about 2.5m (8ft) wide, have been traced for nearly 45m (50yd) along the north-west, and for 108m (120yd) or so on the south-west. The camp is about a third of a mile from the fort at Pen Llysten.

DINAS POWYS South Glamorgan
ST 151709 *Roman earthworks*
A complex of Roman military earthworks has been surveyed here from the air, spreading over most of the common.

DIN LLIGWY Gwynedd
SH 496862 *Fortified village*
A late fourth-century Celtic fortified village built in pentagonal plan, ¾ mile north-west of Llanallgo Church, may have been built by an Anglesey chief. The regular plan and the tidy arrangement of rectangular and cylindrical buildings suggest that the enclosure may have been built with Roman help. The two circular huts were residences, the other buildings workshops, two of them ironsmith sheds. The building on the east wall of the enclosure was the gatehouse. Some of the walling survives to about 1.5m (5ft) and consists of limestone facings upon rubble filling.

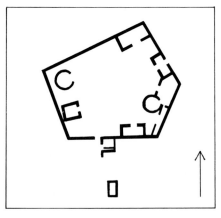

The fortified fourth-century village at Din Lligwy

DINORBEN Clwyd
SH 968757 *Hillfort*
The remains of Dinorben hillfort are swiftly disappearing under quarry activities beside

478

it. The fort was a Bronze Age hillfort of about the ninth century BC. It has been extensively excavated this century, and the work is not yet finished. The hillfort was occupied in Roman times, though it does not seem to have been greatly improved with Roman help. Evidence for timber lacing of the ramparts has been found, as have many Romano-British artefacts, sherds and some traces of buildings of uncertain date; coins of the third and fourth centuries have also been discovered. The site was abandoned for a while and a date for reoccupation has been suggested at c260.

DISCOED Powys
SO 268653 *Fort*
A small rectangular fort, about 135×90m (455×305ft), was recently found as a result of aerial observation on a crest in the upper valley of the river Lugg. There are traces of its defences. It is thought to have been of pre-Flavian date, perhaps built in the early campaign against the Ordovices (AD50s).

DOLAU Powys
SO 018666 *Fort*
About 3 miles north of Castell Collen fort are two adjacent sides of a small 4 acre (1.6ha) fort, or camp, beside the A44. There is little to see except for very slight ramparting.

DOLAUCOTHI Dyfed
SN 664394 *Roman gold mines*
The gold mines at Dolaucothi, near Pumpsaint, are the only ones of the Roman period so far found in Britain. They are also some of the most astonishing of all Roman remains anywhere in the country. Careful excavation over the years, particularly in the past decade or so, under the auspices of the Dolaucothi Research Committee, has enabled us to get a very detailed idea of the workings of a Roman mine. Today, much can be seen. The tunnels leading to the galleries and shafts below, some 43m (145ft) below the ground, were drained by water-wheels, a portion of one of which has been found and is in the National Museum of Wales. Here, criminals and slaves worked out a life sentence in appalling conditions, cramped for hours every day, with little ventilation, breathing in foul air, the working area only lit by oil lamps. Above ground, there was open-cast mining. Vast quantities of water were employed in many processes, and the water was brought along three aqueducts, simple channels cut in the hillside, one of which was 7 miles long. Some are still traceable up the valley of the Cothi. The 7 mile system was capable of moving three million gallons of water in a full day to a series of reservoirs that were sited on the hilltops over the mines. Some of the water was used to break down soft beds of gold-bearing rock by sending it down the slopes on to the soil and vegetation over the rock, carrying it away. The same waters were also used for washing the ore after it had been crushed in special stone mills, and then panned in wooden cradles, one of which has survived. The water was also channelled into baths near the mine-heads for the workers.

The gold mines were almost certainly held by the Roman government and at first operated by Roman army personnel. The first workings started probably in the AD70s, but perhaps by 100 or so, contracts had begun to be let to operators. The works were clearly important economically to the imperial finances, for a fort was built nearby at Pumpsaint to protect them. This fort, built in the 70s, lasted until the Antonine period, during which time it was reduced in size when the Romans felt secure that they needed only a handful of men to control the industry.

The Dolaucothi complex is now owned by the National Trust and is easy to explore by means of sensible signposts and direction arrows. The site is just off the main A482 Llandovery–Lampeter road, on the outskirts of Pumpsaint.

DOLDINNAS Gwynedd
SH 734378 *Practice camps*
Two miles along the road from Tomen-y-Mur to Caer Gai is a series of five practice camps, each with two entrances. They are regarded as being among the best examples of surviving practice camps in Wales.

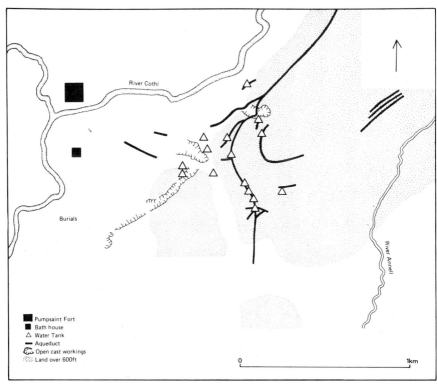

River Cothi

Burials

Pumpsaint Fort
Bath house
△ Water Tank
▬ Aqueduct
Open cast workings
Land over 600ft

River Annell

0   1km

ELY South Glamorgan
ST 147762 *Villa*
A winged corridor villa at Ely, near Cardiff, was built in the second century inside a ditched enclosure, and was renovated in the third century. There were associated farm buildings and an iron smithy. The site was excavated but is no longer visible. Fragments of plaster from walls were found to have been decorated, and pieces of marble flooring were also found.

ERGLODD Dyfed
SN 653903 *Fortlet*
Aerial photographs exposed a fortlet at Erglodd, near Talybont, midway between the forts at Pennal and Pen Llwyn. Examination has shown that it was about ⅝ acre (0.25ha) and lay on a hillock at the northern end of the valley through which the modern A487 runs. There appear to have been two periods: (I) a turf rampart inside a V-shaped ditch enclosure, with evidence of palisading; (II) the rampart was levelled and the ditch filled in, over which a new turf and clay rampart was erected.

ESGAIRPERFYDD Powys
SN 927699 *Marching camp*
The earthworks of a 17 acre (7ha) marching camp here, perhaps of the first century, are still traceable all round, with wide entrances on the four sides.

FFRITH Clwyd
SJ 285552 *Lead mining site*
There was a settlement here, associated with lead mining.

FORDEN GAER Powys
SO 208989 *Fort*
Very little can now be seen of this 7½ acre (3ha) fort which has an interesting history. It lay on the main Roman route (Margary 64) from Caersws to Wroxeter, overlooking the river Severn. Though it could be argued that

(*opposite above*) The gold mines at Dolaucothi and (*below*) the entrance to gold mine at Dolaucothi with (in foreground) part of Roman water-wheel found at the site

it was built during Suetonius' campaign in Wales (58–60), to link Wroxeter fort and the first fort at Caersws raised in the same campaign, the earliest datable evidence for Forden Gaer is the AD70s, that is, under Frontinus or Agricola. The fort was large for an auxiliary cavalry unit, and it was defended by a clay and turf rampart and a ditch 2.5m (8ft) deep in places, which may have been complemented by other ditch systems at some time in the fort's long life.

The fort appears to have been abandoned during Domitian's later years (AD90s), rebuilt in Trajan's reign (98–117), burnt possibly as a result of attack c160, rebuilt again, burnt a second time early in the third century, and rebuilt yet again at least twice, the last time being towards the end of the fourth century. This is a remarkably long history for a fort that does not seem to have had much stonework, which must have meant frequent renovations of the timber and earthwork. The site consists largely of cultivated fields today.

In 1975–6, pupils of Newton High School, under imaginative guidance, discovered a substantial building on the site, with a floor of white clay, some piers of cobble and rough stones interspersed with cobble walling, which had supported roofing of local slate.

GELLIGAER Mid Glamorgan
ST 134971 *Forts*
Gelligaer fort (second) has been described as 'one of the classic military sites of the Roman Empire, providing a text-book example, in the Trajanic stone fort, of the accommodation required by a quingenary cohort of foot' (Boon, G. C. *Wales: an Illustrated Guide to the Ancient Monuments*, 1978, p 34). Sadly, however, although this is true when considering the detailed layout unveiled in excavations between 1899 and 1901, the whole has been back-filled, the stonework has disappeared and only the outline of the ramparting is now visible. The plan, however, was drawn and a comprehensive description prepared by J. Ward in *The Roman Fort of Gelligaer* (1903).

The stone fort was built in the first decade of the second century. It covered 3½ acres (1.5ha) and was intended for a garrison of

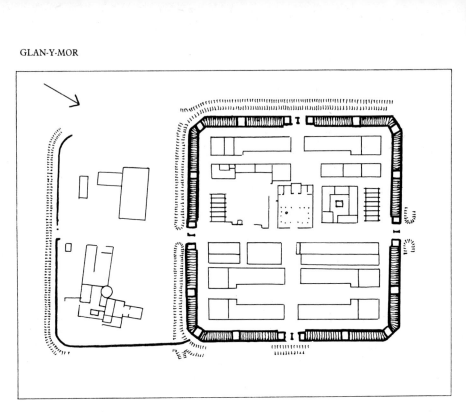

Gelligaer Fort II, with the annexe containing external bath house

five hundred. It was a square fort, with a stone-faced rampart (faced on both sides), surrounded by a single, mainly V-shaped ditch, but here and there, W-shaped. Two gateways (south-west and north-east) opened on to drawbridges over the ditches. Stone turrets were positioned at the four corners and between the corners and the gates, and these were about 5m (16ft) square. Some were built as an integral part of the rampart wall.

There has been discussion as to whether the fort was for infantry or for cavalry and infantry mixed. The barrack remains indicated infantry but left a number of other buildings unsatisfactorily explained, some of which could have been quarters for troops of cavalry, and stables. The *principia* had a courtyard surrounded by an open veranda. Beside the north-west and south-east gates were two granaries, 16 × 7m (17½ × 8yd) internally, which probably held enough stored grain to supply the fort complement

for a year. Outside the fort, on the south-east wall, was an annexe about half the area of the fort, which was used as a parade ground and contained a bath house with painted plaster walls.

The fort was apparently abandoned in Antonine times (138–61), reoccupied soon afterwards and renovated in the early third century, though not necessarily as the result of hostile action. It was held in the fourth century. There was an earlier fort at Gelligaer, of 5½ acres (2ha), next to the later fort, a little higher up the hill. This was probably built in Flavian times, but there is nothing to see today.

GLAN-Y-MOR South Glamorgan
ST 099664 *Administrative Building*
A remarkable discovery has been made at Cold Knap, near Barry, in excavations begun in 1980 on the north side of Porth-kerry Bay by a team sponsored by the Glamorgan–Gwent Archaeological Trust, under its director, G. Dowdell. It is of the remains of a one-phase building of some twenty-two rooms and cellars arranged

482

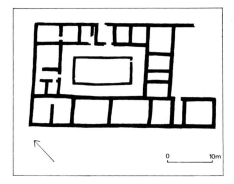

Sketch plan of the administration block discovered at Glan-y-Mor in 1980

round a courtyard, with verandah, the overall dimensions of the block being about 44m (48yd) east–west by 24m (26yd) north–south, with an annexe to the south-east. The absence of domestic fittings suggests an administrative block, and from its site the team believes it may be connected with naval activity. Up to the seventeenth century the area to the south-east used to be a harbour, and if it was a harbour in Roman times, then the block could have been navy offices. The block appears to have been in use for about two centuries (second to fourth). The importance of the discovery led the Welsh Office Ancient Monuments Branch and the local authority jointly to purchase it for conservation and further excavation, and it is being laid out as an ancient monument. This began as a rescue operation in advance of development. Up to the discovery, the received view was that the Roman navy had its south Welsh base at or near Cardiff.

HADNOCK FARM Gwent
SO 536152 *Settlement*
A civilian settlement of many buildings ranging over the second and third centuries at Hadnock Farm, Monmouth, was centred on a number of metal industries, including ironworks. One building had a hypocaust and painted wall plaster. Another contained iron-working apparatus, including a bloom. Also found was a bowl furnace for reworking bronze.

HEN WALIAU Gwynedd
SH 482624 *Enclosure*
About 135m (150yd) to the west of the fort of *Segontium* (Caernarfon) is a remarkable stretch of Roman stone wall, about 6m (20ft) tall in places, associated with a filled-in gate of the same period, in the garden of a private house. This is the visible remains of an extensive enclosure, some 69×50m (230×165ft), which was once thought to be another fort but which is now seen as a storage depot connected with a harbour in the edge of the river Seiont below. The walling is over 2m (6ft) thick. The enclosure probably dates from the second century.

HIRFYNYDD West Glamorgan
SN 828067 *Fortlet*
A fortlet on the Hirfynydd hills may have been a signal station or police post. It was on the road between the forts at Neath and Coelbren Gaer (Margary 622).

HOLT Clwyd
SJ 404546 *Pottery and tilery*
At Holt, on the river Dee, a substantial pottery and tile works run for a time by Legio XX supplied the garrison at Chester legionary fortress. A number of kilns and workers' quarters nearby have been traced. The kilns were of some interest, since they were spread over a large area of about 20 acres (8ha). One group of six kilns was ranged in a bank and they were all provided with heat from one furnace area, probably fired in rotation.

HOLYHEAD MOUNTAIN Gwynedd
SH 218829 *Watchtower*
Excavations in 1980–1 on the summit of Holyhead Mountain, Anglesey, located foundations of a square, stone building, about 6sq m (7sq yd), the walls of which were about 1.25m (4ft) thick. The structure was probably a watchtower, perhaps linked with the fort at Caer Gybi. Coins found by the site included some dating from the end of the fourth century.

LLANDEILO Dyfed
SN 633222 *?Fort*
Aerial photography has revealed two sides of

a rectangular enclosure, about 200×180m (220×198yd), with rounded corners (playing-card shape). This may have been a fort of about 7½ acres (3ha).

LLANDOUGH South Glamorgan
ST 168731 *Villa*
A late Iron Age settlement with a Roman villa superimposed upon it was excavated in 1977-8 at Llandough, by the Glamorgan-Gwent Archaeological Trust, with assistance from the Manpower Services Commission. The remains of the Iron Age farmstead included a vestigial circular building about 7.5m (25ft) across (possibly a round house). The earliest phase of the Roman villa has been dated to the mid second century, and it consisted of a residential block with several rooms and/or passages, one of which had sandstone supports for a hypocaust. The second phase (third century) was more extensive, and it included a bath house with painted wall plaster, two rooms in the central part and remains of a third room. Part of this range was raised over a filled-in ditch of the earlier phase. There was also a long, rectangular building which may have been a barn, 6.5×12.5m (22×42ft), further north but joined to the range by a wall. The site was covered by new building work after 1978.

LLANDOVERY Dyfed
SN 770352 *Fort*
Little remains of the first-century fort here, which overlooks the Towy valley. It began as a 5-6 acre (2-2.5ha) fort, probably built during the campaign of Frontinus in south and west Wales in the mid AD70s against the Silures, though it is held in some quarters that its beginnings may be earlier, cAD50. The fort was defended by a clay bank revetted with stone in the Trajanic period (98-117). It was probably abandoned by the Romans in the second century.

LLANDRINDOD COMMON Powys
SO 0559 to 0560 *Practice camps*
Some 18 practice camps built by legionaries and auxiliaries from nearby Castell Collen fort and elsewhere have been identified at Llandrindod, and most of them can still be

seen in one form or another. There is evidence of *titula*-protected entrances, long stretches of rampart and some of the familiar rounded 'playing card' type corners.

LLANDRINIO Powys
SJ 267135 *?Camp*
Two stretches of parallel ditching, about 11m (12yd) apart, were found here under Severn mud. Fragments of pottery, one of which has been dated to the first half of the second century, are in the Welshpool Museum. The site could be a camp.

LLANDULAS Powys
SN 876404 *Fort*
A 13 acre (5ha) fort, double-ditched and rectangular in plan, Llandulas was built on the side of a ridge overlooking a tributary. M. J. Jones suggests it may be a pre-Flavian fort.

LLANEDEYRN South Glamorgan
ST 199813 *Pottery kiln*
A pottery kiln was found at Llanedeyrn, near Cardiff, following the discovery of a coin hoard of nearly 1100 Roman coins on a new housing estate. The coins ranged from c270 to c273, and included *antoniniani* and several local counterfeits; they are now in the National Museum of Wales. The kiln was associated with third-century sherds.

LLANFAIR CAEREINION Powys
SN 9250 *Fortlet*
A fortification of about ⅝ acre (0.25ha) on Gibbet Hill was excavated in the nineteenth century, and re-examined in 1962. The rampart and ditch are in fair condition, and they appear to be part of an uncompleted fortlet.

LLANFOR Gwynedd
SH 938361 *Fort*
A 9 acre (3.5ha) fort was built at Llanfor in the AD70s, probably by Frontinus, near the confluence of the rivers Dee and Tryweryn at the eastern end of Lake Bala. It was seen by aerial reconnaissance in 1974, and this revealed three ditches and some rampart. Traces of some of the fort's timber buildings were detected, including a granary and

barrack blocks. Further air reconnaissance in 1977 indicated more buildings, and also a polygonal annexe, which may have been a forward stores compound. The fort seems large for an auxiliary unit, but excavation in the future may help to explain its role.

LLANFRYNACH Powys
SO 0625 *Villa*
There was a villa at Llanfrynach, in the Usk valley, not far from the fort at Brecon Gaer. Excavations revealed part of the bath suite which had mosaic flooring.

LLANFRYNACH South Glamorgan
SS 981746 *Enclosure*
A rectangular enclosure at Llanfrynach, near Cowbridge, was examined in the mid 1970s. It was surrounded by a bank. Pottery remains included Samian ware, and a tile with the stamp LEG II AVG was found. Legio II *Augusta* was stationed for some time at the fortress at Caerleon.

LLANIO Dyfed
SN 644564 *Fort: Roman name* Bremia
Llanio fort is identified in the *Ravenna Cosmography* as the fort of *Bremia*. The first fort on the site was built c75. The second fort involved a reduction in size, perhaps about thirty years afterwards. Several phases of timber buildings have been noted in excavations, particularly during the late 1960s and early 1970s. Also found and now visible are the remains of a stone bath house, with some hypocausts; the *tepidarium, frigidarium* and *caldarium* were revealed. Additionally, foundations and parts of a colonnade of a *praetorium* were found, probably dating from the early second century. Artefacts examined suggest that the fort was no longer in use by the middle of the second century. For a period in the early second century the fort was occupied by the second cohort of Asturian cavalry. The remains of the fort are not well cared for, but they can be seen by leave from the owner of Isaf Farm. The excavations of 1969–73 were directed by J. L. Davies, for University College, Aberystwyth.

LLANTWIT MAJOR South Glamorgan
SS 958699 *Villa*
This was one of only a handful of villas built in Wales. It had two principal periods: the first, from the first to the start of the third century, and the second, from the third to

A reconstructed piece of roof, with finial, from Llantwit Major villa

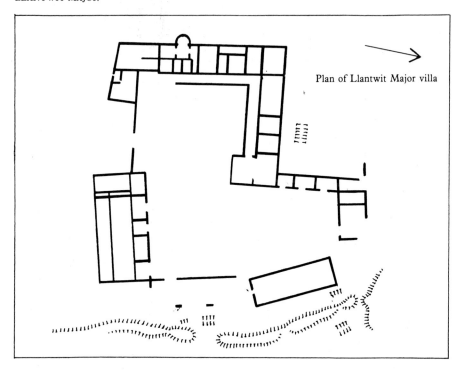

Plan of Llantwit Major villa

Reconstruction of Llantwit Major villa

the late fourth century. The villa began as a simple cottage-type in timber, built on the site of an earlier Iron Age settlement within a ditched enclosure. The timber cottage was then converted to a rectangular stone block, without corridors, sometime in the mid second century. There appears to have been a decline in the villa during the early third century, but in the 270s it received fresh attention. The cottage was greatly enlarged, a bath suite was added, extensions developed at west and east ends and corridors provided. In about 300 a large aisled building was erected to the south-east, about 12m (40ft) from the main ranges; and in the early fourth century, mosaics, painted wall plaster and other decorative features were introduced.

The purpose of the aisled building has been argued for some time. Some authorities call it a *basilica*, which is architecturally right; others believe it was a farm building. Certainly, an iron-working furnace was inserted at one end some time in the fourth century, when the residential part of the villa was abandoned altogether, and the complex administered by an absentee landlord.

LLAWHADEN Dyfed
SN 0719 *Settlement*
There was Roman-style occupation at Llawhaden, marked by enclosures with ditching and finds of Roman coarse pottery. Traces of granaries and other structures were located, and more detailed material may emerge in further work on the site.

LLYS BRYCHAN Dyfed
SN 705255 *Roman-style farm and villa*
This was an interesting Roman-style residence near Llangadog in the Towy valley. Excavated in advance of erecting new farm buildings on a present-day farm, the remains showed the existence of a substantial civilian residence built round three sides of a courtyard. Among the findings were part of the hypocaust, several rooms with stretches of wall 1m (3ft) or more tall surviving, some with paintings, and much pottery. It is believed that the west peninsula of Wales, occupied by the Demetae, was not occupied by the Romans in force because the tribe had 'freely accepted Roman rule'. The residence

may therefore have been the home of a Demetae noble co-operating with the authorities. There are other 'Romanised' farmsteads in this part of Wales (see Cwmbrwyn). The dating of Llys Brychan is put at between 200 and 300.

LOUGHOR West Glamorgan
SS 564979 *Fort: Roman name* Leucarum
For a long time the location of the fort of *Leucarum*, listed in the *Antonine Itinerary* (Iter 12), was not known, but was suspected of lying at or near Loughor, placed as it is on or near the Roman road from Carmarthen to Neath (Margary 60d or another road nearby). Then, in 1969, remnants of a fort of some 5 acres (2ha) were found during excavation at Loughor medieval castle, on the east side of the river Loughor estuary, which was built in the south-east corner of the fort (cf Brough, Pevensey and Portchester for examples of medieval castles placed in old Roman fort enclosures). Loughor fort appears to have had a long history, founded c75 and still in occupation in the early fourth century.

A stone wall was built into the outward face of the rampart, some time in the first quarter of the second century, made of sandstone blocks. Thereafter, the excavations, particularly those of 1972–3, revealed a complicated series of ditch-cutting, filling and re-cutting. Likewise, several phases of both timber and stone internal buildings were revealed, including a succession of granaries and a bath house with concrete floor and drainage channels, with evidence of painted wall plaster (rarely found in auxiliary forts in Wales). Some of the stone walling can be seen in the south of the motte of the medieval castle.

MELIN COURT West Glamorgan
SN 837001 *Camp*
In 1974, a marching camp of about 12 acres (4.8ha) was found at Melin Court, near Clyne, between Neath and Brecon, about 2 miles east-north-east of the marching camp at Blaen-cwm-Bach. Its date is not known but may be guessed as the AD70s. It lies across the track known as Cefn Ffordd, and some lengths of rampart can be seen.

487

MYNYDD CARN GOCH
West Glamorgan SS 609972
Practice camps
Two practice camps were built here by
Roman troops on the ridge of Mynydd Carn
Goch, perhaps in Frontinus' time (mid 70s),
associated with Loughor fort.

NEATH West Glamorgan
SS 748977 *Fort: Roman name* Nidum
This is the fort known as *Nidum* mentioned
in the *Antonine Itinerary* (Iter 12). It was
discovered in 1949, though its existence had
been suspected for many years previously,
since Neath is at the southern seaside end of
the major Roman route south-westwards
from Brecon Gaer, crossing the coast road
from Carmarthen to Cardiff and Caerleon.
The fort is on the west bank of the estuary of
the river Neath, and lies across the present
Neath–Pontadawe road. The fort began as
an earth and timber construction of
Frontinus' time (74–8), but we are not able to
adduce its dimensions. Later, it was rebuilt
on a new alignment and the rampart was of
pink-hued clay. Then in Hadrianic times
(117–38) much of the timber work was converted to stone. Remains of the gateways at
the south and the south-east have survived
and can be seen on the housing estate
nearby, beside Roman Way. The rebuilt fort
was square, and was nearly 6 acres (2.4ha)
internally.

PANT-TEG-UCHAF Dyfed
SN 647485 *Practice camps*
Two practice camps, one of them in an
unfinished state on the north and west, are
probably of Flavian date.

PEN BRYN-Y-EGLWYS Gwynedd
SH 293924 *?Watchtower*
There are remains of what was probably a
watchtower, about 6m (20ft) square, on the
summit of Carmel Head, Anglesey (see
Holyhead Mountain).

PEN LLWYN Dyfed
SN 650806 *Fort*
What appears to be a short-life fort, on a 60m
(200ft) ridge, of about 7 acres (3ha), was
excavated in 1977–8 at Pen Llwyn, Capel

Bangor, and some triple-ditch and rampart
sections were examined. Near the west
corner, evidence was found of a possible
corner tower of timber, including fragments
of the matrix of an 18cm (7in) square timber
post. The fort was occupied probably
between c80 and c130. It is near to a better
known Bronze Age settlement.

PEN LLYSTEN Gwynedd
SH 481449 *Fort*
Pen Llysten began as a 3¾ acre (1.5ha)
auxiliary fort built in AD78 or 79 by Agricola.
The plan has been revealed by excavation
and is said to be the most complete plan of a
timber fort in Wales. It was originally
intended for a mixed contingent of infantry
and cavalry. Its rampart was of gravel and
boulders revetted each side by turf cheeks,
about 4.5m (15ft) wide. The ditch system
was double. The fort appears to have had
angle towers, each on six main upright posts.
In about AD90 it was dismantled. There is
evidence that reconstruction was planned
soon afterwards, on a smaller scale, but this
was abandoned. Then, in about 100, a fortlet
of about 1 acre (0.4ha) was built in the older
fort's north-east corner, defended by a new
rampart on a cobble base. The fortlet was a
police post, and not for a military detachment, though there is some evidence of
living quarters. It had one gateway. The fort
was occupied for about thirty years. In 1976
a fragment of a Samian bowl stamped
PATERCLIM was found in the part of the fort
that is on the modern quarry face, and this
has been identified as Samian ware of
between 100 and 125, which confirms the
dates of occupation.

PEN-MIN-CAE Powys
SO 006539 *Fortlet*
Aerial reconnaissance identified a fortlet of
about ⅓ acre (0.1ha) on the north bank of the
Wye, on a farm. Excavation subsequently
produced some fragments of Samian ware.
The fortlet is midway between Castell
Collen and the fort at Beulah (Caerau).

PENNAL Gwynedd
SH 705001 *Fort*
A nearly square fort 135×123m (450×412ft)

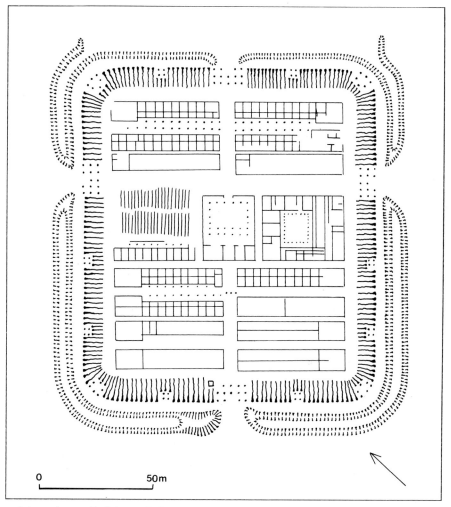

Plan of Pen Llysten fort

of about 4 acres (1.6ha), was built on a spur projecting into the Dyfi valley near a crossing in the river. Marshland protected the site on at least two sides. One road from the fort southwards to the river near Llugwy, and another from the north to Pennal village, were spotted by aerial observation. The buildings in the fort appear to have been chiefly of wood, but there were traces of stonework suggesting a bath house. Pennal was begun in the Flavian period.

PENTRE FARM Clwyd
SJ 254723 *Fort, mine and industrial site*
A complex site on the outskirts of present-day Fflint, known as Pentre Ffwrndau, lies towards the bottom of Halkyn Mountain which edges the shore of the Dee. The Romans mined lead on the mountain slopes from the late first century to the early third. They built a fort there in the AD70s, equipped with a garrison to protect the mining area, as they had done at Charterhouse in Mendip. The fort was later built over. Recent excavations round Pentre Farm have exposed foundations of a residence with villa characteristics, with an outside bath house, which overlay part of the first fort. The residence may have been the official home of the mine overseer. After about 200

489

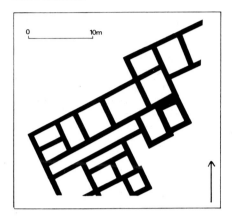

0   10m

The bath house recently discovered at Pentre Farm, near Fflint

the residence was converted into a lead processing works, and was then abandoned altogether.

PEN-Y-COEDCAE Mid Glamorgan
ST 059878 *Marching camps*
Traces of three marching camps remain here; one was 37 acres (15ha) in area.

PEN-Y-CROGBREN Powys
SN 856935 *Fortlet/signal post*
An almost square earthwork fortified enclosure of about ⅛ acre (0.05ha), probably of the second century, lies beside the road from Caersws fort to Pennal fort, south of the deserted village of Dylife. Part of the rampart survives to a height of 1m (3ft). Excavation exposed traces of a timber gate-tower on its single entrance. Dylife was the site of a lead works, and the enclosure may have been erected to protect it, though it is also argued that the enclosure was a signal station on the road.

PEN-Y-DARREN Mid Glamorgan
SO 0506 *Fort*
First discovered as a fort in 1901, Pen-y-Darren was excavated in 1902–4 and again in 1956–7. It covered about 5 acres (2ha) on a steep-sided spur. Raised during the Flavian period, with timber and stone buildings, the fort appears to have ceased to be used after the mid second century.

PEN-Y-GAER Powys
SO 169219 *Fort*
The 3¾ acre (1.5ha) fort here lies halfway between the larger forts at Abergavenny and Brecon Gaer. Erected by Frontinus to control the route through the Usk valley, stone walling was added in Trajan's time (98–117) and the fort was apparently abandoned in the 130s. It was excavated in 1966 and some remains can be seen, particularly on the north side.

PEN-Y-GWRHYD Gwynedd
SH 6655 *Marching camp*
A 9½ acre (4ha) marching camp of rhomboid plan, with one entrance, traces of Pen-y-Gwrhyd can still be seen, chiefly the rampart on the south side. It is off the A4086.

PONT RHYD SARN Gwynedd
SH 860278 *Practice camp*
Traces of a practice camp, occupying approximately 80×50m (265×165ft), have been detected.

PORTH FELEN Gwynedd
SH 145247 *Anchor stock*
In 1974, excavation off the shore at Porth Felen, near Aberdaron, revealed a most interesting Roman anchor stock. It weighed 71kg (156lb) and has been dated to the first century BC, since it is like several similar anchors of that period discovered in the Mediterranean. The anchor is so far the only one of its kind found in British waters, and it is at present in the National Museum of Wales.

PRESTATYN Clwyd
SJ 061817 *Fort*
The adjacent sides of a fort were seen from the air in 1976 and were verified by excavation. It is not yet possible firmly to date the fort, but fragments of a sandstone column of the mid second century were found. There was a civilian settlement to the south-east, first discovered by excavation in the 1930s. The fort lies to the north-east of the harbour area beside Prestatyn. It was probably used for supervision of the lead and silver mines in Halkyn Mountain.

PUMPSAINT Dyfed
SN 656406 *Fort*
Some rescue excavations in the grounds of
The Dolaucothi Arms Hotel in 1972
revealed evidence of an earth and timber
rectangular fort of about 5½ acres (2ha),
built in the AD70s. It was clearly a fort for
controlling the gold mines at Dolaucothi
nearby. The rampart was of turf and clay
and the ditch was W-shaped. There appear
to have been seven building phases in the
fort's interior (one street had had eleven
successive surfaces), and even the alignments
were altered in some phases. At the turn of
the first century, the fort was reduced in size
by more than half, and it was enclosed by a
stone wall. Among the stone buildings put
up at this time or soon after was a granary,
with walls a metre thick. Also found were the
remains of four *fabricae*, with bowl furnaces,
which may have been used for working the
gold from the nearby mines into ingots, bars
or perhaps jewellery. Traces of the *principia*
of the fort were found.

Pumpsaint fort seems to have been
abandoned in the Antonine period (138–61).
Outside, traces have been discovered of a
vicus for personnel working in the mine
complex. These include several yards of
timber waterfronting along the south bank of
the Cothi river.

PYLE Mid Glamorgan
SS 827822 *Milestone*
A rectangular milestone, about 1.35m (4ft
6in) tall, was found in 1845 at Pyle, on the
Roman road from Cardiff to Neath
(Margary 60c). It is dated to Victorinus
(268–70) and is now in Swansea Museum.

ST HARMON Powys
SN 985717 *Marching camp*
A 19 acre (7.7ha) marching camp with
clavicula entrance on the south side is partly
visible.

SARN HELEN Gwynedd
SH 738469 *Stretch of road*
Sarn Helen is the name given to that part of
the Roman road north–south from Caerhun
fort into the mountains that runs across the
hills between Betws-y-Coed to Tomen-y-

Mur fort (Margary 69a). Some of the line of
the road was unconfirmed though suggested
by Margary. The stretch between Rhiwbach
Quarry and the Cwm Penamnen was an
unconfirmed part, but this has now been
given extra evidential support following the
examination of drainage ditches cut across
the road line at Penmachno, which revealed
traces of slate paving edged with a kerb of
boulders.

STACKPOLE WARREN Dyfed
SR 981950 *Circular house*
A Romano-British circular house erected
against a wall was located beside the Bronze
Age standing stone at Stackpole. So far, some
Samian and black burnished ware have been
recovered. Examination is continuing by the
Dyfed Archaeological Trust.

TOMEN-Y-MUR Gwynedd
SH 706386 *Fort*
Placed in an exposed position and
surrounded by magnificent scenery, Tomen-
y-Mur stands on the crossroads where the
old Roman roads from Caernarfon to Caer
Gai (Margary 68) and from Caerhun down
the western edge of Wales to Carmarthen
(Margary 69a, 69b, 69c, 69d) intersected, a
few miles inland from Cardigan Bay, near
Trawsfynydd. The fort was probably built in
AD78 by Frontinus or Agricola (we do not
know which). The first fort occupied about
4 acres (1.6ha), for auxiliary forces (chiefly
cavalry). It was enclosed by a rampart of clay
which may in some places have been revetted
with timber. This was surrounded by
double-ditching. The fort's role changed in
Trajan's time (98–117) when it appears to
have housed infantry only. The ditches were
filled in and a new ditch was cut in the berm.
In Hadrianic times (117–38) it was reduced
in size and given some stone walls (now
vanished). The smaller fort is the rectangle
to the south-east associated with the Norman
motte that stands astride the west wall.

To the north-west the Roman garrisons
built practice camps, and to the north-east a
parade ground which has siege engine platforms (see Hardknott). North of the parade
ground are the remains of a small amphi-

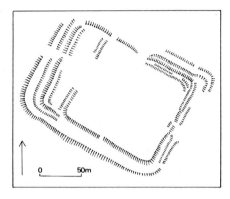

Plan of Tomen-y-Mur fort

theatre. This is the only such building in Roman Britain that is associated with an auxiliary fort. Opinion in some quarters holds that its main role was as a drill ground, and that entertainments within its walls were a secondary feature. Among the many other finds were stone buildings including a bath house, now disappeared, which yielded evidence for sustained pottery and tile making. The fort was abandoned in the early Antonine period.

TRAWSCOED Dyfed
SN 671727 *Fort*
Discovered in 1959, Trawscoed fort, Llanafan, about 4¾ acres (2ha) and built by Frontinus, lies between the forts of Pennal and Llanio. Part of the ditch outside the rampart was cut through rock which was later filled in and acted as a base for the rampart being extended over it. A fresh ditch was cut in front of the rampart, about 1m (3ft) deep, with a cleaning slot. Just beyond, some traces of a timber building were found in 1974. Inside the fort, various changes took place over the fort's relatively short life, before it was evacuated in the early 120s. The modern B4575 road runs through the site.

TWYN-Y-BRIDDALLT Mid Glamorgan
ST 002982 *Marching camp*
A 16 acre (6.5ha) marching camp, with two entrances, was erected here probably in Frontinus's time (mid 70s). There are good sections of outline, and it is possible to see *claviculae* at the entrances.

TY-BRYN Mid Glamorgan
SS 916734 *Farmstead*
A small Romano-British farmstead enclosed by multiple ditches has been investigated at Ty-Bryn, Clemenston. Pottery of the second and third centuries was found, including coarse grey ware.

TY-MAWR HUTS Gwynedd
SH 212820 *Village*
On the south-west slope of Holyhead Mountain, Anglesey, about 2 miles west of Holyhead town, are the remains of an open village of some twenty circular and rectangular huts. There had been more than twice that number. They were built largely of stone slabs, and the circular huts had central hearths. They were occupied between the second and fourth centuries.

USK Gwent
SO 3700 *Legionary fortress and* vicus: *Roman name* Burrium
The fortress at Usk controlled an important route for communications along the narrow valley at the river Usk, and lay midway between the river estuary at Newport and the edge of the uplands at Abergavenny. The first fort at the site was Claudian. It covered 10 acres (4ha) and dates from not before AD49. Shortly after this in the mid 50s, a carefully planned Neronian legionary fortress was established. The rectangular area of 48 acres (20ha) was enclosed by a single bank of turves of about 4.25m (14ft) wide and a ditch 4–4.5m (13–15ft) wide on its north and east sides. To the south a double-ditch system was built in front of the bank and the defences of the west side are unknown. The proximity of the river may well have made only a ditch necessary as a defence. An unusual feature here was the presence of clay ovens set into the outer edge of the fortress ditch.

The east gate of the fortress has been excavated and found to have been about 13.5m (45ft) wide with a double portal flanked by two towers. The defensive ditch continued across the entrance to the fort and so access to the gate was made possible by a timber bridge. Inside the fort, in the area of the east gate, three large granaries have been excavated. These were set on a grid of posts which were placed in parallel trenches. The granaries with their loading bays were fronted by 14.5m (48ft) of cobbled forecourt. Other structures from the interior of the fortress include a set of smaller granaries, a complex building thought to be a tribune's house and possible workshops and store areas. The garrison (possibly Legio XX) was evacuated in the late 60s.

The fortress lost its importance as Caerleon developed only 8 miles away. In the mid 70s, the fortress was demolished and the site was probably used as an auxiliary fort or military works depot; timber buildings containing crucibles and scrap bronze have been traced. The gates give very good evidence of the demolition phase; the posts were deliberately uprooted rather than left to rot in their sockets. The *vicus*, however, continued to be occupied. A rectangular stone building dating from the mid second century has been excavated and three wells were in use until 350. This outdates the occupation of the fort, which appears to have ceased in the third century.

WALTON Powys
SO 257605 *Fort*
A Claudio-Neronian fort was built here, just east of Hindwell Farm. Traces of rampart can be seen, and the ditching, originally about 5m (16½ft) wide and 2.25m (7½ft) deep, was filled in later and re-cut to smaller dimensions. Finds included Claudian coins, a *ballista* bolt and pottery of Claudio-Neronian date. These are in the National Museum of Wales. The fort was erected during the campaign against the Ordovices in mid and north Wales in AD57–8.

WHITTON South Glamorgan
ST 081713 *Farmstead*
A Roman farmstead was excavated at Whitton, St Lythans, under M. G. Jarrett for the Department of the Environment in the late 1960s. It had been discovered in 1956 and was at first thought to be a villa,

but the extensive work of 1965–70 showed it to have been a prosperous farmstead already flourishing when the Romans first arrived in Wales.

The farmstead appears to have a complex story. It began as a group of Iron Age timber round houses inside a native square ditched enclosure of the first half of the first century AD. In early Roman times, rectilinear timber structures were raised over the older buildings, and in the second and third centuries some of these were replaced with stone buildings or newer timber buildings on stone foundations. One of the earlier timber structures on stone foundations was a military-style granary with an area of about 3.6sq m (40sq ft). This was later built over with a stone structure. Remains have also been found of interesting hypocausts, and of two T-shaped corn driers of stone, one of them inside the enclosure and associated with a stone tank. The site has since been destroyed by ploughing.

Y PIGWN Powys
SN 8231 *Marching camps*
A good example of a Roman legionary marching camp can still be seen on the summit of Trecastle Mountain, some 390m (1300ft) above sea level. This is Y Pigwn (The Beacon), a high plateau in the Brecon Beacons range, where in fact there are two marching camps, one of them 25 acres (10ha) inside but differently aligned, the other 37 acres (15ha). The larger camp was the earlier. Both were established in the period c50–75, the second perhaps by Frontinus. Most of the low height ramparting of both camps is visible, and the *clavicula* of the north gate of the smaller camp is well preserved. The camps are on the north side of the Roman road between Brecon Gaer and Llandovery (Margary 62c).

YSTRADFELLTE Powys
SN 924164 *Marching camp*
A 21 acre (8.5ha) marching camp, probably of the AD70s, constructed in a cleared site (which is now heathland) on the Brecon to Coelbren Roman route. It is easily accessible. Much of the low rampart is visible, especially on the south-east.

SCOTLAND

ABERNETHY Tayside
NO 174165 *Temporary camp*
One of the larger temporary camps built by
the Roman army on campaign in Scotland,
Abernethy was raised probably in the year of
Agricola's march to the Tay (*usque ad
Tanaum*), c80. It is rhomboid in shape;
the two longer sides (north and south) had
two gates each, with a single central gate in
the shorter sides. The area of Abernethy was
about 116 acres (46ha). The gates appear to
have been protected by a *titulum*.

ARDOCH Central
NN 839099 *Fort*
Ardoch is a complex site. It has left behind a
most interesting ditch and rampart system.
The first military installation was a fort of
Agricolan (or immediately post-Agricolan)
beginnings, and it was occupied for about
twenty years. Then it was abandoned, but in
the Antonine period it was reoccupied and
altered, as an outpost fort of the Antonine
Wall scheme. It is to this period that much of
the complicated ditch system belongs. The
defences consisted of a series of ditches and
ramparts in parallel, five systems on the east
and north, and an unknown number
(because of destruction) on the west and
south. On the north, there were flattened
areas. Across the east and north series, a
causeway served as the entrance from the
outside, though the fort had gates on the
innermost ramparting, of which traces exist.
  Close to the fort were a number of
marching camps, the traces of some of these
overlap. Two camps were Agricolan or
immediately afterwards, and two much
larger camps, one of about 130 acres (53ha),
date from the time of Severus' campaigning
in Scotland in the early third century.

Ardunie see **Gask Ridge**

AUCHENDAVY Strathclyde
NS 675749 *Antonine Wall fort*
A 3½ acre (1.5ha) fort was erected at
Auchendavy, near Kirkintilloch, as an intermediate fort between Balmuildy and
Castlecary. Little beyond the outline can be
seen today. Inscriptions indicate that the fort
was built by Legio II *Augusta* and that it was
garrisoned by detachments from the legion.

AUCHINHOVE Grampian
NJ 463517 *Temporary camp*
A 30 acre (12ha) temporary camp, probably
of the year of Mons Graupius (AD84),
Auchinhove is the most northerly Agricolan
Roman camp so far found in Scotland. It
appears to have been equipped with
Stracathro-type gates.

BALMUILDY Strathclyde
NS 581718 *Antonine Wall fort*
Balmuildy was one of only two Antonine
Wall forts equipped with stone defences (cf
Castlecary). It was built before the Wall
reached it, attested by the two stone wing
walls which had probably been added in
order to join up with a stonework Antonine
Wall. The plan was changed, however, and
when the Wall builders arrived, the Wall was
an earthen one. The fort was one of the first
of the whole Antonine scheme, and two
inscriptions prove that it was built by Legio
II *Augusta* under the supervision of Lollius
Urbicus, governor of Britain c138–44, who
started the project.
  The fort was nearly 4½ acres (1.8ha), with
buildings of stone and of timber. The
Military Way ran across the fort via the east
and west gates, in front of the central range

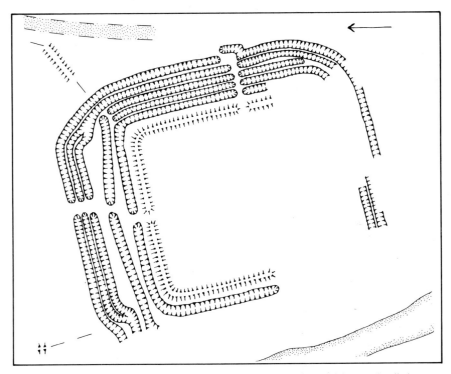

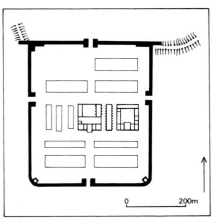

been for artillery pieces, such as *ballista*. The
buildings included a granary with drying
kilns. Just north-west of the fort, the
Antonine Wall extended over the river
Kelvin, with special drainage culverts to let
the waters through. There was a bridge
across the river about 30m (100ft) west of the
Wall.

Balmuildy has been excavated several
times, most recently in the 1970s, and today
there is practically no trace above ground. At
NS 586722 was a temporary camp, of about
12 acres (4.8ha), possibly erected for the
troops building the fort, but this is not
conclusive.

of buildings. The bath house in the north-
east corner was pulled down with care and
the site covered with clay when the fort was
abandoned during the Antonine II period.
The barrack blocks, abandoned at the first
withdrawal c158, were reoccupied c160–1
but reduced in size, presumably to accommodate a smaller garrison. Stone platforms
were erected in two corners which may have

BARBURGH MILL Dumfries & Galloway
NX 903884 *Fortlet*
The interesting Antonine I period fortlet on
the hillock at Barburgh Mill, Closeburn, was
excavated in 1970–1 in advance of quarry
work. It was rhomboid in plan, surrounded
by an inner and outer V-shaped ditch, which,

when cut through, was shown to have a cleaning slot. The rampart was almost obliterated but it was possible to see that it had been 4m (13ft) wide. On its northern side, there had been a timber gate with six posts. Inside, the fortlet was equipped with two main barrack blocks in parallel, north to south. The west block had an officer's two-room suite and four smaller rooms for men. The east block had six more rooms, with a latrine just to the south. The total accommodation was for a century of infantry, ie eighty men plus the commander. The fortlet was built during the 140s and was abandoned c158. There was some evidence that it had been slighted before withdrawal.

BAR HILL Strathclyde
NS 707759 *Antonine Wall fort*
The highest fort along the Antonine Wall, Bar Hill, near Kirkintilloch (off B802 west of Croy), covers just over 3½ acres (1.5ha). Interestingly, it is situated over 30m (100ft) south of the actual Wall, and the Military Way runs between the two. It is the only fort detached from the Wall, except Carriden at the extreme east end. It is almost square, and is surrounded on the west, south and east sides by a double-ditch and a single-ditch on the north. There were gateways on all four sides. The fort was excavated in 1902–5 and again in the 1970s. The first excavations excited great interest, for they revealed the fort's well in which were found coins, amphora, ironwork, broken stone columns and capitals, and underneath all that some iron arrowheads. This indicated Roman dis-

mantling of the fort, probably in the mid 160s. Further coins found on the site suggest that the fort was used again by Roman troops, perhaps to patrol the Lowlands after the pullback from the Antonine frontier. At one time it was considered that the smaller fortlet, traces of which have been found inside the larger, was of first-century, perhaps Agricolan, origin, but it now seems more likely that the smaller structure was raised as an early and temporary fortlet while the main Antonine Wall was being built, as at Duntocher.

Bar Hill is one of the most interesting surviving forts. Among the remains of buildings found were the headquarters building, granary, an L-shaped barrack block (said to have been divided into pairs of rooms to accommodate eight men sharing each), a bath house and latrine, with hypocaust of sandstone pillars and slabs, in the extreme north-west corner, measuring 38×5.5m (125×18ft), and a pottery kiln in which were found quantities of sherds. The excavations have also yielded inscriptions, two of which record the presence of military units of about five hundred men each, the first Cohort of Hamians (a Syrian regiment of archers), which appears to have occupied the fort from c144 to 155, and the first Cohort of Baetasians, infantry men, who were there from c159 to 163. These Baetasians were later transferred to the fort at Maryport.

BAROCHAN HILL Strathclyde
NS 412690 *Fort*
The existence of a fort at Barochan Hill was noted by aerial reconnaissance in 1953 and proved by excavation in 1972. The fort was defended by a rampart of turf and clay. It covered about 3 acres (1.2ha) and was probably erected soon after Agricola's return to Rome, though some authorities believe it had been constructed by Agricola. Remains of interior timber buildings were found, including traces of a barrack block. The fort is on the south side of the Clyde, less than 2 miles from the outpost fortlet at Whitemoss.

BEARSDEN Strathclyde
NS 545721 *Antonine Wall fort*
The fort at Bearsden, New Kilpatrick, has

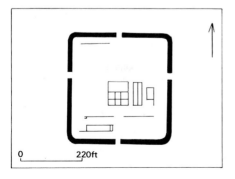

0   220ft

Bar Hill fort

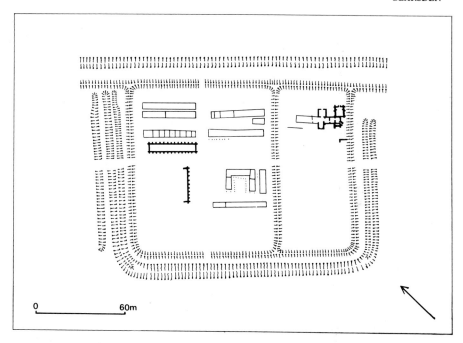

Bearsden fort, with bath house in east annexe

been extensively excavated over the years 1973–81 by a Scottish Development Department team led by D. J. Breeze, and the work has produced many important finds. Dominant among the buildings uncovered, and now preserved for all to see, is the stone bath house and latrine in the annexe on the east side of the fort. Though little more than a layout of foundations and the first few courses of walling, it is of great interest for its various bath-house features, such as the *sudatorium, caldarium, tepidarium* and the drainage system. The *sudatorium* was never completed; it appears to have been pulled down and the space 'used as a mess-room' by the legionaries who were erecting the rest of the bath house.

The fort itself was almost square, and many interesting features were uncovered. The commandant's quarters were ranged round three sides of a rectangle facing south with a verandah (indicated by post holes). A stone granary was located, but no headquarters building has been found. It has been suggested that the garrison for Bearsden was a detachment from a unit at another location, perhaps part of Cohors IV *Gallorum* based at

Castlehill, 1½ miles to the west. The barrack blocks uncovered suggested that both infantry and cavalry were accommodated and this is supported by the discovery of stables. There were also storehouses and workshops. In the annexe, a number of arrowheads and *ballista* bolts were found.

One interesting feature of Bearsden was that the wall-walk along the top of the Antonine Wall rampart on the north side was protected by a wattle breastwork. This was established by analysis of burnt debris which indicated hazel and willow shoots. These are just the kind of scientific proofs that make archaeological investigation so exciting.

Bearsden fort was erected onto the existing Wall, and it was dismantled with noticeable care at the end of the Antonine I period. It was not rebuilt in the Antonine II period. An inscription showed that the fort had been built by men of Legio XX *Valeria Victrix*, but with some auxiliary help.

497

BEATTOCK Dumfries & Galloway
NT 085020 *Temporary camp*
Near Milton (Tassiesholm) fort on the east
bank of the Annan is the site of a 40 acre
(16ha) temporary camp which had
Stracathro-type gates. It was noted from
aerial reconnaissance. Beattock camp was
probably erected in the Agricolan advance
through southern Scotland, c79–84.

BERTHA Tayside
NO 096268 *Fort*
Much remains to discover about Bertha fort,
Almond Bridge, but what is known shows
that it was very probably built in the Flavian
period, perhaps soon after Agricola's time. It
was rectangular in plan, covering just over 9
acres (3.6ha). The ditch was 3.5m (12ft) wide
and nearly 1.75m (6ft) deep, and appears to
have been clay lined. The rampart, about 6m
(20ft) wide at the base, was erected upon
cobble foundations. Bertha was given up in
the withdrawal from Scotland at the turn of
the first century and reoccupied in Antonine
times, suggested by an inscription found
recently at the site. The fort was on the
Roman route from Strageath to Cardean, a
route which passed through the Gask Ridge
area and which included the Gask frontier
watchtowers.

BIRRENS Dumfries & Galloway
NY 218753 *Fort: Roman name* Blatobulgium
Birrens fort began as a military site in
Agricola's period as governor, and a few
traces of this have been discovered underneath subsequent structures. In the
Hadrianic period, before about 128, a second
fort was built here as a northern outpost of
the Wall scheme. This was refurbished in
the early Antonine period (pottery of this era
was discovered in a well during excavations
in the 1960s). The fort then appears to have
been destroyed during the Brigantian revolt
of 155 (see p 117), and it was rebuilt very
soon afterwards. Traces of the Antonine
works can be seen. The fort was finally given
up in the 180s.

BLAINSLIE Borders
NT 552442 *Temporary camps*
A large camp was discovered here in 1973,
about ½ mile to the south of the camp
known at St Leonards. The southern ditch of
the camp, about 360m (400yd) in length, was
found, and parts of the west and east sides.

BOCHASTLE Central
NN 611077 *Fort and camp*
Bochastle fort, near Callander, was built by
Agricola during the Scottish campaigns. It
was one of his 'glen-blocker' forts (see p 85).
The fort was just over 4 acres (1.6ha), and
remains of V-shaped ditching and a length of
what appears to be 'Punic' ditch have been
found, together with artillery platforms.
Near the fort, traces of a temporary camp
which had Stracathro-type gates have also
been detected.

BOONIES Dumfries & Galloway
NY 306900 *Romano-British settlement*
Excavations in the early 1970s at the site of
Boonies, Westerkirk, right beside the river
Esk, opened up an enclosed settlement containing remains of several round, timber
houses, covering several periods, beginning
in the mid first century AD and in occupation
for about a century. The settlement appears
to have expanded over the period from a
single homestead.

BOTHWELLHAUGH Strathclyde
NS 729578 *Fort*
This was one of the forts built in the early
Antonine period in conjunction with the
Antonine Wall. It has been excavated,
notably in the mid 1970s. Finds included
extensive remains of the stonework bath
house, with a fine example of a cold plunge.
The fort was refurbished in the later
Antonine period. Some rampart is visible.

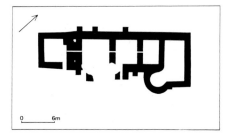

The bath house at Bothwellhaugh fort

498

BROOMHOLM KNOWE
Dumfries & Galloway
NY 378814 *Fort*
Two successive forts were built on this site, near Langholm. The first, smaller fort, was almost certainly part of Agricola's fort building in the early 80s. It was about 2 acres (0.8ha), with an annexe of much the same size, and was defended by a turf rampart about 6.5m (22ft) wide, outside of which were two closely set parallel ditches, with a third, outer, ditch. Broomholm Knowe may have continued in use after the withdrawal from Scotland in the 90s, but early in the second century, a new, larger 3½ acre (1.5ha) fort was built on the site.

BROWNHART LAW Borders
NT 7909 *Signal station*
The signal station at Brownhart Law lies beside the old Dere Street, and was about 16 × 12m (54 × 41ft), with a turf rampart and double-ditching.

BROXMOUTH Lothian
NT 700774 *Iron Age hillfort*
An Iron Age hillfort at Broxmouth, near Dunbar, which continued to be occupied in the second century AD may have had Roman associations.

BUCHLEY Strathclyde
NS 595720 *Enclosure abutting Antonine Wall*
A rectangular enclosure surrounded by a ditch and rampart which abutted onto the south side of the Antonine Wall was detected from the air in 1980. No traces of buildings were found and so far it is not possible to say what purpose the enclosure served. It lies about 270m (300yd) west of the fortlet of Wilderness Plantation.

BURNSWARK Dumfries & Galloway
NY 185787 *Hillfort and practice ground*
This is an unusual site, near Middlebie. It was an Iron Age hillfort, originating from perhaps the sixth century BC (when it may have begun as a Bronze Age site), that was overcome by the Romans. Iron Age round house traces have been found. The fort was used by the Roman army for artillery practice and siege drill. Artillery platforms

have been located nearby, as well as quantities of Roman lead bullets for slings, arrowheads and *ballista* balls. Remains have also been found of two practice camps beside the hillfort. The dating of the use of the hillfort as a kind of artillery range is not definite, but seems to be post-Antonine, perhaps the end of the second century.

CADDER Strathclyde
NS 616726 *Antonine Wall fort*
A 3 acre (1.3ha) fort on the Antonine Wall at Cadder may have been preceded by a late first-century to early second-century enclosure. The Antonine fort was built on this site onto the Wall after the latter had been completed at that point. Cadder fort was the only Antonine Wall fort not to face north; it faced east. Its main buildings in the central range were of stone, and so was the bath house in the north-east corner, but the commandant's house was built of timber, as were the barrack blocks. The fort was equipped with an annexe on the east side in which a second bath house block was constructed.

The garrison for Cadder was a 500-strong cohort of infantry. The fort may have had two occupations in Antonine times. Several inscriptions associated with the fort were recovered; one states tersely that it was built by Legio II *Augusta*. The fort has now been obliterated by quarrying, but it was excavated in depth in the 1920s and details were recorded.

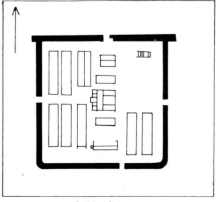

Cadder fort

499

CALLANDER Central
NN 612076 *Marching camps*
There were two marching camps at Callander. One, of 49 acres (20ha), had Stracathro-type gates, and so may be dated to the Agricolan period.

CAMELON Central
NS 8680 *Fort*
'Clyde and Forth . . . are separated only by a narrow neck of land. This neck was now secured by garrisons . . .'. So wrote Tacitus in his summary of the fourth year of Agricola's campaigns in the north. One of the garrisons (for which read forts) was Camelon, some remains of which have recently been the subject of extensive excavation in the suburbs of Falkirk. The site is complex. It began as an Agricolan fort near the river Carron by the extension of Dere Street which went on north into central Scotland. The fort was abandoned at the time of the pullback from Scotland.

Half a century later, when the Antonine Wall scheme was being built, Camelon was reoccupied in order to control Dere Street again. A new fort was built to the north of the old site and partly across it, and the southern part of the old site became an annexe. There is evidence for other structures nearby which are still the subject of examination. The annexe seems to have had some industrial associations: furnaces, hearths and tools have been found. Streets with buildings at more than one level of occupation have also been traced.

CAPPUCK Borders
NT 695213 *Fortlet*
A small fort or fortlet of perhaps only 1 acre (0.4ha) was built here in the period immediately after Agricola. It was erected as a base for an auxiliary unit. The fortlet appears to have been strengthened with stonework on the ramparts in late Domitianic times (c90–6) but about ten years later it was destroyed by fire, either in a raid by the Selgovae or Votadini or from deliberate slighting by the Romans, at perhaps the same time as Newstead. Cappuck was rebuilt in the Antonine period on much the same alignment, and was held until the early third century. Excavations exposed the remains of stone buildings.

CARDEAN Tayside
NO 289460 *Fort*
Cardean, near Airlie, was a Flavian fort of nearly 7 acres (2.8ha), with multiple-ditch and rampart systems on the north and east and a double-ditch and rampart on the south and west. The fort may have been built by Agricola before Mons Graupius, though it is also argued that it was not raised until the time of his successor in AD84–5 who completed the withdrawal from north-east Scotland. The fort has been partly excavated and appears not to have been occupied for more than a few years (cf Inchtuthil). Traces have so far been found of a cavalry-type barrack block, another barrack, a granary and two gates, at the south-east and south-west. Near the fort traces of a marching camp of over 33 acres (13ha), with a V-shaped ditch, have been found.

CARGILL Tayside
NO 166379 *Fort*
The Roman military remains at Cargill are complex, and their story is not yet clarified. There appear to have been two separate Flavian occupations. The first was a small fortlet, immediately south-west of the (later) fort and it was erected (probably by Agricola) to guard a bridge across the river Isla (a branch of the Tay). Further along the Tay, about 2 miles north-west, the great fortress of Inchtuthil was to be constructed in AD85, after Agricola's return to Italy. The Cargill fortlet may have been intended as a protection for traffic heading for the Inchtuthil site. When Inchtuthil was evacuated (unfinished) in AD86 or 87, it is probable that the second structure, a fort, went up at Cargill, presumably to replace it. This fort was defended by a rampart 6m (20ft) wide, in front of which was a V-shaped ditch 3m (10½ft) wide and 2.25m (7½ft) deep, beyond that a second ditch and further out still a third ditch 3.5m (12ft) wide. Remains of some timber buildings have been found inside the fort, including those of a granary.

CARPOW Tayside
NO 208179 *Fortress*
The Severan fortress at Carpow, near Abernethy, was situated on a small plateau on the south shore of the Firth of Tay. The first Roman occupation was a large Agricolan marching camp, and it is thought that Agricola probably crossed the Firth of Tay near Carpow in AD83. Also antedating the fortress was another camp with a ditched enclosure, polygonal in shape, about 64 acres (26ha) in area. Soon after this, the fortress proper was built. It was of 24 acres (9.7ha) and on a parallelogram plan. This would have been too small for a complete legion, and Carpow is normally described as a vexillation fortress. An inscription confirms that building activity was taking place in 212, and stamped tiles attest that the fortress was manned by parts of Legio VI *Victrix* and Legio II *Augusta*. The interior buildings were mostly half-timbered, although the gates appear to have been rebuilt in stone at some time. The *principia* has been located, along with other buildings. Carpow's fortress was short-lived, a common feature of the campaign fortress. By the late third century it seems to have been abandoned.

CARRIDEN Lothian
NT 026808 *Antonine Wall fort: Roman name* Veluniate
The fort at Carriden marks the eastern end of the Antonine Wall fortifications, though the actual linear wall finished a short distance west of the fort, at Bridgness. Carriden fort was built in the late 130s, before the Wall itself was begun. It guarded the south shore of the Forth and was just over 4 acres (1.6ha). A quantity of Roman pottery was found near the east side of the fort in the early 1970s. A short distance east of the fort, a self-governing *vicus* flourished in the mid second century, but it is probable that it was evacuated when the Antonine Wall was finally abandoned in the 160s. The *vicus* was attested by an altar inscription (found in 1956) set up by the inhabitants.

CARZIELD Dumfries & Galloway
NX 9681 *Fort*
A small part of one of the corners can be seen

at the site of this Antonine I period fort which was erected for an *ala* of auxiliary cavalry. It seems to have been abandoned in the 150s.

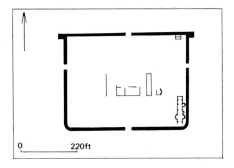

Castlecary fort

CASTLECARY Central
NS 790783 *Antonine Wall fort*
One of only two Antonine Wall forts to have been equipped with stone defences (cf Balmuildy), Castlecary was excavated in 1901–2 and found to cover 3½ acres (1.5ha), surrounded by double-ditching, with an eastern annexe bordered by a single-ditch, through which the modern road passes. Remains discovered included foundations of the headquarters building, granary, barrack blocks, bath house and latrine and what was probably the commandant's house. The fort was enclosed with stone walls and stone gateways. There is a depression with scattered stone blocks where the north gateway stood. Glass and pottery of the late first century were found on site and may suggest that there was a fort here in Agricolan times. Several inscriptions have been found in the fort precincts, some with references to two legions, Legio II and Legio VI, and also to auxiliary units. One inscription is later than the 160s when the fort was abandoned, and this records that a temple was built in the grounds, perhaps between 170 and 185. The fort might have been in use again after about 180. The Edinburgh to Glasgow railway line that runs via Falkirk crosses the fort from south-east to north-west. On either side of the fort are well-preserved stretches of the Antonine Wall.

501

CASTLEDYKES Strathclyde
NS 927445 *Camps and fort*
Castledykes began as a marching camp, which may have been used more as a temporary army base than as an 'overnight' stop. It was built as a 60 acre (24ha) camp in Agricola's time, with Stracathro-type gates. It was given up, then reoccupied when the area was reduced to about 40 acres (16ha) (sometimes called Castledykes II). Beside the camp, an 8 acre (3ha) fort was erected, which remained garrisoned until the early 90s. The fort was repaired and used again in the Antonine period.

CASTLE GREG Lothian
NT 0459 *Fortlet*
A second-century earth and timber fortlet with one gate, probably built in the Antonine period, Castle Greg has well-defined traces today.

CASTLEHILL Strathclyde
NS 524726 *Antonine Wall fort*
A 3½ acre (1.5ha) fort was built on the Antonine Wall at Castlehill, New Kilpatrick, probably early in the building scheme. It was occupied for a time by a cohort of the fourth regiment of Gallic cavalry, as indicated in an inscription. The fort outline has been seen from the air.

CHANNELKIRK Borders
NT 487547 *Marching camp*
One of the huge – 160 acre (65ha) or more – marching camps built by emperor Septimius Severus during his campaign in north-east Scotland in 208-11. (Newstead, St Leonards, Pathhead and Inveresk were others.)

CLEAVEN DYKE Tayside
NO 156408 *Boundary*
A few miles north to north-east of the legionary fortress of Inchtuthil, near Meikleour, the Romans erected a turf wall, flanked it with ditches and put up one watchtower (or possibly more than one). This wall is known as the Cleaven Dyke, and it formed a north-east barrier or boundary for the area immediately north of the fortress. About a mile length has survived but it could have

been much longer. The average width of the wall at the base is 9m (30ft), and the wall is 1.5m (5ft) high for much of its length. The date is not established but may be contemporary with Inchtuthil, ie 85-7.

CLEDDANS Strathclyde
NS 508723 *Antonine Wall fortlet*
The Antonine Wall fortlet at Cleddans, near Duntocher, was discovered by an excavation team in January 1980 under L. J. F. Keppie and J. J. Walker. Its position had been calculated from the fact that the crest on which it stood was the only point between Castlehill and Duntocher forts from which both forts could be seen. The fortlet had been built before the Wall reached the locality. It measured 17.5m (58ft) north–south by 18m (59ft) east–west internally, and was surrounded by a turf rampart on stone base, with entrances on the north and south.

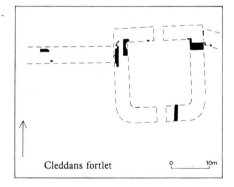

Cleddans fortlet   0   10m

CLEGHORN Strathclyde
NS 910459 *Temporary camp*
About 3 miles south-east of Lanark was a 47 acre (19ha) temporary camp, probably of first-century construction. The existence of the camp was proved by excavation in 1970-1. The camp, an irregular parallelogram in plan, lies on the right bank of the Stobilee, near the suggested route of the Roman road from Bothwellhaugh to Castledykes. Some of the rampart defences can still be seen, particularly in Camp Wood, where part of the south-west to north-east and north-west to south-east sides are clear. The rampart is 3.7m (12ft) wide and nearly 0.8m (2¾ft) tall. The V-shaped ditch was 2m (6ft)

wide and about 0.5m (1½ft) deep. The camp probably had six gates.

CLYDE CROSSING Strathclyde
NS 4274 *Causeway*
Part of a causeway leading from the north of the Clyde, near Dumbuck, probably projecting from the extension road westwards from Old Kilpatrick fort, down to the water edge to join up with a similar causeway on the south side of the river, was examined in 1974 and found to be about 11m (36ft) wide.

COULTER Strathclyde
NT 022359 *Marching camp*
A large marching camp has been identified at Coulter.

CRAIGARNHALL Tayside
NS 757985 *Temporary camp*
Craigarnhall is the site of a 63 acre (25.5ha) temporary camp, with a north side of 330m (1,100ft). The position of the 16m (52ft) wide gateway in the north side was established in excavations of 1973.

CRAIK CROSS HILL
Dumfries & Galloway NT 303047
Signal station
There was a signal station at Craik Cross Hill, beside the Roman road (Margary 89) which in this moorland area was cut into the rock below the peat.

CRAMOND Lothian
NT 192769 *Fort,* vicus *and industrial complex*
On the north side of the village church at Cramond, near Edinburgh, and in the grounds of Cramond House, are extensive remains of Cramond fort and its associated harbour and civilian settlement. The fort was probably begun soon after the departure of Agricola, and the site was well chosen, for it is beside the river Almond where it enters the Firth of Forth, a good place for a harbour and anchorage. Cramond was linked, possibly later on, by road to the centre of the Lowlands, and it may also have been reached by a spur from Dere Street whose main route ended at Inveresk. The fort was rebuilt in the Antonine I period to protect the southern shore of the Firth and the eastern end of the Antonine Wall, and to act as a supply base for the army along the Wall. The civilian settlement began to grow at this time, but may have been abandoned when the fort was given up in the Antonine II period.

When Severus embarked on his campaigns in Scotland in the first years of the third century, Cramond was reoccupied and repaired in both military and civilian capacities. The fort may have been abandoned again by Caracalla. Excavations in the 1970s exposed a bath house which had been altered at least twice. It is hoped that these remains will be displayed. The civilian settlement continued for the rest of the century and even into the fourth, in which time an industrial complex developed within its precincts. This is shown by the discovery of timber sheds that had accommodated various industries, including leather working and shoe making, carpentry and joinery, and iron smithing, which will have served the military personnel when the fort was still in use and the civilian population.

CRAWFORD Strathclyde
NS 953214 *Fort*
Crawford was first built in Flavian times, either by Agricola or soon after his departure. It was sited in the middle of an S-bend in the Clyde. It occupied 1½ acres (0.6ha), and was defended by a double-ditch system, outside which was a further single-ditch system. Crawford is unusual: though playing-card in shape, the arrangement is different from most forts. There is no *retentura* or rear gate; the *praetentura* contains, west to east, two long continuous ranges of buildings side by side, separated by the *via praetoria,* whose functions we do not yet know. The central block consisted of two barracks at west, then one granary, then *principia* (very small), an officers' house and, finally, two more barracks. The fort was built for four *turmae* of cavalry. It was rebuilt and reoccupied in the Antonine I period and then given up altogether.

CROY HILL Strathclyde
NS 734764 *Antonine Wall fort and fortlet*
Practically nothing can now be seen of Croy

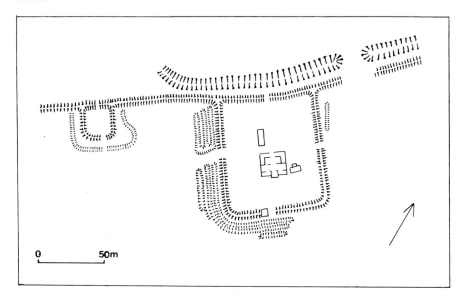

0   50m

Croy Hill fort, with fortlet at left

Hill fort, near Dullatur, at ground level, though outlines are visible from the air. Yet it has been excavated and its history and shape are known. While the small fortlet, occupying about 22×18.5m (73×61ft) about 80m (90yd) to the west of the larger fort, was being built during the early stages of the Antonine Wall scheme, the legionaries undertaking the work occupied a temporary camp on the larger fort site. Then, the larger fort was built on to the Wall which had reached Croy Hill. The Military Way ran through the fort from west to east and then swung sharply north and curved east again to run parallel and close to the Wall. Between the Military Way and the Wall, outside the fort on the east, was a bath house.

Few internal buildings were found in the 2 acre (0.8ha) fort: a headquarters building immediately south of the Military Way, and north of the Way, a granary. Outside the fort, to the south-west, was a vicus, but excavations in the late 1970s failed to discover buildings of the settlement, though there were traces of contemporaneous farming and small-scale industry. The fort was on solid rock. This meant that the ditch in front of the Wall was cut with great

difficulty and there was a stretch where the diggers gave up altogether. The fort was garrisoned by a small legionary detachment, of which it is possible that a few look-out men were posted to the nearby fortlet. An inscription attested Legio VI.

CUPAR Fife
NO 357116 *Temporary camp*
A 63 acre (25.5ha) marching camp was detected here by aerial photography in 1977.

DALGINROSS Tayside
NN 773208 *Camp and forts*
Dalginross, near Comrie, is one of Agricola's 'glen-blocker' sites (see p 85). In this case it blocked the way out of the Highlands via the Earn valley. There were two marching camps, one of which had been used as a construction camp while building the fort. The fort was enclosed by a double-ditch system inside a larger single-ditch enclosure which acted as an annexe.

DALKEITH Lothian
NT 321673 *Fort*
A Flavian fort of 3½ acres (1.5ha) at Elginhaugh, Dalkeith, was recently identified by aerial photographs. The fort lay beside Dere Street, by a crossing of the Esk.

Ground work uncovered remains of a timber building, and confirmed the *via principalis* and part of the *via sagularis* by the west gate. An oven was found behind the rampart just north of the west gate. The fort was probably erected during Agricola's campaigns, and was abandoned soon afterwards.

DALSWINTON Dumfries & Galloway
NX 933849 *Forts and camp*
The Dalswinton site is extremely complex and is not yet fully understood. Aerial photography, so often marvellously clarifying, in this case accentuates the difficulties. P. A. Holder (1982, pp 39, 80) describes a large concentration of military works, all of them Flavian, an apt comment. Out of this we can say that there were marching camps intersecting each other, of which one at least had Stracathro-type gates. Next door to, and superimposing here and there, was an 8½ acre (3.5ha) fort with annexe, built by Agricola, which probably held two part-mounted auxiliary cohorts. This was followed by a larger 10¼ acre (4ha) fort plus annexe built in the late 90s, which housed two cavalry regiments. The whole area was evacuated early in the second century.

DRUMQUHASSIE Central
NS 484874 *Fort*
In 1977, aerial reconnaissance located a fort here, near the south-east corner of Loch Lomond. Its position controlled an entrance to the Highland massif. Trial excavations were undertaken later in the year and in 1978, and these confirmed the existence of a fort of over 3 acres (1.2ha), erected in the late first century AD (suggested from pottery of the period found in one part of the inner ditch). The fort was deliberately dismantled later on. Drumquhassie is in the more westerly line of forts from Barochan Hill to Inchtuthil, raised in the last period of the Agricolan campaign or immediately afterwards. It was one of the 'glen-blockers' (see p 85).

DULLATUR Strathclyde
NS 746767 *Temporary camps*
Near Cumbernauld, just south of Dullatur House, 500m (550yd) south of the Antonine

Wall and about a mile east of Croy Hill fort site, are parts of the ramparts of two rectangular camps, one inside the other. These had been located from the air and were investigated in 1975-7 by L. J. F. Keppie for the Department of the Environment and the Hunterian Museum in Glasgow. The outer, larger camp, which appears to have been the earlier of the two, had two entrances.

DUN Tayside
NO 689595 *Temporary camp*
This is a small temporary camp of about 8 acres (3ha) of the Agricolan or succeeding period, which may have served as a stores depot as well. It lies just north of the Montrose Basin on the south of the Esk. If it was erected by Agricola, and was a depot, it would bear out the description by Tacitus of Agricola's sending ships of the Roman fleet up the North Sea coast to support the land forces moving into north-east Scotland (*Agricola*, xxv).

DUNNING Tayside
NO 023150 *Temporary camp*
A very large camp of Agricolan origin, some 115 acres (46.5ha), was for some time believed to be the site for the battle of Mons Graupius. This was challenged in 1978 by J. K. St Joseph (*Britannia* ix (1978) pp 271-87). The camp has survived in some parts. Over 120m (400ft) of bank and ditch, much of it 1-1.25m (3-4ft) tall, can be seen in Kincladie Wood, on the western side of the B934. The centre gate to the camp on the west side is 25.5m (85ft) wide, and had been protected by a *titulum*. The plan of the camp was almost square.

DUNTOCHER Strathclyde
NS 494727 *Antonine Wall fort*
The second most westerly fort on the Antonine Wall, Duntocher, near Old Kilpatrick, was preceded by a fortlet – about 17.5m (58ft) north–south by 18m (60ft) east–west internally – which was raised during the initial stages of the Wall scheme. A small fort, about ³/₅ acre (0.25ha) and the smallest in the whole scheme, was then built next door to the fortlet. Excavation in the fort has

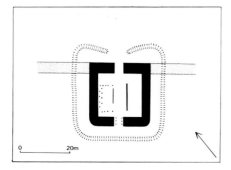

0 ____ 20m

Duntocher fort

revealed a barrack block, about 11×5m (36×16½ft), and part of the walling of a bath house, which had a curved drain with dressed stonework. Both fortlet and fort were completed before the Wall itself reached Duntocher. Interestingly, the fortlet's surrounding ditch has been located on both sides of the Antonine Wall. The fort's garrison was part of a unit. Traces can be seen today. It is off the A810 in Duntocher village.

DURISDEER Dumfries & Galloway
NS 902048 *Fortlet*
The earthwork remains of this fortlet, erected in the Antonine period, are well preserved. Its single entrance was protected by a *titulum*. Durisdeer fortlet is beside a 2 acre (0.8ha) temporary camp at NS 892031.

DURNO Grampian
NJ 699572 *Marching camp*
A large Roman army camp was discovered from the air at Durno in 1975, 6 miles north-west of Inverurie. The camp was about 141 acres (57ha), and ground investigation showed it to be of irregular polygon shape, longer than broad, with four gates protected by *titula*. The camp is in a line of large camps in north-east Scotland that were built by Agricola, south-east to north-west, including Raedykes Normandykes, Durno and Ythan Wells. It has been put forward by its discoverer as the camp out of which the army of Agricola marched to fight the Caledonians at the Battle of Mons Graupius which has been tentatively identified as having been

fought on Bennachie mountain, some 3 miles or so south-west of Durno, between the rivers Don and Urie. The site is the best suggestion so far.

EASSIE Tayside
NO 351469 *Temporary camp*
Aerial reconnaissance identified the outlines of a camp, and its ditching was first confirmed by excavation in 1970. In 1974, over 360m (400yd) of its south side were revealed and the area was established as being about 63 acres (25.5ha). It may have been an Agricolan temporary camp.

EASTER HAPPREW Borders
NT 194400 *Fort*
A Flavian period fort of 3 acres (1.2ha) or so, erected for an auxiliary unit, Easter Happrew was well sited to control routes along the Tweed valley into the Moorfoot Hills, and the road from Newstead to Castledykes in Clydesdale. The fort may have been a base for troops posted elsewhere (Breeze, D. J. 1982, p 45). Excavations revealed the fort to be rhomboid in plan (probably an instance of the occasional inaccuracy of the Roman *groma*), with gates on all sides except the north. It appears to have faced south. The defending turf rampart was 7.5cm (25ft) wide at the base, upon stone, the front 3m (10ft) or so of stone foundation being terraced. Outside the rampart, the single-ditch was about 3.5m (12ft) wide. Though not yet proved, Easter Happrew could have been an Agricolan construction.

ELLISLAND, Dumfries & Galloway
NX 9284 *Temporary camps*
Two marching camps were identified here in the early 1970s, one 112.5×67.5m (375×225ft) and the other 58.5×55.5m (195×185ft).

ESKBANK Lothian
NT 321668 *Temporary camps*
A rescue excavation was carried out at a site in Eskbank, Dalkeith, in advance of housing development, which confirmed the spotting of two successive camps by aerial photography. The first camp may have been

Agricolan: the second is attributed to Severus.

FALKIRK Central
NS 892795 *?Antonine Wall fort*
Excavations along the Wall at this location in 1980 revealed traces of a stone structure with hypocausts. These may be part of a supposed fort on the Antonine Wall, long assumed to have existed at Falkirk. There is no more positive information at present, but the meagre results should, nonetheless, be seen as encouraging.

FENDOCH Tayside
NN 9028 *Fort*
Fendoch fort was about 4½ acres (1.8ha) in area. It was built either by Agricola or immediately after his recall. It lies at the mouth of Sma' Glen, and so may have been a 'glen-blocker'. The site was extensively excavated in the 1930s by Sir Ian Richmond, and its layout recovered in such detail that it has often been regarded as a model for the forts of the period; yet it has differences from others. Fendoch's plan was conventional enough: the centre range consisted of *principia, praetorium,* granaries, *fabrica* and sheds (though Richmond suggested the *fabrica* was in fact a hospital). The *praetentura* to the south consisted of L-shaped barrack blocks and store buildings, and the *retentura* at the north had six barrack blocks. The fort was exceptionally long – nearly double the width – owing to the nature of the site which was largely bogland. It had an annexe on its south side. Fendoch was built for a *cohors milliaria* of 800 men. It was dismantled with some care only a few years after its construction, and was empty by about AD90.

FINAVON Tayside
NO 497574 *Marching camp*
Finavon was a 37 acre (15ha) marching camp built by Agricola during his campaigning in north-east Scotland. Traces of the north-west corner can be seen.

FOUMERKLAND Dumfries & Galloway
NX 915800 *Marching camp*
A square-plan 15 acre (6ha) marching camp

of probable Agricolan origin at Foumerkland may have housed troops policing among the Novantae in south-west Scotland.

GAGIE Tayside
NO 448383 *Marching camp*
The south-east corner of a 10 acre (4ha) marching camp, with a ditch of about 1.5m (5ft) wide, was discovered in 1973.

GARNHALL Central
NS 782780 *Section of Antonine Wall*
Excavation near the Antonine fort of Castlecary in 1976 exposed some rampart and ditch in good condition. It was possible to deduce where two working gangs had reached one another and made a join.

Gask House see **Gask Ridge**

GASK RIDGE
NN 9118 to 0220 (approx) *Line of signal stations and watch towers*
The signal stations and watch towers of the Gask Ridge (see p 86) start on the west side at Parkneuk. There were eleven which, from west to east, were Parkneuk (about 1 mile east of Strageath fort), Raith, Ardunie, Roundlaw, Kirkhill, Muir O'Field, Gask House, Witch Knowe, Moss Side, Thorny Hill and Westmuir. The towers were built either during Agricola's campaigns or immediately afterwards by his successor during the pullback after Mons Graupius. Although eleven are known, there may well have been several more, since the line

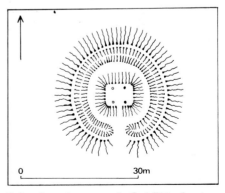

| 0 | 30m |

Parkneuk watch tower on the Gask Ridge frontier

appears to steer straight for the fort at Bertha on the Tay (see also Roundlaw).

GATEHOUSE OF FLEET Dumfries & Galloway NX 595573
Fortlet
A small fortlet for part of an auxiliary unit was erected at Girthon, Gatehouse of Fleet, in Flavian times. Some authorities hold that it is an Agricolan fortlet, established to keep watch upon movements of the Novantae tribe during Agricola's campaigns in Scotland.

GILNOCKIE Dumfries & Galloway
NY 389792 *Marching camp*
A marching camp has been found here, now partly covered by forest.

GIRVAN Strathclyde
NX 188991 *Marching camps*
Aerial photography has revealed two marching camps here. The second, of 10–12 acres (4–5ha) with a V-shaped ditch, was proved in excavations of 1980–1.

GLASGOW BRIDGE Strathclyde
NS 6373 *Antonine Wall fortlet*
It had long been thought that there was a fort or fortlet in this neighbourhood, and in 1954 a possible outline was detected from the air. It replaced the earlier suggested location. The enclosure was less than ¼ acre (0.1ha), suggesting a fortlet rather than a fort. So far, only a single-ditch has been seen, with an entrance on the south-east.

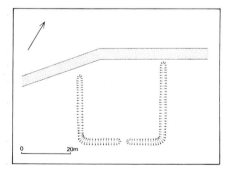

Glasgow Bridge fortlet

GLENLOCHAR Dumfries & Galloway
NX 735645 *Forts,* vicus *and marching camps*
Two successive forts were erected here in Agricolan times (the second may have been just afterwards). The forts appear to have been for cavalry units. Traces of a *vicus* that grew up around the fort have been uncovered. There is also evidence of two successive marching camps, of 22 acres (9ha) and 32 acres (13ha). The second fort was rebuilt in the Antonine period and then abandoned altogether after about 160.

GOURDIE Tayside
NO 115427 *Construction camp*
The 3½ acre (1.5ha) camp at Gourdie has every indication of being a special labour camp for legionaires who built the new stone front grafted onto the earth rampart at the great legionary fortress of Inchtuthil, about 2 miles further south. Aerial photographs showed Gourdie to be square, ditched and divided in half by another ditch. In one half, several small quarry pits have been found in the underlying sandstone from which legionaries took the stone. Gourdie was only one source for the stone: others have yet to be found.

INCHTUTHIL Tayside
NO 1239 *Legionary fortress*
Inchtuthil, lying on a low plateau above the river Tay, demonstrates Roman military planning at its best. This fortress was built after the withdrawal of Agricola in AD84 to play a central role in the campaign against the Caledonians in northern Scotland.

The fortress was rectangular in shape and covered an area of 53 acres (21.5ha). The first set of defences were of earth comprising a ditch and rampart. These fortifications were broken by four gates constructed of timber. The east gate, which has been investigated, had a dual carriageway with passages 4m (13½ft) wide and flanking towers. Outside the fortress defences were a set of earthworks. These probably comprised the camp for the construction party and a compound to the south-east of the fort for the supervising officers. A bath house has also been traced outside the defences.

Although the fort buildings were all of

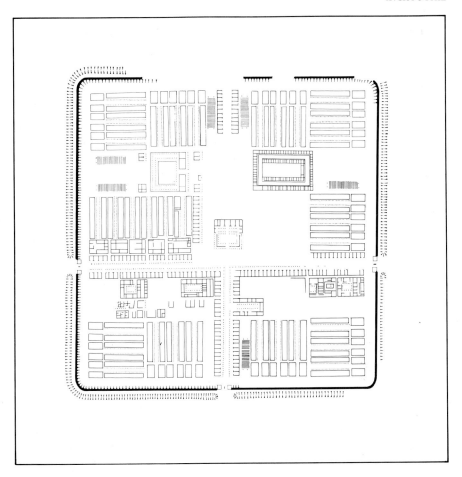

The plan of Inchtuthil fortress

timber, the careful excavations of Sir Ian Richmond and J. K. St Joseph have revealed almost the entire plan of the fortress. Post holes indicate where the timber uprights of the buildings stood. The barracks were laid out with precision in units of six blocks. Each unit of barracks probably housed one cohort. A unit with ten blocks is thought to be that of the larger first cohort. Each barrack building had fourteen *contubernia* which were quite spacious by fortress standards. Also located within the fortress were an unusually small *principia* of 15sq m (160sq ft), granaries, a hospital, houses of tribunes and a surprisingly luxurious house of the *primus pilus* which had a hypocausted room. At some stage during the occupation a stone circuit wall was added to the fortifications outside the earthworks.

The most interesting feature of the fort at Inchtuthil is the manner in which it was abandoned before in fact it was completed. Coin evidence points to abandonment in about AD87, when it must have become apparent that the area could not be held successfully. The fort which had required so much planning and effort in its building was systematically destroyed. The demolition appears to have been carried out in a very orderly way, and nothing was left that could have been of use to the enemy. The stone of the wall and unfinished bath house was

509

stripped and all reusable materials saved. Bent nails were found in profusion: they had been levered out of timbers which could be kept. Pottery and glass were ground and destroyed, wattling was burnt – ash has been traced in the *principia* and even the hospital drain was blocked with gravel. A hoard of about a million unused nails was found buried in the workshop. The withdrawal was complete and final.

INVERAVON Lothian
NS 950796 *Antonine Wall fort*
A small fort on the Antonine Wall probably lay beside the river Avon where the Wall crossed the river. Excavations were carried out in the 1970s, including exploration by sub-aqua club divers in the river, and signs of the rampart base were found. Sections of Wall were also found close by.

INVERESK Lothian
NT 344720 *Fort and* vicus
A fort of several acres was built at Inveresk beside the river Esk by Agricola in the early 80s. It marked the point where two main military roads into the Lowlands of Scotland met, the road from Carlisle via Annandale and the road from Corbridge via Newstead, both having forts erected along the way. Little of this fort remains, but the location is the public gardens of Lewisdale. A second fort was built at Inveresk in the time of Antoninus Pius, as part of the Antonine Wall scheme, though it is several miles east of the first fort (Carriden). The remains of the Antonine structure are under St Michael's Church. Just south of the fort site are remains of the bath house, eg four *pilae* of the hypocaust. The bath house was in an annexe. A road led out of the east gate of the Antonine fort towards a *vicus* of uncertain origin, but probably mid to late second century. The *vicus* site has been excavated and remains found of houses of stone and of timber, some circular and one with a furnace. An inscription at Inveresk recorded the name of an imperial procurator, of the mid second century, one Sabinianus. Pottery finds included a vessel with the graffito VICTORINI on the base.

KAIMS CASTLE Tayside
NN 8612 *Fortlet*
During the years immediately after Mons Graupius (AD84), Roman garrisoning in the centre of Scotland was gradually reduced. A number of small watchtowers and one or two small fortlets were quickly raised in the line between Ardoch and Strageath. Kaims was one fortlet beside this line and soon afterwards it was pulled down. It appears to have been reoccupied in Antonine times. A 24m (80ft) square enclosure with a surrounding ditch, remains of it can still be seen behind Kaims Lodge.

KINNEIL Lothian
NS 977803 *Antonine Wall fortlet*
Recently discovered in excavations in the late 1970s, the Antonine Wall fortlet at Kinneil, near Bo'ness, was found to be 18m (60ft) east to west by 21m (69ft) north to south internally. The north gateway was located, with an entrance about 35m (12ft) wide. The fortlet was defended by a double-ditch. It is clear that the fortlet and the Antonine Wall stretches on either side were erected in the same operation. The excavations exposed much pottery and fragments of green glassware.

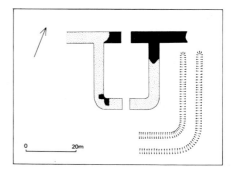

Kinneil fortlet

KINNELL Tayside
NO 615505 *Marching camp*
A 63 acre (25.5ha) marching camp, detected by aerial photography in 1968, was tested by excavation. Two gates, protected by *titula*, were seen. There is evidence of an annexe on the south-east side.

KIRKBUDDO Tayside
NO 4944 *Marching camp*
Traces of a 63 acre (25.5ha) marching camp, probably of Flavian beginnings, sprawl across the woods here, and parts of the rampart and ditching can be seen in clearings.

Kirkhill see **Gask Ridge**

KIRKINTILLOCH Strathclyde
NS 650739 *Antonine Wall fort*
Little work has so far been done at the Kirkintilloch fort site beyond the excavation of what was possibly part of a ditch forming the west side of the fort (or of an annexe). Coins of first century AD have been found at Kirkintilloch but are not enough to establish so early an occupation.

LAKE OF MENTEITH Central
NN 564000 *Fort and camp*
A 'glen-blocking' fort (see p 85) of the time of Agricola, Lake of Menteith was noted by aerial survey in the late 1960s. It was about 6 acres (2.4ha) and was enclosed by double V-shaped ditching. Associated with the fort was a 25 acre (10ha) camp probably erected for the construction gang working on the fort. This camp had Stracathro-type gates. A second, smaller camp of about 13 acres (5ha) has recently been located north of the fort.

LAMINGTON Strathclyde
NS 977307 *Fortlet and temporary camp*
Near the right bank of the Clyde, an 18×15m (59×50ft) fortlet of probable Flavian date was found beside the A702 Coulter to Wandel road. Only part of the fortlet is traceable. To the north has been identified a 20 acre (8ha) temporary camp.

LITTLE CLYDE Strathclyde
NS 994159 *Temporary camp*
A rectangular temporary camp of about 31 acres (12.5ha) was found near the old Roman road from Annandale to Clydesdale. The outline of the rampart surrounds the present Little Clyde Farm. Much of the north rampart and ditch is traceable, with the entrances protected by a *titulum*. The camp may be of Antonine date.

LOCHLANDS Central
Temporary camp
A large temporary camp was detected from the air, lying south of the river Carron, at Lochlands, a few hundred metres north-west of the fort site at Camelon.

LOGIE Tayside
NO 699632 *Marching camp*
A large marching camp with V-shaped ditches has been indicated at Logie. It may be a feature of the Agricolan campaign in the north-east of Scotland.

LOUDOUN HILL Strathclyde
NO 6037 *Fort*
The site is on a slope of Loudoun Hill, in the Irvine valley. The earliest works appear to have been a small 1 acre (0.4ha) fort which was soon replaced by a larger enclosure, and in turn by a 3 acre (1.2ha) fort. Probably these are all Agricolan works. The fort was modified in the period just before the withdrawal in the 90s, and indeed Loudoun may have been an outpost fort of the withdrawal line Glenlochar to Newstead. In the Antonine period Loudoun was reoccupied and the defences were rebuilt.

LURG MOOR Strathclyde
NS 295737 *Antonine Wall outpost fortlet*
One of the outpost fortlets provided at the western end of the Antonine Wall, on the south side of the Clyde, Lurg Moor was just under ½ acre (0.2ha), with gateways on the northern and southern sides. It controlled the Clyde estuary.

LYNE Borders NT 1840
MELDON BRIDGE Borders NT 2040
Military establishments
There are several military establishments around Lyne: two marching camps, one of 49 acres (20ha), of the first Flavian period, a fort of perhaps the Antonine I period and a fortlet which replaced the fort probably in the Antonine II period.

Menteith see **Lake of Menteith**

MIDDLEBIE Dumfries & Galloway
NY 208764 *Marching camp*
A second, smaller marching camp was traced

here in 1973, inside the outlines of a previously discovered larger camp.

MILRIGHAIL Borders
NT 536268 *Marching camp*
A marching camp was seen from the air at Milrighail, near Bowden, in 1976.

MILTON Dumfries & Galloway
NT 093015 *Forts and camps*
Two, possibly three, forts of the first century were built in succession at Milton (Tassieholm) on the ridge in Annandale in Flavian times, the latest being a rebuild and enlargement of the late 80s. In the Antonine I period, a fortlet was erected on the site of the earlier works.

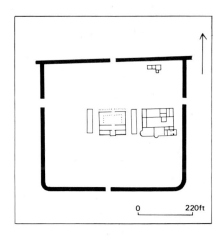

0   220ft

Mumrills fort

MOLLINS Strathclyde
NS 713718 *Fort*
Aerial photography in 1977 revealed a new fort at this location, which is near the Antonine Wall fort of Cadder. The new fort, almost 1 acre (0.4ha) in area, appears to have been early Flavian, built probably in 80–2. It had an annexe of about ½ acre (0.2ha) on one end. Traces of timber buildings were found.

Moss Side see **Gask Ridge**
Muir o'Field see **Gask Ridge**

MUMRILLS Central
NS 918794 *Antonine Wall fort*
Mumrills fort, near Grangemouth, was the largest along the Antonine Wall. It covered just over 7 acres (2.8ha). It was also the fort on the Wall originally built to accommodate cavalry units. Pottery finds have suggested that the first fort there was erected in the late first century, but in any case it was one of the first built along the Forth–Clyde isthmus in the early Antonine I period, and it was completed before the Wall rampart builders reached it in the 140s.

The internal arrangements so far discovered in excavation revealed the timber-built commandant's house and the bath house in the north-east corner. An inscription found at the site attested that Mumrills was occupied by an *ala* of five hundred Tungrian cavalry during the Antonine I period, and by a Thracian cohort of cavalry

in the second, shorter, Antonine period. Although a coin of Marcus Aurelius (emperor 161–80) has been found at the site, it is otherwise evident that the fort was given up in the 160s and demolished. A stretch of Military Way has survived.

NEWSTEAD Borders NT 5734
Fort: Roman name Trimontium
Newstead stood in Selgovian territory near a crossing of the river Tweed below the peaks of the Eildon Hills. Early signs of a series of marching camps were succeeded by three main periods of occupation. The first, very large Agricolan fort of 10½ acres (4.25ha) was of a rare and unusual form, with the more common rectangular shape of the ramparts being staggered. This forced arrivals to approach the gates obliquely, giving the occupants strategic advantage. The fort was surrounded by double-ditching and a rampart. It had two enclosed annexes, one of 7 acres (2.8ha) to the west, another of 20 acres (8ha) to the east.

After about AD90 a second, late Flavian fort was established, which had massive earthen ramparts up to 13.5m (45ft) thick, and covered a huge 13 acre (5ha) area. Not much is known of the interior, other than the existence of one barrack of legionary type in the *praetentura* and another of auxiliary style in the *retentura*. This suggests that Newstead may have acted as a vexillation fortress at

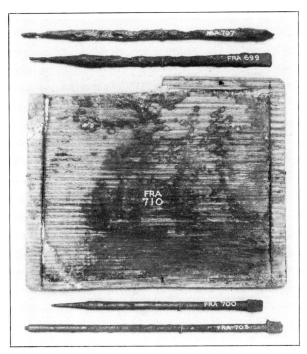

A mid-second-century writing tablet and four iron *styli*, from Newstead fort, Borders (*National Museum of Antiquities of Scotland*)

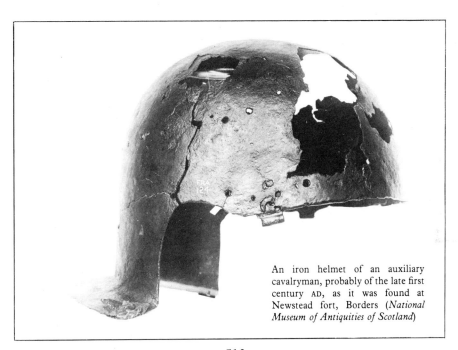

An iron helmet of an auxiliary cavalryman, probably of the late first century AD, as it was found at Newstead fort, Borders (*National Museum of Antiquities of Scotland*)

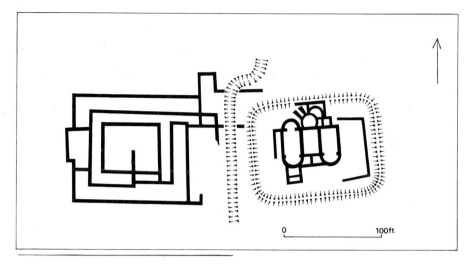

0   100ft

Newstead fort: the *mansio* left and bath house outside

this time, with a mixed legionary and auxiliary garrison. Not much is known of the layout of the later Flavian fort, but fragments of some foundations could show that it had half-timbered buildings resting on stone sills. Modifications to the annexes at this time include the building of a *mansio* and a bath house in the western annexe. The fort was destroyed by fire after about 105, probably in an attack by the Selgovians, since occupation debris – including damaged weapons – does not point to self-destruction.

The third, Antonine period of development saw the construction of two successive forts. The defences were stout, comprising a stone wall, two ditches and a 11m (36ft) wide rampart. The area of the fort was 14¾ acres (6ha), divided into *praetentura* and *retentura* by a stone wall. Twelve barrack blocks have been traced in the *praetentura*, along with a *praetorium*, a *principia* and other buildings. An altar, set up by a centurion of Legio XX and remains of the arms and armour of both legionaries and auxiliaries suggest that Newstead still held a mixed garrison. The bath house in the west annexe was defensively banked in this period.

Stables across the *retentura* of the second Antonine fort suggest that a cavalry unit

occupied the position in this period. Further general alterations occurred, including the demolition of the dividing wall inside the fort and the erection of a cross-hall measuring 15×48m (50×160ft) near the *principia*. The most impressive alterations were to the defences. A triple-ditch system, together with the extension of the rampart to a width of 18m (59ft), rendered the fortifications seemingly impregnable. The date of the final abandonment of Newstead is difficult to ascertain, although it may have been during the reign of Commodus.

NORMANDYKES Grampian
NO 8399 *Marching camp*
This was a large marching camp of about 106–8 acres (43–44ha), erected by Agricola's army in the Scottish campaigns. Part of the eastern rampart can still be seen.

NORTH EILDON Borders
NT 555328 *Signal station*
An Iron Age hillfort of about 40 acres (16ha) was built on the most northerly of three hills in the Eildon range. It was occupied by the Selgovae during the first century, until the Roman army moved into Scotland in AD78–9. The *oppidum* may have been taken by the Romans: evidently it was destroyed, and a signal station was built in the middle of the space. Further down the valley below Agricola built the first fort at Newstead.

514

OAKWOOD Borders
NT 425248 *Fort*
A 3½ acre (1.4ha) fort was discovered here in 1949, beside Ettrick Water. It was built by Agricola c80, and given an annexe soon afterwards. The fort was later renovated, with a puddled clay front to the rampart on three sides. The fort was abandoned in the AD90s. Beside the fort, a temporary camp of about 40 acres (16ha) has also been identified, with internal and external *claviculae.*

OLD KILPATRICK Strathclyde
NS 4673 *Antonine Wall fort*
Old Kilpatrick (12 miles north-west of Glasgow off the A82) was the westernmost fort on the Antonine Wall and covered about 4¾ acres (2ha). It was probably built separately while the Wall itself was being raised gradually from its eastern end at Bridgeness by the Forth. A road led from the fort's western end in an arc to the northern bank of the Clyde and ran along the river, perhaps as far as a harbour at or near Dumbarton. The fort has been built over. In 1969 a stone altar was found in one of the fort ditches. It was set up by the first cohort of the auxiliary troops of the Baetasii, a unit raised in Germany for service in Britain. The Baetasii also served at Bar Hill fort from c159 to 163. Their appearance at Old Kilpatrick may have been for a short spell during a temporary garrisoning of the fort in the governorship of Ulpius Marcellus (see p 120). Pottery found at Old Kilpatrick, dating from the late first century, was once taken to mean that there had been a fort there in Agricola's time, but as yet no other indication of first-century occupation has been revealed.

OUTERWARDS Strathclyde
NS 232666 *Antonine fortlet*
One of the three outpost fortlets protecting the estuary of the river Clyde, Outerwards was a small ⅒ acre (0.04ha) structure, rectangular in plan, with a turf rampart about 3.75m (12ft) wide, and with a timber gateway on the south. The fortlet is on high ground overlooking the estuary and on the route to the most westerly outpost fortlet, Lurg Moor. Outerwards was part of the Antonine Wall scheme. The fortlet probably had two periods of occupation (? Antonine I and II), being demolished and rebuilt.

Parkneuk see **Gask Ridge**

PATHHEAD Lothian
NT 399632 *Temporary camp*
A large temporary camp was erected here, probably in Flavian times. It was nearly 750m (2,500ft) along the east and west sides. A V-shaped ditch about 3.5m (12ft) wide, was excavated.

PENNYMUIR Borders
NT 755140 *Marching camps*
There are three marching camps at Pennymuir, and two of them are among the best preserved in Scotland. The earlier of the two is rectangular, sited beside Dere Street, and is 42 acres (17ha) with a well-preserved rampart. Five gates are visible. The later of the two is smaller, and is inside the earlier, using two sides of the latter's defences. This camp had four gates. The third camp detected nearby is not well preserved. Troops at the Pennymuir camps used the old hillfort at Woden Law for mock sieges.

RAEBURNFOOT Dumfries & Galloway
NY 2599 *Fortlet*
A 1 acre (0.4ha) fortlet of the earlier Antonine period was erected inside an abandoned larger enclosure which may have been Flavian.

RAEDYKES Grampian
NO 8490 *Marching camp*
A marching camp of Agricola's time, Raedykes was 93 acres (38ha) in size, with six gates. There are well-defined stretches of rampart and ditch. The shape may have been planned as a rectangle, but it emerged as a parallelogram, due perhaps to the unsuitability of the ground. It was once suggested as the site for the battle of Mons Graupius.

Raith see **Gask Ridge**

REDSHAWBURN Strathclyde
NT 0213 *Fortlet*
This was a fortlet built probably for a

century of cavalry during the Antonine occupation of Scotland.

ROUGH CASTLE Central
NS 837798 *Antonine Wall fort*
Rough Castle (off the B816 at Bonnybridge, near Falkirk) is among the best preserved of the Antonine Wall forts. It is not a large fort, occupying just over 1½ acres (0.6ha), with an annexe to the east. The Military Way runs through the annexe and the fort, east to west, more or less centrally. The fort is double-ditched, with gateways on all sides, and an east gate leads out of the annexe. The fort was excavated first in 1903, then in the 1930s, 1957–61 and again in the 1970s. Remains established include the commandant's house, barrack blocks, storehouses, granary, the headquarters building with its *basilica*, and in the annexe a bath house. The east side of the annexe was protected by three roughly parallel ditches meeting in a southerly ditch, and inside the inner ditch a curved rampart swept east round to south. The Antonine Wall itself is the northern rampart of the fort and annexe. About 30m (100ft) north-west of the fort's north gateway are the remains of several rows of small pits, about 2 × 1m (7 × 3ft), called *lilia*, which were designed to be covered with scrub and foliage and act as traps for hostile cavalry. An inscription found at Rough showed that the fort was at one time garrisoned by the sixth cohort of the Nervii, under a centurion of Legio XX, though it was not large enough to accommodate the whole cohort.

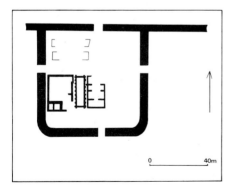

Rough Castle fort

ROUNDLAW Tayside
NN 958189 *Watchtower*
Roundlaw, Trinity Gask, is one of the eleven watchtowers and signal stations built, after Agricola's recall, along the Gask Ridge. The site was excavated after aerial observation in the 1950s. The four corner post holes of the tower had been cut in solid rock. So had the 'Punic'-style ditch round the tower site. The dimensions of the tower were 3.7 × 4.3m (12 × 14ft). There had been a causeway across the ditch to the south to meet the Gask Ridge road. The tower may have reached a height of 6m (20ft).

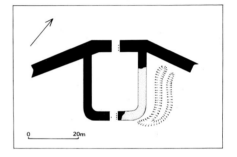

Seabegs Wood fortlet

SEABEGS Central
NS 812792 *Antonine Wall fortlet*
Antonine Wall specialists had for some time expected that a fort or fortlet would be located centrally somewhere in the 3½ miles gap between the forts at Castlecary and Rough Castle, probably near Seabegs Wood, and in 1977 L. J. F. Keppie and J. J. Walker, directing a team for the Hunterian Museum and the University of Glasgow, revealed a fortlet of some 22m (73ft) north–south by 18m (59ft) east–west, with its northern edge on the Wall, at the west of the wood. The fortlet appears to have been built at the time the Vallum was being raised. The ramparts were erected on a cobblestone base. Gateways north and south were inserted, probably guarded by timber towers. There seem to have been two periods of occupation: first in the 140s and then later, when the north gate was reduced or maybe blocked altogether. The Military Way ran due south of the fortlet.

SOUTH SHIELHILL Tayside
NN 856122 *Watchtower*
This is a watchtower on the route between the forts at Ardoch and Strageath. It was erected in the period immediately following Agricola's battle of Mons Graupius. The site lies ½ mile off the Ardoch to Kaims Castle road, near to a quarry. It was surrounded by double-ditching which was seen by aerial observation and confirmed by excavation. The four corner post holes were identified. One had been reinforced with packed gravel.

STRACATHRO Tayside
NO 618658, NO 614655 *Fort and camp*
Stracathro is famous for having had its name given to a particular type of marching camp gates, which have been detected at ten camps in Scotland built in the Agricolan period (see p 166). The gates consisted of a double *clavicula* in the wall line, one being an outward curved extension of ramp and ditch opposite the other outward extension of ramp and ditch which was straight.

The camp (NO 614655) was about 39 acres (16ha) and was erected partly for troops who were building the more permanent fort nearby, and partly for forces patrolling the area generally. The fort (NO 618658) was built with V-shaped ditch defences, and was about 5½ acres (2ha). It may have been built for a cavalry unit, but this is not certain. Traces of timber buildings were found in excavations of the late 1960s

STRAGEATH Tayside
NM 898180 *Fort*
The fort at Strageath was identified some time ago, but an idea of its layout was only gained in the 1950s as a result of aerial observation. This established the lines of some of the fort's defences, but it was not until recent excavations that detailed information about the development of Strageath was gathered.

Strageath was linked with other forts – such as Ardoch – by a road which also provided good communications with stations to the south. The fort was originally a key part of an elaborate signalling system of towers spaced at intervals. Over an 8 mile stretch from Strageath there were eleven

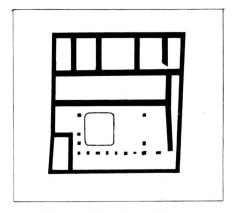

The *principia* at Strageath fort

signalling stations.

Despite difficulties of tracing the outline of the ramparts, owing to plough damage, it has now been established that there were three forts at Strageath. The first fort was Flavian, from which period traces of two pairs of barrack blocks have survived in the north part of the *retentura*. These have irregularly sized *contubernia*, which could give an indication of the nature of the garrison – a cavalry unit seems most likely. Also from this period have been found the outline of the *principia* to the north and a porticoed *praetorium*. To the south is a building that was probably a hospital. An unusual feature is a granary in the *praetentura*.

The site at Strageath was reoccupied early in the Antonine period and the second fort established. The new fort followed the ground plan of the earlier fort in some respects, but also changed the position of some buildings. The Antonine I *praetorium*, for example, was south of the *principia*. In this period a shed of some sort was built beside the *principia*. The final occupation is known as the Antonine II fort. Alterations to the Antonine I fort included the replacement of the road behind the *principia* with a path. At the end of the Antonine II period there is evidence of a systematic demolition of the site.

SUMMERSTON Central
NS 574723 *Fortlet on Antonine Wall*
A university of Glasgow team directed by W.

S. Hanson excavated a site in 1980 at Summerston, ⅔ mile west of Balmuildy, beside the Antonine Wall. It had been identified by aerial photography as a possible temporary camp. A 5 acre (2ha) enclosure was located, and another, smaller enclosure, about 35m (116ft) square. The smaller enclosure has been identified as another Antonine Wall fortlet.

TAMFOURHILL Central
NS 859794 *Temporary camp*
An aerial survey in 1977 showed up traces of a temporary camp at Tamfourhill, Falkirk, about ¼ mile south-west of the Antonine fortlet at Watling Lodge. So far it has not been dated, but it may relate to activities at or around Camelon fort (about 1 mile north) before the Antonine period.

Tassieholm see **Milton**

TENTFIELD PLANTATION Central
NS 8579 *Section of Antonine Wall*
A stretch of the Antonine Wall and Ditch can be seen threading its way through dense undergrowth for several hundred yards, just north of the railway line. There are two signal station mounds along the route.

Thorny Hill see **Gask Ridge**

TOLLPARK Strathclyde
NS 770777 *Antonine Wall structure*
During a search at Tollpark, near Cumbernauld, for the remains of a possible fortlet in 1978, a stone platform one stone thick, about 12×1.75m (40×6ft), was found. It was not the base of a fortlet, and its purpose is not yet understood.

TORWOOD Dumfries & Galloway
NY 1281 *Marching camp*
Some ramparting of a marching camp is visible here.

TWECHAR Strathclyde
NS 697754 *Temporary camp*
A temporary camp was spotted from the air in 1977, about ¼ mile south of the Antonine Wall, and ½ mile or so west-south-west of the Antonine Wall fort at Bar Hill.

WANDEL Strathclyde
NS 944268 *Fortlet and temporary camp*
Very little is left of the 33×31.5m (109× 104ft) trapezoidal fortlet at Wandel, near Crawford, which was enclosed by a single-ditch. The dating has been attributed to the Antonine period. The fortlet's north-west wall fronted on to the Roman road from March Burn to Dolphinton (from Annandale into Clydesdale). David Breeze (1982, p 121) suggests that the fortlet may not have been completed, and it was probably given up in the late first century. Wandel fortlet lies just north of a temporary camp which was excavated in 1970. This camp had a V-shaped ditch, on average 3.35m (11ft) wide. Parts of the rampart can be detected today. The date of the camp is unknown but could fall into the period of the recall of Agricola.

WARD LAW Dumfries & Galloway
NY 024668 *Fort*
There was a hillfort of the Novantae tribe at Ward Law, Caerlaverock. In the Flavian period, a 7 acre (2.8ha) fort was built beside the abandoned hillfort, using some of the hillfort's ditching as part of the new fort's defences. Ward Law may have been used as winter quarters for units of the Agricolan army.

WATERSIDE MAINS Central
NS 869968 *Marching camp*
A marching camp was seen from the air at Waterside Mains, near Alva, in 1977, about 2½ miles north of the Forth river.

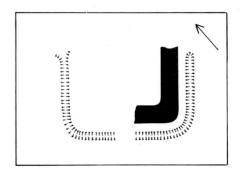

The fort at Watling Lodge

WATLING LODGE Central
NS 862797 *Antonine Wall fortlet*
There was a small fortlet, internally 15.5m (51ft) north–south × 18.5m (61ft) east–west, on the Antonine Wall at Watling Lodge, at the point where the road from the Wall to Camelon joins. A good length of original ditch beside the fort is preserved. This is close to the present road. The site is off the B816, 1 mile west of Falkirk.

WESTERTON Tayside
NN 873146 *Watchtower*
Westerton watchtower, near Muthill, is the northernmost below Strageath in the line of watchtowers erected between Ardoch and Strageath soon after the recall of Agricola. The site was excavated very recently (1980) by the University of Glasgow. The watchtower, rectangular in plan, about 3.5 × 2.5m (12 × 8ft), stood on four corner posts inside a circular 'Punic' ditch-protected enclosure. There are no traces of any rampart.

WESTERWOOD Strathclyde
NS 761773 *Antonine Wall fort*
A 2¼ acre (1ha) fort on the Antonine Wall, Westerwood, near Cumbernauld, is well preserved in outline. Excavations for the Scottish Development Department in 1977–8 exposed stone slabs, dressed stones and brick pieces, which may have come from the fort bath house. There is some discussion about the garrison. The fort was probably too small for a full auxiliary unit. An inscription suggested that the garrison was a detachment from Legio VI, possibly a vexillation. Interestingly, the inscription recorded the unit's centurion and his wife, who had come to Westerwood from York. Westerwood fort was built on to the Antonine Wall after the stretches of the Wall had reached the site.

Westmuir see **Gask Ridge**

WHITEMOSS Strathclyde
NS 418721 *Antonine Wall outpost fortlet*
An outpost fortlet of the Antonine Wall at its western end, Whitemoss, near Old Bishopston, protected the Clyde estuary.

This fortlet was probably garrisoned by cavalry.

WILDERNESS PLANTATION
Strathclyde NS 603723
Antonine Wall fortlet
Detected from the air in the 1950s and excavated in detail in 1965–6, and again later, this fortlet at Wilderness Plantation, near Cadder, was built contemporaneously with the Antonine Wall in one building operation. It was given two ditches, was less than ¼ acre (0.1ha) in area and was erected in the Antonine I period. Timber buildings were later taken down, probably in the Antonine II period, and the inside ground of the fortlet was covered with cobblestones. Quantities of coarse pottery have been recovered from above the cobble floor and below.

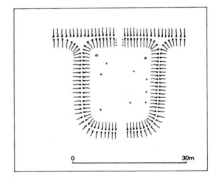

Wilderness Plantation fortlet

Witch Knowe see **Gask Ridge**

WODEN LAW Borders
NT 768125 *Siege works*
One of the relatively few examples of the Roman army on manoeuvres can be seen at Woden Law. This had been an Iron Age hillfort of the Selgovae. In earlier Roman times, at least four temporary camps were erected in the Pennymuir area further down the hill, traces of which can be seen, and it is possible that one or more of the camps were used on a longer term basis, such as for winter quarters. Just below the hillfort, the ramparts and ditches of which are clearly

defined on the hilltop, can be seen equally clearly groups of lines of practice siege works, with stone-packed stretches intended as *ballistaria* (gun platforms). The hillfort had been abandoned before the arrival of the Romans, which suggests that the siege works had nothing to do with taking the hillfort.

WOODHEAD Lothian
NT 384639 *Marching camp*
Woodhead camp was only 3½ acres (1.5ha), with Stracathro-type gates, and is believed to be the smallest Stracathro-type camp in Scotland. It was surrounded by an unusual outwork, polygonal in plan, amounting to nearly 20 acres (8ha), and it is thought that much of the space was given over to intensive growing of timber for fort building in the area. Woodhead lies where Dere Street crossed the Tyne river.

YTHAN WELLS Grampian
NJ 655383 *Marching camps*
Two marching camps have been detected by aerial photography at Ythan Wells. The first, which was Agricolan, had Stracathro-type gates and occupied about 33 acres (13ha). A second, much larger, camp of 110 acres (44.5ha) was built, an elongated rectangle in plan, some of which is superimposed on the earlier camp. The second camp was probably constructed after Agricola's return to Rome.

COUNTY INDEX TO GAZETTEER

The gazetteer entries are here listed alphabetically by county. Hadrian's Wall sites have been grouped together as a special section under 'Hadrian's Wall' and do not appear in the county lists for Tyne & Wear, Northumberland and Cumbria.

SCOTLAND

Scottish sites have been listed alphabetically by region. The forts of the Antonine Wall have been grouped together separately under 'Antonine Wall' and do not appear in the lists for Central, Lothian and Strathclyde regions.

NOTES

ENGLAND

ABBOTSBURY: *Britannia* vi (1975), vii (1976).

ACTON SCOTT: Percival; Rivet (ed); P. Morris.

ALCESTER: *Britannia* ii (1971) to xiii (1982); Arch Ex 1969, 1970; WMANS various issues; Rodwell & Rowley (ed); M. J. Jones.

ALCHESTER: *Britannia* vi (1975); Arch Ex 1974; Oxon. xi (1975); M. J. Jones; Rodwell & Rowley (ed); Antiq J 1932.

ALDBOROUGH: Wacher (1974); *Britannia* i (1970) to vii (1976); DoE booklet; YAJ 1959.

ALDEBY: *East Anglian Archaeology* 1978.

ALDERMASTON: CA 54; Arch Ex 1976; *Britannia* viii (1977).

ALDWINCLE: BNFAS 1971; JRS 1968; CA 9 (1968); *Britannia* vii (1976).

ALFOLDEAN: Winbolt.

ALICE HOLT: Swan; Frere; Collingwood & Richmond; *Britannia* xii (1981).

ALRESFORD: Todd (ed).

ALREWAS: Arch Ex 1974; *Britannia* vi (1975).

ALTON: *Britannia* ix (1978), xii (1981).

AMBERWOOD INCLOSURE: Arch Ex 1970.

AMBLESIDE: *Britannia* i (1970); viii (1977); M. J. Jones; Breeze; Holder; Welsby.

ANCASTER: *Britannia* i (1970), ii (1971), v (1974), vii (1976); Arch Ex 1970; Rodwell & Rowley (ed); P. Morris; M. J. Jones; JRS various issues.

ANGMERING: Rivet (ed); Percival; *Britannia* i (1970), ii (1971).

APETHORPE: Todd (ed); Rivet (ed); Percival.

APPLEFORD: *Britannia* i (1970), v (1974).

ARNE: Swan; *Britannia* vii (1976) to xiii (1982).

ASH: Arch Cant 1915; Kent Arch Rev 1970.

ASHLEY: *Britannia* ii (1971); JRS 1964, 1968.

ASHTEAD: *Britannia* vi (1975); Todd (ed); Rivet (ed).

ASHTON: CA 56; *Britannia* vi (1975), viii (1977), ix (1978), xii (1981).

ASHWELL END: *Britannia* ii (1971).

ASTBURY: M. J. Jones; *Britannia* ii (1971).

ASTON BLANK: *Britannia* xiii (1972); Branigan & Fowler.

ASTON SOMERVILLE: *Britannia* vii (1976), viii (1977); WMANS 1975.

ATWORTH: *Britannia* ii (1971) to vii (1976); Rivet (ed); Branigan & Fowler; P. Morris.

AUGILL BRIDGE: *Britannia* vii (1976).

AYLESBURY: *Britannia* xi (1980), xii (1981).

BADBURY: Arch Ex 1969, 1970; *Britannia* i (1970) to iii (1972); WANHM 1958.

BAGRAW: Daniels.

BALDOCK: Rodwell & Rowley (ed); *Britannia* i (1970) to iv (1973), vii (1976), xii (1981), xiii (1982); Arch Ex 1970, 1971, 1972.

BANCROFT (Bradwell): *Britannia* iii (1972) to xi (1980); CBA Group 9 various years; ABBNO various years; *Excavations at the Bradwell Villa*, 1973-4.

BANWELL: JRS 1968; Percival.

BARBURY CASTLE: CBA Groups 12-13, Newsletter 1970.

BARDOWN: *Britannia* i (1970), ii (1971).

BARHAM: Arch Ex 1970.

BARHOLM: *Britannia* vi (1975); Percival; Todd (ed); P. Morris.

BARKSORE: Kent Arch Rev 1972, 1973.

BARNACK: *Britannia* ii (1971), v (1974); P. Morris.

BARNETBY TOP: *Britannia* vii (1976); Swan.

BARNSLEY PARK: *Britannia* i (1970) to xi (1980); Todd (ed); Branigan & Fowler.

BARNWELL: *Britannia* v (1974).

BARTLOW: *Britannia* iv (1973).

BARTON COURT: *Britannia* v (1974) to viii (1977); Todd (ed); Arch Ex 1976; P. Morris.

BASING: Arch Ex 1969.

BATH: Cunliffe, B. *Roman Bath Discovered* (Routledge & Kegan Paul, 1971); Official Guide, 1978; *Britannia* various issues, esp vii (1976) and x (1979); Rodwell & Rowley (ed).

BAUNTON: *Britannia* xiii (1982); Glevensis 15 (1981).

BAWBURGH: *Britannia* iii (1972).

BAWDRIP: Arch Ex 1971; Branigan & Fowler.

BEADLAM: *Britannia* i (1970), iv (1973), viii (1977); Todd (ed); YAJ xliii (1971).

BEAUFRONT RED HOUSE: *Britannia* vi (1975); CA 46; Arch Ex 1974; Daniels; Holder.

527

BEAUPORT PARK: *Britannia* ii (1971) to x (1979).

BELLSHIEL: SAF 12 (1981); Daniels.

BENWELL: *Britannia* x (1979); Daniels; Breeze & Dobson; Holder.

BERWICK DOWN: Branigan & Fowler.

BEWCASTLE: *Britannia* ix (1978); Daniels; M. J. Jones; Holder; Welsby; Breeze.

BICESTER: CBA Group 9, Newsletter 1979; *Britannia* x (1979), xi (1980).

BIERTON: *Britannia* xi (1980).

BIGBURY: Hawkes; Frere; *Britannia* xii (1981).

BIGNOR: Guide book; *Britannia* xiii (esp. S. S. Frere); Todd (ed).

BINCHESTER: *Britannia* iii (1972), iv (1973), viii (1977) to xi (1980); Holder; Welsby.

BINCOMBE: *Britannia* iii (1972); PDNHAS 1971.

BIRDHOPE: SAF 12 (1981).

BIRDOSWALD: *Britannia* iii (1972), iv (1973), v (1974); Holder; Daniels; Breeze & Dobson.

BISHOPSTONE DOWNS: *Britannia* iv (1973); VCH Wiltshire I (1957).

BITTERNE: *Britannia* xi (1980); Frere; Branigan & Fowler; Rivet; Collingwood & Richmond; Johnston (ed); Welsby.

BLACKDOWN: CBA Groups 12–13, Newsletter 1970; Branigan & Fowler.

BLACKPOOL BRIDGE: Margary.

BLACKWARDINE: WMANS 1975.

BLAKEHOPE: SAF 12 (1981); M. J. Jones; Daniels.

BLAXHALL: *Britannia* v (1974).

BLETSOE: Arch Ex 1970.

BLUNTS GREEN: *Britannia* ii (1972), vi (1975), x (1979); WMANS various issues from 1971.

BOOTHAM STRAY: Holder; Frere.

BOSCOMBE DOWN: Rivet (ed); *Britannia* ii (1971).

BOUGHSPRING: *Britannia* iv (1973), xii (1981); Glevensis 7 (1973), 14 (1980).

BOURTON-on-the-WATER: *Britannia* x (1979), xii (1981), xiii (1982); Glevensis 11 (1977), 12 (1978), 14 (1980), 15 (1981).

BOW BRICKHILL: *Britannia* i (1970), ii (1971), viii (1977) to xii (1981).

BOWES: *Britannia* ii (1971), xii (1981); M. J. Jones; Breeze & Dobson; Holder; Welsby; YAJ 1912.

BOWES MOOR: *Britannia* xii (1981).

BOWNESS-on-SOLWAY: *Britannia* v (1974), viii (1977), xiii (1982); Daniels; Welsby; Holder.

BOX: Percival; Rivet (ed); Branigan & Fowler; VCH Wiltshire I (1957).

BOXMOOR: *Britannia* i (1970), ii (1971); Todd (ed).

BOXTED: *Britannia* i (1970), iv (1973), vii (1976); Todd (ed); Kent Arch Rev 1969.

BRACKLEY: BNFAS 1972; *Britannia* iv (1973).

BRADFIELD: Arch Ex 1970.

BRADING: Local booklet by Margaret Rule; Percival; Rivet (ed); Todd (ed); P. Morris; Rivet.

BRADLEY HILL: Branigan & Fowler; *Britannia* i (1970), ii (1971), iv (1973); P. Morris.

BRADWELL-ON-SEA: Johnston (ed); Johnson (1979).

BRAINTREE: Arch Ex 1974; *Britannia* vi (1975), ix (1978), xii (1981).

BRAMDEAN: VCH Hants I (1900); Rivet (ed).

BRAMPTON: *Britannia* i (1970) to xiii (1982).

BRAMPTON OLD CHURCH: *Britannia* xiii (1982); M. J. Jones; Holder; Breeze & Dobson.

BRANCASTER: *Britannia* i (1970), ii (1971), v (1974), vi (1975), x (1979); Johnson (1979); Arch Ex 1974; Johnston (ed).

BRANTINGHAM: *Britannia* iv (1973); Percival; Rivet (ed); YAJ 1948–51.

BRAUGHING: Rodwell & Rowley (ed); *Britannia* v (1974).

BRAY: *Britannia* i (1970), ii (1971), iii (1972).

BREAGE: Sedgley.

BRENLEY CORNER: Arch Ex 1972; Green.

BRIDGEWORTH: *Britannia* vii (1976).

BRIGHTLINGSEA: Todd (ed); VCH Essex III.

BRIGSTOCK: Collingwood & Richmond; Rivet; Arch Ex 1970; Antiq J 1963.

BRISLINGTON: Branigan & Fowler; TBGAS 1900; Rivet (ed).

BRISTOL: *Britannia* viii (1977).

BRIXWORTH: *Britannia* iii (1972); Todd (ed); Percival.

BROADFIELDS: Arch Ex 1972, 1974; *Britannia* ii (1971), esp. H. Cleere.

BROCKWORTH: *Britannia* v (1974), viii (1977).

BROMHAM: Beds Arch J 1971; Swan; P. Morris; Rivet (ed).

BROMLEY HALL: JRS lix (1969); *Britannia* i (1970).

BROUGH: *Britannia* iv (1973); M. J. Jones; Breeze & Dobson; Holder; Arch Ex 1972; CW lxxvii (1977).

BROUGH-by-BAINBRIDGE: *Britannia* i (1970); Holder; Welsby; M. J. Jones; Breeze & Dobson; *Proceedings of the Leeds Literary and Philosophical Society* various issues.

BROUGH-on-HUMBER: Wacher (1974); *Britannia* various issues, i (1970) to x (1979); Wacher, J. S. *Excavations at Brough, 1958–61* (Society of Antiquities, 1969); Antiq J 1960.

BROUGH-on-NOE: *Britannia* i (1970);

Collingwood & Richmond; M. J. Jones; Holder; Derbys 1965-9.
BROUGHAM: Collingwood & Richmond; M. J. Jones; Breeze; RCHM Westmorland; CW 1932.
BROXTOWE: M. J. Jones.
BUCKNOWLE FARM: *Britannia* vii (1976) to xiii (1982).
BURGH: Arch Ex 1975: *Britannia* vii (1976).
BURGH CASTLE: *Britannia* ii (1971), vi (1975), x (1979); Johnson (1979); Johnston (ed).
BURGH-by-SANDS: *Britannia* viii (1977) to xiii (1982); Daniels; Breeze; Holder.
BURGHWALLIS: *Britannia* iii (1972), v (1974), ix (1978); Welsby.
BURNHAM-on-CROUCH: *Britannia* iv (1973).
BURROW-in-LONSDALE: *Britannia* v (1974); M. J. Jones; CW various issues.
BURWELL: Antiq J 1970; *Britannia* ii (1971), xii (1981).
BUTCOMBE: CBA Groups 12-13, Review 1970; P. Morris; *Britannia* ii (1972), iii (1972), v (1974).
BUXTON: M. J. Jones; Derbys 1916.
CAERMOTE: M. J. Jones; Frere; CW various issues.
CAISTER-on-SEA: Welsby; Rivet; *Norfolk Archaeology* 1962, 1966.
CAISTOR: Antiq J 1960; Rivet; Welsby.
CAISTOR ST EDMUND: Wacher (1974); *Britannia* i (1970), iv (1973), vii (1976), x (1979).
CAMBRIDGE: Rodwell & Rowley (ed); M. J. Jones; *Britannia* i (1970) to vii (1976).
CAMERTON: Branigan & Fowler; *Britannia* i (1970).
CANTERBURY: Wacher (1974); *Britannia* i (1970), iii (1972), v (1974), viii (1977) to xiii (1982); Frere, S. *Roman Canterbury* (London, 1965); other works by Frere; CA 62.
CARDURNOCK: *Britannia* ix (1978), xiii (1982); Daniels.
CARISBROOKE: *Britannia* i (1970); CBA Groups 12-13, Newsletter 1970; P. Morris; Todd (ed); Rivet (ed).
CARLISLE: Wacher (1974); *Britannia* v (1974), vii (1976), viii (1977), ix (1978), x (1979), xii (1981), xiii (1982); Daniels; CW various issues.
CARRAWBURGH: *Britannia* i (1970), ix (1978); Breeze & Dobson; Breeze; Holder; Daniels.
CARSINGTON: *Britannia* xii (1981).
CARVORAN: *Britannia* iii (1972), iv (1973), viii (1977), x (1979); Holder; Breeze; Breeze & Dobson; Collingwood & Richmond; Daniels.
CASTLE DYKES: Percival; Rivet (ed); Todd (ed).
CASTLEFORD: *Britannia* i (1970), vi (1975),

ix (1978), x (1979), xii (1981); CA 45.
CASTLESHAW: *Britannia* ii (1971); M. J. Jones; Holder; T Lancs & Ches AS 1922, 1957, 1963, 1967.
CASTLESTEADS: Breeze & Dobson; Daniels.
CASTOR: *Britannia* i (1970), ii (1971), v (1974), vii (1976), ix (1978), xii (1981); Collingwood & Richmond; Todd (ed); Rivet; Rodwell & Rowley (ed); Rivet (ed).
CATSGORE: *Britannia* i (1970), iii (1972), iv (1973), x (1979), xi (1980); P. Morris; Rivet (ed); Branigan & Fowler; Rivet; PSANHS 1951.
CATTERICK: Wacher (ed); *Britannia* i (1970), vii (1976), xi (1980); Frere; YAJ various issues.
CATTLE HILL: *Britannia* ii (1971), iii (1972); Branigan & Fowler.
CATTY BROOK: *Britannia* v (1974), vi (1975); Arch Ex 1974.
CAVE'S INN: *Britannia* ii (1971), iii (1972), iv (1973), v (1974), vii (1976), ix (1978); Wacher (ed); Welsby; M. J. Jones; WMANS various issues.
CAWTHORN: *Britannia* ix (1978); Holder; SAF 12 (1981); Collingwood & Richmond; YAJ.
CHALK: *Britannia* iii (1972), vii (1976), x (1979), esp. D. E. Johnston's article, 1972.
CHANCTONBURY RING: Green; *Britannia* ix (1978).
CHARLBURY: ABBNO 1982; *Britannia* xiii (1982).
CHARLTON KINGS: *Britannia* xii (1981).
CHARTERHOUSE-on-MENDIP: Rodwell & Rowley (ed); Collingwood & Richmond; Branigan & Fowler; Rivet; M. J. Jones; *Britannia* ii (1971); Holder.
CHEDDAR: PSANHS 1966; Branigan & Fowler; *Britannia* ii (1971).
CHEDWORTH: *Britannia* x (1979) to xiii (1982); *The Roman Villa*, National Trust booklet; TBGAS, lxxviii (1959).
CHELMSFORD: Wacher (1974); M. J. Jones; Arch Ex various issues; VCH Essex III; *Britannia* various issues; Rodwell & Rowley (ed); T Essex AHS 1970, 1972.
CHESTER: Thompson, F. H. *Roman Cheshire*; Strickland; *Britannia* i (1970) to xiii (1982); Holder; M. J. Jones; Welsby.
CHESTERFIELD: *Britannia* vii (1976) to x (1979).
CHESTERHOLM: *Britannia* i (1970), ii (1971), iii (1972), iv (1973), v (1974), vii (1976), ix (1978), x (1979), xii (1981); Daniels; Breeze & Dobson; Holder; Arch Ael various issues.
CHESTER-le-STREET: *Britannia* ii (1971), ix (1978), x (1979), xi (1980); M. J. Jones;

Welsby; Holder; Breeze & Dobson.
CHESTERS: DoE booklet; Daniels; Breeze & Dobson; Holder; *Britannia* ii (1971), vii (1976).
CHESTERTON: *Britannia* ii (1971); WMANS 1969; M. J. Jones.
CHESTERTON-on-FOSSE: *Britannia* i (1970); Rodwell & Rowley (ed).
CHEW GREEN: SAF 12 (1981); Daniels.
CHICHESTER: Wacher (1974); *Chichester Excavations* (Down & Rule) I, 1971; II, 1974; *Britannia* i (1970) to xiii (1982).
CHIGNALL ST JAMES: CBA Calendar, 11 September 1979; Todd (ed); *Britannia* vi (1975) to xiii (1982).
CHILGROVE: Arch 1971, 1972; *Britannia* v (1974) to vii (1976); P. Morris.
CHILSWELL: *Britannia* xi (1980).
CHILVERS COTON: WMANS 1970.
CHURCHILL HOSPITAL: Oxon several issues since 1952; *Britannia* iii (1972), v (1974), viii (1978), xiii (1982); Swan.
CIRENCESTER: Wacher (1974); *Britannia* i (1970) to xiii (1982); Branigan & Fowler; CA 29, 42; Antiq J liii (1973); Antiq J 1962-69, various issues.
CLANVILLE: *Archaeologia* 1898; Todd (ed); Rivet (ed); Percival; P. Morris.
CLAXBY-by-LINCOLN: *Britannia* v (1974).
CLAYDON PIKE: CA, March 1983; *Britannia* xi (1980), xii (1981), xiii (1982); ABBNO various issues.
CLIFFORD: JRS 1973; M. J. Jones.
COBHAM: *Britannia* xi (1980).
COBHAM PARK: Percival; Todd (ed); P. Morris; Arch Cant 1961.
CODDENHAM: Rodwell & Rowley (ed); *Britannia* v (1974), vii (1976), ix (1978); Antiq J 1956.
COLCHESTER: Wacher (1974); various Colchester Borough Council and Colchester Archaeological Trust publications, incl *Roman Colchester*, 1980; *Britannia* i (1970) to xiii (1982).
COLERNE: Rivet (ed).
COLESHILL: *Britannia* x (1979) to xii (1981).
COMBE HAY: Arch Ex 1972: *Britannia* i (1970).
COMB END: *Britannia* iii (1972); Rivet (ed); P. Morris.
COMBLEY: *Britannia* ii (1971), v (1974), vii (1976), xi (1980); Todd (ed).
COOKHAM: *Britannia* i (1970).
CORBRIDGE: DoE booklet; Daniels; *Britannia* ii (1971) to vii (1976); Arch Ael various issues.
COSGROVE: BNFAS 1970; Percival; Green; *Britannia* ii (1971).
COW ROAST: *Britannia* v (1974) to ix (1978); CA 52; Todd (ed).
COX GREEN: Todd (ed); Rivet (ed); Percival.

CRACKENTHORPE: SAF 12 (1981); Holder; Frere.
CRANE GODREVY: CBA Groups 12-13, Newsletter 1969.
CROMHALL: Todd (ed); P. Morris; Branigan & Fowler.
CROSBY-on-EDEN: *Britannia* xii (1981), xiii (1982).
CROWBOROUGH: *Britannia* ix (1978).
CURBRIDGE: CBA Group 9, Newsletter, 1976.
DALTON PARLOURS: *Britannia* viii (1977), ix (1978), x (1979), xii (1981).
DANEBURY: *Britannia* iv (1973); AR 1972.
DANESHILL: *Britannia* xiii (1982).
DARENTH: Todd (ed); P. Morris; Rivet (ed); Percival; Arch Ex 1969; Kent Arch Rev 1970.
DARGUES: SAF 12 (1981); Daniels.
DARTFORD: *Britannia* vi (1975).
DEANSHANGER: Arch Ex 1972; P. Morris; JRS 1958.
DENTON: Todd (ed); Rivet (ed); Percival; P. Morris.
DERBY: *Britannia* ii (1971), iv (1973), v (1974), vi (1975), xi (1980); Arch Ex 1972; Trent Valley Arch Research Committee, Report 7 (1973).
DEWLISH: *Britannia* i (1970) to vii (1976), esp v (1974); PDNHAS 1969 and following; Branigan & Fowler; Percival.
DICKET MEAD: *Britannia* i (1970), ii (1971); Percival; Rivet (ed); Todd (ed); CA 27; P. Morris.
DITCHLEY: Rivet (ed); Percival; Todd (ed); P. Morris; *Britannia* vi (1975).
DODDERHILL: *Britannia* i (1970), ix (1978); M. J. Jones.
DONCASTER: *Britannia* i (1970) to x (1979); Holder; Welsby; M. J. Jones; CA 1971.
DORCHESTER: Wacher (1974); *Britannia* various issues; Branigan & Fowler; *Archaeologia* cv (1976).
DORCHESTER-on-THAMES: *Britannia* iv (1973), xii (1981), xiii (1982); Rodwell & Rowley (ed); Oxon various issues.
DORKING: *Britannia* viii (1977), xii (1981), xiii (1982); Margary.
DOVER: Johnson (1979); B. Philp on the Roman 'Painted House' at Dover in Johnston (ed); *Britannia* ii (1971) to xiii (1982).
DOWNTON: Rivet (ed); Todd (ed); WANHM 1961-3; P. Morris.
DRAGONBY: Collingwood & Richmond; *Britannia* ii (1971), iv (1973); Swan; Antiq J 1970.
DROITWICH: *Britannia* iii (1972), vi (1975) to xii (1981); WMANS various issues; M. J. Jones; Wacher (ed); P. Morris; Rivet; TBAS, 1933, 1938.

DRUMBURGH: *Britannia* vii (1976), xiii (1982); Daniels.

DUBMILL: CW 1954.

DUBMILL POINT: *Britannia* ix (1978), xiii (1982); Daniels.

DUCKLINGTON: *Britannia* v (1974), vii (1976), viii (1977).

DUNCOT: *Britannia* vi (1975).

DUNSTABLE: *Manshead Magazine* 1970; Rivet; *Britannia* ii (1971), viii (1977).

DURRINGTON WALLS: P. Morris; *Britannia* ii (1971).

DYMOCK: *Britannia* i (1970), iii (1972), iv (1973); Glevensis 4 (1969).

EARITH: Arch Ex 1974; P. Morris; *Britannia* vi (1975).

EAST ANTON: Arch Ex 1970; Margary; *Britannia* iii (1972).

EAST BRIDGFORD: Thoroton Soc lxxiii (1969); Collingwood & Richmond; Welsby; M. J. Jones; *Britannia* i (1970).

EAST COKER: Rivet (ed); VCH Somerset I.

EAST GRIMSTEAD: VCH Wiltshire I; Percival; Rivet (ed); Todd (ed); P. Morris.

EAST HOLME: *Britannia* iii (1972), v (1974); Swan.

EASTON: *Britannia* x (1979), xi (1980), xiii (1982); Daniels.

EATON-by-TARPORLEY: *Britannia* xii (1981), xiii (1982).

EBCHESTER: *Britannia* iv (1973); Holder; Breeze & Dobson; M. J. Jones; Welsby; Arch Ael iii (1975).

ECCLES: *Britannia* ii (1971) to v (1974); Todd (ed); P. Morris; Rivet (ed); Percival.

EDLINGTON WOOD: *Britannia* iii (1972).

ELLINGHAM: *Britannia* viii (1977).

ELSLACK: Breeze & Dobson; Holder; Collingwood & Richmond; Welsby; M. J. Jones.

ELSTEAD: Arch Ex 1975.

ELTON: BNFAS, 1970.

EMPINGHAM: Arch Ex 1969, 1970; *Britannia* i (1970), ii (1971), iii (1972) and v (1975).

ENGLETON: Rivet (ed); Todd (ed); *Britannia* ix (1978).

EXETER: Wacher (1974); P. Bidwell, *Roman Exeter* (Exeter Museum, 1980); *Britannia* various issues.

EXNING: JRS 1960; Todd (ed); Rivet (ed); Percival.

FAR COTTON: *Britannia* xi (1980).

FARLEY HEATH: Green; *Britannia* vii (1976).

FARMINGTON: *Britannia* ix (1978); Todd (ed); P. Morris; TBGAS 1969.

FARMOOR: Arch Ex 1974; *Britannia* vi (1975).

FARNHAM: *Britannia* iii (1972).

FARNINGHAM: Arch Ex 1975, 1976; Todd (ed); Rivet (ed).

FEATHERWOOD WEST: Collingwood & Richmond.

FENCOTT: ABBNO 1981.

FINCHAMPSTEAD: *Britannia* vi (1975), vii (1976), ix (1978); Sedgley.

FINGLAND: *Britannia* ii (1971), v (1974), xi (1980), xiii (1982); Breeze.

FINGRINGHOE: Webster (1980); M. J. Jones.

FISHBOURNE: Various works by B. Cunliffe, esp *Excavations at Fishbourne (1961-9)* (Antiq Soc 1971).

FISHTOFT: Lincs Hist Arch Soc J 1976; *Britannia* vi (1975) to viii (1977).

FLITWICK: CBA Group 9, Newsletter 1975; P. Morris.

FLORE: *Britannia* xi (1980).

FOLKESTONE: Rivet (ed); Todd (ed); Percival; Winbolt, S. E. *Roman Folkestone* (London, 1925).

FORDHAM: *Britannia* iv (1973).

FOTHERINGAY: BNFAS 1970; *Britannia* ii (1971).

FOXHOLES: CA 52; *Britannia* vi (1975) to x (1979).

FRAMPTON: *Britannia* ix (1978); Percival; Rivet (ed); RCHM Dorset I (1952).

FRILFORD: *Britannia* vii (1976), xi (1980), xiii (1982); Rivet (ed); Percival

FRING: *Britannia* viii (1977).

FROCESTER: *Britannia* ii (1971), iii (1972), vii (1976) to xiii (1982); TBGAS lxxxix (1970); Todd (ed).

FULLERTON: Rivet (ed); Todd (ed).

GADEBRIDGE: JRS 1967; *Britannia* i (1970), vi (1975); Todd (ed); Percival; P. Morris.

GARDEN HILL: CA 41; *Britannia* iv (1973) to xiii (1982).

GARTON SLACK: Arch Ex 1970, 1971; *Britannia* iii (1972), iv (1973).

GATCOMBE: Branigan, K. *Gatcombe Roman Villa* (British Archaeological Report no 44, 1977); CA 1971; Rodwell & Rowley (ed); *Britannia* various issues.

GAYHURST: Arch Ex 1970; *Britannia* ii (1971).

GAYTON THORPE: *Britannia* vi (1975), vii (1976); Percival; Rivet (ed); Todd (ed); *Norfolk Archaeology* various issues.

GILLALEES: Daniels.

GLASSHOUSE WOOD: WMANS 1971; Arch Ex 1971; *Britannia* viii (1977).

GLOUCESTER: Wacher (1974); Antiq J 1972, 1974, 1975; TBGAS various issues; CA 26; *Britannia* i (1970), ii (1971), iii (1972), vi (1975) to xiii (1982); Branigan & Fowler.

GODMANCHESTER: Rodwell & Rowley (ed);

Britannia i (1970), iii (1972), v (1974), viii (1977), ix (1978), x (1979).

HOLBEANWOOD: *Britannia* ii (1971).

HOLCOMBE: Todd (ed); *Britannia* i (1970), ii (1971), iii (1972); Rivet; Rivet (ed); P. Morris.

HOLME HOUSE: *Britannia* i (1970), ii (1971), iii (1972).

HOLTYE: Arch Ex 1970; Margary.

HOLWAY TEN ACRES: Branigan & Fowler; Britannia iii (1972), iv (1973).

HOOK: Arch Ex 1970.

HORKSTOW: Rivet (ed); *Britannia* iv (1973).

HORNCASTLE: Lincs Hist Arch Soc J 1979; Rivet; *Britannia* x (1979).

HORSTEAD: *Britannia* vi (1975), x (1979).

HORTON KIRBY: *Britannia* iv (1973), v (1974); CA 38; P. Morris; Arch Ex 1972.

HOUSESTEADS: *Britannia* i (1970) to xiii (1982); Daniels; Welsby; Holder; Breeze & Dobson.

HUCCLECOTE: TBGAS 1933; Branigan & Fowler; Rivet (ed).

HUNSBURY: CBA Group 9, Newsletter 1974; *Britannia* iii (1972), v (1974), xi (1980), xiii (1982).

HUNSDON: Herts Arch Rev 1970; *Britannia* iii (1972).

HUNTCLIFF: Collingwood & Richmond; Welsby.

HUNTSHAM: WMANS 1969; JRS 1962, 1965, 1966; Todd (ed); P. Morris.

HUTTONS AMBO: YAR 1977, 1978, 1979; *Britannia* ix (1978), x (1979), xii (1981).

ICKHAM: *Britannia* vi (1925).

ICKLETON: Todd (ed); Rivet (ed); P. Morris.

ICKLINGHAM: Green; *Britannia* iii (1972), v (1974), vi (1975), ix (1978).

IDEN GREEN: Margary.

ILCHESTER: Wacher (1974); *Britannia* various issues, esp vi (1975); Rivet; Rivet (ed); Percival; Branigan & Fowler; Arch Ex 1970, 1971.

ILCHESTER MEAD: *Britannia* i (1970), iv (1973); P. Morris.

ILKLEY: *Britannia* ix (1978); M. J. Jones; Welsby; SAF 12 (1981); Holder; Breeze; Frere; YAJ 1926.

ILLOGAN: JRS 1932; Rivet (ed).

INWORTH: Arch Ex 1971.

IRCHESTER: Rodwell & Rowley (ed); M. J. Jones; Green; *Britannia* i (1970), vii (1976), xiii (1982); Arch J 1967.

ITCHEN ABBASS: VCH Hants I 1900; Rivet (ed); Todd (ed).

IVY CHIMNEYS: *Britannio* xi (1980), xii (1981).

IWERNE: Arch J 1947; Rivet (ed); Todd (ed); P. Morris.

IXWORTH: M. J. Jones; JRS 1953, 1969.

JORDON HILL: Rivet; Green; Branigan & Fowler; *Britannia* vii (1976).

KELVEDON: M. J. Jones; Rodwell & Rowley (ed); *Britannia* various issues, esp v (1974).

KENCHESTER: WMANS 1977; *Britannia* ix (1978), x (1979); Rodwell & Rowley (ed); TBGAS 1972.

KENILWORTH: WMANS 1971; Arch Ex 1971.

KESTON: Kent Arch Rev 1977; *Britannia* v (1974), xii (1982).

KETTERING: *Britannia* i (1970), v (1974); P. Morris.

KEYNSHAM: Collingwood & Richmond; Percival; Todd (ed); Rivet (ed).

KIMMERIDGE: *Britannia* vii (1976), xi (1980); Frere; McWhirr.

KIMPTON: *Britannia* x (1979), xi (1980).

KINGSCOTE: *Britannia* i (1970), viii (1977) to xiii (1982); Glevensis 10 (1976), 15 (1981); Branigan & Fowler; CA, Nov 1979.

KINGSHOLM: *Britannia* iv (1973), vi (1975); Holder; Collingwood & Richmond; Branigan & Fowler.

KING'S LANGLEY: *Britannia* xiii (1982).

KINGS STANLEY: *Britannia* v (1974), ix (1978), x (1979); Glevensis 11 (1977), 12 (1978), 13 (1979).

KING'S WESTON: Branigan & Fowler; *Britannia* ix (1978); TBGAS 1950; Todd (ed); Rivet (ed).

KINGSWORTHY: Rivet (ed); Todd (ed); P. Morris; *Britannia* v (1974).

KINVASTON: JRS 1958; *Britannia* i (1970), v (1974); WMANS 1973; M. J. Jones; TBAS 1951, 1955.

KIRKBRIDE: *Britannia* iii (1972), iv (1973), ix (1978), xiii (1982); Daniels; M. J. Jones; Breeze.

KIRKBY THORE: *Britannia* x (1979); Holder; Breeze & Dobson; Frere; M. J. Jones; CW 1964.

KIRKHAM: M. J. Jones; Arch J 1970.

KIRK SINK: *Britannia* i (1970), v (1974) to vii (1976); Rivet (ed); YAR 1974.

KIRMOND-le-MIRE: Lincs Hist Arch Soc J 1976; *Britannia* vii (1976), viii (1977).

KNAG BURN: *Britannia* vii (1976); Daniels.

KNOWL HILL: Todd (ed); P. Morris; Berks Arch J 38 (1934).

LAKE FARM: Holder; *Britannia* i (1970) to v (1974), xi (1980), xiii (1982); Webster (1980); PDNHAS issues 1965–73.

LAMYATT BEACON: JRS 1961; *Britannia* iii (1972); *Rescue News* 1973; Green.

LANCASTER: *Britannia* ii (1971), iii (1972),

vi (1975), vii (1976), viii (1977), ix (1978), x (1979), xii (1981); Holder; M. J. Jones; Welsby; Breeze; Arch J 1970.

LANCHESTER: Breeze; Collingwood & Richmond; Holder; Welsby; Frere; Arch J cxi (1954).

LANCING DOWN: Green; *Britannia* vii (1976), xii (1982).

LANGTON: *Britannia* vi (1975); P. Morris; Rivet; Todd (ed).

LATIMER: *Britannia* vi (1975); Percival; Todd (ed); P. Morris.

LEASE RIGG: *Britannia* viii (1977) to xii (1981); M. J. Jones.

LEICESTER: Wacher (1974); *Britannia* vii (1976) to xiii (1982); Holder; M. J. Jones.

LEIGH PARK: P. Morris; *Britannia* ii (1971).

LEIGHTON: *Britannia* xi (1980); M. J. Jones; Holder; Frere.

LEINTWARDINE: *Britannia* iii (1972), xii (1981); Holder; Welsby; M. J. Jones; Frere; Woolhope xxxix (1967-9); Arch Ex 1971.

LENHAM: *Britannia* x (1979), xii (1981), xiii (1982); Kent Arch Rev 1979.

LEXDEN: *Colchester Archaeological Group Annual Bulletin* 1971.

LIDGATE: *Antiquity* 1971; Arch Ex 1975; Percival; *Britannia* iii (1972).

LINCOLN: Wacher (1974); *Britannia* various issues from 1970; Holder; Welsby; M. J. Jones; Frere; JRS various issues.

LINLEY: *Britannia* xiii (1982).

LINWOOD: *Antiquity* 1970; *Britannia* i (1970), iv (1973); Arch Ex 1969.

LITTLEBOROUGH: *Britannia* i (1970), ii (1971), v (1974); M. J. Jones.

LITTLECHESTER: *Britannia* i (1970), iv (1973), v (1974), xii (1981); M. J. Jones; Welsby; Derbys 1961, 1967.

LITTLECOTE: *Archaeological Excavations in Littlecote Park* (1978); Todd (ed); Rivet (ed).

LITTLE MILTON: *Britannia* v (1974); Rivet (ed); Percival; JRS 1953.

LITTLE MUNDEN: *Britannia* vi (1975).

LITTLE OAKLEY: *Britannia* xi (1980).

LOCKLEYS: *Britannia* vi (1975); Percival; Rivet (ed); Todd (ed); Antiq J 1938.

LONDON: Marsden; Merrifield; J. Morris; various other papers; various issues of *Britannia*.

LONG BENNINGTON: Lincs Hist Arch Soc J 1976, 1977; Arch Ex 1976; *Britannia* vii (1976), viii (1977).

LONGTHORPE: *Britannia* ii (1971), iii (1972), iv (1973), v (1974), vi (1975); Frere & St Joseph (1974); Holder; M. J. Jones.

LONG WITTENHAM: *Britannia* i (1970),

viii (1977); Arch Ex 1976.

LOW BORROWBRIDGE: M. J. Jones; Welsby; Breeze & Dobson; CW various issues.

LOW HAM: Branigan & Fowler; Rivet; Collingwood & Richmond; Rivet (ed); *Britannia* vii (1976).

LUFTON: PSANHS 107 (1952); Percival; Rivet; Todd (ed).

LUGWARDINE: AW 1973; *Britannia* v (1974).

LULLINGSTONE: Guide Book (G. W. Meates); *Britannia* various issues.

LUNDY ISLAND: *Britannia* i (1970); CA 1969.

LYDIARD TREGOZE: AR 1972.

LYDNEY: *Britannia* xii (1981), xiii (1982); Branigan & Fowler; Green.

LYMPNE: Holder; Welsby; Cunliffe in Johnston (ed).

MAIDEN CASTLE (Cumbria): Collingwood & Richmond.

MAIDEN CASTLE (Dorset): DoE booklet (Wheeler); *Britannia* vii (1976); Green.

MAIDENHATCH: Arch Ex 1970.

MAIDSTONE: *Britannia* iv (1973); Todd (ed); Percival.

MAINS RIGG: *Britannia* iii (1972); CW 1973; Breeze; Daniels.

MALDON: *Colchester Archaeological Group Annual Bulletin* 1972, 1973, 1978.

MALTON: *Britannia* i (1970), ii (1971), iv (1973), v (1974), vi (1975), x (1979); Frere; Holder; Welsby; M. J. Jones; JRS various issues.

MANCETTER: *Britannia* i (1970) to iii (1972), vii (1976) to xiii (1982); WMANS various issues; Rodwell & Rowley (ed); M. J. Jones; Webster; TBAS 1956, 1964, 1973.

MANCHESTER: Bryant, S. *Roman Manchester* (Greater Manchester Archaeological Unit, 1982); *Britannia* vii (1976), x (1979) to xiii (1982); Holder; M. J. Jones.

MANSFIELD WOODHOUSE: Percival; Rivet (ed); P. Morris; Thoroton Soc 1953.

MARTINHOE: Branigan & Fowler; Frere; *Britannia* i (1970), ii (1971), v (1974).

MARYPORT: *Britannia* iv (1973) to viii (1977); M. J. Jones; Daniels; Holder; Welsby; M. G. Jarrett in CW 1976.

MEDBOURNE: *Britannia* i (1970), ix (1978); Rivet; Percival; Arch J 1911.

MELANDRA CASTLE: *Britannia* i (1970), v (1974) to xii (1981); M. J. Jones; Derbys 1969; Holder; Arch J various issues.

MENTLEY FARM: *Britannia* iv (1973).

METCHLEY: *Britannia* i (1970), ii (1971); M. J. Jones; TBAS various issues.

MIDDLE FARM: *Britannia* xiii (1982).

MIDDLETON: Sedgley; Frere.

MIDDLETON STONEY: *Britannia* iii (1972), v (1974), vii (1976); CBA Group 9, Newsletter 2 (1972), 4 (1974).

MIDDLEWICH: *Britannia* i (1970) to vii (1976); Wacher (1974); Rivet.

MILDENHALL: Rodwell & Rowley (ed); Rivet; Wacher (ed); Welsby.

MILECASTLES on HADRIAN'S WALL: All milecastles included are described in C. M. Daniels' 1978 edition of Collingwood Bruce's *The Roman Wall*. Several are also discussed in Breeze & Dobson, including 9, 15, 22, 23, 27, 29, 30, 37, 38, 39, 40, 47, 48, 49, 50, 51, 52, 54, 65, 79: some are also discussed in Collingwood & Richmond (30, 38, 47, 48, 50, 79), and a few in issues of *Britannia* and Arch Ael. For Milecastle 42 (Cawfields) see Daniels; Welsby; Breeze & Dobson.

MILEFORTLET 1 (Biglands): *Britannia* vi (1975), vii (1976), xiii (1982); Daniels.

MILEFORTLET 11 (Silloth): *Britannia* ix (1978), x (1979), xiii (1982); Daniels.

MILEFORTLET 20 (Low Mire): *Britannia* xii (1981), xiii (1982); Daniels; Welsby.

MILEFORTLET 26 (Rise How Bank): Daniels.

MILTON COMMON: Arch Ex 1971; CBA Group 9, Newsletter 1971.

MORESBY: *Britannia* x (1979); Breeze & Dobson; Daniels; Holder.

MOUNT BURES: *Colchester Archaeological Group Annual Bulletin* 1972.

MOUNT WOOD: Group 9, Newsletter 1973.

NANSTALLON: M. J. Jones; *Britannia* i (1970), iii (1972), esp Lady Fox's article; Frere; Branigan & Fowler.

NEATHAM: Rodwell & Rowley (ed); Arch Ex 1970, 1974, 1976.

NETHER DENTON: *Britannia* viii (1977).

NETHERTON: *Britannia* v (1974).

NETHERWILD FARM: JRS 1963; P. Morris; *Britannia* i (1970); Todd (ed).

NEWCASTLE upon TYNE: *Britannia* v (1974), ix (1978), x (1979); Daniels; Welsby; Holder; Breeze.

NEWHAVEN: Arch Ex 1972, 1974; P. Morris.

NEWINGTON: *Britannia* xi (1980).

NEWNHAM: Arch Ex 1972; CBA Group 9, Newsletters, 1974, 1975; *Britannia* iv (1973) to vii (1976).

NEWPORT: Todd (ed); Percival; Frere.

NEWTON-on-TRENT: M. J. Jones; Holder.

NEWTON ST LOE: JRS 1936; Rivet (ed); Percival; Todd (ed).

NORDEN: PDNHAS 1969; *Britannia* iv (1973).

NORTHCHURCH: Herts Arch Rev no 8; Todd (ed); Arch J 1971.

NORTHFLEET: Kent Arch Rev 1977, 1979;

Britannia issues from viii (1977) to xiii (1982).

NORTH LEIGH: Collingwood & Richmond; *Britannia* vii (1976) to xi (1980).

NORTH TAWTON: M. J. Jones; Holder; Branigan & Fowler; Rivet.

NORTH WARNBOROUGH: P. Morris; Rivet (ed); Todd (ed).

NORTHWICH: CBA Group 5, Newsletter 14/15, 1970; *Britannia* i (1970), ii (1972), vi (1975); M. J. Jones.

NORTH WRAXALL: PSAS 1960; Rivet (ed); Todd (ed); P. Morris; *Britannia* ix (1978).

NORTON: Collingwood & Richmond; Rivet; Wacher (1980).

NORTON DISNEY: Rivet (ed); Todd (ed); *Britannia* i (1970); Percival; P. Morris; Antiq J 1937.

ODELL: *Britannia* vi (1975) to ix (1978).

OKEHAMPTON: M. J. Jones; Branigan & Fowler; *Britannia* viii (1977).

OLD BURROW: Branigan & Fowler; Frere; *Britannia* i (1970), iii (1972), v (1974), x (1979).

OLD CARLISLE: M. J. Jones; Welsby; Breeze & Dobson; Breeze; Holder; Arch J cxxxvii (1975); CW various issues.

OLDCROFT: *Britannia* iv (1973); Margary.

OLD DURHAM: P. Morris; Rivet (ed); Arch Ael xxii, xxix, xxxi.

OLD PENRITH: *Britannia* ix (1978); Holder; Breeze & Dobson; Breeze; Welsby; M. J. Jones; CW various issues.

OLD SARUM: Rivet (ed); Webster (1980).

OLD STRATFORD: WMANS 1977.

OLNEY: CBA Group 9, Newsletter 1976.

ORPINGTON: *Britannia* viii (1977), ix (1978), x (1979); Kent Arch Rev 1977, 1978.

OTFORD: *Britannia* iii (1972), vi (1975), ix (1978); Percival; Rivet (ed); P. Morris.

OVERMOIGNE: *Britannia* v (1974); PDNHAS 1973.

OVERSTONE: CBA Group 9, Newsletter 1973; *Britannia* ix (1973).

PAGAN'S HILL: *Britannia* vii (1976); Branigan & Fowler; Rivet; Collingwood & Richmond; Green.

PAPCASTLE: M. J. Jones; Welsby; Frere; Breeze & Dobson; Holder; CW various issues.

PARK STREET: *Britannia* i (1970), ii (1971), viii (1977); Todd (ed); Rivet (ed); Percival.

PENTREHYLING: *Britannia* xiii (1982).

PETERBOROUGH: Arch Ex 1972; *Britannia* iv (1973), vi (1975), ix (1978), x (1979), xiii (1982).

PEVENSEY: Johnston (ed); Johnson (1979); Welsby; *Britannia* i (1970), ii (1971), v (1974).

PIDDINGTON: CA 82; *Britannia* xii (1981).

PIERCEBRIDGE: *Britannia* v (1974) to xiii

(1982); CA 40 (1973); M. J. Jones; Welsby; Holder.

PITNEY: Percival; Todd (ed); Rivet (ed); P. Morris; Branigan & Fowler.

PLUMPTON HEAD: *Britannia* vi (1975); SAF 12 (1981); Frere.

PORTCHESTER: Johnston (ed); Cunliffe, B. *Excavations at Portchester* I & II; *Britannia* i (1970) to iv (1973); Welsby; Collingwood & Richmond; Holder; Johnson (1979).

PORTISHEAD: Branigan & Fowler; *Britannia* iii (1972).

POUNDBURY: *Britannia* i (1970) to viii (1977); PDNHAS 1969.

PRESTON: PDNHAS 1933; Rivet (ed); RCHM Dorset II (1970).

PRIDDY: Branigan & Fowler; *Britannia* iii (1972).

PUCKERIDGE: Arch Ex 1971; Herts Arch Rev 1971, 1972; *Britannia* ii (1971) to iv (1973).

PUNCHBOWL INN: *Britannia* vii (1976).

PURBROOK: *Britannia* vii (1976), ix (1978); JRS 1926.

PURITON: Branigan & Fowler; *Britannia* iii (1972).

QUENTON: BNFAS 1970, 1971; CBA Group 9, Newsletter 1975–7; Arch Ex 1975.

QUERNMORE: *Britannia* ii (1971), iii (1972), iv (1973); Frere.

RADFORD SEMELE: TBGAS 1971; *Britannia* v (1974), vi (1975).

RADWELL: *Britannia* iv (1973).

RAMSDEN: *Britannia* xii (1981).

RANSCOMBE: Arch Ex 1976.

RAPSLEY: *Surrey Archaeological Collections* 1968; Percival; Todd (ed); P. Morris.

RATHAM MILL: *Britannia* xiii (1982).

RAVENGLASS: *Britannia* i (1970), viii (1977); Daniels; Breeze & Dobson; Holder; Welsby; Breeze.

RAVENSBURGH: Hawkes.

RAVENSTONE: *Britannia* xiii (1982).

RECULVER: Johnston (ed); Johnson (1979); Welsby; Kent Arch Rev 1970, 1976.

RED HILL: *Britannia* i (1970), v (1974); Welsby; M. J. Jones.

REYCROSS: Holder; SAF 12 (1981); CW xxxiv (1934).

RHYN PARK: *Britannia* viii (1977), ix (1978), x (1979); Holder; M. J. Jones.

RIBCHESTER: Arch J cxxvii (1970); *Britannia* i (1970), ii (1971), iv (1973), vi (1975), viii (1977), ix (1978), x (1979), xii (1981); Arch Ex 1970, 1972, 1974; Holder; M. J. Jones.

RICHBOROUGH: Johnston (ed); Johnson (1979); Holder; Welsby; DoE Guide.

RISINGHAM: Breeze & Dobson; Breeze;

Holder; Daniels; Welsby.

RIVENHALL: *Britannia* iii (1972), iv (1973), v (1974); Todd (ed); P. Morris.

ROCESTER: M. J. Jones.

ROCHESTER: *Britannia* i (1970), vii (1976), viii (1977); Arch Cant 1905; Arch Ex 1975.

ROCK: P. Morris; Todd (ed); *Britannia* vii (1976).

ROCKBOURNE: Guide book; *Britannia* iii (1972), xi (1980); P. Morris; Todd (ed); Rivet (ed).

ROCKBOURNE DOWN: Collingwood & Richmond; P. Morris; Rivet (ed).

RODMARTON. TBGAS 1972; Percival.

ROMSEY: *Britannia* xii (1981).

ROSSINGTON BRIDGE: Holder; M. J. Jones; JRS lix (1969); Welsby.

ROTHERLEY: Rivet (ed).

ROWLANDS CASTLE: Swan; *Britannia* vii (1976), xii (1981).

RUDCHESTER: *Britannia* iv (1973), vii (1976); Daniels; Breeze; Collingwood & Richmond; CBA Group 3, Newsletter 4, 1973.

RUDSTON: Rivet (ed); Todd (ed); *Britannia* i (1970), ii (1971), iii (1972), iv (1973); P. Morris.

RUSHDEN: CA 31; *Britannia* iii (1972).

SACREWELL: *Northamptonshire Archaeology* 1974; *Britannia* vi (1975).

ST ALBANS: Kenyon, K. and Frere, S. S. *The Roman Theatre of Verulamium* (Official Guide); *Britannia* various issues; Frere, S. S. *Verulamium Excavations* I, II, Soc of Antiq.

ST HILARY: Sedgley.

ST MARTINS (Isles of Scilly): Branigan & Fowler; Arch J cxxiv (1967).

SANDWICH: *Britannia* x (1979), xi (1980) xii (1981).

SANSOM'S PLATT: CBA Group 9, Newsletter 1973.

SAPPERTON: *Britannia* v (1974), vi (1975), viii (1977), ix (1978), xii (1981); Lincs Hist Arch Soc J 1976; P. Morris.

SAUNDERTON: *Britannia* v (1974); P. Morris; Rivet (ed).

SAWLEY: *Britannia* vii (1976); Derbys 1967.

SCALESCEUGH: *Britannia* ii (1971), iii (1972); Holder; Frere; Collingwood & Richmond.

SCAMPTON: Rivet (ed); Todd (ed); *Britannia* v (1974).

SCARBOROUGH: Welsby.

SCARCLIFFE PARK: *Britannia* i (1970), ii (1971); Arch Ex 1970.

SCOLE: *Britannia* v (1974).

SEA MILLS. *Britannia* iv (1973); Arch Ex 1972; Branigar & Fowler.

SEATON: *Britannia* i (1970), viii (1977), x (1979); Arch Ex 1969; P. Morris; Branigan & Fowler.

SHAKENOAK: Brodribb, G. et al. *Excavations at Shakenoak* (privately printed reports); CBA Group 9, Newsletters from 1973.

SHAPWICK: *Britannia* vii (1976), special article; M. J. Jones; Webster (1980).

SHORTLANESEND: *Britannia* xi (1980).

SHOTTLEGATE: *Britannia* iii (1972).

SHREWLEY COMMON: WMANS 1977.

SILCHESTER: Wacher (1974); Guide Book (G. C. Boon); *Britannia* vii (1976) to xiii (1982); Wacher (ed); various works by M. Fulford.

SILLOANS: SAF 12 (1981); Daniels.

SILLSBURN NORTH: Daniels.

SILLSBURN SOUTH: Daniels.

SLACK: *Britannia* i (1970), ii (1971), x (1979); Arch Ex 1970; SAF 12 (1981); Holder; M. J. Jones; Breeze & Dobson; Frere; YAJ various issues.

SNOWFORD BRIDGE: WMANS 1978.

SOBERTON: *Britannia* vii (1976).

SOLDIER'S RING: Collingwood & Richmond.

SOMERTON: *Britannia* x (1979).

SOUTH CADBURY: *Britannia* i (1970); Antiq J 1970; Branigan & Fowler.

SOUTHORPE: *Britannia* ix (1978).

SOUTH SHIELDS: *Britannia* iv (1973), v (1974), vii (1976), viii (1977), xi (1980), xii (1981), xiii (1982); Daniels; Holder; Collingwood & Richmond; Breeze & Dobson.

SOUTHWICK: Todd (ed); *Britannia* xiii (1982).

SPARSHOLT: Arch Ex 1969, 1970, 1971, 1972; CA 1969; Todd (ed); Percival; P. Morris; *Britannia* i (1970) to iv (1973).

SPONG HILL: CBA Group 6, Newsletter 1979; *Britannia* xi (1980), xii (1981).

SPOONLEY WOOD: Branigan & Fowler; Percival; Todd (ed); Rivet (ed).

SPRINGHEAD: *Britannia* i (1970) to iv (1973), viii (1977) to x (1979); Green.

STAINES: CA 52; *Britannia* vii (1976), ix (1978), xi (1980), xii (1981).

STANFORD-in-the-VALE: *Britannia* viii (1977); CBA Group 9, Newsletter 1977.

STANTONBURY: CBA Group 9, Newsletter 1976; ABBNO 1981; *Britannia* xi (1980) to xiii (1982).

STANTON CHAIR: PSIA xxii; Percival; Rivet.

STANTON FITZWARREN: *Britannia* ii (1971); VCH Wiltshire I (1957).

STANWICK: *Britannia* i (1970), iii (1972), iv (1973), v (1974), viii (1977), xiii (1982); DoE booklet.

STANWIX: Breeze; Holder; Daniels; Breeze & Dobson.

STAUNTON-in-the-VALE: *Britannia* ii (1971); Arch Ex 1970.

STIBBINGTON: *Britannia* i (1970).

STOKE BRUERNE: *Britannia* i (1970).

STOKE GIFFORD: *Britannia* ix (1978) to xiii (1982).

STOKE HILL: Branigan & Fowler; Welsby; Arch Ex 1971.

STONE-by-FAVERSHAM: Wilson, R. J. A. *Roman Remains in Britain* (Constable, 1980).

STOWMARKET: *Britannia* x (1979).

STRATFORD SUB CASTLE: Branigan & Fowler; *Britannia* i (1970).

STRETTON-on-FOSSE: Arch Ex 1971; WMANS 1974; *Britannia* iii (1972); vi (1975) to viii (1977).

STRETTON MILL: JRS 1948, 1953; M. J. Jones; Frere; TBAS 1951.

STROUD: Rivet (ed); Todd (ed); P. Morris.

SULEHAY: *Britannia* vi (1975).

SUNNY RIGG: *Britannia* xiii (1982); Daniels.

SUTTON COURTENAY: CBA Group 9, Newsletter 1973, 1974.

SWINDON: *Britannia* v (1974), viii (1977); WANHM various issues.

SWINE HILL: Daniels.

TARRANT HINTON: *Britannia* i (1970) to vi (1975), xi (1980), xii (1981), xiii (1982); Todd (ed); PDNHAS various issues.

TATTERSHALL THORPE: *Britannia* viii (1977), xiii (1982).

TEMPLEBOROUGH: *Britannia* i (1970); M. J. Jones; Frere; Holder; Welsby.

TEMPLE SOWERBY: Sedgley.

TEVERSHAM: *Britannia* xiii (1982).

THE LUNT: Coventry Corporation booklet; *Britannia* ii (1971) to v (1976), xii (1981); M. J. Jones; Birmingham 1966-7, 1973, 1975; CA 4; 24, 28, 44, 63.

THENFORD: BNFAS 1971, 1972; Arch Ex 1972; CBA 9, Newsletter 1973; *Britannia* iii (1972) to v (1974).

THETFORD: *Britannia* xiii (1982).

THEYDON GARNON: *Britannia* viii (1977).

THISTLETON DYER: *Britannia* i (1970); JRS 1961, 1965; Percival; Todd (ed).

THORNBOROUGH: Arch Ex 1972; CBA Group 9, Newsletter 1973; Green.

THORPE AUDLIN: Paper by E. Houlder, Pontefract and District Arch Soc 1982.

THORPE-by-NEWARK: Rodwell & Rowley (ed); Frere; M. J. Jones; Wacher (ed); JRS various issues; Thoroton Soc 1969.

THROP: Collingwood & Richmond; Daniels.

TINTAGEL: Sedgley.

TITSEY PARK: *Britannia* vii (1976); Todd (ed); Green; Rivet.

TOPSHAM: Rivet; Branigan & Fowler; *Britannia* vi (1975).

TOTTERNHOE: JRS xlvii (1957).
TOWCESTER: Rodwell & Rowley (ed); *Britannia* vi (1975) to ix (1978); Rivet.
TREBARVETH: Branigan & Fowler; *Cornish Archaeology* 1969.
TRENT VALE: *Britannia* i (1970), ii (1971); M. J. Jones.
TRETHURGY: Arch Ex 1972; *Britannia* iv (1973), v (1974); CA 40.
TREVETHY: Sedgley.
TROUTBECK: *Britannia* v (1974), xii (1981); SAF 12 (1981); M. J. Jones; Holder.
TURRETS on HADRIAN'S WALL: All turrets included are described in CM Daniels' 1978 edition of Collingwood Bruce's *The Roman Wall*: some are also discussed in Breeze & Dobson, including 12a, 18a, 26, 27a, 29a, 34a, 34b, 35a, 44b, 45a, 48a, 49b, 51b and 52a: some are also discussed in various issues of *Britannia* and Arch Ael.
TWYFORD: *Britannia* viii (1977); Rivet (ed); Todd (ed).
ULEY: *Britannia* viii (1977) to xi (1980); Arch Ex 1976.
UPCHURCH: Kent Arch Rev 1970.
UPPER RAWCLIFFE: *Britannia* x (1979).
UPTON ST LEONARDS: *Britannia* viii (1977), ix (1978); Branigan & Fowler.
WADDON HILL: Holder; M. J. Jones; PDNHAS 1960, 1965, 1970; *Britannia* i (1970), ii (1971), iii (1972).
WAKERLEY: CBA Group 9, Newsletters 1973, 1975; P. Morris; *Britannia* iv (1973) to vi (1975).
WALESBY: *Britannia* ix (1978); Lincs Hist Arch Soc J 1978.
WALL: DoE booklet; WMANS 1969, 1971; *Britannia* ii (1971) to x (1979); TBAS 1964.
WALLSEND: Daniels; *Britannia* vii (1976) to xiii (1982); Holder; Welsby.
WALLTOWN: M. J. Jones; Frere; Shrop Arch Soc 1965-6.
WALTHAM ABBEY: *Britannia* vii (1976), xiii (1982).
WALTON: *Northamptonshire Archaeology* 1974; P. Morris.
WALTON: VCH Suffolk; Johnston (ed); Johnson (1979).
WALTON-le-DALE: *Britannia* xiii (1982).
WANBOROUGH: Wacher (ed); *Britannia* i (1970), ii (1971), vii (1976), viii (1977); M. J. Jones; Rodwell & Rowley (ed); JRS 1955.
WARE: Arch Ex 1974, 1976; *Britannia* vi (1975), viii (1977), ix (1978), x (1979), xii (1981).
WASHINGWELLS: *Britannia* ii (1971); Breeze & Dobson; Daniels; Arch Ael ser 4 1971.
WASPERTON: WMANS 1979; *Britannia* xii (1981), xiii (1982).

WATERCROOK: *Britannia* vi (1975), vii (1976), xi (1980), xii (1981); M. J. Jones; Welsby; CW various issues.
WATER NEWTON: Wacher (1974); M. J. Jones; Frere; *Britannia* v (1974), vii (1976); Rodwell & Rowley (ed).
WATTISFIELD: PSIA xxii, xxv, xxviii.
WEEKLEY: *Britannia* ii (1971), iv (1973), v (1974); BNFAS 1970, 1973.
WEETING: *Britannia* vii (1976), xi (1980).
WELLINGBOROUGH: *Britannia* i (1970) to v (1974); BNFAS 1970.
WELLOW: VCH Somerset I; Percival; Rivet (ed); P. Morris.
WELLS: CA 75; *Britannia* xi (1980), xii (1981).
WELTON WOLD: *Britannia* iii (1972) to viii (1977); Arch Ex 1971, 1976; P. Morris.
WENDENS AMBO: Arch Ex 1971; *Colchester Archaeological Group Annual Bulletin* 1974; Todd (ed).
WEST BLATCHINGDON: Rivet (ed); Percival; Todd (ed); P. Morris.
WEST DEAN: VCH Wiltshire I (1957); Rivet (ed); Todd (ed); Percival; P. Morris.
WEST MEON: Arch J 1907; Todd (ed).
WEST MERSEA: Collingwood & Richmond; Todd (ed); *Britannia* ix (1978).
WEST STOW: Arch Ex 1972; *Britannia* iv (1973).
WHARRAM PERCY: *Britannia* viii (1977) to xiii (1982); Arch Ex 1975, 1976.
WHEELDALE MOOR: Margary.
WHILTON LODGE: *Britannia* iii (1972), iv (1973); Welsby.
WHITCHURCH: *Britannia* viii (1977), ix (1978); Arch Ex 1976; M. J. Jones.
WHITLEY CASTLE: Holder; Collingwood & Richmond; Welsby; Breeze & Dobson.
WHITMINSTER: Glevensis 11 (1977); TBGAS 1971; Branigan & Fowler.
WHITTINGTON COURT: *Britannia* x (1979); Percival; Rivet (ed); TBGAS 1952.
WHITWELL: Arch Ex 1976.
WICKFORD: *Britannia* i (1970), ii (1971), iii (1972); Antiq J 1970; P. Morris.
WICKHAM BUSHES: *Britannia* vi (1975), xi (1980).
WIDFORD: Widford Parish Church Guide.
WIGGINTON: JRS 1966; Rivet (ed); Percival; VCH Oxfordshire I.
WIGSTON PARVA: Arch Ex 1970; M. J. Jones.
WILDERSPOOL: *Britannia* i (1970), vi (1975), viii (1977); Arch Ex 1974, 1976; Frere.
WILMINGTON: *Britannia* vii (1976).
WILSTROP: *Britannia* vii (1976).
WINCHESTER: Wacher (1974); *Britannia* i (1970) to xiii (1982); Antiq J 1968, 1972.
WINDMILL HILL: Arch Ex 1972; P. Morris.

WINGHAM: Antiq J 1943; JRS 1968; Rivet (ed); Todd (ed); P. Morris.
WINTERTON: *Britannia* i (1970) to xiii (1982); Arch Ex 1970, 1971, 1972, 1974; Todd (ed); Rivet (ed); Collingwood & Richmond; P. Morris; Percival.
WITHINGTON: Rivet (ed).
WIVELISCOMBE: M. J. Jones; *Britannia* iii (1972); PSANHS 1958.
WOLLASTON: BNFAS 1971; CBA Group 9, Newsletter 1972; *Britannia* iii (1972), v (1974).
WOOD BURCOTE: CBA Group 9, Newsletter 1975.
WOODCHESTER: *Britannia* v (1974); Todd (ed); Rivet (ed).
WOODEATON: Green; Rivet (ed); Collingwood & Richmond.
WORCESTER: *Britannia* viii (1977) to x (1979); WMANS 1976; Worc Arch Soc 1968.
WORTH: Klein, W. G. 'The Roman temple at Worth', Antiq J 1928; Hawkes; *Britannia* xi (1980).
WORTHY DOWN: *Britannia* xii (1981).
WOUGHTON-on-the-GREEN: CBA Group 9, Newsletters 1974, 1976.
WROXETER: Wacher (1974); *Britannia* ii (1971) to xiii (1982); DoE booklet; Holder; Welsby; M. J. Jones; Antiq J xlvi (1966).
WYCOMB: Branigan & Fowler; *Britannia* i (1970), ii (1971); Green; Glevensis 7 (1973).
WYE: *Britannia* ii (1971).
WYMBUSH: *Britannia* xi (1980), xii (1981).
YARDHOPE: *Britannia* viii (1977).
YEOVIL: Branigan & Fowler; *Britannia* iii (1972), xii (1981); Percival; PSANHS 1928.
YORK: Wacher (1974); RCHM, Roman York; *Britannia* i (1970) to x (1979); CA 1969; Frere; Rivet.

WALES

ABERFFRAW: *Britannia* v (1974), x (1979); M. J. Jones; BBCS xxviii; Holder.
ABERGAVENNY: *Britannia* ii (1971), iv (1973), v (1974); AW 1973; Jarrett.
ARDLEEN: *Britannia* xi (1980); AW 1979.
BIGLIS: GGAT 1978-9; AW 1979; *Britannia* xi (1980).
BEULAH: Jarrett; M. J. Jones; BBCS xvii.
BLAEN-CWM-BACH: *Britannia* vi (1975); Frere; AW 1974.
BRECON GAER: Arch Camb, cxii, cxx; BBCS xxii; Jarrett; Welsby; Holder; M. J. Jones.
BRITHDIR: *Britannia* vi (1975), vii (1976); AW 1975; M. J. Jones; Holder.
BRYN GLAS: Jarrett.
BRYN-Y-CASTELL: *Britannia* xi (1980).
BRYN-Y-GEFEILIAU: M. J. Jones; Jarrett; Arch Camb, cxi; Frere.

CAE GAER: Jarrett.
CAE SUMMERHOUSE: AW 1973; Morgannwg, 1967; P. Morris; *Britannia* v (1974).
CAER GAI: BBCS xiii; Jarrett; M. J. Jones.
CAER GYBI: Ancient Monuments of Anglesey; Jarrett; Welsby.
CAERHUN: Jarrett; Arch Camb lxxx; M. J. Jones; *Britannia* vii (1976); Holder; Welsby.
CAERLEB: Ancient Monuments of Anglesey.
CAERLEON: *Britannia* i (1970), iv (1973), ix (1978), x (1979), xii (1981); M. J. Jones; Frere; Arch Camb various issues.
CAERNARFON: *Britannia* iii (1972), vii (1976), viii (1977) to xi (1980); Jarrett; Holder; Welsby; M. J. Jones.
CAERPHILLY: Arch Camb, cxv; Jarrett; M. J. Jones.
CAERSWS: *Britannia* ix (1978); JRS lvii (1967), lviii (1968); Jarrett; Arch Camb ns iii; M. J. Jones; AW 1976; Holder; Welsby.
CAERWENT: Wacher (1974); *Britannia* iii (1972), vi (1975); Welsh Office booklet; Frere; Arch Ex 1973; AW 1971.
CALDICOT: JRS lvi (1966); *Antiquity* xxxv (1961); *Britannia* ix (1978), xi (1980); AW 1976, 1977.
CAPEL EITHIN: CA 75; *Britannia* xii (1981).
CARDIFF: *Britannia* vi (1975) to xiii (1982); AW 1974-81; M. J. Jones; Welsby; Frere.
CARMARTHEN: *Britannia* i (1970), ii (1971), viii (1977) to xii (1981); M. J. Jones; Wacher (1974); Jarrett; Frere; *Carmarthen Antiquary* v (1964-9).
CARNO: Jarrett.
CASTELL COLLEN: M. J. Jones; Arch Camb lxix (1914), cxiii (1964); Jarrett; Holder; Welsby; *Radnorshire Society Transactions* 1954-7.
CEFN GRAEANOG: *Britannia* ix (1978); P. Morris.
CHEPSTOW: *Britannia* vi (1975); AW 1974.
CLYRO: JRS xlviii (1958), lv (1965); M. J. Jones; Jarrett; Holder.
COED-Y-CAERAU: Jarrett; M. J. Jones.
COELBREN: Arch Camb lxii (1907), xciv (1939), cxii (1963); Jarrett; M. J. Jones.
COLLFRYN: *Britannia* xii (1981), xiii (1982).
COWBRIDGE: *Britannia* ix (1978), xi (1980), xii (1981), xiii (1982); GGAT 1979-80.
CWMBRWYN: P. Morris; Rivet.
DERWYDD: JRS lxvii (1977).
DIN LLIGWY: Ancient Monuments of Anglesey.
DINAS POWYS: AW 1978; *Britannia* x (1979).
DINORBEN: CA 65, 1979; *Britannia* x (1979); Frere; AW 1969.
DISCOED: JRS lix (1969); Jarrett; M. J. Jones.
DOLAU: Jarrett.

DOLAUCOTHI: JRS lix (1969); *Britannia* i (1970), ii (1971), iv (1973); CBA Group 2; AW 1969, 1972.
DOLDINNAS: Jarrett; Holder.
ELY: Rivet (ed); Arch J 1875; P. Morris; Percival.
ERGLODD: AW 1976.
ESGAIRPERFYDD: Holder.
FORDEN GAER: M. J. Jones; Arch Camb lxxxii (1927), lxxxv (1930), cxi (1963); Jarrett; JRS xvii (1927), xix (1929), lxiii (1973); *Britannia* vii (1976); AW 1975; Welsby; Holder.
GELLIGAER: Arch Camb cxii (1963); M. J. Jones; Jarrett; Holder; *Morgannwg* 8 (1964).
GLAN-Y-MOR: CA 75; *Britannia* xii (1981); xiii (1982); GGAT Annual Report 1980–1.
HADNOCK FARM: AW 1977; *Britannia* ix (1978).
HEN WALIAU: Segontium Roman Fort (Welsh Office booklet); Welsby.
HOLT: McWhirr; Collingwood & Richmond; Swan.
HOLYHEAD MOUNTAIN: *Britannia* xii (1981), xiii (1982); AW 1980, 1981.
LLANDEILO: *Britannia* xi (1980); AW 1929.
LLANDOUGH: GGAT 1978–9; AW 1979; *Britannia* xi (1980).
LLANDOVERY: *Britannia* i (1970); Jarrett; M. J. Jones; Holder.
LLANDRINDOD COMMON: Holder; Frere.
LLANDRINIO: *Britannia* ix (1978); AW 1977.
LLANDULAS: M. J. Jones; Jarrett; *Carmarthen Antiquary* iii.
LLANEDEYRN: *Britannia* vii (1976); AW 1975.
LLANFAIR CAEREINION: Jarrett.
LLANFOR: JRS lxvii (1977); M. J. Jones; Holder; *Britannia* vii (1976), ix (1978); AW 1977.
LLANFRYNACH (Powys): Rivet (ed); BBCS xiii.
LLANFRYNACH (South Glamorgan): *Britannia* ix (1978); AW 1976.
LLANIO: Jarrett; AW 1969, 1970, 1972; *Britannia* i (1970), iii (1972), iv (1973), v (1974); M. J. Jones; Holder.
LLANTWIT MAJOR: *Britannia* iii (1972), (1974); AW 1971; Rivet (ed); Frere; Percival; P. Morris; Arch Camb civ (1953).
LLAWHADEN: *Britannia* xii (1981).
LLYS BRYCHAN: *Carmarthen Antiquary* iv (1962); Jarrett.
LOUGHOR: *Britannia* i (1970), ii (1971), iii (1972), v (1974); AW 1970, 1971, 1973; M. J. Jones; Holder; Welsby.
MELIN COURT: *Britannia* vi (1975); AW 1974.
NEATH: BBCS xiii (1950), xiv (1950); Arch Camb cxii (1968); Jarrett.

PANT-TEG-UCHAF: Jarrett.
PEN BRYN-Y-EGLWYS: *Britannia* xiii (1982).
PEN LLWYN: AW 1977; *Britannia* ix (1978).
PEN LLYSTEN: *Britannia* viii (1977); Arch J cxxv (1968); Jarrett; M. J. Jones; Frere.
PEN-MIN-CAE: JRS lxiii (1973).
PENNAL: RCAM (Wales) Merioneth I; Arch Camb 1933; BBCS xvii (1956–8); Jarrett; M. J. Jones; AW 1978.
PENTRE FARM: AW 1977, 1981: *Britannia* viii (1977), ix (1978), x (1979); Flintshire Society 1975–6; *Illustrated London News* February 1977.
PEN-Y-COEDCAE: Jarrett.
PEN-Y-CROGBREN: Jarrett.
PEN-Y-DARREN: Arch Camb lv (1906), cxii (1963); Jarrett; M. J. Jones.
PEN-Y-GAER: Arch Camb 1968; Jarrett; M. J. Jones.
PEN-Y-GWRHYD: JRS xlv (1955); Jarrett; RCAM (Wales) Caernarvons II.
PONT-RHYD-SARN: Jarrett.
PORTH FELEN: AW 1975.
PRESTATYN: AW 1973, 1980, 1981; *Britannia* v (1974), viii (1977), xii (1981).
PUMPSAINT: *Britannia* iv (1973), v (1974), x (1979); M. J. Jones; *Carmarthen Antiquary* ix; AW 1972, 1978; Jarrett; Holder; Arch Ex 1972.
PYLE: Sedgley.
ST HARMON: Holder.
SARN HELEN: *Britannia* xi (1980); AW 1979.
STACKPOLE WARREN: AW 1977; *Britannia* ix (1978).
TOMEN-Y-MUR: M. J. Jones; Holder; Jarrett; Merioneth (1961–4).
TRAWSCOED: JRS li (1961), liii (1963); Jarrett; M. J. Jones; *Britannia* vi (1975); AW 1974.
TWYN-Y-BRIDDALLT: JRS xlix (1954); Jarrett.
TY-BRYN: *Britannia* ix (1978); AW 1976.
USK: *Britannia* i (1970) to vii (1976), xi (1980); Holder; Jarrett; M. J. Jones; CA 10; Arch Ex 1970, 1972; AW 1970, 1972, 1973; *Monmouthshire Antiquities* 1967.
WALTON: JRS lxiii (1973); M. J. Jones; *Transactions of the Radnorshire Society* 1958.
WHITTON: *Morgannwg* x, xiv; *Britannia* ii (1971); Percival; P. Morris; Todd (ed).
Y PIGWN: Holder; Frere.
YSTRADFELLTE: Frere.

SCOTLAND

ABERNETHY: DAES 1974; SAF 12 (1981); Holder.
ARDOCH: *Britannia* i (1970), ii (1971), ix (1978); SAF 12 (1981); DAES various issues;

Breeze & Dobson; Breeze; Arch J cxxi (1964); M. J. Jones; Holder; PSAS various issues.

AUCHENDAVY: *Britannia* x (1979); Breeze & Dobson; Robertson; Holder.

AUCHINHOVE: DAES 1974; SAF 12 (1981); Breeze; Holder.

BALMUILDY: *Britannia* iii (1972), v (1974), vi (1975); Breeze; Breeze & Dobson; RCAHMS Lanarkshire; Holder.

BAR HILL: *Britannia* x (1979), xi (1980), xii (1981); Breeze; Robertson; Breeze & Dobson; Holder.

BARBURGH MILL: *Britannia* v (1974); Breeze; Breeze & Dobson; DAES 1971; Holder.

BAROCHAN HILL: M. J. Jones; Breeze; DAES 1972; *Britannia* iv (1973); SAF 12 (1981).

BEARSDEN: *Britannia* v (1974) to xiii (1982); DAES 1973-81; Breeze & Dobson; Breeze; Holder; Breeze (SDD booklet).

BEATTOCK: *Britannia* ix (1978); DAES 1977; Breeze; SAF 12 (1981).

BERTHA: M. J. Jones; *Britannia* v (1974); DAES 1973; SAF 12 (1981); Breeze.

BIRRENS: *Britannia* i (1970), iii (1972), v (1974); Robertson; Breeze & Dobson; Breeze; Holder; M. J. Jones; JRS various issues; TDGNHAS 1964.

BLAINSLIE: DAES 1974.

BOCHASTLE: M. J. Jones; Breeze; SAF 12 (1981); TGAS xiv (1956).

BOONIES: *Britannia* v (1974); DAES 1973; PSAS cv (1972-4).

BOTHWELLHAUGH: *Britannia* vii (1976), viii (1977); CA 50, 52; Breeze; DAES 1975, 1976.

BROOMHOLM KNOWE: M. J. Jones; JRS lv (1965); Breeze; TDGNHAS 1949-50.

BROWNHART LAW: Daniels (ed.).

BROXMOUTH: *Britannia* xi (1980); DAES 1979.

BUCHLEY: DAES 1980; *Britannia* xii (1981).

BURNSWARK: *Britannia* i (1970), ii (1971), v (1974); DAES 1970; Breeze; Holder; CA 15; Arch J cxv, 1958; Breeze & Dobson.

CADDER: *Britannia* viii (1977); DAES 1974, 1976; Breeze & Dobson; Breeze; RCAHMS Lanarkshire; Robertson.

CALLANDER: DAES 1974; SAF 12 (1981).

CAMELON: DAES 1973, 1974, 1975, 1976, 1977; *Britannia* vi (1975) to x (1979), xiii (1982); CA 50, 55; SAF 12 (1981).

CAPPUCK: DAES 1974; SAF 12 (1981); Breeze & Dobson; Breeze.

CARDEAN: DAES 1970-75; *Britannia* ii (1971) to viii (1977); M. J. Jones; Holder; Breeze; SAF 12 (1981); JRS various issues.

CARGILL: *Britannia* xii (1981), xiii (1982); Breeze.

CARPOW: *Britannia* i (1970), vii (1976), viii (1977), x (1979), xi (1980); DAES various issues; Breeze & Dobson; Holder; SAF 12 (1981).

CARRIDEN: DAES 1972, 1974; *Britannia* vi (1975); JRS xlvii (1957); Breeze & Dobson.

CASTLE GREG: RCAHMS Midlothian and West Lothian.

CASTLECARY: DAES 1974, 1977; Breeze & Dobson; Breeze; Holder; Robertson.

CASTLEDYKES: M. J. Jones; RCAHMS Lanarkshire; Breeze; SAF 12 (1981); Arch Ael 1965.

CASTLEHILL: *Britannia* xii (1981); Breeze & Dobson; Holder; Robertson.

CARZIELD: Breeze; Holder; *Britannia* iii (1972).

CHANNELKIRK: Holder; DAES 1974.

CLEAVEN DYKE: *Britannia* vii (1976); DAES 1975; PSAS lxxiv (1939-40).

CLEDDANS: *Britannia* xi (1980), xii (1981).

CLEGHORN: RCAHMS Lanarkshire; DAES 1971; *Britannia* iii (1972).

CLYDE CROSSING: DAES 1974; *Britannia* iv (1975).

COULTER: DAES 1974.

CRAIGARNHALL: DAES 1974.

CRAIK CROSS HILL: Collingwood & Richmond.

CRAMOND: DAES 1972 to 1982; *Britannia* iii (1972), vii (1976) to xiii (1982); Holder; Breeze; Breeze & Dobson; PSAS 1970.

CRAWFORD: RCAHMS Lanarkshire; JRS lii (1962), liii (1963), lvii (1967); PSAS 1971-2; Breeze; Holder; M. J. Jones; SAF 12 (1981).

CROY HILL: *Britannia* vii (1976) to xiii (1982); DAES 1975-8; Breeze; Robertson; Holder.

CUPAR: DAES 1978; *Britannia* x (1979).

DALGINROSS: DAES 1974; SAF 12 (1981); M. J. Jones; Holder; Breeze; PSAS 1963.

DALKEITH: SAF 12 (1981); *Britannia* xii (1981); PSAS xcviii (1964-6).

DALSWINTON: DAES 1974; JRS xli (1951), xlv (1955), lxiii (1973); M. J. Jones; SAF 12 (1981); Holder; Breeze; TDGNHAS 1957.

DRUMQUHASSIE: *Britannia* ix (1978), x (1979); DAES 1977, 1978; Breeze.

DULLATUR: DAES 1975; *Britannia* vii (1976), viii (1977).

DUN: DAES 1974; SAF 12 (1981).

DUNNING: DAES 1974; SAF 12 (1981).

DUNTOCHER: *Britannia* x (1979), xii (1981); DAES 1978, 1980; Robertson; Breeze & Dobson; Breeze.

DURISDEER: SAF 12 (1981); Holder.

DURNO: *Britannia* ix (1978) (article by J. K. St Joseph).

EASSIE: DAES 1970, 1974.

EASTER HAPPREW: RCAHMS Peebleshire I; M. J. Jones; JRS xlvii (1957), xlviii (1958), li (1961); SAF 12 (1981); Breeze; PSAS 1956.
ELLISLAND: DAES 1974.
ESKBANK: Arch Ex 1972; DAES 1972; Britannia iv (1973); PSAS 1975.
FALKIRK: Britannia viii (1977), xii (1981); DAES 1974; Breeze & Dobson.
FENDOCH: SAF 12 (1981); M. J. Jones; Breeze; Holder.
FINAVON: DAES 1974; SAF 12 (1981); Holder.
FOUMERKLAND: SAF 12 (1981).
GAGIE: DAES 1974.
GARNHALL: DAES 1977; Britannia ix (1978).
GASK RIDGE: TPSNS 1974; Breeze; Breeze & Dobson.
GATEHOUSE of FLEET: SAF 12 (1981); Breeze.
GIRVAN: Britannia xiii (1982).
GLASGOW BRIDGE: JRS xlv (1955); Britannia xii (1981); RCAHMS Lanarkshire.
GLENLOCHAR: JRS xli (1951), xliii (1953), lv (1965); DAES 1974; M. J. Jones; Breeze; SAF 12 (1981); Holder; TDGNHAS 1951-2.
GOURDIE: SAF 12 (1981); Holder.
INCHTUTHIL: JRS various issues; Holder; M. J. Jones; SAF 12 (1981); Breeze; Breeze & Dobson.
INVERAVON: DAES 1973, 1974, 1976; Britannia v (1974), viii (1977); Robertson.
INVERESK: DAES 1976, 1977; Britannia iii (1972), viii (1977), ix (1978), xiii (1982); M. J. Jones; Breeze; Arch Ex 1976; JRS various issues.
KAIMS CASTLE: Breeze; Arch J cxxi (1964).
KINNEIL: Britannia ix (1978), xii (1981), xiii (1982); DAES 1974, 1979, 1980; Robertson.
KINNELL: DAES 1970, 1974.
KIRKINTILLOCH: Britannia vii (1976); DAES 1975; Breeze & Dobson; Breeze; Robertson.
LAKE of MENTEITH: DAES 1972, 1973, 1974; JRS lix (1969); M. J. Jones; Breeze; Holder; SAF 12 (1981).
LAMINGTON: RCAHMS Lanarkshire; SAF 12 (1981); Britannia ix (1978).
LITTLE CLYDE: RCAHMS Lanarkshire.
LOGIE: DAES 1974.
LOUDOUN HILL: JRS xxix (1939), xxxvii (1947), xxxix (1949), xlv (1955); M. J. Jones.
LURG MOOR: DAES 1976.
LYNE: RCAHMS Peebleshire I; SAF 12 (1981); Holder; Breeze; DAES 1975, 1977.
MIDDLEBIE: DAES 1974.
MILRIGHAIL: RCAHMS Roxburghshire; DAES 1977; Britannia ix (1978).

MILTON: SAF 12 (1981); M. J. Jones; Holder; Breeze; TDGNHAS various issues.
MOLLINS: DAES 1978; Britannia ix (1978), x (1979); SAF 12 (1981); RCAHMS Lanarkshire.
MUMRILLS: DAES 1972, 1974; Britannia v (1974), x (1979); Breeze; Holder; Robertson; PSAS 1960.
NEWSTEAD: M. J. Jones; DAES 1974; SAF 12 (1981); Breeze; Breeze & Dobson; Holder; PSAS lxxxiv (1949-50); RCAHMS Roxburghshire II; CA 28.
NORMANDYKES: SAF 12 (1981); Crawford.
OAKWOOD: M. J. Jones; SAF 12 (1981); Breeze; PSAS 1951.
OLD KILPATRICK: DAES 1970; Breeze; Breeze & Dobson; Robertson; Holder.
OUTERWARDS: Britannia ii (1971); DAES 1970, 1971; Breeze; Robertson.
PATHHEAD: DAES 1974; Holder.
PENNYMUIR: RCAHMS Roxburghshire II; Holder.
RAEBURNFOOT: Breeze; Holder; Frere.
RAEDYKES: SAF 12 (1981); PSAS 1916; Crawford; Holder.
REDSHAWBURN: RCAHMS Lanarkshire; Holder; Frere.
ROUGH CASTLE: Britannia vii (1976); DAES 1975; SDD booklet; Breeze & Dobson; Breeze; Robertson; Holder.
ROUNDLAW: DAES 1972; Britannia iv (1973).
SEABEGS: Britannia iv (1973), v (1974), ix (1978), xii (1981), xiii (1982); DAES 1972, 1973, 1977, 1979; CA lvii, 1978.
SHIELHILL: DAES 1974.
STRACATHRO: SAF 12 (1981); M. J. Jones; Breeze; Frere; Britannia i (1970); Holder.
STRAGEATH: DAES 1972 to 1980; Britannia various issues; M. J. Jones; Breeze; SAF 12 (1981); Frere; Holder.
SUMMERSTON: Britannia xii (1981).
TAMFOURHILL: DAES 1977; Britannia ix (1978).
TENTFIELD PLANTATION: Robertson.
TOLLPARK: Britannia xi (1980), xiii (1982).
TWECHAR: DAES 1977; Britannia ix (1978).
WANDEL: RCAHMS Lanarkshire; DAES 1970; JRS li (1961); Breeze; Frere.
WARD LAW: M. J. Jones; Breeze; Holder.
WATERSIDE MAINS: DAES 1977.
WATLING LODGE: Britannia iv (1973), vi (1975); DAES 1972, 1974; Robertson.
WESTERTON: Britannia xii (1981); Breeze.
WESTERWOOD: Britannia vi (1975), vii (1976), x (1979); DAES 1974, 1978, 1979; Breeze & Dobson; Breeze; Robertson.
WHITEMOSS: DAES 1973; Breeze; Robertson.

WILDERNESS PLANTATION: *Britannia* vi (1975), xii (1981); DAES 1974; GAJ iii (1974); Breeze & Dobson; CA 62.

WODEN LAW: RCAHMS Roxburghshire II; Breeze; Holder; Frere.

WOODHEAD: SAF 12 (1981).

YTHAN WELLS: DAES 1974, 1975; SAF 12 (1981); Holder.

GLOSSARY

aedes shrine

agger raised earth foundation of a Roman road

ala auxiliary cavalry regiment, usually of 500 men but sometimes of 1,000

amphora two-handed vessel

apodyterium changing rooms in bath house

ascensus flight of steps in fort or camp rampart

auxilia auxiliary forces, in the form of *cohortes* or *alae* raised among provinces, to assist the legions

ballista long-range stone-throwing catapult used by Roman armies

ballistarium artillery platform

basilica town hall (with central nave and aisles on either side); later, a plan for early Christian churches

caldarium damp heat hot room of a bath house or bath suite

catapulta long-range arrow-firing apparatus used by Roman armies

cella The central room of a Romano-Celtic temple

centuria infantry unit, 80 strong (also known as a century)

christogram monogram of Christ, devised from first two Greek letters (Chi and Rho) of his name

clavicula curved extension; inwards and/or outwards, of a fort or camp rampart and ditch, at an entrance to protect it

civitas a tribal organisation, or state

cohors (Eng. cohort) unit of infantry, legionary or auxiliary

cohors quingenaria a cohort of 500 men

cohors milliaria a cohort of 1,000 men (though less might constitute a milliary cohort)

colonia settlement built for retired legionaries

colonnade row of columns

contubernium strictly, a common war tent, generally for 8 to 10 soldiers, or a room in a barrack-block for same

cursus publicus Government post and transport service

fabrica workshop

forum civic centre and market place

frigidarium cold room of a bath house or bath suite

graffito writing scratched on tile, plaster, pottery, etc.

gyrus small round or oval arena for exercising and training horses and cavalrymen (cf. The Lunt, Baginton)

hypocaust system of central heating by means of hot air circulation under floors and via flues in the walls

insula a block of buildings between two streets

laconicum dry heat (Sauna) hot room of a bath house or bath suite

imbrex semi-cylindrical tile for roof or for linking two *tegulae*

mansio hotel or roadside inn, especially for government officials and staff of *cursus publicus*

mithraeum temple dedicated to Mithras

modius Roman dry measure

mortarium stout, externally flat-based, internally rounded bowl for mixing or crushing food, often surfaced with grit inside

mosaic decorative picture or pavement made up from *tesserae*

nymphaeum fountain house

officina workshop, esp. of mosaicists; also used to mean "school"

onager large *ballista*

oppidum generally, Latin term for Gallic or British main settlement on hilltop or on lower ground defended by dykes *opus signinum* flooring composed of crushed tile and brick with mortar

palaestra exercise yard of public baths, open or covered

palisade upright posts set together in the ground to make a wall

Pelagianism A Christian heresy flourishing in parts of Britain in the late 4th and early 5th centuries, which denied the doctrine of original sin, holding that Man was free to do right or wrong. It emerged as a result of disputes with Augustine and his adherents. Pelagius was a British monk who eventually went to Rome where he argued his heresy. The heresy played some part in the breakdown of order in Britain after the rescript of Honorius (410)

pilae brick or stone pillars supporting the floor of a room having a hypocaust

portal doorway, especially in fort gateway

portico projecting or recessed bay supported on columns, usually forming the centrepiece to a main elevation of a building

praefectus castrorum camp prefect

praetentura front part of Roman fort, in front of *principia* and *praetorium*

praetorium commanding officer's residence in a fort

principia headquarters building in the middle of a fort

retentura rear part of a fort behind the *principia* and *praetorium*

sacellum the shrine in a headquarters building

stokehole small arch leading to furnace for hypocaust

sudatorium dry heat (sweating) hot room of bath house or bath suite

tegula flat tile with flanges on longer edges

tepidarium warm room in a bath house or bath suite

tesserae small cubes of coloured stone, glass or tile used to make up a mosaic or a simpler tessellated pavement

titulum a traverse of earth bank and ditch covering camp entrance

tribunal commanding officer's platform or dais in a *principia* or out on a parade ground

triclinium dining room

turma troop of cavalry, consisting of 32 officers and men

valetudinarium hospital block or sick bay

vexillatio (Eng. vexillation) term to describe a detachment of troops of unspecified strength working independently of the legion or group of auxiliary regiments from which it is drawn

via decumana street leading from rear of *principia* to back gate of fort

via praetoria street leading from *via principalis* (qv) at right angles to front gate of fort

via principalis street crossing a fort from side to side in front of *principia, praetorium* and other centre buildings

via quintana street running across fort behind *principia* and *praetorium*

via sagularis street running round periphery of fort inside the rampart or wall.

BIBLIOGRAPHY

An extensive amount of literature and reference material was studied in the preparation of this book. The lists that follow include every county archaeological journal and other archaeological and antiquarian journal studied, but not the individual volume and page numbers which are easily found in the indexes to the journals concerned. It was my aim to examine every volume that carried references to Romano-British sites specifically, and to Roman Britain more generally, going back where appropriate to issues of the nineteenth century. Also read were numerous special articles on a variety of Romano-British topics, and those that are listed are also page-referenced. The lists also include just about every important work on Roman Britain in the English language, written since the 1950s. There is also a list of the primary ancient sources.

Ancient Sources

All texts are taken from the Loeb Classical Library texts and translations, published by Wm Heinemann Ltd, unless otherwise stated.

Ammianus Marcellinus
Appian, *Roman History*
Caesar, *De Bello Gallico* (Gallic War) (also quoted were extracts from the translation by Rex Warner, Mentor Books, 1960)
Cicero, *Letters to Atticus* (trans. Shackleton Baily, Penguin Classics, 1978)
Dio Cassius, *Roman History*
Diodorus Siculus
Florus
Frontinus, *Stratagems*
Horace, *Odes*
Herodian
Josephus, *The Jewish War* (trans. G. A. Williamson, Penguin Classics, 1970)
Pausanius, *Description of Greece*
Pliny the Younger, *Letters* (trans. Betty Radice, Penguin Classics, 1963)
Scriptores Historiae Augustae (SHA) [includes biographies of Hadrian, Antoninus Pius, Marcus Antoninus (Marcus Aurelius), Commodus (Antoninus), Helvius Pertinax and Septimius Severus]
Statius, *Silvae*
Strabo, *Geography*
Suetonius, *Twelve Caesars* (trans. Robert Graves, Penguin Classics, 1957)
Tacitus, *Agricola* (trans. H. Mattingly, Penguin Classics, 1948)
Tacitus, *Annals* (trans. Michael Grant, Penguin Classics, 1956)
Tacitus, *Histories*
Vegetius, *Epitoma Rei Militaris* (trans. J. Clarke)
Velleius Paterculus
Vitruvius, *De Architectura*

Principal Books

Balsdon, J. P. V. D. *Julius Caesar and Rome* (Penguin, 1967)
Barker, P. *Armies and Enemies of Imperial Rome* (War Games, 1972)
Birley, A. R. *Life in Roman Britain* (rev ed, Batsford, 1981)
Birley, A. R. *The People of Roman Britain* (Batsford, 1979)
Birley, E. *Roman Britain and the Roman Army* (Kendal, 1953)
Brailsford, J. W. *Guide to the Antiquities of Roman Britain* (British Museum, 1964)
Branigan, K. and Fowler, P. *The Roman Westcountry* (David & Charles, 1976)
Breeze, D. J. *The Northern Frontiers of Roman Britain* (Batsford, 1982)

Breeze, D. J. and Dobson, B. *Hadrian's Wall* (Penguin, 1978)

Burnham, B. and Johnson, H. B. (ed) *Invasion and Response: the Case of Roman Britain* (British Archaeological Reports no 73, 1979)

Casey, P. J. (ed) *The End of Roman Britain* (British Archaeological Reports no 71, 1979)

Casson, L. *Travel in the Ancient World* (Toronto, 1974)

Collingwood, R. G. and Myres, J. N. L. *Roman Britain and the English Settlements* (Oxford University Press, 1968 edition)

Collingwood, R. G. and Richmond, I. A. *The Archaeology of Roman Britain* (Methuen, 1969)

Collingwood, R. G. and Wright, R. P. *The Roman Inscriptions of Britain*, vol. 1 (Oxford University Press, 1965)

Crawford, O. G. S. *The Topography of Roman Scotland* (Cambridge University Press, 1949)

Cunliffe, B. and Rowley, T. (ed) *Oppida: the Beginnings of Urbanization in Barbarian Europe* (Oxford, 1976)

Daniels, C. M. (ed) *Collingwood Bruce's Handbook to the Roman Wall* (rev ed, Harold Hill, 1978)

Dyer, J. *Southern England: an Archaeological Guide* (Faber, 1973)

Frere, S. S. *Britannia* (Routledge & Kegan Paul, 1978)

Frere, S. S. and St Joseph J. K. *Roman Britain from the Air* (Cambridge University Press, 1983)

Gelzer, M. *Caesar: Politician and Statesman* (Blackwell, 1969)

Gentry, A. *Roman Military Stone-built Granaries in Britain* (British Archaeological Reports no 32, 1976)

Grant, M. *Julius Caesar* (Weidenfeld & Nicolson, 1968)

Green, M. *The Religions of Civilian Roman Britain* (British Archaeological Reports no 24, 1976)

Grimes, W. F. *Excavations in Roman and Medieval London* (Routledge & Kegan Paul, 1968)

Holder, P. A. *The Roman Army in Britain* (Batsford, 1982)

Houlder, C. *Wales: An Archaeological Guide* (Faber, 1978)

Jarrett, M. G. *The Roman Frontier in Wales* (revision of original work by V. E. Nash-Williams, 1969)

Johnson, S. *Later Roman Britain* (Routledge & Kegan Paul, 1980)

Johnson, S. *The Roman Forts of the Saxon Shore* (Elek, 1979)

Johnston, D. E. *Roman Villas* (Shire Publications, 1979)

Johnston, D. E. (ed) *The Saxon Shore* (CBA Report no 18, 1977)

Jones, A. H. M. *The Later Roman Empire* (Oxford University Press, 1964)

Jones, M. J. *Roman Fort Defences to AD117* (British Archaeological Reports no 21, 1975, rev ed 1977)

Lewis, M. J. P. *Temples in Roman Britain* (Cambridge University Press, 1966)

Liversidge, J. *Britain in the Roman Empire* (Routledge & Kegan Paul, 1968)

Macdonald, G. *The Roman Wall in Scotland* (2nd ed, Oxford University Press, 1934)

McGrail, S. *Rafts, Boats and Ships* (National Maritime Museum and HMSO, 1981)

MacKie, E. W. *Scotland: An Archaeological Guide* (Faber, 1975)

McWhirr, A. *Roman Crafts and Industries* (Shire Publications, 1982)

Margary, I. D. *Roman Roads in Britain* (John Baker, 1973)

Marsden, P. *Roman London* (Thames & Hudson, 1980)

Merrifield, R. *Roman London* (Cassell, 1969)

Morris, J. *Londinium* (Weidenfeld/Book Club Associates, 1982)

Morris, P. *Agricultural Buildings in Roman Britain* (British Archaeological Reports no 70, 1979)

Morrison, J. S. *Long Ships and Round Ships* (National Maritime Museum and HMSO, 1980)

Morrison, J. S. and Williams, R. T. *Greek Oared Ships* (Cambridge University Press, 1967)

Percival, J. *The Roman Villa* (Batsford, 1976)

Phillips, T. R. and Lane, J. (ed) *Roots of Strategy* (The Bodley Head, 1943)

Rainey, A. *Mosaics in Roman Britain* (David & Charles, 1973)

Richmond, I. A. *Roman Britain* (Pelican, 1963)

Rivet, A. L. F. (ed) *The Roman Villa in Britain* (Routledge & Kegan Paul, 1969)

Rivet, A. L. F. *Town and Country in Roman Britain* (Hutchinson, 1975)

Rivet, A. L. F. and Smith, C. *The Place Names of Roman Britain* (Batsford, 1979)

Robertson, A. S. *The Antonine Wall* (rev ed, Glasgow Archaeological Journal, 1979)

Rodwell, W. and Rowley, T. (ed) *Small Towns of Roman Britain* (British Archaeological Reports no 15, 1975)

Salway, P. *The Frontier People of Roman Britain* (Cambridge University Press, 1965)

Salway, P. *Roman Britain* (Oxford University Press, 1981)

Sedgley, J. *The Roman Milestones of Britain* (British Archaeological Reports no 18, 1975)

Somerset Fry, P. *Great Caesar* (Collins, 1974)

Somerset Fry, P. *Rebellion against Rome* (Dalton, 1982)

Strickland, T. J. *New Evidence for Roman Chester* (University of Liverpool, 1978)

Swan, V. *Pottery in Roman Britain* (Shire Publications, 1980)

Todd, M. *Roman Britain, 55BC–AD410* (Fontana, 1981)

Todd, M. (ed) *Studies in the Romano-British Villa* (Leicester University Press, 1978)

Toynbee, J. M. C. *Art in Roman Britain* (Phaidon, 1962)

Wacher, J. S. (ed) *The Civitas Capitals of Roman Britain* (Leicester University Press, 1966)

Wacher, J. S. *The Coming of Rome* (Routledge & Kegan Paul, 1981)

Wacher, J. S. *Roman Britain* (Dent, 1980)

Wacher, J. S. *The Towns of Roman Britain* (Batsford, 1975)

Webster, G. *Boudica* (Batsford, 1978)

Webster, G. *The Roman Army* (Grosvenor Museum, 1973)

Webster, G. *The Roman Invasion of Britain* (Batsford, 1980)

Welsby, D. *The Roman Military Defence of the British Provinces in its Later Phases* (British Archaeological Reports no 101, 1982)

Wheeler, R. E. M. *The Stanwick Fortifications* (Oxford University Press, 1954)

Wilson, R. J. A. *Roman Forts* (Bergstrom, 1980)

Winbolt, S. E. *Britain under the Romans* (Pelican, 1945)

Yawetz, Z. *Julius Caesar and his Public Image* (Thames & Hudson, 1983)

Special Articles

Barker, P. 'Excavations of the baths and basilica at Wroxeter, 1966–74: interim report', *Britannia* vi (1975), pp 106–17.

Barrett, A. A. 'The career of Tiberius Claudius Cogidubnus', *Britannia* x (1979), pp 227–42.

Birley, A. R. 'Petillius Cerialis and the conquest of Brigantia', *Britannia* iv (1973), pp 179–90.

Bogaers, J. E. 'King Cogidubnus in Chichester: another reading of RIB 91', *Britannia* x (1979), pp 243–54.

Boon, G. C. 'Belgic and Roman Silchester', *Archaeologia* cii (1969), pp 1–81.

Breeze, D. J. 'Agricola the builder', SAF 12 (1981), pp 14–24.

Brodribb, G. 'Tile from the Roman bathhouse at Beauport Park', *Britannia* x (1979), pp 129–58.

Carroll, K. K. 'The date of Boudica's revolt', *Britannia* x (1979) pp 197–202.

Clarke, G. 'The Roman villa at Woodchester', *Britannia* xiii (1982), pp 197–228.

Cleere, H. 'The *Classis Britannica*: the Saxon Shore', CBA Report 18 (1977), pp 16–19.

Cleere, H. 'Iron-making in a Roman furnace', *Britannia* ii (1971), pp 203–17.

Cunliffe, B. 'The Roman baths at Bath: excavations 1969–75', *Britannia* vii (1976), pp 1–32.

Crummy, P. 'Colchester: the Roman fortress and the development of the *colonia*', *Britannia* viii (1977), pp 65–106.

Daniels, C. M. 'Problems of the northern Roman frontier', SAF 2 (1970) pp 91–101.

Dobson, B. 'Agricola's life and career', SAF 12 (1981), pp 1–13.

Eichholz, D. 'How long did Vespasian serve in Britain?', *Britannia* iii (1972), pp 149–63.

Field, N. 'Discovery of a Roman fort at Shapwick, near Badbury Rings, Dorset', *Britannia* vii (1976), pp 280-3.

Fox, A. and Ravenhill, W. 'The Roman fort at Nanstallon', *Britannia* iii (1972), pp 78-103.

Frere, S. S. 'The Bignor villa', *Britannia* xiii (1982), pp 135-96.

Frere, S. S. 'The forum and baths at Caistor St Edmund', *Britannia* ii (1971), pp 1-26.

Frere, S. S. 'Hyginus and the first cohort', *Britannia* xi (1980), pp 51-60.

Frere, S. S. and St Joseph, J. K. 'The Roman fortress at Longthorpe', *Britannia* v (1974), pp 1-129.

Gillam, J. P. 'The frontier after Hadrian - a history of the problem', Arch Ael ser 2 (1974), pp 1-15.

Gillam, J. P. 'Possible changes in plan in the course of the construction of the Antonine Wall', SAF 7 (1975), pp 51-6.

Gillam, J. P. 'The Roman forts at Corbridge', Arch Ael ser 2 (1977), pp 47-74.

Guy, C. J. 'Roman circular lead tanks in Britain', *Britannia* xii (1981), pp 271-6.

Hanson, W. S. 'The first Roman occupation of Scotland', in *Roman Frontier Studies 1979* (ed W. S. Hanson and L. J. F. Keppie), British Archaeological Reports International Series 71 (Oxford, 1980)

Hanson, W. S. 'Roman military timber supply', *Britannia* ix (1978), pp 293-306.

Hartley, B. R. 'The Roman occupation of Scotland: evidence of the Samian ware', *Britannia* iii (1972), pp 15-42.

Hawkes, C. F. C. 'Britain and Julius Caesar', Proc Brit Acad lxiii (1977), pp 125-92.

Hebditch, M. and Mellor, J. 'The forum and basilica of Roman Leicester', *Britannia* iv (1973), pp 1-83.

Heighway, C. M. and Parker, A. J. 'The Roman tilery at St Oswald's Priory, Gloucester', *Britannia* xiii (1982), pp 25-74.

Hobley, B. 'An experimental reconstruction of a Roman military turf rampart', in *Roman Frontier Studies* (ed S. Applebaum), Tel Aviv, 1977, pp 21-33.

Hogg, A. H. A. 'The Llantwit Major villa: a reconsideration of the evidence', *Britannia* v (1974), pp 225-50.

Jackson, D. A. 'A Roman lime kiln at Weekley, Northants', *Britannia* iv (1973), pp 128-40.

Jackson, D. A. 'A Roman timber bridge at Aldwincle, Northants', *Britannia* vii (1976), pp 39-72.

Jobey, G. 'Burnswark Hill', TDGNHAS 53 (1979), pp 37-104.

Johnson, S. 'Hayton Roman fort: 1975', *Britannia* ix (1978), pp 57-114.

Johnston, D. E. 'A Roman building at Chalk, near Gravesend', *Britannia* iii (1972), pp 112-48.

Jones, G. D. B. 'The Solway frontier: interim report, 1976-81', *Britannia* xiii (1982), pp 283-98.

Jones, G. D. B. 'The western extension of Hadrian's Wall: Bowness to Cardurnock', *Britannia* vii (1976), pp 236-43.

Jones, M. J. and Gilmour, J. J. 'Lincoln: principia and forum. Preliminary report', *Britannia* xi (1980), pp 61-72.

Keppie, L. J. F. 'The Antonine Wall: 1960-1980', *Britannia* xiii (1982), pp 91-112.

Keppie, L. J. F. 'The building of the Antonine Wall: archaeological and epigraphic evidence', PSAS 105 (1972-5), pp 151-65.

Keppie, L. J. F. 'Some rescue excavations on the line of the Antonine Wall, 1973-6', PSAS 107 (1975-6), pp 61-80.

Knowles, A. K. 'Brampton, Norfolk: an interim report', *Britannia* viii (1977), pp 209-22.

Mann, J. C. 'The northern frontier after AD369', GAJ (1974), pp 34-42.

Manning, W. H. 'Roman timber military gateways', *Britannia* x (1979), pp 19-62.

Margary, I. 'The Fishbourne story', *Britannia* ii (1971), pp 117-21.

Maxwell, G. 'Agricola's campaigns: evidence of the temporary camps', SAF 12 (1981), pp 25-54.

Miles, H. 'The Honeyditches villa, Seaton', *Britannia* viii (1977) pp 107-46.

Milne, G. 'Further evidence from Roman London Bridge', *Britannia* xiii (1982), pp 271-6.

Money, J. H. 'Garden Hill, Sussex: interim report', *Britannia* viii (1977), pp 339-50.

Nash, D. 'Reconstructing Poseidonios' Celtic ethnography: some considerations', *Britannia* vii (1976), pp 111-46.

Neal, D. S. 'The Roman villa at Boxmoor: interim report', *Britannia* i (1970), pp 156-62.

Philp, B. 'The British evidence: Dover', in *The Saxon Shore* (ed D. E. Johnston) CBA Report no 18, 1977, pp 20-1.

Philp, B. 'The forum of Roman London, 1968-9', *Britannia* viii (1977), pp 1-64.

Potter, T. W. 'The Roman occupation of the central fenland', *Britannia* xii (1981), pp 79-134.

Rae, A. and Rae, V. 'The Roman fort at Cramond, Edinburgh', *Britannia* v (1974), pp 163-224.

Reed, N. 'The fifth year of Agricola's campaigns', *Britannia* ii (1971), pp 143-8.

Reed, N. 'The Scottish campaigns of Septimus Severus', PSAS 107 (1975), pp 92-102.

Richmond, I. A. 'The Agricolan fort at Fendoch', PSAS 73 (1938), pp 110-54.

Richmond, I. A. 'Excavations at the Roman fort of Newstead', PSAS 84 (1949), pp 1-37.

Robertson, A. 'Birrens (*Blatobulgium*)', TDGNHAS (1975).

Robertson, A. 'Roman signal stations on the Gask Ridge', TPSNS special issue (1973), pp 14-29.

Rodwell, W. 'The Roman fort at Great Chesterford, Essex', *Britannia* iii (1972), p 290.

St Joseph, J. K. Various articles on air reconnaissance of Roman Britain in JRS.

Stead, I. M. 'Excavations at Winterton Roman villa and other Roman sites in north Lincolnshire' (London, 1976)

Stead, I. M. and Liversidge, J. 'Brantingham Roman villa', *Britannia* iv (1973), pp 84-106.

Steer, K. A. 'The Antonine Wall: 1934-1959', JRS (1960), pp 84-93.

Steer, K. A. 'Roman and native in south Scotland', Arch J cxxi (1964), pp 164-7.

Stevens, C. E. 'Britain between the invasions', in *Aspects of Archaeology in Britain and Beyond* (ed W. F. Grimes) (London, 1951).

Stevens, C. E. '55BC and 54BC', *Antiquity* xxi (1947), pp 4-9.

Thompson, E. A. 'Britain: 406-410 AD', *Britannia* viii (1977), pp 303-18.

Todd, M. 'Small towns of Roman Britain', *Britannia* i (1970), pp 114-30.

Ward, J. H. 'Vortigern and the end of Roman Britain', *Britannia* iii (1972), pp 277-89.

Whittick, G. C. 'Roman lead-mining on Mendip and in north Wales', *Britannia* xiii (1982), pp 113-24.

Wilson, D. R. 'Roman British villas from the air', *Britannia* v (1974), pp 251-61.

Journals

Antiquaries Journal (Antiq J)
Antiquity
Archaeologia
Archaeologia Aeliana (Arch Ael)
Archaeologia Cambrensis (Arch Camb)
Archaeologia Cantiana (Arch Cant)
Archaeological Excavations (DoE) 1961-76 (Arch Ex)
Archaeological Journal (Arch J)
Archaeological Reports, since 1956 (AR)
Archaeology (AW)
Bedfordshire Archaeological Journal (Beds Arch J)
Bedfordshire, Buckinghamshire, Northamptonshire, Oxfordshire, Review of Archaeology (ABBNO)
Bedfordshire Historical Record Society Transactions
Berkshire Archaeological Journal
Birmingham and Warwickshire Archaeological Society Transactions (TBAS)
Bristol and Gloucestershire Archaeological Society Transactions (TBGAS)
Britannia
British Archaeological Association Journal (JBAA)
Bulletin of the Board of Celtic Studies (BBCS)
Caernarvon Historical Society Transactions
Cambridge Antiquarian Society Proceedings (CAS)
Carmarthen Antiquary
Chester Archaeological Society Journal
Clwyd-Powys Archaeological Trust Reports
Cornish Archaeology
Council of British Archaeology Reports (CBA)
Cumberland and Westmorland Antiquarian and Archaeological Society Transactions (CW)

Current Archaeology (issues 1–89) (CA)
Derbyshire Archaeological Journal (Derbys)
Devon Archaeological Society Transactions
Discovery and Excavation in Scotland (DAES)
Dorset Natural History and Archaeological Society Proceedings (PDNHAS)
Dumfriesshire and Galloway Natural History and Antiquarian Society Transactions (TDGNHAS)
Durham and Northumberland Architectural and Archaeological Society Transactions
Dyfed Archaeological Trust Annual Reports (Dyfed)
East Anglian Archaeology
Essex Archaeological and Historical Society Transactions
Glamorgan–Gwent Archaeological Trust Annual Reports (GGAT)
Glasgow Archaeological Journal (GAJ)
Glasgow Archaeological Society Transactions (TGAS)
Glevensis (Gloucestershire)
Hampshire Field Club Proceedings
Herefordshire Archaeology
Hertfordshire Archaeological Review (Herts Arch Rev)
Journal of Roman Studies (JRS)
Kent Archaeological Review (Kent Arch Rev)
Lancashire and Cheshire Antiquarian Society Transactions
Leicestershire Archaeological and Historical Society Transactions
Lichfield and South Staffordshire Archaeological and Historical Society Transactions (TLSSAHS)
Lincolnshire History and Archaeology Society Journal (Lincs Hist Arch Soc)
London and Middlesex Archaeological Society Transactions
Merioneth Historical Society Journal (Merioneth)
Morgannwg (Glamorganshire)
Norfolk Archaeology
Northamptonshire Archaeology
Northamptonshire Federation of Archaeological Societies Bulletin (BNFAS)
North Staffordshire Journal of Field Studies
Oxfordshire Archaeological Unit Newsletter
Oxoniensia (Oxon)
Perthshire Society of Natural Science Transactions (TPSNS)

Proceedings of the British Academy (Proc Brit Acad)
Radnorshire Society Transactions
Records of Buckinghamshire
Roman Frontier Studies
Scottish Archaeological Forum (SAF)
Shropshire Archaeological and Natural History Society Transactions (Shrop Arch Soc)
Society of Antiquaries of Scotland Proceedings (PSAS)
Somerset Archaeological and Natural History Society Proceedings (PSANHS)
Suffolk Institute of Archaeology Proceedings (PSIA)
Surrey Archaeological Collections
Sussex Archaeological Collections
Thoroton Society of Nottinghamshire Transactions (Thoroton Soc)
West Midlands Archaeological News Sheet (WMANS)
Wiltshire Archaeological and Natural History Magazine (WANHM)
Woolhope Field Club (Herefordshire) Transactions (Woolhope)
Worcestershire Archaeological Society Transactions (Worc Arch Soc)
Yorkshire Archaeological Journal (YAJ)
Yorkshire Archaeological Review (YAR)

Maps

Ordnance Survey Map of Roman Britain (HMSO, 1979)
Ordnance Survey Map of Hadrian's Wall (HMSO, 1975)
Ordnance Survey Map of the Antonine Wall (HMSO, 1975)

Other Sources

The county inventories published by the Royal Commission on Historical Monuments (RCHM) (England), Royal Commission on Ancient Monuments (RCAM) (Wales) and Royal Commission on the Ancient and Historical Monuments of Scotland (RCAHMS), and the Victoria County Histories (VCH) of all counties concerned may also be consulted.

A number of official handbooks and leaflets on Romano-British sites contain useful information, including Aldborough, Burgh Castle, Chesters fort, Corbridge Roman Station, Hadrian's Wall, Housesteads fort, Lullingstone villa, Maiden Castle, Pevensey, Portchester, Reculver, and Richborough (Department of the Environment); Ancient Monuments of Anglesey (including Caer Gybi, Holyhead Mountain), Brecon Gaer, Caerleon, Caerwent, Segontium Roman fort (Welsh Office); the Antonine Wall, Bearsden fort (Scottish Development Department).

Many of the sites with visible remains, in private, local authority or other official hands have locally published guidebooks, information sheets etc, and these are entered in the bibliography of references for the gazetteer (pp 527–42).

MUSEUMS

There are many museums in Britain that have collections of Romano-British material, and there are also a number of smaller museums, chiefly on or near sites, that are devoted exclusively to Romano-British displays. The list that follows does not differentiate, and it is not total, but the fifty or so mentioned should provide an evenly distributed choice throughout the UK. Many are under the control of local authorities, and the recent swingeing cuts in local authority expenditure have already begun to affect such museums, reducing opening hours, limiting staff to run them and hampering them in other ways, so that it is no longer possible to provide a realistic list of opening days or times.

Aldborough	Dover	Newport, Isle of Wight
Bath	Edinburgh	Orpington
Brecon	Exeter	Oxford
Caerleon	Falkirk	Peterborough
Cambridge	Fishbourne	Reading
Canterbury	Gloucester	Richborough
Cardiff	Housesteads	Salisbury
Carlisle	Hull	Scarborough
Carmarthen	Ilkley	Sheffield
Chedworth	Kettering	Shrewsbury
Chelmsford	Leicester	Southampton
Chesterholm	Lincoln	Taunton
Chester	Littlecote	Verulamium (St Albans)
Chesters	London: British Museum;	Wall
Chichester	Museum of London	Warwick
Cirencester	Lullingstone	Winchester
Colchester	Maidstone	Worcester
Corbridge	Malton	Yeovil
Doncaster	Newcastle	York
Dorchester	Newport, Gwent	

INDEX OF PEOPLE AND PLACES

SUBJECT INDEX